THE LOEB CLASSICAL LIBRARY

FOUNDED BY JAMES LOEB, LL.D.

EDITED BY

† T. E. PAGE, C.H., LITT.D.

† E. CAPPS, PH.D., LL.D.   † W. H. D. ROUSE, LITT.D.

L. A. POST, M.A.   E. H. WARMINGTON, M.A., F.R.HIST.SOC.

MINOR ATTIC ORATORS

II

TO MY WIFE

MINOR ATTIC ORATORS

IN TWO VOLUMES

II

LYCURGUS   DINARCHUS

DEMADES   HYPERIDES

WITH AN ENGLISH TRANSLATION BY

J. O. BURTT, M.A.

FORMERLY POSTMASTER OF MERTON COLLEGE, OXFORD

LONDON

WILLIAM HEINEMANN LTD

CAMBRIDGE, MASSACHUSETTS

HARVARD UNIVERSITY PRESS

MCMLIV

Printed in Great Britain

CONTENTS OF VOLUME II

MINOR ATTIC ORATORS, II

CONTENTS

MINOR ATTIC ORATORS, II

MINOR ATTIC ORATORS, II

edition, in accordance with the kind permission given, before the text, the preparation of the Budé text, I have relied on Jensen's very full apparatus criticus to the texts of both C. G. Kenyon in the Oxford and . . . . . Budé edition. The possible . . . . so great that the text is adopted with . . . . . no

PREFACE

In preparing the second volume of the *Minor Attic Orators* I have tried to follow as closely as possible the general method of presentation adopted in volume I. The Greek text can best be considered under two heads. (1) The text of Lycurgus, Dinarchus, and Demades is based, for the speeches, on that of Bekker (1823) and, for the fragments, on that of Baiter and Sauppe (1845–1850) ; while the excerpts of Demades, which were not discovered until later, are taken from an article by H. Haupt in *Hermes*, vol. xiii. Various changes have been introduced in the light of more recent criticism ; and in making this revision I have relied chiefly, for Lycurgus, on the critical notes of F. Blass, F. Durrbach, and A. Petrie, for Dinarchus, on those of F. Blass and T. Thalheim, and, for Demades, on those of F. Blass. The resulting text will be found to be rather more conservative than that of the Teubner editions. Though the accompanying notes are necessarily brief, my aim has been to include in them all the important variations in the manuscript tradition and to account for all departures from it. I hope that in cases where my choice of reading may seem questionable the notes will throw sufficient light on the passage to enable the reader to judge it for himself. (2) The text of Hyperides has been taken with scarcely any change from C. Jensen's edition, in accordance with the kind permission given, before the last war, by the proprietors of the Bibliotheca Teubneriana. In preparing the textual notes on this I have relied on Jensen's very full apparatus criticus together with that of F. G. Kenyon in the Oxford, and G. Colin in the Budé, edition. The possibilities of conjectural restoration are here so great that the text adopted will perhaps please no one. Nevertheless, I hope that, set out as it is, the reader will not find it misleading, and that here too the notes will help him to form his own conclusions.

Detailed acknowledgements to the various scholars whose writings I have consulted are out of the question here ; a list is given, in the introduction, of the chief works of reference for the study of these four orators, and to all of these, as well as to some others, I am in varying degrees indebted. In conclusion I must express my thanks to the late Dr. W. H. D. Rouse for encouragement and helpful criticism.

J. O. BURTT

April 1953

INTRODUCTION

THE four orators who figure in this volume all lived
and worked at Athens in the fourth century B.C.
The youngest of them, Dinarchus, who survived into
the third, was not an Athenian citizen and therefore
took no part himself in public life ; but the remaining
three, like their contemporary Demosthenes, stood
in the forefront of Athenian politics during the city's
struggle with Macedon and often met as adversaries
or allies in the law courts or the Assembly. Demades
left no written work behind him and the speech which
has come down to us as his is from the hand of a later
writer. But in the first century B.C. 179 speeches
ascribed to the other three orators were still extant,
of which 127 were considered genuine. From this
body of writing the contents of the present volume
are all that remains.

SOURCES OF THE TEXT

LYCURGUS AND DINARCHUS.—The sources
for Lycurgus, *Against Leocrates*, and for the three
speeches of Dinarchus are two MSS., both of which
appear to be derived from a common archetype now
lost. (1) The chief of these is a thirteenth-century
MS., Codex Crippsianus, Brit. Mus. Burneianus 95
(A). This was bought in Greece by J. M. Cripps

about 1803, was later sold to J. Burney, and is now in the British Museum. It contains, of the orators, Andocides, Isaeus, Dinarchus, Antiphon, and Lycurgus. The scribe who wrote the MS. later revised his work and made a number of corrections (A corr.) in which he generally recorded the reading of the archetype, although he seems occasionally to have relied on his own intelligence. Besides these original corrections, there are others in a different hand which are evidently the conjectures of a later critic (A corr.[2]) ; and there are also places in the text where an unknown corrector has erased one or more letters (A corr. ras.). In spite of these alterations, the text of A still contains many obvious errors, and there are certain passages which are seriously corrupt. From A are derived, directly or indirectly, five other MSS., B, L, M, P, Z, to which more attention was paid by scholars before their dependence on A was proved. The first edition of these authors, that of Aldus (1513), though based on L, contains some variant readings of unknown origin (Ald.). (2) The second source for the text is a MS. of the thirteenth or fourteenth century, Codex Oxoniensis Bodleianus misc. 208 (N). This contains Dinarchus, Antiphon, and part of Lycurgus, i.e. sects. 1-34. 6 (προδοσίας) and sections 98. 5 (τὸν Ποσειδῶνος) to 147. 5 (ἐγκατα[λιπών). Like A, N has been corrected, though less often, by the original scribe (N corr.) and contains a number of later conjectures (N corr.[2]).

DEMADES.—The text of the Ὑπὲρ τῆς Δωδεκαετίας is derived from two sources. (1) The main portion of the speech, i.e. sections 1-17, is preserved in a twelfth-century MS., Codex Palatinus Heidelbergensis 88 (X), which is the chief source for the text of Lysias. It was written at Nicaea and, after various wanderings, came to Heidelberg in 1815. The six later MSS., C, E, I, M, N, T, which were used by Bekker for his edition, are all derived from X. (2) Fifty-seven short extracts of this speech were found in a Palatine MS. by H. Haupt and published by him in 1878. Only the first nine of these belong to sections 1-17, and the text of all (e) is independent of X.

HYPERIDES.—Apart from the brief fragments of the second speech for Lycophron, which came to light in 1905, the extant orations of Hyperides were discovered in Egypt at intervals during the last century. They are contained in four papyri of which the first three referred to here are well written and the fourth inferior. (I) Pap. Ardenianus (A), which was written probably in the first or second century A.D. and contains speeches V, I, and IV, was discovered in two parts, both of which are now in the British Museum (B.M. 108 & 115). (a) The first of these contains V and the beginning of I. It was found torn in pieces and the surviving fragments were only gradually recovered direct from Egypt or from collections of papyri in Europe. Thus, thirty-two were bought at Thebes in 1847 by Harris, six found later by Babington, and thirteen more brought to Paris by Chasles and published by Egger. A single fragment containing the three titles was discovered in London by Blass and published in 1875, six others were brought from Egypt by Tancock and a further four found by Raphael and given to the British Museum. From these fragments the present text of the *Demosthenes* and the first part of the *Lycophron* has been restored by the labours of different scholars. (*b*) The second part, which contains the end of I and the whole of IV, is in good condition. It was acquired in 1848 by Arden and first edited in 1853. (2) Pap. Londiniensis (L), which contains II and, in a different hand, the third epistle of Demosthenes, probably dates from the first century B.C. The discoverer of it is not known, but it was acquired by the British Museum and first published by Kenyon in 1891 (B.M. 134). The roll is badly mutilated. (3) Pap. Parisinus (P) dates from the second century B.C. and contains speech III. Bought in Egypt by Revillout it was first edited by him in 1892 and is now in the Louvre (9331). The beginning and part of the bottom of the roll are damaged. (4) Pap. Stobartianus (S), dating from the second century A.D. and containing VI and an astrological work, was brought from Egypt in 1856 by Stobart in fifteen pieces which were successfully restored by Babington. The papyrus, which is mutilated at the end, is now in the British Museum (B.M. 98).

SELECT BIBLIOGRAPHY

All four orators are discussed briefly by R. C. Jebb, *The Attic Orators*, vol. 2 (1876), by J. F. Dobson, *The Greek Orators* (1929), and more fully by F. Blass, *Attische Beredsamkeit*, vol. iii. 2 (1898). For detailed study the older editions of the Attic orators, which include Lycurgus, Dinarchus and Demades but not Hyperides, are still useful, particularly : I. Bekker (1823), W. S. Dobson (1828), and J. G. Baiter and H. Sauppe (1845–1850). LYCURGUS. F. Blass, Teubner edition (1899), F. Durrbach, Budé edition

INTRODUCTION

(1932), both containing text and apparatus criticus of the *Leocrates* and Fragments and the latter a French transalation ; A. Petrie, *Leocrates*, text and notes (1922). DINARCHUS AND DEMADES. F. Blass, Teubner edition (1888) containing text and apparatus criticus of the speeches but not including the fragments of Dinarchus. HYPERIDES. F. G. Kenyon, Oxford text (1906), C. Jensen, Teubner edition (1917), G. Colin, Budé edition (1946), all containing text and apparatus criticus of the extant works, except that the Budé edition omits the minor fragments though providing a French translation of the speeches. Of the many publications dealing with separate speeches the following may be mentioned as having proved of special value in the preparation of this edition : C. Babington, *Demosthenes* (1850), *Lycophron and Euxenippus* (1853), *Funeral Speech* (1859), all containing text, facsimiles of papyri and English commentary ; F. G. Kenyon, *Philippides and Athenogenes* (1893) with text and English notes and translation ; E. Revillout : " Mémoire sur le discours d'Hypéride contre Athénogène " (in *Revue Egyptologique*, vol. vi., 1892) ; D. Comparetti, *Euxenippus* (1861), *Funeral Speech* (1864), text and Italian commentary ; H. Hess, *Textkritische und erklaerende Beitraege zum Epitaphios des Hypereides* (1938). Owing to the fragmentary state in which the speeches have survived some variation will naturally be found in the texts adopted in these editions.

LYCURGUS

LIFE OF LYCURGUS[a]

LYCURGUS was born at Athens in the early years of the fourth century B.C. and died there, probably in 324, when he was in the late sixties. He did not come into full prominence as a statesman until near the end of his life, when for twelve years he controlled Athenian finances and dominated the politics of the city. He was a man of conservative outlook and strong convictions, deeply sensible of the traditions of his city and anxious to do his utmost to restore her to the position which she had once held. For this task no leader of the time was better fitted. Scrupulously honest and wholeheartedly devoted to the state, Lycurgus practised in his personal life the stern self-denial which he expected from his fellow citizens. His long period of office was spent in an attempt to rid Athens of corruption and fit her for success in her struggle against Macedon.

[a] Sources for the Life of Lycurgus. The chief source for the life of Lycurgus is the Pseudo-Plutarch's biography of him in the *Lives of the Ten Orators*. This seems to be derived from the work of Caecilius of Calacte (first century B.C.), who perhaps drew on the earliest life of Lycurgus, that written by Philiscus just after the orator's death. Fragments of inscriptions survive relating to his work (*CIA* ii. 162, 168, 173, 176, 180, 180b) and the honours paid to him after death (*CIA* ii. 240). Suidas gives a short note on him (*s.v.* " Lycurgus ") which includes a list of his speeches then extant.

LIFE OF LYCURGUS

The details which we possess of his family and early upbringing go far towards explaining the views which he held. He came of a noble clan, the Eteobutadae, in which the priesthood of Apollo Erechtheus and other religious offices were hereditary, and it is probable that he was himself a priest of Apollo, since his son Hagnonides later held this office. The Eteobutadae had produced men of note in the past, among them the Lycurgus who opposed Pisistratus. Of the orator's father Lycophron nothing is known but his name; but his great grandfather Lycomedes had been buried publicly in the Ceramicus and so had his grandfather Lycurgus who was killed by the Thirty.

In his youth Lycurgus studied under both Plato and Isocrates. The former of these no doubt helped to foster his admiration for the disciplined life of Sparta, while to the latter he owed much of his technique as an orator. No evidence exists to show that he took part in public life until he was over fifty. Whether or not in 343 he accompanied Demosthenes on embassies to various Greek cities with a view to forming a league against Philip is not certain; but we are bound to presume some previous activity to explain his rise to eminence in 338 when he succeeded Eubulus as controller of finances. The exact title attaching to this post is not known, but the term of office was four years and Lycurgus remained in power for three such periods, from 338 to 326, during the second of which one of his friends nominally held the appointment, since the law did not allow it to fall to the same man for two consecutive periods. There was a moment of danger in 335, when Alexander, after capturing Thebes, demanded that Lycurgus

3

should be surrendered as an anti-Macedonian with
Demosthenes and eight others. But the demand
was withdrawn on the intercession of Demades, and
soon after the young king set out for the East.

Athens was now left unmolested. The different
parties had attained a measure of agreement. Phocion
and Demades, friends of Macedon, were entrusted
with foreign policy and Lycurgus with finance. He
seems soon to have had his sphere of control ex-
tended ; for his biographer says that he was elected
to supervise preparations for war, and certainly much
of his policy was directed to that end. Not only did
he improve the walls of the city by replacing brick
with stone and digging a ditch round them but he
built up a large supply of arms on the Acropolis and
increased the fleet to four hundred vessels, finishing
the docks and naval arsenal which Eubulus had
begun. Under his direction the method of appointing
generals was altered, thus enabling them to be chosen
from the whole people irrespective of the tribe to
which they belonged, and the Ephebate, a youth
organization lately formed, was reorganized to serve
the needs of the army, so that in it the young men
of Athens could devote their nineteenth and twentieth
years to military training.

But Lycurgus took a broader view of war-prepara-
tion than these measures would suggest : material
improvement must be supported by a strengthening
of moral fibre ; the city must be purged of treason
and the favour of Heaven assured. Lysicles, general
at Chaeronea, was convicted and executed and other
trials followed, including that of Leocrates. As a
prosecutor Lycurgus proved such a determined
patriot that he rarely failed to secure a conviction,

and his laws against malefactors were said to be drafted with a pen dipped in death. Greater encouragement was given to religious cults. In the time of Pericles there had been ten gold figures of Victory on the Acropolis, of which eight were used to meet the expenses of the Peloponnesian war. Only one of these had yet been replaced and Lycurgus now supplied the remaining seven. He also furnished numerous ornaments for processions and laid down various regulations to govern the conduct of sacrifices and the cults of different gods. The extensive building programme, whose military side we have already noticed, included several religious items. A portico was erected at Eleusis, the stadium begun by Philon was completed and the theatre of Dionysus rebuilt in stone instead of wood. As an admirer of Attic drama Lycurgus had an official copy made of the plays of Aeschylus, Sophocles and Euripides to safeguard them against the interpolations of actors.

There seems little doubt that the Athenians appreciated the man who was doing so much to glorify their city, and who, during his time of office, had raised the average annual revenue from six hundred to twelve hundred talents. Hard and outspoken though he was they felt him to be sincere ; and the sight of a noble going about the city summer and winter in the same austere dress helped to strengthen their confidence. Though his enemies often prosecuted him they never had their way, and he was many times crowned and granted statues by the people. He died, probably in 324, and was then accused by his successor Menesaechmus of leaving a deficit in the treasury. But even this last attack was thwarted ; for although the sons of Lycurgus were imprisoned for their father's offence they were soon released, largely through the efforts of Hyperides and the exiled Demosthenes.

We have only one speech on which to assess the merits of Lycurgus as an orator. With ancient critics,[a] who had a better opportunity to judge him, he did not rank very high, and Hermogenes put him second to last among the ten orators. He had however one characteristic which called forth the admiration of Dionysius, who thought him rather harsh on the whole, namely the power to impress his hearers with the seriousness of a particular crime, a quality which comes out well in the speech against Leocrates.

[a] Brief criticisms of Lycurgus as an orator are given by Hermogenes, περὶ ἰδεῶν B p. 418 Sp. (389 W), Dionysius of Halicarnassus, ᾿Αρχαίων κρίσις v. 3 and Dio Chrysostom xviii. 11.

SPEECH AGAINST LEOCRATES

INTRODUCTION

THE speech against Leocrates was delivered in the year 330 [a] and, like those against Lysicles and Autolycus, was connected with the battle of Chaeronea.

Leocrates was an Athenian citizen, evidently of moderate means, since he was a blacksmith [b] by trade and employed a number of slaves in his forge. In 338, on hearing the news that Philip of Macedon had defeated the Athenians at Chaeronea, he took fright and collecting as many of his belongings as he could embarked by night with his mistress on a boat bound for Rhodes. On his arrival there he spread a report that Athens had been partly captured, which caused a minor panic until it was proved false, [c] and later moved to Megara, where he lived for five or six years as a resident alien trading in corn. Meanwhile he sold his property in Athens to his brother-in-law Amyntas, whom he asked to pay his debts and send him his household gods. Apparently he intended to settle permanently in Megara. [d] Then, for a reason which we do not know, he suddenly returned to Athens. If he thought that after eight years his flight was no longer regarded as serious he was

[a] Very shortly before Demosthenes' speech on the Crown (*cf.* Aeschin. iii. 252).
[b] § 58.   [c] §§ 17 *sq.*
[d] § 22.

mistaken ; for, impeached by Lycurgus for treason, he escaped conviction by only one vote.[a]

It is doubtful whether Leocrates had infringed any definite regulation in leaving the city. Lycurgus does indeed describe certain emergency measures passed after the battle and say that he had disregarded them.[b] But Autolycus, an Areopagite, had been sentenced to death for breaking one of them [c] ; and if Leocrates had been in the city when they were passed, and come within their scope, Lycurgus would surely have emphasized the point far more than he does. Probably Leocrates left too soon to be affected by the new provisions, and his prosecutor simply hoped on general grounds to persuade the jury that cowardice of this type amounted to treason. His attitude is therefore more impersonal than that of most Athenian accusers. Instead of a bitter attack on the private life of the defendant we are given what has been described as a sermon on patriotism. It is a sermon with obvious faults : the argument is sometimes unconvincing ; the legendary and historical anecdotes, as well as the long passages of poetry, are seldom strictly relevant ; and many may feel that Lycurgus is regarding in too serious a light a crime committed eight years previously, a view which some of the jury probably shared. But the speech is undoubtedly forceful and bears the stamp of sincerity on it, commanding attention still because it reflects so clearly the convictions of the man who wrote it.

[a] Aeschin. iii. 252.
[b] §§ 16 and 17.
[c] § 53 and Frag. 9.

11

the refutation of them : (1) that he
sailed as a merchant, but the facts dis-
prove this and he had no right to be
sailing then ; (2) that he was responsible for no department of the city's
affairs, but it was the whole city which
he betrayed ; (3) that the action of
one man could not have decided the
city's fate, but it is the quality of the
act which the jury should consider ;
(4) that to leave the city is not treason,
since the Athenians left it before
Salamis, but their conduct cannot be
compared to his.

ΚΑΤΑ ΛΕΩΚΡΑΤΟΥΣ

ΥΠΟΘΕΣΙΣ

Μετὰ τὰ ἐν Χαιρωνείᾳ δεινὰ ψήφισμα ποιεῖ ὁ τῶν Ἀθηναίων δῆμος, ὥστε μήτε τινὰ ἔξω γενέσθαι τῆς πόλεως, μήτε μὴν ἐκθέσθαι παῖδας καὶ γυναῖκας. Λεωκράτης οὖν τις ἐξελθὼν τῆς πόλεως, καὶ ἀφικόμενος ἐν Ῥόδῳ καὶ πάλιν ἐν Μεγάροις, ἦλθεν ἐν Ἀθήναις· καὶ παρρησιαζομένου αὐτοῦ κατηγορίαν ποιεῖται ὁ Λυκοῦργος αὐτοῦ ὡς προδότου. ἡ δὲ στάσις ὅρος ἀντονομάζων· ὁμολογεῖ γὰρ καὶ ὁ Λεωκράτης ἀπολιπεῖν τὴν πόλιν, οὐ μέντοι προδιδόναι. ἄλλοι στοχασμὸν ἀπὸ γνώμης, ὡς τοῦ μὲν ἐξελθεῖν ὁμολογουμένου, ἀμφιβαλλομένης δὲ τῆς προαιρέσεως, ποίᾳ γνώμῃ ἐξῆλθεν, εἴτ' ἐπὶ προδοσίᾳ εἴτ' ἐπὶ ἐμπορίᾳ. ἄλλοι δὲ ἀντίστασιν· λέγει γὰρ οὐκ ἐπὶ προδοσίᾳ τῆς πόλεως ἐξελθεῖν, ἀλλ' ἐπὶ ἐμπορίᾳ. ἔοικε δὲ ἡ τοῦ λόγου ὑπόθεσις τῇ τοῦ κατὰ Αὐτολύκου.

Δικαίαν, ὦ Ἀθηναῖοι, καὶ εὐσεβῆ καὶ ὑπὲρ ὑμῶν καὶ ὑπὲρ τῶν θεῶν τὴν ἀρχὴν τῆς κατη-γορίας Λεωκράτους τοῦ κρινομένου ποιήσομαι. εὔχομαι γὰρ τῇ Ἀθηνᾷ καὶ τοῖς ἄλλοις θεοῖς καὶ τοῖς ἥρωσι τοῖς κατὰ τὴν πόλιν καὶ τὴν χώραν ἱδρυμένοις, εἰ μὲν εἰσήγγελκα Λεωκράτη δικαίως καὶ κρίνω τὸν¹ προδόντ' αὐτῶν² καὶ τοὺς νεὼς καὶ τὰ ἕδη καὶ τὰ τεμένη καὶ τὰς ἐν τοῖς νόμοις [148] τιμὰς καὶ³ θυσίας τὰς ὑπὸ τῶν ὑμετέρων προγόνων 2 παραδεδομένας, ἐμὲ μὲν ἄξιον ἐν τῇ τήμερον ἡμέρᾳ τῶν Λεωκράτους ἀδικημάτων κατήγορον ποιῆσαι,

¹ τὸν om. Ald.
² αὐτῶν Bekker : αὐτὸν Α : αὐτὸν Ν.
³ τιμὰς καὶ add. Ν.

14

AGAINST LEOCRATES

ARGUMENT

AFTER the disaster of Chaeronea the Athenian people passed a decree forbidding persons to leave the city or to remove their wives or children. Now a certain Leocrates left the city and, after going to Rhodes and later Megara, returned to Athens. He made no secret of his story and so was accused of treason by Lycurgus. The case must be classified as an instance of contradictory definition, since Leocrates admits that he left the city but denies that he betrayed it. Others class it as an instance of conjecture as to intention, since it is admitted that the accused left the city, while his purpose in leaving it is doubtful : did he wish to be a traitor or only to trade ? Others think it an instance of counterplea, since he claims that he left the city not with treasonable intentions but for commerce. The subject matter resembles that of the speech against Autolycus.

JUSTICE towards you, Athenians, and reverence for the gods, shall mark the opening of my speech against Leocrates, now here on trial ; so may Athena and those other gods and heroes whose statues are erected in our city and the country round receive this prayer. If I have done justly to prosecute Leocrates, if he whom I now bring to trial has been a traitor to their temples, shrines and precincts, a traitor to the honours which your laws ordain and the sacrificial rituals which your ancestors have handed down, may they make me on this day, in the interest of the city and its people, a worthy accuser of his crimes ; and

15

ὃ καὶ τῷ δήμῳ καὶ τῇ πόλει συμφέρει, ὑμᾶς δ᾽
ὡς ὑπὲρ πατέρων καὶ παίδων καὶ γυναικῶν καὶ
πατρίδος καὶ ἱερῶν βουλευομένους, καὶ ἔχοντας
ὑπὸ τῇ ψήφῳ τὸν προδότην ἁπάντων τούτων,
ἀπαραιτήτους δικαστὰς¹ καὶ νῦν καὶ εἰς τὸν λοιπὸν
χρόνον γενέσθαι τοῖς τὰ τοιαῦτα καὶ τηλικαῦτα
παρανομοῦσιν· εἰ δὲ μήτε τὸν προδόντα τὴν πατρίδα
μήτε τὸν ἐγκαταλιπόντα τὴν πόλιν καὶ τὰ ἱερὰ εἰς
τουτονὶ τὸν ἀγῶνα καθίστημι, σωθῆναι αὐτὸν ἐκ
τοῦ κινδύνου καὶ ὑπὸ τῶν θεῶν καὶ ὑφ᾽ ὑμῶν τῶν
δικαστῶν.

3 Ἐβουλόμην δ᾽ ἄν, ὦ ἄνδρες, ὥσπερ ὠφέλιμόν
ἐστι τῇ πόλει εἶναι τοὺς κρίνοντας ἐν ταύτῃ τοὺς
παρανομοῦντας, οὕτω καὶ φιλάνθρωπον αὐτὸ παρὰ
τοῖς πολλοῖς ὑπειλῆφθαι· νῦν δὲ περιέστηκεν εἰς
τοῦτο, ὥστε τὸν ἰδίᾳ κινδυνεύοντα καὶ ὑπὲρ τῶν
κοινῶν ἀπεχθανόμενον οὐ² φιλόπολιν ἀλλὰ φιλο-
πράγμονα δοκεῖν εἶναι, οὐ δικαίως οὐδὲ συμφερόντως τῇ πόλει. τρία γάρ ἐστι τὰ μέγιστα ἃ
διαφυλάττει καὶ διασῴζει τὴν δημοκρατίαν καὶ τὴν
4 τῆς πόλεως εὐδαιμονίαν, πρῶτον μὲν ἡ τῶν νόμων
τάξις, δεύτερον δ᾽ ἡ τῶν δικαστῶν ψῆφος, τρίτον
δ᾽ ἡ τούτοις τἀδικήματα παραδιδοῦσα³ κρίσις.
ὁ μὲν γὰρ νόμος πέφυκε προλέγειν ἃ μὴ δεῖ πράττειν, ὁ δὲ κατήγορος μηνύειν τοὺς ἐνόχους τοῖς
ἐκ τῶν νόμων ἐπιτιμίοις καθεστῶτας, ὁ δὲ δικαστὴς
κολάζειν τοὺς ὑπ᾽⁴ ἀμφοτέρων τούτων ἀποδει-
χθέντας αὐτῷ, ὥστ᾽ οὔθ᾽ ὁ νόμος οὔθ᾽ ἡ τῶν
δικαστῶν ψῆφος ἄνευ τοῦ παραδώσοντος αὐτοῖς
5 τοὺς ἀδικοῦντας ἰσχύει. ἐγὼ δ᾽, ὦ Ἀθηναῖοι,
εἰδὼς Λεωκράτην φυγόντα μὲν τοὺς ὑπὲρ τῆς

16

may you, who in your deliberation now are defending your fathers, wives and children, your country and your temples, who hold at the mercy of your vote one who has betrayed all these things, be inexorable judges, now and in future, towards all who break the laws on such a scale as this. But if the man whom I am now bringing to trial neither betrayed his country nor forsook his city and its temples, I pray that he may be saved from danger by the gods and you, the members of the jury.

Gentlemen, it is a privilege for the city to have within it those who prosecute transgressors of the law, and I could wish to find among the public an appropriate sense of gratitude. In fact the opposite is true, and anyone who takes the personal risk of unpopularity for our common good is actually regarded as an interferer rather than a patriot, which makes neither for justice nor the state's advantage. For the things which in the main uphold our democracy and preserve the city's prosperity are three in number : first the system of law, second the vote of the jury, and third the method of prosecution by which the crimes are handed over to them. The law exists to lay down what must not be done, the accuser to report those liable to penalties under the law, and the juryman to punish all whom these two agencies have brought to his attention. And thus both law and jury's vote are powerless without an accuser who will hand transgressors over to them. I myself, Athenians, knew that Leocrates avoided the dangers to which

---

[1] Post δικαστὰς codd. μὴ παρέχοντας συγγνώμην habent, del. Taylor.   [2] οὐ A : μὴ N.

[3] παραδιδοῦσα Bekker : παραδοῦσα codd.

[4] ὑπ' in marg. Ald. : ἐπ' codd.

πατρίδος κινδύνους, ἐγκαταλιπόντα δὲ τοὺς αὑτοῦ
πολίτας, προδεδωκότα δὲ πᾶσαν τὴν ὑμετέραν
δύναμιν, ἅπασι δὲ τοῖς γεγραμμένοις ἔνοχον ὄντα,
ταύτην τὴν εἰσαγγελίαν ἐποιησάμην, οὔτε δι'
ἔχθραν οὐδεμίαν οὔτε διὰ φιλονικίαν οὐδ' ἡντινοῦν
τοῦτον τὸν ἀγῶνα προελόμενος, ἀλλ' αἰσχρὸν εἶναι
νομίσας τοῦτον περιορᾶν εἰς τὴν ἀγορὰν ἐμβάλ-
λοντα καὶ τῶν κοινῶν ἱερῶν μετέχοντα, τῆς τε
πατρίδος ὄνειδος καὶ πάντων ὑμῶν γεγενημένον.
6 πολίτου γάρ ἐστι δικαίου μὴ διὰ τὰς ἰδίας ἔχθρας
εἰς τὰς κοινὰς κρίσεις καθιστάναι¹ τοὺς τὴν πόλιν
μηδὲν ἀδικοῦντας, ἀλλὰ τοὺς εἰς τὴν πατρίδα τι
παρανομοῦντας ἰδίους ἐχθροὺς εἶναι νομίζειν, καὶ
τὰ κοινὰ τῶν ἀδικημάτων κοινὰς καὶ τὰς προφάσεις ἔχειν τῆς πρὸς αὐτοὺς διαφορᾶς.
7 Ἅπαντας μὲν οὖν χρὴ νομίζειν μεγάλους εἶναι
τοὺς δημοσίους² ἀγῶνας, μάλιστα δὲ τοῦτον ὑπὲρ
οὗ νῦν μέλλετε τὴν ψῆφον φέρειν. ὅταν μὲν γὰρ
τὰς τῶν παρανόμων γραφὰς δικάζητε, τοῦτο μόνον
ἐπανορθοῦτε καὶ ταύτην τὴν πρᾶξιν κωλύετε, καθ'
ὅσον ἂν τὸ ψήφισμα μέλλῃ βλάπτειν τὴν πόλιν·
ὁ δὲ νῦν ἐνεστηκὼς ἀγὼν οὐ μικρόν τι μέρος
συνέχει τῶν τῆς πόλεως οὐδ' ἐπ' ὀλίγον χρόνον,
ἀλλ' ὑπὲρ ὅλης τῆς πατρίδος καὶ κατὰ παντὸς τοῦ
αἰῶνος ἀείμνηστον καταλείψει τοῖς ἐπιγιγνομένοις³
8 τὴν κρίσιν. οὕτω γάρ ἐστι δεινὸν τὸ γεγενημένον
ἀδίκημα καὶ τηλικοῦτον ἔχει τὸ μέγεθος, ὥστε
μήτε κατηγορίαν [μήτε τιμωρίαν]⁴ ἐνδέχεσθαι
εὑρεῖν ἀξίαν μήτ' ἐν τοῖς νόμοις ὡρίσθαι τιμωρίαν
[ἀξίαν]⁵ τῶν ἁμαρτημάτων. τί γὰρ χρὴ παθεῖν

---

¹ καθιστάναι Stephanus : καθεστάναι codd.
² δημοσίους Taylor : δημίους codd.

18

his country called him and deserted his fellow citizens.
I knew that he had utterly disregarded your authority
and was chargeable with all the articles of the indictment. Therefore I instituted these proceedings.
It was not out of hatred in the least nor with the
slightest wish to be contentious that I undertook this
trial ; but I thought it monstrous to allow this man
to push into the market place and share the public
sacrifices, when he had been a disgrace to his country
and to you all. A just citizen will not let private
enmity induce him to start a public prosecution
against one who does the state no harm. On the
contrary, it is those who break his country's laws
whom he will look on as his personal enemies ; crimes
which affect the public will, in his eyes, offer public
grounds for enmity towards the criminals.

All public trials should therefore rank as important,
but particularly this present one, in which you are
about to cast your vote. For when you give a verdict
on a charge of illegal proposals you merely rectify
one single error, and in preventing the intended
measure your scope depends upon the extent to
which the decree in question will harm the city. But
the present case is not concerned with some trifling
constitutional issue, nor yet with a moment of time ;
our city's whole life is at stake, and this trial will
leave a verdict to posterity to be remembered for
all time. So dangerous is the wrong which has
been done and so far-reaching that no indictment ade-
quate could be devised, nor have the laws defined a
punishment for the crimes. What punishment would

---

³ καταλείψει τοῖς ἐπιγιγνομένοις A : τοῖς ἐπιγιγνομένοις κατα-
λείψειν N.

⁴ μήτε τιμωρίαν secl. Sauppe.   ⁵ ἀξίαν secl. Blass.

τὸν ἐκλιπόντα μὲν τὴν πατρίδα, μὴ βοηθήσαντα
δὲ τοῖς πατρῴοις ἱεροῖς, ἐγκαταλιπόντα δὲ τὰς
τῶν προγόνων θήκας, ἅπασαν δὲ τὴν χώραν[1]
ὑποχείριον τοῖς πολεμίοις παραδόντα; τὸ μὲν γὰρ
μέγιστον καὶ ἔσχατον τῶν τιμημάτων, θάνατος,
ἀναγκαῖον μὲν ἐκ τῶν νόμων ἐπιτίμιον, ἔλαττον
9 δὲ τῶν Λεωκράτους ἀδικημάτων καθέστηκε. παρεῖ-
σθαι δὲ τὴν ὑπὲρ τῶν τοιούτων τιμωρίαν συμβέβηκεν, ὦ ἄνδρες, οὐ διὰ ῥαθυμίαν τῶν τότε νομο-
θετούντων, ἀλλὰ διὰ τὸ μήτ᾽[2] ἐν τοῖς πρότερον
χρόνοις γεγενῆσθαι τοιοῦτον μηδὲν μήτ᾽ ἐν τοῖς
μέλλουσιν ἐπίδοξον εἶναι γενήσεσθαι.[3] διὸ καὶ
[149] μάλιστ᾽, ὦ ἄνδρες, δεῖ ὑμᾶς γενέσθαι μὴ μόνον
τοῦ νῦν ἀδικήματος δικαστάς, ἀλλὰ καὶ νομοθέτας.
ὅσα μὲν γὰρ τῶν ἀδικημάτων νόμος τις διώρικε,
ῥᾴδιον τούτῳ κανόνι χρωμένους κολάζειν τοὺς
παρανομοῦντας· ὅσα δὲ μὴ σφόδρα περιείληφεν, ἑνὶ
ὀνόματι[4] προσαγορεύσας, μείζω δὲ τούτων τις
ἠδίκηκεν, ἅπασι δ᾽ ὁμοίως ἔνοχός ἐστιν, ἀναγκαῖον
τὴν ὑμετέραν κρίσιν καταλείπεσθαι παράδειγμα
10 τοῖς ἐπιγιγνομένοις. εὖ δ᾽ ἴστε, ὦ ἄνδρες, ὅτι οὐ
μόνον τοῦτον νῦν κολάσετε κατεψηφισμένοι, ἀλλὰ
καὶ τοὺς νεωτέρους ἅπαντας ἐπ᾽ ἀρετὴν προτρέψετε.[5] δύο γάρ ἐστι τὰ παιδεύοντα τοὺς νέους,
ἥ τε τῶν ἀδικούντων τιμωρία, καὶ ἡ τοῖς ἀνδράσι
τοῖς ἀγαθοῖς διδομένη δωρεά· πρὸς ἑκάτερον δὲ
τούτων ἀποβλέποντες τὴν μὲν διὰ τὸν φόβον
φεύγουσι, τῆς δὲ διὰ τὴν δόξαν ἐπιθυμοῦσι. διὸ

---

[1] χώραν N : πόλιν A.   [2] μήτ᾽ Bekker : μὴ codd.

suit a man who left his country and refused to guard the temples of his fathers, who abandoned the graves of his ancestors and surrendered the whole country into the hands of the enemy ? The greatest and final penalty, death, though the maximum punishment allowed by law, is too small for the crimes of Leocrates. The reason why the penalty for such offences, gentlemen, has never been recorded is not that the legislators of the past were neglectful ; it is that such things had not happened hitherto and were not expected to happen in the future. It is therefore most essential that you should be not merely judges of this present case but lawmakers besides. For where a crime has been defined by some law, it is easy, with that as a standard, to punish the offender. But where different offences are not specifically included in the law, being covered by a single designation, and where a man has committed crimes worse than these and is equally chargeable with them all, your verdict must be left as a precedent for your successors. I assure you, gentlemen, that if you condemn this man you will do more than merely punish him ; you will be giving all younger men an incentive to right conduct. For there are two influences at work in the education of the young : the punishments suffered by wrongdoers and the reward available to the virtuous. With these alternatives before their eyes they are deterred by fear from the one and attracted by desire for honour to the other.

---

[3] γενήσεσθαι Valckenaer : γεγενῆσθαι codd., qui addunt ὥστε (ὡς A) μήτε κατηγορίαν μήτε τιμωρίαν ἐνδέχεσθαι ἀξίαν, quae verba del. Taylor, coll. § 8.

[4] ἑνὶ ὀνόματι] ἐν ὁ νόμος τι Blass.

[5] προτρέψετε Stephanus : προτρέψητε codd.

δεῖ, ὦ ἄνδρες, προσέχειν τούτῳ τῷ ἀγῶνι καὶ μηδὲν
περὶ πλείονος ποιήσασθαι τοῦ δικαίου.

11 Ποιήσομαι δὲ κἀγὼ τὴν κατηγορίαν δικαίαν,
οὔτε ψευδόμενος οὐδέν, οὔτ' ἔξω τοῦ πράγματος
λέγων. οἱ μὲν γὰρ πλεῖστοι τῶν εἰς ὑμᾶς εἰσιόντων
πάντων ἀτοπώτατον ποιοῦσιν· ἢ γὰρ συμβου-
λεύουσιν ἐνταῦθα περὶ τῶν κοινῶν πραγμάτων ἢ
κατηγοροῦσι καὶ διαβάλλουσι πάντα μᾶλλον ἢ
περὶ οὗ μέλλετε τὴν ψῆφον φέρειν. ἔστι δ' οὐδέ-
τερον τούτων χαλεπόν, οὔθ' ὑπὲρ ὧν μὴ βου-
λεύεσθε¹ γνώμην ἀποφήνασθαι, οὔθ' ὑπὲρ ὧν
12 μηδεὶς ἀπολογήσεται κατηγορίαν εὑρεῖν. ἀλλ' οὐ
δίκαιον ὑμᾶς μὲν ἀξιοῦν δικαίαν τὴν ψῆφον φέρειν,
αὐτοὺς δὲ μὴ δικαίαν τὴν κατηγορίαν ποιεῖσθαι.
τούτων δ' αἴτιοι ὑμεῖς ἐστε, ὦ ἄνδρες· τὴν γὰρ
ἐξουσίαν ταύτην δεδώκατε τοῖς ἐνθάδ' εἰσιοῦσι,
καὶ ταῦτα κάλλιστον ἔχοντες τῶν Ἑλλήνων παράδειγμα τὸ ἐν Ἀρείῳ πάγῳ συνέδριον, ὃ τοσοῦτον
διαφέρει τῶν ἄλλων δικαστηρίων ὥστε καὶ παρ'
αὐτοῖς ὁμολογεῖσθαι τοῖς ἁλισκομένοις δικαίαν
13 ποιεῖσθαι τὴν κρίσιν. πρὸς ὃ δεῖ καὶ ὑμᾶς ἀποβλέποντας μὴ ἐπιτρέπειν τοῖς ἔξω τοῦ πράγματος
λέγουσιν· οὕτω γὰρ ἔσται τοῖς τε κρινομένοις ἄνευ
διαβολῆς ὁ ἀγών, καὶ τοῖς διώκουσιν ἥκιστα συκοφαντεῖν, καὶ ὑμῖν εὐορκοτάτην ⟨τὴν⟩² ψῆφον
ἐνεγκεῖν. ἀδύνατον γάρ ἐστι [ἄνευ τοῦ λόγου]
⟨τοὺς⟩³ μὴ δικαίως δεδιδαγμένους δικαίαν θέσθαι
τὴν ψῆφον.

14 Δεῖ δ', ὦ ἄνδρες, μηδὲ ταῦτα λαθεῖν ὑμᾶς, ὅτι
οὐχ ὅμοιός ἐστιν ὁ ἀγὼν περὶ τούτου καὶ τῶν

You must therefore give your minds to the trial on hand and let your first consideration be justice.

In my speech also justice shall come first ; on no occasion will I have recourse to falsehoods or irrelevance. Most of the speakers who come before you behave in the strangest possible manner, either giving you advice from the platform on public affairs or wasting their charges and calumnies on any subject except the one on which you are going to vote. Either course is easy, whether they choose to express an opinion on questions about which you are not deliberating or else to invent a charge to which no one is going to reply. But it is wrong that they should ask for justice from you when you give your vote and yet be unjust themselves in handling the prosecution. And yet the blame for this is yours, gentlemen ; for you have granted this freedom to speakers appearing before you, although you have, in the council of the Areopagus, the finest model in Greece : a court so superior to others that even the men convicted in it admit that its judgements are just. Let it be your pattern, and, like it, do not give way to speakers who digress from the point. If you take this advice, defendants will receive an unbiased hearing, accusers will be least able to give false information, and you will best be able to make the verdict in keeping with your oath. For those who have not been rightly informed cannot give their verdict rightly.

A further point for you to notice, gentlemen, is this : the trial of Leocrates is not comparable with that of

---

¹ βουλεύεσθε in marg. Ald. : βούλεσθε codd.
² τὴν add. Bekker.
³ τοὺς addidi (ἄνευ τοῦ λόγου ut gloss. secluso) monente L. A. Post : post τοῦ add. τοιούτου Nicolai : alii alia.

ἄλλων ἰδιωτῶν. περὶ μὲν γὰρ ἀγνῶτος ἀνθρώπου
τοῖς Ἕλλησιν ἐν ὑμῖν αὐτοῖς ἐδοκεῖτ' ἂν ἢ καλῶς
ἢ καὶ φαύλως ἐψηφίσθαι· περὶ δὲ τούτου ὅ τι ἂν
βουλεύσησθε, παρὰ πᾶσι τοῖς Ἕλλησιν ἔσται
λόγος, οἳ ἴσασι[1] τὰ τῶν προγόνων τῶν ὑμετέρων
ἔργα ἐναντιώτατα τοῖς τούτῳ διαπεπραγμένοις
ὄντα. ἐπιφανὴς γάρ[2] ἐστι διὰ τὸν ἔκπλουν τὸν
εἰς Ῥόδον καὶ τὴν ἀπαγγελίαν[3] ἣν ἐποιήσατο καθ'
ὑμῶν πρός τε τὴν πόλιν τὴν τῶν Ῥοδίων, καὶ τῶν
15 ἐμπόρων τοῖς ἐπιδημοῦσιν ἐκεῖ, οἳ πᾶσαν τὴν
οἰκουμένην περιπλέοντες δι' ἐργασίαν ἀπήγγελλον
ἅμα περὶ τῆς πόλεως ἃ Λεωκράτους ἠκηκόεσαν.[4]
ὥστε περὶ πολλοῦ ποιητέον ἐστὶν ὀρθῶς βουλεύσασθαι περὶ αὐτοῦ. εὖ γὰρ ἴστε, ὦ Ἀθηναῖοι,
ὅτι ᾧ πλεῖστον διαφέρετε τῶν ἄλλων ἀνθρώπων,
τῷ πρός τε τοὺς θεοὺς εὐσεβῶς καὶ πρὸς τοὺς
γονέας ὁσίως καὶ πρὸς τὴν πατρίδα φιλοτίμως
ἔχειν, τούτου[5] πλεῖστον ἀμελεῖν δόξαιτ'[6] ἂν εἰ τὴν
παρ' ὑμῶν οὗτος διαφύγοι τιμωρίαν.

16 Δέομαι δ' ὑμῶν, ὦ Ἀθηναῖοι, ἀκοῦσαί μου τῆς
κατηγορίας διὰ τέλους καὶ μὴ ἄχθεσθαι ἐὰν
ἄρξωμαι ἀπὸ τῶν τῇ πόλει τότε συμβάντων, ἀλλὰ
τοῖς αἰτίοις ὀργίζεσθαι[7] δι'[8] οὓς ἀναγκάζομαι νῦν
μεμνῆσθαι περὶ αὐτῶν. γεγενημένης γὰρ τῆς ἐν
Χαιρωνείᾳ μάχης, καὶ συνδραμόντων ἁπάντων
ὑμῶν εἰς τὴν ἐκκλησίαν, ἐψηφίσατο ὁ δῆμος
παῖδας μὲν καὶ γυναῖκας ἐκ τῶν ἀγρῶν εἰς τὰ
τείχη κατακομίζειν, τοὺς δὲ στρατηγοὺς τάττειν

---

[1] Verba οἳ ἴσασι . . . ὄντα, quae codd. post ἠκηκόεσαν
habent, huc transtulit Franke.
[2] γάρ Bekker : τε γάρ codd.
[3] ἀπαγγελίαν Taylor : ἐπαγγελίαν codd.

other ordinary men. For if the defendant were unknown in Greece, your verdict, whether good or bad,
would be a matter solely for yourselves to contem-
plate. But where this man is concerned, whatever
judgement you may give will be discussed by every
Greek, since it is common knowledge that the conduct
of your ancestors was just the opposite of his. He
won notoriety by his voyage to Rhodes and the discreditable report of you which he made officially to
the Rhodians and to those merchants residing there ;
merchants who sailed round the whole Greek world
on their business and passed on the news of Athens
which they had heard from Leocrates. It is important
therefore to reach a correct verdict upon him. For
you must realize, Athenians, that you would be held
to have neglected the virtues which chiefly distinguish
you from the rest of mankind, piety towards the
gods, reverence for your ancestors and ambition for
your country, if this man were to escape punishment
at your hands.

I am asking you, Athenians, to listen to my
accusation to the end and not to be impatient if I
begin with the history of Athens at the time under
discussion ; you may reserve your anger for the men
whose fault it is that I am now compelled to recall
those happenings. After the battle of Chaeronea
you all gathered hastily to the Assembly, and the
people decreed that the women and children should
be brought from the countryside inside the walls and

---

[4] ἠκηκόεσαν Es : ἀκηκόεσαν N A corr. : ἀκηκόασιν A pr.
    [5] τούτου Reiske : τούτῳ codd.
    [6] δόξαιτ' N corr. : δόξοιτ' N pr. A.
    [7] ὀργίζεσθαι A N pr. : ὀργίζεσθε N corr.
    [8] δι' οὓς Coraes : καὶ δι' οὓς codd.

25

εἰς τὰς φυλακὰς τῶν Ἀθηναίων καὶ τῶν ἄλλων
τῶν οἰκούντων Ἀθήνησι, καθ' ὅ τι ἂν αὐτοῖς δοκῇ.
17 Λεωκράτης δὲ τούτων οὐδενὸς φροντίσας, συσκευασάμενος ἃ εἶχε χρήματα, μετὰ τῶν οἰκετῶν
ἐπὶ τὸν λέμβον κατεκόμισε, τῆς νεὼς ἤδη περὶ
[150] τὴν ἀκτὴν ἐξορμούσης,[1] καὶ περὶ δείλην ὀψίαν
αὐτὸς μετὰ τῆς ἑταίρας Εἰρηνίδος κατὰ μέσην τὴν
ἀκτὴν διὰ τῆς πυλίδος ἐξελθὼν πρὸς τὴν ναῦν
προσέπλευσε καὶ ᾤχετο φεύγων, οὔτε τοὺς λιμένας
τῆς πόλεως ἐλεῶν ἐξ ὧν ἀνήγετο, οὔτε τὰ τείχη
τῆς πατρίδος αἰσχυνόμενος ὧν τὴν φυλακὴν ἔρημον τὸ καθ' αὑτὸν μέρος κατέλιπεν· οὐδὲ[2] τὴν
ἀκρόπολιν καὶ τὸ ἱερὸν τοῦ Διὸς τοῦ σωτῆρος καὶ
τῆς Ἀθηνᾶς τῆς σωτείρας ἀφορῶν καὶ προδι-
δοὺς ἐφοβήθη, οὓς αὐτίκα σώσοντας[3] ἑαυτὸν ἐκ
18 τῶν κινδύνων ἐπικαλεῖται. καταχθεὶς δὲ καὶ ἀφικόμενος εἰς Ῥόδον, ὥσπερ τῇ πατρίδι μεγάλας
εὐτυχίας εὐαγγελιζόμενος, ἀπήγγειλεν[4] ὡς τὸ μὲν
ἄστυ τῆς πόλεως ἑαλωκὸς καταλίποι, τὸν δὲ
Πειραιέα πολιορκούμενον, αὐτὸς δὲ μόνος δια-
σωθεὶς ἥκοι· καὶ οὐκ ᾐσχύνθη τὴν τῆς πατρίδος
ἀτυχίαν αὐτοῦ σωτηρίαν προσαγορεύσας. οὕτω
δὲ σφόδρα ταῦτ' ἐπίστευσαν οἱ Ῥόδιοι ὥστε
τριήρεις πληρώσαντες τὰ πλοῖα κατῆγον, καὶ τῶν
ἐμπόρων καὶ τῶν ναυκλήρων οἱ παρεσκευασμένοι
δεῦρο πλεῖν αὐτοῦ τὸν σῖτον ἐξείλοντο καὶ τἆλλα
19 χρήματα διὰ τοῦτον. καὶ ὅτι ταῦτ' ἀληθῆ λέγω,
ἀναγνώσεται ὑμῖν τὰς μαρτυρίας ἁπάντων, πρῶτον
μὲν τὰς τῶν γειτόνων καὶ τῶν ἐν τῷ τόπῳ τούτῳ

---

[1] ἐξορμούσης Taylor : ἐξορμώσης codd.
[2] οὐδὲ Heinrich : οὔτε codd.
[3] σώσοντας N : σώσαντας A.

that the generals should appoint any Athenians or
other residents at Athens to defence duties as they
thought fit.[a] Leocrates ignored all these provisions.
He collected what belongings he had and with his
slaves' assistance placed them in the ship's boat, the
ship itself being already anchored off the shore.
Late in the evening he went out himself with his
mistress Irenis through the postern gate on to the
open beach and sailed out to the ship. And so he
disappeared, a deserter, untouched by pity for the
city's harbours from which he was putting out to sea,
and unashamed in face of the walls which, for his
own part, he left undefended. Looking back at the
Acropolis and the temple of Zeus the Saviour and
Athena the Protectress, which he had betrayed, he
had no fear, though he will presently call upon these
gods to save him from danger. He landed and entered
Rhodes, where, as if he were bringing good news of
great successes for his country, he announced that the
main city had been captured when he left it, that
the Piraeus was blockaded and that he was the only
one who had escaped, feeling no shame at speaking
of his country's ruin as the occasion of his own safety.
The Rhodians took his news so seriously that they
manned triremes and brought in their merchantmen ;
and the traders and shipowners who had intended to
sail to Athens unloaded their corn and other cargoes
there, because of Leocrates. To prove the truth of
this account the clerk shall read you the evidence of
all concerned : first the testimony of the neighbours
and the men living in this district who know that the

[a] The proposer of this measure was Hyperides, *cf.* § 41.
See Life of Hyperides and Hyperides, fragment 18, note.

---

[4] ἀπήγγειλεν N : ἀπήγγελλεν A.

κατοικούντων, οἳ τοῦτον ἴσασιν ἐν τῷ πολέμῳ
φυγόντα[1] καὶ ἐκπλεύσαντα Ἀθήνηθεν, ἔπειτα τῶν
παραγενομένων εἰς Ῥόδον ὅτε Λεωκράτης ταῦτ᾽
ἀπήγγελλε, μετὰ δὲ ταῦτα τὴν Φυρκίνου μαρτυρίαν,
ὃν καὶ ὑμῶν ⟨ἴσασιν⟩[2] οἱ πολλοὶ κατηγοροῦντα ἐν
τῷ δήμῳ τούτου, ὡς καὶ μεγάλα καταβεβλαφὼς[3]
εἴη τὴν πεντηκοστήν, μετέχων αὐτῆς.[4]

20   Πρὸ δὲ τοῦ ἀναβαίνειν τοὺς μάρτυρας βραχέα
βούλομαι διαλεχθῆναι ὑμῖν. οὐ γὰρ ἀγνοεῖτε, ὦ
ἄνδρες, οὔτε τὰς παρασκευὰς τῶν κρινομένων οὔτε
τὰς δεήσεις τῶν ἐξαιτουμένων, ἀλλ᾽ ἀκριβῶς ἐπίστασθε ὅτι χρημάτων ἕνεκα καὶ χάριτος πολλοὶ
ἐπείσθησαν τῶν μαρτύρων ἢ ἀμνημονεῖν ἢ μὴ
ἐλθεῖν ἢ ἑτέραν πρόφασιν εὑρεῖν. ἀξιοῦτε οὖν τοὺς
μάρτυρας ἀναβαίνειν καὶ μὴ[5] ὀκνεῖν, μηδὲ περὶ
πλείονος ποιεῖσθαι τὰς χάριτας ὑμῶν καὶ τῆς
πόλεως, ἀλλ᾽ ἀποδιδόναι τῇ πατρίδι τἀληθῆ καὶ
τὰ δίκαια, καὶ μὴ λείπειν τὴν τάξιν ταύτην μηδὲ[6]
μιμεῖσθαι Λεωκράτην, ἢ λαβόντας τὰ ἱερὰ κατὰ
τὸν νόμον ἐξομόσασθαι. ἐὰν δὲ μηδέτερον τούτων
ποιῶσιν, ὑπὲρ ὑμῶν καὶ τῶν νόμων καὶ τῆς δημοκρατίας κλητεύσομεν[7] αὐτούς. λέγε τὰς μαρτυρίας.

----

[1] φυγόντα F. A. Wolf : φεύγοντα codd.
[2] ἴσασιν hic add. Ald., idem post τούτου N corr.[2].
[3] καταβεβλαφὼς Jenicke : καὶ βλάβους codd. : βεβλαφὼς
Sauppe.
[4] αὐτῆς N : αὐτοῖς A.
[5] καὶ μὴ Blass : μηδὲ codd.
[6] μηδὲ N : καὶ μὴ A corr. : καὶ A pr.
[7] κλητεύσομεν N : κλητεύσωμεν A.

----

[a] The πεντηκοστή, a 2 per cent tax on imports and exports,
was let out by the πωληταί to the highest bidder, usually a

28

defendant ran away during the war and sailed from
Athens, next that of the people present at Rhodes
when Leocrates was delivering this news, and finally
the evidence of Phyrcinus, whom most of you know
as the accuser of Leocrates in the Assembly for
having seriously harmed the two per cent tax in
which he had an interest.[a]

But before the witnesses come up I want to say
a few words to you. You are well acquainted, gentlemen, with the tricks of defendants and with the requests made by others asking pardon for them. You
know too well that desire for bribes and favours
induces many witnesses to forget what they know,
to fail to appear, or to contrive some other excuse.
Ask the witnesses therefore to come up without
hesitation and not to put offered favours before your
interests and the state. Ask them to pay their
country the debt of truth and justice which they
owe and not to follow the example of Leocrates by
failing in this duty. Otherwise let them swear the
oath of disclaimer with their hands on the sacrifice.[b]
If they refuse both these alternatives, we will summons them in the interest of yourselves, our laws and
our democracy. Read the evidence.

company. Leocrates was evidently a member of such a
company, and by frightening away trade from Athens
diminished the returns from the tax. *Cf.* Andocid. i. 133.

 [b] At Athens depositions bearing on a case were submitted
in writing to a magistrate at a preliminary inquiry (ἀνάκρισις),
and no fresh evidence was allowed at the trial itself. But if
a witness refused to appear at the ἀνάκρισις he might be
called to the trial by either party, on pain of a 1000 drachma
fine, to vouch for the truth of a written statement which the
clerk would read out to him. If he professed ignorance he
had to support his claim with a solemn oath (ἐξωμοσία).
See Isae. ix. 18 ; Aeschin. i. 45 ; Dem. xix. 176, etc.

ΜΑΡΤΥΡΙΑΙ

21 Μετὰ ταῦτα τοίνυν, ὦ ἄνδρες, ἐπειδὴ χρόνος
ἐγένετο, καὶ ἀφικνεῖτο Ἀθήνηθεν πλοῖα εἰς τὴν
Ῥόδον, καὶ φανερὸν ἦν ὅτι οὐδὲν δεινὸν ἐγεγόνει
περὶ τὴν πόλιν, φοβηθεὶς ἐκπλεῖ πάλιν ἐκ τῆς
Ῥόδου καὶ ἀφικνεῖται εἰς Μέγαρα· καὶ ᾤκει ἐν
Μεγάροις πλείω ἢ πέντε ἔτη προστάτην ἔχων
Μεγαρέα, οὐδὲ τὰ ὅρια τῆς χώρας αἰσχυνόμενος,
ἀλλ' ἐν[1] γειτόνων τῆς ἐκθρεψάσης αὐτὸν πατρίδος
22 μετοικῶν. καὶ οὕτως αὐτοῦ κατεγνώκει ἀίδιον
φυγὴν ὥστε μεταπεμψάμενος ἐντεῦθεν Ἀμύνταν
τὸν τὴν ἀδελφὴν ἔχοντα αὐτοῦ. τὴν πρεσβυτέραν
καὶ τῶν φίλων Ἀντιγένην Ξυπεταιόνα,[2] καὶ δεηθεὶς
τοῦ κηδεστοῦ πρίασθαι παρ' αὐτοῦ τἀνδράποδα
καὶ τὴν οἰκίαν, ἀποδόσθαι ταλάντου, κἀπὸ τούτου
προσέταξε τοῖς τε χρήσταις ἀποδοῦναι τὰ ὀφειλόμενα καὶ τοὺς ἐράνους διενεγκεῖν, τὸ δὲ λοιπὸν
23 αὐτῷ ἀποδοῦναι. διοικήσας δὲ ταῦτα πάντα ὁ
Ἀμύντας αὐτὸς πάλιν ἀποδίδοται τἀνδράποδα
πέντε καὶ τριάκοντα μνῶν Τιμοχάρει Ἀχαρνεῖ
τῷ τὴν νεωτέραν ἔχοντι τούτου ἀδελφήν· ἀργύριον
δὲ οὐκ ἔχων δοῦναι ὁ Τιμοχάρης, συνθήκας ποιη-
σάμενος καὶ θέμενος παρὰ Λυσικλεῖ μίαν μνᾶν[3]
τόκον ἔφερε τῷ Ἀμύντᾳ. ἵνα δὲ μὴ λόγον οἴησθε[4]
εἶναι ἀλλ' εἰδῆτε τὴν ἀλήθειαν, ἀναγνώσεται καὶ
τούτων ὑμῖν τὰς μαρτυρίας. εἰ μὲν οὖν ζῶν

---

[1] ἐν N corr.[2] : ἐκ N pr. A.

[2] Ξυπεταιόνα Rehdantz : Ξυπετεόνα N pr. : Ξυπετεῶνα N corr.[2] A.

[3] μίαν μνᾶν] ci. ἡμιμναῖον Maetzner, δραχμὴν τῆς μνᾶς Es, μίαν τῆς μνᾶς Blass.

Evidence

To resume then, gentlemen. After this, time passed, merchant ships from Athens continued to arrive at Rhodes, and it was clear that no disaster had overtaken the city. So Leocrates grew alarmed, and embarking again, left Rhodes for Megara. He stayed at Megara for over five years with a Megarian as his patron, unashamed at living on the boundaries of Attica, an alien on the borders of the land that nurtured him. He had condemned himself so finally to a lifetime of exile that he sent for Amyntas, the husband of his elder sister, and Antigenes of Xypete, a friend of his, to come to him from Athens, and asked his brother-in-law to buy his house and slaves from him, selling them to him for a talent. Out of this sum he arranged that his debts should be settled, his loans paid off [a] and the balance restored to him. After concluding all this business Amyntas resold the slaves himself for thirty-five minas to Timochares of Acharnae who had married Leocrates' younger sister. Timochares had no ready money for the purchase and so drew up an agreement which he lodged with Lysicles [b] and paid Amyntas interest of one mina. To convince you that this is fact, lest you should think it idle talk, the clerk shall read you the evidence relating to these points also. If Amyntas

---

[a] For these loans compare Hyp. iii. 7 and note.
[b] A Lysicles of Leuconoë, possibly a banker, is mentioned in a similar connexion in Hyp. iii. 9. The rate of interest here given (a mina per month) amounts to $34\frac{3}{7}\%$, which is very high, even though from 12% to 18% was a normal rate for Greeks. Hence the text has been suspected, but none of the emendations can be regarded as certain.

---

[4] οἴησθε Ald. : οἴεσθε codd.

ἐτύγχανεν ὁ Ἀμύντας, ἐκεῖνον ⟨ἂν⟩[1] αὐτὸν παρει-
[151] χόμην· νυνὶ δ' ὑμῖν καλῶ τοὺς συνειδότας. καί
μοι λέγε ταύτην τὴν μαρτυρίαν, ὡς ἐπρίατο παρὰ
Λεωκράτους ἐν Μεγάροις τὰ ἀνδράποδα Ἀμύντας
καὶ τὴν οἰκίαν.

ΜΑΡΤΥΡΙΑ

24 Ἀκούσατε δὲ καὶ ὡς ἀπέλαβε τετταράκοντα
μνᾶς παρ' Ἀμύντου Φιλόμηλος Χολαργεὺς καὶ
Μενέλαος ὁ πρεσβεύσας ὡς[2] βασιλέα.

ΜΑΡΤΥΡΙΑ[3]

Λαβὲ δέ μοι καὶ τὴν Τιμοχάρους τοῦ πριαμένου
τἀνδράποδα παρ' Ἀμύντου πέντε καὶ τριάκοντα
μνῶν, καὶ τὰς συνθήκας.

ΜΑΡΤΥΡΙΑ. ΣΥΝΘΗΚΑΙ

25 Τῶν μὲν μαρτύρων ἀκηκόατε, ὦ ἄνδρες· ἄξιον
δ' ἐστὶν ἐφ' οἷς μέλλω λέγειν ἀγανακτῆσαι καὶ
μισῆσαι τουτονὶ Λεωκράτην. οὐ γὰρ ἐξήρκεσε
τὸ σῶμα τὸ ἑαυτοῦ καὶ τὰ χρήματα μόνον ὑπεκθέσθαι, ἀλλὰ καὶ τὰ ἱερὰ τὰ πατρῷα, ἃ τοῖς ὑμετέροις νομίμοις καὶ πατρίοις[4] ἔθεσιν οἱ πρόγονοι
παρέδοσαν αὐτῷ ἱδρυσάμενοι, ταῦτα μετεπέμψατο
εἰς Μέγαρα καὶ ἐξήγαγεν ἐκ τῆς χώρας, οὐδὲ τὴν
ἐπωνυμίαν τῶν πατρῴων ἱερῶν φοβηθείς, ὅτι ἐκ
τῆς πατρίδος αὐτὰ κινήσας συμφεύγειν αὐτῷ,

---

[1] ἂν add. Bekker.
[2] ὡς Blass : εἰς N : πρὸς A.

had been still alive I should have produced him in person ; since he is not, I am summoning for you the men who know the facts. Please read me this evidence showing that Amyntas bought the slaves and house from Leocrates at Megara.

Evidence

Now hear how Philomelos of Cholargus and Mene-laüs, once an envoy to the King, received from Amyntas forty minas owed them.

Evidence

Please take the evidence of Timochares who bought the slaves from Amyntas for thirty-five minas, and also his agreement.

Evidence. Agreement

You have heard the witnesses, gentlemen. What I am now going to say will give you good reason for indignation and hatred of this man Leocrates. For he was not content simply to remove his own person and his goods. There were the sacred images of his family which his forbears established and which, in keeping with your customs and ancestral tradition, they afterwards entrusted to him. These too he had sent to Megara. He took them out of the country without a qualm at the name " ancestral images " or at the thought that he had uprooted them from their country and expected them to share his exile, to

---

[3] ΜΑΡΤΥΡΙΑ Bekker : ΜΑΡΤΥΡΙΑΙ NA.
[4] πατρίοις Dobree : πατρῴοις codd.

ἐκλείποντα[1] τοὺς νεὼς καὶ τὴν χώραν ἣν κατεῖχεν,[2]
ἠξίωσε, καὶ ἱδρῦσθαι[3] ἐπὶ ξένης καὶ ἀλλοτρίας,
καὶ εἶναι ὀθνεῖα τῇ χώρᾳ καὶ τοῖς νομίμοις τοῖς
26 κατὰ τὴν Μεγαρέων πόλιν εἰθισμένοις. καὶ οἱ
μὲν πατέρες ὑμῶν †τὴν Ἀθηνᾶν ὡς τὴν χώραν
εἰληχυῖαν†[4] [ὁμώνυμον αὐτῇ] τὴν πατρίδα προσ-
ηγόρευον Ἀθήνας, ἵν' οἱ τιμῶντες τὴν θεὸν τὴν
ὁμώνυμον αὐτῇ[5] πόλιν μὴ ἐγκαταλίπωσι· Λεωκράτης δ' οὔτε νομίμων οὔτε πατρίδος[6] οὔθ' ἱερῶν
φροντίσας τὸ καθ' ἑαυτὸν ἐξαγώγιμον ὑμῖν καὶ
τὴν παρὰ τῶν θεῶν βοήθειαν ἐποίησε. καὶ οὐκ
ἐξήρκεσεν αὐτῷ τοσαῦτα καὶ τηλικαῦτα τὴν πόλιν
ἀδικῆσαι, ἀλλ' οἰκῶν ἐν Μεγάροις, οἷς παρ' ὑμῶν
ἐξεκομίσατο χρήμασιν ἀφορμῇ χρώμενος, ἐκ τῆς
Ἠπείρου παρὰ Κλεοπάτρας εἰς Λευκάδα ἐσιτήγει
27 καὶ ἐκεῖθεν εἰς Κόρινθον. καίτοι, ὦ ἄνδρες, καὶ
περὶ τούτων οἱ ὑμέτεροι νόμοι τὰς ἐσχάτας τιμωρίας ὁρίζουσιν, ἐάν τις Ἀθηναίων ἄλλοσέ ποι
σιτηγήσῃ ἢ ὡς ὑμᾶς. ἔπειτα τὸν προδόντα μὲν
ἐν τῷ πολέμῳ, σιτηγήσαντα δὲ παρὰ τοὺς νόμους,
μὴ φροντίσαντα δὲ μήτε ἱερῶν μήτε πατρίδος μήτε
νόμων, τοῦτον ἔχοντες ἐπὶ[7] τῇ ὑμετέρᾳ ψήφῳ οὐκ
ἀποκτενεῖτε καὶ παράδειγμα τοῖς ἄλλοις[8] ποιήσετε;

---

[1] ἐκλείποντα] ἐκλιπόντα Coraes.
[2] κατεῖχεν Blass : κατεῖχον codd.
[3] ἱδρῦσθαι Bekker : ἱδρύσασθαι codd.
[4] Verba τὴν . . . εἰληχυῖαν obelis inclusi : ὁμώνυμον αὐτῇ
secl. Heinrich : verba τὴν Ἀθηνᾶν usque ad αὐτῇ delenda
ci. Bekker : τιμῶντες ante τὴν Ἀθηνᾶν add. Taylor : τῇ
Ἀθηνᾷ . . . εἰληχυίᾳ Coraes : ὡς τὴν χώραν τῆς Ἀθηνᾶς εἰλη-
χυίας Blass.
[5] αὐτῇ] secl. Schoene : αὐτὴν Rehdantz.

leave the temples and the land which they had
occupied and be established in a strange and uncon-
genial place, as aliens to the soil and to the rites
traditionally observed in Megara. Your fathers,
⟨honouring⟩[a] Athena as the deity to whom their land
had been allotted, called their native city Athens, so
that men who revered the goddess should not desert
the city which bore her name. By disregarding
custom, country, and sacred images Leocrates did all
in his power to cause even your divine protection to
be exported. Moreover, to have wronged the city on
this enormous scale was not enough for him. Living
at Megara and using as capital the money which he
had withdrawn from Athens he shipped corn, bought
from Cleopatra,[b] from Epirus to Leucas and from
there to Corinth. And yet, gentlemen, in cases of
this sort your laws lay down the most severe penalties
if an Athenian transports corn to any place other
than your city. When therefore a man has been a
traitor in war and has broken the laws in transporting
corn, when he has had no regard for sacred things and
none for his country or the laws, if you have him at
the mercy of your vote, will you not execute him and
make an example of him to others? If you do not it

[a] In order to give what must be the general sense of this
corrupt passage I have translated Taylor's suggested addition of τιμῶντες before τὴν 'Αθηνᾶν and ignored the words
ὁμώνυμον αὐτῇ. But the Greek text cannot be restored with
certainty.

[b] Cleopatra, the sister of Alexander the Great, was married
to Alexander of Epirus in 336 and must now have been
acting as regent for her husband while he was at war in Italy.

---

[6] πατρίδος Frohberger : πατρῴων codd.
[7] ἐπὶ N : ἐν A : ὑπὸ Herwerden (coll. §§ 2, 115).
[8] τοῖς ἄλλοις N : τοῖς ἄλλοις ἀνθρώποις A.

πάντων ἄρ' ἀνθρώπων ῥᾳθυμότατοι ἔσεσθε, καὶ
ἥκιστα ἐπὶ τοῖς δεινοῖς ὀργιζόμενοι.

28   Καὶ ταῦτα δ', ὦ ἄνδρες, ἐμοῦ θεωρήσατε ὡς
δικαίαν τὴν ἐξέτασιν ποιουμένου περὶ τούτων. οὐ
γὰρ οἶμαι δεῖν ὑμᾶς ὑπὲρ τηλικούτων ἀδικημάτων
εἰκάζοντας ἀλλὰ τὴν ἀλήθειαν εἰδότας ψηφίζε-
σθαι, καὶ τοὺς μάρτυρας μὴ δώσοντας ἔλεγχον
μαρτυρεῖν ἀλλὰ δεδωκότας. προὐκαλεσάμην[1] γὰρ
αὐτοὺς πρόκλησιν ὑπὲρ τούτων ἁπάντων γράψας
καὶ ἀξιῶν βασανίζειν τοὺς τούτου οἰκέτας, ᾗ[2] προκλήσεις προκαλεῖσθαι ἄξιόν ἐστιν. καί μοι λέγε
ταύτην.

ΠΡΟΚΛΗΣΙΣ

29   Ἀκούετε, ὦ ἄνδρες, τῆς προκλήσεως. ἅμα
τοίνυν ταύτην Λεωκράτης[3] οὐκ ἐδέχετο καὶ κατε-
μαρτύρει αὐτοῦ ὅτι προδότης τῆς πατρίδος ἐστίν·
ὁ γὰρ τὸν παρὰ τῶν[4] συνειδότων ἔλεγχον φυγὼν
ὡμολόγηκεν ἀληθῆ εἶναι τὰ εἰσηγγελμένα. τίς
γὰρ ὑμῶν οὐκ οἶδεν ὅτι περὶ τῶν ἀμφισβητου-
μένων πολὺ δοκεῖ δικαιότατον καὶ δημοτικώτατον[5]
εἶναι, ὅταν οἰκέται ἢ θεράπαιναι συνειδῶσιν ἃ δεῖ,
τούτους ἐλέγχειν καὶ βασανίζειν, καὶ τοῖς ἔργοις
μᾶλλον ἢ τοῖς λόγοις πιστεύειν, ἄλλως τε καὶ περὶ
πραγμάτων κοινῶν καὶ μεγάλων καὶ συμφερόντων
30 τῇ πόλει; ἐγὼ τοίνυν τοσοῦτον ἀφέστηκα τοῦ
ἀδίκως τὴν εἰσαγγελίαν κατὰ Λεωκράτους ποιή-

---

[1] προὐκαλεσάμην Taylor : παρεκαλεσάμην codd.
[2] ᾗ προκλήσεις προκαλεῖσθαι ἄξιόν ἐστιν Jernstedt : η προκλήσεις προκλήσοι ἄξιόν ἐστι N : om. A dimidio versu post
οἰκέτας vacuo relicto : ἧς ἀκοῦσαι ἄξιόν ἐστιν Blass.
[3] Λεωκράτης Ald. : ἃ σωκράτης codd.
[4] τὸν παρὰ τῶν Schoemann : τὸν πάντων A : τῶν πάντων N.
[5] δημοτικώτατον Ernesti : δημοτικὸν codd.

will show an apathy and lack of righteous indignation completely without parallel.

Consider these further proofs that my inquiry into this question has been just ; for it is my opinion that in dealing with such serious crimes you must base your vote, not on conjecture, but on certainty ; and I hold that witnesses must prove their good faith before, not after, they give their evidence. I submitted to the defence a written challenge on all these points and demanded the slaves of Leocrates for torture, according to the right procedure for making challenges. Please read the challenge.

Challenge

You hear the challenge, gentlemen. By the very act of refusing to accept this Leocrates condemned himself as a traitor to his country. For whoever refuses to allow the testing of those who share his secrets has confessed that the charges of the indictment are true. Every one of you knows that in matters of dispute it is considered by far the justest and most democratic course, when there are male or female slaves, who possess the necessary information, to examine these by torture and so have facts to go upon instead of hearsay, particularly when the case concerns the public and is of vital interest to the state.[a] Certainly I cannot be called unjust in my

[a] The right of torturing slave witnesses does not seem often to have been exercised, and it is doubtful whether evidence obtained in this way was really very highly rated. No man was bound to submit his slaves for examination, and accusers often demanded them in such a way as to ensure a refusal which gave them an additional argument against the defendant. To strengthen their position they

σασθαι, ὅσον ἐγὼ μὲν ἐβουλόμην τοῖς ἰδίοις
κινδύνοις[1] ἐν τοῖς Λεωκράτους οἰκέταις καὶ θεραπαίναις βασανισθεῖσι τὸν ἔλεγχον γενέσθαι, οὑτοσὶ
δὲ διὰ τὸ συνειδέναι ἑαυτῷ[2] οὐχ ὑπέμεινεν ἀλλ᾽
ἔφυγε. καίτοι, ὦ ἄνδρες, πολὺ θᾶττον οἱ Λεωκράτους οἰκέται καὶ θεράπαιναι τῶν γενομένων[3] ἄν
31 τι ἠρνήθησαν ἢ τὰ μὴ ὄντα τοῦ αὐτῶν δεσπότου
[152] κατεψεύσαντο. χωρὶς τοίνυν τούτων Λεωκράτης
ἀναβοήσεται αὐτίκα ὡς ἰδιώτης ὤν, καὶ ὑπὸ τῆς
τοῦ ῥήτορος καὶ συκοφάντου δεινότητος ἀναρπαζό-
μενος· ἐγὼ δ᾽ ἡγοῦμαι πάντας ὑμᾶς εἰδέναι ὅτι τῶν
μὲν δεινῶν καὶ συκοφαντεῖν ἐπιχειρούντων ἔργον
ἐστὶν ἅμα τοῦτο προαιρεῖσθαι καὶ ζητεῖν τὰ
χωρία ταῦτα, ἐν οἷς τοὺς παραλογισμοὺς κατὰ
τῶν ἀγωνιζομένων ποιήσονται, τῶν δὲ δικαίως
τὰς κρίσεις ἐνισταμένων καὶ τοὺς ἐνόχους ταῖς
ἀραῖς ἀκριβῶς ἀποδεικνύντων τἀναντία φαίνεσθαι
32 τούτοις ποιοῦντας, ὥσπερ ἡμεῖς.[4] οὑτωσὶ δὲ
διαλογίζεσθε περὶ τούτων παρ᾽ ὑμῖν αὐτοῖς. τίνας
ἀδύνατον ἦν τῇ δεινότητι καὶ ταῖς παρασκευαῖς
ταῖς τοῦ λόγου παραγαγεῖν; κατὰ φύσιν τοίνυν
βασανιζόμενοι πᾶσαν τὴν ἀλήθειαν περὶ πάντων
τῶν ἀδικημάτων ἔμελλον φράσειν οἱ οἰκέται καὶ
αἱ θεράπαιναι. ἀλλὰ τούτους Λεωκράτης[5] παραδοῦναι ἔφυγε, καὶ ταῦτα οὐκ ἀλλοτρίους ἀλλ᾽
33 αὑτοῦ ὄντας. τίνας δὲ δυνατὸν εἶναι δοκεῖ τοῖς

---

[1] τοῖς ἰδίοις κινδύνοις Reiske : τοὺς ἰδίους κινδύνους codd.
[2] ἑαυτῷ N : ἑαυτὸν A.
[3] γενομένων Bekker : λεγομένων codd.
[4] ἡμεῖς N : ὑμεῖς A.
[5] Λεωκράτης Thalheim : ὁ Λεωκράτης codd.

---

naturally tried, as Lycurgus does here, to impress the jury

prosecution of Leocrates. I was even willing at my
own risk to let the proof rest on the torture of his
male and female slaves, but the defendant, realizing
his guilt, rejected the offer instead of accepting it.
And yet, gentlemen, the male and female slaves of
Leocrates would have been far readier to deny any of
the real facts than to invent lies against their master.
Apart from this, Leocrates will presently proclaim
that he is a simple citizen and is falling a prey to the
cunning of an orator and false informer. But I am
sure you all know well the characteristic behaviour
of those unscrupulous men who try to lay false information ; for when they choose their part they look
for vantage-points on which to quibble against those
on trial, whereas the man whose aims in going to
law are honest, who brings proofs to bear against
those who come under the herald's curse,[a] does just
the opposite, as I myself am doing. Look at the
present case yourselves in this way. Which people
could not have been misled by cunning or a deceptive
argument ? The male and female slaves. Naturally,
when tortured, they would have told the whole truth
about all the offences. But it was just these persons
whom Leocrates refused to hand over, though they
were his and no one else's. On the other hand which

---

with the value of such evidence (*cf.* Isae. viii. 12 etc.) : but
Antiphon must be nearer the mark when he points out that
a man on the rack would say anything to gratify his torturers
(Antiph. v. 32).

[a] Before meetings of the Assembly and the Council a curse
was pronounced by the herald against all who might be
acting treasonably against the state (see Dem. xix. 70).

λόγοις ψυχαγωγῆσαι, καὶ τὴν ὑγρότητα αὐτῶν
τοῦ ἤθους τοῖς δακρύοις εἰς ἔλεον προαγαγέσθαι;
τοὺς δικαστάς. ἐνταῦθα Λεωκράτης ὁ προδότης
τῆς πατρίδος ἐλήλυθεν, οὐδὲν ἕτερον ἢ φοβούμενος
μὴ ἐκ τῆς αὐτῆς οἰκίας οἵ τ᾽ ἐξελέγχοντες τῷ
ἔργῳ καὶ ὁ ἐξελεγχόμενος γένηται. τί γὰρ ἔδει
προφάσεων ἢ λόγων ἢ σκήψεως;[1] ἁπλοῦν τὸ
34 δίκαιον, ῥᾴδιον τὸ ἀληθές, βραχὺς ὁ ἔλεγχος. εἰ
μὲν ὁμολογεῖ τὰ ἐν τῇ εἰσαγγελίᾳ ἀληθῆ καὶ ὅσια
εἶναι, τί οὐ τῆς ἐκ τῶν νόμων τιμωρίας τυγχάνει;
εἰ δὲ μή φησι ταῦτα ἀληθῆ εἶναι, τί οὐ παραδέδωκε
τοὺς οἰκέτας καὶ τὰς θεραπαίνας; προσήκει[2] γὰρ
τὸν ὑπὲρ προδοσίας[3] κινδυνεύοντα καὶ παραδιδόναι[4]
βασανίζειν καὶ μηδένα τῶν ἀκριβεστάτων ἐλέγχων
35 φεύγειν. ἀλλ᾽ οὐδὲν τούτων ἔπραξεν. ἀλλὰ
καταμεμαρτυρηκὼς ἑαυτοῦ ὅτι προδότης ἐστὶ τῆς
πατρίδος καὶ τῶν ἱερῶν καὶ τῶν νόμων, ἀξιώσει
ὑμᾶς ἐναντία ταῖς αὐτοῦ ὁμολογίαις καὶ μαρτυ-
ρίαις ψηφίσασθαι. καὶ πῶς δίκαιόν ἐστι τὸν
τὴν ἐξουσίαν τῆς ἀπολογίας αὐτοῦ ἐξ ἄλλων τε
πολλῶν καὶ ἐκ τοῦ μὴ δέξασθαι τὰ δίκαια περιηρη-
μένον, τοῦτον ἐᾶσαι ὑμᾶς αὐτοὺς ὑπὲρ τῶν ὁμολογουμένων ἀδικημάτων ἐξαπατῆσαι;
36 Περὶ μὲν οὖν τῆς προκλήσεως καὶ τοῦ ἀδικήματος, ὅτι ὁμολογούμενόν ἐστιν, ἱκανῶς ὑμᾶς
ἡγοῦμαι, ὦ ἄνδρες, μεμαθηκέναι· ἐν οἷς δὲ καιροῖς
καὶ ἡλίκοις κινδύνοις τὴν πόλιν οὖσαν Λεωκράτης
προδέδωκεν ἀναμνῆσαι ὑμᾶς βούλομαι. καί μοι
λαβὲ τὸ ψήφισμα, γραμματεῦ, τὸ Ὑπερείδου καὶ
ἀνάγιγνωσκε.

people could he probably impose upon by arguments, appealing to their softer side by his tears and so winning their sympathy ? The jury. Leocrates, the betrayer of his country, has come into court with only one fear, namely that the witnesses who by certain proofs expose the criminal will be produced from the same household as the man whom they expose. What was the use of pretexts, pleas, excuses ? Justice is plain, the truth easy and the proof brief. If he admits that the articles of the indictment are true and right, why does he not suffer punishment as the laws require? But if he claims that they are false, why has he not handed over his male and female slaves ? When a man is up for treason he should submit his slaves for torture, without evading a single one of the most searching tests. Leocrates did nothing of the sort. Though he has condemned himself as a traitor to his country, a traitor to his gods and to the laws, he will ask you when you vote to contradict his own admissions and his own evidence. How can it be right, when a man has refused a fair offer and in many other ways also has robbed himself of the means of defence, for you to let him mislead your judgement on crimes to which he has confessed ?

So much for the challenge and the crime. I think you have been shown well enough, gentlemen, that that part is beyond dispute. I want now to remind you what emergencies, what great dangers the city was facing when Leocrates turned traitor to it. Please take the decree of Hyperides, clerk, and read it.

---

[1] σκήψεως A : σκέψεως N.
[2] προσήκει] προσῆκεν Blass.
[3] Post προδοσίας usque ad § 98 mancus N.
[4] Post παραδιδόναι codd. καὶ habent, secl. Taylor.

37 Ἀκούετε τοῦ ψηφίσματος, ὦ ἄνδρες, ὅτι τὴν
βουλὴν τοὺς πεντακοσίους καταβαίνειν εἰς Πειραιᾶ
χρηματιοῦσαν περὶ φυλακῆς τοῦ Πειραιέως ἐν
τοῖς ὅπλοις ἔδοξε, καὶ πράττειν διεσκευασμένην
ὅ τι ἂν δοκῇ τῷ δήμῳ συμφέρον εἶναι. καίτοι,
ὦ ἄνδρες, εἰ οἱ ἀφειμένοι[1] τοῦ στρατεύεσθαι ἕνεκα
τοῦ βουλεύεσθαι ὑπὲρ τῆς πόλεως ἐν τῇ τῶν
στρατιωτῶν τάξει διέτριβον, ἆρ᾽ ὑμῖν δοκοῦσι
μικροὶ καὶ οἱ τυχόντες φόβοι τότε τὴν πόλιν
38 κατασχεῖν; ἐν οἷς Λεωκράτης οὑτοσὶ καὶ αὐτὸς
ἐκ τῆς πόλεως ἀποδρὰς ᾤχετο, καὶ τὰ χρήματα
τὰ ὑπάρχοντα ἐξεκόμισε, καὶ ⟨τὰ⟩[2] ἱερὰ τὰ πατρῷα
μετεπέμψατο, καὶ εἰς τοσοῦτον προδοσίας ἦλθεν
ὥστε κατὰ τὴν τούτου[3] προαίρεσιν ἔρημοι μὲν ἦσαν
οἱ νεώ,[4] ἔρημοι δ᾽ αἱ φυλακαὶ τῶν τειχῶν, ἐξελέ-
39 λειπτο δ᾽ ἡ πόλις καὶ ἡ χώρα. καίτοι κατ᾽ ἐκείνους
τοὺς χρόνους, ὦ ἄνδρες, τίς οὐκ ἂν τὴν πόλιν
ἠλέησεν, οὐ μόνον πολίτης ἀλλὰ καὶ ξένος ἐν τοῖς
ἔμπροσθεν χρόνοις ἐπιδεδημηκώς; τίς δ᾽ ἦν
οὕτως ἢ μισόδημος τότ᾽ ἢ μισαθήναιος, ὅστις
ἐδυνήθη ἂν ἄτακτον αὐτὸν[5] ὑπομεῖναι ἰδεῖν; ἡνίκα
ἡ μὲν ἧττα καὶ τὸ γεγονὸς πάθος τῷ ⟨δήμῳ⟩[6]
προσήγγελτο, ὀρθὴ δ᾽ ἦν ἡ πόλις ἐπὶ[7] τοῖς συμ-
βεβηκόσιν, αἱ δ᾽ ἐλπίδες τῆς σωτηρίας τῷ δήμῳ
ἐν τοῖς ὑπὲρ πεντήκοντ᾽ ἔτη γεγονόσι καθειστή-
40 κεσαν, ὁρᾶν δ᾽ ἦν ἐπὶ μὲν τῶν θυρῶν γυναῖκας

---

[1] ἀφειμένοι A. G. Becker (coll. § 40): ἀφιέμενοι codd.
[2] τὰ add. Halm.   [3] τούτου Thalheim : αὐτοῦ codd.
[4] νεώ Blass (coll. §§ 1, 25, etc.): ναοί codd. qui τῶν ἱερέων
add. : secl. Heinrich.

42

Decree

You hear the decree, gentlemen. It provided that the Council of Five Hundred should go down to the Piraeus armed, to consult for the protection of that harbour, and that it should hold itself ready to do whatever seemed to be in the people's interest. And yet, if the men who had been exempted from military service so that they might deliberate upon the city's affairs were then playing the part of soldiers, do you think that the alarms which had taken hold upon the city were any trivial or ordinary fears? Yet it was then that this man Leocrates made off himself—a runaway from the city; it was then that he conveyed to safety his available property and sent back for the sacred images of his family. To such a pitch did he carry his treason that, so far as his decision went, the temples were abandoned, the posts on the wall unmanned and the town and country left deserted. And yet in those days, gentlemen, who would not have pitied the city, even though he were not a citizen but only an alien who had lived among us in previous years? Surely there was no one whose hatred of the people or of Athens was so intense that he could have endured to see himself remain outside the army. When the defeat and consequent disaster had been reported to the people and the city was tense with alarm at the news, the people's hope of safety had come to rest with the men of over fifty. Free women could be seen crouching at the doors in

---

[5] αὐτὸν Baiter et Sauppe : ἑαυτὸν Ald. : τὸν αὐτὸν codd.
[6] δήμῳ add. Ald. ; προσήγγελτο Es : τῷ προσηγγέλλετο codd. : pro τῷ, ἀρτίως Blass : στρατοπέδῳ add. Meier, στρατῷ Petrie. [7] ἐπὶ Bekker : ἐν codd.

LYCURGUS

[153] ἐλευθέρας, περιφόβους κατεπτηχυίας καὶ πυνθανο-
μένας εἰ ζῶσι, τὰς μὲν ὑπὲρ ἀνδρός, τὰς δ᾽ ὑπὲρ
πατρός, τὰς δ᾽ ὑπὲρ ἀδελφῶν, ἀναξίως αὑτῶν καὶ
τῆς πόλεως ὁρωμένας, τῶν δ᾽ ἀνδρῶν[1] τοὺς τοῖς
σώμασιν ἀπειρηκότας καὶ ταῖς ἡλικίαις[2] πρεσβυ-
τέρους καὶ ὑπὸ τῶν νόμων τοῦ στρατεύεσθαι ἀφειμένους[3] ἰδεῖν ἦν καθ᾽ ὅλην τὴν[4] πόλιν τότ᾽ ἐπὶ
γήρως ὁδῷ περιφθειρομένους,[5] διπλᾶ τὰ ἱμάτια[6]
41 ἐμπεπορπημένους; πολλῶν δὲ καὶ δεινῶν κατὰ
τὴν πόλιν γιγνομένων, καὶ πάντων τῶν πολιτῶν
τὰ μέγιστα ἠτυχηκότων, μάλιστ᾽ ἄν τις ἤλγησε
καὶ ἐδάκρυσεν ἐπὶ ταῖς τῆς πόλεως συμφοραῖς,
ἡνίχ᾽ ὁρᾶν ἦν τὸν δῆμον ψηφισάμενον τοὺς μὲν
δούλους ἐλευθέρους, τοὺς δὲ ξένους Ἀθηναίους,
τοὺς δ᾽ ἀτίμους ἐπιτίμους[7]· ὃς πρότερον[8] ἐπὶ τῷ
42 αὐτόχθων εἶναι καὶ ἐλεύθερος ἐσεμνύνετο. τοσαύτη
δ᾽ ἡ πόλις ἐκέχρητο μεταβολῇ ὥστε πρότερον μὲν
ὑπὲρ τῆς τῶν ἄλλων Ἑλλήνων ἐλευθερίας ἀγωνίζεσθαι, ἐν δὲ τοῖς τότε χρόνοις ἀγαπᾶν, ἐὰν ὑπὲρ
τῆς αὑτῶν σωτηρίας ἀσφαλῶς δύνηται διακινδυνεῦσαι,[9] καὶ πρότερον μὲν πολλῆς χώρας τῶν βαρβάρων ἐπάρχειν, τότε δὲ πρὸς Μακεδόνας ὑπὲρ
τῆς ἰδίας κινδυνεύειν· καὶ τὸν δῆμον ὃν πρότερον
Λακεδαιμόνιοι καὶ Πελοποννήσιοι καὶ οἱ τὴν
Ἀσίαν κατοικοῦντες Ἕλληνες βοηθὸν ἐπεκαλοῦντο,
οὗτος ἐδεῖτο τῶν ἐξ Ἄνδρου καὶ Κέω καὶ Τροζῆνος[10]

---

1 Verba τῶν δ᾽ ἀνδρῶν usque ad ἐμπεπορπημένους cit. Suidas
(s.v. πεπορπημένος).
2 ταῖς ἡλικίαις Suidas : τὰς ἡλικίας codd.
3 ἀφειμένους Suidas : ἀφειμένους codd.
4 τὴν et τότ᾽ Suidas : om. codd.
5 ὁδῷ περιφθειρομένους Suidas : οὐδῷ διαφθειρομένους codd.
6 τὰ ἱμάτια] om. Suidas : θαιμάτια Blass.

terror inquiring for the safety of their husbands, fathers or brothers, offering a spectacle degrading to themselves and to the city. The men who had out-lived their stength and were advanced in life, exempt by law from service in the field, could be seen throughout the city, now on the threshold of the grave, wretchedly scurrying with their cloaks pinned double round them. Many sufferings were being visited upon the city ; every citizen had felt mis-fortune at its worst ; but the sight which would most surely have stirred the onlooker and moved him to tears over the sorrows of Athens was to see the people vote that slaves should be released, that aliens should become Athenians and the disfranchised regain their rights *a* : the nation that once proudly claimed to be indigenous and free. The city had suffered a change indeed. She who used once to champion the freedom of her fellow Greeks was now content if she could safely meet the dangers that her own defence entailed. In the past she had ruled a wide extent of foreign land ; now she was disputing with Macedon for her own. The people whom Lacedaemonians and Peloponnesians, whom the Greeks of Asia used once to summon to their help,*b* were now entreating men of Andros, Ceos, Troezen and Epidaurus to send

---

a For this proposal of Hyperides compare § 16 and note.

b Two notable occasions when Athens sent help to Sparta were the Third Messenian War (464 B.C.) and the campaign of Mantinea (362 B.C.). She had assisted the Asiatic Greeks in the revolt of Aristagoras (c. 498 B.C.) and at the time of the Delian League.

---

⁷ ἐπιτίμους Dobree : ἐντίμους codd.

⁸ πρότερον Osann : πρῶτον codd. : πρὸ τοῦ Reiske.

⁹ διακινδυνεῦσαι M : κινδυνεῦσαι A.

¹⁰ Τροζῆνος Blass : Τροιζῆνος codd.

καὶ Ἐπιδαύρου ἐπικουρίαν αὑτῷ μεταπέμψασθαι.
43 ὥστε, ὦ ἄνδρες, τὸν ἐν τοῖς τοιούτοις φόβοις καὶ
τηλικούτοις κινδύνοις καὶ τοσαύτῃ αἰσχύνῃ ἐγκαταλιπόντα[1] τὴν πόλιν, καὶ μήτε ⟨τὰ⟩[2] ὅπλα θέμενον
ὑπὲρ τῆς πατρίδος μήτε τὸ σῶμα παρασχόντα
τάξαι τοῖς στρατηγοῖς, ἀλλὰ φυγόντα καὶ προδόντα
τὴν τοῦ δήμου σωτηρίαν, τίς ἂν ἢ δικαστὴς φιλόπολις καὶ εὐσεβεῖν βουλόμενος ψήφῳ ἀπολύσειεν,
ἢ ῥήτωρ κληθεὶς τῷ προδότῃ τῆς πόλεως βοηθήσειε,
τὸν οὐδὲ συμπενθῆσαι τὰς τῆς πατρίδος συμφορὰς
τολμήσαντα, οὐδὲ συμβεβλημένον οὐδὲν εἰς τὴν
44 τῆς πόλεως καὶ τοῦ δήμου σωτηρίαν; καίτοι κατ᾽
ἐκείνους τοὺς χρόνους οὐκ ἔστιν ἥτις ἡλικία οὐ
παρέσχεν[3] ἑαυτὴν εἰς τὴν τῆς πόλεως σωτηρίαν,
ὅθ᾽ ἡ μὲν χώρα τὰ δένδρα συνεβάλλετο, οἱ δὲ
τετελευτηκότες τὰς θήκας, οἱ δὲ νεῴ[4] τὰ ὅπλα.
ἐπεμελοῦντο γὰρ οἱ μὲν τῆς τῶν τειχῶν κατα-
σκευῆς, οἱ δὲ τῆς τῶν τάφρων, οἱ δὲ τῆς χαρακώ-
σεως· οὐδεὶς δ᾽ ἦν ἀργὸς τῶν ἐν τῇ πόλει. ἐφ᾽
ὧν οὐδενὸς τὸ σῶμα τὸ ἑαυτοῦ παρέσχε[5] τάξαι
45 Λεωκράτης. ὧν εἰκὸς ὑμᾶς ἀναμνησθέντας τὸν
μηδὲ συνενεγκεῖν[6] μηδ᾽ ἐπ᾽ ἐκφορὰν ἐλθεῖν ἀξιώσαντα τῶν ὑπὲρ τῆς ἐλευθερίας καὶ τοῦ δήμου
σωτηρίας ἐν Χαιρωνείᾳ τελευτησάντων θανάτῳ
ζημιῶσαι ὡς τὸ ἐπὶ τούτῳ μέρος ἀτάφων ἐκείνων
τῶν ἀνδρῶν γεγενημένων· ὧν οὗτος οὐδὲ τὰς θήκας
παριὼν ᾐσχύνθη, ὀγδόῳ ἔτει τὴν πατρίδα αὐτῶν
προσαγορεύων.
46 Περὶ ὧν, ὦ ἄνδρες, μικρῷ πλείω βούλομαι
διελθεῖν, καὶ ὑμῶν ἀκοῦσαι δέομαι καὶ μὴ νομίζειν

them aid. Therefore, gentlemen, if at a time of fears like these, a time of such great danger and disgrace, there was a deserter from the city, a man who neither took up arms in his country's defence nor submitted his person to the generals for enrolment but ran away and betrayed the safety of the people, what patriotic juryman with any scruples would vote for his acquittal ? What advocate summoned into court would help a traitor to his city ? He had not even the grace to share our grief at the misfortunes of his country, and he has made no contribution towards the defence of Athens and our democracy. Yet men of every age offered their services for the city's defence on that occasion when the land was giving up its trees, the dead their gravestones, and the temples arms. Some set themselves to building walls, others to making ditches and palisades. Not a man in the city was idle. Leocrates did not offer himself to be enrolled for a single one of these tasks. You would do well to remember this and punish with death this man who did not even deign to help collect the bodies or attend the funeral of those who at Chaeronea died for freedom and the safety of our people ; for had it rested with him those men would be unburied. He was not even ashamed to pass their graves when he greeted their country eight years after.

I wish to say a few words more about these men, gentlemen, and I ask you to listen and not regard

---

¹ ἐγκαταλιπόντα Ald. : ἐγκαταλείποντα codd.
² τὰ add. Es.
³ παρέσχεν Blass (coll. §§ 43, 57, etc.): παρέσχετο codd.
⁴ νεῲ Melanchthon : νέοι codd.
⁵ παρέσχε Bekker: παρέσχετο codd.
⁶ συνενεγκεῖν Z : ξυνεγκεῖν A : συνεξενεγκεῖν Dobree.

ἀλλοτρίους εἶναι τοὺς τοιούτους ⟨λόγους⟩[1] τῶν
δημοσίων ἀγώνων[2]· αἱ γὰρ τῶν ἀγαθῶν ἀνδρῶν
εὐλογίαι τὸν ἔλεγχον σαφῆ κατὰ τῶν τἀναντία
ἐπιτηδευόντων ποιοῦσιν. ἔτι δὲ καὶ δίκαιον τὸν
ἔπαινον, ὃς μόνος ἆθλον τῶν κινδύνων τοῖς ἀγαθοῖς
ἀνδράσιν ἐστί, τοῦτον, ἐπειδὴ καὶ ἐκεῖνοι εἰς τὴν
κοινὴν σωτηρίαν τῆς πόλεως τὰς ψυχὰς ⟨τὰς⟩[3]
αὐτῶν ἀνήλωσαν,[4] ἐν τοῖς δημοσίοις καὶ κοινοῖς
47 ἀγῶσι τῆς πόλεως μὴ παραλείπειν.[5] ἐκεῖνοι γὰρ
τοῖς πολεμίοις ἀπήντησαν ἐπὶ τοῖς ὁρίοις τῆς
Βοιωτίας ὑπὲρ τῆς τῶν Ἑλλήνων ἐλευθερίας
μαχούμενοι, οὐκ ἐν[6] τοῖς τείχεσι τὰς ἐλπίδας τῆς
σωτηρίας ἔχοντες, οὐδὲ τὴν χώραν κακῶς ποιεῖν
προέμενοι τοῖς ἐχθροῖς, ἀλλὰ τὴν μὲν αὑτῶν
ἀνδρείαν ἀσφαλεστέραν φυλακὴν εἶναι νομίζοντες
τῶν λιθίνων περιβόλων, τὴν δὲ θρέψασαν αὐτοὺς
48 αἰσχυνόμενοι περιορᾶν πορθουμένην, εἰκότως· ὥσπερ γὰρ πρὸς τοὺς φύσει γεννήσαντας καὶ τοὺς
ποιητοὺς τῶν πατέρων οὐχ ὁμοίως ἔχουσιν
ἅπαντες ταῖς εὐνοίαις, οὕτω καὶ πρὸς τὰς χώρας τὰς
[154] μὴ φύσει προσηκούσας, ἀλλ' ὕστερον ἐπικτήτους
γενομένας καταδεέστερον διάκεινται. τοιαύταις δὲ
γνώμαις χρησάμενοι καὶ τοῖς ἀρίστοις ἀνδράσιν ἐξ
ἴσου τῶν κινδύνων μετασχόντες, οὐχ ὁμοίως τῆς
τύχης ἐκοινώνησαν· τῆς γὰρ ἀρετῆς οὐ ζῶντες
ἀπολαύουσιν, ἀλλὰ τελευτήσαντες τὴν δόξαν καταλελοίπασιν,[7] οὐχ ἡττηθέντες, ἀλλ' ἀποθανόντες
ἔνθαπερ ἐτάχθησαν[8] ὑπὲρ τῆς ἐλευθερίας ἀμύνον-
49 τες. εἰ δὲ δεῖ καὶ παραδοξότατον μὲν εἰπεῖν,
ἀληθὲς δέ, ἐκεῖνοι νικῶντες ἀπέθανον. ἃ[9] γὰρ

---

[1] λόγους add. Reiske.
[2] ἀγώνων Reiske : ἀγῶνας codd.

such pleas as out of keeping with public trials. For the praise of brave men provides an unanswerable refutation of all whose conduct is opposed to theirs. And it is fair too that that praise which is to them the only reward for danger should be remembered at the public trials in which the entire city shares, since it was for her safety as a whole that they forfeited their lives. Those men encountered the enemy on the borders of Boeotia, to fight for the freedom of Greece. They neither rested their hopes of safety on city walls nor surrendered their lands for the foe to devastate. Believing that their own courage was a surer protection than battlements of stone, they held it a disgrace to see the land that reared them wasted. And they were right. Men do not hold their foster parents so dear as their own fathers, and so towards countries which are not their own but which have been adopted during their lifetime they feel a weaker loyalty. In such a spirit did these men bear their share of dangers with a courage unsurpassed ; but their prowess was not equalled by their fortune. For they have not lived to reap the enjoyment of their valour ; they died and have bequeathed their glory in its stead. Unconquered, they fell at their posts in the defence of freedom, and if I may use a paradox but one which yet conveys the truth, they triumphed in their death.

---

³ τὰς add. Baiter et Sauppe.
⁴ ἀνήλωσαν Muretus : ἀνάλωσαν codd.
⁵ παραλείπειν Es : παραλιπεῖν codd.
⁶ ἐν Es : ἐπὶ codd.
⁷ καταλελοίπασιν Bekker : ἐγκαταλελοίπασιν codd.
⁸ ἔνθαπερ ἐτάχθησαν Markland : ἔνθα παρετάχθησαν codd.
⁹ ἃ . . . ταῦτ' ἀμφότερα Coraes : τὰ . . . ταῦτα γὰρ ἀμφότερα codd. : τὰ γὰρ . . . ταῦτ' ἄρα Rehdantz.

49

ἆθλα τοῦ πολέμου τοῖς ἀγαθοῖς ἀνδράσιν ἐστίν,
ἐλευθερία καὶ ἀρετή, ταῦτ' ἀμφότερα τοῖς τελευ-
τήσασιν ὑπάρχει. ἔπειτα δ' οὐδ' οἷόν τ' ἐστὶν
εἰπεῖν ἡττῆσθαι τοὺς[1] ταῖς διανοίαις μὴ πτήξαντας
τὸν τῶν ἐπιόντων φόβον. μόνους γὰρ τοὺς ἐν
τοῖς πολέμοις καλῶς ἀποθνήσκοντας οὐδ' ἂν εἷς
ἡττῆσθαι δικαίως φήσειε· τὴν γὰρ δουλείαν φεύγοντες εὐκλεᾶ θάνατον αἱροῦνται. ἐδήλωσε δ' ἡ
50 τούτων τῶν ἀνδρῶν ἀρετή· μόνοι γὰρ τῶν ἀπάντων
τὴν τῆς Ἑλλάδος ἐλευθερίαν ἐν τοῖς ἑαυτῶν σώμασιν εἶχον. ἅμα γὰρ οὗτοί τε τὸν βίον μετήλλαξαν καὶ τὰ τῆς Ἑλλάδος εἰς δουλείαν μετέπεσεν·
συνετάφη γὰρ τοῖς τούτων σώμασιν ἡ τῶν ἄλλων
Ἑλλήνων ἐλευθερία. ὅθεν καὶ φανερὸν πᾶσιν
ἐποίησαν οὐκ ἰδίᾳ πολεμοῦντες ἀλλ' ὑπὲρ κοινῆς
ἐλευθερίας προκινδυνεύοντες. ὥστε, ὦ ἄνδρες,
οὐκ ⟨ἂν⟩[2] αἰσχυνθείην εἰπὼν στέφανον τῆς πατρίδος
51 εἶναι τὰς ἐκείνων ψυχάς. καὶ δι' ἃ οὐκ ἀλόγως[3]
ἐπετήδευον ἐπίστασθε, ὦ Ἀθηναῖοι, μόνοι τῶν
Ἑλλήνων τοὺς ἀγαθοὺς ἄνδρας τιμᾶν· εὑρήσετε
δὲ παρὰ μὲν τοῖς ἄλλοις ἐν ταῖς ἀγοραῖς ἀθλητὰς
ἀνακειμένους, παρ' ὑμῖν δὲ στρατηγοὺς ἀγαθοὺς
καὶ τοὺς τὸν τύραννον ἀποκτείναντας. καὶ τοιούτους μὲν ἄνδρας οὐδ' ἐξ ἁπάσης τῆς Ἑλλάδος
ὀλίγους εὑρεῖν ῥᾴδιον, τοὺς δὲ τοὺς στεφανίτας
ἀγῶνας νενικηκότας εὐπετῶς πολλαχόθεν ἔστι
γεγονότας ἰδεῖν. ὥσπερ τοίνυν τοῖς εὐεργέταις
μεγίστας τιμὰς ἀπονέμετε, οὕτω δίκαιον[4] καὶ τοὺς

---

[1] ἡττῆσθαι τοὺς Taylor : ἥττης αἰτίους τοὺς codd.
[2] ἂν add. Bekker.
[3] Post ἀλόγως add. ἀνδρείαν Blass.
[4] δίκαιον] δίκαιοι Blass, qui καὶ secl.

For liberty and courage, the prizes offered to brave
men in war, are both in the possession of the dead ;
neither can we say that men have been defeated
whose spirits did not flinch at the aggressor's threat.
For it is only those who meet an honourable end in war
whom no man justly could call beaten, since by the
choosing of a noble death they are escaping slavery.
The courage of these men has made this plain. They
alone among us all held in their persons the liberty of
Greece. For at the very moment when they passed
away her lot was changed to servitude. With the
bodies of these men was buried the freedom of every
other Greek, and thus they proved it to the world
that they were fighting for no private ends but facing
danger for our common liberty. I therefore say without misgiving that their lives have been a laurel
wreath for Athens. They had good reason for their
conduct,[a] since you, Athenians, alone among Greeks
know how to honour valiant men. In other cities,
you will find, it is the athletes who have their statues
in the market place, whereas in yours it is victorious
generals and the slayers of the tyrants : men whose
like it is hard to find though we search the whole of
Greece for but a few, whereas the winners of contests
for a wreath have come from many places and can
easily be seen. It is then only right, since you pay
the highest honours to your benefactors, that you

---

[a] The text of this passage has been suspected because (a)
the words δι' ἅ are difficult to understand ; (b) there is no
object for ἐπετήδευον. But (a) δι' ἅ can be taken to refer to
what follows in this sense : " Moreover,—and here is the
justification for their conduct,—you alone know, etc." ; (b)
although ἐπιτηδεύω normally takes an object, at least the
present participle can be used absolutely. I have therefore
ventured to leave the text as it stands.

τὴν πατρίδα καταισχύνοντας καὶ προδιδόντας ταῖς
ἐσχάταις τιμωρίαις κολάζειν.

52 Σκέψασθε δ', ὦ ἄνδρες, ὅτι οὐδ' ἐν¹ ὑμῖν ἐστιν
ἀποψηφίσασθαι Λεωκράτους τουτουί, τὰ δίκαια
ποιοῦσι. τὸ γὰρ ἀδίκημα τοῦτο κεκριμένον ἐστὶ
καὶ κατεγνωσμένον. ἡ μὲν γὰρ ἐν² Ἀρείῳ πάγῳ
βουλή (καὶ μηδείς μοι θορυβήσῃ· ταύτην γὰρ ὑπολαμβάνω μεγίστην τότε γενέσθαι τῇ πόλει σωτηρίαν) τοὺς φυγόντας³ τὴν πατρίδα καὶ ἐγκαταλιπόντας τότε τοῖς πολεμίοις⁴ λαβοῦσα ἀπέκτεινε.
καίτοι, ὦ ἄνδρες, μὴ νομίζετε τοὺς τὰ τῶν ἄλλων
φονικὰ ἀδικήματα ὁσιώτατα δικάζοντας αὐτοὺς ἂν
εἴς τινα τῶν πολιτῶν τοιοῦτόν τι παρανομῆσαι.

53 ἀλλὰ μὴν Αὐτολύκου μὲν⁵ ὑμεῖς κατεψηφίσασθε,
μείναντος μὲν αὐτοῦ ἐν τοῖς κινδύνοις, ἔχοντος δ'
αἰτίαν τοὺς υἱεῖς καὶ τὴν γυναῖκα ὑπεκθέσθαι, καὶ
ἐτιμωρήσασθε.⁶ καίτοι εἰ τὸν τοὺς ἀχρήστους εἰς
τὸν πόλεμον ὑπεκθέσθαι αἰτίαν ἔχοντα ἐτιμωρήσασθε, τί δεῖ πάσχειν ὅστις ἀνὴρ ὢν οὐκ ἀπέδωκε
τὰ τροφεῖα τῇ πατρίδι; ἔτι δὲ ὁ δῆμος δεινὸν
ἡγησάμενος εἶναι τὸ γιγνόμενον ἐψηφίσατο ἐνόχους
εἶναι τῇ προδοσίᾳ τοὺς φεύγοντας τὸν ὑπὲρ τῆς
πατρίδος κίνδυνον, ἀξίους εἶναι νομίζων τῆς

54 ἐσχάτης τιμωρίας. ἃ δὴ κατέγνωσται μὲν παρὰ
τῷ δικαιοτάτῳ συνεδρίῳ, κατεψήφισται δ' ὑφ'
ὑμῶν τῶν δικάζειν λαχόντων, ὁμολογεῖται δὲ παρὰ

¹ οὐδ' ἐν Taylor : οὐδὲν codd. : οὐδ' ἐφ' Bekker.
² ἐν Bekker : ἐπ' codd.
³ φυγόντας A. G. Becker : φεύγοντας codd.
⁴ τοῖς πολεμίοις Bekker : τοὺς πολεμίους codd. : ὡς πολεμίους Ald.   ⁵ μὲν] γε Gebauer.

should also punish with the utmost rigour those who dishonour and betray their country.

You should bear in mind, gentlemen, that it is not even in your power, unless you go beyond your rights, to acquit this man Leocrates, since his offence has had judgement passed upon it and a vote of condemnation too. For the council of the Areopagus ;—(No one need interrupt me. That council was, in my opinion, the greatest bulwark of the city at the time ;) —seized and executed men who then had fled from their country and abandoned it to the enemy. You must not think, gentlemen, that these councillors who are so scrupulous in trying other men for homicide would themselves have taken the life of any citizen unlawfully. Moreover you condemned Autolycus [a] and punished him because, though he himself had faced the dangers, he was charged with secretly sending his wife and sons away. Yet if you punished him when his only crime was that he had sent away persons useless for war, what should your verdict be on one who, though a man, did not pay his country the price of his nurture ? The people also, who looked with horror upon what was taking place, decreed that those who were evading the danger which their country's defence involved were liable for treason, meriting in their belief the extreme penalty. When therefore certain actions have been censured by the most impartial council and condemned by you who were the judges appointed by lot, when they have been recognized by the people as demanding the severest

[a] For the trial of Autolycus compare Lycurg. frag. 9 and note.

---

[6] καὶ ἐτιμωρήσασθε] del. Dobree.

τῷ δήμῳ τῆς μεγίστης ἄξια εἶναι τιμωρίας, τούτοις ὑμεῖς ἐναντία ψηφιεῖσθε; πάντων ἄρ'[1]
ἀνθρώπων ἔσεσθε ἀγνωμονέστατοι καὶ ἐλαχίστους
ἕξετε τοὺς ὑπὲρ ὑμῶν αὐτῶν κινδυνεύοντας.

55 Ὡς μὲν οὖν ἔνοχός ἐστι τοῖς εἰσηγγελμένοις
ἅπασιν, ὦ ἄνδρες, Λεωκράτης φανερόν ἐστι·
πυνθάνομαι δ' αὐτὸν ἐπιχειρήσειν ὑμᾶς ἐξαπατᾶν
λέγοντα, ὡς ἔμπορος ἐξέπλευσε καὶ κατὰ ταύτην
τὴν ἐργασίαν ἀπεδήμησεν εἰς Ῥόδον. ἐὰν οὖν
ταῦτα λέγῃ, ἐνθυμεῖσθ' ᾧ[2] ῥᾳδίως λήψεσθ' αὐτὸν
[155] ψευδόμενον. πρῶτον μὲν γὰρ οὐκ ἐκ τῆς ἀκτῆς
κατὰ τὴν πυλίδα ἐμβαίνουσιν οἱ κατ' ἐμπορίαν
πλέοντες ἀλλ' εἴσω[3] τοῦ λιμένος, ὑπὸ πάντων τῶν
φίλων ὁρώμενοι καὶ ἀποστελλόμενοι· ἔπειτα οὐ
μετὰ τῆς ἑταίρας καὶ τῶν θεραπαινῶν ἀλλὰ μόνοι[4]
56 μετὰ παιδὸς τοῦ διακονοῦντος. πρὸς δὲ τούτοις
τί προσῆκεν ἐν Μεγάροις τὸν Ἀθηναῖον ὡς[5]
ἔμπορον πέντε ἔτη κατοικεῖν καὶ τὰ ἱερὰ τὰ πατρῷα[6]
μετακομίζεσθαι καὶ τὴν οἰκίαν τὴν ἐνθάδε πωλεῖν,
εἰ μὴ κατεγνώκει τε αὐτοῦ προδεδωκέναι τὴν
πατρίδα καὶ μεγάλα πάντας ἠδικηκέναι; ὃ καὶ
πάντων γένοιτ' ἂν ἀτοπώτατον, εἰ περὶ ὧν αὐτὸς
προσεδόκα τεύξεσθαι τιμωρίας, ταῦθ' ὑμεῖς ἀπολύσαιτε[7] κύριοι γενόμενοι τῆς ψήφου. χωρὶς δὲ
τούτων οὐχ ἡγοῦμαι δεῖν ἀποδέχεσθαι ταύτην τὴν
57 ἀπολογίαν. πῶς γὰρ οὐ δεινὸν τοὺς μὲν ἐπ'
ἐμπορίαν[8] ἀποδημοῦντας σπεύδειν ἐπὶ τὴν τῆς
πόλεως βοήθειαν, τοῦτον δὲ μόνον ἐν τοῖς τότε
καιροῖς καὶ κατ' ἐργασίαν ἐκπλεῖν, ἡνίκα οὐδ' ἂν

---

[1] ἄρ' Heinrich (còll. §§ 27, 78) : γὰρ codd.
[2] ᾧ] ὡς Baiter.   [3] εἴσω Sauppe : εἰσὶ codd. : ἐκ Ald.
[4] μόνοι Ald. : μόνος codd.   [5] ὥς] del. Bekker.

punishment, will you give a verdict which opposes all
these views ? If you do, you will be the most un-
conscionable of men and will have few indeed ready
to risk themselves in your defence.

It is now clear, gentlemen, that Leocrates is liable
under all the articles of the indictment. He will, I
gather, try to mislead you by saying that it was merely
as a merchant that he departed on this voyage and
that the pursuance of this calling took him from his
home to Rhodes. So if he says this, please take note
how you may easily expose his lies. The first point
is that men travelling as merchants do not leave by
the postern on the beach ; they embark inside the
harbour with all their friends watching to see them
off. Secondly, they go alone with their attendant
slave, not with their mistress and her maids. Besides,
what need had this Athenian to stay five years in
Megara as a merchant ? What need had he to
send for the sacred images of his family or to sell
his house in Athens ? The answer is that he had
condemned himself as a traitor to his country, as a
criminal who had greatly wronged us all. It would
be incongruous indeed if you, with the decision in
your power, were to dismiss this charge on which he
was himself expecting punishment. But quite apart
from these objections, we need not, I think, admit
this line of defence. For surely it is outrageous, when
men abroad on business were hurrying to the city's
help, that Leocrates alone should sail away at such a
time for purposes of trade, since no one would then

---

⁶ πατρῷα Schoemann : πάτρια codd.

⁷ ἀπολύσαιτε Dobree : ἀπολύσετε codd.

⁸ ἐπ' ἐμπορίαν edd. : ἐπὶ ἐμπορίαν codd. : ἐπὶ ἐμπορίᾳ
Stephanus : κατ' ἐμπορίαν Es.

εἷς προσκτήσασθαι οὐδὲν ἂν ἐζήτησεν, ἀλλὰ τὰ
ὑπάρχοντα μόνον διαφυλάξαι; ἡδέως δ' ἂν αὐτοῦ
πυθοίμην τίν' ἐμπορίαν εἰσάγων χρησιμώτερος
ἐγένετο ἂν τῇ πόλει τοῦ παρασχεῖν τὸ σῶμα τάξαι
τοῖς στρατηγοῖς καὶ τοὺς ἐπιόντας ἀμύνασθαι μεθ'
ὑμῶν μαχόμενος. ἐγὼ μὲν οὐδεμίαν ὁρῶ τηλι-
58 καύτην οὖσαν βοήθειαν. ἄξιον δ' ἐστὶν οὐ μόνον
αὐτῷ διὰ τὴν πρᾶξιν ὀργίζεσθαι ταύτην, ἀλλὰ καὶ
διὰ τὸν λόγον τοῦτον· φανερῶς γὰρ ψεύδεσθαι
τετόλμηκεν. οὔτε γὰρ πρότερον οὐδεπώποτε
ἐγένετο ἐπὶ ταύτης τῆς ἐργασίας, ἀλλ' ἐκέκτητο
χαλκοτύπους, οὔτε τότ' ἐκπλεύσας οὐδὲν εἰσήγαγεν
ἐκ Μεγάρων, ἐξ ἔτη συνεχῶς ἀποδημήσας. ἔτι
δὲ καὶ ⟨τῆς⟩[1] πεντηκοστῆς μετέχων ἐτύγχανεν,
ἣν οὐκ ἂν καταλιπὼν κατ' ἐμπορίαν ἀπεδήμει.[2]
ὥστ' ἂν μέν τι περὶ τούτων λέγῃ, οὐδ' ὑμᾶς ἐπιτρέψειν αὐτῷ νομίζω.

59 Ἥξει δ' ἴσως ἐπ' ἐκεῖνον τὸν λόγον φερόμενος,
ὃν αὐτῷ συμβεβουλεύκασί τινες τῶν συνηγόρων,
ὡς οὐκ ἔνοχός ἐστι τῇ προδοσίᾳ· οὔτε γὰρ νεωρίων
κύριος οὔτε πυλῶν οὔτε στρατοπέδων οὔθ' ὅλως
τῶν τῆς πόλεως οὐδενός. ἐγὼ δ' ἡγοῦμαι τοὺς
μὲν τούτων κυρίους μέρος ἄν τι προδοῦναι τῆς
ὑμετέρας δυνάμεως, τουτονὶ δ' ὅλην ἔκδοτον
ποιῆσαι τὴν πόλιν. ἔτι δ' οἱ μὲν τοὺς ζῶντας
μόνον ἀδικοῦσι προδιδόντες, οὗτος δὲ καὶ τοὺς
τετελευτηκότας [καὶ τὰ ἐν τῇ χώρᾳ ἱερά,][3] τῶν
60 πατρῴων νομίμων ἀποστερῶν. καὶ ὑπὸ μὲν
ἐκείνων προδοθεῖσαν οἰκεῖσθαι ἂν συνέβαινε δούλην

have thought of adding to his wealth. Men's only care was to preserve what they already had. I should like Leocrates to tell me what merchandise he could have brought us to render him more useful than he would have been, had he presented himself before the generals for enrolment and had resisted the invaders by fighting at your sides. Personally I know no help to equal this. He deserves your anger for this conduct and for his explanation too, since he has not hesitated to tell a blatant lie. For he never previously carried on this trade, being in fact a master smith ; and subsequently, after his departure, he imported nothing to us from Megara, though he was away for six years without a break. Besides, he had, as it happens, an interest in the two per cent tax,[a] which he would never have left to live abroad on business. So if he says a word about these matters, I do not doubt that you will stop him.

He will perhaps in his impetuosity raise the argument, suggested to him by certain of his advocates, that he is not liable on a charge of treason, since he was not responsible for dockyards, gates or camps, nor in fact for any of the city's concerns. My own view is that those in charge of these positions could have betrayed a part of your defences only, whereas it was the whole city which Leocrates surrendered. Again, it is the living only whom men of their kind harm, but Leocrates has wronged the dead as well, depriving them of their ancestral rites. Had the city been betrayed by them it would have been inhabited though en-

---

[a] For the two per cent tax see § 19 and note.

[1] τῆς add. Heinrich.
[2] ἀπεδήμει, ut vid., A corr. : ἐπεδήμει cett.
[3] καὶ . . . ἱερά del. Herwerden.

LYCURGUS

οὖσαν τὴν πόλιν, ὃν δὲ[11] τρόπον οὗτος ἐξέλιπεν, ἀοίκητον ἂν γενέσθαι. ἔτι δ' ἐκ μὲν τοῦ κακῶς πράττειν τὰς πόλεις μεταβολῆς τυχεῖν ἐπὶ τὸ βέλτιον εἰκός ἐστιν, ἐκ δὲ τοῦ παντάπασι γενέσθαι ἀναστάτους[2] καὶ τῶν κοινῶν ἐλπίδων στερηθῆναι. ὥσπερ γὰρ ἀνθρώπῳ ζῶντι μὲν ἐλπὶς ἐκ τοῦ κακῶς πρᾶξαι μεταπεσεῖν, τελευτήσαντι δὲ συναναιρεῖται[3] πάντα δι' ὧν ἄν τις εὐδαιμονήσειεν, οὕτω καὶ περὶ τὰς πόλεις συμβαίνει πέρας ἔχειν 61 τὴν ἀτυχίαν, ὅταν ἀνάστατοι γένωνται. εἰ γὰρ δεῖ τὴν ἀλήθειαν εἰπεῖν, πόλεώς ἐστι θάνατος ἀνάστατον γενέσθαι. τεκμήριον δὲ μέγιστον· ἡμῶν γὰρ ἡ πόλις τὸ μὲν παλαιὸν ὑπὸ τῶν τυράννων κατεδουλώθη, τὸ δ' ὕστερον ὑπὸ τῶν τριάκοντα, καὶ ὑπὸ Λακεδαιμονίων τὰ τείχη καθῃρέθη· καὶ ἐκ τούτων ὅμως ἀμφοτέρων ἠλευθερώθημεν καὶ τῆς τῶν Ἑλλήνων εὐδαιμονίας ἠξιώθημεν προστάται 62 γενέσθαι. ἀλλ' οὐχ ὅσαι πώποτ' ἀνάστατοι γεγόνασι. τοῦτο μὲν γάρ, εἰ καὶ παλαιότερον εἰπεῖν ἐστι, τὴν Τροίαν τίς οὐκ ἀκήκοεν ὅτι μεγίστη γεγενημένη τῶν τότε πόλεων καὶ πάσης ἐπάρξασα τῆς Ἀσίας, ὡς ἅπαξ ὑπὸ τῶν Ἑλλήνων κατεσκάφη, τὸν αἰῶνα ἀοίκητός ἐστι; τοῦτο δὲ Μεσσήνην[4] πεντακοσίοις ἔτεσιν ὕστερον ἐκ τῶν τυχόντων ἀνθρώπων συνοικισθεῖσαν; 63 Ἴσως οὖν τῶν συνηγόρων αὐτῷ τολμήσει τις

---

[1] δὲ, quod supra post δούλην habent codd., huc transtulit Reiske.

[2] ἀναστάτους Reiske : ἀνάστατον codd.

[3] συναναιρεῖται] συνανήρηται Blass.

[4] Μεσσήνην Melanchthon : Μεσήνην codd.

58

slaved, but left as this man left it, it would have been deserted. Moreover, after suffering hardships cities may well expect to see a change to better times, but with complete destruction even the hopes common to every city are taken from them. A man, if he but lives, has still a prospect of change from evil fortunes, but at his death there perishes with him every means by which prosperity could come. And so it is with cities ; their misfortune reaches its limit when they are destroyed. Indeed, the plain fact is that for a city destruction is like death. Let us take the clearest illustration. Our city was enslaved[a] in earlier times by the tyrants and later by the Thirty, when the walls were demolished by the Spartans. Yet we were freed from both these evils and the Greeks approved us as the guardians of their welfare. Not so with any city which has ever been destroyed. First, though it is to quote a rather early case, remember Troy. Who has not heard how, after being the greatest city of her time and ruling the whole of Asia, she was deserted for ever when once the Greeks had razed her ? Think of Messene too, established again as a city five hundred years after from men of indiscriminate origin.[b]

Perhaps one of his advocates will dare to belittle

[a] By the Pisistratids from c. 560 to 510 and by the Thirty from 404 to 403. The walls were destroyed in 404.

[b] If by these words Lycurgus means five hundred years after it was destroyed, as he presumably does, he is being very inaccurate. Messene was founded in 369 by Epaminondas and its previous destruction is most naturally assigned to the Second Messenian War (mid-seventh century). Even the beginning of the First Messenian War, in which the Spartans conquered the country, cannot be placed much earlier than 720, i.e. only 350 years before. See Dinarch. i. 73 and note.

εἰπεῖν, μικρὸν τὸ πρᾶγμα ποιῶν, ὡς οὐδὲν ἂν παρ᾽
[156] ἕνα ἄνθρωπον ἐγένετο τούτων· καὶ οὐκ αἰσχύνονται[1] τοιαύτην ἀπολογίαν ποιούμενοι πρὸς ὑμᾶς,
ἐφ᾽ ᾗ δικαίως ἂν ἀποθάνοιεν. εἰ μὲν γὰρ ὁμολο-
γοῦσι τὴν πατρίδα αὐτὸν ἐκλιπεῖν, τοῦτο συγχωρή-
σαντες ὑμᾶς ἐῶντων[2] διαγνῶναι περὶ τοῦ μεγέθους·
εἰ δ᾽ ὅλως μηδὲν τούτων πεποίηκεν, οὐ μανία δή
που τοῦτο λέγειν, ὡς οὐδὲν ἂν γένοιτο[3] παρὰ
64 τοῦτον;[4] ἡγοῦμαι δ᾽ ἔγωγε, ὦ ἄνδρες, τοὐναντίον
τούτοις, παρὰ τοῦτον εἶναι τῇ πόλει τὴν σωτηρίαν.
ἡ γὰρ πόλις οἰκεῖται κατὰ τὴν ἰδίαν ἑκάστου
μοῖραν φυλαττομένη· ὅταν οὖν ταύτην ἐφ᾽ ἑνός τις
παρίδῃ,[5] λέληθεν ἑαυτὸν ἐφ᾽ ἁπάντων τοῦτο
πεποιηκώς. καίτοι ῥᾴδιόν ἐστιν, ὦ ἄνδρες, πρὸς
τὰς τῶν ἀρχαίων νομοθετῶν διανοίας ἀποβλέψαντας
65 τὴν ἀλήθειαν εὑρεῖν. ἐκεῖνοι γὰρ οὐ τῷ μὲν
ἑκατὸν τάλαντα κλέψαντι θάνατον ἔταξαν, τῷ δὲ
δέκα δραχμὰς ἔλαττον ἐπιτίμιον· οὐδὲ τὸν μὲν
μεγάλα ἱεροσυλήσαντα ἀπέκτεινον,[6] τὸν δὲ μικρὰ
ἐλάττονι τιμωρίᾳ ἐκόλαζον· οὐδὲ τὸν μὲν οἰκέτην
ἀποκτείναντα ἀργυρίῳ ἐζημίουν, τὸν δὲ ἐλεύθερον
εἷργον τῶν νόμων[7] ἀλλ᾽ ὁμοίως ἐπὶ πᾶσι καὶ τοῖς
ἐλαχίστοις παρανομήμασι θάνατον ὥρισαν εἶναι τὴν
66 ζημίαν. οὐ γὰρ πρὸς τὸ ἴδιον ἕκαστος αὐτῶν
ἀπέβλεπε τοῦ γεγενημένου πράγματος, οὐδ᾽ ἐντεῦθεν τὸ μέγεθος τῶν ἁμαρτημάτων ἐλάμβανον,
ἀλλ᾽ αὐτὸ ἐσκόπουν τοῦτο, εἰ πέφυκε τὸ ἀδίκημα

---

[1] αἰσχύνονται] αἰσχυνοῦνται Es.
[2] ἐώντων Es : ἐάτωσαν codd.
[3] ἂν γένοιτο Halm : ἂν γένηται codd. : ἂν γίγνοιτο Blass : γεγένηται aut ἂν ἐγένετο Bekker.

the offence and say that none of these misfortunes
could have resulted from the action of one man.
They are not ashamed to make before you the kind
of plea for which they deserve to die. For if they
admit that he deserted his country, once they have
granted this, let them leave it to you to determine the seriousness of the offence ; and even if
he has committed none of these crimes, surely it is
madness to say that this one man could cause no
harm. Personally, gentlemen, I think the opposite
is true : the safety of the city rested with this man.
For the city's life continues only if each one guards
her by personally doing his duty ; and if a man
neglects his duty in a single aspect, he has, un-
wittingly, neglected it entirely. But it is easy,
gentlemen, to ascertain the truth by referring to the
attitude of the early lawgivers. It was not their way,
when prescribing the death penalty for the thief who
stole a hundred talents, to approve a punishment less
severe for one who took ten drachmas. Again with
sacrilege : for a great offence they inflicted death,
and for a small one too they had no milder punishment. They did not differentiate between him who
killed a slave and him who killed a free man, by
fining one and outlawing the other. For all breaches
of the law alike, however small, they fixed upon the
death penalty, making no special allowances, in their
assessment of the magnitude of crimes, for the
individual circumstances of each. On one point only
they insisted : was the crime such that, if it became

---

⁴ τοῦτον Ald. : τοῦτο codd.

⁵ παρίδῃ Ald. : παρίδοι codd.

⁶ ἀπέκτεινον Coraes : ἀπέκτειναν codd.

⁷ νόμων] νομίμων Stephanus.

τοῦτο ἐπὶ πλεῖον ἐλθὸν μέγα βλάπτειν τοὺς ἀνθρώπους. καὶ γὰρ ἄτοπον ἄλλως πως περὶ τούτου
ἐξετάζειν. φέρε γάρ, ὦ ἄνδρες, εἴ τις ἕνα νόμον
εἰς τὸ Μητρῷον ἐλθὼν ἐξαλείψειεν, εἶτ᾽ ἀπολογοῖτο
ὡς οὐδὲν παρὰ τοῦτον τῇ πόλει ἐστίν, ἆρ᾽ οὐκ ἂν
ἀπεκτείνατ᾽ αὐτόν; ἐγὼ μὲν οἶμαι δικαίως, εἴπερ
67 ἐμέλλετε καὶ τοὺς ἄλλους σῴζειν. τὸν αὐτὸν
τοίνυν τρόπον κολαστέον ἐστὶ τοῦτον, εἰ μέλλετε
τοὺς ἄλλους πολίτας βελτίους ποιήσειν· καὶ οὐ
τοῦτο λογιεῖσθε, εἰ εἷς ἐστι μόνος ἄνθρωπος,[1] ἀλλ᾽
εἰς τὸ πρᾶγμα.[2] ἐγὼ μὲν γὰρ ἡγοῦμαι τὸ μὴ
πολλοὺς τοιούτους γενέσθαι ἡμέτερον εὐτύχημα
εἶναι, τοῦτον μέντοι διὰ τοῦτο[3] μείζονος τιμωρίας
ἄξιον εἶναι τυχεῖν, ὅτι μόνος τῶν ἄλλων πολιτῶν
οὐ κοινὴν ἀλλ᾽ ἰδίαν τὴν σωτηρίαν ἐζήτησεν.

68 Ἀγανακτῶ δὲ μάλιστα, ὦ ἄνδρες, ἐπειδὰν
ἀκούσω τῶν μετὰ τούτου τινὸς λέγοντος ὡς οὐκ
ἔστι τοῦτο προδιδόναι, εἴ τις ᾤχετο ἐκ τῆς πόλεως·
καὶ γὰρ οἱ πρόγονοί ποθ᾽ ὑμῶν[4] τὴν πόλιν καταλιπόντες, ὅτε πρὸς Ξέρξην ἐπολέμουν, εἰς Σαλαμῖνα
διέβησαν. καὶ οὕτως ἐστὶν ἀνόητος καὶ παντάπασιν ὑμῶν καταπεφρονηκὼς ὥστε τὸ κάλλιστον
τῶν ἔργων πρὸς τὸ αἴσχιστον συμβαλεῖν ἠξίωσε.

69 ποῦ γὰρ οὐ περιβόητος ἐκείνων τῶν ἀνδρῶν ἡ
ἀρετὴ γέγονε; τίς δ᾽ οὕτως ἢ φθονερός ἐστιν ἢ
παντάπασιν ἀφιλότιμος, ὃς οὐκ ἂν εὔξαιτο τῶν
ἐκείνοις πεπραγμένων μετασχεῖν; οὐ γὰρ τὴν
πόλιν ἐξέλιπον ἀλλὰ τὸν τόπον μετήλλαξαν, πρὸς
70 τὸν ἐπιόντα κίνδυνον καλῶς βουλευσάμενοι. Ἐτεό-

---

[1] ἄνθρωπος Blass : ὁ ἄνθρωπος codd.
[2] εἰς τὸ πρᾶγμα] obelis inclusit Blass : οἷον τὸ πρᾶγμα
Bekker : alii alia.   [3] διὰ τοῦτο] om. A pr., secl. Blass.

more widespread, it would do serious harm to society?
And it is absurd to face this question in any other
way. Just imagine, gentlemen. Suppose someone
had entered the Metroön[a] and erased one law and then
excused himself on the grounds that the city was not
endangered by the loss of just this one. Would you
not have killed him ? I think you would have been
justified in doing so, at least if you intended to save
the other laws. The same applies here : you must
punish this man with death if you intend to make the
other citizens better, oblivious of the fact that he is
only one. You must consider the act. There are not
many like him. In my opinion we have our good
fortune to thank for that ; but Leocrates, I think,
deserves a more severe punishment on this account,
since he alone of his fellow citizens sought safety for
himself rather than for the city.

Nothing angers me so much, gentlemen, as to hear
some person among his supporters saying that to have
left the city is not treason, since your ancestors once
left it when they crossed to Salamis during their war
with Xerxes : a critic so senseless and contemptuous
of you that he has presumed to confuse the most
honourable action with the most base. For where
have men not proclaimed the valour of those heroes ?
Who is so grudging, who so completely without spirit,
that he would not wish to have shared in their
exploits ? They did not desert Athens ; they simply
changed the scene, making an honourable decision
in the face of the growing menace. Eteonicus the

---

[a] The Metroön or temple of Cybele, which stood in the
market place, contained the state archives. *Cf.* Dem. xix. 129.

---

[4] ὑμῶν A pr. : ἡμῶν cett.

νικος μὲν γὰρ ὁ Λακεδαιμόνιος καὶ Ἀδείμαντος ὁ
Κορίνθιος καὶ τὸ Αἰγινητῶν ναυτικὸν ὑπὸ νύκτα τὴν
σωτηρίαν αὐτοῖς ἔμελλον πορίζεσθαι· ἐγκαταλειπό-
μενοι δ' οἱ πρόγονοι ὑπὸ πάντων τῶν Ἑλλήνων
βίᾳ καὶ τοὺς ἄλλους ἠλευθέρωσαν, ἀναγκάσαντες
ἐν Σαλαμῖνι μεθ' αὐτῶν[1] πρὸς τοὺς βαρβάρους
ναυμαχεῖν. μόνοι δ' ἀμφοτέρων περιγεγόνασι,
καὶ τῶν πολεμίων καὶ τῶν συμμάχων, ὡς ἑκατέρων
προσῆκε, τοὺς μὲν εὐεργετοῦντες, τοὺς δὲ μαχόμενοι νικῶντες. ἆρά γ' ὅμοιοι[2] τῷ φεύγοντι τὴν
71 πατρίδα τεττάρων ἡμερῶν πλοῦν εἰς Ῥόδον; ἦ
που ταχέως ἂν ἠνέσχετό τις ἐκείνων τῶν ἀνδρῶν
τοιοῦτον ἔργον, ἀλλ' οὐκ ἂν κατέλευσαν τὸν κατ-
αισχύνοντα τὴν αὐτῶν[3] ἀριστείαν.[4] οὕτω γοῦν
ἐφίλουν τὴν πατρίδα πάντες ὥστε τὸν παρὰ Ξέρξου
πρεσβευτὴν Ἀλέξανδρον, φίλον ὄντα αὐτοῖς πρότερον, ὅτι γῆν καὶ ὕδωρ ᾔτησε, μικροῦ δεῖν κατέλευσαν. ὅπου δὲ καὶ τοῦ λόγου τιμωρίαν ἠξίουν
λαμβάνειν, ἦ που τὸν ἔργῳ παραδόντα τὴν πόλιν
ὑποχείριον τοῖς πολεμίοις οὐ μεγάλαις ἂν ζημίαις
[157] ἐκόλασαν. τοιγαροῦν τοιαύταις χρώμενοι γνώμαις,
72

---

[1] μεθ' αὐτῶν Taylor : μετ' αὐτῶν codd.
[2] ὅμοιοι Hauptmann : ὅμοιον codd.
[3] αὐτῶν edd. : αὑτῶν A corr.[2] : αὐτῷ A pr.
[4] ἀριστείαν A corr.[2] : ἀρίστην A pr. : ἀρετήν Blass.

---

[a] There are at least two mistakes in this account. (1) The
Spartan general was Eurybiadas. (2) The Aeginetans supported the Athenians' policy, since a withdrawal to the
isthmus of Corinth would have entailed the surrender of their
island. See Herod. viii. 74. Even the Athenian claim that
Adimantus wished, or, as Herodotus (viii. 94) records it,

Spartan, Adimantus the Corinthian and the Aeginetan fleet intended, under cover of night, to seek safety for themselves.[a] Our ancestors, though they were being deserted by all the Greeks, forcibly liberated themselves and the others too by making them assist at Salamis in the naval battle against the Persians, and so triumphed unaided over both enemy and ally, in a way appropriate to each, conferring a favour upon one and defeating the other in battle. A fit comparison indeed to make with the man who escapes from his country on a four days' voyage to Rhodes ! Do you imagine that any one of those heroes would have been ready to condone such an act ? Would they not have stoned to death one who was disgracing their valour ? At least they all loved their country so much that they nearly stoned to death Alexander,[b] the envoy from Xerxes, formerly their friend, because he demanded earth and water. If they thought it right to exact vengeance for a speech, are we to believe that they would not have visited with severe punishment a man who in fact delivered his country into the hands of the enemy ? It was because they held such beliefs as these that

actually attempted, to flee is now regarded as a misrepresentation of the fact that the Corinthians were dispatched before the battle to oppose the Egyptian ships which had blocked the western end of the bay.

[b] Alexander of Macedon was conquered by Mardonius in 492 B.C. This account of him does not tally with that of Herodotus (viii. 136) in which he is portrayed as a friend of the Athenians who, though pressed into the service of Persia, only visited them after Salamis to offer favourable terms and was not " nearly stoned to death." The only stoning described by Herodotus was the execution of a certain Lycidas who proposed that the Athenians should accept terms from Persia (Herod. ix. 5).

ἐνενήκοντα[1] μὲν ἔτη τῶν Ἑλλήνων ἡγεμόνες
κατέστησαν, Φοινίκην δὲ καὶ Κιλικίαν ἐπόρθησαν,
ἐπ' Εὐρυμέδοντι δὲ καὶ πεζομαχοῦντες καὶ ναυ-
μαχοῦντες ἐνίκησαν, ἑκατὸν δὲ τριήρεις τῶν βαρβάρων αἰχμαλώτους ἔλαβον, ἅπασαν δὲ τὴν Ἀσίαν
73 κακῶς ποιοῦντες περιέπλευσαν. καὶ τὸ κεφάλαιον
τῆς νίκης, οὐ τὸ ἐν Σαλαμῖνι τρόπαιον ἀγαπήσαν-
τες ἔστησαν,[2] ἀλλ' ὅρους τοῖς βαρβάροις πήξαντες
τοὺς εἰς τὴν ἐλευθερίαν τῆς Ἑλλάδος, καὶ τούτους
κωλύσαντες ὑπερβαίνειν, συνθήκας ἐποιήσαντο,
μακρῷ μὲν πλοίῳ μὴ πλεῖν ἐντὸς Κυανέων καὶ
Φασήλιδος,[3] τοὺς δ' Ἕλληνας αὐτονόμους εἶναι,
μὴ μόνον τοὺς τὴν Εὐρώπην ἀλλὰ καὶ τοὺς τὴν
74 Ἀσίαν κατοικοῦντας. καίτοι οἴεσθ' ἄν, εἰ τῇ Λεωκράτους διανοίᾳ χρησάμενοι πάντες ἔφυγον, τούτων
ἄν τι γενέσθαι τῶν καλῶν ἔργων, ἢ ταύτην ἂν ἔτι
τὴν χώραν κατοικεῖν ὑμᾶς; χρὴ τοίνυν, ὦ ἄνδρες,
ὥσπερ τοὺς ἀγαθοὺς ἐπαινεῖτε καὶ τιμᾶτε, οὕτω
καὶ τοὺς κακοὺς μισεῖν τε καὶ κολάζειν, ἄλλως
τε καὶ Λεωκράτην, ὃς οὔτε ἔδεισεν οὔτε ᾐσχύνθη
ὑμᾶς.
75 Καίτοι ὑμεῖς τίνα τρόπον νενομίκατε περὶ τούτων
καὶ πῶς ἔχετε ταῖς διανοίαις, θεωρήσατε. ἄξιον

---

[1] ἐνενήκοντα] ἑβδομήκοντα Taylor (coll. Isocrat. iv. 106).
[2] ἔστησαν] del. Maetzner, Blass.
[3] Φασήλιδος Victorius : Φάσιδος codd.

---

[a] Estimates of other orators range from 73 years (Dem. ix.
23) to 65 years (Isocr. xii. 56), but in view of the inaccuracy of
Lycurgus on historical matters it does not seem necessary
to accept Taylor's suggestion to read " seventy " instead of

for ninety years they were leaders of the Greeks.[a]
They ravaged Phoenicia and Cilicia, triumphed by
land and sea at the Eurymedon, captured a hundred
barbarian triremes and sailed round the whole of Asia
wasting it. And to crown their victory : not content
with erecting the trophy in Salamis, they fixed for
the Persian the boundaries necessary for Greek freedom and prevented his overstepping them, making
an agreement that he should not sail his warships
between the Cyaneae and Phaselis and that the
Greeks should be free not only if they lived in Europe
but in Asia too.[b] Do you think that if they had all
adopted the attitude of Leocrates and fled, any of
these glorious things would have been done or that
you would still be living in this country ? Then,
gentlemen, as you praise and honour brave men so
too you must hate and punish cowards, and particularly Leocrates who showed no fear or respect towards
you.

Consider too what your traditional views have been
in this respect and what your present feelings are.

" ninety." The maximum possible length for the period
would be 85 years, from the battle of Marathon in 490 B.C. to
that of Aegospotami in 405.

[b] Lycurgus seems to be referring in exaggerated terms to
the campaign in which the Athenians won a naval victory off
Cyprus (v. Thucyd. i. 112). That he connects it with the
battle of the Eurymedon which took place some eighteen
years earlier (c. 467 B.C.) need not surprise us, in view of his
other inaccuracies (cf. §§ 62 and 70). The agreement in
question is the so-called Peace of Callias (c. 448 B.C.), about
which nothing certain is known. His account of the sea
limit agrees substantially with that of other orators (e.g. Isocr.
xii. 59 ; Dem. xix. 273), but the old triumphs over Persia
were exaggerated in the fourth century and the statement
that the Asiatic Greeks were guaranteed autonomy is certainly false.

γὰρ ὅμως καίπερ πρὸς εἰδότας διελθεῖν· ἐγκώμιον
γὰρ νὴ τὴν Ἀθηνᾶν εἰσι τῆς πόλεως οἱ παλαιοὶ
νόμοι καὶ τὰ ἔθη τῶν ἐξ ἀρχῆς ταῦτα κατασκευ-
ασάντων, οἷς ἂν προσέχητε, τὰ δίκαια ποιήσετε
καὶ πᾶσιν ἀνθρώποις σεμνοὶ καὶ ἄξιοι τῆς πόλεως
76 δόξετ' εἶναι. ὑμῖν γὰρ ἔστιν ὅρκος, ὃν ὀμνύουσι
πάντες οἱ πολῖται, ἐπειδὰν εἰς τὸ ληξιαρχικὸν
γραμματεῖον ἐγγραφῶσι καὶ ἔφηβοι γένωνται,
μήτε τὰ ἱερὰ ὅπλα καταισχυνεῖν¹ μήτε τὴν τάξιν
λείψειν, ἀμυνεῖν¹ δὲ τῇ πατρίδι καὶ ἀμείνω παρα-
δώσειν. ὃν εἰ μὲν ὀμώμοκε Λεωκράτης, φανερῶς
ἐπιώρκηκε, καὶ οὐ μόνον ὑμᾶς ἠδίκηκεν, ἀλλὰ
καὶ εἰς τὸ θεῖον ἠσέβηκεν²· εἰ δὲ μὴ ὀμώμοκεν
εὐθὺς δῆλός ἐστι παρασκευασάμενος³ ⟨ὡς⟩⁴ οὐδὲν
ποιήσων⁵ τῶν δεόντων, ἀνθ' ὧν δικαίως ἂν αὐτὸν
καὶ ὑπὲρ ὑμῶν καὶ ὑπὲρ τῶν θεῶν τιμωρήσαισθε.⁶
77 βούλομαι δ' ὑμᾶς ἀκοῦσαι τοῦ ὅρκου. λέγε,
γραμματεῦ.

ΟΡΚΟΣ.⁷—⟨Οὐκ αἰσχυνῶ τὰ ἱερὰ ὅπλα, οὐδὲ λείψω
τὸν παραστάτην ὅπου ἂν στοιχήσω· ἀμυνῶ δὲ καὶ
ὑπὲρ ἱερῶν καὶ ὁσίων καὶ οὐκ ἐλάττω παραδώσω τὴν
πατρίδα, πλείω δὲ καὶ ἀρείω κατά τε ἐμαυτὸν καὶ μετὰ
ἁπάντων, καὶ εὐηκοήσω τῶν ἀεὶ κραινόντων ἐμφρόνως.

¹ καταισχυνεῖν . . . ἀμυνεῖν Stephanus: καταισχύνειν . . .
ἀμύνειν codd.
² ἠσέβηκεν Ald. : ἠσέβησεν A.
³ παρασκευασάμενος A pr. : παρεσκευασμένος cett.
⁴ ὡς add. Es.
⁵ ποιήσων Frohberger : ποιήσειν codd.
⁶ τιμωρήσαισθε Ducas : τιμωρήσεσθε A pr. : τιμωρήσοισθε
A corr.
⁷ Iurisiurandi formulam, quam om. codd., addidi ex in-

It is as well that I should remind you though you
know already. For by Athena, in the ancient laws
and in the principles of those who drew them up in
the beginning we have indeed a panegyric on the
city. You have but to observe them to do right and
all men will respect you as worthy of her. There is
an oath which you take, sworn by all citizens when,
as ephebi,[a] they are enrolled on the register of the
deme, not to disgrace your sacred arms, not to desert
your post in the ranks, but to defend your country
and to hand it on better than you found it. If Leocrates has sworn this oath he has clearly perjured
himself and, quite apart from wronging you, has behaved impiously towards the god. But if he has not
sworn it, it becomes immediately plain that he has
been playing tricks in the hope of evading his duty;
and for this you would be justified in punishing him,
on your own and Heaven's behalf. I want you to
hear the oath. Read, clerk.

THE OATH.—I will not bring dishonour on my sacred arms
nor will I abandon my comrade wherever I shall be stationed.
I will defend the rights of gods and men and will not leave my
country smaller, when I die, but greater and better, so far
as I am able by myself and with the help of all. I will respect

---

[a] The Ephebate, an organization for training the young
men of Athens, chiefly in military matters, had existed since
the fifth century but was reorganized by Lycurgus (v. Life of
Lycurgus). The oath was taken in the temple of Aglaurus,
daughter of Cecrops (cf. Herod. viii. 53; Dem. xix. 303),
probably at the age of eighteen when the youth underwent
an examination (δοκιμασία) and had his name entered on
the deme register. He was then an ephebus until the age of
twenty. Cf. Aristot. Ath. Pol. 42.

---

scriptione saec. iv A.C. Acharnis inventa. Cf. Stobaeum,
Florileg. xliii. 48 et Pollucem viii, 105 sq.

καὶ τῶν θεσμῶν τῶν ἱδρυμένων καὶ οὓς ἂν τὸ λοιπὸν
ἱδρύσωνται ἐμφρόνως· ἐὰν δέ τις ἀναιρεῖ, οὐκ ἐπι-
τρέψω κατά τε ἐμαυτὸν καὶ μετὰ πάντων, καὶ τιμήσω
ἱερὰ τὰ πάτρια. ἴστορες θεοὶ Ἄγραυλος, Ἑστία,
Ἐννώ, Ἐννάλιος, Ἄρης καὶ Ἀθηνᾶ Ἀρεία, Ζεύς,
Θαλλώ, Αὐξώ, Ἡγεμόνη, Ἡρακλῆς, ὅροι τῆς πατρίδος,
πυροί, κριθαί, ἄμπελοι, ἐλάαι, συκαῖ . . .⟩

Καλός γ᾽, ὦ ἄνδρες, καὶ ὅσιος ὁ ὅρκος. παρὰ
τοῦτον τοίνυν ἅπαντα πεποίηκε Λεωκράτης. καίτοι
πῶς ἂν ἄνθρωπος γένοιτο ἀνοσιώτερος ἢ μᾶλλον
προδότης τῆς πατρίδος; τίνα δ᾽ ἂν τρόπον ὅπλα
καταισχύνειέ τις μᾶλλον ἢ εἰ λαβεῖν μὴ θέλοι[1] καὶ
τοὺς πολεμίους ἀμύνασθαι; πῶς δ᾽ οὐ καὶ τὸν
παραστάτην καὶ τὴν τάξιν λέλοιπεν ὁ μηδὲ τάξαι
78 τὸ σῶμα παρασχών; ποῦ δ᾽ ὑπὲρ ὁσίων καὶ ἱερῶν
ἤμυνεν ἂν ὁ μηδένα κίνδυνον ὑπομείνας; τίνι δ᾽
ἂν τὴν πατρίδα προὔδωκε μείζονι[2] προδοσίᾳ; τὸ
γὰρ τούτου μέρος ἐκλελειμμένη τοῖς πολεμίοις
ὑποχείριός ἐστιν. εἶτα τοῦτον οὐκ ἀποκτενεῖτε
τὸν ἁπάσαις ταῖς ἀδικίαις ἔνοχον ὄντα; τίνας
οὖν τιμωρήσεσθε; τοὺς ἔν τι τούτων ἡμαρτηκότας;
ῥᾴδιον ἔσται παρ᾽ ὑμῖν ἄρα μεγάλα ἀδικεῖν, εἰ
φανεῖσθε ἐπὶ τοῖς μικροῖς μᾶλλον ὀργιζόμενοι.

79 Καὶ μήν, ὦ ἄνδρες, καὶ τοῦθ᾽ ὑμᾶς δεῖ μαθεῖν,
ὅτι τὸ συνέχον τὴν δημοκρατίαν ὅρκος ἐστί. τρία

---

[1] θέλοι Ald. : θέλη A pr. : θέλει A corr.
[2] προὔδωκε μείζονι] παρέδωκε μείζονα Wesseling.

---

[a] The inscription from which the text of this oath is taken,
found in 1932 at Acharnae, contains also a variant version
of the next oath which Lycurgus quotes (§ 81). For the full
text and notes on it see M. N. Tod, *Greek Historical Inscriptions*, ii. 204. Agraulus (more commonly called Aglaurus)
had a temple on the north side of the Acropolis, in which the

the rulers of the time duly and the existing ordinances duly and all others which may be established in the future. And if anyone seeks to destroy the ordinances I will oppose him so far as I am able by myself and with the help of all. I will honour the cults of my fathers. Witnesses to this shall be the gods Agraulus, Hestia, Enyo, Enyalius, Ares, Athena the Warrior, Zeus, Thallo, Auxo, Hegemone, Heracles, and the boundaries of my native land, wheat, barley, vines, olive-trees, fig-trees. . . .*a*

It is a fine and solemn oath, gentlemen ; an oath which Leocrates has broken in all that he has done. How could a man be more impious or a greater traitor to his country ? How could he disgrace his arms more than by refusing to take them up and resist the enemy ? Is there any doubt that a man has deserted the soldier at his side and left his post, if he did not even offer his person for enlistment ? How could anyone have defended the rights of men and gods who did not face a single danger ? What greater treachery could he have shown towards his country, which, for all that he has done to save it, is left at the mercy of the enemy ? Then will you not kill this man who is answerable for every crime ? If not, whom will you punish ? Those guilty of only one such act ? It will be easy then to commit serious offences among you, if you show that the smaller ones arouse your anger more.

There is a further point which you should notice, gentlemen. The power which keeps our democracy together is the oath. For there are three things of

Ephebate oath was taken. For Enyo the goddess of war compare *Iliad* v. 333. Enyalius, though his name was often applied to Ares, was regarded by some as a separate God. Thallo (Growth) was one of the Horae, Auxo and Hegemone (Increase and Guidance) two of the Graces. The concluding words of the list are lost.

γάρ ἐστιν ἐξ ὧν ἡ πολιτεία συνέστηκεν, ὁ ἄρχων,
ὁ δικαστής, ὁ ἰδιώτης. τούτων τοίνυν ἕκαστος
ταύτην πίστιν δίδωσιν, εἰκότως· τοὺς μὲν γὰρ
ἀνθρώπους πολλοὶ ἤδη ἐξαπατήσαντες καὶ δια-
λαθόντες οὐ μόνον τῶν παρόντων κινδύνων ἀπελύ-
θησαν, ἀλλὰ καὶ τὸν ἄλλον χρόνον ἀθῷοι τῶν
ἀδικημάτων τούτων εἰσί· τοὺς δὲ θεοὺς οὔτ᾽ ἂν
ἐπιορκήσας τις λάθοι οὔτ᾽ ἂν ἐκφύγοι τὴν ἀπ᾽
αὐτῶν τιμωρίαν, ἀλλ᾽ εἰ μὴ αὐτός, οἱ παῖδές γε
καὶ τὸ γένος ἅπαν τὸ τοῦ ἐπιορκήσαντος μεγάλοις
80 ἀτυχήμασι περιπίπτει. διόπερ, ὦ ἄνδρες δικασταί,
ταύτην πίστιν ἔδοσαν αὑτοῖς ἐν Πλαταιαῖς πάντες
οἱ Ἕλληνες, ὅτ᾽ ἔμελλον παραταξάμενοι μάχεσθαι
πρὸς τὴν Ξέρξου δύναμιν, οὐ παρ᾽ αὑτῶν εὑρόντες,
ἀλλὰ μιμησάμενοι τὸν παρ᾽ ὑμῖν εἰθισμένον ὅρκον.
ὃν ἄξιόν ἐστιν ἀκοῦσαι· καὶ γὰρ παλαιῶν ὄντων
τῶν τότε πεπραγμένων ὅμως ἱκανῶς¹ ἔστιν ἐν
[158] τοῖς γεγραμμένοις ἰδεῖν τὴν ἐκείνων ἀρετήν. καί
μοι ἀναγίγνωσκε αὐτόν.

81   ΟΡΚΟΣ.²—Οὐ ποιήσομαι περὶ πλείονος τὸ ζῆν τῆς
ἐλευθερίας οὐδ᾽ ἐγκαταλείψω³ τοὺς ἡγεμόνας οὔτε
ζῶντας οὔτε ἀποθανόντας, ἀλλὰ τοὺς ἐν τῇ μάχῃ τε-
λευτήσαντας τῶν συμμάχων ἅπαντας θάψω. καὶ κρα-
τήσας τῷ πολέμῳ τοὺς βαρβάρους τῶν μὲν μαχεσα-
μένων ὑπὲρ τῆς Ἑλλάδος πόλεων οὐδεμίαν ἀνάστατον
ποιήσω, τὰς δὲ τὰ τοῦ βαρβάρου προελομένας ἁπάσας
δεκατεύσω. καὶ τῶν ἱερῶν τῶν ἐμπρησθέντων καὶ
καταβληθέντων ὑπὸ τῶν βαρβάρων οὐδὲν ἀνοικοδο-
μήσω παντάπασιν, ἀλλ᾽ ὑπόμνημα τοῖς ἐπιγιγνομένοις
ἐάσω καταλείπεσθαι τῆς τῶν βαρβάρων ἀσεβείας.

82   Οὕτω τοίνυν, ὦ ἄνδρες, σφόδρα ἐνέμειναν ἐν

which the state is built up : the archon, the juryman
and the private citizen. Each of these gives this oath
as a pledge, and rightly so. For human beings have
often been deceived. Many criminals evade them,
escaping the dangers of the moment, yes, and even
remaining unpunished for these crimes for the remainder of their lives. But the gods no one who
broke his oath would deceive. No one would escape
their vengeance. If the perjured man does not suffer
himself, at least his children and all his family are
overtaken by dire misfortunes. It was for this reason,
gentlemen of the jury, that all the Greeks exchanged
this pledge at Plataea, before taking up their posts to
fight against the power of Xerxes. The formula was
not their own but borrowed from the oath which is
traditional among you. It would be well for you to
hear it ; for though the events of that time are ancient
history now we can discern clearly enough, in these
recorded words, the courage of our forbears. Please
read the oath.

THE OATH.—I will not hold life dearer than freedom nor
will I abandon my leaders whether they are alive or dead.
I will bury all allies killed in the battle. If I conquer the
barbarians in war I will not destroy any of the cities which
have fought for Greece but I will consecrate a tenth of all
those which sided with the barbarian. I will not rebuild a
single one of the shrines which the barbarians have burnt
and razed but will allow them to remain for future generations as a memorial of the barbarians' impiety.

They stood by this oath so firmly, gentlemen, that

---

[1] ἱκανῶς Coraes : ἰσχνῶς codd. : ἴχνος M. Haupt et mox
τῆς ἐκείνων ἀρετῆς.

[2] Huius iurisiurandi formulam, aliquanto breviorem, tra-
dit Diodorus xi. 29.

[3] οὐδ' ἐγκαταλείψω Sauppe : οὐδὲ καταλείψω codd.

τούτῳ πάντες ὥστε καὶ τὴν παρὰ τῶν θεῶν εὔνοιαν
μεθ᾽ ἑαυτῶν ἔσχον βοηθόν, καὶ πάντων ⟨τῶν⟩[1]
Ἑλλήνων ἀνδρῶν ἀγαθῶν γενομένων πρὸς τὸν κίνδυνον, μάλιστα ἡ πόλις ὑμῶν εὐδοκίμησεν. ὃ καὶ
πάντων ἂν εἴη δεινότατον, τοὺς μὲν προγόνους ὑμῶν
ἀποθνήσκειν τολμᾶν ὥστε μὴ τὴν πόλιν ἀδοξεῖν,
ὑμᾶς δὲ μὴ κολάζειν τοὺς καταισχύναντας αὐτήν,
ἀλλὰ περιορᾶν τὴν κοινὴν καὶ μετὰ πολλῶν πόνων
συνειλεγμένην εὔκλειαν, ταύτην διὰ τὴν τῶν τοιούτων ἀνδρῶν πονηρίαν καταλυομένην.

83 Καίτοι, ὦ ἄνδρες, μόνοις ὑμῖν τῶν Ἑλλήνων
οὐκ ἔστιν οὐδὲν τούτων περιιδεῖν. βούλομαι δὲ
μικρὰ τῶν παλαιῶν ὑμῖν διελθεῖν, οἷς παραδείγμασι
χρώμενοι καὶ περὶ τούτων καὶ περὶ τῶν ἄλλων
βέλτιον βουλεύσεσθε. τοῦτο γὰρ ἔχει μέγιστον ἡ
πόλις ὑμῶν ἀγαθόν, ὅτι τῶν καλῶν ἔργων παράδειγμα τοῖς Ἕλλησι γέγονεν· ὅσον γὰρ τῷ χρόνῳ
πασῶν ἐστιν ἀρχαιοτάτη, τοσοῦτον οἱ πρόγονοι
ἡμῶν τῶν ἄλλων ἀνθρώπων ἀρετῇ διενηνόχασιν.

84 [2]ἐπὶ[3] Κόδρου γὰρ βασιλεύοντος Πελοποννησίοις
γενομένης ἀφορίας κατὰ τὴν χώραν αὐτῶν[4] ἔδοξε
στρατεύειν ἐπὶ τὴν πόλιν ἡμῶν, καὶ ἡμῶν τοὺς προγόνους ἐξαναστήσαντας κατανείμασθαι τὴν χώραν.
καὶ πρῶτον μὲν εἰς Δελφοὺς ἀποστείλαντες τὸν
θεὸν ἐπηρώτων εἰ λήψονται[5] τὰς Ἀθήνας· ἀνελόν-
τος δὲ τοῦ θεοῦ αὐτοῖς ὅτι τὴν πόλιν αἱρήσουσιν
ἂν μὴ τὸν βασιλέα τὸν Ἀθηναίων Κόδρον ἀπο-
85 κτείνωσιν, ἐστράτευον ἐπὶ τὰς Ἀθήνας. Κλεό-
μαντις δὲ τῶν Δελφῶν τις πυθόμενος τὸ χρη-

---

[1] τῶν add. Baiter et Sauppe.

they had the favour of the gods on their side to help them; and, though all the Greeks proved courageous in the hour of danger, your city won the most renown. Your ancestors faced death to save the city from shame ; nothing could then be worse than for you to pardon those who have disgraced her and allowed our national glory, won through many hardships, to perish by the wickedness of men like this.

Consider, gentlemen : you are the only Greeks for whom it is impossible to ignore any of these crimes. Let me remind you of a few past episodes ; and if you take them as examples you will reach a better verdict in the present case and in others also. The greatest virtue of your city is that she has set the Greeks an example of noble conduct. In age [a] she surpasses every city, and in valour too our ancestors have no less surpassed their fellows. Remember the reign of Codrus.[b] The Peloponnesians, whose crops had failed at home, decided to march against our city and, expelling our ancestors, to divide the land amongst themselves. They sent first to Delphi and asked the god if they were going to capture Athens, and when he replied that they would take the city so long as they did not kill Codrus, the king of the Athenians, they marched out against Athens. But a Delphian Cleomantis, learning of the oracle, secretly

---

[a] *Cf.* § 41 and § 100.
[b] The story of Codrus is told, with minor variations, by other ancient writers, *e.g.* by Velleius Paterculus i. 2, but the version here given by Lycurgus is the earliest extant.

---

[2] Suidas (s.v. Εὐγενέστερος) multa ex hac narratione citat.
[3] ἐπὶ om. Suidas.   [4] αὐτῶν] πᾶσαν Suidas.
[5] λήψονται Suidas : ἐπιλήψονται codd.

στήριον δι' ἀπορρήτων ἐξήγγειλε[1] τοῖς Ἀθηναίοις·
οὕτως οἱ πρόγονοι ἡμῶν, ὡς ἔοικε, καὶ τοὺς
ἔξωθεν ἀνθρώπους εὔνους ἔχοντες διετέλουν. ἐμ-
βαλόντων δὲ τῶν Πελοποννησίων εἰς τὴν Ἀττικήν,
τί ποιοῦσιν οἱ πρόγονοι ἡμῶν,[2] ὦ ἄνδρες δικασταί;
οὐ καταλιπόντες τὴν χώραν ὥσπερ Λεωκράτης
ᾤχοντο οὐδ' ἔκδοτον τὴν θρεψαμένην καὶ τὰ ἱερὰ
τοῖς πολεμίοις παρέδοσαν, ἀλλ' ὀλίγοι ὄντες κατακλησθέντες[3] ἐπολιορκοῦντο καὶ διεκαρτέρουν εἰς
86 τὴν πατρίδα. καὶ οὕτως ἦσαν, ὦ ἄνδρες, γενναῖοι
οἱ τότε βασιλεύοντες ὥστε προῃροῦντο ἀποθνῄ-
σκειν ὑπὲρ τῆς τῶν ἀρχομένων σωτηρίας μᾶλλον
ἢ ζῶντες ἑτέραν μεταλλάξαι[4] χώραν. φασὶ γοῦν
τὸν Κόδρον παραγγείλαντα τοῖς Ἀθηναίοις προσέχειν ὅταν τελευτήσῃ τὸν βίον, λαβόντα πτωχικὴν
στολὴν ὅπως ἂν ἀπατήσῃ τοὺς πολεμίους, κατὰ
τὰς πύλας ὑποδύντα φρύγανα συλλέγειν πρὸ τῆς
πόλεως, προσελθόντων δ' αὐτῷ δυοῖν ἀνδρῶν ἐκ
τοῦ στρατοπέδου καὶ τὰ κατὰ τὴν πόλιν πυνθανο-
μένων, τὸν ἕτερον αὐτῶν ἀποκτεῖναι τῷ δρεπάνῳ
87 παίσαντα[5] τὸν δὲ περιλελειμμένον, παροξυνθέντα
τῷ Κόδρῳ καὶ νομίσαντα πτωχὸν εἶναι, σπασά-
μενον τὸ ξίφος ἀποκτεῖναι τὸν Κόδρον. τούτων
δὲ γενομένων οἱ μὲν Ἀθηναῖοι κήρυκα πέμψαντες
ἠξίουν δοῦναι τὸν βασιλέα θάψαι, λέγοντες αὐτοῖς
ἅπασαν τὴν ἀλήθειαν· οἱ δὲ Πελοποννήσιοι τοῦτον
μὲν ἀπέδοσαν, γνόντες δ' ὡς οὐκέτι δυνατὸν
αὐτοῖς τὴν χώραν κατασχεῖν ἀπεχώρησαν. τῷ δὲ
Κλεομάντει τῷ Δελφῷ ἡ πόλις αὐτῷ τε καὶ

76

told the Athenians. Such, it seems, was the goodwill which our ancestors always inspired even among aliens. And when the Peloponnesians invaded Attica, what did our ancestors do, gentlemen of the jury ? They did not desert their country and retire as Leocrates did, nor surrender to the enemy the land that reared them and its temples. No. Though they were few in number, shut inside the walls, they endured the hardships of a siege to preserve their country. And such was the nobility, gentlemen, of those kings of old that they preferred to die for the safety of their subjects rather than to purchase life by the adoption of another country. That at least is true of Codrus, who, they say, told the Athenians to note the time of his death and, taking a beggar's clothes to deceive the enemy, slipped out by the gates and began to collect firewood in front of the town. When two men from the camp approached him and inquired about conditions in the city he killed one of them with a blow of his sickle. The survivor, it is said, enraged with Codrus and thinking him a beggar drew his sword and killed him. Then the Athenians sent a herald and asked to have their king given over for burial, telling the enemy the whole truth ; and the Peloponnesians restored the body but retreated, aware that it was no longer open to them to secure the country. To Cleomantis of Delphi the city made a grant of maintenance in the Prytaneum for himself

---

1 ἐξήγγειλε Bekker : ἐξήγγελλε A.

2 ἡμῶν Bekker : ὑμῶν codd.

3 κατακλησθέντες Es : κατακλεισθέντες codd.

4 Post μεταλλάξαι habent τὴν codd., del. Budaeus : τινα Reiske.

5 παίσαντα Blass : πεσόντα A pr. : προσπεσόντα A corr.² : πλήξαντα Suidas.

ἐκγόνοις ἐν πρυτανείῳ ἀΐδιον σίτησιν ἔδοσαν.
88 ἆρά γ'¹ ὁμοίως ἐφίλουν τὴν πατρίδα Λεωκράτει
[159] οἱ τότε βασιλεύοντες, οἳ γε προῃροῦντο τοὺς
πολεμίους ἐξαπατῶντες ἀποθνήσκειν ὑπὲρ αὐτῆς
καὶ τὴν ἰδίαν ψυχὴν ἀντὶ τῆς κοινῆς σωτηρίας
ἀντικαταλλάττεσθαι; τοιγαροῦν μονώτατοι ἐπώ-
νυμοι τῆς χώρας εἰσὶν ἰσοθέων τιμῶν τετυχηκότες,
εἰκότως· ὑπὲρ ἧς γὰρ οὕτω σφόδρα ἐσπούδαζον,
δικαίως ταύτης² καὶ τεθνεῶτες ἐκληρονόμουν.
89 ἀλλὰ Λεωκράτης οὔτε ζῶν οὔτε τεθνεὼς δικαίως
ἂν αὐτῆς μετάσχοι, μονώτατος ⟨δ'⟩³ ἂν προσή-
κόντως ἐξορισθείη τῆς χώρας, ἣν ἐγκαταλιπὼν
τοῖς πολεμίοις ᾤχετο· οὐδὲ γὰρ καλὸν τὴν αὐτὴν
καλύπτειν τοὺς τῇ ἀρετῇ διαφέροντας καὶ τὸν
κάκιστον πάντων ἀνθρώπων.

90   Καίτοι γ' ἐπεχείρησεν εἰπεῖν, ὃ καὶ νῦν ἴσως
ἐρεῖ πρὸς ὑμᾶς, ὡς οὐκ ἄν ποτε ὑπέμεινε⁴ τὸν
ἀγῶνα τοῦτον συνειδὼς ἑαυτῷ τοιοῦτόν τι δια-
πεπραγμένῳ· ὥσπερ οὐ πάντας καὶ τοὺς κλέπτοντας καὶ ἱεροσυλοῦντας τούτῳ τῷ τεκμηρίῳ
χρωμένους. οὐ γὰρ τοῦ πράγματός ἐστι σημεῖον
ὡς οὐ πεποιήκασιν, ἀλλὰ τῆς ἀναιδείας ἣν ἔχουσιν.
οὐ γὰρ τοῦτο δεῖ λέγειν, ἀλλ' ὡς οὐκ ἐξέπλευσεν,
οὐδὲ τὴν πόλιν ἐγκατέλιπεν, οὐδ' ἐν Μεγάροις
91 κατῴκησε· ταῦτά ἐστι τεκμήρια τοῦ πράγματος,
ἐπεὶ τό γ'⁵ ἐλθεῖν τοῦτον, οἶμαι θεόν τινα αὐτὸν
ἐπ' αὐτὴν ἀγαγεῖν τὴν τιμωρίαν, ἵν' ἐπειδὴ τὸν
εὐκλεᾶ κίνδυνον ἔφυγε, τοῦ ἀκλεοῦς καὶ ἀδόξου
θανάτου τύχοι, καὶ οὓς προὔδωκε, τούτοις ὑποχείριον αὐτὸν καταστήσειεν. ἑτέρωθι μὲν γὰρ
78

and his descendants for ever. Is there any re-
semblance between Leocrates' love for his country
and the love of those ancient kings who preferred to
die for her and outwit the foe, giving their own life
in exchange for the people's safety? It is for this
reason that they and only they have given the land
their name and received honours like the gods, as is
their due. For they were entitled, even after death,
to a share in the country which they so zealously
preserved. But Leocrates, whether alive or dead,
would have no claim to a portion in it; he of all men
deserves to be cast out from the country which he
abandoned to the enemy by his flight. For it is un-
fitting that the same ground should cover heroes and
the most cowardly of mankind.

Yet he contended (and perhaps he will say this to
you now also) that he would not have faced this trial
if he had been conscious of committing a crime like
this. As if all thieves and temple-robbers did not
use this argument! It is an argument which goes to
prove their shamelessness rather than the fact of their
innocence. That is not the point at issue; we need
the assurance that he did not sail, that he did not
leave the city or settle at Megara. These are the
facts by which the truth can be established. As for
his appearance in court: surely some god brought
him specially for punishment, so that, after shirking
an honourable danger, he might meet a death of
disgrace and shame and place himself at the mercy
of the men he betrayed. If misfortune befalls him in

---

[1] ἆρά γ' Coraes : ὁρᾶτε codd.
[2] ταύτης Es : ταύτην codd.   [3] δ' add. Ald.
[4] ὑπέμεινε Schaub : ὑπομεῖναι codd.
[5] τό γ' Coraes : γε τὸ codd.

ἀτυχῶν οὔπω δῆλον εἰ διὰ ταῦτα δίκην δίδωσιν·
ἐνταῦθα δὲ παρ' οἷς προὔδωκε φανερόν ἐστιν ὅτι
τῶν αὑτοῦ παρανομημάτων ὑπέχει ταύτην τὴν
92 τιμωρίαν. οἱ γὰρ θεοὶ οὐδὲν πρότερον ποιοῦσιν[1]
ἢ τῶν πονηρῶν ἀνθρώπων τὴν διάνοιαν παράγουσι·
καί μοι δοκοῦσι τῶν ἀρχαίων τινὲς ποιητῶν
ὥσπερ χρησμοὺς γράψαντες τοῖς ἐπιγιγνομένοις[2]
τάδε τὰ ἰαμβεῖα καταλιπεῖν·

ὅταν γὰρ ὀργὴ δαιμόνων βλάπτῃ τινά,
τοῦτ' αὐτὸ πρῶτον, ἐξαφαιρεῖται[3] φρενῶν
τὸν νοῦν τὸν ἐσθλόν, εἰς δὲ τὴν χείρω τρέπει
γνώμην, ἵν' εἰδῇ μηδὲν ὧν ἁμαρτάνει.

93 τίς γὰρ οὐ μέμνηται τῶν πρεσβυτέρων ἢ τῶν
νεωτέρων οὐκ ἀκήκοε Καλλίστρατον, οὗ θάνατον
ἡ πόλις κατέγνω, τοῦτον φυγόντα καὶ τοῦ θεοῦ
τοῦ ἐν Δελφοῖς ἀκούσαντα ὅτι ἂν ἔλθῃ Ἀθήναζε
τεύξεται τῶν νόμων, ἀφικόμενον καὶ ἐπὶ τὸν βωμὸν
τῶν δώδεκα θεῶν καταφυγόντα, καὶ οὐδὲν ἧττον
ὑπὸ τῆς πόλεως ἀποθανόντα; δικαίως· τὸ γὰρ
τῶν νόμων τοῖς ἠδικηκόσι τυχεῖν τιμωρία ἐστίν.
ὁ δέ γε θεὸς ὀρθῶς ἀπέδωκε τοῖς ἠδικημένοις
κολάσαι τὸν αἴτιον· δεινὸν γὰρ ἂν εἴη, εἰ ταὐτὰ
σημεῖα τοῖς εὐσεβέσι καὶ τοῖς κακούργοις φαίνοιτο.[4]
94 Ἡγοῦμαι δ' ἔγωγ', ὦ ἄνδρες, τὴν τῶν θεῶν

---

[1] ποιοῦσιν] del. Bekker.
[2] ἐπιγιγνομένοις Bekker : ἐπιγενομένοις codd.
[3] ἐξαφαιρεῖται Ald. : ἐξαιρεῖται codd.
[4] φαίνοιτο Heinrich : φαίνονται codd.

---

[a] The authorship of these verses is not known.
[b] Callistratus, an orator whom Demosthenes much admired,

some other place it is hardly clear if this is the crime for which he is being punished. But here, among the men whom he betrayed, it is obvious that his own transgressions of the law have brought upon him this reward. For the first step taken by the gods in the case of wicked men is to unhinge their reason; and personally I value as the utterance of an oracle these lines, composed by ancient poets and handed down to posterity [a]:

> When gods in anger seek a mortal's harm,
> First they deprive him of his sanity,
> And fashion of his mind a baser instrument,
> That he may have no knowledge when he errs.

Who does not know the fate of Callistratus,[b] which the older among you remember and the younger have heard recounted, the man condemned to death by the city? How he fled and later, hearing from the god at Delphi that if he returned to Athens he would have fair treatment by the laws, came back and taking refuge at the altar of the twelve gods was none the less put to death by the state, and rightly so, for " fair treatment by the laws " is, in the case of wrongdoers, punishment. And thus the god too acted rightly in allowing those who had been wronged to punish the offender. For it would be an unseemly thing if revelations made to good men were the same as those vouchsafed to malefactors.

It is my belief, gentlemen, that the guidance of

was instrumental in building up the Second Athenian Confederacy. After a raid by Alexander of Pherae on the Piraeus he was condemned to death by the Athenians (361 B.C.); and, though at first he fled to Methone, he returned later and the sentence was carried out. His name is mentioned by Hyperides (iv. 1).

ἐπιμέλειαν πάσας μὲν τὰς ἀνθρωπίνας πράξεις
ἐπισκοπεῖν, μάλιστα δὲ τὴν περὶ τοὺς γονέας καὶ
τοὺς τετελευτηκότας καὶ τὴν πρὸς αὐτοὺς εὐσέ-
βειαν, εἰκότως· παρ᾽ ὧν γὰρ τὴν ἀρχὴν τοῦ ζῆν
εἰλήφαμεν καὶ πλεῖστα ἀγαθὰ πεπόνθαμεν, εἰς
τούτους μὴ ὅτι ἁμαρτεῖν, ἀλλὰ μὴ¹ εὐεργετοῦντας
τὸν αὐτῶν βίον καταναλῶσαι μέγιστον ἀσέβημά
95 ἐστι. λέγεται γοῦν² ἐν Σικελίᾳ (εἰ γὰρ καὶ μυ-
θωδέστερόν ἐστιν, ἀλλ᾽ ἁρμόσει καὶ ὑμῖν ἅπασι
τοῖς νεωτέροις ἀκοῦσαι) ἐκ τῆς Αἴτνης ῥύακα πυρὸς
γενέσθαι· τοῦτον δὲ ῥεῖν φασιν ἐπί ⟨τε⟩³ τὴν ἄλλην
χώραν, καὶ δὴ καὶ πρὸς πόλιν τινὰ τῶν ἐκεῖ κατ-
οικουμένων. τοὺς μὲν οὖν ἄλλους ὁρμῆσαι πρὸς
φυγὴν τὴν αὑτῶν σωτηρίαν ζητοῦντας, ἕνα δέ
τινα τῶν νεωτέρων, ὁρῶντα τὸν πατέρα πρεσβύ-
τερον ὄντα καὶ οὐχὶ δυνάμενον ἀποχωρεῖν ἀλλὰ
96 ἐγκαταλαμβανόμενον, ἀράμενον φέρειν. φορτίου
δ᾽ οἶμαι προσγενομένου καὶ αὐτὸς ἐγκατελήφθη.
ὅθεν δὴ καὶ ἄξιον θεωρῆσαι τὸ θεῖον, ὅτι τοῖς
[160] ἀνδράσι τοῖς ἀγαθοῖς εὐμενῶς ἔχει. λέγεται γὰρ
κύκλῳ τὸν τόπον ἐκεῖνον περιρρυῆναι⁴ τὸ πῦρ καὶ
σωθῆναι τούτους μόνους, ἀφ᾽ ὧν καὶ τὸ χωρίον
ἔτι καὶ νῦν προσαγορεύεσθαι⁵ τῶν εὐσεβῶν⁶ χῶρον·
τοὺς δὲ ταχεῖαν τὴν ἀποχώρησιν ποιησαμένους
καὶ τοὺς ἑαυτῶν γονέας⁷ ἐγκαταλιπόντας ἅπαντας⁸
97 ἀπολέσθαι. ὥστε καὶ ὑμᾶς δεῖν τὴν παρὰ ⟨τῶν⟩⁹
θεῶν ἔχοντας μαρτυρίαν ὁμογνωμόνως τοῦτον
κολάζειν, τὸν ἅπασι τοῖς μεγίστοις ἀδικήμασιν
ἔνοχον ὄντα κατὰ τὸ ἑαυτοῦ μέρος. τοὺς μὲν γὰρ

---

¹ ἀλλὰ μὴ Bekker : ἀλλ᾽ ὅτι μὴ codd.
² γοῦν Maetzner : οὖν codd.   ³ τε add. Baiter.
⁴ περιρρυῆναι Es : περιρρεῦσαι codd.

82

the gods presides over all human affairs and more
especially, as is to be expected, over our duty towards
our parents, towards the dead and towards the gods
themselves. For in our dealings with those to whom
we owe our being, at whose hands we have enjoyed
the greatest benefits, it is the utmost sacrilege that
we should fail, not merely to do our duty, but even
to dedicate our lives to their service. Let me take
an illustration. There is a story that in Sicily,—
the tale, though half a legend, will, for the younger
ones among you, be well worth the hearing,—a
stream of fire burst forth from Etna. This stream, so
the story goes, flowing over the countryside, drew
near a certain city of the Sicilians. Most men, thinking of their own safety, took to flight ; but one of
the youths, seeing that his father, now advanced in
years, could not escape and was being overtaken by
the fire, lifted him up and carried him. Hindered no
doubt by the additional weight of his burden, he too
was overtaken. And now let us observe the mercy
shown by God towards good men. For we are told
that the fire spread round that spot in a ring and
only those two men were saved, so that the place is
still called the Place of the Pious, while those who
had fled in haste, leaving their parents to their fate,
were all consumed. You too, therefore, following
that divine example, should punish with one accord
this man who spared no pains to show himself in all
respects the greatest criminal, depriving the gods of

---

⁵ προσαγορεύεσθαι Reiske : προσαγορεῦσαι codd.
⁶ εὐσεβῶν Ald. : ἀσεβῶν codd.
⁷ γονέας hic et in § 97 Es : γονεῖς codd.
⁸ ἐγκαταλιπόντας ἅπαντας Pinzger : ἅπαντας ἐγκαταλιπόντας
codd.   ⁹ τῶν add. Sauppe.

θεοὺς τὰς[1] πατρίους τιμὰς ἀπεστέρησε,[2] τοὺς δὲ
γονέας τοῖς πολεμίοις ἐγκατάλιπε, τοὺς δὲ τετελευτηκότας τῶν νομίμων οὐκ εἴασε τυχεῖν.

98 Καίτοι σκέψασθε, ὦ ἄνδρες· οὐ γὰρ ἀποστήσομαι
τῶν παλαιῶν· ἐφ᾽ οἷς γὰρ ἐκεῖνοι ποιοῦντες ἐφι-
λοτιμοῦντο, ταῦτα δικαίως ἂν ὑμεῖς ἀκούσαντες
ἀποδέχοισθε. φασὶ γὰρ Εὔμολπον τὸν Ποσειδῶνος[3] καὶ Χιόνης μετὰ Θρᾳκῶν ἐλθεῖν τῆς χώρας
ταύτης ἀμφισβητοῦντα, τυχεῖν δὲ κατ᾽ ἐκείνους
τοὺς χρόνους βασιλεύοντα Ἐρεχθέα, γυναῖκα

99 ἔχοντα Πραξιθέαν τὴν Κηφισοῦ θυγατέρα. μεγάλου δὲ στρατοπέδου μέλλοντος αὐτοῖς εἰσβάλλειν
εἰς τὴν χώραν, εἰς Δελφοὺς ἰὼν ἠρώτα τὸν θεὸν
τί ποιῶν ἂν νίκην λάβοι παρὰ τῶν πολεμίων.
χρήσαντος δ᾽ αὐτῷ τοῦ θεοῦ, τὴν θυγατέρα εἰ
θύσειε πρὸ τοῦ συμβαλεῖν τὼ στρατοπέδω,[4]
κρατήσειν τῶν πολεμίων, ὁ δὲ[5] τῷ θεῷ πειθόμενος
τοῦτ᾽ ἔπραξε, καὶ τοὺς ἐπιστρατευομένους ἐκ τῆς

100 χώρας ἐξέβαλε. διὸ καὶ δικαίως ἄν τις Εὐριπίδην
ἐπαινέσειεν, ὅτι τά τ᾽ ἄλλ᾽ ὢν[6] ἀγαθὸς ποιητὴς
καὶ τοῦτον τὸν μῦθον προείλετο ποιῆσαι, ἡγού-
μενος κάλλιστον ἂν γενέσθαι τοῖς πολίταις παράδειγμα τὰς ἐκείνων πράξεις, πρὸς ἃς ἀποβλέποντας
καὶ θεωροῦντας συνεθίζεσθαι ταῖς ψυχαῖς τὸ τὴν

---

[1] τὰς Reiske : τοὺς codd.
[2] ἀπεστέρησε Blass : ἀπεστέρηκε codd.
[3] A verbis τὸν Ποσειδῶνος rursus incipit N.
[4] τὼ στρατοπέδω Taylor : τῷ στρατοπέδῳ codd.
[5] ὁ δὲ Ald. : ὡς δὲ codd.
[6] ὢν] ἦν Bekker.

---

[a] Eumolpus, legendary ancestor of the Eumolpides of

their traditional cults, abandoning his parents to the enemy and denying the dead their dues.

Here is another story, gentlemen. Again I shall be speaking of our ancestors, since it is only right that you should hear of the deeds in which they took a pride and give them your approval. The tradition is that Eumolpus, the son of Posidon and Chione, came with the Thracians to claim this country during the reign of Erechtheus who was married to Praxithea, the daughter of Cephisus.[a] As a large army was about to invade their country, he went to Delphi and asked the god by what means he could assure a victory over the enemy. The god's answer to him was that if he sacrificed his daughter before the two sides engaged he would defeat the enemy; and, submitting to the god, he did this and drove the invaders from the country. We have therefore good reason to thank Euripides, because, apart from his other merits as a poet, he chose this subject for a play,[b] believing that in the conduct of those people the citizens would have a fine example which they could keep before them and so implant in their hearts

Eleusis, was credited with the founding of the Mysteries. The passage of Euripides quoted in § 100 is the earliest extant source for the tradition that he was a Thracian. According to Apollodorus, Eleusis, being at war with Athens, called in Eumolpus, whereupon the Athenian king Erechtheus consulted the god and learned that he must sacrifice one daughter in order to obtain a victory. He therefore offered up his youngest, the others committing suicide in sympathy, and so was enabled to kill Eumolpus in battle (Apollod. iii. 15. 4).

[b] The *Erechtheus* of Euripides is now lost. Apart from the passage quoted by Lycurgus, a few other fragments have been preserved, including one of 34 lines given by Stobaeus, *Florileg.* iii. 18.

LYCURGUS

πατρίδα φιλεῖν. ἄξιον δ᾽, ὦ ἄνδρες δικασταί, καὶ
τῶν ἰαμβείων ἀκοῦσαι, ἃ πεποίηκε λέγουσαν τὴν
μητέρα τῆς παιδός. ὄψεσθε γὰρ ἐν αὐτοῖς μεγαλο-
ψυχίαν καὶ γενναιότητα ἀξίαν καὶ τῆς πόλεως
καὶ τοῦ γενέσθαι Κηφισοῦ θυγατέρα.

ΡΗΣΙΣ ΕΥΡΙΠΙΔΟΥ

τὰς χάριτας ὅστις εὐγενῶς χαρίζεται,
ἥδιον ἐν βροτοῖσιν· οἳ δὲ δρῶσι μέν,
χρόνῳ δὲ δρῶσι, δυσγενέστερον[1] . . .
ἐγὼ δὲ δώσω τὴν ἐμὴν παῖδα κτανεῖν.
λογίζομαι δὲ πολλά· πρῶτα μὲν πόλιν   5
οὐκ ἄν τιν᾽ ἄλλην τῆσδε βελτίω λαβεῖν·
²ᾗ πρῶτα μὲν λεὼς οὐκ ἐπακτὸς ἄλλοθεν,
αὐτόχθονες δ᾽ ἔφυμεν· αἱ δ᾽ ἄλλαι πόλεις
πεσσῶν ὁμοίαις[3] διαφοραῖς ἐκτισμέναι[4]
ἄλλαι παρ᾽ ἄλλων εἰσὶν εἰσαγώγιμοι.   10
ὅστις δ᾽ ἀπ᾽ ἄλλης πόλεος[5] οἰκήσῃ[6] πόλιν,
ἁρμὸς πονηρὸς ὥσπερ ἐν ξύλῳ παγείς,
λόγῳ πολίτης ἐστί, τοῖς δ᾽ ἔργοισιν οὔ.
ἔπειτα τέκνα τοῦδ᾽ ἕκατι[7] τίκτομεν,
ὡς θεῶν τε βωμοὺς πατρίδα τε ῥυώμεθα.[8]   15
πόλεως δ᾽ ἁπάσης τοὔνομ᾽ ἕν,[9] πολλοὶ[10] δέ νιν
ναίουσι· τούτους πῶς διαφθεῖραί με χρή,
ἐξὸν πρὸ πάντων μίαν ὑπερδοῦναι θανεῖν;
εἴπερ γὰρ ἀριθμὸν οἶδα καὶ τοὐλάσσονος
τὸ μεῖζον οὑνὸς[11] οἶκος οὐ πλεῖον σθένει   20

---

[1] ⟨δρῶσι⟩ δυσγενέστερον Heinrich: δυσγενέστερον ⟨λέγω⟩
Meineke.
[2] Vv. 7–10 cit. Plut. *Mor.* 604 D–E.
[3] ὁμοίαις] ὁμοίως Plut., Ald.
[4] διαφοραῖς ἐκτίσμεναι] διαφορηθεῖσαι βολαῖς Plut.

86

a love of their country. You must hear the iambic lines, gentlemen of the jury, which, in the play, are spoken by the mother of the girl. You will find in them a greatness of spirit and a nobility worthy of Athens and a daughter of Cephisus.

Speech from Euripides

He wins men's hearts who with a ready hand
Confers his favours; he who in the doing
Delays and falters is less generous.
But I consent to give my child to die
For many reasons: first there is no state
I count more worthy to accept my gift
Than Athens, peopled by no alien race.
For we are of this soil, while other towns,
Formed as by hazard in a game of draughts,
Take their inhabitants from divers parts.
He who adopts a city, having left
Some other town, resembles a bad peg
Fixed into wood of better quality,
A citizen in name but not in fact.
And secondly: it is that we may guard
Our country and the altars of the gods
That we get children for ourselves at all.
This city, though it bears a single name,
Holds many people in it. Should I then
Destroy all these, when it is in my power
To give one girl to die on their behalf?
The mere ability to count, and tell
The greater from the less, convinces me
That this, the ruin of one person's home,
Is of less consequence and brings less grief

---

5 πόλεος et in v. 21 Grotius : πόλεως codd.
    6 οἰκήσῃ Meineke : οἰκίζει codd.
  7 ἕκατι Matthiae : ἕνεκα codd. : ἕκητι Ald.
  8 ῥυώμεθα Ald. : ῥυόμεθα NA.
    9 ἕν Grotius : ἐν codd.
   10 πολλοὶ Musgrave : πολλοῖς codd.
11 οὑνὸς Emperius : ἑνὸς codd. : οὑμὸς Bekker.

87

πταίσας ἁπάσης πόλεος, οὐδ᾽ ἴσον φέρει.
εἰ δ᾽ ἦν ἐν οἴκοις ἀντὶ θηλειῶν[1] στάχυς

ἄρσην, πόλιν δὲ πολεμία κατεῖχε φλόξ,
οὐκ ἄν νιν[2] ἐξέπεμπον εἰς μάχην δορός,
θάνατον προταρβοῦσ᾽· ἀλλ᾽ ἔμοιγ᾽ εἴη[3] τέκνα,   25
⟨ἃ⟩[4] καὶ μάχοιτο καὶ μετ᾽ ἀνδράσιν πρέποι,
μὴ σχήματ᾽[5] ἄλλως ἐν πόλει πεφυκότα.
τὰ μητέρων δὲ δάκρυ᾽ ὅταν πέμπῃ τέκνα,
πολλοὺς ἐθήλυν᾽ εἰς μάχην ὁρμωμένους.
μισῶ γυναῖκας αἵτινες πρὸ τοῦ καλοῦ   30
ζῆν παῖδας εἵλοντ᾽ ἢ[6] παρῄνεσαν κακά.
καὶ μὴν θανόντες γ᾽ ἐν μάχῃ πολλῶν μέτα
τύμβον τε κοινὸν ἔλαχον εὔκλειάν τ᾽ ἴσην·
τῇ ᾽μῇ δὲ παιδὶ στέφανος εἷς μιᾷ μόνῃ
πόλεως θανούσῃ[7] τῆσδ᾽ ὕπερ δοθήσεται.   35
καὶ τὴν τεκοῦσαν καὶ σὲ δύο θ᾽ ὁμοσπόρω[8]
σώσει· τί[9] τούτων οὐχὶ δέξασθαι καλόν;
τὴν οὐκ ἐμὴν πλὴν ⟨ἢ⟩[10] φύσει δώσω κόρην
θῦσαι πρὸ γαίας. εἰ γὰρ αἱρεθήσεται
πόλις, τί παίδων τῶν ἐμῶν μέτεστί μοι;   40
οὐκοῦν ἅπαντα τοὐν γ᾽[11] ἐμοὶ σωθήσεται·
ἄρξουσιν ἄλλοι, τήνδ᾽ ἐγὼ σώσω πόλιν.
ἐκεῖνο δ᾽ οὗ τὸ[12] πλεῖστον ἐν κοινῷ μέρος,
οὐκ ἔσθ᾽ ἑκούσης τῆς ἐμῆς ψυχῆς ἄτερ,[13]
προγόνων παλαιὰ[14] θέσμι᾽ ὅστις[15] ἐκβαλεῖ[16]·   45

---

[1] θηλειῶν Grotius : θηλέων codd.
[2] ἄν νιν Matthiae : ἂν μὴν NA : ἂν μιν Ald.
[3] εἴη Ald. : ἐστι codd.   [4] ἃ add. Ald.
[5] σχήματ᾽ Scaliger : σχήματα δ᾽ codd.
[6] εἵλοντ᾽ ἢ Matthiae : εἵλοντο καὶ codd.

Than would result if the whole city fell.
If I had sons at home instead of girls,
When hostile flames beset the city's walls,
Should I not send them forth into the fight,
Though fearing for them ?   May my children then
Fight also, vie with men, and not become
Mere shapes of vanity within the state.
And yet, when mothers send their sons to war
With tears, they often daunt them as they leave.
I hate the women who above all else
Prefer their sons to live and put this thought
Before their honour, urging cowardice.
But if they fall in battle they obtain
A common grave and glory which they share
With many others ;   whereas she, my child,
By dying for this city will attain
A garland destined solely for herself.
And she will save her mother and you too
And both her sisters.   Is it right to scorn
Honours like these ?   Except in nature's way
This girl whom I shall give for sacrifice
To save her native land is not my own.
And if the city falls, what further chance
Shall I have left me to enjoy my child ?
So far as rests with me, all shall be saved.
Let others rule in Athens ;   I will be
Her saviour, and without my wish no man
Shall harm what most concerns our common good,
The ancient laws our fathers handed down.

---

[7] εἰς μιᾷ μόνῃ . . . θανούσῃ Tyrwhitt :   ἢ (ἡ N) μία μόνη
. . . θανοῦσα codd.

[8] ὁμοσπόρῳ Bekker :   ὁμοσπόρων codd.

[9] σώσει· τί Melanchthon :   ὡς εἴ τι codd.

[10] ἢ add. Wagner.

[11] ἅπαντα τοὖν γ' Heinrich (iam ἅπαντα τοὖν Reiske) :
ἅπαντας γοῦν τ' codd.

[12] ἐκεῖνο δ' οὖ τὸ Ald. :   ἐκεῖνο δ' οὐ NA.

[13] ἄτερ] ἄνερ Valckenaer :   ἀνήρ Bothe.

[14] παλαιὰ Ald. :   πάλαι NA.

[15] θέσμι' ὅστις Reiske :   θέσμιά τις NA.

[16] ἐκβαλεῖ Ald. :   ἐκβάλλει codd.

οὐδ' ἀντ' ἐλάας¹ χρυσέας τε Γοργόνος
τρίαιναν ὀρθὴν στᾶσαν ἐν πόλεως βάθροις
Εὔμολπος οὐδὲ Θρῇξ² ἀναστέψει³ λεὼς
στεφάνοισι, Παλλὰς δ' οὐδαμοῦ τιμήσεται.
χρῆσθ', ὦ πολῖται, τοῖς ἐμοῖς λοχεύμασιν,   50
σῴζεσθε,⁴ νικᾶτ'· ἀντὶ γὰρ ψυχῆς μιᾶς
οὐκ ἔσθ' ὅπως οὐ τήνδ' ἐγώ⁵ σώσω πόλιν.
ὦ πατρίς, εἴθε πάντες οἳ ναίουσί σε
οὕτω φιλοῖεν ὡς ἐγώ· καὶ ῥᾳδίως
οἰκοῖμεν ἄν σε, κοὐδὲν ἂν πάσχοις κακόν.   55

101   Ταῦτα, ὦ ἄνδρες, τοὺς πατέρας ὑμῶν ἐπαίδευε.
φύσει γὰρ οὐσῶν φιλοτέκνων πασῶν τῶν γυναικῶν,
ταύτην ἐποίησε τὴν πατρίδα μᾶλλον τῶν παίδων
φιλοῦσαν, ἐνδεικνύμενος ὅτι εἴπερ αἱ γυναῖκες
τοῦτο τολμήσουσι ποιεῖν, τούς γ' ἄνδρας ἀνυπέρ-
βλητόν τινα δεῖ τὴν εὔνοιαν ὑπὲρ τῆς πατρίδος
ἔχειν, καὶ μὴ φεύγειν αὐτὴν ἐγκαταλιπόντας μηδὲ
καταισχύνειν πρὸς ἅπαντας τοὺς Ἕλληνας, ὥσπερ
Λεωκράτης.

102   Βούλομαι δ' ὑμῖν καὶ τὸν Ὅμηρον παρασχέσθαι
ἐπαινῶν.⁶   οὕτω γὰρ ὑπέλαβον ὑμῶν οἱ πατέρες
σπουδαῖον εἶναι ποιητὴν ὥστε νόμον ἔθεντο καθ'
ἑκάστην πεντετηρίδα⁷ τῶν Παναθηναίων μόνου τῶν
ἄλλων ποιητῶν ῥαψῳδεῖσθαι τὰ ἔπη, ἐπίδειξιν
ποιούμενοι πρὸς τοὺς Ἕλληνας ὅτι τὰ κάλλιστα

¹ ἀντ' ἐλάας Dobree : ἂν τελείας codd.
² Θρῇξ Dindorf : Θρᾷξ codd.
³ ἀναστέψει Musgrave : ἀναστρέψει codd.
⁴ Post σῴζεσθε habent καὶ codd., om. Ald.
⁵ οὐ τήνδ' ἐγὼ Ald. : ὑμῖν τήνδ' ἐγὼ οὐ codd.

Eumolpus and his slavish Thracian train
Shall set no trident in our midst or deck
It round with garlands, where the olive tree
And Gorgon's golden head have been revered;
Nor shall Athena meet with utter scorn.
Come, citizens, and use my travail's fruit
To save yourselves and conquer, knowing well
That I could never hesitate to save
This city for the sake of one poor life.
My country, were the love of all your sons
As great as mine ! You could not suffer ill,
And we possessing you would live secure.

On these verses, gentlemen, your fathers were
brought up. All women are by nature fond of
children, but this one Euripides portrayed as loving
her country more than her offspring and made it clear
that, if women bring themselves to act like this, men
should show towards their country a devotion which
cannot be surpassed, not forsake it and flee, as
Leocrates did, nor disgrace it before the whole of
Greece.

I want also to recommend Homer to you. In your
fathers' eyes he was a poet of such worth that they
passed a law that every four years at the Panathenaea
he alone of all the poets should have his works
recited [a]; and thus they showed the Greeks their

[a] The law that Homer should be recited at the festival of
the Great Panathenaea, held in the third year of each
Olympiad, may fairly safely be assigned to the time of the
Pisistratids (c. 560 to 510 B.C.). It is not mentioned in connexion with Pisistratus himself, though he is credited by
a number of ancient authorities with the establishment of
a definite text of Homer (cf. Cicero, de Orat. iii. 34), but
according to [Plat.] Hipparchus 228 B, his son Hipparchus
did provide for recitations at the festival.

---

[6] τὸν Ὅμηρον . . . ἐπαινῶν] τῶν Ὁμήρου . . . ἐπῶν Reiske.
[7] πεντετηρίδα Dobree : πενταετηρίδα codd.

τῶν ἔργων προῃροῦντο. εἰκότως· οἱ μὲν γὰρ
νόμοι διὰ τὴν συντομίαν οὐ διδάσκουσιν ἀλλ' ἐπι-
τάττουσιν ἃ δεῖ ποιεῖν, οἱ δὲ ποιηταὶ μιμούμενοι
τὸν ἀνθρώπινον βίον, τὰ κάλλιστα τῶν ἔργων
[162] ἐκλεξάμενοι, μετὰ λόγου καὶ ἀποδείξεως τοὺς
103 ἀνθρώπους συμπείθουσιν. Ἕκτωρ γὰρ τοῖς Τρωσὶ
παρακελευόμενος ὑπὲρ τῆς πατρίδος τάδ' εἴρηκεν·

> ἀλλὰ μάχεσθ' ἐπὶ νηυσὶ διαμπερές.[1] ὃς δέ κεν
>   ὑμέων
> βλήμενος ἠὲ τυπεὶς θάνατον καὶ πότμον ἐπίσπῃ,
> τεθνάτω. οὔ οἱ ἀεικὲς ἀμυνομένῳ περὶ πάτρης
> τεθνάμεν· ἀλλ' ἄλοχός τε σόη καὶ νήπια τέκνα,[2]
> καὶ κλῆρος καὶ οἶκος[3] ἀκήρατος, εἴ κεν Ἀχαιοὶ
> οἴχωνται σὺν νηυσὶ φίλην ἐς πατρίδα γαῖαν.

104 τούτων τῶν ἐπῶν ἀκούοντες, ὦ ἄνδρες, οἱ πρόγονοι ὑμῶν καὶ τὰ τοιαῦτα τῶν ἔργων ζηλοῦντες
οὕτως ἔσχον πρὸς ἀρετὴν ὥστ' οὐ μόνον ὑπὲρ τῆς
αὑτῶν πατρίδος, ἀλλὰ καὶ πάσης ⟨τῆς⟩[4] Ἑλλάδος
ὡς κοινῆς ἤθελον ἀποθνήσκειν. οἱ γοῦν [ἐν][5]
Μαραθῶνι παραταξάμενοι τοῖς βαρβάροις τὸν ἐξ
ἁπάσης τῆς Ἀσίας στόλον ἐκράτησαν, τοῖς ἰδίοις
κινδύνοις κοινὴν ἄδειαν ἅπασι τοῖς Ἕλλησι κτώ-
μενοι, οὐκ ἐπὶ τῇ δόξῃ μέγα φρονοῦντες ἀλλ' ἐπὶ
τῷ ταύτης ἄξια πράττειν, τῶν μὲν Ἑλλήνων
προστάτας, τῶν δὲ βαρβάρων δεσπότας ἑαυτοὺς
καθιστάντες· οὐ γὰρ λόγῳ τὴν ἀρετὴν ἐπετήδευον
105 ἀλλ' ἔργῳ πᾶσιν ἐνεδείκνυντο.[6] τοιγαροῦν οὕτως

---

[1] διαμπερές] ἀολλέες Ilias. xv. 494.

admiration for the noblest deeds. They were right to do so. Laws are too brief to give instruction : they merely state the things that must be done ; but poets, depicting life itself, select the noblest actions and so through argument and demonstration convert men's hearts. Thus Hector, while exhorting the Trojans to defend their country, speaks these words :

Fight on unresting by the ships ; and if some meet their fate
By wound of dart, or battling hand to hand, then let them die.
To fall in combat for your country's sake is no disgrace ;
For wife and child will live unharmed, and home and plot last on,
If once the Achaeans leave and sail their ships to their own land.

These are the lines, gentlemen, to which your forefathers listened, and such are the deeds which they emulated. Thus they developed such courage that they were ready to die, not for their country alone, but for the whole of Greece as a land in whose heritage they shared. Certainly those who confronted the barbarians at Marathon, by defeating an army from the whole of Asia, won, at their own peril, security for every Greek alike. They gave themselves no credit for glory but valued rather conduct deserving of it, whereby they made themselves the champions of the Greeks and lords of the barbarians. Their pursuit of valour was no idle boast ; they displayed it in action to the world. Mark how the men

---

² καὶ νήπια τέκνα] καὶ παῖδες ὀπίσσω ibid. 497.
³ καὶ κλῆρος καὶ οἶκος] καὶ οἶκος καὶ κλῆρος ibid. 498.
⁴ τῆς add. Blume.
⁵ ἐν del. Es.
⁶ ἐνεδείκνυντο Cohn : ἀνεδείκνυντο N : ἐπεδείκνυντο A.

ἦσαν ἄνδρες σπουδαῖοι καὶ κοινῇ καὶ ἰδίᾳ οἱ τότε
τὴν πόλιν οἰκοῦντες ὥστε τοῖς ἀνδρειοτάτοις
Λακεδαιμονίοις ἐν τοῖς ἔμπροσθεν χρόνοις πολε-
μοῦσι πρὸς Μεσσηνίους ἀνεῖλεν ὁ θεός, παρ' ἡμῶν
ἡγεμόνα λαβεῖν καὶ νικήσειν τοὺς ἐναντίους. καίτοι εἰ τοῖν ἀφ' Ἡρακλέους γεγενημένοιν,[1] οἳ ἀεὶ
βασιλεύουσιν ἐν Σπάρτῃ, τοὺς παρ' ἡμῶν ἡγεμόνας ἀμείνους ὁ θεὸς ἔκρινε, πῶς οὐκ ἀνυπέρ-
106 βλητον χρὴ τὴν ἐκείνων ἀρετὴν νομίζειν; τίς γὰρ
οὐκ οἶδε τῶν Ἑλλήνων ὅτι Τυρταῖον στρατηγὸν
ἔλαβον παρὰ τῆς πόλεως, μεθ' οὗ καὶ τῶν πολεμίων
ἐκράτησαν καὶ τὴν περὶ τοὺς νέους ἐπιμέλειαν
συνετάξαντο, οὐ μόνον εἰς τὸν παρόντα κίνδυνον
ἀλλ' εἰς ἅπαντα τὸν αἰῶνα βουλευσάμενοι καλῶς;
κατέλιπε γὰρ αὐτοῖς ἐλεγεῖα ποιήσας, ὧν ἀκούοντες
107 παιδεύονται πρὸς ἀνδρείαν· καὶ περὶ τοὺς ἄλλους
ποιητὰς οὐδένα λόγον ἔχοντες περὶ τούτου οὕτω
σφόδρα ἐσπουδάκασιν ὥστε νόμον ἔθεντο, ὅταν ἐν
τοῖς ὅπλοις ἐξεστρατευμένοι[2] ὦσι,[3] καλεῖν ἐπὶ τὴν
τοῦ βασιλέως σκηνὴν ἀκουσομένους τῶν Τυρταίου
ποιημάτων ἅπαντας, νομίζοντες οὕτως ἂν αὐτοὺς
μάλιστα πρὸ τῆς πατρίδος ἐθέλειν ἀποθνήσκειν.
χρήσιμον δ' ἐστὶ καὶ τούτων ἀκοῦσαι τῶν ἐλε-

---

[1] τοῖν . . . γεγενημένοιν Bursian : τοῖς . . . γεγενημένοις
codd. : τῶν . . . γεγενημένων Ald.

[2] ἐξεστρατευμένοι Es : ἐκστρατευόμενοι codd.

who lived at Athens then excelled in public, and in
private life ; so greatly that when in days gone by
the Spartans, so renowned for courage, were at war
with the Messenians the god advised them to take a
leader from us ; for so they would defeat their
enemies. And yet if the god decided that the
leaders sent from Athens were better than the two
descendants of Heracles who in succession reign at
Sparta, must we not conclude that nothing could sur-
pass the valour of our ancestors ? Does any Greek
not know that they took Tyrtaeus from our city *a* to be
their leader and with him defeated their enemies and
established their system of training for the young,
thus wisely providing for the immediate danger and
for their whole future too ? For Tyrtaeus left them
elegiac poems by his own hand, and through listening
to these they are trained to be brave. Though they
have no regard for other poets, they valued his works
so highly that they passed a law which provides that
their men, after taking the field, shall be summoned
to the king's tent to hear the verses of Tyrtaeus all
together, holding that this of all things would make
them most ready to die for their country. It will be
profitable for you to hear these elegiac verses too,

---

a Tyrtaeus, of whose date nothing certain is known, is
generally thought to have lived at the time of the Second
Messenian War (*c.* 640 B.C.). The tradition that he came
from Athens, though open to question, is at least as old as
Plato, who in the *Laws* asserts simply that he was an Athenian
(Plat. *Leg.* i. 629 A). Pausanias tells the story, agreeing
substantially with Lycurgus but adding that Tyrtaeus was a
lame schoolmaster whom the Athenians were willing to let
go since he was not regarded as in any way outstanding
(Paus. iv. 15. 3).

---

³ ὦσι A. G. Becker : εἰσί codd.

γείων, ἵν᾽ ἐπίστησθε οἷα ποιοῦντες εὐδοκίμουν παρ᾽
ἐκείνοις.

τεθνάμεναι γὰρ καλὸν ἐνὶ προμάχοισι πεσόντα
   ἄνδρ᾽ ἀγαθόν, περὶ ᾗ πατρίδι μαρνάμενον.
τὴν δ᾽ αὑτοῦ προλιπόντα πόλιν καὶ πίονας
   ἀγρούς
   πτωχεύειν πάντων ἔστ᾽ ἀνιηρότατον,
πλαζόμενον σὺν μητρὶ φίλῃ καὶ πατρὶ γέροντι   5
   παισί τε σὺν μικροῖς κουριδίῃ τ᾽ ἀλόχῳ.
ἐχθρὸς μὲν γὰρ τοῖσι μετέσσεται, οὕς κεν ἵκηται
   χρημοσύνῃ[1] τ᾽ εἴκων καὶ στυγερῇ πενίῃ,
αἰσχύνει δὲ[2] γένος, κατὰ δ᾽ ἀγλαὸν εἶδος ἐλέγχει,
   πᾶσα δ᾽ ἀτιμίη καὶ κακότης ἕπεται.   10
εἰ δ᾽[3] οὕτως ἀνδρός τοι ἀλωμένου οὐδεμί᾽ ὤρη
   γίγνεται οὐδ᾽ αἰδώς, οὔτ᾽ ὀπίσω γένεος,[4]
θυμῷ γῆς περὶ τῆσδε μαχώμεθα, καὶ περὶ παίδων
   θνήσκωμεν ψυχέων[5] μηκέτι φειδόμενοι.
[163] ὦ νέοι, ἀλλὰ μάχεσθε παρ᾽ ἀλλήλοισι μένον-
   τες,   15
   μηδὲ φυγῆς αἰσχρῆς[6] ἄρχετε μηδὲ φόβου,
ἀλλὰ μέγαν ποιεῖσθε καὶ ἄλκιμον ἐν φρεσὶ θυ-
   μόν,
   μηδὲ φιλοψυχεῖτ᾽ ἀνδράσι μαρνάμενοι·
τοὺς δὲ παλαιοτέρους, ὧν οὐκέτι γούνατ᾽ ἐλα-
   φρά,
   μὴ καταλείποντες φεύγετε, τοὺς γεραιούς.   20
αἰσχρὸν γὰρ δὴ τοῦτο, μετὰ προμάχοισι πεσόντα
   κεῖσθαι πρόσθε νέων ἄνδρα παλαιότερον,
ἤδη λευκὸν ἔχοντα κάρη πολιόν τε γένειον,
   θυμὸν ἀποπνείοντ᾽ ἄλκιμον ἐν κονίῃ,

that you may know what sort of conduct brought men fame among the Spartans.[a]

Nobly comes death to him who in the van
    Fighting for fatherland has made his stand.
Shame and despite attend the coward's flight,
    Who, leaving native town and fruitful land,
Wanders, a homeless beggar, with his kin,
    True wife, old father, mother, tender child.
Unwelcome will he be where'er he goes,
    Bowed down with hardship and by want defiled.
Bringing his house dishonour, he belies
    His noble mien, a prey to fear and shame.
Thus roams the waif unpitied and unloved,
    He and the line that after bears his name.
Be stalwart then. Think not of life or limb ;
    Shielding our land and children let us die.
Youths, brave the fight together. Be not first
    To yield to craven cowardice and fly.
Make large your hearts within you. Undismayed
    Engage in battle with grown men. Be bold ;
And standing fast forsake not those whose feet
    No longer keep their swiftness. Guard the old.
For shame it is to see an elder fall,
    Down in the forefront, smitten in the strife,
Before the youths, with grey beard, hair grown white,
    To breathe out in the dust his valiant life,

[a] Alternative versions of these lines will be found in the *Oxford Book of Greek Verse in Translation* (no. 97) and in the Loeb *Elegy and Iambus* (vol. i., no. 258).

---

[1] χρημοσύνη Bergk : χρησμοσύνη codd.
[2] δὲ Hartung : τε codd.
[3] εἰ δ' Francke : εἴθ' codd.
[4] γένεος Ahrens : τέλος codd. : εἰσοπίσω τελέθει Ald.
[5] ψυχέων Ald. : ψυχάων codd.
[6] αἰσχρῆς Sauppe : αἰσχρᾶς codd.

αἱματόεντ' αἰδοῖα φίλαις ἐν χερσὶν ἔχοντα   25
(αἰσχρὰ τά γ'[1] ὀφθαλμοῖς καὶ νεμεσητὸν ἰδεῖν)
καὶ χρόα γυμνωθέντα. νέοισι δὲ πάντ' ἐπέοικεν,
ὄφρ' ἐρατῆς ἥβης ἀγλαὸν ἄνθος ἔχῃ·
ἀνδράσι μὲν θηητὸς[2] ἰδεῖν, ἐρατὸς δὲ γυναιξὶν
ζωὸς ἐών, καλὸς δ' ἐν προμάχοισι πεσών.   30
ἀλλά τις εὖ διαβὰς μενέτω ποσὶν ἀμφοτέροισιν
στηριχθεὶς ἐπὶ γῆς, χεῖλος ὀδοῦσι δακών.

108 καλά γ', ὦ ἄνδρες, καὶ χρήσιμα τοῖς βουλομένοις
προσέχειν. οὕτω τοίνυν εἶχον πρὸς ἀνδρείαν οἱ
τούτων ἀκούοντες ὥστε πρὸς τὴν πόλιν ἡμῶν περὶ
τῆς ἡγεμονίας ἀμφισβητεῖν, εἰκότως· τὰ γὰρ
κάλλιστα τῶν ἔργων ἀμφοτέροις ἦν κατειργασμένα.
οἱ μὲν γὰρ πρόγονοι τοὺς βαρβάρους ἐνίκησαν, οἳ
πρῶτοι τῆς Ἀττικῆς ἐπέβησαν, καὶ καταφανῆ
ἐποίησαν τὴν ἀνδρείαν τοῦ πλούτου καὶ τὴν ἀρετὴν
τοῦ πλήθους περιγιγνομένην· Λακεδαιμόνιοι δ' ἐν
Θερμοπύλαις παραταξάμενοι ταῖς μὲν τύχαις οὐχ[3]
ὁμοίαις[4] ἐχρήσαντο, τῇ δ' ἀνδρείᾳ πολὺ πάντων δι-
109 ήνεγκαν. τοιγαροῦν ἐπὶ τοῖς ἠρίοις[5] μαρτύρια ἔστιν
ἰδεῖν τῆς ἀρετῆς αὐτῶν ἀναγεγραμμένα ἀληθῆ
πρὸς ἅπαντας τοὺς Ἕλληνας, ἐκείνοις μέν·

ὦ ξεῖν', ἄγγειλον Λακεδαιμονίοις ὅτι τῇδε
κείμεθα τοῖς κείνων πειθόμενοι νομίμοις,

τοῖς δ' ὑμετέροις προγόνοις·

Ἑλλήνων προμαχοῦντες Ἀθηναῖοι Μαραθῶνι
χρυσοφόρων Μήδων ἐστόρεσαν δύναμιν.

---

[1] τά γ'] τάδ' Baiter et Sauppe : τά τ' G. Hermann.   [2] θηητὸς Reiske : θνητοῖσιν codd.
[3] οὐχ add. N.   [4] ὁμοίαις Bekker : ὁμοίως codd.

Clasping his bloody groin with clinging hands,
   (Fit sight indeed to kindle wrath and shame!)
His body bared. But those whom youth's sweet flower
   Adorns unfaded nothing can defame.
Honour of men is theirs, in life, and women's love ;
   Fair are they too when in the van laid low.
Then clench your teeth and, with both feet astride,
   Firm planted on the ground withstand the foe.

They are fine lines, gentlemen, and a lesson too for those who wish to heed them. Such was the courage of the men who used to hear them that they disputed with our city for supremacy ; no matter for surprise, since the most gallant feats had been performed by either people. Your ancestors defeated the barbarians who first set foot in Attica, demonstrating clearly the superiority of valour over wealth and courage over numbers. The Spartans took the field at Thermopylae, and, though their fortune was less happy, in bravery they far surpassed all rivals. And so over their graves a testimony to their courage can be seen, faithfully engraved for every Greek to read : to the Spartans :

   Go tell the Spartans, thou who passest by,
     That here obedient to their laws we lie.

And to your ancestors :

   Athenians, guarding Greece, subdued in fight,
     At Marathon the gilded Persians' might.[a]

[a] Both epigrams are by Simonides of Ceos (*c.* 560-470 B.C.). The well-known version of the first given here is that of W. L. Bowles, which has been somewhat modified in the *Oxford Book of Greek Verse in Translation* (no. 212). Strabo, who quotes the original (Strabo ix. iv.), agrees with the wording given by Lycurgus, except that for the first three

---

[5] ἠρίοις Wurm : ὁρίοις τοῦ βίου codd.

LYCURGUS

110 Ταῦτα, ὦ Ἀθηναῖοι, καὶ μνημονεύεσθαι καλὰ καὶ
τοῖς πράξασιν[1] ἔπαινος καὶ τῇ πόλει δόξα ἀείμνη-
στος. ἀλλ᾽ οὐχ ὁ Λεωκράτης πεποίηκεν, ἀλλ᾽ ἑκὼν
τὴν ἐξ ἅπαντος τοῦ αἰῶνος συνηθροισμένην τῇ
πόλει δόξαν κατῄσχυνεν. ἐὰν μὲν οὖν αὐτὸν ἀποκτείνητε, δόξετε πᾶσι τοῖς Ἕλλησι καὶ ὑμεῖς τὰ
τοιαῦτα τῶν ἔργων μισεῖν· εἰ δὲ μή, καὶ τοὺς προγόνους τῆς παλαιᾶς δόξης ἀποστερήσετε καὶ τοὺς
ἄλλους πολίτας μεγάλα βλάψετε. οἱ γὰρ ἐκείνους
μὴ θαυμάζοντες τοῦτον πειράσονται μιμεῖσθαι,
νομίζοντες ἐκεῖνα μὲν παρὰ τοῖς παλαιοῖς[2] εὐδοκιμεῖν, παρ᾽ ὑμῖν δ᾽[3] ἀναίδειαν καὶ προδοσίαν καὶ
δειλίαν κεκρίσθαι κάλλιστον.

111 Εἰ ⟨δὲ⟩[4] μὴ δύνασθε ὑπ᾽ ἐμοῦ διδαχθῆναι ὃν
τρόπον δεῖ πρὸς τοὺς τοιούτους ἔχειν, σκέψασθε
ἐκείνους τίνα τρόπον ἐλάμβανον παρ᾽ αὐτῶν τὴν τι-
μωρίαν· ὥσπερ γὰρ τὰ καλὰ τῶν ἔργων ἠπίσταντο
ἐπιτηδεύειν, οὕτω καὶ τὰ πονηρὰ προῃροῦντο
κολάζειν. ἐκεῖνοι γάρ, ὦ ἄνδρες, θεωρήσατε ὡς
ὠργίζοντο τοῖς προδόταις καὶ κοινοὺς ἐχθροὺς
112 ἐνόμιζον εἶναι τῆς πόλεως. Φρυνίχου γὰρ ἀπο-
[164] σφαγέντος νύκτωρ παρὰ τὴν κρήνην τὴν ἐν τοῖς

---

[1] τοῖς πράξασιν Taylor : ταῖς πράξεσιν codd.
[2] τοῖς παλαιοῖς Taylor : τοῖς πολεμίοις codd.
[3] παρ᾽ ὑμῖν δ᾽ Blass : παρὰ δ᾽ ὑμῖν A : παρ᾽ ὑμῖν N.
[4] δὲ add. Stephanus.

---

words he has: ὦ ξέν᾽ ἀπάγγειλον. Herodotus (vii. 228) has
a slightly different version :

ὦ ξεῖν᾽ ἀγγέλλειν Λακεδαιμονίοις, ὅτι τῇδε
κείμεθα τοῖς κείνων ῥήμασι πειθόμενοι.

Cicero's Latin translation was as follows (*Tusc. Disp.* i. 42) :

Dic, hospes, Spartae nos te hic vidisse iacentes
dum sanctis patriae legibus obsequimur.

These are noble lines for us to remember, Athenians; they are a tribute to those whose deeds they record and an undying glory to the city. But Leocrates has not acted thus. Deliberately he sullied that honour which the city has accumulated from the earliest times. Therefore if you kill him all Greeks will believe that you too hate such acts as his. If not, you will rob your forbears of their long-lived renown, and will do grievous harm to your fellow citizens. For those who do not admire our ancestors will try to imitate Leocrates believing, that although among men of the past the old virtues had a place of honour, in your eyes shamelessness, treachery and cowardice are held in most esteem.

If I am unable to show you what your attitude towards such men should be, remember your ancestors and the methods of punishment which they employed against them. Capable as they were of the noblest actions, they were no less ready to punish what was base. Think of them, gentlemen; think how enraged they were with traitors and how they looked on them as common enemies of the city. You remember when Phrynichus ^{a} was murdered at night beside the

---

^{a} Phrynichus, commander of the Athenian fleet at Samos, took part in the Revolution of the Four Hundred in 411 B.C. According to Thucydides (viii. 92) he was murdered in the market place in broad daylight (ἐν τῇ ἀγορᾷ πληθούσῃ) by an unknown hand, after returning from a mission to Sparta which had failed. But the account of Lysias (xiii. 71) agrees in the main with that of Lycurgus. The spring was probably in the market place. Critias was later chief of the Thirty.

οἰσύοις ὑπὸ Ἀπολλοδώρου καὶ Θρασυβούλου, καὶ
τούτων ληφθέντων καὶ εἰς τὸ δεσμωτήριον ἀπο-
τεθέντων ὑπὸ τῶν τοῦ Φρυνίχου φίλων, αἰσθόμενος ὁ δῆμος τὸ γεγονὸς τούς τε εἰρχθέντας
ἐξήγαγε,[1] καὶ βασάνων γενομένων ἀνέκρινε, καὶ
ζητῶν τὸ πρᾶγμα εὗρε τὸν μὲν Φρύνιχον προδιδόντα
τὴν πόλιν, τοὺς δ' ἀποκτείναντας αὐτὸν ἀδίκως
113 εἰρχθέντας· καὶ ψηφίζεται ὁ δῆμος Κριτίου εἰπόντος
τὸν μὲν νεκρὸν κρίνειν προδοσίας, κἂν δόξῃ προδότης ὢν ἐν τῇ χώρᾳ τεθάφθαι, τά τε[2] ὀστᾶ αὐτοῦ
ἀνορύξαι καὶ ἐξορίσαι ἔξω τῆς Ἀττικῆς, ὅπως
ἂν μὴ κέηται ἐν τῇ χώρᾳ μηδὲ τὰ ὀστᾶ τοῦ τὴν
χώραν καὶ τὴν πόλιν προδιδόντος. ἐψηφίσαντο
114 δὲ[3] καὶ ἐὰν ἀπολογῶνταί τινες ὑπὲρ[4] τοῦ τετελευ-
τηκότος, ἐὰν ἁλῷ ὁ τεθνηκώς, ἐνόχους εἶναι καὶ
τούτους τοῖς αὐτοῖς ἐπιτιμίοις· οὕτως οὐδὲ βοηθεῖν
τοῖς τοὺς ἄλλους ἐγκαταλείπουσιν ἡγοῦντο δίκαιον
εἶναι, ἀλλ' ὁμοίως ἂν προδοῦναι τὴν πόλιν καὶ
τὸν διασῴζοντα τὸν προδότην. τοιγαροῦν οὕτω
μισοῦντες τοὺς ἀδικοῦντας καὶ τὰ τοιαῦτα κατ'
αὐτῶν ψηφιζόμενοι ἀσφαλῶς ἐκ τῶν κινδύνων ἀπ-
ηλλάττοντο. λαβὲ δ' αὐτοῖς τὸ ψήφισμα, γραμματεῦ, καὶ ἀνάγνωθι.

ΨΗΦΙΣΜΑ

115 Ἀκούετε, ὦ ἄνδρες, τούτου τοῦ ψηφίσματος.
ἔπειτα ἐκεῖνοι μὲν τὰ τοῦ προδότου ὀστᾶ ἀνορύξ-
αντες ἐκ τῆς Ἀττικῆς ἐξώρισαν καὶ τοὺς ἀπολογουμένους ὑπὲρ αὐτοῦ Ἀρίσταρχον καὶ Ἀλεξικλέα

---

[1] αἰσθόμενος . . . ἐξήγαγε Coraes : αἰσθανόμενος . . . ἐσῆγε
codd.
[2] τε] γε Jacob.

fountain in the osier beds by Apollodorus and Thrasybulus, who were later caught and put in the prison by the friends of Phrynichus. The people noted what had happened and, releasing the prisoners, held an inquiry after torture. On investigation they found that Phrynichus had been trying to betray the city and that his murderers had been unjustly imprisoned. They decreed publicly, on the motion of Critias, that the dead man should be tried for treason, and that if it were found that this was a tratior who had been buried in the country, his bones should be dug up and removed from Attica,[a] so that the land should not have lying in it even the bones of one who had betrayed his country and his city. They decreed also that if any persons defended the dead man and he were found guilty, they should be liable to the same punishment as he. Thus, in their view, it was wrong even to assist men who had deserted others ; and to try to save the traitor would be to betray the city no less than he. In this way then, by hating wrongdoers and by passing such measures against them, they brought themselves safely out of dangers. Produce the decree for them, clerk, and read it.

The Decree

You hear this decree, gentlemen. After it was passed your ancestors dug up the traitor's bones and cast them out of Attica ; they killed his defenders, Aristarchus and Alexicles, and even refused them

---

[a] A law existed to the effect that a man condemned for treason should not be buried in Attica (see Xen. *Hell.* i. 7. 22).

---

[3] Post δὲ habent τινες codd., del. Heinrich.
[4] ὑπὲρ Herwerden : περὶ codd.

ἀπέκτειναν καὶ οὐδ' ἐν τῇ χώρᾳ ταφῆναι ἐπέτρεψαν·
ὑμεῖς δ' αὐτὸ τὸ σῶμα τὸ προδεδωκὸς τὴν πόλιν
ζῶν καὶ ὑποχείριον ἔχοντες τῇ ψήφῳ, ἀτιμώρητον
116 ἐάσετε; καὶ τοσοῦτόν γ' ἔσεσθε[1] τῶν προγόνων
χείρους ὅσον ἐκεῖνοι μὲν τοὺς λόγῳ μόνον τῷ
προδότῃ βοηθήσαντας ταῖς ἐσχάταις τιμωρίαις
μετῆλθον, ὑμεῖς δὲ αὐτὸν τὸν ἔργῳ καὶ οὐ λόγῳ
τὸν δῆμον ἐγκαταλιπόντα ὡς οὐδὲν ἀδικοῦντα
ἀφήσετε; μὴ δῆτα, ὦ ἄνδρες δικασταί, ⟨οὔτε γὰρ
ὅσιον⟩[2] ὑμῖν οὔτε[3] πάτριον, ἀναξίως ὑμῶν αὐτῶν
ψηφίζεσθε. καὶ γὰρ εἰ μὲν ἕν τι τοιοῦτον γεγονὸς
ἦν ψήφισμα, εἶχεν ἄν τις εἰπεῖν ὡς δι' ὀργὴν
μᾶλλον ἢ δι' ἀλήθειαν ἐποιήσαντο· ὅταν δὲ παρὰ
πάντων ὁμοίως εἰληφότες ὦσι τὴν αὐτὴν τιμωρίαν,
πῶς οὐκ εὔδηλον ὅτι φύσει πᾶσι τοῖς τοιούτοις
117 ἔργοις ἐπολέμουν; Ἵππαρχον γὰρ τὸν Χάρμου,[4]
οὐχ ὑπομείναντα τὴν περὶ τῆς προδοσίας ἐν τῷ
δήμῳ κρίσιν ἀλλ' ἔρημον τὸν ἀγῶνα ἐάσαντα,
θανάτῳ τοῦτον ζημιώσαντες, ἐπειδὴ τῆς ἀδικίας
οὐκ ἔλαβον τὸ σῶμα ὅμηρον, τὴν εἰκόνα αὐτοῦ ἐξ
ἀκροπόλεως καθελόντες καὶ συγχωνεύσαντες καὶ
ποιήσαντες στήλην, ἐψηφίσαντο εἰς ταύτην ἀνα-
γράφειν τοὺς ἀλιτηρίους καὶ τοὺς προδότας· καὶ
αὐτὸς ὁ Ἵππαρχος ἐν ταύτῃ τῇ στήλῃ ἀναγέ-
118 γραπται, καὶ οἱ ἄλλοι δὲ προδόται. καί μοι λαβὲ
πρῶτον μὲν τὸ ψήφισμα, καθ' ὃ ἡ εἰκὼν τοῦ
Ἱππάρχου τοῦ προδότου ἐξ ἀκροπόλεως καθῃρέθη,
ἔπειτα τῆς στήλης τὸ ὑπόγραμμα καὶ τοὺς ὕστερον

[1] γ' ἔσεσθε Gebauer : ἔσεσθέ γε codd.
[2] οὔτε γὰρ ὅσιον add. Petrie : οὔτε γὰρ ἔμφυτον ci. Blass.

burial in the country. Will you then, who have the very person who has betrayed the city alive and at the mercy of your vote, let him go unpunished ? Your ancestors inflicted the extreme penalty on men who simply lent the traitor verbal help. Will you fall so short of their example as to let go as innocent the man who abandoned the state in deed as well as word ? Do not do it, gentlemen of the jury. Do not give a verdict unworthy of yourselves ; for it would be both impious and contrary to your traditions. If only one such decree were recorded, we might have said that anger rather than real conviction had prompted it. But when the same punishment was meted out by them to all alike it is surely plain that our ancestors were by nature bound to make war on all such crimes. When Hipparchus, the son of Charmus,[a] did not stand his trial for treason before the people but let the case go by default, they sentenced him to death. Then, as they did not secure his person to answer for the crime, they took down his statue from the Acropolis and, melting it down, made a pillar of it, on which they decreed that the names of sinners and traitors should be inscribed. Hipparchus himself has his name recorded on this pillar and all other traitors too. Clerk, please take the decree which authorized the statue of Hipparchus to be taken down from the Acropolis and then the inscription at the base of the

---

[a] Lycurgus appears to be the sole authority for this story. Hipparchus, a relation of the Pisistratids, was the first Athenian to be ostracized (cf. Arist. Ath. Pol. 22 and Plut. Nic. 11).

---

[3] οὔτε] οὔτω Ald.

[4] Χάρμου Harpocration (s.v. Ἵππαρχος. Cf. Aristot. Ath. Pol. 22. 4) : Τιμάρχου codd.

προσαναγραφέντας[1] προδότας εἰς ταύτην τὴν στήλην, καὶ ἀναγίγνωσκε, γραμματεῦ.

119 Τί δοκοῦσιν ὑμῖν, ὦ ἄνδρες; ἆρά γ' ὁμοίως
ὑμῖν περὶ τῶν ἀδικούντων γιγνώσκειν, καὶ οὐκ,
ἐπειδὴ καὶ τὸ σῶμα οὐκ ἐδύναντο ὑποχείριον [τοῦ
προδότου][2] λαβεῖν, τὸ μνημεῖον τοῦ προδότου
ἀνελόντες ταῖς ἐνδεχομέναις τιμωρίαις ἐκόλασαν;
οὐχ ὅπως τὸν χαλκοῦν ἀνδριάντα συγχωνεύσειαν,
ἀλλ' ἵνα τοῖς ἐπιγιγνομένοις παράδειγμα εἰς τὸν
λοιπὸν χρόνον ὡς εἶχον πρὸς τοὺς προδότας
καταλίποιεν.

120 Λαβὲ δ' αὐτοῖς καὶ τὸ ἕτερον ψήφισμα ⟨τὸ⟩[3]
περὶ τῶν εἰς Δεκέλειαν μεταστάντων, ὅτε ὁ δῆμος
ὑπὸ Λακεδαιμονίων ἐπολιορκεῖτο, ὅπως εἰδῶσιν
ὅτι περὶ τῶν προδοτῶν οἱ πρόγονοι ὁμοίας καὶ
ἀκολούθους ἀλλήλαις τὰς τιμωρίας ἐποιοῦντο.
ἀναγίγνωσκε, γραμματεῦ.

121 Ἀκούετε, ὦ ἄνδρες, καὶ τούτου τοῦ ψηφίσματος,
[165] ὅτι τῶν ἐν τῷ πολέμῳ μεταστάντων εἰς Δεκέλειαν
κατέγνωσαν, καὶ ἐψηφίσαντο, ἐάν τις αὐτῶν
ἐπανιὼν ἁλίσκηται, ἀπαγαγεῖν Ἀθηναίων τὸν
βουλόμενον πρὸς τοὺς θεσμοθέτας, παραλαβόντας
δὲ παραδοῦναι τῷ ἐπὶ τοῦ ὀρύγματος. ἔπειτα
ἐκεῖνοι μὲν τοὺς ἐν αὐτῇ τῇ χώρᾳ μεταστάντας

---

[1] προσαναγραφέντας Taylor : προαναγραφέντας codd.
[2] τοῦ προδότου del. Es.
[3] τὸ add. Thalheim.

pillar with the names of the traitors later engraved
upon it and read them out.

Decree and Text of Inscription on the Pillar

What is your impression of them, gentlemen? Had
they the same attitude as yourselves towards wrongdoers? Or did they, by obliterating the memorial of
the traitor, since they could not command his person,
punish him with all the means at their disposal?
The simple fact of melting down the bronze statue
was not enough for them; they wished to leave to
their successors a lasting memorial of their attitude
to traitors.

Let the jury hear the other decree, clerk, relating
to the men who withdrew to Decelea [a] when the
people were besieged by the Spartans, so that they
will realize that the punishments inflicted by our ancestors on traitors were uniform and self-consistent.
Read it.

Decree

You hear this decree too, gentlemen. It says that
they condemned any who moved to Decelea in wartime and laid it down that those who were caught
returning should be led by any Athenian who cared
to do so to the Thesmothetae who should take them
into custody and hand them over to the executioner.[b]
If they dealt thus with men who merely changed their

---

[a] Decelea, a town in the North of Attica, was occupied by the
Peloponnesians in 413 B.C. and therefore served as a haven
for deserters from Athens. Lycurgus seems to be the only
writer who mentions this decree.
[b] Literally: "the man in charge of the pit." τὸ ὄρυγμα
is the same as τὸ βάραθρον, the cleft into which criminals at
Athens were thrown.

οὕτως ἐκόλαζον, ὑμεῖς δὲ τὸν ἐκ τῆς πόλεως καὶ
τῆς χώρας ἐν τῷ πολέμῳ φυγόντα εἰς Ῥόδον καὶ
προδόντα τὸν δῆμον οὐκ ἀποκτενεῖτε; πῶς οὖν
δόξετε ἀπόγονοι εἶναι ἐκείνων τῶν ἀνδρῶν;

122 Ἄξιον τοίνυν ἀκοῦσαι καὶ ⟨τοῦ⟩[1] περὶ τοῦ ἐν
Σαλαμῖνι τελευτήσαντος γενομένου ψηφίσματος,
ὃν ἡ βουλή, ὅτι λόγῳ μόνον ἐνεχείρει προδιδόναι
τὴν πόλιν, περιελομένη τοὺς στεφάνους αὐτοχειρὶ
ἀπέκτεινεν. γενναῖον δ᾽, ὦ ἄνδρες, τὸ ψήφισμα καὶ
ἄξιον τῶν ὑμετέρων προγόνων, δικαίως· εὐγενεῖς[2]
γὰρ οὐ μόνον τὰς ψυχὰς ἀλλὰ καὶ τὰς τῶν ἀδικούντων τιμωρίας ἐκέκτηντο.

ΨΗΦΙΣΜΑ[3]

123 Τί οὖν, ὦ ἄνδρες; ἆρά γ᾽ ὑμῖν δοκεῖ βουλομένοις μιμεῖσθαι τοὺς προγόνους πάτριον εἶναι
Λεωκράτην μὴ οὐκ[4] ἀποκτεῖναι; ὁπότε γὰρ
ἐκεῖνοι ἀνάστατον τὴν πόλιν οὖσαν τὸν λόγῳ μόνον
προδιδόντα οὕτως ἀπέκτειναν, τί ὑμᾶς προσήκει
τὸν ἔργῳ καὶ οὐ λόγῳ τὴν οἰκουμένην ἐκλιπόντα
ποιῆσαι; ἆρ᾽ οὐχ ὑπερβαλέσθαι ἐκείνους ταῖς
τιμωρίαις;[5] καὶ ὅτ᾽ ἐκεῖνοι τοὺς ἐπιχειρήσαντας[6]
τῆς παρὰ τοῦ δήμου σωτηρίας[6] ἀποστερεῖν οὕτως
ἐκόλασαν, τί ὑμᾶς προσήκει τὸν αὐτοῦ[7] τοῦ δήμου
τὴν σωτηρίαν προδόντα ποιῆσαι; καὶ ὅτε ὑπὲρ

---

[1] τοῦ add. Reiske.
[2] εὐγενεῖς Dobree : συγγενεῖς codd.
[3] Titulum, quem supra post ἀπέκτεινεν habet N, om. alii
codd., huc transtulit Rehdantz.
[4] οὐκ add. N.
[5] ταῖς τιμωρίαις Stephanus : τῆς τιμωρίας codd.
[6] Post ἐπιχειρήσαντας Reiske ἑαυτούς, post σωτηρίας Blass
τὴν πόλιν add.   [7] αὐτοῦ Z : αὐτὴν NA.

place in Attica, how will you treat Leocrates who in wartime fled from his city and his country to Rhodes and deserted the state ? Will you not kill him ? If you do not, how can you pass as the descendants of those men ?

You ought also to hear the decree relating to the man executed in Salamis.[a] Though he had only attempted to speak treason against the city, the Council, after removing their crowns, killed him with their own hands. It is an admirable decree, gentlemen, and well worthy of your ancestors. Their nobility, revealed in their characters, was shown too in their punishment of criminals.

Decree

What is your view, gentlemen ? Do you think that if you wish to emulate your forefathers, it is in keeping to allow Leocrates to live ? When they dispatched like that one who merely betrayed with his lips a city already desolate, how ought you, whose city prospered at the time, to treat the man who did in very fact desert it ? Ought you not to outdo them in severity ? When they chastised so sternly those who tried to rob them of the security which the people offered,[b] how ought you to treat a traitor to the people's own safety ? And if they,

---

[a] Lycurgus is probably alluding to the stoning of Lycidas (see note on § 71), which Herodotus (ix. 5) puts after Salamis. Demosthenes (xviii. 204), though apparently alluding to the same story, calls the traitor Cyrsilus and places the incident before the battle.

[b] i.e. those who deserted to Decelea. The sense seems to demand an object for ἀποστερεῖν. Hence the proposals by Reiske and Blass to supply one.

τῆς δόξης ἐκεῖνοι τοὺς αἰτίους ἐτιμωροῦντο, τί
ὑμᾶς ὑπὲρ τῆς πατρίδος προσήκει ποιεῖν;

124 Ἱκανὰ μὲν οὖν καὶ ταῦτα τὴν τῶν προγόνων
γνῶναι διάνοιαν, ὡς εἶχον πρὸς τοὺς παρανομοῦντας
εἰς τὴν πόλιν· οὐ μὴν ἀλλ' ἔτι βούλομαι τῆς
στήλης ἀκοῦσαι ὑμᾶς τῆς ἐν τῷ βουλευτηρίῳ περὶ
τῶν προδοτῶν καὶ τῶν τὸν δῆμον καταλυόντων·
τὸ γὰρ μετὰ πολλῶν παραδειγμάτων διδάσκειν
ῥᾳδίαν ὑμῖν τὴν κρίσιν καθίστησι. μετὰ γὰρ τοὺς
τριάκοντα οἱ πατέρες ὑμῶν, πεπονθότες ὑπὸ τῶν
πολιτῶν οἷα οὐδεὶς πώποτε τῶν Ἑλλήνων ἠξίωσε,[1]
καὶ μόλις εἰς τὴν ἑαυτῶν κατεληλυθότες, ἁπάσας
τὰς ὁδοὺς τῶν ἀδικημάτων ἐνέφραξαν, πεπειραμένοι
καὶ εἰδότες τὰς ἀρχὰς καὶ τὰς ἐφόδους τῶν τὸν
125 δῆμον προδιδόντων. ἐψηφίσαντο γὰρ καὶ ὤμοσαν,
ἐάν τις τυραννίδι ἐπιτιθῆται[2] ἢ τὴν πόλιν προδιδῷ
ἢ τὸν δῆμον καταλύῃ, τὸν αἰσθανόμενον καθαρὸν
εἶναι ἀποκτείναντα, καὶ κρεῖττον ἔδοξεν αὐτοῖς
τοὺς τὴν αἰτίαν ἔχοντας τεθνάναι μᾶλλον ἢ πειρα-
θέντας μετὰ ἀληθείας αὐτοὺς δουλεύειν· ἀρχὴν γὰρ
οὕτως ᾤοντο δεῖν ζῆν τοὺς πολίτας, ὥστε μηδ'
εἰς ὑποψίαν ἐλθεῖν μηδένα τούτων τῶν ἀδικημάτων.
καί μοι λαβὲ τὸ ψήφισμα.

ΨΗΦΙΣΜΑ

126 Ταῦτα, ὦ ἄνδρες, ἔγραψαν εἰς τὴν στήλην, καὶ
ταύτην ἔστησαν εἰς τὸ βουλευτήριον, ὑπόμνημα

---

[1] ἠξίωσε] del. Dobree.

from considerations of honour only, took vengeance
on criminals in this way, how should you react when
your country is at stake ?

These instances suffice to show you the attitude of
our ancestors towards those who broke the city's
laws. Nevertheless I want also to remind you of the
pillar in the Council Chamber which commemorates
traitors and enemies of democracy. For if my point
is backed by frequent illustrations, I am rendering
your verdict easy. After the rule of the Thirty, your
fathers, who had suffered from citizens what no other
Greek had ever thought fit to inflict and had barely
managed to return to their country, barred all the
paths to crime, having learnt by experience the
principles and methods followed by men who wished
to overthrow democracy. For they established it
by decree and oath that anyone who found a person
aspiring to tyranny or attempting to betray the city
or overthrow the democracy should be guiltless if he
killed him.[a] They thought it better that imagined
culprits should perish than that they themselves
should have a real experience of slavery, holding that
citizens must simply live in such a manner as to
avoid the very suspicion of any of these crimes.
Please take the decree.

Decree

These words, gentlemen, they inscribed on the
pillar, erecting it in the Council Chamber as a

---

[a] The decree of Demophantus is mentioned below (§ 127).
It was passed in 410 B.C. on the restoration of the democracy
and not, so far as is known, re-enacted after the downfall of
the Thirty. It is quoted in full by Andocides (i. 96 sq.).

---

² ἐπιτιθῆται Bekker : ἐπιθῆται codd.

LYCURGUS

τοῖς καθ᾽ ἑκάστην ἡμέραν συνιοῦσι καὶ βουλευομένοις ὑπὲρ τῆς πατρίδος, ὡς δεῖ πρὸς τοὺς
τοιούτους ἔχειν. καὶ διὰ τοῦτο ἄν τις αἴσθηται
μόνον μέλλοντας αὐτοὺς τούτων τι ποιεῖν, ἀπο-
κτενεῖν¹ συνώμοσαν, εἰκότως· τῶν μὲν γὰρ ἄλλων
ἀδικημάτων ὑστέρας δεῖ τετάχθαι τὰς τιμωρίας,
προδοσίας δὲ καὶ δήμου καταλύσεως προτέρας.
εἰ γὰρ προήσεσθε² τοῦτον τὸν καιρόν, ἐν ᾧ μέλλουσιν ἐκεῖνοι κατὰ τῆς πατρίδος φαῦλόν τι πράττειν,
οὐκ ἔστιν ὑμῖν μετὰ ταῦτα δίκην παρ᾽ αὐτῶν
ἀδικούντων λαβεῖν· κρείττους γὰρ ἤδη γίγνονται
τῆς παρὰ τῶν ἀδικουμένων τιμωρίας.

127 Ἐνθυμεῖσθε τοίνυν, ὦ ἄνδρες, τῆς προνοίας
ταύτης καὶ τῶν ἔργων ἀξίως, καὶ μὴ ἐπιλανθάνεσθε
ἐν τῇ ψήφῳ οἵων ἀνδρῶν ἔκγονοί ἐστε, ἀλλὰ
παρακελεύεσθε ὑμῖν αὐτοῖς, ὅπως ὅμοια ἐκείνοις
καὶ ἀκόλουθα ἐν τῇ τήμερον ἡμέρᾳ ἐψηφισμένοι
ἐκ τοῦ δικαστηρίου ἐξίητε. ὑπομνήματα δ᾽ ἔχετε
καὶ παραδείγματα τῆς ἐκείνων τιμωρίας τὰ ἐν
τοῖς περὶ τῶν ἀδικούντων ψηφίσμασιν ὡρισμένα·
διομωμόκατε δ᾽ ἐν τῷ ψηφίσματι τῷ Δημοφάντου
κτενεῖν³ τὸν τὴν πατρίδα προδιδόντα καὶ λόγῳ
[166] καὶ ἔργῳ καὶ χειρὶ καὶ ψήφῳ. μὴ γὰρ οἴεσθε
τῶν μὲν οὐσιῶν, ἃς ἂν οἱ πρόγονοι καταλίπωσι,
κληρονόμοι εἶναι, τῶν δ᾽ ὅρκων καὶ τῆς πίστεως,
ἣν δόντες οἱ πατέρες ὑμῶν ὅμηρον τοῖς θεοῖς τῆς
κοινῆς εὐδαιμονίας τῆς πόλεως μετεῖχον, ταύτης
δὲ μὴ κληρονομεῖν.

128 Οὐ μόνον τοίνυν ἡ πόλις ὑμῶν οὕτως ἔσχε πρὸς

---

¹ ἀποκτενεῖν Cobet : ἀποκτείνειν codd.
² προήσεσθε Taylor : ποιήσεσθε codd.
³ κτενεῖν Cobet : κτείνειν codd.

112

reminder to those who daily met in council over affairs of state what their attitude to men like this should be, and hence they swore a common oath to kill them if they saw them even contemplating such conduct. Naturally enough. For where other offences are concerned, the punishment should follow on the crime ; but in cases of treason or the overthrow of a democracy it should precede it. If you let slip the moment when the criminals are contemplating some treasonable act against their country, you cannot afterwards bring them to justice for their crimes, since by then they are too powerful to be punished by those whom they have wronged.

Let this foresight, gentlemen, and these actions be the inspiration to you that they should. Remember, when you vote, the temper of your forbears, and urge each other to bring in to-day, before you leave the court, a verdict modelled to their pattern. You have memorials, you have examples of the punishments they meted out, embodied in the decrees concerning criminals. You have sworn in the decree of Demophantus to kill the man who betrays his country, whether by word or deed, hand or vote. I say " you " ; for you must not think that, as heirs to the riches bequeathed by your ancestors, you can yet renounce your share in their oaths or in the pledge your fathers gave as a security to the gods, thereby enjoying the prosperity of their city.

Your city was not alone in dealing thus with traitors.

113

τοὺς προδιδόντας ἀλλὰ καὶ Λακεδαιμόνιοι. καὶ μή
μοι ἀχθεσθῆτε, ὦ ἄνδρες, εἰ πολλάκις μέμνημαι
τῶν ἀνδρῶν τούτων· καλὸν γάρ ἐστ᾽ ἐκ[1] πόλεως
εὐνομουμένης περὶ τῶν δικαίων παραδείγματα λαμβάνειν, ἵν᾽ ἀσφαλέστερον[2] ἕκαστος ὑμῶν τὴν δικαίαν καὶ τὴν εὔορκον ψῆφον θῆται.[3] Παυσανίαν
γὰρ τὸν βασιλέα αὐτῶν προδιδόντα τῷ Πέρσῃ τὴν
Ἑλλάδα λαβόντες, ἐπειδὴ ἔφθασε καταφυγὼν εἰς
τὸ τῆς Χαλκιοίκου ἱερόν, τὴν θύραν ἀποικοδομήσαντες,[4] καὶ τὴν ὀροφὴν ἀποσκευάσαντες, καὶ κύκλῳ περιστρατοπεδεύσαντες, οὐ πρότερον ἀπῆλθον
129 πρὶν ἢ τῷ λιμῷ ἀπέκτειναν, καὶ πᾶσιν ἐπίσημον
ἐποίησαν τὴν τιμωρίαν,[5] ὅτι οὐδ᾽ αἱ παρὰ τῶν
θεῶν ἐπικουρίαι τοῖς προδόταις βοηθοῦσιν, εἰκό-
τως· οὐδὲν γὰρ πρότερον ἀδικοῦσιν[6] ἢ περὶ τοὺς
θεοὺς ἀσεβοῦσι τῶν πατρίων[7] νομίμων αὐτοὺς[8] ἀπο-
στεροῦντες. μέγιστον δὲ τῶν ἐκεῖ γεγενημένων
τεκμήριόν ἐστιν ὃ μέλλω λέγειν· νόμον γὰρ ἔθεντο
περὶ ἁπάντων τῶν μὴ ᾽θελόντων ὑπὲρ τῆς πατρίδος
κινδυνεύειν, διαρρήδην λέγοντα ἀποθνήσκειν, εἰς
αὐτὸ τοῦτο τὴν τιμωρίαν τάξαντες, εἰς ὃ μάλιστα
φοβούμενοι τυγχάνουσι, καὶ τὴν ἐκ τοῦ πολέμου
σωτηρίαν ὑπεύθυνον ἐποίησαν κινδύνῳ μετ᾽ αἰσχύνης. ἵνα δ᾽ εἰδῆτε ὅτι οὐ λόγον ἀναπόδεικτον

---

[1] ἐστ᾽ ἐκ Blass : ἐστιν ἐκ N : ἐστι cett.
[2] ἵν᾽ ἀσφαλέστερον Blass : ἀσφαλέστερον γὰρ codd.
[3] θῆται] θήσεται Schaub.
[4] ἀποικοδομήσαντες Duker : ἀνοικοδομήσαντες codd.
[5] τὴν τιμωρίαν] del. Heinrich : τῇ τιμωρίᾳ Morus.

114

The Spartans were the same. Please do not think me tedious, gentlemen, if I allude often to these men. We shall be well advised to take examples of just conduct from a city which has good laws, and so be surer that each of you will give a just verdict in keeping with his oath. The Spartans, you remember, caught their king Pausanias trying to betray Greece to the Persians. He escaped in time into the temple of the Brazen House, but they walled up the door, took off the roof and mounted guard in a circle round it, remaining at their posts until they had starved him to death and made his punishment a proof to all that even divine assistance is not vouchsafed to traitors.[a] And it is right that it should not be ; for impiety towards the gods is the first crime by which they show their wickedness, since they deprive them of their traditional cults. But I have yet to give you the best illustration of the prevailing practice at Sparta. They passed a law, covering all who refused to risk their lives for their country, which expressly stated that they should be put to death. Thus the punishment which they laid down was the very fate which traitors most fear ; survival after war was to be subject to a scrutiny which might involve disgrace and death. Let me convince you

---

[a] Pausanias was, in actual fact, regent for Pleistarchus, not king (Herod. ix. 10). Though he led the Greeks at Plataea and was afterwards commander of the allied fleet he was later deposed on a charge of Medism and attempted subversion of the Spartan constitution. For the full story of his last days see Thucyd. i. 94-134.

---

[6] ἀδικοῦσιν] del. Bekker.
[7] πατρίων Sauppe : πατρῴων codd.
[8] αὐτοὺς Schulze : ἑαυτοὺς codd.

LYCURGUS

εἴρηκα, ἀλλὰ μετ' ἀληθείας[1] παραδείγματα, φέρε
αὐτοῖς τὸν νόμον.

130 Ἐνθυμεῖσθε δὴ ὡς καλὸς ὁ νόμος, ὦ ἄνδρες,
καὶ σύμφορος οὐ μόνον ἐκείνοις ἀλλὰ καὶ τοῖς
ἄλλοις ἀνθρώποις. ὁ γὰρ παρὰ τῶν πολιτῶν
φόβος ἰσχυρὸς ὢν ἀναγκάσει τοὺς πρὸς τοὺς
πολεμίους κινδύνους ὑπομένειν· τίς γὰρ ὁρῶν
θανάτω ζημιούμενον τὸν προδότην ἐν τοῖς κινδύνοις
ἐκλείψει τὴν πατρίδα; ἢ τίς παρὰ τὸ συμφέρον
τῆς πόλεως φιλοψυχήσει, εἰδὼς ὑποκειμένην αὐτῷ
⟨ταύτην⟩[2] τιμωρίαν; οὐδεμίαν γὰρ ἄλλην δεῖ
ζημίαν εἶναι τῆς δειλίας ἢ θάνατον· εἰδότες γὰρ
ὅτι δυοῖν κινδύνοιν ὑποκειμένοιν ἀναγκαῖον ἔσται
θατέρου μετασχεῖν, πολὺ μᾶλλον αἱρήσονται τὸν
πρὸς τοὺς πολεμίους ἢ τὸν πρὸς τοὺς νόμους καὶ
τοὺς πολίτας.

131 Τοσούτω δ' ἂν δικαιότερον οὗτος ἀποθάνοι τῶν
ἐκ τῶν στρατοπέδων φευγόντων,[3] ὅσον οἱ μὲν εἰς
τὴν πόλιν ἥκουσιν ὡς ὑπὲρ ταύτης μαχούμενοι ἢ
κοινῇ μετὰ τῶν ἄλλων πολιτῶν συνατυχήσοντες,[4]
οὑτοσὶ δ' ἐκ τῆς πατρίδος ἔφυγεν, ἰδίᾳ τὴν σωτηρίαν ποριζόμενος, οὐδ' ὑπὲρ τῆς ἰδίας ἑστίας
ἀμύνεσθαι τολμήσας, ἀλλὰ μόνος οὗτος τῶν πάντων
ἀνθρώπων καὶ τὰ τῆς φύσεως οἰκεῖα καὶ ἀναγκαῖα
προδέδωκεν, ἃ καὶ τοῖς ἀλόγοις ζῴοις μέγιστα
132 καὶ σπουδαιότατα διείληπται. τὰ γοῦν[5] πετεινά,
ἃ[6] μάλιστα πέφυκε πρὸς τάχος,[7] ἔστιν ἰδεῖν ὑπὲρ

---

[1] Post ἀληθείας add. ὑμῖν N.
[2] ταύτην add. Scheibe.

that what I have said can be proved and that my examples are genuine. Produce the law for them.

The Law of the Spartans

See what an admirable law this is, gentlemen, and how expedient it would be for other peoples too besides the Spartans. The fear of one's own community is a strong thing and will compel men to face danger against an enemy ; no one will forsake his country in times of peril when he sees that a traitor is punished with death. No one will turn coward when his city needs him, if he knows that the punishment in store for him is this. For death is the one fitting penalty for cowardice ; since, when men know that there are two alternative dangers of which they must face one, they will choose to meet the enemy far rather than stand out against the law and their fellow citizens.

Leocrates is much more deserving of death than deserters from the army. They return to the city ready to defend it or to meet disaster in company with their fellow citizens, while he fled from his country and provided for his own safety, not daring to protect his hearth and home. He alone of men has betrayed even the natural ties of kinship and blood which the unthinking beasts themselves hold dearest and most sacred. Birds at least, which by nature are best fitted for a swift escape, can be seen

---

³ φευγόντων] φυγόντων Es.

⁴ συνατυχήσοντες Dobree : συνατυχοῦντες codd.

⁵ Post γοῦν codd. ζῷα habent, del. G. Hermann.

⁶ ἅ, quod infra post τάχος habent codd., huc transtulit Reiske.

⁷ τάχος] τὸ τάχος NA : τὸ om. cett.

τῆς αὑτῶν νεοττιᾶς ἐθέλοντα ἀποθνήσκειν· ὅθεν
καὶ τῶν ποιητῶν τινες εἰρήκασιν·

οὐδ' ἀγρία γὰρ ὄρνις, ἣν πλάσῃ δόμον,
ἄλλην[1] νεοσσοὺς ἠξίωσεν ἐντεκεῖν.[2]

ἀλλὰ Λεωκράτης τοσοῦτον ὑπερβέβληκε δειλίᾳ
ὥστε τὴν πατρίδα τοῖς πολεμίοις ἐγκατέλιπε.
133 τοιγαροῦν οὐδεμία πόλις αὐτὸν εἴασε παρ' αὑτῇ
μετοικεῖν, ἀλλὰ μᾶλλον τῶν ἀνδροφόνων[3] ἤλαυνεν,
εἰκότως· οἱ μὲν γὰρ φόνου φεύγοντες εἰς ἑτέραν
πόλιν μεταστάντες οὐκ ἔχουσιν ἐχθροὺς τοὺς ὑπο-
δεξαμένους, τοῦτον δὲ τίς ἂν ὑποδέξαιτο πόλις;
ὃς γὰρ ὑπὲρ τῆς αὑτοῦ πατρίδος οὐκ ἐβοήθησε,
ταχύ γ' ἂν ὑπὲρ τῆς ἀλλοτρίας κίνδυνόν τιν' ὑπο-
μείνειεν. κακοὶ γὰρ καὶ πολῖται καὶ ξένοι καὶ
ἰδίᾳ φίλοι οἱ τοιοῦτοι τῶν ἀνθρώπων εἰσίν, οἳ τῶν
μὲν ἀγαθῶν τῶν τῆς πόλεως μεθέξουσιν, ἐν δὲ
134 ταῖς ἀτυχίαις οὐδὲ βοηθείας ἀξιώσουσι. καίτοι
[167] τὸν ὑπὸ τῶν μηδὲν ἀδικουμένων μισούμενον καὶ
ἐξελαυνόμενον τί δεῖ παθεῖν ὑφ' ὑμῶν τῶν τὰ δει-
νότατα πεπονθότων; ἆρ' οὐ τῆς ἐσχάτης τιμωρίας
τυγχάνειν; καὶ μήν, ὦ ἄνδρες, τῶν πώποτε προδοτῶν δικαιότατ' ἂν Λεωκράτης, εἴ τις μείζων
εἴη τιμωρία θανάτου, ταύτην ὑπόσχοι. οἱ μὲν γὰρ
ἄλλοι προδόται, μέλλοντες ἀδικεῖν ὅταν ληφθῶσι,[4]
τιμωρίαν ὑπέχουσιν· οὗτος δὲ μόνος διαπεπραγμένος ὅπερ ἐπεχείρησε, τὴν πόλιν ἐγκαταλιπὼν
κρίνεται.

135   Θαυμάζω δὲ καὶ τῶν συνηγορεῖν αὐτῷ μελλόν-

---

[1] ἄλλην Coraes : ἄλλῃ codd.
[2] ἠξίωσεν ἐντεκεῖν Scaliger : ἐντεκεῖν ἠξίωσεν codd.
[3] τῶν ἀνδροφόνων N corr.[2] : τὸν ἀνδροφόνον NA.

accepting death in defence of their brood. Hence the words of the old poets [a] :

> Nor does the wild fowl let another's brood
> Be laid within the nest that she has built.

But the cowardice of Leocrates has so passed all bounds that he left his country to the enemy. That is why no city let him reside within it as an alien. He was naturally expelled more quickly than a murderer. Exiles for murder who move into another city do not meet with enmity among their hosts ; but what city could admit Leocrates ? One who refused to help his own country would indeed be likely to face danger for another's ! Such men are bad, whether as citizens, guests, or personal friends ; for they will enjoy the advantages offered by the state but will not consent to assist it too, in times of difficulty. Consider : he is hated and expelled by those without a reason to resent him ; what treatment should he get from you who have had the utmost provocation ? Should it not be the extreme penalty ? Indeed, gentlemen, if there were any punishment worse than death, Leocrates of all the traitors that have ever been would most deserve to undergo it. For other traitors are punished, though, when they are caught, their crime has yet to be committed. The defendant, alone of all men, by deserting the city, has, at the time of his trial, accomplished what he undertook to do.

I am amazed at the advocates who are going to

---

[a] The authorship of these lines is not known.

[1] ὅταν ληφθῶσι Contius : ὅταν μὴ ληφθῶσι N pr. A : ὅταν ἢ (vel δὴ) ληφθῶσι N corr.[2].

119

των, διὰ τι ποτε τοῦτον ἀξιώσουσιν ἀποφυγεῖν.
πότερον διὰ τὴν πρὸς αὐτοὺς φιλίαν; ἀλλ' ἔμοιγε
δοκοῦσι δικαίως οὐκ ἂν χάριτος τυχεῖν ἀλλ' ἀποθανεῖν, ὅτι χρῆσθαι τούτῳ τολμῶσι. πρὶν μὲν
γὰρ τοῦτο πρᾶξαι Λεωκράτην ἄδηλον ἦν ὁποῖοί
τινες ὄντες ἐτύγχανον, νῦν δὲ πᾶσι φανερὸν ὅτι
τοῖς αὐτοῖς ἤθεσι χρώμενοι τὴν πρὸς τοῦτον φιλίαν
διαφυλάττουσιν, ὥστε πολὺ πρότερον ὑπὲρ αὑτῶν
αὐτοῖς ἐστιν ἀπολογητέον ἢ τοῦτον παρ' ὑμῶν
ἐξαιτητέον.

136 Ἡγοῦμαι δ' ἔγωγε καὶ τὸν πατέρα αὐτῷ τὸν
τετελευτηκότα, εἴ τις ἄρ' ἔστιν αἴσθησις τοῖς ἐκεῖ
περὶ τῶν ἐνθάδε γιγνομένων, ἁπάντων ἂν χαλεπώτατον γενέσθαι δικαστήν, οὗ τὴν χαλκῆν εἰκόνα
ἔκδοτον κατέλιπε τοῖς πολεμίοις ἐν τῷ τοῦ Διὸς
⟨τοῦ⟩[1] σωτῆρος ἱεροσυλῆσαι καὶ αἰκίσασθαι, καὶ
ἣν ἐκεῖνος ἔστησε μνημεῖον τῆς αὑτοῦ μετριότητος,
ταύτην αὐτὸς ἐπονείδιστον ἐποίησε· τοιούτου γὰρ
137 υἱοῦ πατὴρ προσαγορεύεται. διὸ καὶ πολλοί μοι
προσεληλύθασιν, ὦ ἄνδρες, ἐρωτῶντες διὰ τί οὐκ
ἐνέγραψα τοῦτο εἰς τὴν εἰσαγγελίαν, προδεδωκέναι
τὴν εἰκόνα τὴν τοῦ πατρὸς τὴν ἐν τῷ τοῦ Διὸς
τοῦ σωτῆρος ἀνακειμένην. ἐγὼ δ', ὦ ἄνδρες, οὐκ
ἠγνόουν τοῦτο τἀδίκημ' ἄξιον ⟨ὂν⟩[2] τῆς μεγίστης
τιμωρίας, ἀλλ' οὐχ ἡγούμην δεῖν περὶ προδοσίας
τοῦτον κρίνων ὄνομα Διὸς σωτῆρος ἐπιγράψαι
πρὸς τὴν εἰσαγγελίαν.

138 Ἐκπέπληγμαι δὲ μάλιστα ἐπὶ τοῖς μήτε γένει
μήτε φιλίᾳ μηδὲν προσήκουσι, μισθοῦ δὲ συναπο-
λογουμένοις ἀεὶ τοῖς κρινομένοις, εἰ λελήθασιν ὑμᾶς

defend him. Whatever justification, I wonder, will they find for his acquittal? Will it be his friendship with themselves? In my own view they are not entitled to indulgence but deserve to die for daring to be intimate with him. Though their attitude was not obvious, before Leocrates acted as he did, it is clear to everyone now, since they maintain their friendship with him, that they uphold the same principles as he does and should therefore far rather be required to plead their own defence than be allowed to win your pardon for him.

I believe myself that if the dead really do have any knowledge of earthly affairs, his own father, now no more, would be a sterner judge than any other; since he it was whose bronze statue Leocrates left behind him in the temple of Zeus the Saviour, abandoned to the enemy for them to steal or mutilate. He turned that statue, which his father erected as a memorial of his own uprightness, into an object of reproach, since it commemorates a man now famed as father of a son like this. It is with this in mind, gentlemen, that many have approached me and asked why I did not include in the indictment the charge that he had betrayed his father's statue, dedicated in the temple of Zeus the Saviour. Gentlemen, I fully realized that this offence called for the most severe punishment, but I did not think it right, when prosecuting the defendant for treason, to add the name of Zeus the Saviour to the bill of indictment.

What astounds me most of all is, that though you are dealing with men who have no ties of blood or friendship with him but who always champion defendants for a fee, you do not realize that they

---

1 τοῦ add. Ald.   2 ὄν add. Bekker.

τῆς ἐσχάτης ὀργῆς δικαίως ἂν τυγχάνοντες. τὸ γὰρ
ὑπὲρ τῶν ἀδικησάντων[1] ἀπολογεῖσθαι τεκμήριόν
ἐστιν ὅτι καὶ τῶν πεπραγμένων οἱ τοιοῦτοι[2] ἂν
μετάσχοιεν. οὐ γὰρ δεῖ[3] καθ' ὑμῶν γεγενῆσθαι
δεινὸν ἀλλ' ὑπὲρ ὑμῶν καὶ τῶν νόμων καὶ τῆς
δημοκρατίας.

139 Καίτοι τινὲς αὐτῶν οὐκέτι[4] τοῖς λόγοις ὑμᾶς
παρακρούσασθαι ζητοῦσιν, ἀλλ' ἤδη ταῖς αὑτῶν
λῃτουργίαις[5] ἐξαιτεῖσθαι τοὺς κρινομένους ἀξιώ-
σουσιν· ἐφ' οἷς ἔγωγε καὶ μάλιστ' ἀγανακτῶ. εἰς
γὰρ τὸν ἴδιον οἶκον αὐτὰς περιποιησάμενοι, κοινὰς
χάριτας ὑμᾶς ἀπαιτοῦσιν. οὐ γὰρ εἴ τις ἱπποτρόφηκεν[6] ἢ κεχορήγηκε λαμπρῶς ἢ τῶν ἄλλων τῶν
τοιούτων τι δεδαπάνηκεν, ἄξιός ἐστι παρ' ὑμῶν
τοιαύτης χάριτος (ἐπὶ τούτοις γὰρ αὐτὸς μόνος
στεφανοῦται, τοὺς ἄλλους οὐδὲν ὠφελῶν), ἀλλ'
εἴ τις τετριηράρχηκε λαμπρῶς ἢ τείχη τῇ πατρίδι
περιέβαλεν ἢ πρὸς τὴν κοινὴν σωτηρίαν ἐκ τῶν
140 ἰδίων συνευπόρησε· ταῦτα γάρ ἐστι κοινῶς ὑπὲρ
ὑμῶν ἁπάντων, καὶ ἐν μὲν τούτοις ἔστιν ἰδεῖν τὴν
ἀρετὴν τῶν ἐπιδεδωκότων, ἐν ἐκείνοις δὲ τὴν
εὐπορίαν μόνον[7] τῶν δεδαπανηκότων. ἡγοῦμαι δ'
ἔγωγε οὐδέν[8] οὕτω μεγάλα τὴν πόλιν εὐηργετη-
κέναι, ὥστ' ἐξαίρετον ἀξιοῦν λαμβάνειν χάριν τὴν
κατὰ τῶν προδιδόντων τιμωρίαν, οὐδ' οὕτως
ἀνόητον ὥστε φιλοτιμεῖσθαι μὲν πρὸς τὴν πόλιν,

---

[1] ἀδικησάντων Bekker : ἀδικημάτων codd.
[2] οἱ τοιοῦτοι] τοῖς τοιούτοις Blass.
[3] δεῖ Bekker : δὴ codd.
[4] οὐκέτι Reiske : οὐκ ἐπὶ codd.
[5] λῃτουργίαις Blass : λειτουργίαις codd.
[6] ἱπποτρόφηκεν Es : ἱπποτετρόφηκεν codd.
[7] μόνον A corr. : μόνων N : om. A pr., Blass.
[8] Post οὐδέν' codd. ἂν habent, del. Franke.

deserve to feel your anger in its fullest violence. If they and their kind defend the criminals it is proof that they would associate themselves with the actual crimes. It is to defend you, in the interests of democracy and law, not to oppose you, that a speaker should have acquired his skill.

Some of them indeed are no longer using arguments to try to deceive you; they will even cite their own public services in favour of the defendants. These I particularly resent. For having performed the services for the advancement of their own families, they are now asking you for public token of thanks. Horsebreeding,[a] a handsome payment for a chorus, and other expensive gestures, do not entitle a man to any such recognition from you, since for these acts he alone is crowned, conferring no benefit on others. To earn your gratitude he must, instead, have been distinguished as a trierarch, or built walls to protect his city, or subscribed generously from his own property for the public safety. These are services to the state: they affect the welfare of you all and prove the loyalty of the donors, while the others are evidence of nothing but the wealth of those who have spent the money. I do not believe that anyone has done the city so great a service that he can claim the acquittal of traitors as a special privilege for himself; nor do I believe that anyone, with ambitions for the city's honour, is so unthinking as to help Leocrates,

[a] On horsebreeding see note to Hyp. i. 16. The public service of equipping a chorus was imposed on richer citizens who were nominated from each tribe in turn. The trierarch had to contribute towards the equipment and maintenance of a ship, of which the state supplied the hull and usually the oars and rigging. He was also responsible for the command of it. For further details see note on Hyp. frag. 43.

τούτῳ δὲ βοηθεῖν ὃς αὐτοῦ πρώτου τὰς φιλοτιμίας
ἠφάνισεν· εἰ μὴ νὴ Δία μὴ ταὐτὰ τῇ πατρίδι καὶ
τούτοις ἐστὶ συμφέροντα.

141 Ἐχρῆν μὲν οὖν, ὦ ἄνδρες, εἰ καὶ περὶ οὐδενὸς
ἄλλου νόμιμόν ἐστι παῖδας καὶ γυναῖκας παρα-
καθισαμένους ἑαυτοῖς τοὺς δικαστὰς δικάζειν, ἀλλ'
οὖν γε περὶ προδοσίας κρίνοντας οὕτως ὅσιον
εἶναι τοῦτο πράττειν, ὅπως ὁπόσοι τοῦ κινδύνου
μετεῖχον ἐν ὀφθαλμοῖς ὄντες, καὶ ὁρώμενοι καὶ
ἀναμιμνήσκοντες ὅτι τοῦ κοινοῦ παρὰ πᾶσιν ἐλέου
[168] οὐκ ἠξιώθησαν, πικροτέρας τὰς γνώσεις κατὰ τοῦ
ἀδικοῦντος παρεσκεύαζον.[1] ἐπειδὴ δ' οὐ νόμιμον
οὐδ' εἰθισμένον ἐστίν, ἀλλ' ἀναγκαῖον ὑμᾶς ὑπὲρ
ἐκείνων δικάζειν, τιμωρησάμενοι γοῦν[2] Λεωκράτη
καὶ ἀποκτείναντες αὐτὸν ἀπαγγείλατε τοῖς ὑμετέροις αὐτῶν παισὶ καὶ γυναιξὶν ὅτι ὑποχείριον

142 λαβόντες τὸν προδότην αὐτῶν ἐτιμωρήσασθε. καὶ
γὰρ δεινὸν καὶ σχέτλιον, ὅταν νομίζῃ δεῖν Λεωκράτης ἴσον ἔχειν ὁ φυγὼν ἐν τῇ τῶν μεινάντων[3]
πόλει, καὶ ὁ μὴ κινδυνεύσας ἐν τῇ τῶν παρα-
ταξαμένων, καὶ ὁ μὴ διαφυλάξας ἐν τῇ τῶν σωσάντων, ἀλλ' ἥκῃ[4] ἱερῶν θυσιῶν[5] ἀγορᾶς νόμων
πολιτείας μεθέξων, ὑπὲρ ὧν τοῦ μὴ καταλυθῆναι
χίλιοι τῶν ὑμετέρων πολιτῶν ἐν Χαιρωνείᾳ ἐτε-
λεύτησαν καὶ δημοσίᾳ αὐτοὺς ἡ πόλις ἔθαψαν[6]·
ὧν οὗτος οὐδὲ τὰ ἐλεγεῖα τὰ ἐπιγεγραμμένα τοῖς
μνημείοις ἐπανιὼν εἰς τὴν πόλιν ἠδέσθη, ἀλλ'
οὕτως ἀναιδῶς ἐν τοῖς ὀφθαλμοῖς τῶν πενθησάν-
των τὰς ἐκείνων συμφορὰς ἡγεῖται δεῖν ἀναστρέφε-

---

[1] παρεσκεύαζον Es : παρασκευάζωσιν NA corr. : παρασκευά-
ζουσι A pr.   [2] γοῦν Jenicke : οὖν codd.
[3] μεινάντων Taylor : σωσάντων codd.

124

by whom he, first and foremost, had those ambitions frustrated ; unless indeed such people have interests other than their country's.

Though it may not be customary at any other time for members of the jury to set their wives and children beside them in the court, at least in a trial for treason this practice ought to have been sanctioned, so as to bring into full view all those who shared in the danger, as a reminder that they had not been thought deserving of the pity which is their universal right, and make the jury reach a sterner verdict on the man who wronged them. Since, however, custom and tradition have not sanctioned this and you must act on their behalf, at least avenge yourselves upon Leocrates by putting him to death, and so report to your own wives and children that when you had their betrayer in your power you took vengeance upon him. It is an outrageous scandal for Leocrates to think that he, the runaway, should take his place in the city of those who stood their ground, the deserter among men who fought in battle, the one who left his post among those who saved their country ; it is outrageous that he is returning to have access to your cults and sacrifices, to your market, your laws and constitution, when to save these from destruction a thousand of your citizens fell at Chaeronea and received public burial from the city. Yet Leocrates, on his way back to Athens, even braved the epitaphs engraved on their memorials, shamelessly presuming to exhibit himself, in the way he does, before the eyes of those who mourn their loss.

----

⁴ ἤκῃ Stephanus : ἤκει codd.
⁵ θυσιῶν Taylor : οὐσιῶν codd. : ὁσίων Reiske.
⁶ ἔθαψαν] ἔθαψεν Taylor, sed cf. § 87 ἔδοσαν.

143 σθαι. καὶ αὐτίκα μάλ' ὑμᾶς ἀξιώσει ἀκούειν
αὐτοῦ ἀπολογουμένου κατὰ τοὺς νόμους· ὑμεῖς δ'
ἐρωτᾶτε αὐτὸν ποίους· οὓς ἐγκαταλιπὼν ᾤχετο.
καὶ ἐᾶσαι[1] αὐτὸν οἰκεῖν ἐν τοῖς τείχεσι τῆς πατρί-
δος· ποίοις; ἃ μόνος[2] τῶν πολιτῶν[3] οὐ συνδιε-
φύλαξε. καὶ ἐπικαλεῖται τοὺς θεοὺς σώσοντας
αὐτὸν ἐκ τῶν κινδύνων· τίνας; οὐχ ὧν τοὺς νεὼς
καὶ τὰ ἕδη καὶ τὰ τεμένη προὔδωκε; καὶ δεήσεται
καὶ ἱκετεύσει ἐλεῆσαι αὐτόν· τίνων; οὐχ οἷς τὸν
αὐτὸν ἔρανον[4] εἰς τὴν σωτηρίαν εἰσενεγκεῖν οὐκ
ἐτόλμησε; Ῥοδίους ἱκετευέτω· τὴν γὰρ ἀσφάλειαν
144 ἐν τῇ ἐκείνων πόλει μᾶλλον ἢ ἐν τῇ ἑαυτοῦ πατρίδι
ἐνόμισεν εἶναι. ποία δ' ἡλικία δικαίως ἂν τοῦτον
ἐλεήσειε; πότερον ἡ τῶν πρεσβυτέρων; ἀλλ'
οὐδὲ γηροτροφηθῆναι οὐδ' ἐν ἐλευθέρῳ ⟨τῷ⟩[5]
ἐδάφει τῆς πατρίδος αὐτοῖς ταφῆναι τὸ καθ' αὑτὸν
μέρος παρέδωκεν. ἀλλ' ἡ τῶν νεωτέρων; καὶ
τίς ⟨ἂν⟩[6] ἀναμνησθεὶς τῶν ἡλικιωτῶν τῶν ἐν
Χαιρωνείᾳ ἑαυτῷ[7] συμπαραταξαμένων καὶ τῶν
κινδύνων τῶν αὐτῶν μετασχόντων, σώσειε τὸν
τὰς ἐκείνων θήκας προδεδωκότα, καὶ τῇ αὐτῇ
ψήφῳ τῶν μὲν ὑπὲρ τῆς ἐλευθερίας τελευτησάντων
παράνοιαν[8] καταγνοίη, τὸν δ' ἐγκαταλιπόντα[9] τὴν
145 πατρίδα ὡς εὖ φρονοῦντα ἀθῷον ἀφείη; ἐξουσίαν
ἄρα δώσετε τῷ βουλομένῳ καὶ λόγῳ καὶ ἔργῳ τὸν
δῆμον καὶ ὑμᾶς κακῶς ποιεῖν. οὐ γὰρ μόνον νῦν
οἱ φεύγοντες κατέρχονται, ὅταν ὁ ἐγκαταλιπὼν

---

[1] ἐᾶσαι Reiske : ἐάσετε codd.
[2] ποίοις; ἃ μόνος Reiske : ποιησάμενοι codd.

He will shortly beg you to hear him plead his defence
according to the laws. Ask him what laws. The ones
he deserted in his flight. He will beg you to let him
live within the walls of his native city. Which walls ?
Those which he, alone of Athenians, did not help to
defend. He will call on the gods to save him from
danger. Who are they ? Are they not the gods
whose temples, altars and precincts he betrayed ?
He will beg and pray you to pity him. To whom is
this prayer addressed if not to men who made a
contribution to safety which he had not the courage
to make ? Let him make his plea to the Rhodians,
since he thought their city safer than his own country.
Would any men, no matter what their age, be justified
in pitying him ? Take the older generation. He did
his best to deny them so much as a safe old age or
even a grave in the free soil of their native land. What
of the younger men ? Would any of them, remembering their contemporaries, comrades in arms at Chaeronea who shared the same dangers, absolve the man
who has betrayed the graves they lie in ? Would
they, in the same vote, denounce as mad those who
died for freedom and let Leocrates who deserted his
country go unpunished as a sane man ? By such
means you will grant to all who wish it the power to
injure the state and yourselves whether by word or
deed. This is no simple matter of an exile's coming

---

³ Post πολίτων N pr. A corr. οἷς habent, N corr.² A pr. οὖς,
del. Bekker.

⁴ τὸν αὐτὸν ἔρανον Scaliger : τῶν αὐτῶν ἐράνων codd.

⁵ τῷ add. Dobree.

⁶ ἄν add. Schaub.

⁷ ἑαυτῷ Morus : ἑαυτοῖς codd.

⁸ παράνοιαν Reiske : παρανοίας codd.

⁹ δ' ἐγκαταλιπόντα Bekker : δὲ καταλιπόντα codd.

τὴν πόλιν καὶ φυγὴν αὐτὸς ἑαυτοῦ καταγνοὺς καὶ
οἰκήσας ἐν Μεγάροις ἐπὶ προστάτου πλείω πέντ'
ἢ ἓξ ἔτη[1] ἐν τῇ χώρᾳ καὶ ἐν τῇ πόλει ἀναστρέφηται,
ἀλλὰ καὶ ὁ μηλόβοτον τὴν Ἀττικὴν ἀνεῖναι[2]
φανερᾷ τῇ ψήφῳ καταψηφισάμενος, οὗτος ἐν
ταύτῃ τῇ χώρᾳ σύνοικος ὑμῶν γίγνεται.[3]

146 Βούλομαι δ' ἔτι βραχέα πρὸς ὑμᾶς εἰπὼν κατα-
βῆναι, καὶ τὸ ψήφισμα τοῦ δήμου παρασχόμενος,
ὃ περὶ εὐσεβείας ἐποιήσατο· χρήσιμον γὰρ ὑμῖν
ἐστι τοῖς μέλλουσι τὴν ψῆφον φέρειν. καί μοι
λέγε αὐτό.[4]

ΨΗΦΙΣΜΑ

Ἐγὼ τοίνυν μηνύω τὸν ἀφανίζοντα ταῦτα πάντα
πρὸς ὑμᾶς τοὺς κυρίους ὄντας κολάσαι, ὑμέτερον
δ' ἐστὶ καὶ ὑπὲρ ὑμῶν καὶ ὑπὲρ τῶν θεῶν τιμωρήσασθαι Λεωκράτην. τὰ γὰρ ἀδικήματα, ἕως μὲν
ἂν ᾖ ἄκριτα, παρὰ τοῖς πράξασίν ἐστιν, ἐπειδὰν
δὲ κρίσις γένηται, παρὰ τοῖς μὴ δικαίως ἐπεξ-
ελθοῦσιν. εὖ δ' ἴστε, ὦ ἄνδρες, ὅτι νῦν κρύβδην
ψηφιζόμενος ἕκαστος ὑμῶν φανερὰν ποιήσει τὴν
147 αὑτοῦ διάνοιαν τοῖς θεοῖς. ἡγοῦμαι δ', ὦ ἄνδρες,
ὑπὲρ ἁπάντων τῶν μεγίστων καὶ δεινοτάτων
ἀδικημάτων μίαν ὑμᾶς ψῆφον ἐν τῇ τήμερον ἡμέρᾳ
φέρειν, οἷς ἅπασιν ἔνοχον ὄντα Λεωκράτην ἔστιν
ἰδεῖν, προδοσίας μὲν ὅτι τὴν πόλιν ἐγκαταλιπὼν[5]
τοῖς πολεμίοις ὑποχείριον ἐποίησε, δήμου δὲ καταλύσεως ὅτι οὐχ ὑπέμεινε τὸν ὑπὲρ τῆς ἐλευθερίας
[169] κίνδυνον, ἀσεβείας δ' ὅτι τοῦ τὰ τεμένη τέμνεσθαι
καὶ τοὺς νεὼς κατασκάπτεσθαι τὸ καθ' ἑαυτὸν

---

[1] ἔτη Ald. : τῇ codd.   [2] ἀνεῖναι Baiter : εἶναι codd.
[3] γίγνεται Rehdantz : γένηται codd. : γεγένηται Thalheim.

128

back; the deserter of his city, who condemned himself to banishment and lived for more than five or six years in Megara with a sponsor, is now at large in Attica and in the city. It means that one who openly gave his vote for abandoning Attica to be a sheepwalk is in this country resident among you.

Before I leave the platform I want to add a few remarks and to read you the decree relating to piety which the people drew up. It has a message for you who are on the point of giving your verdict. Please read it.

The Decree

My part consists in exposing one who is doing away with all these principles, to you who are empowered to chastise him; it remains for you, as a service to yourselves and Heaven, to take vengeance on Leocrates. For while crimes remain untried the guilt rests with those who committed them, but once the trial has taken place it falls on all who did not mete out justice. Do not forget, gentlemen, that each of you now, though giving his vote in secret, will openly proclaim his attitude to the gods. I believe, gentlemen, that all the greatest and most atrocious crimes are to-day included within the scope of your single verdict; for Leocrates can be shown to have committed them all. He is guilty of treason, since he left the city and surrendered it to the enemy; guilty of overthrowing the democracy, because he did not face the danger which is the price of freedom; guilty of impiety, because he has done all in his power to have the sacred precincts ravaged and the

---

[4] αὐτό Baiter et Sauppe : τὸ αὐτὸ ψήφισμα codd.
[5] Post ἐγκαταλιπὼν N mancus.

γέγονεν αἴτιος, τοκέων δὲ κακώσεως[1] τὰ μνημεῖα
αὐτῶν ἀφανίζων καὶ τῶν νομίμων ἀποστερῶν,
λιποταξίου[2] δὲ καὶ ἀστρατείας οὐ παρασχὼν τὸ
148 σῶμα τάξαι τοῖς στρατηγοῖς. ἔπειτα τούτου τις
ἀποψηφιεῖται, καὶ συγγνώμην ἕξει τῶν κατὰ
προαίρεσιν ἀδικημάτων; καὶ τίς οὕτως[3] ἐστὶν
ἀνόητος ὥστε τοῦτον σῴζων[4] τὴν ἑαυτοῦ σωτηρίαν
προέσθαι τοῖς ἐγκαταλιπεῖν βουλομένοις, καὶ
τοῦτον ἐλεήσας αὐτὸς ἀνηλέητος[5] ὑπὸ τῶν πολεμίων ἀπολέσθαι προαιρήσεται, καὶ τῷ προδότῃ
τῆς πατρίδος χάριν θέμενος ὑπεύθυνος εἶναι τῇ
παρὰ τῶν θεῶν τιμωρίᾳ;
149 Ἐγὼ μὲν οὖν καὶ τῇ πατρίδι βοηθῶν καὶ τοῖς
ἱεροῖς καὶ τοῖς νόμοις ἀποδέδωκα τὸν ἀγῶνα
ὀρθῶς καὶ δικαίως, οὔτε τὸν ἄλλον τούτου βίον
διαβαλὼν οὔτ' ἔξω τοῦ πράγματος οὐδὲν κατηγο-
ρήσας· ὑμῶν δ' ἕκαστον χρὴ νομίζειν τὸν Λεωκράτους ἀποψηφιζόμενον θάνατον τῆς πατρίδος
καὶ ἀνδραποδισμὸν[6] καταψηφίζεσθαι, καὶ δυοῖν
καδίσκοιν κειμένοιν τὸν μὲν προδοσίας, τὸν δὲ
σωτηρίας εἶναι, καὶ[7] τὰς ψήφους φέρεσθαι τὰς
μὲν ὑπὲρ ἀναστάσεως τῆς πατρίδος, τὰς δ' ὑπὲρ
150 ἀσφαλείας καὶ τῆς ἐν τῇ πόλει εὐδαιμονίας. ἐὰν
μὲν Λεωκράτην ἀπολύσητε, προδιδόναι τὴν πόλιν
καὶ τὰ ἱερὰ καὶ τὰς ναῦς ψηφιεῖσθε· ἐὰν δὲ τοῦτον
ἀποκτείνητε, διαφυλάττειν καὶ σῴζειν τὴν πατρίδα
καὶ τὰς προσόδους καὶ τὴν εὐδαιμονίαν παρακελεύσεσθε.[8] νομίζοντες οὖν, ὦ Ἀθηναῖοι, ἱκετεύειν
ὑμῶν τὴν χώραν καὶ τὰ δένδρα, δεῖσθαι τοὺς

---

[1] Post κακώσεως codd. ὅτι habent, del. Morus.
[2] λιποταξίου Es : λειποταξίου codd.
[3] τίς οὕτως Dobree : τοσοῦτον codd.

temples destroyed. He is guilty too of injuring his forbears, for he effaced their memorials and deprived them of their rites, and guilty of desertion and refusal to serve, since he did not submit his person to the leaders for enrolment. Shall this man then find someone to acquit him or pardon his deliberate misdeeds ? Who is so senseless as to choose to save Leocrates at the cost of leaving his own security at the mercy of men who wish to be deserters, to choose to pity him at the cost of being killed himself without pity by his enemies, or to grant a favour to the betrayer of his country and so expose himself to the vengeance of the gods ?

My task has been to assist my country, its temples and its laws. I have conducted the trial rightly and justly without slandering the private life of the defendant or digressing from the subject of my indictment. It is now for each of you to reflect that the absolver of Leocrates condemns his country to death and slavery, that of the two caskets before you one stands for treason and the other for deliverance, that the votes cast into one are given for the destruction of your country and the rest for safety and prosperity in Athens. If you acquit Leocrates, you will vote for the betrayal of the city, of its temples and its fleet. But if you kill him, you will be encouraging others to preserve your country with its revenues and its prosperity. Imagine then, Athenians, that the country and its trees are appealing to you, that the

---

[4] σώζων Ald. : σώζοντα codd.
[5] ἀνηλέητος Bekker : ἀνελέητος codd.
[6] ἀνδραποδισμὸν Bekker : ἀνδραπόδων codd.
[7] εἶναι, καὶ Emperius : εἵνεκα codd.
[8] παρακελεύσεσθε Ald. : παρακελεύεσθε codd.

λιμένας ⟨καὶ⟩[1] τὰ νεώρια καὶ τὰ τείχη τῆς πόλεως,
ἀξιοῦν δὲ καὶ τοὺς νεὼς καὶ τὰ ἱερὰ βοηθεῖν αὐτοῖς,
παράδειγμα ποιήσατε Λεωκράτη, ἀναμνησθέντες
τῶν κατηγορημένων, ὅτι[2] οὐ πλέον ἰσχύει παρ'
ὑμῖν ἔλεος οὐδὲ δάκρυα τῆς ὑπὲρ τῶν νόμων καὶ
τοῦ δήμου σωτηρίας.[3]

[1] καὶ add. Scheibe.
[2] Ante ὅτι habent καὶ codd., del. Morus.
[3] σωτηρίας] τιμωρίας Reiske.

harbours, dockyards and walls of the city are begging you for protection, yes, and the temples and sanctuaries too. Bear in mind the charges brought and make of Leocrates a proof that with you tears and compassion have not more weight than the salvation of the laws and people.

FRAGMENTS

INTRODUCTION

Besides the speech against Leocrates at least thirteen[a] published orations of Lycurgus are recorded which, though extant for centuries after his death, are now lost. Only a few fragments of these have come down to us, almost all embodied in the writings of other authors. Most of them are short sentences or phrases, often even single words, quoted by Harpocration and Suidas, who as compilers of dictionaries were more interested in vocabulary than in subject matter. Two have survived independently in papyri, and for the others we are indebted mainly to Stobaeus, who included them in his anthology of Greek literature published about A.D. 500, or to Rutilius Lupus, who lived in the first century and in his treatise on

[a] Possibly even fourteen or fifteen. Suidas, in his note on Lycurgus, gives the titles of fourteen speeches which he regards as genuine, provided that we understand his phrase Ἀπολογία πρὸς τὸν αὐτὸν [sc. Δημάδην] ὑπὲρ τῶν εὐθυνῶν as referring to one speech not two (see note on Lycurg. frag. 3). All these but three (κατὰ Δημάδου, πρὸς τὰς Μαντείας, περὶ τῆς Ἱερωσύνης) are mentioned by Harpocration, who refers in addition to four fresh titles : (1) Ἀπολογισμὸς ὧν πεπολίτευται, (2) Κροκωνίδων διαδικασία, (3) κατὰ Κηφισοδότου, (4) κατὰ Δεξίππου. Of these no. 4 is probably the work of Lysias and no. 3 an alternative title to κατὰ Δημάδου. Thus Harpocration contributes at most two new speeches, giving us a total of sixteen including the *Leocrates*. It is possible that no. 2 refers to περὶ τῆς Ἱερωσύνης, in which case the total would be only fifteen.

FRAGMENTS

figures of speech included as illustrations passages
from the works of Greek orators translated into Latin.

In this volume the titles are arranged according to
the classification given by Blass in *Attische Beredsamkeit* and all fragments except single words are included.
The bracketed numbers in the margin are those
assigned to the fragments by Sauppe.

A.

1. ΑΠΟΛΟΓΙΣΜΟΣ ΩΝ ΠΕΠΟΛΙΤΕΥΤΑΙ

[102] Nam, cum iuventus concitata temere arma caperet
et quietos Thessalos manu lacessere conaretur, ego[1]
senatum coegi auctoritate sua comprimere adule-
scentium violentiam. Ego quaestoribus interminatus
sum ne sumptum stipendio praeberent. Ego arma-
mentario patefacto restiti atque efferri arma prohibui.
Itaque unius opera mea non concitatum bellum non
necessarium scitis. (Rutil. Lup. i. 7.)

This title, cited four times by Harpocration, presents a
problem, since it is not included by Suidas in his list of
speeches of Lycurgus. Despite this it seems best to regard
it as denoting a distinct speech. It is strange that Suidas
should have omitted it, but his list includes apparently only
fourteen speeches, and, as the Pseudo-Plutarch (*Lycurg.* 39)
credits Lycurgus with fifteen, there is room for one more.
A less likely solution is to accept this as an alternative title
for one of those speeches which Suidas does mention. If
we take this course there are three possibilities. (1) It may,
as Sauppe held, refer to the *Defence against Demades*
(no. 3). But (*a*) Harpocration quotes this elsewhere under

2. ΠΕΡΙ ΤΗΣ ΔΙΟΙΚΗΣΕΩΣ

[24] 1. Τρεῖς δοκιμασίαι κατὰ τὸν νόμον γίγνονται·

---

[1] *ego* Scheibe : *iure ego* codd.

A. *On his own administration*

1. DEFENCE OF HIS POLICY

For when the young men in their enthusiasm were thoughtlessly taking up arms and seeking to provoke the peaceful Thessalians, I compelled the Council to use its authority and restrain their violence. It was I who by my threats forbade the treasurers to grant a subsidy for soldiers' pay. It was I who stood firm when the arsenal was opened and refused to have arms taken out. It was thus entirely my doing, as you perceive, that an unnecessary war was avoided.

the title used by Suidas, which suggests that he is here referring to a different speech, (*b*) a passage in the Pseudo-Plutarch (*Lycurg.* 31), which seems to bear on the present speech, says that Menesaechmus, not Demades, was the prosecutor. (2). If Suidas intended the phrase " On the Accounts " as the title of a different speech from the *Defence against Demades*, which is unlikely,[a] we might identify this speech with that. (3) This speech may be the same as *On his Administration* (no. 2) ; but the latter title too is used by Harpocration elsewhere. The above fragment was assigned to the speech by Sauppe.

2. ON HIS ADMINISTRATION

1. The law provides for three types of examina-

[a] See the notes on the introduction to the fragments and on fragment 3.

μία μὲν ἦν οἱ ἐννέα ἄρχοντες δοκιμάζονται, ἑτέρα
δὲ ἦν οἱ ῥήτορες, τρίτη δὲ ἦν οἱ στρατηγοί.
Harpocration, *s.v.* δοκιμασθείς.

[29] 2. Ἀλλὰ μὴν καὶ Καλλισθένην ἑκατὸν μναῖς
ἐστεφανώσατε. Harpocration, *s.v.* στεφανῶν τοὺς
νενικηκότας.

[30] 3. Ἐκ τῶν ἱερῶν ὧν ἡμεῖς ἐπετροπεύσαμεν.
Bekker, *Anecdota* 145. 30.

4. Πολλῶν δὲ χρημάτων ἐξοδιασμὸν εἰληφότων.
Lex. rhetor. Reitzensteinii Ind. lect. Rost. 1892/3, p. 4.

[22] 5. Ἀγαθῆς τύχης νεώς. Harpocration.

[27] 6. Γείτονας τοῦ ὀχείου. Harpocration, *s.v.* ὀ-
χεῖον.

3. ΠΡΟΣ ΔΗΜΑΔΗΝ ΑΠΟΛΟΓΙΑ
ΥΠΕΡ ΤΩΝ ΕΥΘΥΝΩΝ

[21] Τοὺς ἑτέρους τραγῳδοὺς ἀγωνιεῖται. Harpocration.

The speech is cited by Harpocration as " Against
Demades " ; the full title is given by Suidas. It has been
thought that " On the Accounts " may be intended as the
title of a distinct speech. But Blass points out that Suidas

tion : one to which the nine archons submit, another applying to orators and a third to generals.

2. But you awarded Callisthenes a crown worth a hundred minas.

3. From the sacred funds which we administered.

4. After much money had been paid out.

5. A temple of good fortune.

6. Neighbours of the breeding place.

The date of this speech is not certain, though it may perhaps have been delivered in 330 B.C., after Lycurgus had completed his first five years of administration.[a] Dinarchus wrote a speech entitled κατὰ Λυκούργου εὐθυνῶν, to which this may possibly be the answer (v. Dinarch. frag. 4). Δοκιμασία was less restricted in its application than fragment 1 implies. According to Harpocration Lycurgus himself referred in this very speech to a δοκιμασία of knights (cf. Aristot. Ath. Pol. 49). For δοκιμασία of archons see Ath. Pol. 55, of orators Aeschines i. 28, and of generals Dinarch. i. 71, though in the last mentioned passage the actual word is not used. Callisthenes is perhaps the man mentioned by Demosthenes (Dem. xviii. 37 ; xx. 33).

3. DEFENCE AGAINST DEMADES ON THE ACCOUNTS

He will play tragic parts made for others.

has arranged the speeches in his list in groups, according as the title begins with κατά, πρὸς or περί ; and, if ὑπὲρ τῶν Εὐθυνῶν were a distinct title, it would be out of place in the middle of the πρὸς group. The date and circumstances of the speech are not known. It was identified by Sauppe with no. 1 ; but see the note on the latter. The quotation was explained by Didymus as a saying which referred to people who seek to adapt themselves to a rôle beyond their powers.

[a] See Koehler, Hermes i.

B.

4. ΚΑΤΑ ΜΕΝΕΣΑΙΧΜΟΥ sive ΔΗΛΙΑΚΟΣ

1. ["Οτι δὲ ἀληθῆ λέγω,] ὦ ἄνδρες δικαστ[αί],
ὅτι οὐδ' οἷόν τέ ἐστι[ν] θῦσαι, ὡς Μενέσαιχμος
λέγει, εἰ δὲ μὴ ἀσέβημα γίγνεται, ἀναγνώσεται
ὑμῖν Θεογένους μαρτυρίαν τοῦ κηρυκεύσαντος
Διοδώρῳ, ὃς οἶδεν θύσαντος ἰδιώτου [τιν]ὸς οὐ
παρόντος [Διο]δώρου καὶ θέντος . . . Berlin Pap.
11748.

2. Καὶ θαλλὸν μέγαν κοσμήσαντας[1] ἁπάντων,
ὧν κατ' ἐκείνους τοὺς καιροὺς αἱ ὧραι φέρουσιν,
ἀνατιθέναι τῷ Ἀπόλλωνι ἔμπροσθεν τῶν θυρῶν,
εἰρεσιώνην ὀνομάσαντας, ἀπαρχὰς ποιησαμένους
τῶν γιγνομένων πάντων ἐκ τῆς γῆς, ὅτι τὴν
ἀφορίαν ἡμῶν τῆς χώρας ἱκετηρία ἡ παρὰ τῷ
Ἀπόλλωνι τεθεῖσα ἔπαυσεν. καὶ οὕτως οἱ πρόγονοι ἡμῶν λέγονται ἕκαστος κατὰ τὴν ἰδίαν θύραν
θεῖναι τὴν ἱκετηρίαν τῷ Ἀπόλλωνι, τὴν νῦν
εἰρεσιώνην. Λέξεις Patmiacae.

[84] 3. Καὶ ἡμεῖς Πυανόψια ταύτην τὴν ἑορτὴν κα-
λοῦμεν, οἱ δ' ἄλλοι Ἕλληνες Πανόψια,[2] ὅτι πάντες εἶδον τοὺς κάρπους τῇ ὄψει. Harpocration, s.v.
Πυανόψια.

[87] 4. Καὶ γὰρ νῦν πολλὰς καὶ μεγάλας ὑμῖν τιμὰς
ὀφείλω· καὶ ζηλῶ παρὰ πᾶσιν Ἕλλησι μαντευο-
μένοις τὸν Δία προηροσίαν ποιήσασθαι. Suidas,
s.v. Προηροσία.

---

[1] κοσμήσαντας edd. : κοσμήσαντες cod.
[2] Πανοψία Bekker : Πανοψίαν codd.

B. *Religious cases*

4. AGAINST MENESAECHMUS (DELIAN SPEECH)

1. To prove, gentlemen of the jury, that I am right in saying that it is impossible to sacrifice in the way Menesaechmus suggests, as it involves an act of impiety, the clerk shall read you the evidence of Theogenes, the herald of Diodorus, who knows that if a private person sacrifices when Diodorus is not present and places . . .

2. After adorning a big olive branch with all the plants that the seasons yield at this time of year they dedicated it to Apollo in front of their doors, calling it *eiresione* and intending it as an offering of first fruits of all that the earth yields, because the suppliant bough offered to Apollo had stopped the barrenness of our land. And so our ancestors are said to have placed before Appolo, each by his own door, the suppliant bough which is the same as the *eiresione* to-day.

3. We call this festival Pyanopsia, but the other Greeks call it Panopsia because everyone has seen the fruits with his own eyes.

4. For I now owe you many great honours and I am anxious to offer Proerosia [a] before all the Greeks . . .

Harpocration and Suidas both use the bare title " Against Menesaechmus," but it is clear from their comments that the speech dealt with Apollo and Delos, and therefore the " Delian Speech " of the papyrus is almost certainly an alternative title. The date of the speech is not known. Menesaechmus, who had been head of an Athenian embassy sent to Delos, was impeached by Lycurgus for impiety

---

[a] Proerosia was a sacrifice offered by Athens on behalf of the whole of Greece before the time of tillage.

LYCURGUS

because he had failed to observe the proper ritual in sacrificing to Apollo. Dinarchus is credited with a speech prosecuting him (v. Dinarchus, frag. 23). The verdict is not known, but Menesaechmus remained an enemy of Lycurgus until his

5. ΠΕΡΙ ΤΗΣ ΙΕΡΕΙΑΣ

[31] 1. Εἰ μὲν ὑπὲρ ἰδίου τινὸς ἦν ὁ ἀγών, ἐδεόμην ἂν ὑμῶν μετ᾽ εὐνοίας ἀκοῦσαί μου . . . νυνὶ δὲ αὐτοὺς ὑμᾶς οἶμαι τοῦτο ποιήσειν καὶ χωρὶς παρακλήσεως τῆς ἐμῆς. Harpocration, s.v. παράκλησις.

2. Ἔτι τοίνυν ἔφη πάντων ὕστατα ταῦτα θύεσθαι καὶ ἐπιτελεώματα εἶναι τῶν ἄλλων θυσιῶν. Harpocration, s.v. ἐπιτελεοῦν, ἐπιτελέωμα.

[51] 3. Ὥστε προστεταγμένον ὑπὸ[1] ψηφίσματος καὶ τὴν ἱερείαν συσσημαίνεσθαι τὰ γραμματεῖα. Suidas, s.v. συσσημαίνεσθαι.

4. Ὡς περὶ εἴκοσιν ἀνθρώποις. Priscian xviii. 267, p. 346 Hertz.

6. ΠΕΡΙ ΤΗΣ ΙΕΡΩΣΥΝΗΣ

[53] Τὴν τοίνυν ἀρχαιοτάτην θυσίαν διὰ τὴν ἄνοδον τῆς θεοῦ, ὀνομασθεῖσαν δὲ Προχαριστήρια, διὰ τὴν βλάστησιν τῶν φυομένων.[2] Suidas, s.v. προχαριστήρια.

---

[1] ὑπὸ Blass : ἐπὶ codd.
[2] Post φυομένων add. ἀγομένην Sauppe.

death. Diodorus was priest of Apollo at Delos. Fragment 2 is assigned to Lycurgus on the evidence of the *Etym. Magn.* (*s.v.* εἰρεσιώνη). The Pyanopsia was an Attic festival to Apollo, celebrated the 7th of Pyanopsion, when a dish of beans and other vegetables was offered to the god. The name is wrongly explained as being derived from κύαμος a bean and ἕψω I boil. The last part of fragment 4 is unintelligible as it stands.

5. ON THE PRIESTESS

1. If this case were concerned with some private matter, I should ask you to give me a sympathetic hearing . . . as it is I think you will do this without any appeal on my part.

2. Furthermore he said that these sacrifices were the last of all to be performed and were a completion of the other sacrifices.

3. So that it has been laid down by decree that the priestess also must add her seal to the registers.

4. About twenty men.

The date of the speech is not known. Harpocration quotes several words from it, and it appears from his comments that it concerned the priestess of Athena Polias. The office was hereditary in the clan of the Eteobutadae to which Lycurgus belonged.

6. ON THE PRIESTHOOD

The most ancient sacrifice celebrating the ascent of the goddess and called Procharisteria is to ensure the growth of the fruits of the earth.

The title is preserved by Suidas only, who says that the Procharisteria was a feast observed in early spring by Athenians in office. Date and circumstances not known.

LYCURGUS

7. ΚΡΟΚΩΝΙΔΩΝ ΔΙΑΔΙΚΑΣΙΑ ΠΡΟΣ ΚΟΙΡΩΝΙΔΑΣ

Title known from Harpocration, who is doubtful whether to assign the speech to Lycurgus or Philinus, and from Athenaeus, who definitely attributes it to Philinus (v. Athen. x. 425 b). Date and circumstances not known. Sauppe identified this

8. ΠΡΟΣ ΤΑΣ ΜΑΝΤΕΙΑΣ sive ΠΕΡΙ ΤΩΝ ΜΑΝΤΕΙΩΝ

[78] Δεῖ δὲ τἆλλα ἐν δημοκρατίᾳ σοι εἰπεῖν. ἑνὸς δὲ οὐκ ἔστι σοι· κακῶς γὰρ αὐτοῦ προέστης. ἐφ' οἷς[1] καυχᾷ, οἱ ἄλλοι αἰσχύνονται. Suidas, s.v. καυχᾷ.

C.

9. ΚΑΤ' ΑΥΤΟΛΥΚΟΥ

[15] 1. Πολλῶν δὲ καὶ μεγάλων ἀγώνων εἰσεληλυθότων, οὐδέποτε περὶ τηλικούτου δικάσοντες ἥκετε.[2] Schol. Dem. liv. 1. [Cornutus], τέχνη ῥητ. 7, p. 353. 24 Hammer.

[17] 2. Ἀλλὰ καὶ μηλόβοτον τὴν χώραν ἀνῆκε. Suidas, s.v. μηλόβοτος χώρα.

The date of this speech is probably 338 B.C., since it was connected with the battle of Chaeronea. Autolycus was an

10. ΚΑΤΑ ΛΥΣΙΚΛΕΟΥΣ

[75] 1. Ἐστρατήγεις, ὦ Λυσίκλεις, καὶ χιλίων μὲν

---

[1] οἷς Blass : ὡς codd.
[2] τηλικούτου δικάσοντες ἥκετε Schol. Dem. : μειζόνων ἥκετε δικάσοντες [Cornutus].

146

7. SUIT OF THE CROCONIDAE AGAINST THE COERONIDAE (?)

speech with the last, since Harpocration quotes the word προχαριστήρια from it. However if this view is correct it is surprising that Suidas included " On the Priesthood " among the genuine works of Lycurgus. The Croconidae and Coeronidae were two clans connected with Eleusis.

8. ON THE ORACLES

I must tell you the other features of a democracy, in one of which you have no part, since you but ill represented it. You take a pride in what causes shame to others.

Suidas mentions the speech under both titles. Date and circumstances not known. The first words of the fragment are corrupt and the translation given is doubtful.

C. *Political cases*

9. AGAINST AUTOLYCUS

1. Many important cases have come before you, but you have never come to judge one so important as this.

2. But he abandoned the country to be pasturage for sheep.

Areopagite who was prosecuted and condemned for removing his wife and children to a safe place at the time of the battle (see Harpocration, *s.v.* Αὐτόλυκος and Lycurg. *Against Leocrates* §§ 53 and 145).

10. AGAINST LYSICLES

1. You were our general, Lysicles. A thousand

147

LYCURGUS

πολιτῶν τετελευτηκότων, δισχιλίων δ' αἰχμαλώτων γεγονότων, τροπαίου δὲ κατὰ τῆς πόλεως
ἑστηκότος, τῆς δ' Ἑλλάδος ἁπάσης δουλευούσης,
καὶ τούτων ἁπάντων γεγενημένων σοῦ ἡγουμένου
καὶ στρατηγοῦντος, τολμᾷς ζῆν καὶ τὸ τοῦ ἡλίου
φῶς ὁρᾶν καὶ εἰς τὴν ἀγόραν ἐμβάλλειν, ὑπόμνημα
γεγονὼς αἰσχύνης καὶ ὀνείδους τῇ πατρίδι. Diodor.
Sic. xvi. 88. Gemistus Pletho, *Hellen.* ii. 21 Reiske.

[77]   2. Ἐπὶ Δηλίῳ μάχη. Harpocration.

[105]   3. In praesentia, iudices, iniussu populi quae im-
probissime gesserit, reticebo ; de falsis eius litteris,
quas ad senatum miserit, nihil dicam ; quae[1] illi
saepe interminati sitis, omittam ; nam et haec vobis
nota sunt, et quae novissime multo indigniora com-
misit, quam primum cognoscenda. (Rutil. Lup. ii. 11.)

The date is probably 338 B.C., or soon after. Lysicles, one
of the Athenian generals at Chaeronea, was prosecuted by
Lycurgus and condemned to death for his conduct (*v.* Diodor.
Sic. xvi. 88). At Delium in Boeotia the Athenians under

11 et 12. ΚΑΤΑ ΛΥΚΟΦΡΟΝΟΣ Α΄, Β΄

[61]   1. Θαυμάζω δὲ ἔγωγε,[2] εἰ τοὺς ⟨μὲν⟩[3] ἀνδρα-
ποδιστάς, ⟨τοὺς⟩[3] τῶν οἰκετῶν μόνον ἡμᾶς ἀπο-
στεροῦντας, θανάτῳ ζημιοῦμεν.[4] Harpocration, *s.v.*
ἀνδραποδιστής.

[70]   2. Οὐ γὰρ ὅσιον ⟨τὸν⟩[5] τοὺς ⟨μὲν⟩[5] γεγραμ-
μένους νόμους, δι' ὧν ἡ δημοκρατία σῴζεται,

[1] *quae* add. Ald.
[2] ἔγωγε Blass : ἐγώ codd.

148

citizens have fallen and two thousand have been made prisoners; a trophy has been set up in triumph over the city, and the whole of Greece is in slavery. All these things have happened while you have held command as general, and still you dare to live and look on the light of the sun and push into the market place, though you have become a reminder of shame and disgrace to your country.

2. A battle at Delium.

3. For the present, gentlemen, I shall ignore the unscrupulous things which he did without the authorization of the people. I shall say nothing of the false letter which he sent to the Council, nor shall I mention the frequent occasions on which you threatened him. For you are familiar with these facts and should now lose no time in hearing of his latest crimes far more outrageous than these.

Hippocrates were beaten by the Boeotians in 424 B.C. (v. Thucyd. iv. 96). Sauppe suggests that Lycurgus was here comparing Lysicles with Hippocrates. Fragment 3 was referred to this speech by Kiessling and to no. 13 by Sauppe.

11 and 12. AGAINST LYCOPHRON I AND II

1. It is surprising to me that when we inflict the death penalty on slave-dealers who only rob us of our servants . . .

2. For it is not decent to let a man go unpunished, when he is breaking the laws by which democracy is

---

³ μὲν et τοὺς add. Blass.
⁴ ζημιοῦμεν Dobree : ζημιοῦν codd.
⁵ τὸν et μὲν add. Bernhardy.

παραβαίνοντα, ἑτέρων δὲ μοχθηρῶν εἰσηγητὴν[1]
ἐθῶν καὶ νομοθέτην γενόμενον, ἀτιμώρητον ἀφεῖναι.
Suidas, *s.v.* μοχθηρία.

[99]   3. Ὅταν γυνὴ ὁμονοίας τῆς πρὸς ⟨τὸν⟩[2] ἄνδρα
στερηθῇ, ἀβίωτος ὁ καταλειπόμενος γίγνεται βίος.
Stobaeus, *Florileg.* lxviii. 35.

13. ΚΑΤ' ΑΡΙΣΤΟΓΕΙΤΟΝΟΣ

The date is about 325 B.C., *i.e.* shortly before the trial, in
323 B.C., of the orators bribed by Harpalus (*v.* Dinarch. ii. 13).
For Aristogiton, who was a notorious sycophant, see the
introduction to Dinarchus' speech against him. In this trial

14. ΚΑΤΑ ΔΗΜΑΔΟΥ sive ΚΑΤΑ ΚΗΦΙ-
ΣΟΔΟΤΟΥ ΠΕΡΙ ΤΩΝ ΔΗΜΑΔΟΥ ΤΙΜΩΝ

[91]   1. ⟨Ἐγὼ δὲ ἐὰν μὴ⟩[3] καὶ παράνομον τὸ ψήφισμα ἐπιδείξω καὶ ἀσύμφορον καὶ ἀνάξιον τὸν
ἄνδρα δωρεᾶς. [Cornutus], τέχνη ῥητ. 167, p. 381
Hammer.

2. Περικλῆς δὲ ὁ Σάμον καὶ Εὔβοιαν καὶ Αἴ-
γιναν ἑλών, καὶ τὰ προπύλαια καὶ τὸ ᾠδεῖον
καὶ τὸ Ἑκατόμπεδον οἰκοδομήσας, καὶ μύρια
τάλαντα ἀργυρίου εἰς τὴν Ἀκρόπολιν ἀνενεγκών,
θαλλοῦ στεφάνῳ ἐστεφανώθη. Λέξεις *Patmiacae.*

---

[1] εἰσηγητὴν Cobet : ἐξηγητὴν codd.
[2] τὸν add. Blass.

preserved and has been a promulgator and a legislator of bad new usages.

3. When a woman is deprived of the good understanding between herself and her husband her life henceforward is impossible.

For the date of this trial and the circumstances see the introduction to Hyperides, *Defence of Lycophron*. Athenaeus specifically mentions the first speech and Harpocration the second (*v.* Athen. vi. 267 a ; Harpocr. *s.v.* ὀρκάνη).

13. AGAINST ARISTOGITON

Lycurgus and Demosthenes were prosecutors (*v.* [Dem.] xxv. 1). Two speeches against Aristogiton relating to it are included among the works of Demosthenes ([Dem.] xxv. and xxvi.), but were regarded by Dionysius as spurious. The first however may well be genuine (*v.* arg. to [Dem.] xxv. § 7). Aristogiton was found guilty (Dinarch. ii. 13). Fragment 3 of no. 10 was assigned by Sauppe to this speech.

14. AGAINST DEMADES or AGAINST CEPHISODOTUS ON THE HONOURS TO DEMADES

1. As for myself, if I do not show that the decree is illegal and inexpedient and that the man is unworthy of a reward . . .

2. Pericles, who took Samos, Euboea and Aegina, who built the Propylaea, the Odeum and the Hecatompedon, and who deposited ten thousand talents of silver in the Acropolis, was crowned with a wreath of olive.

---

³ ἐγὼ δὲ ἐὰν μὴ add. Sauppe.

[18]   3. Φίλιππον . . . προπίνειν κέρατι τούτοις οἷς
ἐφιλοφρονεῖτο.   Athen. xi. 476 d.

[104]   4. Cuius omnes corporis partes ad nequitiam sunt
appositissimae :   oculi   ad   petulantem   lasciviam,
manus ad rapinam, venter ad aviditatem, membra,[1]
quae non[2] possumus honeste appellare, ad omne
genus corruptelae, pedes[3] ad fugam : prorsus ut aut
ex hoc vitia, aut ipse ex vitiis ortus videatur. (Rutil.
Lup. i. 18.)

The speech is referred to as " Against Demades " by
Suidas and Athenaeus and " Against Cephisodotus " by
Harpocration. Its full title is preserved in fragment 2. The
date must be about 334 B.C. Cephisodotus proposed that
Demades should be honoured for twice saving Athens from
the anger of Alexander, *i.e.* after his descents on Greece in
336 and 335 B.C. Lycurgus and Polyeuctus prosecuted him

D.

15. ΚΑΤΑ ΙΣΧΥΡΙΟΥ

16. [ΚΑΤΑ ΔΕΞΙΠΠΟΥ]

E. ΑΠΑΡΑΣΗΜΑ

[96]   1. Ὅσοι τοῖς ἀπὸ τῆς φύσεως ἀγαθοῖς ἐπὶ τὰ

---

[1] *membra* Ruhnken : *virilis naturae membra* codd.
[2] *non* add. Ald.

152

3. He says that Philip pledged with a horn those to whom he felt friendly.

4. A man whose body is finely adapted to vice in every part : the eyes for wanton lust, the hands for robbery, the stomach for greed, the parts which we cannot decently name for every form of corruption, and the feet for flight.[3] So that it seems as if vices owe their origin to him or else he himself has arisen out of vices.

for this but were defeated, and Demades was granted a bronze statue in the Agora and free meals in the Prytaneum (*v.* Dinarch. i. 101). Sauppe connected the speech *Against Demades* with the Euthycrates case in which he claimed that Lycurgus helped Hyperides (*cf.* Hyp. frag. 19), but this is a less satisfactory explanation. Fragments 1 and 4 have been referred to this speech because their subject matter seems appropriate.

D. *Miscellaneous speeches*

15. AGAINST ISCHYRIAS

The title is given as Πρὸς Ἰσχυρίαν by Suidas and κατὰ Ἰσχυρίου by Harpocration. Date and circumstances not known.

16. [AGAINST DEXIPPUS]

This title is given by Harpocration but Sauppe's alteration of Lycurgus to Lysias is probably justified.

E. *Fragments of uncertain origin*

1. Whenever men use the gifts of nature for baser

---

³ *pedes* Stanger : *pes* codd.

LYCURGUS

χείρω χρῶνται, τούτοις πολέμια τὰ εὐτυχήματά
ἐστιν· ὡς εἴ τις ἀνδρεῖος ὢν λήζεσθαι μᾶλλον ἢ
στρατεύεσθαι προῄρηται, ἢ ἰσχυρὸς ὢν λωποδυτεῖν
μᾶλλον ἢ . . . συμβουλεύειν, ἢ καλὸς ὢν μοι-
χεύειν μᾶλλον ἢ γαμεῖν, οὗτος τῶν ἀπὸ τῆς
φύσεως ἀγαθῶν ὑπαρξάντων προδότης ἐστίν. Stobaeus, *Florileg.* ii. 31.

[97]   2. Ζηλωτὸν ἴσως ὁ πλοῦτος· τίμιον μέντοι καὶ
θαυμαστὸν ἡ δικαιοσύνη. Stobaeus, *Florileg.* ix. 50.

[98]   3. Δεῖ φίλοις καὶ τοῖς οἰκείοις βοηθεῖν ἄχρι
τοῦ μὴ ἐπιορκεῖν. Stobaeus, *Florileg.* xxvii. 10.

[100]   4. Οὐ τὸ πλουτεῖν καλόν, ἀλλὰ τὸ ἐκ καλῶν
πλουτεῖν. Stobaeus, *Florileg.* xciv. 17.

[101]   5. Nemo enim nocens sine summo maerore est,
iudices, sed multa simul eum perturbant : quod adest,
sollicitudinis plenum, quod futurum est, formidolo-
sum, lex paratum supplicium ostentans, vitia ex
vitiis coacta, occasionem arguendi maleficii captans
inimicus : quae cotidiano eius animum vehementer
excruciant. (Rutil. Lup. i. 2.)

[103]   6. At mihi non[1] mirum videtur, quod tam excelsum
boni[2] gradum homo summi laboris escenderit.[3] Nam
cui praesto est strenua[4] voluntas, industrius sit
necesse est ; industriam[5] vero scientia consequitur ;
ex scientia copia et facultas ingenii nascitur ; ex qua
facultate verae[6] facile felicitas laudis oritur.   Neque

---

[1] *non* add. Sauppe.
[2] *boni*] *honoris* Ruhnken.
[3] *escenderit* Ruhnken : *excederit* codd.
[4] *strenua* Sauppe : *tua* codd.
[5] *industriam* Durrbach : *industrium* codd.

154

purposes, good fortune proves to be their enemy. For example, if a brave man prefers the life of a brigand to that of a soldier, or if a strong man chooses to be a highwayman [a] . . . rather than an advocate, or a handsome man chooses adultery in preference to marriage, he is a betrayer of the good things bestowed on him by nature.

2. Wealth, no doubt, calls for envy, but goodness inspires honour and admiration.

3. We must help our friends and relatives as far as we can without perjury.

4. Mere wealth does not claim respect but only wealth acquired in honourable ways.

5. For the guilty man, gentlemen of the jury, always experiences the deepest sorrow. In fact he is the victim of many cares at once : the present is full of anxiety, the future of terror ; the law confronts him, holding out a punishment ever ready ; crimes which have grown out of crimes ; an enemy seizing a chance to prove his guilt. These thoughts torture his mind unmercifully day by day.

6. It does not surprise me that a man of the greatest diligence has risen to so high a degree of fortune. For a man of strong will power must of necessity be industrious, and industry leads to knowledge. From knowledge comes fluency and oratorical power, a gift which results naturally in the attainment

---

[a] Some words have clearly dropped out here. An honourable calling is needed for the strong, and a disreputable one for the clever man, who might be an advocate. Meier suggested : " . . . a highwayman rather than a wrestler, or if a clever speaker elects to be an informer rather than an advocate."

---

[6] *verae* Frotscher : *vera et* codd.

LYCURGUS

enim temere[1] diligens studium virtutis fructus fortunae fallit. (Rutil. Lup. i. 13.)

[106] 7. Sed vos, iudices, vos haec facere debetis. Nam cum in sententiis ferundis nocentibus remisse parcatis, vos impiorum[2] studium ad peccandum[3] excitatis. (Rutil. Lup. ii. 18.)

[1] *temere* Ald. : *tenere* codd.
[2] *impiorum* Sauppe : *in forum* codd.
[3] *peccandum* Stephanus : *spectatum* codd.

156

of true renown. For fortune's reward does not lightly disappoint the resolute pursuit of virtue.

7. But it is you, gentlemen of the jury, you who ought to do this. For whenever, in giving your vote, you indulgently spare the guilty, you are yourselves arousing the desire of wicked men for crime.

DINARCHUS

LIFE OF DINARCHUS [a]

DINARCHUS, son of Sostratus and last of the ten Attic orators, was born at Corinth about 361 B.C. and, while still young, moved to Athens where he studied under Theophrastus and Demetrius of Phalerum. Being an alien he could take no personal part in the politics of the city ; but he gradually made a name for himself as a writer of speeches for others, and in the notorious Harpalus case, when most of the leading orators were suspect, was employed by the prosecution.

It was after the death of Alexander, when Demosthenes and his great contemporaries were either dead or in exile, that Dinarchus had his most successful period ; and for some fifteen years, during which Cassander controlled Athens, he continued to prosper in his profession, amassing considerable wealth. In 307 however, after the liberation of Athens by Demetrius Poliorcetes, he was accused of supporting

---

[a] Sources for the Life of Dinarchus. The chief source, from which nearly all the available details concerning the life and work of Dinarchus come, is the essay on him written by Dionysius of Halicarnassus. A brief notice of his life is given in chapter 2 of this, and from it is derived the Pseudo-Plutarch's biography in the *Lives of the Ten Orators*. Suidas gives a short note on him (*s.v.* " Dinarchus "), of which the latter part relates to a different person of the same name.

DINARCHUS

the late oligarchy, and fearing that his riches would prove a source of trouble, sold most of his property and retired to Chalcis in Euboea. There he remained for fifteen years continuing to make money until at last, in 292, an old man with failing eye-sight, he was permitted with some other exiles to return to Athens. There, we are told, while lodging with a friend Proxenus, he lost a sum of money, and since his host declined to look for it, brought an action against him; on which occasion, for the first time in his life, he spoke himself in court. It is unlikely that he lived much longer, but the date and circumstances of his death are not known.

Dinarchus was not a great orator. Some ancient critics thought highly of his work, Demetrius of Magnesia even comparing him favourably with Hyperides. But Dionysius of Halicarnassus, who has left us an essay on the subject, had a poorer opinion of his merits, and this is shared by most modern readers. Though we should bear in mind that the authenticity of the speech against Demosthenes was questioned in antiquity, and that even if genuine, all three extant speeches are early compositions, it remains true that, despite his long career as a writer, Dinarchus developed no marked characteristics of his own, being content to imitate with moderate success the style of other orators, particularly that of Demosthenes. The two descriptions of himself which he thus earned as ἄγροικος Δημοσθένης [a] and κρίθινος Δημοσθένης [b] (a rustic Demosthenes and a small-beer Demosthenes) convey an impression of his abilities which is probably not unfair.

[a] Dion. Hal. *Dinarch.* 8.
[b] Hermogenes, περὶ ἰδεῶν B, p. 384 W.

I
SPEECH AGAINST DEMO-
STHENES

INTRODUCTION

The Harpalus Affair [a]

THE three extant speeches of Dinarchus all bear on one important trial, which took place in 323 B.C.,[b] when a number of prominent Athenian citizens were prosecuted for taking bribes from Harpalus. Harpalus was a Macedonian noble, who on the death of Philip in 336 was recalled from exile by Alexander and, being physically unsuited for war, appointed treasurer. Accompanying the king on his Persian campaign he deserted before the battle of Issus; but, pardoned and reinstated in office, he was left in charge of the Persian treasures at Ecbatana.[c] When the army proceeded eastwards Harpalus thus

[a] Sources for the Harpalus Affair. The whole story is briefly told by Diodorus (xvii. 108), and references to it occur in the *Lives of the Ten Orators* (*e.g. Vit. X Or.* 846 A, 848 F, 850 c). Further details included here are derived in the main from Plutarch's Life of Demosthenes (Plut. *Dem.* 857 B *sq.*), the speech of Hyperides against Demosthenes and the three speeches of Dinarchus. Although the history of this affair is obscure in many particulars, the salient points in the story are summarized in the above account.

[b] The exact chronology cannot be determined. The arrival of Harpalus in Athens certainly took place in 324; and, in view of the time required for the intervening events, January 323 would seem to be the earliest date which can reasonably be assigned to the trial itself.

[c] Arrian, *Anab.* iii. 6. 6 and 19. 7.

remained behind and indulged himself with despotic
liberty, believing that Alexander would not return.
On realizing his error he fled with five thousand
talents to Greece, where he hoped for a welcome at
Athens. Having made a gift of corn to the city during
a time of shortage he had recently been made an
Athenian citizen ; and as the leading statesmen
were determined opponents of Macedon, they might
well be expected to harbour a powerful ally. Accordingly, early in 324, Harpalus appeared off Cape
Sunium with thirty ships and six thousand mercenaries, only to be rebuffed ; Demosthenes, who had
now adopted a more compromising attitude to
Macedon, proposed a decree forbidding him to land.
Withdrawing, therefore, to Cape Taenarum he again
approached the city, this time as a suppliant with only
one or two ships and no escort. Being granted permission to enter, he appeared before the people,
declaring that he would be their ally.

It was not long before messages came from Antipater and Olympias, and from Philoxenus governor
of Cilicia,[a] demanding the surrender of the treasurer.
The Athenians, however, on the advice of Demosthenes, refused to give him up before receiving word
from Alexander himself but in the mean time arrested
him and deposited his money on the Acropolis. It
was at this point that suspicion fell on certain well-
known citizens. While proposing the decree which
authorized the seizure of Harpalus Demosthenes
asked him publicly how much money he had brought
with him. The answer was seven hundred talents ;
yet on the following day, when the money was
deposited on the Acropolis, it was found to amount

[a] *Cf.* Diodor. xvii. 108 ; Hyp. v. col. 8.

to no more than three hundred and fifty.[a] No proper inquiry was made to account for the missing sum, a piece of negligence for which Demosthenes seems to have been to blame, and a short time later Harpalus eluded his guards and escaped to Crete, where he was subsequently murdered.

At Athens grave dissatisfaction was felt at these proceedings ; for it seemed obvious that Harpalus had ensured his escape by extensive bribery. Demosthenes proposed that the council of the Areopagus should hold an inquiry to discover what men had received money from Harpalus ; and knowing that he was himself suspected, he expressed his willingness to submit to the death penalty if he were proved guilty. After six months the Areopagus published its conclusions in the form of a bare list of names with a sum of money imputed to each. This list, the length of which is not recorded, included the names of Demosthenes, Demades, Philocles, Aristogiton, Aristonicus,[b] Hagnonides,[c] Polyeuctus of Sphettus and Cephisophon.[d] The suspects were prosecuted, before a jury of fifteen hundred, by ten chosen accusers [e] of whom we have the names of six : Stratocles, Hyperides, Menesaechmus, Pytheas, Himeraeus and Procles (or perhaps Patrocles).[f] Demosthenes, Demades and Aristonicus were condemned ; Aristogiton and perhaps Hagnonides and Philocles [g] were acquitted ; the verdict on the others is not known.

        [a] *Vit. X Or.*, *Dem.* 846 B.
        [b] Dion. Hal. *Dinarch.* 10.
        [c] Hyp. v. col. 40 and note.
        [d] Dinarch. i. 45.
        [e] Dinarch. ii. 6.
     [f] Dinarch. i. 1 ; *Vit. X Or.*, *Dem.* 846 c.
     [g] See Dinarch. *Against Philocles*, Introd.

DINARCHUS

The Speech of Dinarchus

Demosthenes was the first statesman to come up for trial in connexion with the Harpalus affair, having been reported by the Areopagus as the recipient of twenty talents. Stratocles spoke first and was followed by the orator for whom Dinarchus composed his speech. The identity of this person is not known, but in view of the fact that he spoke second and at considerable length, we may assume that he was a citizen of some importance. Hyperides and Pytheas [a] need not be considered, since they composed for themselves; nothing is known of Procles, and it seems reasonable to assume that he and the four unnamed accusers were of no great standing. The choice would therefore appear to lie between Menesaechmus and Himeraeus, but in the absence of further evidence no definite conclusion can be reached. The order in which the remaining speeches were delivered is not known. Demosthenes was condemned to pay a fine of fifty talents, and being unable to do this, was imprisoned. Later, however, with the connivance of some of his guards, he escaped to Aegina, whence the Athenians recalled him on the death of Alexander a few months after.

The speech of Dinarchus is in the main disappointing. He has some telling passages and sometimes a striking phrase; but though the attack is vigorous, no logical sequence can be traced in the argument and much that he says seems unconvincing. Stratocles had no doubt anticipated everything pertinent to the case,[b] and the second speaker was compelled to

---

[a] Dion. Hal. *Isaeus* 4; Rutil. Lup. i. 11.
[b] See Dinarch. i. 1.

resort to excessive abuse and arguments used by
Aeschines years before. The genuineness of this
oration was doubted in antiquity, and it may not
therefore give quite a fair impression of the writer's
ability.

AGAINST DEMOSTHENES

...

ANALYSIS

sometimes acquitted by the people, but the reports are not thereby proved false. The Areopagus has often condemned men at the instigation of Demosthenes.

§§ 64-71. For their own sakes the jury must condemn Demosthenes. He has made the relations of Athens with Alexander difficult.

§§ 72-83. Statesmen are responsible for a city's prosperity or misfortune. Let the jury consider Thebes and Athens. They cannot afford to retain Demosthenes in view of his record.

§§ 84-104. They must support the Areopagus and ensure the city's safety. Demosthenes has rendered none of the services expected of an orator, but has in fact favoured Macedon.

§§ 104-114. Appeal to the jury to condemn Demosthenes, who has grown great at their expense. They must not be influenced by his prayers or his witnesses.

ΚΑΤΑ ΔΗΜΟΣΘΕΝΟΥΣ

[90] Ὁ μὲν δημαγωγὸς ὑμῖν, ὦ Ἀθηναῖοι, καὶ θανάτου
τετιμημένος ἑαυτῷ ἐὰν ἐξελεγχθῇ ὁτιοῦν εἰληφὼς
παρ᾽ Ἁρπάλου, οὗτος φανερῶς ἐξελήλεγκται δῶρ᾽
εἰληφὼς παρὰ τούτων, οἷς ἐναντία πράττειν ἔφη
τὸν ἄλλον χρόνον. πολλῶν δ᾽ ὑπὸ Στρατοκλέους
εἰρημένων καὶ τῶν πλείστων προκατειλημμένων
κατηγορημάτων, καὶ περὶ μὲν αὐτῆς τῆς ἀποφάσεως
τῆς ἐξ Ἀρείου πάγου βουλῆς δικαίας καὶ ἀληθεῖς
ἀποδείξεις εἰρηκυίας, περὶ δὲ τῶν ἀκολούθων τούτοις Στρατοκλέους εἰρηκότος καὶ τὰ ψηφίσματ᾽
2 ἀνεγνωκότος ἤδη τὰ περὶ τούτων, ὑπόλοιπον ἡμῖν,
ὦ Ἀθηναῖοι, καὶ ταῦτ᾽ ἀγωνιζομένοις ἀγῶνα τηλικοῦτον ἡλίκος οὐδεπώποτε γέγονε τῇ πόλει, κοινῇ
πᾶσιν ὑμῖν παρακελεύεσθαι, πρῶτον μὲν τοῖς
λοιποῖς ἡμῖν συγγνώμην ἔχειν, ἂν τῶν αὐτῶν
ἐνίοις περιπίπτωμεν—οὐ γὰρ ἵν᾽ ἐνοχλῶμεν ὑμᾶς,
ἀλλ᾽ ἵν᾽ ὀργίζεσθαι μᾶλλον παροξύνωμεν,[1] δὶς περὶ
τῶν αὐτῶν ἐροῦμεν—, ἔπειτα μὴ προΐεσθαι τὰ
κοινὰ τῆς πόλεως ἁπάσης δίκαια, μηδὲ τὴν κοινὴν
σωτηρίαν ἀντικαταλλάξασθαι τῶν τοῦ κρινομένου
3 λόγων. ὁρᾶτε γάρ, ὦ Ἀθηναῖοι, ὅτι παρὰ μὲν ὑμῖν

---

[1] ὀργίζεσθαι μᾶλλον παροξύνωμεν Thalheim: ὀργίζησθε μᾶλλον
παροξύνωμεν A pr. (παροξυνόμενοι A corr.²): μᾶλλον ὀργίζησθε
παροξύνωμεν N pr. (ὀργίζησθαι (sic) N corr.²): παροξύν. del.
Finke: ὀργίζ. del. Blass. Alii alia.

172

AGAINST DEMOSTHENES

THIS popular leader of yours, Athenians, who has imposed on himself a sentence of death should he be proved to have taken even the smallest sum from Harpalus, has been clearly convicted of taking bribes from those very men whom he formerly professed to oppose. Much has already been said by Stratocles [a] and most of the charges have now been made ; as regards the report itself the Areopagus has expressed opinions which are both just and true, while with events succeeding this Stratocles has already dealt and read the decrees relating to them. It remains for us, Athenians, especially when contesting a case never paralleled in the experience of the city, to make a general exhortation to you all. May we ask you first to pardon those of us who have still to speak if there are certain points which we raise again ; our aim is not to weary you by alluding twice to the same matters but to arouse your anger all the more. Secondly, may we ask you not to surrender the rights enjoyed by the whole city or to barter away our common security in exchange for the arguments of the defendant. You are aware, Athenians, that

[a] Stratocles the orator, who proposed that special honours should be paid to Lycurgus after his death (*Vit. X Or.*, *Lycurg.* 852 A), may possibly be the same man as the general of that name who served at Chaeronea.

Δημοσθένης οὑτοσὶ κρίνεται, παρὰ δὲ τοῖς ἄλλοις
ὑμεῖς· οἳ σκοποῦσι τίνα ποτὲ γνώμην ἕξετε περὶ
τῶν τῇ πατρίδι συμφερόντων, καὶ πότερον τὰς
ἰδίας τούτων δωροδοκίας καὶ πονηρίας ἀναδέξεσθ᾽[1]
εἰς ὑμᾶς αὐτούς, ἢ φανερὸν πᾶσιν ἀνθρώποις ποιήσετε διότι μισεῖτε τοὺς κατὰ τῆς πολιτείας δῶρα
λαμβάνοντας, καὶ οὐχ ἵν᾽ ἀφῆτε ζητεῖν προσετάξατε
τῇ ἐξ Ἀρείου πάγου βουλῇ, ἀλλ᾽ ἵν᾽ ἀποφηνάντων
τούτων ὑμεῖς τιμωρήσησθε τῶν ἀδικημάτων ἀξίως.
4 νυνὶ τοίνυν τοῦτ᾽ ἐφ᾽ ὑμῖν ἐστι. ψηφισαμένου γὰρ
τοῦ δήμου δίκαιον ψήφισμα, καὶ πάντων τῶν πολιτῶν βουλομένων εὑρεῖν τίνες εἰσὶ τῶν ῥητόρων οἱ
τολμήσαντες ἐπὶ διαβολῇ καὶ κινδύνῳ τῆς πόλεως
χρήματα παρ᾽ Ἁρπάλου λαβεῖν, καὶ πρὸς τούτοις
⟨ἐν⟩[2] ψηφίσματι γράψαντος, ὦ Δημόσθενες, σοῦ
καὶ ἑτέρων πολλῶν, ζητεῖν τὴν βουλὴν περὶ αὐτῶν,
ὡς αὐτῇ πάτριόν ἐστιν, εἴ τινες εἰλήφασι παρ᾽
5 Ἁρπάλου χρυσίον, ζητεῖ ἡ βουλή, οὐκ ἐκ τῶν προκλήσεων μαθοῦσα τὸ δίκαιον, οὐδὲ τὴν ἀλήθειαν
καὶ τὴν πίστιν τὴν περὶ[3] αὐτῆς[4] ἐπὶ σοῦ καταλῦσαι
βουλομένη, ἀλλ᾽, ὅπερ καὶ αὐτοὶ οἱ Ἀρεοπαγῖται
εἶπον, προορῶσα ⟨μὲν⟩[5] ἡ βουλή, ὦ ἄνδρες, τὴν
τούτων ἰσχὺν καὶ τὴν ἐν τῷ λέγειν καὶ πράττειν
δύναμιν, οὐκ οἰομένη δὲ δεῖν οὐδεμίαν ὑπολογί-
ζεσθαι τῶν περὶ αὐτῆς[6] ἐσομένων βλασφημιῶν, εἴ
τις μέλλει τῇ πατρίδι αὐτῆς[7] αἰτία μοχθηρὰ καὶ
6 κίνδυνος ἔσεσθαι. τούτων ὡς ἐδόκει τῷ δήμῳ

---

[1] ἀναδέξεσθε Stephanus : ἀναδέχεσθε codd.
[2] ἐν add. Blass : ψηφίσματι A pr. : ψήφισμά τι A corr. :
ψη . . . . . . N pr. : ψήφισμα N corr.[2] : del. Thalheim.
[3] περὶ] προτέραν Rosenberg : πατρίαν Blass.
[4] αὐτῆς Bekker : αὑτῆς codd.
[5] μὲν add. Reiske.   [6] αὐτῆς Bekker : αὑτῆς codd.

whereas this man Demosthenes is here for judgement before you, you are on trial before your fellows. For they are waiting to see what kind of conclusion you will reach about your country's interests : are you going to welcome into your midst the private venality and corruption of these people, or will you make it universally known that you hate men who accept bribes against their city and that, in ordering the Areopagus to make its inquiry, your intention was not to acquit the culprits but rather, when the councillors had made their report, to exact punishment in a manner appropriate to the crimes ? This decision then rests with you now. For when the people passed a lawful decree and every citizen wished to discover which of the politicians had dared to accept money from Harpalus to the discredit and danger of the city ; when, moreover, you, Demosthenes, and many others had proposed in a decree that the Areopagus, according to its traditional right, should hold an inquiry to discover if any of them had received gold from Harpalus, the Areopagus began its investigation. In reaching a just decision it paid no heed to your challenges, Demosthenes, nor did it wish to pervert the truth or destroy its own reputation on your account. On the contrary, gentlemen, although, as the Areopagites themselves said, the council realized beforehand the strength of these men and their influence as orators and statesmen, it did not consider that if incrimination or danger was threatening its country it ought to be influenced by any misrepresentation likely to be published about itself. Though this investigation has been conducted, in the people's

---

⁷ αὐτῆς] αὐτοῖς, cum BL, Bekker : αὐτῇ Baiter : τις Blass, qui τις post εἰ seclusit.

DINARCHUS

καλῶς καὶ συμφερόντως πεπραγμένων, αἰτίαι νῦν
καὶ προκλήσεις καὶ συκοφαντίαι παρὰ Δημοσθένους
ἤκουσιν, ἐπειδὴ οὗτος ἀποπέφανται εἴκοσι τάλαντα
ἔχων χρυσίου· καὶ ἡ τῶν ἐκ προνοίας φόνων ἀξιό-
πιστος οὖσα βουλὴ τὸ δίκαιον καὶ τἀληθὲς[1] εὑρεῖν,
καὶ κυρία δικάσαι τε περὶ τοῦ σώματος καὶ τῆς
[91] ψυχῆς ἑκάστου τῶν πολιτῶν, καὶ τοῖς μὲν βιαίῳ
θανάτῳ τετελευτηκόσι βοηθῆσαι, τοὺς δὲ παράνομόν
τι τῶν ἐν τῇ πόλει διαπεπραγμένους ἐκβαλεῖν ἢ
θανάτῳ ζημιῶσαι, νῦν ἐπὶ τοῖς κατὰ Δημοσθένους ἀποπεφασμένοις χρήμασιν ἄκυρος ἔσται τοῦ
δικαίου;

7 Ναί· κατέψευσται γὰρ ἡ βουλὴ Δημοσθένους·
τουτὶ γάρ ἐστιν ὑπερβολὴ τοῦ πράγματος. σοῦ
κατέψευσται καὶ Δημάδου; καθ᾽ ὧν οὐδὲ τἀληθὲς
εἰπεῖν, ὡς ἔοικεν, ἀσφαλές ἐστιν; οἳ πολλὰ πρότερον τῶν κοινῶν ἐκείνῃ ζητεῖν προσετάξατε καὶ
διὰ τὰς γενομένας ζητήσεις ἐπῃνέσατε; οὓς δ᾽
ἡ πόλις ἅπασα οὐ δύναται ἀναγκάσαι τὰ δίκαια
ποιεῖν, κατὰ τούτων ἡ βουλὴ ψευδεῖς ἀποφάσεις
8 πεποίηται; ὦ Ἡράκλεις. διὰ τί οὖν ἐν τῷ δήμῳ
συνεχώρεις, ὦ Δημόσθενες, ἐὰν ἀποφήνῃ ⟨κατὰ⟩[2]
σοῦ ἡ βουλή, θάνατον ἑαυτῷ τὴν ζημίαν; καὶ διὰ
τί πολλοὺς ἀνῄρηκας σὺ ταῖς τῆς βουλῆς ἰσχυρι-
ζόμενος ἀποφάσεσιν; ἢ ποῖ[3] νῦν ἐλθὼν ὁ δῆμος ἢ
τίσι προστάξας ζητεῖν περὶ τῶν ἀφανῶν καὶ με-

---

[1] τἀληθὲς Blass : ἀληθὲς codd.
[2] Aut κατὰ addendum (cf. § 7) aut σὲ pro σοῦ legendum
(cf. § 61) coni. Wolf.   [3] ποῖ Reiske : ποῦ codd.

---

[a] After the restoration of the democracy in 403 B.C. the

176

opinion, both fairly and profitably, accusations, challenges, and calumnies are proceeding from Demosthenes, since he has been listed as the holder of twenty talents of gold. Will that council then which, in cases of wilful murder, is trustworthy enough to arrive at truth and justice and is empowered to pass judgement in matters of life and death on each of the citizens, to take up the cause of those who have met a violent end and banish or execute any in the city who have broken the law,[a] be powerless now to administer justice over the money credited to Demosthenes ?

It will ; for the council has told lies against Demosthenes. This is the crowning argument in his case. It has told lies, has it, against you and Demades : men against whom it is evidently not even safe to speak the truth ; though you previously instructed the Areopagus to investigate many public matters and expressed approval of it for the inquiries which it had held ? Are the indictments which the council has made against these men false when the whole city cannot compel them to do right ? Great Heavens ! Then why, Demosthenes, did you agree in the Assembly to a penalty of death for yourself, if the report of the council should turn out against you ? And why have you yourself ruined many others by insisting on the findings of the council ? To what authority should the people now refer, or to whom should it entrust the inquiry in the event of mysterious or momentous

Areopagus played a more important part in public affairs than in the preceding half-century. It dealt with all cases of voluntary homicide and sometimes with political cases also, when it could act either on its own initiative (*cf.* § 63 and Dem. xviii. 133) or in response to the people's request, as in the present instance. See § 50.

9 γάλων ἀδικημάτων εὕρῃ τὴν ἀλήθειαν; τὸ μὲν
γὰρ συνέδριον, τὸ πρότερον δοκοῦν εἶναι πιστόν,
σὺ καταλύεις, ὁ δημοτικὸς εἶναι φάσκων, ᾧ τὴν
τῶν σωμάτων φυλακὴν ὁ δῆμος παρακαταθήκην
ἔδωκεν, ᾧ τὴν πολιτείαν καὶ δημοκρατίαν πολλάκις
ἐγκεχείρικεν, ὃ¹ διαπεφύλαχε² τὸ σὸν σῶμα τοῦ
βλασφημεῖν περὶ αὐτοῦ μέλλοντος πολλάκις, ὡς σὺ
φῄς, ἐπιβουλευθέν, ὃ φυλάττει τὰς ἀπορρήτους
διαθήκας,³ ἐν αἷς τὰ τῆς πόλεως σωτήρια κεῖται.

10 Δίκαια μὲν οὖν, δίκαια τρόπον γέ τινα πάσχει τὸ
συνέδριον· εἰρήσεται γὰρ ἃ γιγνώσκω. δυοῖν γὰρ
θάτερον ἐχρῆν αὐτούς, ἢ καὶ τὴν προτέραν ζήτησιν
τὴν ὑπὲρ τῶν τριακοσίων ταλάντων τῶν παρὰ τοῦ
Περσῶν βασιλέως ἀφικομένων ζητεῖν, καθάπερ
συνέταξεν ὁ δῆμος, ἵνα τότε δόντος δίκην τοῦ
θηρίου τούτου, καὶ τῶν μερισαμένων ἐκεῖνα τὰ
χρήματα φανερῶν γενομένων, καὶ τῆς περὶ Θηβαίους προδοσίας ἐξελεγχθείσης ἣν οὗτος προδέδωκεν, ἀπηλλάγμεθα τούτου τοῦ δημαγωγοῦ δίκην
11 ἀξίαν δόντος· ἤ, εἰ ταῦθ' ὑμεῖς ἐβούλεσθε Δημο-

---

¹ ὃ N : ᾧ A.
² διαπεφύλαχε Wolf : διαπεφύλακε codd.
³ διαθήκας] ἀποθήκας N : θήκας Wolf.

ᵃ The exact nature of these mystic deposits, on which the
welfare of the community was thought to depend, is not
known ; they were probably oracles.

ᵇ After Alexander's accession Darius subsidized several
Greek states to oppose him. Three hundred talents offered
by him to Athens and officially refused were said to have been
accepted by Demosthenes to be used in the king's interest.
Cf. § 18 ; Aeschin. iii. 239 (who gives the sum which Demosthenes appropriated as seventy talents) ; Diodor. xvii. 4.

ᶜ In 335 B.C., owing to a report that Alexander, who was

crimes, if it is to discover the truth ? For the council which formerly commanded confidence is being discredited by you, who claim to be the people's man, though it is a body to which the people gave in trust the protection of their lives, to whose charge they have often committed their constitution and democracy, a council which, destined though you were to malign it, has safeguarded your life, according to your own account so often threatened, and which keeps the mystic deposits *a* whereby the safety of the city is preserved.

Now in one respect—for I shall speak my mind— the Areopagus fully deserves this treatment. It was faced with two alternatives. One would have been, in accordance with the people's instructions, to conduct the previous investigation over the three hundred talents which came from the Persian king *b* ; in which case this monster would have been convicted and the names of those who shared the money published ; the betrayal of Thebes, for which Demosthenes was responsible,*c* would have been exposed, and we, exacting from this demagogue the punishment he deserved, would have been rid of him. Alternatively, if it was your wish to forgive Demo-

fighting the Triballi, had been killed, Thebes revolted against Macedonian domination encouraged by Demosthenes and others who assisted them to procure arms. When they applied for assistance to the Peloponnese and Athens, the Peloponnesians sent an army as far as the Isthmus, while Athens voted help but awaited the turn of events. Meanwhile Thebes was taken by Alexander and destroyed. Dinarchus, who goes into greater detail later (§§ 18-22), maintains that for ten talents of the Persian money Demosthenes could have secured the help of the Peloponnesian army but was too miserly to do so. *Cf.* Diodor. xvii. 8 ; Aeschin. iii. 239-240.

σθένει συγχωρεῖν καὶ πολλοὺς ἐν τῇ πόλει τοὺς καθ᾽
ὑμῶν δωροδοκήσοντας εἶναι, τὴν περὶ τῶν νῦν
ἀποπεφασμένων ζήτησιν χρημάτων μὴ προσδέχε-
σθαι, πεῖραν ὑμῶν ἐν τοῖς πρότερον εἰληφότας· ὅπου
γ᾽[1] οὕτω καλῶς καὶ δικαίως τῆς ἀποφάσεως τῆς
κατὰ τούτου καὶ τῶν ἄλλων νυνὶ γεγενημένης, καὶ
τῆς ἐξ Ἀρείου πάγου βουλῆς οὔτε τὴν Δημοσθένους
οὔτε τὴν Δημάδου δύναμιν ὑποστειλαμένης, ἀλλὰ
τὸ δίκαιον αὐτὸ καὶ τἀληθὲς προυργιαίτερον πε-
12 ποιημένης, οὐδὲν ἧττον περιέρχεται Δημοσθένης
περί τε τῆς βουλῆς βλασφημῶν καὶ περὶ ἑαυτοῦ
λέγων οἷσπερ ἴσως[2] καὶ πρὸς ὑμᾶς αὐτίκα χρήσεται
λόγοις ἐξαπατῶν ὑμᾶς, ὡς " ἐγὼ Θηβαίους ὑμῖν
ἐποίησα συμμάχους." οὔκ· ἀλλὰ τὸ κοινῇ συμφέρον ἀμφοτέραις ἐλυμήνω ταῖς πόλεσιν, ὦ Δημόσθενες. " ἐγὼ παρέταξα πάντας εἰς Χαιρώνειαν."
οὔκ· ἀλλ᾽ ἔλιπες μόνος αὐτὸς τὴν ἐκεῖ τάξιν. " ἐγὼ
13 πολλὰς ὑπὲρ ὑμῶν ἐπρέσβευσα πρεσβείας." ἐφ᾽
αἷς[3] οὐκ οἶδ᾽ ὅ τι ποτ᾽ ἂν ἐποίησεν ἢ τίνας ἂν εἶπε
λόγους, εἰ συνέβη κατορθῶσαι αὐτῷ[4] ἃ συνεβού-
λευσεν, ὃς[5] ἐπὶ τοῖς τοιούτοις ἀτυχήμασι καὶ κακοῖς
ἅπασαν ἐπεληλυθὼς τὴν οἰκουμένην ὅμως ἀξιοῖ
δωρεὰς αὑτῷ[6] δεδόσθαι τὰς μεγίστας, λαμβάνειν
δῶρα κατὰ τῆς πατρίδος καὶ λέγειν καὶ πράττειν

---

[1] γε Ald. : γὰρ codd.
[2] οἷσπερ ἴσως N corr.[2] : οἷς περισσῶς N pr. A.
[3] αἷς Reiske : οἷς codd.
[4] αὐτῷ N : αὑτῷ A.　　　　[5] ὃς Taylor : ὁ codd.
[6] αὑτῷ Bekker : αὐτῷ codd.

sthenes for these offences and to have in the city a large number of people who would take bribes against you, the council ought, having tested your wishes in the previous cases, to have refused to undertake an investigation over the payments of money recently reported. For despite the excellence and the justice of this recent report, which incriminates Demosthenes and the rest of them, and despite the fact that the Areopagus has not deferred to the power of Demosthenes or Demades but has regarded justice and truth as more important, Demosthenes goes round none the less maligning the council and telling the same stories about himself with which he will probably try to mislead you presently. " I made the Thebans your allies."[a] No, Demosthenes, you impaired the common interest of both our states. " I brought everyone into line at Chaeronea." On the contrary you yourself were the only one to leave the line at Chaeronea.[b] " I served on many embassies on your behalf." One wonders what he would have done or what he would have said if the course that he had recommended on these missions had proved successful, when, after touring the whole Greek world to negotiate such disasters and mistakes, he still claims to have been granted the greatest privileges, namely those of accepting bribes against his country and saying and doing whatever he wishes against the public

---

[a] In making this claim Demosthenes was referring to events just before the battle of Chaeronea when he won Thebes over to Athens by offering her more liberal terms than Philip. For his defence of this policy see Dem. xviii. 153 *sq.*
[b] The charge of cowardice in battle is often brought against Demosthenes by Aeschines (*e.g.* iii. 175) ; it is mentioned by Plutarch (Plut. *Dem.* 855 A) and in the *Lives of the Ten Orators* (*Vit. X Or.* 845 F).

14 κατὰ τοῦ δήμου ἃ ἂν βούληται. καὶ Τιμοθέῳ[1] μέν,
ὦ Ἀθηναῖοι, Πελοπόννησον περιπλεύσαντι καὶ τὴν
ἐν Κερκύρᾳ ναυμαχίαν νικήσαντι Λακεδαιμονίους
καὶ Κόνωνος υἱεῖ τοῦ τοὺς Ἕλληνας ἐλευθερώσαντος
καὶ Σάμον λαβόντι[2] καὶ Μεθώνην καὶ Πύδναν καὶ
Ποτείδαιαν καὶ πρὸς ταύταις ἑτέρας εἴκοσι πόλεις,
οὐκ ἐποιήσασθ᾽ ὑπόλογον, οὐδὲ τῆς τότ᾽ ἐνεστώσης
κρίσεως οὐδὲ τῶν ὅρκων, οὓς ὀμωμοκότες ἐφέρετε
[92] τὴν ψῆφον, ἀντικατηλλάξασθε[3] τὰς τοιαύτας εὐεργεσίας, ἀλλ᾽ ἑκατὸν ταλάντων ἐτιμήσατε, ὅτι χρήματ᾽
αὐτὸν ⟨Ἀριστοφῶν⟩[4] ἔφη παρὰ Χίων εἰληφέναι καὶ
15 Ῥοδίων· τὸν δὲ κατάπτυστον τοῦτον καὶ Σκύθην—
ἐξάγομαι γάρ—, ὃν οὐχ εἷς ἀνὴρ ἀλλὰ πᾶσ᾽ ἡ ἐξ
Ἀρείου πάγου βουλὴ ζητήσασ᾽ ἀποπέφαγκε χρήματ᾽
ἔχειν καθ᾽ ὑμῶν, καὶ ὃς ἀποπέφανται μισθαρνῶν
καὶ δωροδοκῶν κατὰ τῆς πόλεως καὶ ταῦτ᾽ ἐξελήλεγκται, τοῦτον οὐ τιμωρησάμενοι παράδειγμα
ποιήσετε τοῖς ἄλλοις; ὃς οὐκ ἐκ τῶν βασιλικῶν
μόνον εἰληφὼς χρυσίον φανερός ἐστιν, ἀλλὰ καὶ
ἐξ αὐτῆς τῆς πόλεως κεχρηματισμένος· ὁ νῦν οὐδὲ
τῶν ὑφ᾽ Ἁρπάλου κομισθέντων χρημάτων εἰς τὴν
16 πόλιν ἀποσχόμενος. καίτοι τί μέρος ἐστὶ τῶν ὑπὸ

---

[1] Cf. Dinarch. iii. 17.
[2] λαβόντι ex orat. III Sauppe : λαβόντος codd.
[3] ἀντικατηλλάξασθε Ald. : ἀντικαταλλάξασθαι codd.
[4] αὐτὸν Ἀριστοφῶν ex orat. III Gruter : αὐτὸς codd.

[a] The following passage is repeated almost word for word
in the speech against Philocles (Dinarch. iii. 17). Timotheüs,
an Athenian general and a friend of Isocrates, who recounts
his exploits (Isocr. xv. 107-113), sailed round the Peloponnese and gained a victory at Corcyra in 375 B.C. In 365 he took
Samos, which was occupied by a Persian garrison, after a
ten months' siege (Dem. xv. 9). Thence he moved to Thrace
and mastered several Chalcidian cities, of which Dinarchus

182

interest. You made no allowance for Timotheüs,[a]
Athenians, although he sailed round the Peloponnese
and defeated the Lacedaemonians in a naval battle
at Corcyra, and was the son of Conon [b] too who
liberated Greece. Though he captured Samos,
Methone, Pydna, Potidaea, and twenty other cities
besides, you did not permit such services to outweigh
the trial which you were then conducting or the oaths
that governed your vote ; instead you fined him a
hundred talents because Aristophon said that he had
accepted money from the Chians and Rhodians.
Will you then absolve this abominable wretch, this
Scythian,—really I cannot contain myself,—whom
no mere individual but the whole Areopagus has
shown, after inquiry, to be in possession of money to
your detriment, whose bribery and corruption against
the city have been revealed and established beyond
doubt ? Will you not punish him and make him an
example to others ? He is known not only to have
taken gold from the royal treasuries[c] but also to
have enriched himself at the city's own expense, since
he did not even withhold his hand from the money
lately brought to her by Harpalus. Yet the embassies

here mentions three. In 356 he was sent out with two others
to reinforce the fleet of Chares who was trying to crush an
allied revolt ; but in a sea battle near Chios he failed to help
Chares, owing to stormy weather, and was therefore prosecuted by him for bribery. Timotheüs was not popular owing
to his haughty behaviour ; and being fined the unprecedented
amount of a hundred talents, which he could not pay, he
went into exile in Chalcis.   *Cf.* Isocr. xv. 131.

  [b] Conon, a general in the Peloponnesian war who fought
at Aegospotami, was later joint commander of the Persian
fleet. In this capacity he rendered a service to Athens by
defeating the Spartan Pisander in a naval battle off Cnidus
in 394 B.C.   [c] See note on § 10.

Τιμοθέου πεπραγμένων ἀγαθῶν ἃς Δημοσθένης
ἐπρέσβευσεν εἰς Θήβας πρεσβείας; ἢ τίς οὐκ ἂν
καταγελάσειεν ὑμῶν τῶν τούτου[1] τολμώντων
ἀκούειν, ἀντιθεὶς ἐφ᾽ αἷς οὗτος σεμνύνεται πράξεσιν
ἐκείνας ἃς Τιμόθεος ὑμᾶς καὶ Κόνων εὐεργέτησαν;
ἀλλὰ γὰρ οὐ πρὸς τοῦτο τὸ κάθαρμα παραβάλλειν
δεῖ τοὺς ἄξια καὶ τῆς πόλεως καὶ τῶν προγόνων
ὑπὲρ ὑμῶν πράξαντας. παρασχόμενος οὖν τὸ ψήφισμα τὸ Τιμοθέῳ γενόμενον πάλιν ἐπὶ τοὺς περὶ
τούτου λόγους βαδιοῦμαι. λέγε.

ΨΗΦΙΣΜΑ[2]

17 Ὁ τοιοῦτος, ὦ Δημόσθενες, πολίτης, ὃς δικαίως
ἂν καὶ συγγνώμης καὶ χάριτος ἐτύγχανε παρὰ τῶν
ἐν ἐκείνοις τοῖς χρόνοις συμπεπολιτευμένων, οὐ
λόγοις ἀλλ᾽ ἔργοις μεγάλα τὴν πόλιν ἀγαθὰ ποιήσας,
καὶ διαμείνας ἐπὶ τῆς ⟨αὑτῆς⟩[3] πολιτείας καὶ οὐκ
ἄνω καὶ κάτω μεταβαλόμενος ὥσπερ σύ, ἐτελεύ-
τησεν οὐ τηλικαύτας τὸν δῆμον αἰτήσας δωρεὰς
ὥστε τῶν νόμων εἶναι κρείττων, οὐδ᾽ οἰόμενος δεῖν
τοὺς ὀμωμοκότας κατὰ τοὺς νόμους οἴσειν τὴν
ψῆφον ἄλλο τι προὐργιαίτερον ποιεῖσθαι τῆς εὐσεβείας, ἀλλ᾽ ὑπομένων καὶ κρίνεσθαι,[4] εἰ δόξειε τοῖς
δικασταῖς, καὶ οὐ καιροὺς λέγων, οὐδ᾽ ἕτερα φρονῶν
καὶ δημηγορῶν.

18 Οὐκ ἀποκτενεῖτε, ἄνδρες Ἀθηναῖοι, τὸν μιαρὸν
τοῦτον ἄνθρωπον, ὃς πρὸς ἑτέροις πολλοῖς καὶ
μεγάλοις ἁμαρτήμασι καὶ τὴν Θηβαίων πόλιν περι-

---

[1] τούτου Reiske : τοῦτο codd.
[2] ΨΗΦΙΣΜΑ om. NA.
[3] αὑτῆς add. Cobet.

to Thebes which Demosthenes undertook are equivalent to a mere fraction of Timotheüs' services ; and which of you, contrasting with the exploits on which Demosthenes prides himself those which Timotheüs and Conon performed on your behalf, would not laugh to scorn all who consented to listen to this man ? But then there should be no comparison made between this outcast and the men who in your interests acted worthily of the city and your ancestors. I will therefore cite the decree which was passed concerning Timotheüs and then return to my review of the defendant. Read.

Decree

This citizen, Demosthenes, of such a character, who might well have gained the pardon and gratitude of his colleagues in the public life of those days, since he had rendered great services to the city, not in word only but in deed, and had always remained true to the same policy rather than changing to and fro as you have done, met his death without begging the people for such extensive favours as would set him above the laws or thinking that men who had sworn to vote in accordance with the law should consider anything more important than their word ; he was ready even for condemnation, if the jury decided upon it, and did not plead the inclemency of circumstance or express in public opinions which he did not hold.

Will you not execute this accursed wretch, Athenians, who, in addition to many other crucial blunders, stood by while the Thebans' city was de-

---

⁴ Post κρίνεσθαι lacunam indicavit Blass : κατακρίνεσθαι Wolf.

DINARCHUS

εἶδεν ἀνάστατον γενομένην, τριακόσια τάλαντα
λαβὼν εἰς τὴν ἐκείνων σωτηρίαν παρὰ τοῦ Περσῶν
βασιλέως, καὶ Ἀρκάδων ἡκόντων εἰς Ἰσθμὸν καὶ
τὴν μὲν παρ' Ἀντιπάτρου πρεσβείαν ἄπρακτον
ἀποστειλάντων, τὴν δὲ παρὰ Θηβαίων τῶν ταλαιπώρων προσδεξαμένων, οἳ κατὰ θάλατταν μόλις
ἀφίκοντο πρὸς ἐκείνους, ἱκετηρίαν ἔχοντες καὶ
κηρύκεια συμπεπλεγμένα, ὡς ἔφασαν, ἐκ τῶν
19 θαλλῶν, ἐροῦντες τοῖς Ἀρκάσιν ὅτι οὐ τὴν πρὸς
τοὺς Ἕλληνας φιλίαν Θηβαῖοι διαλῦσαι βουλόμενοι
τοῖς πράγμασιν ἐπανέστησαν, οὐδ' ἐναντίον τῶν
Ἑλλήνων οὐδὲν πράξοντες, ἀλλὰ τὰ παρ' αὐτοῖς¹
ὑπὸ τῶν Μακεδόνων ἐν τῇ πόλει γιγνόμενα² φέρειν
οὐκέτι δυνάμενοι, οὐδὲ τὴν δουλείαν ὑπομένειν, οὐδὲ
τὰς ὕβρεις ὁρᾶν τὰς³ εἰς τὰ ἐλεύθερα σώματα γιγνο-
20 μένας,—οἷς ἑτοίμων γενομένων τῶν Ἀρκάδων
βοηθεῖν, καὶ ἐλεησάντων ἐν οἷς⁴ ἦσαν κακοῖς, καὶ
φανερὸν ποιησάντων ὅτι τοῖς μὲν σώμασι μετ'
Ἀλεξάνδρου διὰ τοὺς καιροὺς ἀκολουθεῖν ἠναγκά-
ζοντο, ταῖς δ' εὐνοίαις μετὰ Θηβαίων καὶ τῆς τῶν
Ἑλλήνων ἐλευθερίας ἦσαν, καὶ τοῦ στρατηγοῦ
αὐτῶν Ἀστύλου ὠνίου ὄντος, ὥσπερ καὶ Στρατοκλῆς εἶπε, καὶ δέκα τάλαντ' αἰτοῦντος ὥστ'
ἀγαγεῖν τὴν βοήθειαν τοῖς Θηβαίοις, καὶ τῶν πρε-
σβευτῶν ὡς τοῦτον ἐλθόντων, ὃν ᾔδεσαν ἔχοντα τὸ
βασιλικὸν χρυσίον, καὶ δεομένων καὶ ἱκετευόντων
δοῦναι τὰ χρήματ' εἰς τὴν τῆς πόλεως σωτηρίαν,
21 οὐκ ἐτόλμησεν ὁ μιαρὸς οὗτος καὶ ἀσεβὴς καὶ
αἰσχροκερδὴς ἀπὸ τῶν πολλῶν χρημάτων ὧν εἶχε
δέκα μόνον τάλαντα δοῦναι, τοσαύτας ὁρῶν ἐλπίδας
ὑποφαινούσας εἰς τὴν Θηβαίων σωτηρίαν, ἀλλὰ

¹ αὐτοῖς Bekker : αὑτοῖς codd.

stroyed, though he had accepted three hundred
talents from the Persian King for their protection ;
though the Arcadians,[a] arriving at the Isthmus, had
dismissed with a rebuff the envoys of Antipater and
welcomed those from the unhappy Thebans who had
reached them with difficulty by sea, bearing a suppliant's staff and heralds' wands, plaited, they said,
from olive shoots ? They came to assure the Arcadians
that no wish to break their friendship with the Greeks
had led the Thebans to a revolution, nor did they
intend to do anything to the detriment of Greece ;
but they were no longer able to countenance at home
the behaviour of the Macedonians in the city, to endure slavery, or to witness the outrages perpetrated
against the persons of free men. The Arcadians were
ready to help them and, sympathizing with their
misfortunes, explained that, though they were compelled through force of circumstance to serve Alexander with their persons, in spirit they sided always
with the Thebans and the cause of Greek liberty.
Since their leader, Astylus, was open to bribery, as
Stratocles said, and wanted ten talents as the price
of helping the Thebans, the envoys approached
Demosthenes who, as they knew, held the King's
gold and earnestly begged him to spend the money
to save their city. But this hard-hearted and impious
miser could not bring himself to expend, from his
great resources, ten paltry talents, though he saw
such high hopes dawning for the salvation of Thebes.

[a] See note on § 10.

---

[2] γιγνόμενα Blass : γενόμενα NA : γινόμενα, cum ZM, Bekker.
[3] ὁρᾶν τὰς Bekker : ὁρῶντες codd.
[4] οἷς] οἴοις Maetzner.

187

περιεῖδεν ἑτέρους δόντας τοῦτο τὸ ἀργύριον, ὥσπερ
καὶ Στρατοκλῆς εἶπεν, ὑπὲρ τοῦ πάλιν ἀπελθεῖν
οἴκαδε τοὺς ἐξεληλυθότας Ἀρκάδων καὶ μὴ βοη-
[93] θῆσαι τοῖς Θηβαίοις. ἆρ' ὑμῖν δοκεῖ μικρῶν κακῶν
22 ἢ τῶν τυχόντων ὅλῃ τῇ Ἑλλάδι αἴτιος γεγενῆσθαι
Δημοσθένης καὶ ἡ τούτου φιλαργυρία; ἢ προσήκειν αὐτὸν ὑφ' ὑμῶν ἐλέου τινὸς τυγχάνειν τοιαῦτα
διαπεπραγμένον, ἀλλ' οὐ τῆς ἐσχάτης τιμωρίας καὶ
ὑπὲρ τῶν νῦν καὶ ὑπὲρ τῶν πρότερον γεγενημένων
ἀδικημάτων; ἀκούσονται τὴν κρίσιν, ὦ Ἀθηναῖοι,
τὴν ὑφ' ὑμῶν ἐν τῇ τήμερον ἡμέρᾳ γεγενημένην
πάντες ἄνθρωποι· θεωρήσουσιν ὑμᾶς τοὺς κρίνοντας,
ὅπως χρῆσθε¹ τῷ τὰ τοιαῦτα διαπεπραγμένῳ.
23 ὑμεῖς ἔσθ' οἱ διὰ πολλῷ τῶν ὑπὸ τούτου πεπραγμένων ἀδικημάτων ἐλάττω μεγάλας καὶ ἀπαραιτήτους ἐνίοις ἐπιτεθηκότες τιμωρίας. ὑμεῖς
Μένωνα μὲν τὸν μυλωθρὸν ἀπεκτείνατε, διότι παῖδ'
ἐλεύθερον ἐκ Πελλήνης ἔσχεν ἐν τῷ μυλῶνι²·
Θεμίστιον δὲ τὸν Ἀφιδναῖον, διότι τὴν Ῥοδίαν
κιθαρίστριαν ὕβρισεν Ἐλευσινίοις, θανάτῳ ἐζημιώ-
σατε, Εὐθύμαχον δέ, διότι τὴν Ὀλυνθίαν παιδίσκην
24 ἔστησεν ἐπ' οἰκήματος. διὰ δὲ τοῦτον τὸν προδότην παῖδες καὶ γυναῖκες αἱ Θηβαίων ἐπὶ τὰς
σκηνὰς τῶν βαρβάρων διενεμήθησαν, πόλις ἀστυ-
γείτων καὶ σύμμαχος ἐκ μέσης τῆς Ἑλλάδος ἀνήρ-
πασται, ἀροῦται καὶ σπείρεται τὸ Θηβαίων ἄστυ
τῶν κοινωνησάντων ὑμῖν τοῦ πρὸς Φίλιππον πολέμου. ἀροῦται, φημί, καὶ σπείρεται· καὶ οὐκ
ἠλέησε, φημί, ὁ μιαρὸς οὗτος πόλιν οἰκτρῶς οὕτως
ἀπολλυμένην, εἰς ἣν ἐπρέσβευσεν ὑφ' ὑμῶν ἀπο-
σταλείς, ἧς³ ὁμόσπονδος καὶ ὁμοτράπεζος πολλάκις
γέγονεν, ἣν αὐτός φησι σύμμαχον ἡμῖν ποιῆσαι.

Instead, as Stratocles said, he allowed others to provide this sum to induce those of the Arcadians who had marched out to return home and deny their help to Thebes. Do you consider that the evils for which Demosthenes and his avarice have been responsible are trivial or of little import for the whole of Greece ? Do you think that he deserves any pity at your hands after committing such offences ? Should he not rather suffer the extreme penalty to atone for his crimes, both past and present ? The verdict given by you to-day, Athenians, will be heard by all mankind, who will observe how you, the judges, treat the man with such a record. You are the people who, for crimes far smaller than those Demosthenes has committed, have inflicted on men severe and irrevocable penalties. It was you who killed Menon the miller, because he kept a free boy from Pellene in his mill. You punished with death Themistius of Aphidna, because he assaulted the Rhodian lyre-player at the Eleusinian festival, and Euthymachus, because he put the Olynthian girl in a brothel. But through this traitor children and women, the wives of the Thebans, were distributed among the tents of the barbarians, a neighbouring and allied city has been torn up from the midst of Greece and the site of Thebes is being ploughed and sown, the city of men who shared with you the war against Philip. Yes, it is being ploughed and sown. And this unfeeling wretch showed no compassion for a city thus lamentably destroyed, though he visited it as an envoy representing you and has often shared the meat and drink of its citizens, claiming himself that he made it our

---

¹ χρῆσθε] χρήσεσθε Rosenberg : κέχρησθε Blass.
² μυλῶνι Sauppe : μύλωνι codd.   ³ ἧς Wolf : οἷς codd.

ἀλλὰ πρὸς οὓς εὐτυχοῦντας πολλάκις ἦλθε, τούτους
25 ἀτυχοῦντας προδέδωκεν. κἀκεῖνοι ⟨μέν⟩,[1] ὡς οἱ
πρεσβύτεροι λέγουσι, καταλελυμένης τῆς δημοκρατίας τῆς παρ' ἡμῖν καὶ συνάγοντος ἐν Θήβαις
Θρασυβούλου τοὺς φυγάδας ἐπὶ[2] τὴν Φυλῆς κατάληψιν, καὶ Λακεδαιμονίων ἰσχυόντων[3] καὶ ἀπαγο-
ρευόντων μηδέν' Ἀθηναίων ὑποδέχεσθαι μηδ' ἐκ-
πέμπειν, ὅμως συνέπραττον τῷ δήμῳ τὴν κάθοδον
καὶ τὸ πολλάκις ἀνεγνωσμένον παρ' ὑμῖν ἐψηφίσαντο ψήφισμα, [μὴ][4] περιορᾶν ἐάν τις ὅπλα διὰ
τῆς χώρας [τῆς][5] Ἀθηναίων[6] ἔχων πορεύηται·
26 οὗτος δὲ ὁ κοινὸν αὑτὸν τοῖς συμμάχοις, ὡς αὐτίκα
φήσει,[7] παρέχων οὐδὲν τοιοῦτον ἔπραξεν, οὐδὲ τῶν
χρημάτων ὧν ἔλαβεν εἰς τὴν τούτων σωτηρίαν
οὐδὲν ἠθέλησε προέσθαι. ὧν ὑμεῖς, ὦ ἄνδρες,
μνησθέντες, καὶ τὰ ἀτυχήματα τὰ γιγνόμενα διὰ
τοὺς προδότας θεωρήσαντες ἐν ταῖς Ὀλυνθίων καὶ
Θηβαίων συμφοραῖς, ὑπὲρ ὑμῶν αὐτῶν ὀρθῶς νυνὶ
βουλεύεσθε, καὶ τοὺς δωροδοκεῖν ἐθέλοντας κατὰ
τῆς πατρίδος ἀνελόντες ἐν ὑμῖν αὐτοῖς καὶ τοῖς
27 θεοῖς τὰς ἐλπίδας τῆς σωτηρίας ἔχετε. μόνως
γὰρ οὕτως, ἄνδρες[8] Ἀθηναῖοι, μόνως καὶ τοὺς
ἄλλους ποιήσετε βελτίους, ἐὰν τοὺς ἐνδόξους τῶν
πονηρῶν ἐξελέγξαντες κολάσητε τῶν ἀδικημάτων[9]
ἀξίως. τοὺς μὲν γὰρ τυχόντας τῶν κρινομένων,
ὅταν ἁλῶσιν, οὐδεὶς οἶδεν οὐδὲ ζητεῖ πυθέσθαι τί

---

[1] μέν add. Bekker.
[2] ἐπὶ Bekker : ἔτι N pr. A : διά τε N corr.[2]
[3] ἰσχυόντων Wolf : ἰσχόντων codd.
[4] μὴ del. Sauppe : ret. Blass, qui ὁρᾶν pro περιορᾶν scripsit.
[5] τῆς del. Sauppe : τις (deleto τις post ἐάν) Vogel, Blass.
[6] Ἀθηναίων] Θηβαίων Reiske.
[7] φήσει Wolf : φησί codd.

ally. But those to whom he often resorted in their prosperity he has betrayed in their misfortune. The Thebans, so our elders tell us, when the democracy in our city had been overthrown and Thrasybulus was assembling the exiles in Thebes ready for the seizure of Phyle,[a] although the Spartans were strong and forbade them to admit or let out any Athenian, helped the democrats to return and passed that decree which has so often been read before you, stating that they would turn a blind eye if any Athenian marched through their territory bearing arms. This man who fraternizes, as he will presently tell you, with our allies, behaved very differently ; he would not part with any of the money which he had received for their protection. Remember these things, gentlemen ; consider the disasters caused by traitors in the downfall of Olynthus and of Thebes ; decide wisely now in your interest ; destroy those who are ready to take bribes against their country and so rest your hopes of safety on yourselves and on the gods. For there is only one way, Athenians, in which you will reform the rest of mankind, only one way : to expose those criminals who are notable men and punish them as their crimes deserve. In the case of the average defendant no one knows or troubles to inquire, when he is convicted, what has been his sentence. But with

[a] Thrasybulus and Anytus, exiled by the Thirty, were received in Thebes. After seizing and holding the fortress of Phyle in Attica in 404 B.C., they subsequently occupied the Piraeus and, with the intervention of Sparta, brought about the restoration of democracy in Athens.

---

[8] ἄνδρες (hic et passim in orat. I) N : ὦ ἄνδρες (hic et in §§ 29, 80, 83, 108) A.
[9] τῶν ἀδικημάτων N : τῆς πονηρίας A.

DINARCHUS

πεπόνθασι· τοὺς δ᾽ ἐνδόξους πάντες πυνθάνονται,
καὶ τοὺς δικάζοντας ἐπαινοῦσιν, ὅταν τὸ δίκαιον μὴ
προῶνται ταῖς τῶν κρινομένων δόξαις. ἀνάγνωθι
τὸ ψήφισμα τὸ Θηβαίων. λέγε τὰς μαρτυρίας.
ἀναγίγνωσκε τὰς ἐπιστολάς.

ΨΗΦΙΣΜΑ. ΜΑΡΤΥΡΙΑΙ. ΕΠΙΣΤΟΛΑΙ

28 Μισθωτὸς οὗτος, ὦ ᾿Αθηναῖοι, μισθωτὸς οὗτός[1]
ἐστι παλαιός. οὗτος ἦν ὁ τὴν πρεσβείαν τὴν παρὰ
Φιλίππου πορευομένην ὡς ἡμᾶς ἐκ Θηβῶν καλέσας,
καὶ τοῦ λυθῆναι τὸν πρῶτον πόλεμον αἴτιος γενό-
μενος· οὗτος Φιλοκράτει συναπελογεῖτο[2] τῷ γράψαντι πρὸς Φίλιππον εἰρήνην, δι᾽ ἣν ὑμεῖς ἐκεῖνον
ἐξεβάλετε, καὶ ζεύγη τοῖς πρέσβεσιν ἐμισθώσατο
τοῖς μετ᾽ ᾿Αντιπάτρου δεῦρ᾽ ἐλθοῦσιν, ἀναλαμβάνων
αὐτοὺς καὶ τὸ κολακεύειν τοὺς Μακεδόνας πρῶτος
29 εἰς τὴν πόλιν εἰσάγων. μὴ ἀφῆτε, ἄνδρες ᾿Αθη-
ναῖοι, μὴ ἀφῆτε τὸν ἐπὶ τοῖς τῆς πόλεως καὶ τῶν
[94] ἄλλων ῾Ελλήνων ἀτυχήμασιν ἐπιγεγραμμένον ἀτιμώρητον, εἰλημμένον ἐπ᾽ αὐτοφώρῳ δῶρα ἔχοντα
κατὰ τῆς πόλεως, μηδὲ τῆς ἀγαθῆς τύχης ὑμᾶς[3]
ἐπὶ τὸ βέλτιον ἀγούσης, καὶ τὸν μὲν ἕτερον τῶν τὴν
πατρίδα λελυμασμένων ἐκ τῆς πόλεως ἐκβεβλη-
κυίας, τοῦτον δ᾽ ὑμῖν ἀποκτεῖναι παραδούσης,
αὐτοὶ τοῖς πᾶσι συμφέρουσιν ἐναντιωθῆτε, ἀλλὰ
μετοιωνίσασθε τὰς τῆς πόλεως πράξεις, εἰς τού-

---

[1] οὗτός] del. Blass.
[2] συναπελογεῖτο Wurm : συνανελογεῖτο codd. : συνανεκοινο-
λογεῖτο Ald.   [3] ὑμᾶς Sauppe : ἡμᾶς codd.

---

[a] The first war with Macedon (349–346 B.C.) was under-
taken by Athens and Olynthus against Philip. Even before
Olynthus was taken the king made overtures of peace, and

192

men of note everyone hears the news and praises the
jury, when they have not sacrificed the interests of
justice in deference to the reputation of the defendants. Read the Theban decree. Cite the evidence.
Read the letters.

Decree. Evidence. Letters

This man is a hireling, Athenians, a hireling of long
standing. It was he who summoned from Thebes the
embassy coming to us from Philip and was responsible
for finishing the first war.[a] He helped to defend
Philocrates who proposed the peace with Philip and
was exiled by you in consequence, he hired a carriage
for the envoys who came here with Antipater, and
by attaching them to himself, first introduced into
the city the custom of flattering Macedon. Do not
acquit him, Athenians. Do not let go unpunished
this man who has endorsed the misfortunes of his
country and the rest of Greece, when he has been
caught with bribes against the city in his very hands.
Now that good fortune is improving your lot and,
after expelling from the city one of the two who have
defiled their country, has surrendered this other to
you for execution, do not oppose all our interests yourselves but rather bring happier omens to our state

it was Philocrates who proposed in Athens that these negotia-
tions should begin. However, after the fall of Olynthus in
348, the Athenians tried to unite other Greek states against
Philip, and it was not until this attempt had failed that
Demosthenes acquiesced in peace proposals. In 347 he
defended Philocrates, who was accused of illegality in making
his first peace proposals, and himself served on an embassy
to Macedon. The final peace was signed in 346, when Antipater and Parmenio came to Athens as Philip's envoys.
Philocrates was prosecuted by Hyperides in 343 for being
bribed by Philip and went into exile. *Cf*. Hyp. frag. 16.

30 τοὺς τοὺς ἡγεμόνας τὰς ἀποτυχίας τρέψαντες. εἰς
ποῖον γὰρ καιρὸν ἀποθήσεσθε τοῦτον ὑπολαβόντες
χρήσιμον ὑμῖν αὐτοῖς ἔσεσθαι; ἔχοι τις ἂν εἰπεῖν ἢ
ὑμῶν ἢ τῶν περιεστηκότων, εἰς ποῖα οὗτος πράγματα εἰσελθὼν ἢ ἴδια ἢ κοινὰ οὐκ ἀνατέτροφεν;[1]
οὐκ εἰς μὲν τὴν Ἀριστάρχου οἰκίαν εἰσελθών,
βουλεύσας μετ᾽ ἐκείνου τὸν Νικοδήμῳ θάνατον
κατασκευασθέντα, ὃν ἴστε πάντες, ἐξέβαλε τὸν
Ἀρίσταρχον ἐπὶ ταῖς αἰσχίσταις αἰτίαις; καὶ
τοιούτῳ φίλῳ Δημοσθένει ἐχρήσατο, ὥστε δαίμονα
αὐτῷ τοῦτον καὶ τῶν γεγενημένων συμφορῶν ἡγε-
31 μόνα νομίσαι προσελθεῖν; οὐκ ἐπειδὴ τῷ δήμῳ
συμβουλεύειν ἤρξατο, ὡς μήποτε ὤφελεν—ἀφήσω
γὰρ αὐτοῦ τὰ ἴδια· ὁ γὰρ χρόνος οὐκ ἐπιδέχεται
μακρολογεῖν—, ἀγαθὸν μὲν ἁπλῶς εἰπεῖν οὐδὲν
γέγονε τῇ πόλει, ἐν κινδύνοις δὲ καὶ κακοῖς καὶ
ἀδοξίᾳ πᾶσ᾽ ἡ Ἑλλάς, οὐ μόνον ἡ πόλις, καθέστηκε;
καί, πλείστοις καιροῖς ἐν ταῖς δημηγορίαις χρώμενος, ἅπαντας ἀφῆκε τοὺς ὑπὲρ ὑμῶν καιρούς;
καὶ ἐν οἷς[2] τις ἂν φιλόπολις ἀνὴρ καὶ κηδεμὼν
προείλετό τι πρᾶξαι, τοσοῦτον ἐδέησεν ὁ δημαγωγὸς καὶ χρήσιμος αὐτίκα φήσων ὑμῖν γεγενῆσθαι πρᾶξίν τινα προφέρειν, ὥστε καὶ τοὺς
πράττοντας ὑπὲρ ὑμῶν τι τῆς αὐτοῦ τύχης ἀν-

---

[1] ἀνατέτροφεν Blass : ἀνατέτραφεν codd.
[2] καὶ ἐν οἷς A corr.[2] : ἐν οἷς A pr. N, Thalheim, qui post
πρᾶξαι interpunxit et δὲ post τοσοῦτον addidit.

---

[a] This story is told more fully by Aeschines (i. 171 ; ii. 148
and 166), who says that Aristarchus son of Moschus was a
wealthy orphan, half mad, from whom Demosthenes, pretending to have taken a fancy to him personally, extracted
three talents. He asserts that together they contrived to

affairs and divert our misfortunes on to the heads of these leaders. Against what occasion will you reserve Demosthenes in the belief that he will prove useful to you ? Could any one of you, or of the bystanders, say what public or private affairs he has not ruined by his contact with them ? After gaining access to the home of Aristarchus [a] and planning with him the death of Nicodemus which they contrived, an affair of which you all know the details, did he not banish Aristarchus on the most shameful charges ? And did not Aristarchus find in Demosthenes such a friend as to make him think that this was some evil spirit which had visited him and the originator of all his misfortunes ? Is it not true that once this man began to advise the city, and would he had never done so,— I shall pass over his private affairs, for time does not permit me to speak at length,—absolutely no good has befallen it ; indeed not only the city but the whole of Greece has been involved in dangers, misfortunes, and dishonour ? Is it not true that he has had many opportunities while speaking to you and yet let slip every opportunity to help you ? On those occasions when a patriot with any regard for the city would have chosen to make some move, this demagogue, who will presently say that he has been of service to you, was so far from showing signs of action that he even infected with his own ill-luck the men who were doing something to further your interests.

murder, with great brutality, Nicodemus of Aphidna who had once prosecuted Demosthenes for desertion ; as the result of which crime Aristarchus went into exile. Demosthenes himself mentions the murder in his speech against Midias, where he claims that Midias went about casting suspicion on him and persuaded the relatives of Nicodemus to do likewise (Dem. xxi. 104). *Cf.* Athen. xiii. 592 f.

32 ἔπλησεν. ἀπῆρε Χαρίδημος πρὸς τὸν Περσῶν
βασιλέα, χρήσιμος ὑμῖν οὐ λόγοις ἀλλ' ἔργοις βουλόμενος γενέσθαι, καὶ τοῖς ἰδίοις τοῖς αὐτοῦ κινδύνοις ὑμῖν καὶ τοῖς ἄλλοις Ἕλλησι βουλόμενος τὴν
σωτηρίαν παρασκευάσαι· περιιὼν οὗτος¹ κατὰ τὴν
ἀγορὰν ἐλογοποίει καὶ τῶν πραττομένων εἰσεποίει
κοινωνὸν αὑτόν· οὕτω κατέστρεψεν ἡ τύχη ταῦτα
33 ὥστ' ἐναντία² γενέσθαι³ τοῖς προσδοκωμένοις. ἐξέπλευσεν Ἐφιάλτης, μισῶν μὲν τοῦτον, ἀναγκα-
ζόμενος δὲ τῶν πραγμάτων κοινωνεῖν· ἀφείλετο
καὶ τοῦτον ἡ τύχη τῆς πόλεως. Εὐθύδικος προ-
ῃρεῖτο τὰς ὑπὲρ τοῦ δήμου πράξεις· ἔφη τούτῳ
Δημοσθένης φίλος εἶναι· ⟨καὶ⟩⁴ οὗτος ἀπώλετο.
καὶ ταῦθ' ὑμεῖς ὁρῶντες καὶ ἐπιστάμενοι πολὺ
βέλτιον ἢ ἐγὼ οὐ λογίζεσθε, οὐ σκοπεῖσθε πρὸς
ὑμᾶς αὐτούς, τεκμαιρόμενοι τὰ μέλλοντα ἐκ τῶν
γεγενημένων, ὅτι οὐδὲν οὗτος χρήσιμος ἀλλ' ἢ τοῖς
34 ἐχθροῖς κατὰ τῆς πόλεως⁵ . . .; . . . συστῆσαι
κατασκευὴν ἑτέραν οἵα ἐπ' Ἄγιδος⁶ ἐγένετο, ὅτε

¹ οὗτος A : οὕτως N.
² ὥστ' ἐναντία Baiter : ὡς τἀναντία codd.
³ γενέσθαι Blass : γίνεσθαι A : γίγνεσθαι N.
⁴ καὶ add. Reiske.
⁵ Post πόλεως lacunam indicavit Maetzner, post ἐγένετο
Sauppe.
⁶ ἐπ' Ἄγιδος Wesseling : ἐπ' Αἰγὸς codd. : ἔναγχος Cobet.

ᵃ Charidemus of Oreos in Euboea was made an Athenian
citizen for his services as a soldier (Dem. xxiii. 151). He went
to Persia in 335 B.C., having been banished from Athens on
the orders of Alexander (Arrian i. 10. 6), and after being well
received at first by Darius, fell under suspicion two years
later and was executed (Diodor. xvii. 30).

Charidemus[a] set out to visit the Persian King, wishing to do you some practical service apart from mere talking, and anxious at his own peril to win safety for you and every Greek. Demosthenes went round the market making speeches and associating himself with the project. So completely did fortune wreck this plan that it turned out in just the opposite way to what was expected. Ephialtes put to sea. Admittedly he hated Demosthenes but he was compelled to have a partner in public affairs. Fortune robbed the city of this man too.[b] Euthydicus[c] elected to work for the people. Demosthenes claimed to be his friend. He too was lost. Do not these facts, which you see and know better than I do, give you cause for thought? Do they not make you weigh up your future prospects in the light of the past and reflect in your own minds that this man is of no use except to our enemies, against the interests of the city . . . ? . . . to raise such another force as we had in the time of Agis,[d] when the Spartans took the

---

[b] The facts are here distorted. Ephialtes, one of the orators whose surrender was demanded by Alexander in 335 B.C. (Arrian i. 104), was a supporter of Demosthenes and, according to the Pseudo-Plutarch, brought back money for the demagogues from the Persian court (*Vit. X Or.* 847 F and 848 E). He was killed while helping the Persians to defend Halicarnassus against Alexander (Diodor. xvii. 27).

[c] No details are known of Euthydicus. He seems to be mentioned as an Athenian patriot together with Ephialtes and Lycurgus in the third letter of Demosthenes (Dem. *Ep.* iii. 31), where however the MSS. have Εὔδικον.

[d] While Alexander was in the East, Agis the Third of Sparta rose against Macedon with the help of Darius in 333 B.C. In 331 he headed an army raised by various Greek states but was refused the support of Athens, on the advice of Demosthenes. Defeated near Megalopolis by Antipater he was killed in battle (Diodor. xvii. 48 and 62).

Λακεδαιμόνιοι μὲν ἅπαντες ἐξεστράτευσαν, ᾿Αχαιοὶ
δὲ καὶ ᾿Ηλεῖοι τῶν πραγμάτων ἐκοινώνουν, ὑπῆρχον
δὲ ξένοι μύριοι, ᾿Αλέξανδρος δ᾽, ὡς οἱ[1] λέγοντες, ἐν
᾿Ινδοῖς ἦν, ἡ δ᾽ ῾Ελλὰς ἅπασα διὰ τοὺς ἐν ἑκάστῃ
τῶν πόλεων προδότας ἀχθομένη τοῖς παροῦσι πράγμασιν ἠσμένει μεταβολήν τινα τῶν κακῶν τῶν
35 περιεστηκότων. τί οὖν; ἐν τούτοις τοῖς καιροῖς
Δημοσθένης τίς ἦν, ὁ τοῦ συμβουλεῦσαι καὶ γράψαι
κύριος καὶ φήσων αὐτίκα δὴ μισεῖν τὰ καθεστῶτα
πράγματα; ἐῶ γὰρ τοὺς ἄλλους κινδύνους. ἔγραψάς
τι περὶ τούτων[2] [κινδύνων];[3] συνεβούλευσας; ἐπό-
ρισας χρήματα; μικρόν τι χρήσιμος ἐγένου τοῖς
ὑπὲρ τῆς κοινῆς σωτηρίας πράττουσιν; οὐδ᾽
ὁτιοῦν, ἀλλὰ περιῄεις κατασκευάζων λογοποιούς,
καὶ παρ᾽ αὑτῷ γράφων ἐπιστολήν, καὶ καταισχύνων
36 τὴν τῆς πόλεως δόξαν, ἐκ τῶν δακτύλων ἀναψά-
μενος περιεπορεύετο, τρυφῶν ἐν τοῖς τῆς πόλεως
κακοῖς, καὶ ἐπὶ φορείου κατακομιζόμενος τὴν εἰς
Πειραιᾶ ὁδόν, καὶ τὰς τῶν πενήτων ἀπορίας
ὀνειδίζων. εἶθ᾽ οὗτος εἰς τοὺς μέλλοντας ὑμῖν καιροὺς ἔσται χρήσιμος, παραβεβηκὼς ἅπαντας τοὺς
παρεληλυθότας; τοιούτων, ὦ δέσποιν᾽ ᾿Αθηνᾶ καὶ
Ζεῦ σῶτερ, συμβούλων καὶ ἡγεμόνων ὤφελον τυ-
[95] χεῖν οἱ πολεμήσαντες τῇ πόλει,[4] καὶ μηδεπώποτε[5]
βελτιόνων.
37 Οὐκ ἀναμνήσεσθε, ὦ ἄνδρες, τὰς τῶν πρεσβυτέρων πράξεις; οἳ μεγάλων καὶ πολλῶν κινδύνων
καταλαμβανόντων τὴν πόλιν ἀξίως τῆς πατρίδος
καὶ τῆς αὐτῶν ἐλευθερίας καὶ τῆς δόξης τῆς

---

[1] ὡς οἱ] ὡς ἦσαν οἱ Reiske.
[2] τούτων Bekker : του τῶν A : τῷ . . . τῶν, ut vid., N pr.
(τῷ eras.).   [3] κινδύνων del. Bekker.

field together and Achaeans and men of Elis were
taking their part in the campaign with ten thousand
mercenaries also ; when Alexander was in India,[a]
according to report, and the whole of Greece, owing
to the traitors in every city, was dissatisfied with the
existing state of things and hoped for some release
from the misfortunes that beset her. In that hour,—
for I need not dwell on other crises,—what was the
behaviour of this Demosthenes who had the power
to give advice and make proposals, who will shortly
tell you that he hates our present circumstances ?
On these matters, Demosthenes, did you offer any
proposal, any advice ? Did you contribute money ?
Were you of the smallest value to the men safeguarding us all ? Not the least ; you went round suborning
speechwriters. He wrote a letter at home, defiling
the city's honour, and walked about dangling it from
his finger ends, living in luxury during the city's misfortunes, travelling down the road to the Piraeus in
a litter and reproaching the needy for their poverty.
Is this man then going to prove useful to you on
future occasions, when he has let slip every opportunity
in the past ? By our lady Athena and Zeus the
Saviour, I could wish that the enemies of Athens had
lighted upon counsellors and leaders like him and
never better.

Let me remind you, gentlemen, of the conduct of
your forbears, who, at a time when many grave perils
beset the city, faced danger in the interests of the

---

[a] Alexander was, in fact, in Persia.

---

4 τῇ πόλει Stephanus : τὴν πόλιν codd.
5 μηδεπώποτε Blass : μηδέποτε codd.

δικαίας[1] ὑπὲρ τῶν τοῦ δημοσίου συμφερόντων
ἐκινδύνευσαν; ὧν τοὺς μὲν ἀρχαίους ἐκείνους
μακρὸν ἂν εἴη λέγειν, Ἀριστείδην καὶ Θεμιστοκλέα,
τοὺς ὀρθώσαντας τὰ τείχη τῆς πόλεως καὶ τοὺς
φόρους εἰς ἀκρόπολιν ἀνενεγκόντας παρ' ἑκόντων
38 καὶ βουλομένων τῶν Ἑλλήνων· ἀλλὰ ταυτὶ τὰ
μικρὸν πρὸ τῆς ἡμετέρας ἡλικίας γεγενημένα ὑπὸ
Κεφάλου τοῦ ῥήτορος καὶ Θράσωνος τοῦ Ἐρχιέως[2]
καὶ Ἡλείου[3] ⟨καὶ⟩[4] Φορμισίου καὶ ἑτέρων ἀνδρῶν
ἀγαθῶν, ὧν ἐνίων ἔτι καὶ νῦν ζῇ τὰ σώματα. τούτων γὰρ οἱ μὲν φρουρουμένης ὑπὸ Λακεδαιμονίων
τῆς Καδμείας βοηθήσαντες τοῖς εἰς Θήβας κατιοῦσι
τῶν φυγάδων τοῖς ἰδίοις κινδύνοις ἠλευθέρωσαν
πόλιν ἀστυγείτονα καὶ πολὺν χρόνον δουλεύουσαν,
39 οἱ δὲ πείσαντος[5] ἐξελθεῖν ὑμῶν τοὺς προγόνους
Κεφάλου τοῦ τὸ[6] ψήφισμα γράψαντος, ὃς οὐ κατα-
πλαγεὶς τὴν Λακεδαιμονίων δύναμιν, οὐδὲ λογισά-
μενος ὅτι τὸ κινδυνεύειν καὶ τὸ γράφειν ὑπὲρ τῆς
πόλεως ἐπισφαλές ἐστιν, ἔγραψεν ἐξιέναι βοηθήσοντας Ἀθηναίους τοῖς κατειληφόσι τῶν φυγάδων
Θήβας· καὶ ἐξελθόντων ἐκεῖσε τῶν ὑμετέρων
πατέρων ὀλίγαις ἡμέραις ἐξεβλήθη ὁ τῶν[7] Λακεδαιμονίων φρούραρχος, ἠλευθέρωντο[8] Θηβαῖοι, διε-
πέπρακτο ἡ πόλις ἡ ὑμετέρα ἄξια τῶν προγόνων.
40 ἐκεῖνοι ἦσαν, ἐκεῖνοι, ὦ Ἀθηναῖοι, ἄξιοι σύμβουλοι

---

[1] δικαίας] παλαιᾶς Bekker : alii alia.
[2] Ἐρχιέως Weidner : Ἐρχιέως codd.
[3] Ἡλείου Reiske : Ἡλιοῦ NA.
[4] καὶ add. Bergk.
[5] πείσαντος Blass : πείσαντες codd.
[6] τοῦ τὸ Blass : τούτου codd. : τοῦτο τὸ Bekker.
[7] τῶν om. N.
[8] ἠλευθέρωντο Bekker : ἠλευθεροῦντο codd.

people, in a manner worthy of their country and their well-earned reputation, as befitted free men. Time does not permit me to deal with those figures of the past, Aristides and Themistocles : the men who built the city's walls and carried up to the Acropolis the tribute paid by the willing and even eager Greeks. But you will recall what was done, shortly before our own time, by Cephalus the orator, Thrason of Herchia, Eleus and Phormisius and other fine men, some of whom are still alive to-day.[a] Some of them, when the Cadmea was garrisoned by Spartans, assisted the exiles who returned to Thebes and at their own risk set free a neighbouring city, long enslaved.[b] Others lent aid when your ancestors were persuaded to take the field by Cephalus, who proposed the decree and who, undaunted by the might of Sparta and regardless of the risks either of military or political action, moved that the Athenians should march out to help the exiles who had taken Thebes. Your fathers did march out and in a few days the commander of the Spartan garrison was expelled, the Thebans had been freed and your city had acted worthily of your ancestors. They were counsellors, Athenians, they

[a] Cephalus assisted in the overthrow of the Thirty in 403 B.C. His reputation as an orator is acknowledged by Demosthenes (xviii. 219). Cf. Dinarch. i. 76. Of the other three men little is known. Thrason is mentioned as a Theban proxenus by Aeschines (iii. 139) ; Eleus is perhaps the trierarch (c. 323) whose name appears in an inscription (I.G. ii. 812, b. 14) ; Phormisius is a mere name. Cf. Aristotle, Ath. Pol. 34. 3.

[b] In 382 B.C. Thebes was betrayed to Sparta and many leading men were exiled. These took refuge at Athens, with whose help in 378 they soon overthrew the new government and ejected the Spartan garrison from the city (Diodor. xv. 25).

καὶ ἡγεμόνες ὑμῶν καὶ τοῦ δήμου· μὰ Δί᾽ οὐ τὰ
τοιαῦτα κινάδη, οἳ πεποιήκασι μὲν οὐδὲν οὐδὲ
πράξουσιν ἀγαθὸν ὑπὲρ τῆς πόλεως, τὴν δὲ αὑτῶν
ἀσφάλειαν τηροῦντες καὶ πανταχόθεν[1] ἀργυριζόμε-
νοι καὶ πεποιηκότες τὴν πόλιν ἀδοξοτέραν ἑαυτῶν,
καὶ νῦν εἰλημμένοι δῶρα καθ᾽ ὑμῶν εἰληφότες,
παρακρούονται ὑμᾶς, καὶ ἀξιοῦσι τοιοῦτοι γεγενημένοι περὶ τῆς ἑαυτῶν πλεονεξίας παραγγέλλειν.
οὓς χρῆν[2] τεθνάναι πάλαι κατὰ τὸ ἑαυτῶν ψήφισμα,[3]
τοιαῦτα διαπεπραγμένους.

41 Οὐκ αἰσχύνεσθε, ἄνδρες Ἀθηναῖοι, τὴν κατὰ
Δημοσθένους τιμωρίαν ἐκ τῶν ἡμετέρων λόγων
μόνων ἡγούμενοι δεῖν κρίνειν; οὐκ ἴστε τοῦτον
αὐτοὶ δωροδόκον ὄντα καὶ κλέπτην καὶ προδότην
τῶν[4] φίλων, καὶ τῆς πόλεως ἀνάξιον καὶ αὐτὸν καὶ
τὴν περὶ τοῦτον τύχην γεγενημένην; ἀπὸ ποίων
ψηφισμάτων οὗτος ἢ ποίων νόμων οὐκ εἴληφεν
42 ἀργύριον; εἰσί τινες ἐν τῷ δικαστηρίῳ τῶν ἐν τοῖς
τριακοσίοις γεγενημένων, ὅθ᾽ οὗτος ἐτίθει τὸν περὶ
τῶν τριηράρχων νόμον; οὐ φράσετε τοῖς πλησίον
ὅτι τρία τάλαντα λαβὼν μετέγραφε καὶ μετεσκεύαζε
τὸν νόμον καθ᾽ ἑκάστην ἐκκλησίαν, καὶ τὰ μὲν
ἐπώλει ὧν εἰλήφει τὴν τιμήν, τὰ δ᾽ ἀποδόμενος οὐκ
43 ἐβεβαίου; εἴπατέ μοι πρὸς Διός, ὦ ἄνδρες, προῖκα
τοῦτον οἴεσθε γράψαι Διφίλῳ τὴν ἐν πρυτανείῳ

---

[1] πανταχόθεν Blass : πάντοθεν codd.
[2] χρῆν Bekker : χρὴ codd.
[3] πάλαι κατὰ τὸ ἑαυτῶν ψήφισμα N : κατὰ τὸ ἑαυτῶν ψήφισμα
πάλαι A.
[4] τῶν om. A.

---

[a] For the trierarch law see note on Hyp. frag. 43.
[b] Little is known of the various men mentioned in this

were leaders such as yourselves and the state deserve. How different from rogues like this who neither have done nor will do the city any service but watch over their own safety and treat everything as a source of income. They have made the city more infamous than themselves, and now, convicted of taking bribes against you, they deceive you and presume, after conduct such as this, to talk to you about their own aggrandizement. They ought, by the terms of their own decree, to have been put to death long ago for doing such things.

Are you not ashamed, Athenians, that you should think our speeches the only evidence you have on which to determine the punishment of Demosthenes ? Do you not know yourselves that this man is open to bribes and is both a robber and a traitor to his friends ; that neither he nor the fortune which has gone with him is fit for the city ? Are there any decrees or any laws which have not brought him money ? Are there any people in the court who were among those included in the three hundred when Demosthenes brought in his law concerning the trierarchs ? [a] Then tell your neighbours that he accepted three talents and used to alter and re-draft the law for every sitting of the Assembly, in some cases taking money over points for which he had been paid already, in others failing to honour the sales which he had made. Really, gentlemen, tell me : do you think he got nothing for proposing that Diphilus [b] should have

section. Diphilus was perhaps the son of Diopithes, trierarch in 325/4 and 323/2 B.C. (*CIA* ii. 809 d, 53 and 811 b, 104). For Chaerephilus, a dealer in salt fish, compare Hyp. frags. 34 and 35. The three names following his are those of his sons. All four were evidently put in the deme of Paeania, Pamphilus and Phidippus being mentioned as

σίτησιν, καὶ τὴν εἰς τὴν ἀγορὰν ἀνατεθησομένην[1]
εἰκόνα; ἢ τὸ ποιῆσαι πολίτας ὑμετέρους[2] Χαιρέ-
φιλον καὶ Φείδωνα καὶ Πάμφιλον καὶ Φείδιππον,[3]
ἢ πάλιν Ἐπιγένην καὶ Κόνωνα τοὺς τραπεζίτας;
ἢ τὸ χαλκοῦς ἐν ἀγορᾷ στῆσαι Βηρισάδην[4] καὶ
Σάτυρον καὶ Γόργιππον τοὺς ἐκ τοῦ Πόντου[5] τυράννους, παρ᾽ ὧν αὐτῷ χίλιοι μέδιμνοι[6] τοῦ ἐνιαυτοῦ
πυρῶν ἀποστέλλονται τῷ οὐδ᾽ ὅποι[7] καταφύγῃ αὐ-
44 τίκα φήσοντι εἶναι; ἢ τὸ γράψαι Ταυροσθένην
Ἀθηναῖον εἶναι, ⟨τὸν⟩[8] τοὺς μὲν αὐτοῦ πολίτας
καταδουλωσάμενον, τῆς δ᾽ Εὐβοίας ὅλης μετὰ τοῦ
ἀδελφοῦ Καλλίου προδότην Φιλίππῳ γεγενημένον;
ὃν οὐκ ἐῶσιν οἱ νόμοι τῆς Ἀθηναίων χώρας ἐπι-
βαίνειν, εἰ δὲ μή, τοῖς αὐτοῖς ἔνοχον εἶναι κελεύουσιν
οἷσπερ ἄν τις τῶν φευγόντων ἐξ Ἀρείου πάγου
κατίῃ.[9] καὶ τοῦτον οὗτος ὁ δημοτικὸς ὑμέτερον
45 ἔγραψε πολίτην εἶναι. περὶ τούτων οὖν μάρτυρας
ὑμῖν δεῖ καλεῖν, ἢ περὶ τῶν ἄλλων ὅσους οὗτος
γέγραφε προξένους εἶναι καὶ Ἀθηναίους; ⟨εἶτα⟩,[10]
[96] πρὸς τῆς Ἀθηνᾶς, οἴεσθ᾽ αὐτὸν ἀργύριον μὲν

---

1. ἀνατεθησομένην Reiske : ἀναθησομένην codd.
2. ὑμετέρους (coll. § 44) Blass : ὑμᾶς codd.
3. Φείδιππον Bergk : Φίλιππον codd.
4. Βηρισάδην Ald. : Βιρισάδην codd. : Παιρισάδην Thalheim.
5. ἐκ τοῦ Πόντου Baiter : ἐκ τούτων codd. : ἐχθίστους Ald.
6. μέδιμνοι Gibbon : μόδιοι codd.
7. ὅποι N : ὅπῃ A.   8. τὸν add. Baiter.
9. κατίῃ N : κατίοι A.   10. εἶτα add. Gebauer.

---

members of it in inscriptions (*CIA* ii. 172 and 811 d, 142).
Cf. also Athen. iii. 119 *sq.* and viii. 339 d. Berisades is probably the same man as Paerisades, a king of Bosporus to
whom Demosthenes refers (xxxiv. 8) ; Satyrus was his son.

a Dinarchus, like Aeschines, is distorting the facts. (*Cf.*
Aeschin. iii. 85 *sq.* and schol. *ad loc.*). The cities of Euboea

meals at the Prytaneum or for that statue to be put up in the market ? Nothing for conferring Athenian citizenship on Chaerephilus, Phidon, Pamphilus, and Phidippus, or again on Epigenes and Conon the bankers ? Nothing for putting up in the market bronze statues of Berisades, Satyrus and Gorgippus the tyrants from the Pontus, from whom he receives a thousand medimni of wheat a year—this man who will presently tell you that there is nowhere for him to take refuge. Did he get nothing for proposing that Taurosthenes [a] should become an Athenian, though he had enslaved his fellow citizens and, with his brother Callias, betrayed the whole of Euboea to Philip ? Taurosthenes whom the laws forbid to set foot on Athenian soil, providing that if he does so he shall be liable to the same penalties as an exile who returns after being sentenced by the Areopagus. This was the man who Demosthenes the democrat proposed should be your fellow citizen. Is there any need then for me to call up witnesses for you so far as these men are concerned or any of the others whom he has proposed as proxeni or citizens ? I ask you in Athena's name : do you imagine that when he gladly

had entered the Athenian alliance in 357 B.C., but in 348 they revolted, probably owing to the intrigues of Philip with whom Athens was now at war over Olynthus. Taurosthenes and Callias commanded the army of Chalcis and the Athenians lost control of the island. In 343 however they transferred the allegiance of Chalcis to Athens, and a few years later—the exact date is not certain—were made Athenian citizens on the motion of Demosthenes (*cf.* Hyp. v., col. 20), whom Aeschines says they bribed.

χαίρειν λαμβάνοντα, χρυσίου δ' εἴκοσι τάλαντ' οὐκ
ἂν λαβεῖν; ἢ κατὰ μικρὸν μὲν δωροδοκεῖν, ἀθρόον
δ' οὐκ ἂν προσδέξασθαι τοσοῦτον λῆμμα; ἢ τὴν
ἐξ Ἀρείου πάγου βουλὴν Δημοσθένην καὶ Δημάδην
καὶ Κηφισοφῶντα ζητήσασαν ἓξ μῆνας ἀδίκως εἰς
ὑμᾶς πεποιῆσθαι τὰς ἀποφάσεις;

46 Πολλοί, ὦ ἄνδρες, πολλοὶ τῶν πολιτῶν καὶ τῶν
ἄλλων Ἑλλήνων, ὅπερ καὶ πρότερον εἶπον, θεω-
ροῦσιν ὑμᾶς πῶς τοῦτον δικάσετε τὸν ἀγῶνα, καὶ
πότερον εἰσαγωγίμους καὶ τὰς τῶν¹ ἄλλων δωροδοκίας ποιήσετε, ἢ ἀνέδην ἐξέσται δῶρα λαμβάνειν
καθ' ὑμῶν, καὶ τὰ πρότερον δοκοῦντα πιστὰ καὶ
βέβαι' εἶναι νῦν ἄπιστα διὰ τὴν Δημοσθένους
κρίσιν γενήσεται, ὃν ἐκ τῶν ἄλλων προσῆκεν ἀπολωλέναι τῶν πεπολιτευμένων αὐτῷ, ὃς ἁπάσαις
ταῖς ἀραῖς ταῖς ἐν τῇ πόλει γιγνομέναις² ἔνοχος
47 καθέστηκεν, ἐπιωρκηκὼς μὲν τὰς σεμνὰς θεὰς ἐν
Ἀρείῳ πάγῳ καὶ τοὺς ἄλλους θεοὺς οὓς ἐκεῖ δι-
όμνυσθαι νόμιμόν ἐστι, κατάρατος δὲ καθ' ἑκάστην
ἐκκλησίαν γιγνόμενος,³ ἐξεληλεγμένος δῶρα κατὰ
τῆς πόλεως εἰληφώς, ἐξηπατηκὼς δὲ καὶ τὸν δῆμον καὶ τὴν βουλὴν παρὰ τὴν ἀράν, καὶ ἕτερα
μὲν λέγων ἕτερα δὲ φρονῶν, ἰδίᾳ δὲ συμβεβουλευ-
κὼς Ἀριστάρχῳ δεινὰς καὶ παρανόμους συμβουλάς,
ἀνθ' ὧν—εἴπερ ἐστί που δικαία τιμωρία κατὰ τῶν

accepts silver he would refuse twenty talents of gold ? Do you think that though he takes money in dribblets, he would not accept as a lump sum so great a fee, or that the Areopagus, which spent six months inquiring over Demosthenes, Demades, and Cephisophon,[a] has been unjust over the reports submitted to you ?

Gentlemen, you have very many witnesses, as I said before, among citizens and other Greeks, watching to see how you will judge this trial ; are you, they wonder, going to bring within the scope of the courts the venal actions of other men, or will there be complete freedom to accept bribes against you ? Will the things which so far have been held trustworthy and sure now cease to be so on account of the trial of Demosthenes ? On his past record he ought to have been put to death, and he is liable to all the curses known to the city, having broken the oaths he took on the Areopagus, in the names of the holy goddesses and the other deities by whom it is customary to swear there, and making himself accursed at every sitting of the Assembly. He has been proved to have taken bribes against Athens, has cheated the people and the council in defiance of the curse, professing views he does not hold, and in private has recommended to Aristarchus a course both cruel and unlawful.[b] For these misdeeds, if there is any power to exact a just punishment from perjurers and

---

[a] This is probably the same Cephisophon, a politician of the time, as is mentioned by Demosthenes (Dem. xviii. 21 and xix. 293).   [b] Cf. § 30 and note.

---

[1] τὰς τῶν A : τὰς κατὰ τῶν N.
[2] γιγνομέναις Blass : γενομέναις codd.
[3] γιγνόμενος Blass : γενόμενος A pr. N : γινόμενος A corr.

DINARCHUS

ἐπιόρκων καὶ πονηρῶν, ὥσπερ ἔστι—δώσει δίκην
οὗτος ἐν τῇ τήμερον ἡμέρᾳ. ἀκούσατ', ἄνδρες δικασταί, τῆς ἀρᾶς.

ΑΡΑ

48 Ἀλλ' ὅμως, ἄνδρες δικασταί, οὕτω Δημοσθένης
τῷ ψεύδεσθαι καὶ μηδὲν ὑγιὲς λέγειν ἑτοίμως
χρῆται, καὶ οὔτ' αἰσχύνης οὔτ' ἐλέγχου οὔτ' ἀρᾶς
οὐδὲν αὐτῷ μέλει, ὥστε καὶ περὶ ἐμοῦ τολμήσει
λέγειν, ὡς ἀκούω, ὡς ἄρα κἀμοῦ κατέγνω πρότερον
ἡ βουλή· καὶ ποιῶ πάντων ἀτοπώτατον, ὡς οὗτός
φησι, πρότερον μὲν ἐναντίον τῇ τῆς βουλῆς ἀποφάσει ἀγῶνα ἀπολογούμενος ὑπὲρ ἐμαυτοῦ, νυνὶ δὲ
συνηγορῶν αὐτῇ, κατηγορῶν τούτου περὶ τῆς γε-
49 γενημένης ἀποφάσεως· πρᾶγμα κατασκευάζων οὐ
γεγενημένον, ἀλλὰ ψεύδεσθαι πρὸς ὑμᾶς[1] τολμῶν.
ἵν' οὖν, ἐὰν ἐπὶ τοῦτον ἴῃ τὸν λόγον, μὴ ἐπιτρέπητ'
αὐτῷ, ἀλλ' εἰδῆτ' ἀκριβῶς ὅτι οὔτε μ' ἀπέφηνεν ἡ
βουλὴ οὔτ' ἐμέλλησεν, ἠδικήθην δὲ ὑφ' ἑνὸς ἀνθρώπου πονηροῦ καὶ δίκην δεδωκότος παρ' ὑμῖν,
ἀκούσατέ μου βραχέα· ἔπειτ' ἐπὶ τοῦτον πάλιν
βαδιοῦμαι.

50 Ἀνάγκη τὴν βουλήν, ὦ ἄνδρες, τὴν ἐξ Ἀρείου
πάγου κατὰ δύο τρόπους ποιεῖσθαι τὰς ἀποφάσεις
πάσας. τίνας τούτους; ἤτοι αὐτὴν προελομένην
καὶ ζητήσασαν, ἢ τοῦ δήμου προστάξαντος αὐτῇ.
χωρὶς τούτων οὐκ ἔστιν ὅντιν' ἂν[2] τρόπον ποιήσειεν.
εἰ μὲν τοίνυν φῄς, ὦ μιαρὸν σὺ θηρίον, τοῦ δήμου

---

[1] πρὸς ὑμᾶς Baiter et Sauppe : πρός τινας codd.
[2] ὅντιν' ἂν Baiter et Sauppe : ὅντινα codd.

208

criminals—as there surely is—this man shall pay to-day. Gentlemen of the jury, listen to the curse.[a]

The Curse

Despite this, gentlemen of the jury, Demosthenes is so ready with his lies and utterly unsound assertions, so oblivious of shame, exposure, or curse, that he will dare to say of me, I gather, that I too was previously condemned by the council. According to him I am behaving with the utmost inconsistency, because in the past I opposed the council's report and pleaded my own case, whereas I am now serving as its advocate and accusing him over the report before us to-day. This is a story of his own invention, not based on fact, and he is impudent enough to lie to you. So to make sure that, if he embarks upon this story, you will pay no attention to him but will realize fully that the council did not report me and was in no danger of doing so,—the truth being that I suffered at the hands of a man of low character who has been convicted before you,—let me explain briefly. Then I will come back to Demosthenes.

The council of the Areopagus is bound, gentlemen, to follow one of two methods in making all its reports. What are these methods? Its inquiry is made either on its own initiative or in obedience to the people's instructions.[b] Apart from these two, there is no other procedure it could follow. If then you tell us, you abominable brute, that the council followed the

---

[a] For the curse pronounced by the herald before each sitting of the Council and Assembly on all who might be acting treasonably against the state compare Lycurg. *Leocr.* 31.

[b] See note on § 6.

προστάξαντος ζητήσασαν τὴν βουλὴν περὶ ἐμοῦ
51 ποιήσασθαι τὴν ἀπόφασιν, δεῖξον τὸ ψήφισμα, καὶ
τίνες ἐγένοντό μου κατήγοροι γενομένης τῆς ἀποφάσεως, ὥσπερ νῦν ἀμφότερα γέγονε, καὶ ψήφισμα
καθ᾽ ὃ ἐζήτησεν ἡ βουλή, καὶ κατήγοροι χειρο-
τονήσαντος τοῦ δήμου, παρ᾽ ὧν νῦν οἱ δικασταὶ
τἀδικήματα πυνθάνονται. κἂν ᾖ ταῦτα ἀληθῆ,
ἀποθνήσκειν ἕτοιμός εἰμι. εἰ δ᾽ αὐτὴν προελομένην ἀποφῆναί με φῇς, παράσχου μάρτυρας τοὺς
Ἀρεοπαγίτας, ὥσπερ ἐγὼ παρέξομαι ὅτι οὐκ
52 ἀπεφάνθην. καταψευσάμενον μέντοι κἀμοῦ καὶ τῆς
βουλῆς ὥσπερ σὺ καὶ πονηρὸν καὶ προδότην ἕν᾽¹
εἰσαγγείλας, καὶ ἐξελέγξας ἐν πεντακοσίοις καὶ
δισχιλίοις τῶν πολιτῶν ὅτι μισθώσας αὐτὸν Πυ-
θοκλεῖ² κατ᾽ ἐμοῦ ταῦτ᾽ ἔπραξεν, ἐτιμωρησάμην
μετὰ τῶν τότε δικασάντων. λαβέ μοι σὺ τὴν μαρτυρίαν, ἣν καὶ πρότερον παρεσχόμην μαρτυρου-
μένην τοῖς δικασταῖς καὶ οὐδεὶς ἐπεσκήψατο ὡς
ψευδεῖ οὔσῃ, ἣν καὶ νῦν παρέξομαι. λέγε τὴν
μαρτυρίαν.

53 Εἶτ᾽ οὐ δεινόν, ὦ Ἀθηναῖοι, εἰ, ὅτι μὲν εἷς ἀνὴρ
ἔφησε Πιστίας Ἀρεοπαγίτης ὢν ἀδικεῖν με, κατα-
[97] ψευδόμενος κἀμοῦ³ καὶ τῆς βουλῆς, ἴσχυσεν ἂν τὸ
ψεῦδος τῆς ἀληθείας μᾶλλον, εἰ⁴ διὰ τὴν ἀσθένειαν
τὴν τότε καὶ τὴν ἐρημίαν τὴν ἐμὴν ἐπιστεύθησαν
αἱ κατ᾽ ἐμοῦ ψευδεῖς γενόμεναι⁵ κατασκευαί· ἐπειδὴ

---

¹ ἕν᾽ Blass : ὃν A pr. (del. ras.) N : ὄντ᾽ Franke.
² Πυθοκλεῖ N : Τιμοκλεῖ A.
³ κἀμοῦ A corr.² : κατ᾽ ἐμοῦ A pr. N.
⁴ εἰ Gebauer : καὶ codd.
⁵ γενόμεναι Blass : γινόμεναι codd.

people's instructions in making its inquiry and publishing the report on me, show me the decree and tell me who were my accusers after the report was made. Compare the present case, where you have both : a decree which authorized the council's inquiry, and accusers, elected by the people, who are now giving the jury an account of the crimes. If your story is true, I am prepared to die. But if you claim that the council took the initiative in reporting me, produce the Areopagites as witnesses, just as I myself shall produce them to show that I was not reported, to show in fact that, after impeaching one rogue and traitor who, like you, had maligned the council and myself, I proved before two thousand five hundred citizens that he had hired himself to Pythocles [a] in making this attack upon me, and so avenged myself with the help of those then serving on the jury. Clerk, please take the deposition. I laid it before the jury previously as evidence and no one questioned its veracity. So I will produce it now. Read the deposition.

Deposition

Is it not an anomaly, Athenians, that on that occasion, because one man, Pistias an Areopagite,[b] told lies against the council and myself and said that I was a criminal, falsehood would have prevailed over truth, if through my weakness and isolation at the time the trumped up lies against me had been believed ;

[a] Pythocles was an Athenian orator who, in company with Aeschines, attacked Demosthenes unsuccessfully after Chaeronea. *Cf.* Dem. xviii. 285.

[b] Nothing else is known of Pistias except that Dinarchus composed a speech against him, the title of which appears in the list of his genuine public orations preserved by Dionysius.

DINARCHUS

δὲ τἀληθὲς παρὰ πάσης τῆς ἐξ Ἀρείου πάγου βουλῆς ὁμολογεῖται, Δημοσθένην εἰληφέναι εἴκοσι τάλαντα χρυσίου καθ᾿ ὑμῶν καὶ ταῦτα πεποιηκότ᾿
ἀδικεῖν, καὶ ὁ δημαγωγὸς ὑμῖν, ἐν ᾧ τὰς ἐλπίδας
54 ἔχουσί τινες, ἐπ᾿ αὐτοφώρῳ χρήματα λαμβάνων
εἴληπται, νῦν τὰ νόμιμα τἀκεῖθεν καὶ τὰ δίκαια καὶ
τἀληθῆ ἀσθενέστερα γενήσεται τῶν Δημοσθένους
λόγων, καὶ ἰσχύσει μᾶλλον τῆς ἀληθείας ἡ παρὰ
τούτου ῥηθησομένη κατὰ τοῦ συνεδρίου διαβολή,
ὡς ἄρα πολλοὺς ἡ βουλὴ ἀποπέφαγκεν ἀδικεῖν τὸν
δῆμον, οἳ ἀποπεφεύγασιν εἰσελθόντες εἰς τὸ δικαστήριον, καὶ ἡ βουλὴ ἐπ᾿ ἐνίων τὸ πέμπτον μέρος
οὐ μετείληφε τῶν ψήφων; τοῦτο δὲ ὃν τρόπον
55 γίγνεται, ῥᾳδίως ἅπαντες μαθήσεσθε. ἡ βουλή,
ὦ ἄνδρες, ζητεῖ τὰ προσταχθένθ᾿ ὑφ᾿ ὑμῶν καὶ τὰ
γεγενημένα παρ᾿ αὑτοῖς[1] ἀδικήματ᾿ οὐχ ὡς ὑμεῖς
—καί μοι μὴ ὀργισθῆτε— δικάζειν ἐνίοτε εἴθισθε,
τῇ συγγνώμῃ πλέον ἢ τῷ δικαίῳ ἀπονέμοντες, ἀλλ᾿
ἁπλῶς τὸν ἔνοχον ὄντα τοῖς ζητουμένοις ⟨ἀπο-
φαίνει⟩[2] καὶ τὸν ὁποιονοῦν ἠδικηκότα ⟨παρὰ⟩[3] τὰ
πάτρια, νομίζουσα τὸν ἐν τοῖς μικροῖς συνεθιζό-
μενον ἀδικεῖν τοῦτον τὰ μεγάλα τῶν ἀδικημάτων
56 εὐχερέστερον προσδέξεσθαι. διόπερ τὸν παρ᾿
αὑτῶν ἀποστερήσαντα τὸ ναῦλον τὸν πορθμέα ζη-
μιώσασα πρὸς ὑμᾶς ἀπέφηνε· πάλιν τὸν τὴν πεντε-
δραχμίαν ἐπὶ τῷ τοῦ μὴ παρόντος ὀνόματι λαβεῖν

---

[1] αὑτοῖς Bekker : αὐτοῖς codd.
[2] ἀποφαίνει add. Wolf.
[3] παρὰ add. Blass.

---

[a] It appears from Hyperides (v., col. 26), who seems to be
referring to the same case, that Dinarchus is here alluding
to the dole made to Athenians to enable them to attend the
212

whereas now, when the fact is admitted by the whole Areopagus that Demosthenes has taken twenty talents of gold against your interests, and is therefore a criminal, and that your popular leader, in whom some men place their hopes, has been caught in the act of taking bribes, the customs of the Areopagus and truth and justice are going to prove weaker than Demosthenes' word? Truth will be overridden by the slanderous statement he intends to make against the council, namely that many of those reported by it as a menace to the people have, on coming into court, been acquitted, in some cases the council failing to secure a fifth part of the votes. There is an explanation for this which you will easily follow. The council, gentlemen, has its own method of inquiring into the cases which you assign to it and the crimes committed within its own body. Unlike yourselves,—and you need not take offence at this,— who are sometimes apt when judging to give more weight to mercy than to justice, it simply reports anyone who is liable to the charges in question or has broken any traditional rule of conduct; believing that if a person is in the habit of committing small offences he will more easily involve himself in serious crimes. Consequently when one of its number robbed the ferryman of his fare it fined him and reported him to you. Again, when someone claimed the five drachma allowance [a] in the

theatre. The normal price of a seat was one-third of a drachma only, but as the fund was apparently drawn upon for other purposes also, it is perhaps not surprising that the sum mentioned here is larger. *Cf.* Libanius, *arg. ad Demosthenem* i. The portion mentioned in the following sentence was an allowance of sacrificial meat made to members of the Areopagus.

ἀξιώσαντα, καὶ τοῦτον ὑμῖν ἀπέφηνε, καὶ τὸν τὴν
μερίδα τὴν ἐξ Ἀρείου πάγου τολμήσαντ' ἀποδόσθαι παρὰ τὰ νόμιμα τὸν αὐτὸν τρόπον ζημιώσας·
57 ἐξέβαλε. τούτους ὑμεῖς κρίναντες ἀφήκατε, οὐ τῆς
ἐξ Ἀρείου πάγου βουλῆς καταγιγνώσκοντες ψεύδεσθαι, ἀλλὰ τῇ συγγνώμῃ μᾶλλον ἢ τῷ δικαίῳ
προσθέμενοι, καὶ τὴν τιμωρίαν μείζω νομίζοντες
εἶναι τῆς ὑπὸ τῶν κρινομένων γεγενημένης ἁμαρ-
τίας. ἦ που ἄρα ἡ βουλή, Δημόσθενες, τὰ ψευδῆ
ἀπέφηνεν; οὐ δήπου. τούτους μέντοι, ὦ ἄνδρες,
καὶ τοιούτους ἑτέρους ἀδικεῖν παρ' ἑαυτοῖς[1] ἀπο-
58 φηνάσης τῆς βουλῆς ὑμεῖς ἀφήκατε. Πολύευκτον
δὲ τὸν Κυδαντίδην τοῦ δήμου προστάξαντος ζητῆσαι
τὴν βουλήν, εἰ συνέρχεται τοῖς φυγάσιν εἰς Μέγαρα,
καὶ ζητήσασαν ἀποφῆναι πρὸς ὑμᾶς, ἀπέφηνεν ἡ
βουλὴ συνιέναι. κατηγόρους εἵλεσθε κατὰ τὸν
νόμον, εἰσῆλθεν εἰς τὸ δικαστήριον, ἀπελύσαθ'
ὑμεῖς, ὁμολογοῦντος τοῦ[2] Πολυεύκτου βαδίζειν εἰς
Μέγαρ' ὡς τὸν Νικοφάνην· ἔχειν γὰρ τὴν αὑτοῦ
μητέρα τοῦτον. οὐδὲν οὖν ἄτοπον οὐδὲ δεινὸν
ἐφαίνεθ' ὑμῖν ποιεῖν τῷ τῆς μητρὸς ἀνδρὶ διαλεγό-
μενος ἠτυχηκότι καὶ συνευπορῶν, καθ' ὅσον δυνατὸς
59 ἦν, ἀπεστερημένῳ τῆς πατρίδος. αὕτη, Δημόσθενες, τῆς βουλῆς ἡ ἀπόφασις οὐκ ἐξηλέγχθη
ψευδὴς οὖσα, ἀληθινῆς δὲ αὐτῆς οὔσης ἔδοξε τοῖς
δικασταῖς ἀφεῖναι[3] τὸν Πολύευκτον· τὸ μὲν γὰρ
ἀληθὲς τῇ βουλῇ προσετάχθη ζητεῖν, τὸ δὲ συγγνώμης ἄξιόν φημι[4] τὸ δικαστήριον ἔκρινε. διὰ

---

[1] ἑαυτοῖς Blass : ἑαυτῆς codd. : ἑαυτῇ Reiske.
[2] τοῦ om. A.   [3] ἀφεῖναι Blass : ἀφιέναι codd.

name of an absentee, it reported him also to you. Similarly it fined and expelled the man who presumed to break the rule and sell the Areopagite portion. You tried these men and acquitted them. You were not thereby convicting the Areopagus of error ; but you were more concerned with sympathy than justice, and thought the punishment too severe for the offence which the defendants had committed. Do you imagine then, Demosthenes, that the council made a false report ? Of course it did not. Nevertheless, gentlemen, you acquitted these men and others like them, though the council reported that they were guilty of breaking its rules. In the case of Polyeuctus of Cydantidae,[a] when the people instructed the council to inquire whether he was accompanying the exiles to Megara and to report back after the investigation, it reported that he was doing so. You chose accusers as the law prescribes : Polyeuctus came into court and you acquitted him, on his admitting that he was going to Megara to Nicophanes who, he said, was married to his mother. So you did not consider that he was doing anything strange or reprehensible in keeping in touch with his mother's husband who was in difficulties, or in assisting him, so far as he could, while he was banished from the country. The report of the council, Demosthenes, was not proved false ; it was quite true, but the jury decided to acquit Polyeuctus. The council was instructed to discover the truth, yet, as I say, the court decided whether it was a case for pardon. Is that

---

[a] For Polyeuctus of Cydantidae, the accuser of Euxenippus, *cf.* Hyp. iv. 4, Introduction.

---

[a] φημι] ἢ μὴ Reiske.

τοῦτ᾽ οὐ πιστευτέον τῇ βουλῇ περὶ τῶν γιγνομένων[1]
ἀποφάσεων, ἐπειδή σε καὶ τοὺς μετὰ σοῦ τὸ χρυσίον
60 ἔχοντας ἀποπέφαγκε; δεινὸν μέντ᾽ ἂν εἴη. δεῖξον
γὰρ τοῖς δικασταῖς σύ, Δημόσθενες, νυνὶ ὡς τούτων τι τῶν ἁμαρτημάτων[2] ὅμοιόν ἐστι τοῖς σοῖς
ἀδικήμασι, καὶ ὡς τὸ δῶρα λαμβάνειν κατὰ τῆς
πατρίδος συγγνώμης ἐστὶν ἄξιον, ὥστ᾽ ἀποφύγοις
ἂν παρὰ τούτοις εἰκότως. ἀλλ᾽ οἱ νόμοι περὶ μὲν
τῶν ἄλλων ἀδικημάτων τῶν εἰς ἀργυρίου λόγον
ἀνηκόντων διπλῆν τὴν βλάβην ὀφλεῖν[3] κελεύουσι,
περὶ δὲ τῶν δωροδοκούντων δύο μόνον τιμήματα
πεποιήκασιν, ἢ θάνατον, ἵνα ταύτης τυχὼν τῆς
ζημίας ὁ λαβὼν παράδειγμα γένηται τοῖς ἄλλοις,
ἢ δεκαπλοῦν τοῦ ἐξ ἀρχῆς λήμματος τὸ τίμημα
τῶν δώρων, ἵνα μὴ λυσιτελήσῃ[4] τοῖς τοῦτο τολμῶσι
ποιεῖν.

[98]
61 Ἡ τοῦτο μὲν οὐκ ἐπιχειρήσεις λέγειν, ὅτι δὲ τῶν
προτέρων[5] ἀποφανθέντων ὑπὸ τῆς βουλῆς, τοῖς μὲν
ἄλλοις ὡμολογηκέναι συμβέβηκεν ἀξίαν εἶναι τὴν
τῆς βουλῆς ζημίαν,[6] σοὶ δὲ μόνῳ τὰ[7] περὶ αὐτῆς
ἠναντιῶσθαι. ἀλλὰ μόνος σὺ τῶν πώποτ᾽ ἀποπεφασμένων ἠξίωσας ἑκὼν σεαυτῷ τούτους κριτὰς
καὶ ζητητὰς γενέσθαι, καὶ ἔγραψας κατὰ σαυτοῦ
τὸ ψήφισμα, καὶ τὸν δῆμον ἐποίησω μάρτυρα τῶν
ὡμολογημένων, ὁρισάμενος σεαυτῷ ζημίαν εἶναι
θάνατον, ἐὰν ἀποφήνῃ ⟨σ᾽⟩[8] ἡ βουλὴ τῶν χρημάτων
εἰληφότα τι τῶν εἰς τὴν χώραν ὑφ᾽ Ἁρπάλου
62 κομισθέντων. ἀλλὰ μὴν πρότερον ἔγραψας σύ, ὦ

---

[1] γιγνομένων Blass : γινομένων N : γενομένων A.
[2] ἁμαρτημάτων Sauppe : ἡμαρτηκότων codd.
[3] ὀφλεῖν Meier : ὀφείλειν codd.

216

any reason for distrusting the council over the present
reports in which it has stated that you and your confederates are in possession of the gold ? That would
be disgraceful. Convince the jury now, Demosthenes,
that any of those crimes ranks with yours and that to
take bribes against one's country is a pardonable act
which would justify these men in acquitting you.
For other pecuniary offences the laws prescribe
damages twice as great as the sum involved,[a] but in
cases of bribery they have laid down two penalties
only : either death, to ensure that by meeting with
this punishment the guilty man is an example to
others, or a fine for bribery ten times as great as the
original bribe, so that men who dare to commit this
offence shall not gain by it.

Perhaps you will not attempt to argue thus, Demosthenes, but will say that of those whom the council has
reported up till now the rest have admitted that the
penalty which it imposed was deserved, whereas you
alone have protested against it. But you alone, of all
those ever reported, asked these men of your own accord to be your judges and court of inquiry. You proposed the decree against yourself and made the people
witness of the agreement, defining the penalty for
yourself as death, if the council should report that
you had taken any of the money brought into the
country by Harpalus. And yet in the past, Demo-

---

[a] A misleading statement. *Cf.* Hyp. v., col. 24, where the
contrast made is between a simple and a tenfold fine. A fine
was doubled only if it had not been paid before a specific
date. *Cf.* Dinarch. ii. 17 and Aristotle, *Ath. Pol.* 54.

---

⁴ λυσιτελήσῃ Blass : λυσιτελὴς ᾖ N A pr. : λυσιτελὲς ᾖ A corr.
⁵ πρότερον Scaliger : προτέρων codd.
⁶ ζημίαν A pr. : ζήτησιν A corr. N.
⁷ τὰ] del. Dobree.   ⁸ σ᾽ add. Blass.

Δημόσθενες, κατὰ πάντων τούτων καὶ τῶν ἄλλων
Ἀθηναίων κυρίαν εἶναι τὴν ἐξ Ἀρείου πάγου βουλὴν κολάσαι τὸν παρὰ τοὺς νόμους πλημμελοῦντα,
χρωμένην τοῖς πατρίοις¹ νόμοις· καὶ παρέδωκας σὺ
καὶ ἐνεχείρισας τὴν πόλιν ἅπασαν ταύτῃ, ἣν αὐτίκα
φήσεις ὀλιγαρχικὴν εἶναι· καὶ τεθνᾶσι κατὰ τὸ σὸν
ψήφισμα δύο τῶν πολιτῶν, πατὴρ καὶ υἱός, παρα-
63 δοθέντες τῷ ἐπὶ τῷ ὀρύγματι· ἐδέθη τῶν ἀφ'
Ἁρμοδίου γεγονότων εἷς κατα τὸ σὸν πρόσταγμα·
ἐστρέβλωσαν Ἀντιφῶντα καὶ ἀπέκτειναν οὗτοι τῇ
τῆς βουλῆς ἀποφάσει πεισθέντες· ἐξέβαλες σὺ
Χαρῖνον² ἐκ τῆς πόλεως ἐπὶ προδοσίᾳ κατὰ τὰς τῆς
βουλῆς ἀποφάσεις καὶ τιμωρίας. κατὰ δὲ σαυτοῦ
καὶ ταῦτα γράψας αὐτὸς τὸ ψήφισμ' ἀκυροῖς; καὶ
ποῦ ταῦτα δίκαια ἢ νόμιμά ἐστι;

64 Μαρτύρομαι τὰς σεμνὰς θεάς, ἄνδρες Ἀθηναῖοι,
καὶ τὸν τόπον ὃν ἐκεῖναι κατέχουσι, καὶ τοὺς ἥρωας
τοὺς ἐγχωρίους, καὶ τὴν Ἀθηνᾶν τὴν Πολιάδα³
καὶ τοὺς ἄλλους θεοὺς οἳ τὴν χώραν καὶ τὴν πόλιν
ἡμῶν εἰλήχασιν, ὅτι τοῦ δήμου παραδεδωκότος
ὑμῖν τιμωρήσασθαι⁴ τὸν εἰληφότα τι τῶν⁵ . . .
κατὰ τῆς πατρίδος, τὸν λελυμασμένον καὶ ἐφθαρ-
κότα τὴν τῆς πόλεως εὐδαιμονίαν, τὸν περικεχαρα-
κωμένην προδεδωκότα⁶ τὴν πατρίδα ταῖς αὑτοῦ

¹ πατρίοις Wolf : πατρῴοις codd.
² Χαρῖνον Rohdewald : Ἀρχίνον codd.
³ Πολιάδα Wolf : πολίτιδα codd.
⁴ τιμωρήσασθαι A: Τιμωρήσ. τε N pr. : τιμωρήσατε N corr.² :
οὐκ ἐτιμωρήσασθε Ald.
⁵ Post τῶν nonnihil excidisse videtur : κομισθέντων χρημάτων supplendum ci. Blass (coll. § 70).
⁶ προδεδωκότα Schmidt : παραδεδωκότα codd.

ᵃ Demosthenes (xviii. 132) confirms this and says that

sthenes, you proposed that the council of the Areopagus should have power over all these men, and the rest of Athens too, to enforce the laws of the land and punish any who transgressed them. It was you who surrendered the whole city into the hands of this council which you will presently tell us is oligarchic. By the terms of your decree the death sentence has been inflicted on two citizens, a father and a son, who were given over to the executioner. One of the descendants of Harmodius was imprisoned in pursuance of your order. These gentlemen, acting on the council's report, tortured and killed Antiphon.[a] You expelled Charinus [b] from the city for treason on the strength of the council's reports and punishments. After proposing this treatment for yourself also, are you now overriding the decree of your own accord? Surely that is neither just nor lawful.

I summon as my witnesses, Athenians, the awful goddesses and their abode, the heroes of the land, Athena Polias, and those other gods who have obtained our city and countryside as their home, to show that when the people has consigned to you for punishment one who, against his country's interests, has accepted a part of the ⟨imported money⟩,[c] one who has defiled and ruined the city's prosperity and betrayed that country which he claimed to have forti-

a Antiphon promised Philip that he would burn the dockyards in the Piraeus. Demosthenes caught him there and brought him before the people, who at first acquitted him. But the Areopagus intervened and he was later executed.

b Charinus, a figure of little importance, is mentioned as a traitor in the speech against Theocrines, which was attributed by Dionysius to Dinarchus but has survived among the works of Demosthenes ([Dem.] lviii. 38).

c The sense of this passage is clear, though the Greek wording leaves room for doubt.

DINARCHUS

65 συμβουλίαις, [ὃν]¹ οἱ μὲν ἐχθροὶ καὶ κακόνοι τῇ
πόλει² ζῆν ἂν βούλοιντο, συμφορὰν ἡγούμενοι τῆς
πόλεως εἶναι, ὅσοι δὲ εὖνοι τοῖς ὑμετέροις πράγμασι, καὶ μεταπεσούσης τῆς τύχης ἐλπίζουσιν ἐπὶ
τὸ βέλτιον ἂν τὰ τῆς πόλεως πράγματ᾽ ἐλθεῖν, τὴν
ἀξίαν δίκην δόντα τῶν πεπραγμένων ἀπολωλέναι
βούλονται, καὶ ταῦτ᾽ εὔχονται τοῖς θεοῖς· οὓς κἀγὼ
συμπαρακαλῶ σῶσαι τὴν πατρίδα, κινδυνεύουσαν
ὁρῶν ὑπὲρ σωτηρίας, ὑπὲρ παίδων, ὑπὲρ γυναικῶν,
ὑπὲρ δόξης, ὑπὲρ τῶν ἄλλων ἀγαθῶν ἁπάντων.
66 τί γὰρ ἐροῦμεν, ὦ Ἀθηναῖοι, πρὸς τοὺς περιεστηκότας ἐξελθόντες ἐκ τοῦ δικαστηρίου, ἐάν, ὃ μὴ
γένοιτο, παρακρουσθῆτε ὑπὸ τῆς τούτου γοητείας;
τίσιν ὀφθαλμοῖς ἕκαστος ὑμῶν τὴν πατρῴαν ἑστίαν
οἴκαδ᾽ ἀπελθὼν ἰδεῖν τολμήσει,³ ἀπολελυκότες μὲν
τὸν προδότην τὸν πρῶτον εἰς τὸν ἴδιον οἶκον εἰσεν-
εγκάμενον τὸ δεδωροδοκημένον χρυσίον, κατεγνω-
κότες δὲ μηδὲν ἀληθὲς μήτε⁴ ζητεῖν μήθ᾽ εὑρίσκειν
τὸ παρὰ πᾶσιν ἀνθρώποις εἶναι σεμνότατον νομιζό-
67 μενον συνέδριον; τίνας δ᾽, ὦ Ἀθηναῖοι,—σκοπεῖτε
γὰρ πρὸς ὑμᾶς αὐτούς—, τίνας τὰς ἐλπίδας ἕξομεν,
ἐὰν κίνδυνός τις καταλάβῃ τὴν πόλιν, τὸ μὲν δῶρα
λαμβάνειν κατὰ τῆς πατρίδος ἀσφαλὲς εἶναι πεποιηκότες, τὸ δὲ τὴν φυλακὴν ἔχον συνέδριον τῆς
πόλεως ἐν τοῖς τοιούτοις κινδύνοις ἀδόκιμον κατα-
68 στήσαντες; τί δ᾽ ἐάν—τιθῶμεν⁵ γὰρ ταῦτα—, ἐὰν
κατὰ τὸ ψήφισμα τὸ Δημοσθένους ἀπαιτῇ πέμψας
ἡμᾶς Ἀλέξανδρος τὸ χρυσίον τὸ κομισθὲν εἰς τὴν

¹ ὃν del. Thalheim.
² τῇ πόλει Kleyn : τῆς πόλεως codd.
³ τολμήσει Bekker : τολμήσειε N : τολμήσειεν A.
⁴ μήτε Bekker : μηδὲ codd.

fied by his diplomacy,[a] enemies, and those who bear
the city ill will, would wish him alive, counting this a
disaster for Athens ; but all who favour your concerns
and hope that with a turn of fortune the city's prospects may improve wish that this man may die and
pay the penalty merited by his conduct, and such is
the burden of their prayers. I also join in praying
the gods to save our country, which I see to be in
danger of forfeiting its safety, its women and children,
its honour, and every other thing of worth. What
shall we say to the bystanders, Athenians, when we
come out of the court, if you are deceived, as I pray
you may not be, by the wizardry of this man ? What
will be the feelings of you all, when, on your return,
you presume to look upon your fathers' hearths, after
acquitting the traitor who first brought into his own
home the gold of bribery ; after convicting as utterly
false, in both its inquiry and its conclusion, the body
which all men hold in the greatest awe ? What hopes,
Athenians,—picture for yourselves,—what hopes
shall we have if some danger overtakes the city,
when we have made it a safe thing to take bribes
against one's country and have robbed of its status
the body which kept watch over the city in such times
of crisis ? Or again,—let us suppose this to happen,—
what if Alexander, in pursuance of Demosthenes'
decree,[b] sends and asks us for the gold brought into

[a] An allusion to some words of Demosthenes in the speech
on the Crown (Dem. xviii. 299).

[b] Demosthenes had proposed that the money should be
kept on the Acropolis until Alexander sent for it.

[5] τί δ᾽ ἐάν,—τιθῶμεν Funkhaenel : τί δέ, ἀντιθῶμεν A : τί δαὶ
ἀντιθῶμεν N.

χώραν ὑφ' Ἁρπάλου, καὶ πρὸς τῷ γεγενῆσθαι τὴν
τῆς βουλῆς ἀπόφασιν τοὺς παῖδας καταπέμψῃ πρὸς
ἡμᾶς τοὺς νῦν ὡς ἑαυτὸν ἀνακεκομισμένους, καὶ
τούτων ἀξιοῖ πυνθάνεσθαι τὴν ἀλήθειαν ἡμᾶς,[1] πρὸς
69 θεῶν, ὦ ἄνδρες, τί ἐροῦμεν; γράψεις[2] σύ, Δημόσθενες, πολεμεῖν ἡμᾶς, ἐπειδὴ καὶ τοὺς πρότερον
[99] πολέμους καλῶς διῴκησας; καὶ πότερόν ἐστι
δικαιότερον, ἂν ταῦτα δόξῃ καὶ τοῖς ἄλλοις Ἀθηναίοις, εἰς τὸν πόλεμον ὑπάρχειν μετὰ τῶν ἄλλων
καὶ τὸ παρὰ σοῦ χρυσίον, ἢ τοὺς μὲν ἄλλους ἀπὸ
τῶν ἰδίων κτημάτων ἕκαστον εἰσφέρειν, καὶ κατα-
χωνεύειν τὸν ἴδιον κόσμον τῶν γυναικῶν, καὶ τὰ
ἐκπώματα, καὶ πάντα τὰ ἐν τῇ χώρᾳ ἀναθήματα
τῶν θεῶν, ὥσπερ ἔφησθα σὺ γράψειν,[3] αὐτὸς εἰσ-
ενεγκὼν πεντήκοντα δραχμὰς ἀπὸ τῆς οἰκίας τῆς
ἐν Πειραιεῖ, καὶ τῆς ἐν ἄστει; τοσοῦτον γὰρ κατὰ
τὴν προτέραν εἰσφορὰν εἰσενηνοχώς, εἴκοσι τάλαντ'
70 ἔχεις. ἢ πολεμεῖν μὲν οὐ γράψεις, ἀποδιδόναι δὲ
κατὰ τὸ γεγραμμένον ὑπὸ σοῦ ψήφισμα κελεύσεις[4]
Ἀλεξάνδρῳ τὸ κεκομισμένον χρυσίον; οὐκοῦν
ὑπὲρ σοῦ τὸν δῆμον ἀποδιδόναι δεήσει. καὶ ποῦ
τοῦτ' ἐστὶ δίκαιον ἢ κοινὸν ἢ δημοτικόν, τοὺς μὲν
ἐργαζομένους εἰσφέρειν, σὲ δ' ἁρπάζειν καὶ κλέπτειν;[5] καὶ τοὺς μὲν φανερὰν κεκτῆσθαι τὴν οὐσίαν
καὶ ἀπὸ ταύτης εἰσφέρειν, σὲ δὲ πλείω ἢ πεντήκοντα καὶ ἑκατὸν τάλαντα, τὰ μὲν ἐκ τῶν βασιλικῶν, τὰ δ' ἐκ τῶν Ἀλεξάνδρου πραγμάτων,
εἰληφέναι, μηδὲν δὲ φανερὸν ἐν τῇ πόλει κεκτῆσθαι, ἀλλὰ διεσκευάσθαι πρὸς τὸν δῆμον ὡς οὐ πι-

---

[1] ἡμᾶς Baiter et Sauppe : ὑμᾶς codd.

the country by Harpalus, and, over and above the
fact that the council has made a report, sends down
here the slaves which have now been returned to
him and asks us to find out the truth from them ;
what in Heaven's name shall we say, gentlemen ?
Will you propose, Demosthenes, that we go to war,
in view of your success with the previous wars ? Suppose the rest of Athens decides on this, which is fairer :
for your gold to be available for war along with other
people's or for others to contribute from their own
property, melting down the personal ornaments of
their wives, the cups and all the country's store of
offerings to the gods, as you said you would suggest,
though you yourself paid in fifty drachmas from your
houses in Piraeus and the city ? That has been your
contribution under the last levy though now you have
twenty talents. Perhaps you will not advocate war
but advise us to follow out the decree which you
proposed and give back to Alexander the gold brought
to us ? If so, it will be for your sake that the people
have to restore it. It is surely neither just nor fair
nor democratic that those who work should contribute,
while you plunder and steal ; that some should make
no secret of the property they hold and make contributions proportionate to it, while you who have
received more than a hundred and fifty talents, either
from the King's money [a] or from your association
with Alexander, have no declared property in the
city but have fortified yourself against the people as

---

[a] See note on § 10.

---

[2] γράψεις Stephanus : γράφεις codd.
[3] γράψειν Stephanus : γράφειν codd.
[4] κελεύσεις Stephanus : κελεύεις codd.
[5] καὶ κλέπτειν add. N.

71 στεύοντα τοῖς ἑαυτῷ πολιτευομένοις; καὶ τοὺς μὲν
νόμους προλέγειν τῷ ῥήτορι καὶ τῷ στρατηγῷ,
⟨τῷ⟩¹ τὴν παρὰ τοῦ δήμου πίστιν ἀξιοῦντι λαμβάνειν, παιδοποιεῖσθαι κατὰ τοὺς νόμους, γῆν ἐντὸς
ὅρων κεκτῆσθαι, πάσας τὰς δικαίας πίστεις παρα-
καταθέμενον οὕτως ἀξιοῦν προεστάναι τοῦ δήμου·
σὲ δὲ τὴν ⟨μὲν⟩² πατρῴαν γῆν πεπρακέναι, τοὺς
δ' οὐ γεγενημένους υἱεῖς σαυτῷ προσποιεῖσθαι παρὰ
τοὺς νόμους τῶν ἐν ταῖς κρίσεσιν ἕνεκα γιγνομένων
ὅρκων, ἐπιτάττειν δὲ τοῖς ἄλλοις στρατεύεσθαι
λιπόντ' αὐτὸν τὴν κοινὴν τάξιν.

72 ῏Ω Ἀθηναῖοι, παρὰ τί οἴεσθε τὰς πόλεις τοτὲ
μὲν εὖ τοτὲ δὲ φαύλως πράττειν; οὐδὲν εὑρήσετ'
ἄλλο πλὴν παρὰ τοὺς συμβούλους καὶ τοὺς ἡγεμόνας. ἐπιβλέψατε δ' ἐπὶ τὴν Θηβαίων πόλιν.
ἐγένετο³ πόλις,⁴ ἐγένετο μεγίστη· καὶ τίνων τυ-
χοῦσα ἡγεμόνων καὶ στρατηγῶν; ἅπαντες ἂν
ὁμολογήσαιεν ⟨οἱ⟩⁵ πρεσβύτεροι, παρ' ὧνπερ κἀγὼ
τοὺς λόγους ἀκούων ἐρῶ, ὅτε Πελοπίδας, ὥς φασιν,

73 ἡγεῖτο τοῦ ἱεροῦ λόχου⁶ καὶ Ἐπαμινώνδας ἐστρα-

---

¹ τῷ add. Reiske. ² μὲν add. Blass.
³ πότε ante ἐγένετο add. Stephanus, ante καὶ τίνων Blass.
⁴ Verba πόλις, ἐγένετο del. Dobree.
⁵ οἱ add. Reiske.
⁶ λόχου A corr.² : λόγου A pr. N.

---

^a A reference to the oath whereby a man called down
imprecations on his children, swearing that he was not guilty
of a certain action. Demosthenes had lost his only child, a
daughter, in 336 (Aeschin. iii. 77); and if he had other
children now, they were adopted or by a hetaera. *Cf.*
Athen. xiii. 592 e.

^b Pelopidas and Epaminondas were the chief Theban

though you had no confidence in your own conduct of affairs. Is it right, when the laws demand that the orator or general who expects to get the people's confidence shall observe the laws in begetting children, shall own land within our boundaries, shall give all the lawful pledges and only thus lay claim to be the people's leader, that you should have sold the land inherited from your father or be claiming as yours children which are not your own, thus breaking the laws which govern oaths in court,*a* and be ordering others to fight when you deserted the citizens' ranks yourself?

What do you think it is, Athenians, that makes cities vary between good and evil fortunes? You will find only one cause : the counsellors and leaders. Take Thebes. It was a city ; it became supreme. Under what leaders and generals? All the older men, on whose authority I shall give you the story, would admit that it was when Pelopidas,*b* so they have it, led the Sacred Band *c* and Epaminondas and

generals during their city's period of greatness (371–362 B.C.). In 371 they defeated Sparta at Leuctra and, in response to an appeal from the Arcadians who then rose against Sparta, entered the Peloponnese in 370. Here they refounded the town of Messenê which the Spartans had destroyed at the end of the 8th century B.C. (Diodor. xv. 56 and 62-66). Epaminondas conducted three further invasions of the Peloponnese, penetrating Laconia, but never actually taking Sparta. It was probably during the second of these that he founded Megalopolis, the new capital of Arcadia ; in the third he was killed at Mantinea (362 B.C.).

c The Sacred Band was a company of 300 picked soldiers maintained by the state. They first attracted attention by defeating a Spartan force in 375 B.C. and played a large part in the victory of Leuctra. At Chaeronea they fought to the last man and were buried by the highway from Phocis to Thebes with the figure of a lion over their tomb.

τήγει καὶ οἱ μετὰ τούτων, τότε τὴν ἐν Λεύκτροις
μάχην ἐνίκησεν ἡ τῶν Θηβαίων πόλις, τότ' εἰς τὴν
ἀπόρθητον νομιζομένην εἶναι Λακεδαιμονίων χώραν
εἰσέβαλον, κατ' ἐκείνους τοὺς χρόνους πολλὰ καὶ
καλὰ διεπράξαντ' ἔργα, Μεσσήνην τετρακοσιοστῷ
ἔτει κατῴκισαν, Ἀρκάδας αὐτονόμους ἐποίησαν,
74 ἔνδοξοι παρὰ πᾶσιν ἦσαν. πότε δ' αὖ τοὐναντίον
ταπεινὰ καὶ τοῦ φρονήματος ἀνάξια διεπράξαντο;
ὅτ' ἐδωροδόκει μὲν λαμβάνων χρήματα παρὰ
Φιλίππου Τιμόλαος ὁ τούτου φίλος, ἐπὶ δὲ τοῖς
ξένοις τοῖς εἰς Ἄμφισσαν συλλεγεῖσι Πρόξενος ὁ
προδότης ἐγένετο, ἡγεμὼν δὲ τῆς φάλαγγος κατέστη Θεαγένης, ἄνθρωπος ἀτυχὴς καὶ δωροδόκος
ὥσπερ οὗτος. τότε διὰ τρεῖς γ' ἀνθρώπους οὓς
εἶπον ἅπασ' ἡ πόλις ἐκ τῶν Ἑλλήνων[1] ἀπώλετο
καὶ διεφθάρη. οὐ γὰρ ψεῦδός ἐστιν ἀλλὰ καὶ λίαν
ἀληθὲς τὸ τοὺς ἡγεμόνας αἰτίους ἁπάντων γίγνεσθαι καὶ τῶν ἀγαθῶν καὶ τῶν ἐναντίων τοῖς πολί-
75 ταις. θεωρήσατε δὴ πάλιν καὶ ἐπὶ τῆς ἡμετέρας
πόλεως, τὸν αὐτὸν τρόπον ἐξετάσαντες. ἡ πόλις
ἡμῶν ἦν μεγάλη καὶ ἔνδοξος παρὰ τοῖς Ἕλλησι καὶ
τῶν προγόνων ἀξία, μετά γε τὰς ἀρχαίας ἐκείνας
πράξεις, ὅτε Κόνων, ὡς οἱ πρεσβύτεροι λέγουσιν,
ἐνίκησε τὴν ἐν Κνίδῳ ναυμαχίαν, ὅτ' Ἰφικράτης
ἀνεῖλε τὴν Λακεδαιμονίων μόραν,[2] ὅτε Χαβρίας ἐν
Νάξῳ κατεναυμάχησε τὰς Λακεδαιμονίων τριήρεις,

---

[1] (ἐκ?) τῶν Ἑλλήνων A pr.: μετὰ τῶν Ἑλλήνων ἁπάντων A
corr.: μετὰ τῶν ἄλλων Ἑλλήνων N.

their compeers were in command. It was then that
Thebes won the battle of Leuctra, then that they
invaded the Spartans' country which, it was thought,
could not be ravaged. During that period they
accomplished many fine achievements: founded
Messene in the four hundredth[a] year after its fall,
gave the Arcadians self-government, and won a
universal reputation. On the other hand when was
their achievement despicable and unworthy of their
spirit? When Timolaüs,[b] the friend of Demosthenes,
was corrupted and took bribes from Philip, when the
traitor Proxenus commanded the mercenaries enlisted
at Amphissa and Theagenes was placed in command
of the phalanx, a man of ill luck and, like the defendant
here, open to bribes. Then, because of the three men
whom I have mentioned, the whole city was destroyed
and blotted from the face of Greece. Far from being
false it is only too true that leaders are responsible for
all the citizens' good fortunes and for the reverse.
Think again, this time of Athens, with the same
points in mind. Our city was great, renowned in
Greece, and worthy of our forbears, apart from the
well-known exploits of the past, at the time when
Conon triumphed, as our elders tell us, in the naval
battle at Cnidus; when Iphicrates destroyed the
Spartan company, when Chabrias defeated the
Spartan triremes at sea off Naxos, when Timotheüs

---

[a] Messenia was first conquered about the year 700 B.C.,
so that the figure 400th is a very rough estimate; 300th
would be nearer. *Cf.* Lycurg. *Leocr.* 62 and note.
[b] The three men mentioned in this sentence were Theban
generals at the battle of Chaeronea.

---

² μόραν Scaliger : μοῖραν codd.

ὅτε Τιμόθεος τὴν ἐν Κερκύρᾳ ναυμαχίαν ἐνίκησε.
76 τότε, ὦ Ἀθηναῖοι, τότε οἱ μὲν πρότερον ὄντες
λαμπροὶ διὰ τοὺς ἡγεμόνας Λακεδαιμόνιοι καὶ
ὑπὸ τοῖς ἐκείνων ἤθεσι τραφέντες ταπεινοὶ πρὸς
τὴν πόλιν ἡμῶν ἦκον, δεόμενοι τῆς παρὰ τῶν προγόνων ἡμῶν σωτηρίας, ὁ δὲ καταλυθεὶς ὑπ' ἐκείνων
[100] δῆμος διὰ τοὺς τότε γενομένους παρ' ἡμῖν¹ συμβούλους πάλιν ἡγεμὼν ἦν τῶν Ἑλλήνων, δικαίως
οἶμαι, στρατηγῶν μὲν τοιούτων τετυχηκὼς οἵων
εἶπον ἀρτίως, συμβούλους δ' ἔχων Ἀρχῖνον καὶ
Κέφαλον τὸν Κολλυτέα. μία γὰρ αὕτη σωτηρία
καὶ πόλεως καὶ ἔθνους ἐστί, τὸ προστατῶν ἀνδρῶν
77 ἀγαθῶν καὶ συμβούλων σπουδαίων τυχεῖν. διόπερ,
ὦ Ἀθηναῖοι, δεῖ ταῦθ' ὑμᾶς ὁρῶντας καὶ λογιζο-
μένους μὴ μὰ Δία τὸν πλείω χρόνον τῆς Δημοσθένους δωροδοκίας καὶ ἀτυχίας κοινωνεῖν, μηδ' ἐν
τούτῳ τὰς ἐλπίδας τῆς σωτηρίας ἔχειν, μηδ' οἴεσθαι
ἀπορήσειν ἀνδρῶν ἀγαθῶν καὶ συμβούλων σπουδαίων, ἀλλὰ τὴν τῶν προγόνων λαβόντας ὀργὴν τὸν
ἐπ' αὐτοφώρῳ κλέπτην εἰλημμένον καὶ προδότην,
τὸν οὐκ ἀπεχόμενον τῶν εἰς τὴν πόλιν ἀφικνου-
μένων χρημάτων, τὸν εἰς τὰς δεινοτάτας ἀτυχίας
ἐμβεβληκότα τὴν πόλιν, τὸν τῆς Ἑλλάδος ἀλιτήριον
ἀποκτείναντας² ἐξόριστον ἐκ τῆς πόλεως ποιῆσαι,
καὶ μεταβαλέσθαι³ τὴν τῆς πόλεως τύχην ἐᾶσαι,
καὶ προσδοκῆσαι τούτων γενομένων βέλτιον πρά-
ξειν.

¹ ἡμῖν Sauppe : ὑμῖν codd.

won the sea battle off Corcyra.^a That was the time, Athenians, when the Spartans, once famous through the leaders in whose ways they had been schooled, came humbly to our city and begged our ancestors to save them ; and the democracy which they had overthrown was made by the counsellors, whom we then had, the first power in Greece again : deservedly, in my belief ; for they had found generals of the type I have just mentioned and had as advisers Archinus and Cephalus of Collytus.^b For the only salvation of a city or a nation is to find brave men to lead it and wise counsellors. It follows then, Athenians, that if you fully recognize this fact you should not surely be parties in future to Demosthenes' corruption and ill-luck or rest your hopes of security on him ; you need not think that you will lack brave men or wise advisers. Let the anger of your forefathers be yours. Put to death this robber taken in the act, this traitor who does not withhold his hands from the gold brought into Athens but has cast the city into the direst misfortunes, this arch-criminal of Greece. Have his body cast beyond the city's borders, give her fortunes a chance to mend, and then, with this accomplished, expect a happier lot.

^a For the exploits of Conon and Timotheüs compare § 14 and note. In 391 B.C. the Athenian general Iphicrates, on going to the relief of Corinth, surprised and almost annihilated a Spartan company. The defeat of the Spartan fleet by Chabrias took place in 376 and won supremacy in the Aegean for Athens for over fifty years (Xen. *Hell.* v. 4. 61 ; Dem. xx. 77).

^b Like Cephalus, who is mentioned above (§ 38), Archinus took a leading part in the overthrow of the Thirty in 403.

² Post ἀποκτείναντας add. δεῖ N A pr., del. A corr. ras.
³ μεταβαλέσθαι A corr.² : μεταβάλλεσθαι A pr. N.

78 Ἀκούσατε, ὦ Ἀθηναῖοι, κἀκείνου τοῦ ψηφίσματος τοῦ γραφέντος ὑπὸ Δημοσθένους, ὃ¹ τε-
ταραγμένης τῆς πόλεως μετὰ τὴν ἐν Χαιρωνείᾳ
μάχην ἔγραψεν ὁ δημοτικὸς οὗτος, καὶ τῆς μαντείας
τῆς ἐλθούσης ἐκ Δωδώνης παρὰ τοῦ Διὸς τοῦ
Δωδωναίου· σαφῶς γὰρ ὑμῖν πάλαι προείρηκε
φυλάττεσθαι τοὺς ἡγεμόνας καὶ τοὺς συμβούλους.
λέγε τὴν μαντείαν πρῶτον.

MANTEIA

79 λέγε δὴ τὸ καλὸν ψήφισμα τούτου.

ΨΗΦΙΣΜΑΤΟΣ ΜΕΡΟΣ

δημοτικός γ᾽ ὁ διατάττων ἑαυτὸν μέν, ἐπειδὴ ἀνδρεῖος καὶ εὔψυχός ἐστιν, ἐν τοῖς ὅπλοις μένειν,
οὓς δ᾽ ἂν οὗτος² ἀποδοκιμάσῃ τῶν πολιτῶν, ἐπὶ τὰ
ἔργα ἀπιέναι, καὶ ἐάν τι ἄλλο τούτῳ δόξῃ ἐπιτή-
δειον εἶναι, τοῦτο ποιεῖν. λέγε τὰ λοιπά.

ΤΟ ΛΟΙΠΟΝ ΤΟΥ ΨΗΦΙΣΜΑΤΟΣ

80 ἀκούετε, ἄνδρες δικασταί. ἀπιέναι φησὶ τὸ ψή-
φισμα³ τὰς ᾑρημένας⁴ πρεσβείας. ἐπειδὴ ⟨γὰρ⟩⁵
ἤκουσε μετὰ τὴν μάχην τὴν ἐν Χαιρωνείᾳ Φίλιππον
εἰς τὴν χώραν ἡμῶν μέλλειν εἰσβάλλειν, αὐτὸς ἑαυτὸν πρεσβευτὴν κατασκευάσας, ἵν᾽ ἐκ τῆς πόλεως
ἀποδραίη, ⟨ᾤχετο⟩⁶ συσκευασάμενος ⟨ἐκ⟩⁷ τῆς
διοικήσεως ὀκτὼ τάλαντα, οὐδὲν φροντίσας τῆς

---

¹ ὃ A corr. ras. : ὅτ. N pr. : ὅτε A pr. N corr.
² οὗτος N : αὐτὸς A.   ³ τὸ ψήφισμα] del. Bekker.
⁴ ᾑρημένας Wolf : εἰρημένας codd.
⁵ γὰρ add. Reiske.
⁶ ᾤχετο hic add. Blass (iam infra post τάλαντα suppleverat
Maetzner).   ⁷ ἐκ add. Wurm.

I want you also, Athenians, to hear that other decree moved by Demosthenes,[a] the decree which this democratic statesman proposed when the city was in disorder after the battle of Chaeronea, and also the oracle sent from Dodona from Dodonian Zeus; for it has long been warning you clearly to beware of your leaders and advisers. Read the oracle first.

Oracle

Read that splendid decree of his.

Part of the Decree

A fine democrat indeed who arranges for himself, being a brave and courageous man, to remain in arms, while he orders the citizens whom he rejects for service to go off to their work or to do anything else he thinks is called for. Read the rest.

Rest of the Decree

Listen to that, gentlemen of the jury. The decree says that the chosen embassies shall set out. When, after the battle of Chaeronea, he heard that Philip intended to invade our country he appointed himself an envoy, so as to escape from the city, and went off,[b] after scraping together eight talents from the treasury, without a thought about the plight we were

---

[a] One of the several decrees relating to defence proposed by Demosthenes after Chaeronea; the oracle is mentioned in the speech on the False Embassy (Dem. xix. 297 *sq.*).

[b] Dinarchus is perhaps referring to the fact that after Chaeronea Demosthenes was appointed a commissioner for corn (σιτώνης) and went abroad to procure it (*cf.* Dem. xviii. 248). Alternatively when appeals for help were made by Athens to some of the islands (*cf.* Lycurg. *Leocr.* 42) Demosthenes may have served as an envoy.

τότε παρούσης ἀπορίας, ἡνίχ᾽ οἱ ἄλλοι πάντες ἐκ
τῶν ἰδίων ἐπεδίδοσαν εἰς τὴν ὑμετέραν σωτη-
81 ρίαν. τοιοῦτος ὑμῖν ὁ σύμβουλος, καὶ δύο ταύτας
μόνας ἐν τῷ βίῳ[1] Δημοσθένης πεποίηται ἀπο-
δημίας, μετὰ τὴν μάχην ὅτ᾽ ἀπεδίδρασκεν ἐκ τῆς
πόλεως, καὶ νῦν εἰς Ὀλυμπίαν, ἐπεὶ Νικάνορι διὰ
τῆς ἀρχεθεωρίας ἐντυχεῖν ἐβούλετο. ἄξιόν γε
τούτῳ παρακαταθέσθαι τὴν πόλιν καὶ ἐπιτρέψαι[2]
κινδυνεύειν μέλλοντας, ὃς ὅτε μὲν ἔδει μάχεσθαι
μετὰ τῶν ἄλλων τοῖς πολεμίοις, λιπὼν τὴν τάξιν
ᾤχετο ἀπιὼν οἴκαδε, ἐπειδὴ δὲ προσῆκεν οἴκοι
κινδυνεύειν μετὰ τῶν ἄλλων, πρεσβευτὴν αὐτὸς
αὑτὸν προβαλόμενος[3] ᾤχετο ἐκ τῆς πόλεως ἀπο-
82 δράς, ἐπειδὴ δὲ πρεσβεύειν ἔδει περὶ τῆς εἰρήνης,
οὐκ ἂν ἔφασκεν ἐκ τῆς πόλεως ἐξελθεῖν οὐδὲ τὸν
ἕτερον πόδα, ἐπειδὴ δὲ τοὺς φυγάδας Ἀλέξανδρον
ἔφασαν κατάγειν καὶ Νικάνωρ εἰς Ὀλυμπίαν ἧκεν,
ἀρχεθεωρὸν αὑτὸν ἐπέδωκε[4] τῇ βουλῇ. τοιοῦτος
οὗτος, ἐν μὲν ταῖς παρατάξεσιν οἰκουρός, ἐν δὲ τοῖς
οἴκοι μένουσι πρεσβευτής, ἐν δὲ τοῖς πρεσβευταῖς
δραπέτης ἐστίν.

Λέγε δὴ[5] . . . καὶ τὸ περὶ ζητήσεως τῶν χρη-

---

[1] ἐν τῷ βίῳ] delendum ci. Maetzner, qui post μάχην interpunxit.
[2] ἐπιτρέψαι A : ἐπιτρέψειν N.
[3] προβαλόμενος A corr. ras. : προβαλόμενος A pr. N.
[4] ἐπέδωκε Scaliger : ἀπέδωκε codd.
[5] Post δὴ lacunam susp. Maetzner, infra post ὑμῶν Weil.

---

[a] This statement is wholly incorrect and Dinarchus appears
to be contradicting himself, since in § 12 of this speech he
does not attempt to refute Demosthenes' claim to have
served on many embassies. By excluding the words " in his
life " and placing a colon after " battle " Maetzner would

in, at a time when everyone else was contributing from his own money to ensure your protection. That is the character of your adviser. Demosthenes has made only these two journeys abroad in his life [a] : one after the battle when he ran away from the city, and another just recently to Olympia when he wanted to use the presidency of the sacred embassy as a means of meeting Nicanor.[b] A right thing indeed to entrust the city to this man's charge, when danger confronts us ! When it was time to fight against the enemy, side by side with his fellows, he left his post and made for home ; yet when he should have stayed at home to face danger with them, he offered himself as an envoy and ran away and left the city. When ambassadors were needed for the peace he said he would not move a foot to leave the city ; yet when it was reported that Alexander was restoring the exiles and Nicanor came to Olympia he offered himself to the council as president of the sacred embassy. These are the parts he plays : on the field of battle he is a stay-at-home, when others stay at home he is an ambassador, among ambassadors he is a runaway.

Now read the . . .[c] and the decree relating to the

---

alter the sense to : " Demosthenes has made only these two journeys abroad since the battle of Chaeronea."

[b] Demosthenes was the chief Athenian religious envoy at the Olympic games in 324 B.C. when Nicanor presented Alexander's decree demanding that exiles should be allowed to return to all Greek cities except Thebes. *Cf.* Diodor. xviii. 8 ; Hyp. v., col. 18.

[c] That some words have dropped out of the text here is evident from the fact that two decrees are to be read and compared ; moreover the executions mentioned in § 83 could have no connexion with the decree relating to the money of Harpalus, since in this case Demosthenes himself was the first to be tried (§ 106),

μάτων ψήφισμα, ἃ[1] ἔγραψε Δημοσθένης τῇ ἐξ
Ἀρείου πάγου βουλῇ περὶ αὑτοῦ τε καὶ ὑμῶν, ἵνα
παρ᾽ ἄλληλα θεωρήσαντες εἰδῆτε τὴν Δημοσθένους
ἀπόνοιαν.

ΨΗΦΙΣΜΑ

83 ἔγραψας σὺ τοῦτο, Δημόσθενες; ἔγραψας· οὐκ
ἔστιν ἀντειπεῖν. ἐγένετο ἡ βουλὴ κυρία σοῦ προστάξαντος; ἐγένετο. τεθνᾶσι τῶν πολιτῶν ἄνδρες;
τεθνᾶσι. κύριον ἦν τὸ σὸν ψήφισμα κατ᾽ ἐκείνων;
ἀδύνατον ἀντειπεῖν.

Λέγε δὴ πάλιν ὃ Δημοσθένης κατὰ Δημοσθένους
ἔγραψε. προσέχετε, ὦ ἄνδρες.

ΨΗΦΙΣΜΑ

84 ἡ βουλὴ εὕρηκε Δημοσθένην. τί δεῖ πολλῶν λόγων;
ἀποπέφαγκεν, ὦ Ἀθηναῖοι. τὸ μὲν τοίνυν δίκαιον
[101] ἦν ὑφ᾽ ἑαυτοῦ κεκριμένον εὐθὺς ἀποθνῄσκειν· ἐπειδὴ δ᾽ εἰς τὰς ὑμετέρας ἥκει χεῖρας τῶν[2] ὑπὲρ τοῦ
δήμου συνειλεγμένων καὶ τῶν ὀμωμοκότων[2] πείσεσθαι[3] τοῖς νόμοις καὶ τοῖς τοῦ δήμου ψηφίσμασι,
τί ποιήσετε; προήσεσθε τὴν πρὸς τοὺς θεοὺς εὐσέ-
βειαν καὶ τὰ παρὰ πᾶσιν ἀνθρώποις δίκαια νομι-
85 ζόμενα; μή, ὦ Ἀθηναῖοι, μή· αἰσχρὸν γὰρ καὶ
δεινόν, ἑτέρους μὲν ὑπὸ τῶν Δημοσθένους ψηφισμάτων, οὐδὲν ὄντας τούτου χείρους οὐδὲ τοσαῦτ᾽
ἠδικηκότας ὅσαπερ οὗτος, ἀπολωλέναι, τουτονὶ δὲ
καταφρονοῦντα ὑμῶν καὶ τῶν νόμων ἀτιμώρητον
ἐν τῇ πόλει περιιέναι, αὐτὸν ὑφ᾽ ἑαυτοῦ καὶ τῶν

¹ ἃ Maetzner : ὃ codd.

234

inquiry over the money proposed by Demosthenes for the Areopagus and affecting both himself and you. I want you by comparing them together to realize that he is demented.

Decree

Did you propose this, Demosthenes ? You did ; you cannot deny it. Was the council given authority on your motion ? It was. Have some of the citizens been executed ? They have. Did your decree have power over them ? You cannot deny that it did.

Read the decree again which Demosthenes proposed against Demosthenes. Let me have your attention, gentlemen.

Decree

The council has found Demosthenes guilty. Need we enlarge on this ? It has made its report on him, Athenians. Justice demanded that, having been self-condemned, he should immediately be put to death. But now that he has fallen into the hands of you who have been assembled by the people and have sworn to obey the laws and the people's decrees, what will you do ? Will you ignore the claims of piety towards the gods and the justice recognized by the world ? No, Athenians, do not do so. It would be an utter disgrace if, when others no worse, and even less guilty, than Demosthenes have been destroyed by his decrees, he, with his contempt for you and the laws, should be at large unpunished in the city, when by his own motion and the decrees which he proposed

---

² τῶν . . . συνειλεγμένων . . . τῶν ὀμωμοκότων Stephanus (συνειλεγμένων iam Ald.): τοὺς . . . συνειλεγμένους . . . τοὺς ὀμωμοκότας codd.   ³ πείσεσθαι Baiter: πείθεσθαι codd.

ψηφισμάτων ὧν ἔγραψεν ἑαλωκότα. ταὐτὸ¹ συνέδριον, ὦ Ἀθηναῖοι, καὶ ὁ αὐτὸς τόπος, καὶ ταὐτὰ¹
86 δίκαια. ὁ αὐτὸς ῥήτωρ ἐκείνοις τ' αἴτιος ἐγένετο
τῶν συμβάντων κακῶν καὶ αὑτῷ τῶν νῦν συμβη-
σομένων. ἐπέτρεψεν [ὁ]² αὐτὸς οὗτος ἐν τῷ δήμῳ
τῷ συνεδρίῳ τούτῳ κρῖναι περὶ αὐτοῦ, μάρτυρας
ὑμᾶς πεποιημένος. ἔθετο συνθήκας μετὰ τοῦ δήμου, γράψας τὸ ψήφισμα καθ' ἑαυτοῦ παρὰ τὴν
μητέρα³ τῶν θεῶν, ἣ πάντων τῶν ἐν τοῖς γράμμασι
δικαίων φύλαξ τῇ πόλει καθέστηκε. διὸ καὶ οὐχ
ὅσιον ὑμῖν ἐστι ταύτας ἀκύρους ποιεῖν, οὐδὲ τοὺς
θεοὺς ὀμωμοκόσι περὶ ταύτης τῆς κρίσεως ταῖς
αὐτῶν τῶν θεῶν πράξεσιν ἐναντίαν τὴν ψῆφον
87 ἐνεγκεῖν. κρίσεως⁴ Ποσειδῶν ἀποτυχὼν τῆς⁵ ὑπὲρ
Ἁλιρροθίου πρὸς Ἄρη γενομένης⁵ ἐνέμεινεν· ⟨ἐνέ-
μειναν⟩⁶ αὐταὶ αἱ σεμναὶ θεαὶ τῇ πρὸς Ὀρέστην
ἐν τούτῳ τῷ συνεδρίῳ κρίσει γενομένῃ καὶ τῇ
τούτου ἀληθείᾳ συνοίκους ἑαυτὰς εἰς τὸν λοιπὸν
χρόνον κατέστησαν. ὑμεῖς δὲ τί ποιήσετε οἱ πάντων
εἶναι φάσκοντες εὐσεβέστατοι;⁷ τὴν τοῦ συνεδρίου
γνώμην⁸ ἄκυρον καταστήσετε τῇ Δημοσθένους ἐπ-
ακολουθήσαντες πονηρίᾳ; οὐκ, ἐὰν σωφρονῆτε, ὦ

<hr/>

¹ ταὐτὸ . . ταὐτὰ Dobree : τουτὶ τὸ . . . ταυτὰ τὰ
codd.
² ὁ del. Kleyn.
³ τὴν μητέρα] τῇ μητρὶ Reiske.
⁴ κρίσεως Blass : κρίσει codd.
⁵ τῆς . . . γενομένης N A pr. ; τοῖς . . . γενομένοις A
corr.² : τῇ γενομένῃ Bekker.
236

he has been convicted. The same council, Athenians, the same place, the same rights have been in question. The same orator was responsible for the misfortunes which overtook them and those which will soon overtake him. He himself in the Assembly instructed this council to judge his case, after calling on you as his witnesses. He made an agreement with the people and proposed the decree against himself, to be kept by the mother of the gods,[a] who is the city's guardian of all written contracts. It would thus be impious for you to invalidate this or, after swearing by the gods in the present trial, to give a vote which did not conform with the actions of the gods themselves. When Posidon lost his suit against Ares over Halirrothius he abode by the decision.[b] The awful goddesses too, in their case against Orestes,[c] abode by the judgement of this council, associating themselves for the future with its reputation for truth. How will you act with your claim to unrivalled piety? Will you annul the decision of the council and follow the bad example of Demosthenes? You will not, Athenians, if you

---

[a] Dinarchus is alluding to the Metroön, in which the state archives were kept. *Cf.* Lycurg. *Leocr.* 66 and note.

[b] According to tradition, Halirrothius, son of Posidon, was killed by Ares for trying to seduce his daughter Alcippe. Posidon accused Ares before the Areopagus but failed to secure his conviction. *Cf.* Apollodorus iii. 14. 2.

[c] Orestes, pursued by the Furies, was said to have been given protection by Athena, who allowed the Areopagus to try his case and herself gave the casting vote which acquitted him. *Cf.* Aeschylus, *Eum.* 443 *sq.* ; Pausanias i. 28. 5.

---

[6] ἐνέμειναν hic add. Sauppe, infra post γενομένη Reiske.
[7] εὐσεβέστατοι N : εὐσεβέστεροι A.
[8] γνώμην A : γνῶσιν N.

88 Ἀθηναῖοι· οὐ γὰρ περὶ μικρῶν οὐδὲ τῶν τυχόντων
ἐν τῇ τήμερον ἡμέρᾳ δικάζετε, ἀλλὰ περὶ σωτηρίας
τῆς πόλεως ἁπάσης καὶ πρὸς τούτοις περὶ δωροδοκίας, ἔθους πονηροῦ καὶ πράγματος ἀλυσιτελοῦς
ὑμῖν καὶ πάντας ἀνθρώπους ἀπολωλεκότος. ⟨δ⟩[1]
εἰ μέν, καθ᾽ ὅσον ἐστὲ δυνατοί, ἐκβαλεῖτ᾽ ἐκ τῆς
πόλεως καὶ παύσετε τοὺς ῥᾳδίως καθ᾽ ὑμῶν χρήματα λαμβάνοντας, σωθησόμεθα θεῶν βουλομένων·
εἰ δ᾽ ἐπιτρέψετε τοῖς ῥήτορσι πωλεῖν ὑμᾶς αὐτούς,
περιόψεσθε τὴν πόλιν ἀνατραπεῖσαν ὑπὸ τούτων.

89 Ἔγραψεν αὐτὸς ἐν τῷ δήμῳ Δημοσθένης, ὡς
δηλονότι δικαίου τοῦ πράγματος ὄντος, φυλάττειν
Ἀλεξάνδρῳ τὰ εἰς τὴν Ἀττικὴν ἀφικόμενα μετὰ
Ἁρπάλου χρήματα. οὕτως οὖν, ὦ ἄριστε, εἰπέ
μοι, φυλάξομεν,[2] ἐὰν σὺ μὲν εἴκοσι τάλαντα λαβὼν
ἔχῃς ἰδίᾳ,[3] ἕτερος δὲ πεντεκαίδεκα, Δημάδης δ᾽
ἑξακισχιλίους χρυσοῦ στατῆρας, ἕτεροι δ᾽ ὅσα δή
ποτε ἀποπεφασμένοι εἰσί; τέτταρα[4] γὰρ τάλαντ᾽
ἐστὶ καὶ ἑξήκοντα ἤδη εὑρημένα, ὧν οἴεσθε τὴν
90 αἰτίαν τούτοις δεῖν[5] ἀναθεῖναι. καὶ πότερα κάλλιόν
ἐστι, πρὸς δὲ δικαιότερον, ἅπαντ᾽ ἐν τῷ κοινῷ
φυλάττεσθαι, ἕως ἄν τι δίκαιον ὁ δῆμος βουλεύ-
σηται, ἢ τοὺς ῥήτορας καὶ τῶν στρατηγῶν ἐνίους
διηρπακότας ἔχειν; ἐγὼ μὲν γὰρ οἶμαι τὸ μὲν ἐν
τῷ κοινῷ φυλάττειν παρὰ πάντων ὁμολογούμενον
εἶναι δίκαιον, τὸ δὲ τούτους ἔχειν μηδέν᾽ ἂν εἰπεῖν
ὡς ἔστι καλῶς ἔχον.

91 Πολλοὺς οὗτος εἴρηκε[6] καὶ παντοδαποὺς λόγους,

---

[1] δ add. Reiske.   [2] φυλάξομεν A : φυλάξωμεν N.
[3] ἰδίᾳ Wurm : ἴδια codd.
[4] τέτταρα A corr.[2] : τετρακόσια A pr. N : διακόσια Thalheim.

238

remain in your senses. This is no small or incidental matter that you are deciding to-day; the question at issue is the safety of the whole city and also bribery, an evil habit and a practice which is harmful to you and has always brought men to ruin. If you do everything in your power to rid the city of this vice and to suppress those who gladly take bribes against you, we shall be saved, with Heaven's consent. But if you allow the orators to sell you, you will stand by and see them wreck the city.

Demosthenes himself proposed in the Assembly, clearly implying that it was a just step to take, that we should keep for Alexander the money brought into Attica with Harpalus.[a] Tell me, sir: are we going to keep it under present conditions, when you have taken twenty talents for personal use, someone else fifteen, Demades six thousand gold staters, and the others the various sums that have been credited to them? For sixty-four talents have already been traced, for which, you must conclude, gentlemen, that these men are to be held responsible. Which is the more honourable alternative, which the more just: that all the money should be kept in the treasury until the people has reached some fair decision, or that the orators and certain of the generals should seize and keep it? Personally I think that to keep it in the treasury is the course which all would admit to be just, while no one would consider it fair for these men to retain it.

The statements made by the defendant, gentlemen,

---

[a] See § 68 and note.

[5] τούτοις δεῖν (δεῖν post οἴεσθε iam Reiske) Blass : τουτοισὶν codd.

[6] εἴρηκε Dobree : ἐρεῖ codd., ret. Wurm.

ὦ ἄνδρες, καὶ οὐδεπώποτε[1] τοὺς αὐτούς. ὁρᾷ γὰρ
ὑμᾶς τὸν ἅπαντα χρόνον ἐλπίσι κεναῖς καὶ ψευδέσι
λόγοις ἐξηπατημένους ὑφ᾽ ἑαυτοῦ, καὶ μέχρι[2] ἂν τούτου μνημονεύοντας τὰς ὑποσχέσεις μέχρι[2] ἂν ῥη-
θῶσιν. εἰ μὲν οὖν ἔτι δεῖ τὴν πόλιν τῆς Δημοσθένους πονηρίας καὶ ἀτυχίας ἀπολαύειν, ἵνα πλείω[3]
κακοδαιμονῶμεν— οὐ[4] γὰρ ἔχω τί ἄλλο εἴπω—
92 στερκτέον ⟨ἂν⟩[5] εἴη τοῖς συμβαίνουσιν· εἰ δέ τι[6]
κηδόμεθα τῆς πατρίδος καὶ τοὺς πονηροὺς καὶ
δωροδόκους μισοῦμεν καὶ μετοιωνίσασθαι τὴν τύχην
καὶ μεταλλάξασθαι βουλόμεθα, οὐ προετέον[7] ἐστὶν
[102] ὑμᾶς αὐτούς, ὦ Ἀθηναῖοι, ταῖς τοῦ μιαροῦ καὶ
γόητος τούτου δεήσεσιν, οὐδὲ προσδεκτέον τοὺς
οἴκτους καὶ τοὺς φενακισμοὺς ⟨τοὺς⟩[8] τούτου·
ἱκανὴν γὰρ εἰλήφατε πεῖραν αὐτοῦ καὶ τῶν ἔργων
93 καὶ τῶν λόγων καὶ τῆς τύχης. τίς οὕτως εὔελπις
ὑμῶν ἐστιν, ὦ Ἀθηναῖοι, τίς οὕτως ἀλόγιστος, τίς
τῶν προγεγενημένων καὶ νῦν ἐνεστηκότων πραγμάτων ἄπειρος, ὅστις[9] ἐλπίζει τὸν ἐκ τοσαύτης
εὐδαιμονίας εἰς τοσαύτην ἀδοξίαν καταστήσαντα
τὴν πόλιν, δι᾽ ἡντιναδήποτε αἰτίαν ἢ τύχην—ἐῶ γὰρ
τοῦτο—νῦν,[10] ἐπειδὴ πρὸς ταῖς ἄλλαις ἀπορίαις καὶ
τοῖς περιεστηκόσιν ἡμᾶς κινδύνοις καὶ ἡ τῶν ἐξ
αὐτῆς τῆς πόλεως δωροδοκία προσγέγονε, καὶ περὶ
αἰσχρᾶς αἰτίας κοινῇ πάντες ἀγωνιζόμεθα καὶ περὶ
τοῦ μὴ δοκεῖν τὰ ἰδίᾳ[11] παρά τισιν ὄντα χρήματα
κοινῇ τὸν δῆμον ἔχειν, τηνικαῦτα συμβουλεύοντα
94 καὶ διοικοῦντα τοῦτον σώσειν ὑμᾶς; ἐῶ γὰρ τἆλλα
ὅσα μεταβαλλόμενος ἐν τοῖς πράγμασι καὶ δημη-

---

[1] οὐδεπώποτε] οὐδέποτε Wurm.
[2] μέχρι Blass : μέχρις codd.
[3] πλείω N : πλέον A.   [4] οὐ N : οὐδὲ A.

240

have been numerous and very varied but never con-
sistent. For he realizes that all along you have been
cheated by him with empty hopes and lying assertions and that you remember his promises only so long
as they are being uttered. If then the city must go
on enjoying the fruits of Demosthenes' wickedness
and ill-fortune, that we may still be plagued by an
evil genius,—I can find no other word for it,—we
should acquiesce in the present state of affairs. But
if we have any regard for our country, if we hate
wicked and corrupt men and want our fortune to
change for the better, you must not surrender yourselves, Athenians, to the prayers of this accursed
juggler or lend an ear to his laments and quackeries.
You have had enough experience of him, his speeches,
his actions, and his luck. Which of you is so hopeful,
Athenians, or so irrational, which of you is so unversed
in past or present history, as to expect that a man
who reduced the city, through whatever fault or
fortune,—I am not concerned with that,—from such
great prosperity to such utter disgrace, will save us
now by serving as a counsellor and administrator ?
For besides the other difficulties and dangers which
beset us we have now corruption also, of men right
in the city, and are one and all striving to clear ourselves of a shameful charge, lest the people be
thought to hold in their own name the money which
certain individuals are keeping for themselves. I am
not citing other instances of his continual change of

---

⁵ ἄν add. Bekker.   ⁶ δέ τι Baiter : δ' ἔτι codd.
          ⁷ προετέον Wolf : προσεκτέον codd.
⁸ τοὺς add. Baiter et Sauppe.   ⁹ ὅστις Ald. : τίς codd.
          ¹⁰ τοῦτο—νῦν, Gebauer : τοῦτο νῦν—codd.
          ¹¹ ἰδίᾳ Bekker : ἰδία A corr.² : ἴδια A pr. N.

γορῶν οὐδὲν ὑγιὲς διατετέλεκε,[1] καὶ τοτὲ μὲν
γράφων καὶ ἀπαγορεύων μηδένα νομίζειν ἄλλον
θεὸν ἢ τοὺς παραδεδομένους, τοτὲ δὲ λέγων ὡς οὐ
δεῖ τὸν δῆμον ἀμφισβητεῖν τῶν ἐν τῷ[2] οὐρανῷ
τιμῶν Ἀλεξάνδρῳ, ὅταν δὲ μέλλῃ κριθήσεσθαι
παρ' ὑμῖν, Καλλιμέδοντα εἰσαγγέλλων συνιέναι ἐν
Μεγάροις τοῖς φυγάσιν ἐπὶ καταλύσει τοῦ δήμου,
καὶ ταύτην τὴν εἰσαγγελίαν εὐθὺς παραχρῆμα ἀν-
95 αιρούμενος, ἐν δὲ τῇ ἐκκλησίᾳ ταύτῃ τῇ πρώτῃ
γεγενημένῃ προσάγων καὶ κατασκευάζων ψευδῆ
μηνυτὴν ὡς ἐπιβουλευομένων τῶν νεωρίων, καὶ
περὶ τούτων γράφων μὲν οὐδέν, αἰτίας δ' ἕνεκα
τοῦ παρόντος ἀγῶνος παρασκευάζων· τούτων γὰρ
ἁπάντων ὑμεῖς τούτῳ μάρτυρές ἐστε. γόης οὗτος,
ἄνδρες Ἀθηναῖοι, καὶ μιαρὸς ἄνθρωπός ἐστι, καὶ
οὔτε τῷ γένει τῆς πόλεως πολίτης οὔτε τοῖς πε-
96 πολιτευμένοις αὐτῷ καὶ πεπραγμένοις· ποῖαι γὰρ
τριήρεις εἰσὶ κατεσκευασμέναι διὰ τοῦτον, ὥσπερ
ἐπὶ Εὐβούλου, τῇ πόλει; ἢ ποῖοι νεώσοικοι τούτου
πολιτευομένου γεγόνασι; πότε οὗτος ἢ διὰ ψηφίσματος ἢ νόμου ἐπηνώρθωσε τὸ ἱππικόν; τίνα
κατεσκεύασε δύναμιν τοιούτων καιρῶν παραγενομένων μετὰ τὴν ἐν Χαιρωνείᾳ μάχην, ἢ πεζὴν εἰς
ναυτικήν; τίς ἀνενήνεκται[3] τῇ θεῷ κόσμος εἰς
ἀκρόπολιν ὑπὸ τούτου; τί κατεσκεύακεν οἰκοδό-
μημα Δημοσθένης ἐν τῷ ἐμπορίῳ τῷ ὑμετέρῳ ἢ

---

[1] διατετέλεκε N : τετέλεκε A.
[2] τῷ add. N.
[3] ἀνενήνεκται Bekker : ἀνήνεκται codd.

---

[a] Demosthenes had merely said : " Let him be the son of
Zeus and Posidon too if he likes." *Cf.* Hyp. v., col. 31.
[b] Athens, unlike most Greek cities, refused to obey Alex-

policy or of the pernicious speeches which he has consistently made. At one time he made a proposal forbidding anyone to believe in any but the accepted gods and at another said that the people must not question the grant of divine honours to Alexander [a]; and again when he was on the point of being tried before you, he impeached Callimedon for consorting with the exiles [b] in Megara with intent to overthrow the democracy, and directly after countermanded the impeachment and brought forward at the recent sitting of the Assembly a false witness whom he had primed to say that there was a plot afoot threatening the docks. In all this he offered no proposals but simply furnished us with charges for the present trial, since on all these points you are witnesses against him. This man is a juggler, Athenians, and a black-guard, not entitled to be a citizen of Athens, either by virtue of his birth or of his political record. Where are the triremes which Demosthenes, like Eubulus [c] in his time, has supplied to the city ? Where are the dockyards built under his administration ? When did he improve the cavalry either by decree or law ? Despite such opportunities as were offered after the battle of Chaeronea, did he raise a single force either for land or sea ? What ornament for the goddess has he carried up to the Acropolis ? What building has Demosthenes put up, either in your exchange, or in

ander's order for the restoration of exiles (*cf.* note on § 81). Callimedon, a politician with pro-Macedonian sympathies, nicknamed the Crab, is mentioned several times by Plutarch (*e.g.* Plut. *Dem.* 27).

[c] For the confidence inspired by Eubulus, son of Spin-tharus, who controlled Athenian finances from 354 to 350 B.C., and perhaps for a further period also, compare Aeschin. iii. 25.

ἐν τῷ ἄστει ἢ ἄλλοθί που τῆς χώρας; οὐδεὶς ἂν[1]
97 οὐδαμοῦ δείξειεν. ἔπειτα τὸν ἐν μὲν[2] ταῖς πολεμι-
καῖς πράξεσιν ἄπιστον γεγενημένον, ἐν δὲ ταῖς κατὰ
τὴν πόλιν οἰκονομίαις ἄχρηστον, περιεορακότα δὲ
τοὺς ἀντιπολιτευομένους ἅπαντα διαπεπραγμένους[3]
ὅσ᾽ ἐβουλήθησαν, μεταβεβλημένον δ᾽ αὐτὸν καὶ
τὰς ὑπὲρ τοῦ δήμου πράξεις ἐγκαταλελοιπότα,
98 τοῦτον περιποιῆσαι βουλήσεσθε;[4] οὐκ, ἐὰν σωφρονῆτε καὶ καλῶς καὶ ὑπὲρ ὑμῶν αὐτῶν καὶ τῆς
πόλεως βουλεύησθε[5]· ἀλλὰ δέξεσθε[6] τὴν ἀγαθὴν
τύχην, ἢ τιμωρήσασθαι παρέδωκε τῶν ῥητόρων
τοὺς τὴν πόλιν διὰ τὴν αὐτῶν δωροδοκίαν ταπεινὴν
πεποιηκότας, καὶ φυλάξεσθε,[7] καθάπερ οἱ θεοὶ
προειρήκασιν ὑμῖν ἐν ταῖς μαντείαις πολλάκις, τοὺς
τοιούτους ἡγεμόνας καὶ συμβούλους. ἀκούσατε δ᾽
αὐτῆς τῆς μαντείας. λέγε τὴν μαντείαν.

MANTEIA

99 Πῶς οὖν μίαν γνώμην ἕξομεν, ὦ Ἀθηναῖοι;
πῶς ὁμονοήσομεν[8] ἅπαντες ὑπὲρ τῶν κοινῇ συμφερόντων, ὅταν οἱ ἡγεμόνες καὶ οἱ δημαγωγοὶ
χρήματα λαμβάνοντες προϊῶνται τὰ τῆς πατρίδος
συμφέροντα, καὶ ὑμεῖς μὲν καὶ ὁ δῆμος ἅπας κιν-
δυνεύῃ περὶ τοῦ ἐδάφους τοῦ τῆς πόλεως καὶ
τῶν ἱερῶν τῶν πατρῴων καὶ παίδων καὶ γυναικῶν,
οἱ δὲ διηλλαγμένοι πρὸς αὐτοὺς ἐν μὲν ταῖς ἐκ-
κλησίαις λοιδορῶνται καὶ προσκρούσιν ἀλλήλοις
ἐξεπίτηδες, ἰδίᾳ δὲ ταυτὰ[9] πράττωσιν ἐξαπατῶντες

---

[1] ἂν Stephanus : οὖν codd.   [2] ἐν μὲν Blass : μὲν ἐν codd.
[3] διαπεπραγμένους A corr.[2] : δὲ πεπραγμένους A pr. N.

244

the city, or anywhere else in the country ? Not a
man could point to one anywhere. Very well ; if
a person has proved untrustworthy in military matters
and useless in the business of the city, if he has idly
watched his opponents accomplish everything they
wished, changing his own position and neglecting to
pursue the people's interests, will you wish to preserve him ? Not if you are prudent and make the
right decision for yourselves and Athens. No ; you
will welcome the good fortune which gave up to you
for punishment those orators who, through their own
bribery, have humiliated the city, and will beware, as
the gods have often cautioned you in oracles, against
the leaders and counsellors of this type. Listen to the
oracle itself. Read the oracle.[a]

Oracle

How then shall we be of one mind, Athenians ?
How shall we agree upon the interests of the state
when our leaders and demagogues take bribes and
betray their country's interests, when you yourselves
and the whole people are in danger of losing the very
foundations of Athens, together with your fathers'
temples and your wives and children, while they have
conspired together, so that in the assemblies they
purposely abuse and lose their tempers with each
other, though in private they are united and thus

<hr />

[a] *Cf.* § 78.

4 βουλήσεσθε Dobree : βούλεσθε codd.
5 βουλεύησθε A corr. : βουλεύεσθε A pr. N.
6 δέξεσθε Dobree : δέξασθε codd.
7 φυλάξεσθε Dobree : φυλάξασθε codd.
8 ὁμονοήσομεν A : ὁμονοήσωμεν N.
9 ταὐτὰ Wolf : τὰ αὐτὰ N ; ταῦτα A.

100
[103] ὑμᾶς τοὺς ῥᾶστα πειθομένους τοῖς τούτων λόγοις;
τί γάρ ἐστι ῥήτορος δημοτικοῦ καὶ μισοῦντος τοὺς
κατὰ τῆς πόλεως λέγοντας καὶ γράφοντας; ἢ τί φασι
τοὺς πρὸ ὑμῶν[1] γεγενημένους, ὦ Δημόσθενες καὶ
Πολύευκτε, διατελεῖν ποιοῦντας; καὶ ταῦτ’ οὐδενὸς
δεινοῦ τότε τὴν πόλιν περιεστηκότος. οὐ κρίνειν
ἀλλήλους; οὐκ εἰσαγγέλλειν; οὐ γράφεσθαι παρανόμων; ἔστιν οὖν ὅ τι πεποιήκατε τούτων ὑμεῖς
οἱ φάσκοντες τοῦ δήμου κήδεσθαι καὶ τὴν σωτηρίαν
101 ὑμῖν ἐν τῇ τούτων εἶναι ψήφῳ; γέγραψαι ψήφισμα,
Δημόσθενες, πολλῶν ὄντων καὶ δεινῶν παρανόμων
ὧν Δημάδης γέγραφε; κεκώλυκας τινὰ πρᾶξιν ὧν
ἐκεῖνος προελόμενος κατὰ τοῦ δήμου πεπολίτευται;
οὐδ’ ἡντινοῦν. εἰσήγγελκας τὸν παρὰ τὰ[2] τοῦ δήμου
ψηφίσματα[2] καὶ τοὺς νόμους πολλὰ διαπεπραγμένον; οὐδεπώποτε,[3] ἀλλὰ περιεῖδες αὐτὸν ἐν τῇ ἀγορᾷ
χαλκοῦν σταθέντα καὶ τῆς ἐν[4] πρυτανείῳ σιτήσεως
κεκοινωνηκότα τοῖς Ἁρμοδίου καὶ Ἀριστογείτονος
102 ἀπογόνοις. ἔπειτα ποῦ τῆς εὐνοίας τῆς σῆς ὁ
δῆμος ἔλαβε πεῖραν, ἢ ποῦ τὴν τοῦ ῥήτορος βοήθειαν καὶ δύναμιν ἐξεταζομένην εἴδομεν; ἢ ἐνταῦθα φήσετ’ εἶναι δεινοί, εἰ παρακρούεσθε[5] τούτους
ἀεὶ λέγοντες ὡς οὐκ ἔστιν ἔξω τῆς πατρίδος ὑμῖν
ἐξελθεῖν, οὐκ ἔστιν ἄλλη καταφυγὴ χωρὶς τῆς ἡμετέρας εὐνοίας; φανεροὺς ἐχρῆν γεγενημένους ἀντι-
πράττοντας καὶ λόγῳ καὶ ἔργῳ τοῖς κατὰ τοῦ δήμου
γραφομένοις ψηφίσμασιν, οὕτω πείθειν τούτους λέ-

---

[1] ὑμῶν Reiske : ἡμῶν codd.
[2] τὰ . . . ψηφίσματα Reiske : τὸ . . . ψήφισμα codd.
[3] οὐδεπώποτε A : οὐδέποτε N.
[4] ἐν πρυτανείῳ A (cf. § 43) : ἐν τῷ πρυτανείῳ N.
[5] παρακρούεσθε Blass : παρακρούσησθε N : παρακρούσετε A :
παρακρούετε Dobree.

246

deceive you, who are so ready to lend an ear to what
they say. What is the duty of a democratic orator,
hating those who menace the city by speech or bill?
What are we told, Demosthenes and Polyeuctus,
about your predecessors? What did they always do,
even though no danger threatened the city at the
time? Did they not summon each other for trial;
bring in impeachments? Did they not indict each
other for illegal proposals? Have you, who profess
to have the people at heart, and maintain that your
safety rests upon this jury's vote, done a single one
of these things? Have you denounced a decree,
Demosthenes, despite the many outrageous and
illegal measures which Demades has proposed? Have
you prevented any political step among those which
he has taken on his own initiative against the interests of the state? Not a single one. Have you
impeached this man who has often acted contrary to
the decrees of the people and the laws? Never.
You allowed him to have his statue set up in bronze
in the market and to share entertainment in the
Prytaneum with the descendants of Harmodius and
Aristogiton.[a] In what way then did the people
sample your goodwill, where did we see proof of the
orator's protecting power? Or will you all maintain
that herein lie your powers: to cheat these men by
persisting that you cannot leave the country, that you
have no other refuge than our goodwill? You ought
first to have made it clear that in speech and action
you opposed the decrees brought forward against
the people's interests and then sought to convince

---

[a] These honours were paid to Demades about 335 B.C. in
recognition of his mission to Alexander after the destruction
of Thebes. *Cf.* Life of Demades.

γοντας ὡς οὐκ ἔστιν ὑμῖν οὐδεμία σωτηρία χωρὶς
103 τῆς παρὰ τοῦ δήμου βοηθείας. ὑμεῖς δ᾽ ἐν τοῖς
ἔξω τὰς ἐλπίδας ἔχετε, ἁμιλλώμενοι ταῖς κολα-
κείαις πρὸς τοὺς ὁμολογοῦντας ὑπὲρ Ἀλεξάνδρου
πράττειν καὶ δῶρ᾽ εἰληφέναι παρὰ τῶν αὐτῶν ὧνπερ
νῦν ἀποπέφαγκεν ὑμᾶς ἡ βουλή, καὶ σύ, πάντων
ἐναντίον τῶν Ἑλλήνων[1] διειλεγμένος Νικάνορι καὶ
κεχρηματικὼς [ἐν Ὀλυμπίᾳ][2] περὶ ὧν ἐβουλήθης,
ἐλεεινὸν νῦν σεαυτὸν κατασκευάζεις προδότης ὢν
καὶ δωροδόκος, ὡς ἐπιλησομένους[3] τούτους τῆς σῆς
πονηρίας, καὶ οὐ δώσων δίκην ὑπὲρ ὧν εἴληψαι
104 πεποιηκώς, τοσούτῳ τολμηρότερον Δημάδου, ὥσθ᾽
ὁ μὲν προειρηκὼς ἐν τῷ δήμῳ τὸν αὑτοῦ τρόπον
καὶ τὴν ἀπόνοιαν, καὶ ὁμολογῶν λαμβάνειν καὶ
λήψεσθαι, ὅμως οὐ τετόλμηκε τούτοις[4] δεῖξαι[5] τὸ
πρόσωπον, οὐδ᾽ ἐναντία τῇ τῆς βουλῆς ἀποφάσει
λέγειν ἠξίωσε—καίτοι οὐκ ἔγραψεν ἐκεῖνος περὶ
αὑτοῦ κυρίαν εἶναι τὴν βουλήν, οὐδὲ θάνατον ὡρί-
σατο, ἐὰν ἀποφανθῇ χρήματ᾽ εἰληφώς—σὺ δ᾽ οὕτω
σφόδρα πεπίστευκας τοῖς σεαυτοῦ λόγοις καὶ κατα-
πεφρόνηκας τῆς τούτων εὐηθείας, ὥστε πείσειν
οἴει τοὺς δικαστὰς ὡς μόνου σοῦ κατέψευσται τὸ
συνέδριον καὶ μόνον οὐκ εἰληφότα σε τὸ χρυσίον
ἀποπέφαγκεν. καὶ τίς ἂν ταῦτα πεισθείη;
105 Ὁρᾶτε, ὦ Ἀθηναῖοι, τί μέλλετε ποιεῖν. παρειλή-
φατε παρὰ τοῦ δήμου τὸ πρᾶγμα, τὸ γεγενημένον
εἰδότος,[6] τιμωρίας δ᾽ ἕνεκα τῆς κατὰ τῶν ἐνόχων

---

[1] ἐναντίον τῶν Ἑλλήνων Maetzner : ἐναντίων τῶν Ἑλλήνων N :
τῶν Ἑλλήνων ἐναντίον A.
[2] ἐν Ὀλυμπίᾳ del. Kleyn.
[3] ἐπιλησομένους Stephanus : ἐπιμελησομένους codd.
[4] τετόλμηκε τούτοις N : τετόλμηκεν αὐτοῖς A.

these men that your claim to have no means of safety but the assistance offered by the people was true. But you place your hopes abroad and compete in flattery with those who admit that they are serving Alexander and have taken bribes from the same sources as those from which you are reported by the council to have received them. And you, Demosthenes, after conversing with Nicanor in front of all the Greeks and settling everything you wanted, now make yourself out to be in need of pity, traitor though you are and a receiver of bribes ; as if these men will forget your wickedness, as if you will not pay the penalty for the crimes at which you have been caught. You are acting more boldly than Demades to this extent, that though he has given warning in the Assembly of his desperate character and admits that he accepts money and will continue to do so, still he has not dared to show his face before these men and did not presume to dispute the council's report ; moreover he did not propose that the council should have authority over him or lay down the death penalty if he should be proved to have taken bribes. But you have such complete confidence in your own arguments and such a contempt for these men's simplicity that you expect to persuade the jury that in your case only has the council's statement been false and that you alone of those whom it reported have not accepted the gold. Who could believe that ?

Let me explain, Athenians, what you are going to do. You have taken over the case from the people, who know the facts ; and to undergo the punishment,

---

⁵ δεῖξαι A : ἐνδεῖξαι N.
⁶ εἰδότος Emperius : εἶδος codd. : ἤδη Ald.

ὄντων ταῖς ἀποφάσεσι[1] Δημοσθένης εἰσάγεται
πρῶτος. κατηγορήκαμεν ἡμεῖς, ⟨οὐδὲν⟩[2] οὐδενὶ
106 καταχαρισάμενοι τῶν κοινῶν δικαίων. πότερ' ἀμε-
λήσαντες τῶν γεγενημένων ἁπάντων ἀφήσετε τὸν
πρῶτον εἰσεληλυθότα πρὸς ὑμᾶς, καὶ τὰ δίκαια
[τὰ][3] παρὰ τῷ δήμῳ καὶ τῇ βουλῇ τῇ ἐξ Ἀρείου
πάγου δόξαντ' εἶναι καὶ τοῖς ἄλλοις ἅπασιν ἀνθρώποις, ταῦθ' ὑμεῖς οἱ κύριοι πάντων λύσετε, καὶ τὴν
107 πονηρίαν αὐτοὶ τὴν τούτων ἀναδέξεσθε; ἢ πᾶσιν
ἀνθρώποις παράδειγμα ἐξοίσετε κοινὸν ὑπὲρ τῆς
πόλεως, ὅτι μισεῖτε τοὺς προδότας καὶ τοὺς χρημάτων ἕνεκα προϊεμένους τὰ τοῦ δήμου συμφέροντα; ταῦτα γὰρ ἅπαντ' ἐστὶν ἐφ' ὑμῖν νῦν, καὶ
πεντακόσιοι καὶ χίλιοι ὄντες τὴν ἁπάσης τῆς πόλεως
σωτηρίαν ἐν ταῖς χερσὶν ἔχετε, καὶ ἡ τήμερον
ἡμέρα καὶ ἡ ὑμετέρα ψῆφος πολλὴν ἀσφάλειαν τῇ[4]
πόλει καταστήσει τὰ δίκαια ὑμῶν ἐθελόντων κρίνειν, ἢ μοχθηρὰς ἐλπίδας ποιήσετε πάντας ἔχειν
τοιαῦθ' ὑμῶν ἔθη καθιστάντων.

108   Οὐ καταπληκτέον ἐστίν, ἄνδρες Ἀθηναῖοι, οὐδὲ
[104] προετέον, ἐὰν σωφρονῆτε, τοῖς Δημοσθένους ἐλέοις
τὴν κοινὴν καὶ δικαίαν ὑπὲρ τῆς πόλεως ἀπολογίαν.
οὐδεὶς γὰρ ὑμῶν ἠνάγκαζε τοῦτον τὰ μὴ προσήκοντα χρήματα λαμβάνειν[5] καθ' ὑμῶν, πολλῷ πλείω
τῶν ἱκανῶν δι' ὑμᾶς ἕτερα κεκτημένον, οὐδ' ἀπολογεῖσθαι[6] νῦν ὑπὲρ τῶν ὡμολογημένων ἀδικημάτων, γράψαντα καθ' ἑαυτοῦ θάνατον τὴν ζημίαν·
ἀλλ' ἡ ἐκ τοῦ ἄλλου βίου ἔμφυτος αἰσχροκέρδεια
καὶ πονηρία ταῦτ' εἰς τὴν κεφαλὴν αὐτῷ τέτροφε.[7]

---

[1] Post ἀποφάσεσι punctum habet Blass.
[2] οὐδὲν add. Reiske.
[3] τὰ del. Sauppe.

due to those whose names appear in the reports, Demosthenes is brought in first. We have made our accusation and have allowed no private interest on the part of any to stand in the way of common justice. Will you disregard all that has passed and acquit the first man up before you ? Will you, with full power at your command, reject what seemed just both to the people and the Areopagus, and indeed to everyone, and take upon yourselves these men's depravity ? Or will you, for the city's sake, give a demonstration to all alike of the hatred you bear towards traitors and those who, through love of gain, betray the people's interests ? All this now lies in your control, and the fifteen hundred of you hold the city's safety in your hands. Your verdict of to-day will either bring to Athens great security, if you are willing to make a just decision, or else, if you endorse such practices as this, drive all men to despondency.

You must not be cowed, Athenians, or by losing your self-control give up the city's just defence, which touches all alike, in deference to Demosthenes' entreaties. For none of you compelled this man to take the money, to which he had no right, against your own interests, when he has acquired, with your assistance, much more than enough besides, nor to defend himself now when the crimes have been acknowledged and he has proposed the death penalty for himself. But the avarice and wickedness, fostered in him by his whole mode of life, have brought this

---

[4] τῇ A : ἐν τῇ N.

[5] λαμβάνειν Wolf : λαμβάνοντα codd. : λαμβάνειν τὰ Ald.

[6] ἀπολογεῖσθαι A pr. : ἀπολεῖσθαι A corr. ras. N.

[7] τέτροφε Blass : τέτραφε codd.

DINARCHUS

109 μὴ οὖν ἄχθεσθ᾽ αὐτοῦ κλαίοντος καὶ ὀδυρομένου·
πολὺ γὰρ ἂν δικαιότερον ἐλεήσαιτε[1] τὴν χώραν, ἣν
οὗτος καθίστησιν εἰς τοὺς κινδύνους τοιαῦτα πράττων, ἢ τοὺς ἐξ αὐτῆς γεγενημένους ὑμᾶς ἱκετεύει,
παραστησαμένη τὰ ὑμέτερα τέκνα καὶ γυναῖκας,
τιμωρήσασθαι τὸν προδότην καὶ σῴζειν ἑαυτήν,
ὑπὲρ ἧς οἱ πρόγονοι πολλοὺς καὶ καλοὺς[2] κινδύνους
ὑπομείναντες ἐλευθέραν ὑμῖν αὐτὴν παραδεδώκασιν,
ἐν ᾗ πολλὰ καὶ καλὰ παραδείγματα λέλειπται τῆς
110 τῶν τελευτησάντων ἀρετῆς. εἰς ταύτην ἀποβλέψαντας, ὦ Ἀθηναῖοι, καὶ τὰς ἐν αὐτῇ γιγνομένας
πατρίους θυσίας καὶ τὰς τῶν προγόνων θήκας
φέρειν δεῖ τοὺς εὖ φρονοῦντας τὴν ψῆφον. καὶ
ὅταν Δημοσθένης ἐξαπατῆσαι βουλόμενος καὶ παρα-
κρουόμενος ὑμᾶς[3] οἰκτίζηται καὶ δακρύῃ, ὑμεῖς
εἰς τὸ τῆς πόλεως σῶμ᾽ ἀποβλέψαντες καὶ τὴν
πρότερον δόξαν ὑπάρχουσαν[4] αὐτῇ ἀντίθετε, πότερον ἡ πόλις ἐλεεινοτέρα διὰ τοῦτον γέγονεν ἢ διὰ
111 τὴν πόλιν Δημοσθένης. εὑρήσετε γὰρ τοῦτον μὲν
λαμπρὸν ἐξ οὗ προσελήλυθε πρὸς[5] τὸ πολιτεύεσθαι
γεγενημένον, καὶ ἀντὶ μὲν λογογράφου καὶ μισθοῦ
τὰς δίκας λέγοντος ὑπὲρ Κτησίππου καὶ Φορμίωνος
καὶ ἑτέρων πολλῶν πλουσιώτατον[6] ὄντα τῶν ἐν τῇ
πόλει, ἀντὶ δ᾽ ἀγνῶτος καὶ οὐδεμίαν πατρικὴν
δόξαν παρὰ τῶν προγόνων παρειληφότος ἔνδοξον
γεγενημένον, τὴν δὲ πόλιν οὐκ ἀξίως ἑαυτῆς οὐδὲ
τῆς τῶν προγόνων δόξης διακειμένην. ἀφέντες

---

[1] ἐλεήσαιτε Dobree : ἐλεήσετε codd.
[2] καὶ καλοὺς] del. Baiter.
[3] ὑμᾶς A : ἡμᾶς N.
[4] ὑπάρχουσαν αὐτῇ N : αὐτῇ ὑπάρχουσαν A.

252

on his head. So do not be concerned when he weeps and laments. You might, with far more justice, pity the country, which this man is exposing to danger by behaving as he has, and which is begging you, who are its sons, in the names of your wives and children, to take vengeance on the traitor and save it : the land which your ancestors, after facing many noble combats for it, have handed on to you free ; in which many noble examples have been left us of the courage of those who gave their lives. It is this land, Athenians, the sacrifices traditional in it, and its ancestral sepulchres to which right-thinking men must turn their thoughts when they give their vote. And when Demosthenes wishes to cheat you and cunningly turns pathetic, shedding tears, you must think of the city's person, and the glory which it once possessed, and judge between two alternatives : which has become the more deserving of pity : the city because of Demosthenes or Demosthenes because of the city ? You will find that this man has become famous since he entered politics ; that from being a speechwriter and a paid advocate, in the service of Ctesippus, Phormio and many others,[a] he has become the richest man in Athens ; that after being an unknown figure, inheriting no family honour from his ancestors, he is now famous, while the city has reached a pass unworthy of herself or the honour of

[a] Demosthenes was acting in the interests of Ctesippus, son of Chabrias, when he attacked the Law of Leptines in 355 B.C. The Phormio referred to is possibly the freedman of the banker Pasion whom he defended in 350. *Cf.* Dem. xx. and xxxvi.

---

5 προσελήλυθε πρὸς N : προσελήλυθεν εἰς A.
6 πλουσιώτατον N : πλουσιώτερον A.

οὖν τοὺς ἐλέους καὶ τοὺς φενακισμοὺς τοὺς τούτου
τὴν ὁσίαν καὶ δικαίαν φέρετε ψῆφον, καὶ σκοπεῖτε
τὸ τῇ πατρίδι συμφέρον, μὴ τὸ¹ Δημοσθένει· τοῦτο
γάρ ἐστι καλῶν κἀγαθῶν δικαστῶν ἔργον.

112 Καὶ ὅταν ἀναβαίνῃ τις συνηγορήσων Δημοσθένει,
λογίζεσθ' ὅτι οὗτος ὁ ἄνθρωπος, εἰ μὲν μὴ ἔνοχος
ὢν ταῖς μελλούσαις ἀποφάσεσιν ἀναβαίνει, κακό-
νους ἐστὶ τῇ πολιτείᾳ, καὶ τοὺς ἐπὶ τῷ δήμῳ δῶρα
λαμβάνοντας οὐ βουλόμενος δίκην δοῦναι καὶ τὴν
κοινὴν τῶν ὑμετέρων σωμάτων φυλακήν, ἐφ' ᾗ
τέτακται τὸ ἐν Ἀρείῳ πάγῳ συνέδριον, καταλυθῆναι βούλεται καὶ συγκεχύσθαι πάντα τὰ ἐν τῇ
πόλει δίκαια· εἰ δὲ ῥήτωρ ἢ στρατηγός, οἳ τὴν
προσδοκωμένην καθ' αὑτῶν ἀπόφασιν ἄπιστον βουλόμενοι γενέσθαι συνηγοροῦσιν, οὐ προσεκτέον ὑμῖν
ἐστι τοῖς τούτων λόγοις, εἰδότας ὅτι ἐκ πάντων
τούτων γεγένηται² συνεργία περὶ τὸν Ἁρπάλου
113 κατάπλουν καὶ τὴν ἄφεσιν. νομίσαντες οὖν, ὦ
Ἀθηναῖοι, καθ' ὑμῶν πάντας τούτους ἀναβαίνειν
καὶ κοινοὺς ἐχθροὺς εἶναι τῶν νόμων καὶ τῆς
πόλεως ἁπάσης, μὴ ἀποδέχεσθ' αὐτῶν, ἀλλὰ κε-
λεύετ' ἀπολογεῖσθαι περὶ τῶν κατηγορημένων· μηδὲ
τὴν αὐτοῦ τούτου μανίαν, ὃς μέγα φρονεῖ ἐπὶ τῷ
δύνασθαι λέγειν, καὶ ἐπειδὰν φανερὸς³ ὑμῖν γένηται
δωροδοκῶν, ἔτι μᾶλλον ἐξελήλεγκται φενακίζων
ὑμᾶς, ⟨ἀλλὰ⟩⁴ τιμωρήσασθε ὑμῶν αὐτῶν καὶ τῆς
πόλεως ἀξίως. εἰ δὲ μή, μιᾷ ψήφῳ καὶ ἑνὶ ἀγῶνι
πάντας τοὺς ἀποπεφασμένους καὶ τοὺς μέλλοντας
ἀφέντες εἰς ὑμᾶς αὐτοὺς καὶ τὸν δῆμον τὴν τούτων

¹ τὸ A : τῷ N.   ² γεγένηται Maetzner : γίνεται codd.

our forbears. Therefore ignore this man's entreaties and deceptions, bring in the verdict that is just and right, having regard for your country's interest, as befits an honourable jury, not the welfare of Demosthenes.

And whenever anyone comes forward to speak for him, bear in mind that he who does so, even if not involved in the reports we are about to hear, is hostile to the constitution, unwilling to see punished those who take bribes against the people and anxious that the general protection of your persons, for which the Areopagus is responsible, should be abolished and every right in the city overwhelmed; whereas, if it is some orator or general, one of those participating in the defence because they wish to discredit the report, which they expect will reflect against themselves, you must give their arguments no credence, knowing as you do that all these men collaborated over the landing of Harpalus and his release. You must realize then, Athenians, that when these men come forward, they do so against your interests, being enemies alike of the laws and the entire city. Do not tolerate them; insist that their defence answers the charges. And do not countenance his own fury either; for he prides himself on his powers as an orator and, since he is known to have taken bribes against you, has been proved an even greater fraud. No, punish him in a manner befitting yourselves and the city. If you do not, by one verdict and at one trial you will release all who have been reported, and all who ever will be, and will bring these men's corruption upon yourselves and upon the

---

[3] φανερὸς A : φανερῶς N.
[4] ἀλλὰ add. Reiske.

DINARCHUS

δωροδοκίαν τρέψετε, κἂν¹ ὕστερον ἐγκαλῆτε² τοῖς
ἀφεῖσιν, ὅτε οὐδὲν ἔσται πλέον ὑμῖν.

114 Ἐγὼ μὲν οὖν, ὅσον εἰς τὸ μέρος τοὐμὸν τῆς κατηγορίας ἥκει, βεβοήθηκα, τἆλλα πάντα παριδὼν
πλὴν τοῦ δικαίου καὶ τοῦ συμφέροντος ὑμῖν. οὐκ
ἐγκαταλέλοιπα τὴν πόλιν, οὐ χάριν προὐργιαιτέραν
τῆς τοῦ δήμου χειροτονίας ἐποιησάμην. ἀξιῶ δὲ
καὶ ὑμᾶς τὴν αὐτὴν γνώμην ἔχειν, παραδίδωμι τὸ
ὕδωρ τοῖς ἄλλοις κατηγόροις.³

¹ κἂν N corr. A corr.: κα. N pr.: καὶ A pr.: κᾆθ' Blass.
² ἐγκαλῆτε N corr. A corr.: ἐγκαλ.τε N pr.: ἐγκαλεῖτε
A pr. Blass.
³ κατὰ δημοσθένους subicit N.

people, even though, afterwards, you may prosecute those who acquitted them, when it will avail you nothing.

I have now played my full part in assisting the prosecution and have shown regard for nothing but justice and your interests. I have not deserted the city or given more weight to personal favour than to the people's vote. With an appeal to you to show the same spirit I now hand over the water to the other prosecutors.

II
SPEECH AGAINST ARI-
STOGITON

DINARCHUS

. . . . all the . . . . . .

INTRODUCTION

ARISTOGITON was an Athenian orator [a] of Demosthenes' time who had a reputation for impudence and
profligacy and was nicknamed the Dog.[b] His father
Cydimachus went into exile as a debtor to the state
and died in prison in Euboea ; and Aristogiton, who
inherited the debt and was imprisoned for it, refused
to pay the expenses of the funeral.[c] Henceforward
he was seldom free from debt and, according to
Dinarchus,[d] spent most of his life in gaol, where he
finally died. Nevertheless he managed to obtrude
himself into public affairs, and after Chaeronea in 338
B.C. even prosecuted Demosthenes and Hyperides.[e]
Some years later he was himself indicted by Lycurgus[f]
for exercising civic rights while still a public debtor,
and the two speeches against Aristogiton which have
survived under the name of Demosthenes were delivered in this trial.

After the escape of Harpalus from Athens Aristogiton was said by the Areopagus to have received
twenty minas from him.[g] By the time that his case

[a] Athenaeus credits him with a speech against Phrynê, and
Suidas with seven others, but the latter's note on him is con-
fused (Athen. xiii. 591 e ; Suid. s.v. " Aristogiton ").
[b] [Dem.] xxv. 40. [c] § 8. [d] § 2.
[e] Cf. Hyp. frag. 18.
[f] Cf. Lycurg. frag. 13.
[g] § 1. 20 minas were equivalent to about £80.

was heard the people had had ample opportunity to vent their anger, since Demosthenes and Demades had already been condemned, and he was consequently acquitted, partly no doubt because the sum assigned to him was so trivial.

The following speech, short though it is, may well have been the first for the prosecution. There is no reference to a previous accuser, and, as all the important evidence had already been given in connexion with the earlier cases, there was little new to be said.

ANALYSIS

ΚΑΤΑ ΑΡΙΣΤΟΓΕΙΤΟΝΟΣ

[105] Πάνθ᾽, ὡς ἔοικεν, ὦ Ἀθηναῖοι, προσδοκητέα ἐστὶ
καὶ ἀκοῦσαι καὶ ἰδεῖν ἐν ταῖς γεγενημέναις ἀπο-
φάσεσι· θαυμασιώτατον δὲ πάντων, ὡς ἐμοὶ δοκεῖ,
τὸ νῦν γιγνόμενον. ὁ γὰρ πονηρότατος τῶν ἐν τῇ
πόλει, μᾶλλον δὲ καὶ τῶν ἄλλων ἀνθρώπων,
Ἀριστογείτων διαδικασόμενος ἥκει τῇ ἐξ Ἀρείου
πάγου βουλῇ περὶ ἀληθείας καὶ δικαιοσύνης, καὶ
νυνὶ μείζονα κίνδυνον ἢ τὴν ἀπόφασιν πεποιημένη
βουλὴ κινδυνεύει ἢ ὁ δῶρα λαμβάνων καθ᾽ ὑμῶν
καὶ τὴν ὑπὲρ τῶν δικαίων παρρησίαν ἀποδόμενος
2 εἴκοσι μνῶν. τούτῳ μέν γε καινὸν οὐδὲν οὐδὲ
δεινόν, ἐὰν ἁλῷ, συμβήσεται· καὶ γὰρ θανάτου
ἄξια πολλὰ πρότερον ἕτερα διαπέπρακται, καὶ ἐν
τῷ δεσμωτηρίῳ πλείω χρόνον ἢ ἔξω διατέτριφε,
καὶ ὀφείλων τῷ δημοσίῳ κατὰ τῶν ἐπιτίμων γέ-
γραφεν οὐκ ἐξὸν αὐτῷ, καὶ ἕτερα πολλὰ καὶ δεινὰ
πεποίηκε, περὶ ὧν ὑμεῖς ἀκριβέστερον[1] ἐμοῦ γιγνώ-
σκετε· τῇ δὲ βουλῇ τὸ δόξαι ψευδῆ[2] κατ᾽ Ἀριστογείτονος ἀποφαίνειν καὶ τοῦτον ἐκείνης παρ᾽ ὑμῖν
ὑποληφθῆναι δικαιότερα λέγειν τῶν αἰσχίστων καὶ
3 δεινοτάτων ἐστίν. διόπερ, ὦ Ἀθηναῖοι, οὗτός μοι
δοκεῖ, τὸν ἀγῶνα αὐτῷ ἀσφαλῆ εἶναι νομίζων, δια-

---

[1] ὑμεῖς ἀκριβέστερον N : ἀκριβέστερον ὑμεῖς A.
[2] ψευδῆ A corr. ras. : τὰ ψευδῆ, ut vid., A pr. : καὶ ψευδῆ N.

AGAINST ARISTOGITON

THERE is nothing, it appears, Athenians, which we must not expect either to hear or see in connexion with the reports which have been made ; but the most remarkable fact of all, in my opinion, confronts us now. The worst character in the city, I should say in the whole world, Aristogiton, has come to pit himself in law against the Areopagus on the subject of truth and justice ; and the council which has made the report is now in greater danger than this man who takes bribes against you and who sold for twenty minas the right of free speech in the cause of justice. It will be no new or alarming experience for the defendant if he is convicted, for he has committed in the past many other crimes meriting the death penalty and has spent more time in prison than out of it. While he has been in debt to the state he has prosecuted men with citizen rights, though not entitled to do so, and has committed numerous other offences of which you have a more exact knowledge than I. It is a most shameful and monstrous thing for this council to be suspected of making a false report against Aristogiton and for him to be considered among you as having more justice on his side than it has. For this reason, Athenians, thinking that the trial holds no dangers for him, this man is

πειρασόμενος ἥκειν τῆς ὑμετέρας γνώμης. ἅπαντα
γὰρ αὐτῷ πολλάκις τὰ δεινὰ συμβέβηκε, πλὴν τοῦ
ἀποθανεῖν· τοῦτο δ᾿, ἂν θεὸς θέλῃ καὶ ὑμεῖς σωφρονῆτε, ἐν τῇ τήμερον ἡμέρᾳ συμβήσεται. οὐ
γὰρ δὴ μὰ τὸν Ἡρακλέα βελτίω γενήσεσθαι αὐτὸν
προσδοκᾶτε συγγνώμης νυνὶ τυγχάνοντα παρ᾿ ὑμῶν,
οὐδὲ τὸ λοιπὸν ἀφέξεσθαι τοῦ λαμβάνειν χρήματα
καθ᾿ ὑμῶν, ἐὰν νῦν ἀφῆτε αὐτόν. πονηρίαν γὰρ
ἀρχομένην μὲν κωλῦσαι τάχ᾿ ἄν¹ τις κολάζων
δυνηθείη, ἐγκαταγεγηρακυῖαν δὲ καὶ γεγευμένην²
τῶν εἰθισμένων τιμωριῶν ἀδύνατον εἶναι λέγουσιν.
4 εἰ μὲν οὖν ἐγγενήσεσθαι βούλεσθε δευσοποιὸν ἐν
τῇ πόλει πονηρίαν, διαφυλάττειν ὑμᾶς Ἀριστογείτονα δεῖ, καὶ ἐὰν ὅ τι ἂν [τις]³ βούληται ἐν τῇ
πόλει διαπράττεσθαι· εἰ δὲ τοὺς πονηροὺς καὶ
καταράτους ἀνθρώπους μισεῖτε καὶ ἔστιν ὑμῖν ὀργὴ
καὶ μνήμη τῶν πρότερον ὑπὸ τούτου πεπραγμένων,
ἀποκτείνατε τοῦτον, ὃς παρ᾿ Ἁρπάλου λαβεῖν χρήματα ἐτόλμησεν, ὃν ᾔσθεθ᾿ ἥκειν καταληψόμενον
τὴν πόλιν ὑμῶν,⁴ καὶ τὰς προφάσεις καὶ τοὺς
φενακισμοὺς ἐκκόψατε αὐτοῦ· τούτοις γὰρ ἥκει
πιστεύων πρὸς ὑμᾶς.

5 Ἆρ᾿ ἴσθ᾿ ὅτι τῆς Ἁρπάλου ἀφίξεως δυσχεροῦς
οὔσης ἐκεῖνο συμβέβηκεν εὐτύχημα τῇ πόλει, διότι
πεῖραν εἰλήφατ᾿ ἀκριβῆ τῶν ἕνεκ᾿ ἀργυρίου καὶ
χρυσίου προϊεμένων πάντα τοῖς τῆς πόλεως ἐχθροῖς; μὴ καταρραθυμήσητε, ὦ Ἀθηναῖοι, μηδ᾿
ἀπείπητε τιμωρούμενοι τοὺς πονηρούς, ἀλλ᾿ ἐκ-
καθάρατε, καθ᾿ ὅσον δυνατόν ἐστι, τὴν δωροδοκίαν
ἐκ τῆς πόλεως. καὶ μὴ τῶν παρ᾿ ἐμοῦ λόγων
ἀκούειν ζητήσητε, φανερῶν ὑμῖν γεγενημένων τῶν
ἀδικημάτων κατὰ⁵ τῶν ὑπὸ τῆς βουλῆς ἀποπε-

coming forward, I believe, to test your attitude. He
has often undergone all sorts of suffering short of
death, which, if God so wills it and you are wise,
he will undergo to-day. For you must assume, by
Heracles, that there will be no improvement in him
if he is pardoned by you now, and that in future he
will not abstain from taking bribes against you if you
now acquit him. For when wickedness is in its
infancy perhaps it can be checked by punishment,
but when it has grown old and has sampled the usual
penalties, it is said to be incurable. If therefore you
wish depravity to grow up ingrained in Athens, you
should preserve Aristogiton and allow him to act
there as he pleases. But if you hate the wicked and
accursed and can recall with resentment what this
man has done in the past, kill him, for he dared to
take money from Harpalus, who he knew was coming
to seize your city. Cut short his excuses and deceptive arguments, on which he now depends when
he appears before you.

Do you realize that, awkward though the arrival
of Harpalus was, it has been an advantage to the
city in one respect, because it has given you a sure
means of testing those who give up everything to the
enemies of Athens for a payment of silver or gold ?
Do not be lax, Athenians, or weary of punishing
the guilty ; purge the city of bribery to the utmost
of your ability. Do not ask for arguments from me
when you see that the crimes have been plainly
attributed to those whom the council has reported.

---

¹ τάχ’ ἄν Bekker : τάχα codd.
² γεγευμένην B, Bekker : γεγενημένην NA.
³ τις del. Bekker.   ⁴ ὑμῶν A : ἡμῶν N.
⁵ κατὰ N A pr. : ἐκ A corr.²

267

6 φασμένων. [ἢ διὰ τοὺς τοῦ κρινομένου προγόνους
καὶ[1] τὴν αὐτοῦ μετριότητα, καὶ ὅτι ὑμᾶς πολλὰ
καὶ ἰδίᾳ καὶ δημοσίᾳ ἀγαθὰ εἴργασται, ἄξιόν ἐστιν[2]
αὐτοῦ φείσασθαι;][3] τί γὰρ ἀγνοεῖτε δι᾽ ὃ δεῖσθε
λόγων ἀκούειν κατὰ τοῦ νῦν κρινομένου; πότερ᾽
ἡ τῆς βουλῆς ἀπόφασις, ἐὰν μὲν ἡμεῖς οἱ κατήγοροι
δέκα ὄντες τὸ ὕδωρ ἀναλώσωμεν ἅπαν καὶ ἀναβοή-
σωμεν ὡς δεινόν ἐστιν ἀφεῖσθαι τοὺς εἰλημμένους
ἔχοντας ἐπ᾽ αὐτοφώρῳ δῶρα κατὰ τῆς πατρίδος,
ἀληθὴς καὶ δικαία ἔσται[4] ἡ κατ᾽ Ἀριστογείτονος
7 [ἀπόφασις][5]· ἐὰν δ᾽ ἕκαστος ἡμῶν, ὡς εἰδότων
ὑμῶν πάντα οὐδὲν ἧττον ἡμῶν τὰ δίκαια περὶ του-
[106] τωνὶ τῶν ἀγώνων, βραχέα εἰπὼν καταβῇ, ψευδής,
καὶ οὐ δικαίως[6] παρὰ τῶν Ἀρεοπαγιτῶν γεγενημένη;[7] ἢ τὸ δῶρα λαμβάνειν ἐπὶ προδοσίᾳ τῶν
τῆς πόλεως συμφερόντων οὐκ ἴσθ᾽ ὅτι τῶν δεινοτάτων ἐστὶ καὶ τῶν πλεῖστα κακὰ τὰς πόλεις
ἐργαζομένων.

8 Ἀλλ᾽ αὐτὸς ὁ κρινόμενος νὴ Δία μέτριος τὸν
τρόπον, καὶ προγόνων χρηστῶν, καὶ πολλὰ ἡμᾶς
καὶ ἰδίᾳ καὶ δημοσίᾳ καλὰ εἰργασμένος, ὥστε διὰ
ταῦτ᾽[8] ἄξιόν ἐστιν αὐτοῦ φείσασθαι; καὶ τίς ὑμῶν
οὐ πολλάκις ἀκήκοεν, ὅτι Κυδιμάχου μὲν τοῦ
πατρὸς τοῦ Ἀριστογείτονος θανάτου καταγνωσθέν-
τος καὶ φυγόντος ἐκ ταύτης τῆς πόλεως ὁ χρηστὸς
οὗτος υἱὸς περιεῖδε τὸν αὐτοῦ πατέρα καὶ ζῶντα

---

[1] καὶ A : καὶ διὰ N.
[2] ἐστιν om. A.
[3] Verba ἢ διὰ usque ad φείσασθαι del. Bekker, coll. § 8 init.
[4] ἔσται ἡ κατ᾽ Ἀριστογείτονος ἀπόφασις N : ἡ κατ᾽ Ἀριστογείτονος ἔσται ἀπόφασις A : quae omnia del. Dobree ; infra,
ante παρὰ τῶν Ἀρεοπαγιτῶν, habet Blass.
[5] ἀπόφασις del. Maetzner.

[Or ought you to spare the defendant on account of his ancestry and his moderation, or because he has done you many public and private services ?] *a* What information do you lack that makes you ask for arguments against the defendant here before you ? What if we, the accusers, all ten of us, use up all the water in our clocks and proclaim that it is a terrible thing to release men who have been caught with bribes against the city in their very hands ; will that make the council's report against Aristogiton true and just ? Or suppose that each of us assumes that you are just as well aware as we on which side justice lies in the present trials, and so leaves the platform after a short speech ; will the report then be a false one, unjustly made by the Areopagites ? Or don't you realize that to take bribes in order to betray the city's interests is one of the greatest crimes causing the most irreparable harm to cities ?

No doubt I shall be told that the defendant is himself a man of sober character coming of a good family, that he has done you many noble services in private and in public life and that therefore you are justified in sparing him. You must all have often heard that, when Aristogiton's father Cydimachus was condemned to death and fled from the city, this admirable son allowed his own father to lack the bare

---

a This sentence was excluded from the text by Bekker. It is out of place in the argument here and its substance is given at the beginning of § 8.

---

⁶ οὐ δικαίως Hug : οὐδεὶς ὡς N A pr. : οὐδεὶς ταύτῃ πιστεύσει ὡς A corr.² : ἄδικος Blass.
⁷ γεγενημένη Blass : γεγενημένη codd.
⁸ ταῦτ' Blass : τοῦτ' codd.

τῶν ἀναγκαίων σπανίζοντα καὶ τελευτήσαντα οὐ
τυχόντα τῶν νομίμων, ἅπερ αὐτοῦ πολλάκις κατ-
9 εμαρτυρεῖτο· αὐτὸν δὲ τοῦτον, ὅτ᾽ εἰς τὸ δεσμωτήριον τὸ πρῶτον ἀπήχθη—πολλάκις γὰρ ἴστε τοῦτο
δήπου γεγενημένον—, τοιαῦτα τολμήσαντα ποιεῖν
αὐτοῦ,[1] ὥστ᾽ ἐκείνους ἀποψηφίσασθαι μήτε πῦρ
ἐναύειν τούτῳ μήτε συσσιτεῖν μηδένα μήτε θυσιῶν
τῶν γιγνομένων κοινωνεῖν; καίτοι, ὦ Ἀθηναῖοι,
τίνα χρὴ τοῦτον νομίζειν ἔχειν διάνοιαν, ὃς διὰ μὲν
10 πονηρίαν εἰς τὸ δεσμωτήριον ἐνέπεσεν, ἐκεῖ δ᾽ ὢν
παρὰ τοῖς ἐκ τῶν ἄλλων ἀνθρώπων κακούργοις
ἀπηγμένοις[2] οὕτως εἶναι πονηρὸς ἔδοξεν, ὥστε μηδ᾽
ἐκεῖ[3] τῶν ἴσων ἀξιοῦσθαι τοῖς ἄλλοις, ἀλλὰ κλέπτην
ὥς φασι ληφθέντα τουτονὶ παρ᾽ ἐκείνοις, εἰ ἦν
ἕτερός τις τόπος ἀνοσιώτερος ἵνα ἐξῆν ἀπάγειν
τοὺς ἐκ[4] δεσμωτηρίου κλέπτοντας, εἰς ἐκεῖνον ἂν
τοῦτο τὸ θηρίον ἀπαχθῆναι; καὶ ταῦθ᾽, ὅπερ[5]
ἀρτίως εἶπον, τίς οὐκ οἶδε καταμαρτυρηθέντ᾽
Ἀριστογείτονος, ὅτ᾽ ἐμπορίου ἐπιμελητὴς λαχὼν
ἀπεδοκιμάσθη ὑπὸ τῶν τότε δικαζόντων ἄρχειν
11 ταύτην τὴν[6] ἀρχήν; ἔπειτ᾽ εἰρωνεύεσθε πρὸς ὑμᾶς
αὐτούς, καὶ περὶ Ἀριστογείτονος μέλλοντες φέρειν
τὴν ψῆφον ἐλεεῖτε, ὃς τὸν αὐτοῦ πατέρα κακῶς
διατιθέμενον ὑπὸ τοῦ[7] λιμοῦ οὐκ ἠλέησεν; ἔπειτα
παρ᾽ ἡμῶν ἔτι λόγους ἀκούειν βούλεσθε περὶ τῆς
Ἀριστογείτονος τιμήσεως, ὃν ἴστε ἀκριβῶς ὅτι

---

[1] αὐτοῦ Wurm : αὐτούς codd.
[2] ἀπηγμένοις Wurm : ἀνηγμένοις codd.
[3] ἐκεῖ Dobree : ἐκείνοις codd.
[4] ἐκ A : ἐκ τοῦ N.
[5] ὅπερ Blass : ἅπερ codd.
[6] ταύτην τὴν Baiter et Sauppe : αὐτὴν τὴν N : τὴν αὐτὴν A.
[7] τοῦ om. A.

necessities of life, while he survived, and do without
a proper burial when he died : a fact for which evidence was often brought against him ; or again, that
the man himself, on being taken to prison for the
first time,—no doubt you realize that he has often
been imprisoned—dared to behave in such a way
there that the inmates voted that no one should
either light a fire for him or sit at meals or share the
usual sacrifices with him. Reflect, Athenians ; what
sort of character must we suppose this man to
have, who was thrown into prison for criminal conduct and when he was there, among those who had
been segregated from the rest of the world as felons,
was looked upon as so debased that even there he
was not thought worthy of the same treatment as
the rest ? It is said, in fact, that he was caught
thieving among them and that, if there had been any
other place more degraded where they could have
isolated men who stole in prison, this monster would
have been conducted there. These facts, as I said
just now, were established by evidence against
Aristogiton, as is well known, when the lot fell to him
to be custodian of the exchange but he was rejected
by those who then decided the appointment to that
office.[a] Do you then feign ignorance among yourselves and give way to pity when the man concerning
whom you are about to vote is Aristogiton, who did
not pity his own father when reduced to starvation ?
Do you still wish to hear us talk about the damages
he must pay, when you know quite well that his

---

[a] The custodians of the exchange were responsible for
seeing that the laws governing import and export trade were
observed. Like most magistrates, they were appointed by
lot but were submitted to an examination in court (δοκιμασία)
before taking office and could be rejected if unsuitable.

δικαίως ἂν καὶ ἐκ τοῦ ἄλλου βίου καὶ ἐκ τῶν νῦν
αὐτῷ πεπραγμένων τῆς ἐσχάτης τύχοι τιμωρίας;
12 οὐκ Ἀριστογείτων ἐστίν, ὦ Ἀθηναῖοι, ὁ κατὰ τῆς
ἱερείας τῆς Ἀρτέμιδος τῆς Βραυρωνίας[1] καὶ τῶν
οἰκείων αὐτῆς τοιαῦτα γράψας καὶ ψευσάμενος,
ὥσθ' ὑμᾶς, ἐπειδὴ τὴν ἀλήθειαν ἐπύθεσθε παρὰ
τῶν κατηγόρων, πέντε ταλάντων τιμῆσαι τούτῳ,[2]
ὅσονπερ ἦν ἐπὶ τῇ τῶν παρανόμων γραφῇ τίμημα
ἐπιγεγραμμένον; οὐχ[3] οὗτος πρὶν ἐκτῖσαι τοῦτο,
συκοφαντῶν τὸν ἐντυγχάνοντα ὑμῶν καὶ λέγων καὶ
γράφων ἐν τῷ δήμῳ διατετέλεκε, καὶ καταφρονῶν
ἁπασῶν τῶν τιμωριῶν αἳ κατὰ τῶν ἀδικούντων
13 ἐν τοῖς νόμοις εἰσὶ γεγραμμέναι; οὐ τὸ τελευταῖον
οὗτος ἐνδειχθεὶς ὑπὸ Λυκούργου, καὶ ἐξελεγχθεὶς
ὀφείλων τῷ δημοσίῳ λέγειν οὐκ ἐξὸν αὐτῷ, καὶ
παραδοθεὶς τοῖς ἕνδεκα κατὰ τοὺς νόμους, περι-
πατῶν ἔμπροσθεν τῶν δικαστηρίων[4] . . . καὶ εἰς
τὴν προεδρίαν τῶν[5] πρυτάνεων ἐκάθιζεν;[6]
14 Εἶτ', ὦ ἄνδρες Ἀθηναῖοι, ὃν οἱ νόμοι μὲν πολλάκις ὑμῖν παραδεδώκασι τιμωρήσασθαι κατεψηφισμένον[7] ὑπὸ τῶν πολιτῶν ἐνδειχθέντα,[8] φυλάξαι
δ'[9] οὔθ' οἱ ἕνδεκα δεδύνηνται οὔτε τὸ δεσμωτήριον,
τούτῳ βουλήσεσθε συμβούλῳ χρῆσθαι; καὶ ὁ μὲν
νόμος εὐξάμενον[10] κελεύει τὸν κήρυκα μετ' εὐφημίας
πολλῆς, οὕτως ὑμῖν τὸ βουλεύεσθαι περὶ τῶν πραγμάτων παραδιδόναι· ὑμεῖς δὲ τὸν ἀνόσιον καὶ περὶ

---

[1] Βραυρωνίας Markland : βαυβρωνίας NA.
[2] τούτῳ N : τοῦτον A.
[3] οὐχ Schmidt : ὁ codd., ret. Bekker (del. τοῦτο).
[4] Post δικαστηρίων intercidisse ὤφθη vel ἑωρᾶτο susp. Reiske.   [5] τῶν A : τὴν N.
[6] ἐκάθιζεν] ἐγκαθίζων Reiske.
[7] Post κατεψηφισμένον Sauppe δ' addidit.

whole life, as well as his recent conduct, justifies the extreme penalty ? Was it not Aristogiton, Athenians, who made in writing such lying assertions about the priestess of Artemis Brauronia [a] and her relatives, that when you discovered the truth from his accusers, you fined him five talents, a sum equal to the fine set down in an indictment for illegal proposals ? Has he not persisted in maligning every one of you he meets, though he has not yet paid up, and in speaking and proposing measures in the Assembly, regardless of all the penalties against wrongdoers which the laws prescribe ? And finally, when an information was lodged against him by Lycurgus,[b] and he was convicted, a debtor to the state without the right to speak in public, when he had been handed over to the Eleven in accordance with the laws, ⟨was he not seen⟩ [c] walking about in the front of the lawcourts, and used he not to sit on the seat of the Prytanes ?

Well then, Athenians, if a man has often been committed to you lawfully for punishment, condemned on information lodged by citizens, if neither the Eleven nor the prison have been able to restrain him, will you want to use him as a counsellor ? The law demands that the herald shall first pray, amid dead silence, before he surrenders to you the task of deliberating on public affairs. Will you then allow an

---

[a] The shrine of Artemis at Brauron in Attica was supposed to contain the image of the goddess brought from the Tauri by Iphigenia. There was also a temple of Artemis Brauronia, called τὸ ἱερὸν κυνηγέσιον, on the Acropolis (*cf. arg. ad Demosthenem* xxv. ; Paus. i. 23. 7).

[b] *Cf.* Lycurg. frag. 13 and note.

[c] Reiske's emendation is followed here.

---

8 ἐνδειχθέντα Ald.: διδαχθέντες NA: καὶ ἀπαχθέντα Sauppe.
9 δ' del. Sauppe.   10 εὐξάμενον A : εὐξάμενος N.

273

πάντας πονηρὸν καὶ μάλιστα περὶ τὸν ἑαυτοῦ πατέρα γεγενημένον, τοῦτον μεθ' ὑμῶν καὶ μετὰ τῶν
ὑμετέρων οἰκείων καὶ συγγενῶν ἐάσετε πολιτεύ-
15 εσθαι; καὶ Δημάδῃ μὲν καὶ Δημοσθένει οὐδεμίαν
ᾤεσθε δεῖν συγγνώμην ἔχειν, ὅτι δῶρα καθ' ὑμῶν
ἐξηλέγχθησαν λαμβάνοντες, ἀλλ' ἐτιμωρήσασθε,
καὶ δικαίως, οἷς εἰ μὴ πάντα ἀλλὰ πολλά γε συνῇστε[1] χρήσιμα πεπολιτευμένοις[2]· τὸν δὲ κατάρατον
τοῦτον, ὃς ἀγαθὸν μὲν ὑμᾶς οὐδεπώποτε πεποίηκεν[3]
[107] ἐξ οὗ πρὸς τὴν πόλιν προσελήλυθε, κακὸν δ' ὅ τι
δυνατός ἐστιν, ἀφήσετε; καὶ τίς οὐκ ἂν ἐγκαλέ-
σειεν ὑμῖν τοῖς τοῦτον προσδεχομένοις[4] σύμβουλον;
ὅταν γὰρ ἄνθρωπος γνώριμον καὶ φανερὰν[5] καὶ
περιβόητον τὴν πονηρίαν παρὰ πᾶσι τοῖς πολίταις
ἔχων ἐν ὑμῖν[6] δημηγορῇ, τότε τοὺς ἀκούοντας ὑμᾶς
οἱ περιεστηκότες θαυμάσουσι, πότερα[7] βελτίους οὐκ
ἔχετε συμβούλους ἢ καὶ χαίρετε τῶν τοιούτων
16 ἀκούοντες. χρὴ δ', ὦ Ἀθηναῖοι, ὥσπερ οἱ πρῶτοι
νομοθέται περὶ τῶν ἐν τῷ δήμῳ λεγόντων τοῖς
προγόνοις ὑμῶν[8] ἐνομοθέτησαν, οὕτω καὶ ὑμᾶς
ζητεῖν ἀκούειν, ἵνα βελτίους τοὺς προσιόντας ὑμῖν
ποιήσητε. πῶς οὖν ἐκεῖνοι περὶ τούτων ἐγίγνωσκον;
πρῶτον μὲν καθ' ἑκάστην ⟨ἐκκλησίαν⟩[9] δημοσίᾳ
κατὰ τῶν πονηρῶν ἀρὰς ποιούμενοι, εἴ τις δῶρα
λαμβάνων μετὰ ταῦτα λέγει καὶ γιγνώσκει περὶ τῶν
πραγμάτων, ἐξώλη τοῦτον εἶναι· ὧν οὗτος νῦν
17 ἐστιν Ἀριστογείτων· ἔπειτ' ἐν τοῖς νόμοις δώρων
γραφὰς ποιήσαντες, καὶ κατὰ μόνου τούτου τῶν

---

[1] συνῇστε Hirschig : σύνιστε codd.
[2] πεπολιτευμένοις N : πολιτευομένοις A.
[3] οὐδεπώποτε πεποίηκεν Maetzner : οὐδέποτε πεποίηκεν N :
πεποίηκεν οὐδεπώποτε A.

274

impious wretch, who has proved wicked in his dealings
with everyone, and in particular his own father, to
share in citizenship with you, with your families and
kinsmen ? After rejecting all thought of pardon for
Demades and Demosthenes, because they were
proved to have been taking bribes against you, and
punishing them,—quite rightly, though you knew
that they had served you during their administration,
certainly in many respects if not in everything,—
will you acquit this accursed man who has not done
you a service ever since he has been in politics but has
been the greatest possible menace ? Would not
everyone reproach you if you accepted such a person
as your adviser ? For when you are addressed by a
man whose wickedness is both notorious and un-
deniable and a byword among all Athenians, the
bystanders will wonder whether you who listen to
him have no better advisers or whether you enjoy
hearing such people. Like the early lawgivers,
Athenians, who made laws to deal with those addressing your ancestors in the Assembly, you too should
try, by your behaviour as listeners, to make the
speakers who come before you better. What was
the attitude of the lawgivers to these men ? In the
first place, at every sitting of the Assembly they
publicly proclaimed curses against wrongdoers, calling
down destruction on any who, after accepting bribes,
made speeches or proposals upon state affairs, and to
that class Aristogiton now belongs. Secondly, they
provided in the laws for indictments for bribery, and

---

⁴ προσδεχομένοις N : δεχομένοις A.
⁵ γνώριμον καὶ φανερὰν Reiske : γνώριμος καὶ φανερὸς codd.
⁶ ἐν ὑμῖν om. A.   ⁷ πότερα N : πότερον A.
⁸ ὑμῶν N : ἡμῶν A.   ⁹ ἐκκλησίαν add. Dobree.

275

ἀδικημάτων δεκαπλασίαν ἐπιθέντες[1] τοῦ τιμήματος
τὴν ἔκτισιν, ἡγούμενοι τὸν τιμὴν λαμβάνοντα τῶν
ἐν τῷ δήμῳ ῥηθήσεσθαι μελλόντων λόγων, τοῦτον
οὐχ ὑπὲρ τῶν τοῦ δήμου βελτίστων ἀλλ' ὑπὲρ τῶν
τοῖς δοῦσι συμφερόντων δημηγορεῖν· Ἀριστογείτονα
τοίνυν ἡ βουλὴ ἀποπέφαγκε· πρὸς δὲ τούτοις ἀνακρίνοντες[2] τοὺς τῶν κοινῶν τι μέλλοντας διοικεῖν,
τίς ἐστι[3] τὸν ἴδιον τρόπον, εἰ γονέας εὖ ποιεῖ, εἰ
τὰς στρατείας ὑπὲρ τῆς πόλεως ἐστράτευται,
18 εἰ ἱερὰ[4] πατρῷά ἐστιν, εἰ τὰ τέλη τελεῖ· ὧν οὐδὲν
ἂν ἔχοι δεῖξαι[5] συμβεβηκὸς Ἀριστογείτων αὑτῷ.
ἀντὶ μὲν γὰρ τοῦ γονέας εὖ ποιεῖν κακῶς οὗτος τὸν
ἑαυτοῦ πατέρα πεποίηκεν· ὅτε δ' ὑμεῖς ἐστρα-
τεύεσθε πάντες, οὗτος ἦν ἐν τῷ δεσμωτηρίῳ· τοσοῦτον δ' ἀπολέλοιπε τοῦ πατρὸς μνῆμά τι ἔχειν,
ὦ Ἀθηναῖοι, δεῖξαι, ὥστ' οὐδ' ἐν Ἐρετρίᾳ τοῦ
πατρὸς αὑτοῦ τελευτήσαντος ἐκεῖ τὰ νομιζόμενα
ἐποίησεν αὑτῷ· τῶν δ' ἄλλων Ἀθηναίων εἰσφερόν-
των ἐκ τῶν ἰδίων, οὗτος οὐδὲ[6] τῶν δημοσίων καὶ
19 ὧν ὦφλε τὸ ἀργύριον ἅπαν ἐκτέτεικεν. ἁπλῶς δ'
εἰπεῖν, ἐναντία τοῖς νόμοις ἅπασι πράττων διατετέλεκε, καὶ τοῦτον μόνον ἡ ἐξ Ἀρείου πάγου βουλὴ
τοῖς ἐζητηκόσι καὶ εἰδόσιν ἀποπέφαγκεν· οὐ γὰρ
παρ' ἐκείνης ὑμεῖς πυθόμενοι τοῦτον ἴστε πονηρὸν
καὶ ἄδικον ὄντα, ἀλλ' ἕκαστος ὑμῶν ἀκριβῶς οἶδε
τὴν τούτου πονηρίαν. ὥστε τὸ πολλάκις λεγόμενον
ἀληθὲς εἰπεῖν ἐστιν, ὅτι περὶ μὲν τούτου τὴν ψῆφον

---

[1] ἐπιθέντες Fuhr : ἐπιτιθέντες codd.
[2] ἀνακρίνοντες (coll. ποιούμενοι § 16) Blass : ἀνακρίναντες
codd.
[3] ἐστι Reiske : ἔσται codd.
[4] ἱερὰ] ἡρία Valesius.
[5] δεῖξαι hic N : post αὑτῷ A.

this is the only offence for which they imposed a payment equal to ten times the assessment of damages,[a] in the belief that one who is ready to be paid for the opinions which he is going to express in the Assembly has at heart, when he is speaking, not the interests of the people but the welfare of those who have paid him. Now the council has reported Aristogiton as guilty of this. Moreover, when choosing a man for public office they used to ask what his personal character was, whether he treated his parents well, whether he had served the city in the field, whether he had an ancestral cult or paid taxes. Aristogiton could not claim one of these qualifications for himself. So far from treating his parents well this man has ill-treated his own father. When you were all serving in the army he was in prison ; and, far from being able to point to any memorial of his father, Athenians, he did not give him a proper funeral even in Eretria where he died.[b] While other Athenians are contributing from their own purses this man has not even paid up all the money to defray the public debts which he incurred. In fact he has never ceased to contravene all the laws, and his is the one case of those on which the Areopagus has reported where you had inquired yourselves and already knew the answer. For your knowledge that this man is a rogue and a criminal was not gained from the council ; you are all very well aware of his wickedness, and hence the statement so often made applies here also, namely that, while you are passing judgement on the de-

---

[a] Cf. note on I. 60. Aristotle (*Ath. Pol.* 54) states that theft was punished in the same way.

[b] Cf. [Dem.] xxv. 54.

<hr>

[6] οὐδὲ N : οὐδ' ἐκ A.

ὑμεῖς μέλλετε φέρειν, περὶ δ' ὑμῶν οἱ περιεστηκότες
καὶ οἱ ἄλλοι πάντες.

20   Διὸ καὶ σωφρόνων ἐστὶ δικαστῶν, ὦ Ἀθηναῖοι,
μηθ' ὑμῖν αὐτοῖς ἐναντίαν ἐνεγκεῖν τὴν ψῆφον μήτε
πᾶσι τοῖς ἄλλοις Ἀθηναίοις, ἀλλ' ὁμοθυμαδὸν
καταψηφισαμένους πάντας παραδοῦναι τοῖς ἐπὶ
τοῦτο τεταγμένοις θανάτῳ ζημιῶσαι, καὶ μὴ προέσθαι καὶ μὴ προδοῦναι τὴν ὁσίαν[1] καὶ τὴν εὔορκον
ψῆφον, ἀναμνησθέντας ὅτι τούτου κατέγνωκεν ἡ
βουλὴ δῶρα λαμβάνειν καθ' ὑμῶν, τούτου κατέγνωκεν ὁ πατὴρ καὶ ζῶν καὶ τελευτήσας ἀδικεῖν
ἑαυτόν, [καὶ][2] ἵνα τὸ πραότατον[3] εἴπω τῶν ὀνο-
μάτων, τούτου καταχειροτονήσας ὁ δῆμος παρα-
21 δέδωκεν[4] ὑμῖν τιμωρήσασθαι, οὗτος πολλὰ κακὰ
διαπεπραγμένος ἐπὶ τοιούτοις εἴληπται πράγμασι
νῦν ἀδικῶν, ἐφ' οἷς αἰσχρόν ἐστιν ὑμῖν τοῖς δικά-
ζουσιν ἀτιμώρητον ἐᾶσαι τοῦτον. τίνα γὰρ τρόπον,
ὦ Ἀθηναῖοι, περὶ τῶν ἄλλων ἀποφάσεων οἴσετε
τὴν ψῆφον; ἢ διὰ τίνας προφάσεις τῶν ἤδη κεκρι-
μένων ἔσεσθε κατεψηφισμένοι; ἢ διὰ τί τὸ μὲν
ἀποφαίνειν τὴν βουλὴν τοὺς εἰληφότας τὰ χρήματα
φανεῖσθε[5] σπουδάζοντες, τὸ δὲ τιμωρεῖσθαι τοὺς
22 ἀποπεφασμένους ἐῶντες; μὴ γὰρ ἰδίους τοὺς[6]
ἀγῶνας τούτους ὑπολάβητε εἶναι κατὰ τῶν νῦν
ἀποπεφασμένων μόνων, ἀλλὰ κοινοὺς καὶ κατὰ[7]
τῶν ἄλλων ἀνθρώπων. δωροδοκία γὰρ καὶ προ-
δοσία κρινομένη παρ' ὑμῖν δυοῖν θάτερον ἐκ[8] τοῦ
λοιποῦ χρόνου ποιήσει τοὺς ἄλλους, ἢ χρήματα
[108] λαμβάνειν καθ' ὑμῶν θαρροῦντας ὡς οὐ δώσοντας

---

[1] ὁσίαν Bekker : θείαν codd.
[2] καὶ del. Emperius.
[3] πραότατον Reiske : πραότερον codd.

fendant, the bystanders and everyone besides are
passing judgement on you.

Therefore it is your duty as a sensible jury,
Athenians, not to vote against yourselves or the rest
of Athens ; you should sentence him unanimously
to be handed over to the executioners for the death
penalty. Do not be traitors and fail to give the honest
verdict demanded by your oath. Remember that
this man has been convicted by the council of taking
bribes against you, convicted of ill-treating him, to
use the mildest term, by his father during his life and
after his death, condemned by the people's vote and
handed over to you for punishment. Remember that
this man has caused a deal of harm and has now been
caught doing wrong in circumstances which make it
shameful for you, his judges, to release him unpunished. For if you do so, how are you going to
vote on the other reports, Athenians ? What justification will you give for having condemned those men
whom you have already tried ? What reason will you
have, when you were clearly anxious for the council
to report those who had taken the money, for failing
obviously to punish the men whose names they submit ? You must not imagine that these trials are
private issues concerning no one but the men reported ; they are public and concern the rest of us
as well. A case of bribery and treason tried before
you will affect others in the future in two possible
ways : either it will make them accept bribes against
you unhesitatingly in the knowledge that they will

---

⁴ παραδέδωκεν N : παρέδωκεν A.
⁵ φανεῖσθε Dobree : φαίνεσθε codd.
⁶ τοὺς om. A.   ⁷ κατὰ N A corr. : ἀπὸ A pr.
⁸ ἐκ N A pr. : ἐπὶ A corr.²

DINARCHUS

δίκην, ἢ φοβεῖσθαι τὸ λαμβάνειν ὡς τῆς τιμωρίας
τοῖς ληφθεῖσιν ἀξίας γενησομένης τῶν ἀδικημάτων.
23 οὐκ ἴσθ', ὅτι καὶ νῦν ὁ φόβος ὁ παρ' ὑμῶν τοὺς
ὁρμῶντας ἐπὶ τὰ καθ' ὑμῶν[1] ἥκοντα χρήματα [νῦν][2]
ἀνείργει καὶ ποιεῖ πολλάκις ἀπὸ τοῦ λήμματος
ἀποστρέφειν; καὶ τὸ ψήφισμα τοῦ δήμου, τὸ
ζητεῖν τὴν βουλὴν περὶ τούτων τῶν χρημάτων
προστάττον,[3] οὐδὲ τοὺς κεκομικότας τὸ χρυσίον
24 εἰς τὴν χώραν ὁμολογεῖν πεποίηκε; καλῶς γάρ,
ὦ Ἀθηναῖοι, καλῶς οἱ πρόγονοι περὶ τούτων ψηφι-
σάμενοι στήλην εἰς ἀκρόπολιν ἀνήνεγκαν, ὅτε φασὶν
Ἄρθμιον τὸν Πυθώνακτος τὸν Ζελείτην κομίσαι
τὸ χρυσίον ἐκ Μήδων ἐπὶ διαφθορᾷ τῶν Ἑλλήνων.
πρὶν γὰρ λαβεῖν τινας καὶ δοῦναι τοῦ τρόπου πεῖραν,
φυγὴν τοῦ κομίσαντος τὸ χρυσίον καταγνόντες,
ἐξήλασαν αὐτὸν ἐξ ἁπάσης τῆς χώρας. καὶ ταῦθ',
ὥσπερ εἶπον, εἰς τὴν ἀκρόπολιν εἰς στήλην χαλκῆν
γράψαντες ἀνέθεσαν, παράδειγμα ὑμῖν τοῖς ἐπιγιγνομένοις καθιστάντες, καὶ νομίζοντες τὸν ὁπωσοῦν
χρήματα λαμβάνοντα οὐχ ὑπὲρ τῆς πόλεως ἀλλ'
25 ὑπὲρ τῶν διδόντων βουλεύεσθαι. καὶ μόνῳ τούτῳ
προσέγραψαν τὴν αἰτίαν δι' ἣν ὁ δῆμος ἐξέβαλεν
αὐτὸν ἐκ τῆς πόλεως, γράψαντες διαρρήδην·
Ἄρθμιον τὸν Πυθώνακτος τὸν Ζελείτην πολέμιον
εἶναι τοῦ δήμου καὶ τῶν συμμάχων, αὐτὸν καὶ
γένος, καὶ φεύγειν Ἀθήνας ὅτι τὸν ἐκ Μήδων

[1] ὑμῶν N : ἡμῶν A. [2] νῦν del. Bekker.
[3] προστάττον Reiske : πρός τ' αὐτόν codd.

280

not be brought to justice, or it will make them afraid
to take them, since they will know that those who
are caught will be punished in a manner suited to
the crime. Do you not know that now the fear of
what you will do restrains those who are grasping
for the money offered for use against you and often
makes them turn their backs on the bribe, and that
the people's decree, ordering the council to inquire
about this money, has prevented even those who
brought the gold into the country from admitting
their action? It was a noble decree, Athenians, a
noble decree of your ancestors on this question, providing for a pillar on the Acropolis at the time when
Arthmius, son of Pithonax, the Zelite, is said to have
brought the gold from the Persians to corrupt the
Greeks.[a] For before anyone had accepted it or given
proof of his character they sentenced the man who
had brought the gold to exile and banished him completely from the country. This decision, as I said,
they engraved on a bronze pillar and set up on the
Acropolis as a lesson for you their descendants; for
they believed that the man who accepted money in
any way at all had in mind the interests of the donors
rather than those of the city. His was the only case
in which they added the reason why the people
banished him from the city, explicitly writing on the
pillar that Arthmius, son of Pithonax, the Zelite, was
an enemy of the people and its allies, he and his descendants, and was exiled from Athens because he had

---

[a] Demosthenes (ix. 42 and xix. 271) refers to this pillar.
Arthmius of Zelea was an Athenian proxenus. He was sent
by Artaxerxes to the Peloponnesus, probably in 461, to stir
up war against the Athenians, who had been assisting a
revolt in Egypt. (*Cf.* Thucyd. i. 109; Diodor. xi. 74. 5;
Aeschin. iii. 258.)

χρυσὸν ἤγαγεν εἰς Πελοπόννησον. καίτοι εἰ τὸν
ἐν Πελοποννήσῳ χρυσὸν ὁ δῆμος πολλῶν κακῶν
αἴτιον ἡγεῖτο τοῖς Ἕλλησιν εἶναι, πῶς χρὴ ῥαθύμως
ἔχειν ὁρῶντας ἐν αὐτῇ[1] τῇ πόλει δωροδοκίαν
γιγνομένην; καί μοι σκοπεῖτε ταύτην τὴν στήλην.

ΣΤΗΛΗ

26 καίτοι, ὦ Ἀθηναῖοι, τί ἂν οἴεσθ' ἐκείνους τοὺς
ἄνδρας ποιῆσαι[2] λαβόντας ἢ στρατηγὸν ἢ ῥήτορα
πολίτην ἑαυτῶν δῶρα δεχόμενον ἐπὶ τοῖς τῆς πατρίδος συμφέρουσιν, οἳ τὸν ἀλλότριον καὶ τῷ γένει
καὶ τῇ φύσει τῆς Ἑλλάδος ἄνθρωπον οὕτω δικαίως
καὶ σωφρόνως ἐξήλασαν [ἐκ Πελοποννήσου πά-
σης];[3] τοιγάρτοι τῆς πόλεως καὶ τῶν προγόνων
ἀξίως ἐκινδύνευσαν πρὸς τὸν βάρβαρον.[4]

---

[1] αὐτῇ Dobree : ταύτῃ codd.
[2] ποιῆσαι hic N : supra post οἴεσθε A.

brought the Persian gold to the Peloponnese. And yet if the people regarded the gold in the Peloponnese as a source of great danger to Greece, how can we remain unmoved at the sight of bribery in the city itself? Please attend to the inscription on the pillar.

Inscription

Now what do you think those men would have done, Athenians, if they had caught a general or an orator, one of their own citizens, accepting bribes against the interests of their country, when they so justly and wisely expelled a man who was alien to Greece in birth and character? That is the reason why they faced danger against the barbarian worthily of the city and their ancestors.[a]

[a] The conclusion of the speech is lost.

---

[3] ἐκ Πελοποννήσου πάσης del. Bekker.
[4] κατὰ ἀριστογείτονος subicit N : deesse quaedam putant Baiter et Sauppe.

III
SPEECH AGAINST PHILOCLES

INTRODUCTION

PHILOCLES, like Demosthenes and Aristogiton, was one of the accused in the Harpalus case.[a] Of his life nothing certain is known apart from the details contained in the following speech, from which we learn that as general in charge of Munichia he allowed Harpalus to enter the Piraeus. Though he had served as hipparch three or four times and as general more than ten,[b] he was refused the post of Supervisor of the Ephebi (κοσμητής)[c]; a failure which, in the absence of date, it seems reasonable to connect with his coming under suspicion before the present trial, since in normal times he appears to have been a highly respected man.[d]

Though doubt exists regarding the judgement passed on Philocles, it seems likely that he was acquitted. In the third epistle of Demosthenes we are plainly told that he was condemned,[e] but this statement conflicts with inscriptional evidence that a certain Philocles, son of Phormio, of the deme Eroeadae, was crowned in the year 324/3 B.C., at the

---

[a] See Dinarch. *Against Demosthenes* : Introd. (The Harpalus Affair).

[b] Dinarch. iii. 12.

[c] Dinarch. iii. 15.

[d] Dinarch. iii. 12.

[e] Dem. *Ep.* iii. 31. The authenticity of the letter is open to question.

end of his year of office as κοσμητής.[a] If the Philocles there mentioned is the same man as the Philocles whom Dinarchus is attacking, as seems probable, he must have been acquitted, as he could not otherwise have held the post. The evidence of the inscription can then be reconciled with the orator's statement [b] by the assumption that Philocles was rejected as κοσμητής while the trial was pending but finally accepted after being acquitted. In so far as this conclusion discounts the direct testimony of the epistle it must be regarded as tentative,[c] but to allow that Philocles was condemned and conclude that the inscription relates to a different person seems on the whole a less satisfactory line to follow.

[a] Ἐφ. Ἀρχ. (1918), pp. 73 sq. Cf. Rev. Phil. (N.F.), xiv. (1936), pp. 74 sq.
[b] Dinarch. iii. 15.
[c] See Treves in Pauly-Wissowa, s.v. " Philocles."

ANALYSIS

ΚΑΤΑ ΦΙΛΟΚΛΕΟΥΣ

Τί χρὴ λέγειν πρὸς τῶν θεῶν περὶ τοιούτων ἀνθρώπων,[1] ἢ πῶς[2] χρήσεσθε τῇ τούτου πονηρίᾳ; ὃς οὐχ ἅπαξ ἀλλὰ τρὶς ἐξεληλεγμένος ὑπὸ τῆς ἐξ Ἀρείου πάγου βουλῆς, ὡς ὑμεῖς ἅπαντες ἴστε καὶ νῦν ἐν τῷ δήμῳ ἠκούετε, καὶ ἐψευσμένος ἁπάντων Ἀθηναίων ἐναντίον καὶ τῶν περιεστηκότων, φάσκων κωλύσειν Ἅρπαλον εἰς τὸν Πειραιᾶ καταπλεῦσαι,[3] στρατηγὸς ὑφ' ὑμῶν ἐπὶ τὴν Μουνιχίαν 2 καὶ τὰ νεώρια κεχειροτονημένος, καὶ δῶρα τολμήσας λαβεῖν κατὰ πάντων ὑμῶν καὶ τῆς χώρας καὶ παίδων καὶ γυναικῶν, καὶ ἐπιωρκηκὼς ὃν ὤμοσεν ὅρκον μεταξὺ τοῦ ἕδους καὶ τῆς τραπέζης, καὶ γράψας καθ' ἑαυτοῦ ψήφισμα, καὶ θανάτου τιμησάμενος ἐὰν εἰλήφῃ[4] τι τῶν χρημάτων ὧν Ἅρπαλος 3 εἰς τὴν χώραν ἐκόμισεν, ὅμως ἐτόλμησεν εἰς τοὺς εἰδότας ὑμᾶς ἐξεληλεγμένον ἑαυτὸν ἅπασι τούτοις ἔνοχον γεγενημένον ἐλθεῖν καὶ δεῖξαι ἑαυτόν, οὐ τῷ δικαίῳ πιστεύσων, ὦ Ἀθηναῖοι,[5] —τί γὰρ τούτῳ δικαιοσύνης μέτεστιν;—ἀλλὰ τῇ τόλμῃ καὶ[6] τῇ ἀναιδείᾳ, ᾗ χρώμενος πρότερον μὲν ἠξίωσε καταφρονήσας ὑμῶν καὶ τῶν ἐν τῇ πόλει δικαίων τὰ

---

[1] τοιούτων ἀνθρώπων N : τοιούτου ἀνθρώπου A.
[2] ἢ πῶς Bekker : ὅπως codd.

AGAINST PHILOCLES

WHAT in Heaven's name are we to say about such
men as this? How will you deal with the wickedness
of Philocles, who has been convicted by the Areopagus
not once only but three times, as you all know, and
as you were recently informed in the Assembly? He
has lied before all the Athenians and the surrounding
crowd, saying that he would prevent Harpalus from
putting into the Piraeus, when he had been appointed
by you as general in command of Munichia and the
dockyards, and he dared to take bribes against you
all, against your country and your wives and children;
he has broken the oath which he swore between the
statue of Athena and the table; and he proposed a
decree against himself imposing the death penalty
on him if he had accepted any of the money which
Harpalus brought into the country. Yet despite
this he dared to come and show himself to you when
you knew that he had been proved answerable on
all these counts. It is not justice on which he is
relying, Athenians; for what has he to do with
justice? No, it is audacity and effrontery, in virtue
of which he has seen fit to take bribes in the past,
to the utter disregard of yourselves and the course

---

³ καταπλεῦσαι Bekker : καταπλεύσειν codd.
⁴ εἰλήφῃ Bekker : εἴληφέ codd.
⁵ ὦ 'Αθηναῖοι om. A.   ⁶ καὶ add. A corr.²

χρήματα λαβεῖν, νυνὶ δὲ ἀπολογησόμενος ἥκει
ὡς οὐδὲν τούτων διαπέπρακται· τοσοῦτον τῆς
4 ὑμετέρας ῥᾳθυμίας καταπεφρόνηκε. καὶ ὁ μὲν
κοινὸς τῆς πόλεως νόμος, ἐάν τις ⟨ἑνὸς⟩¹ ἐναντίον
[109] τῶν πολιτῶν ὁμολογήσας τι παραβῇ τοῦτον ἔνοχον
εἶναι κελεύει τῷ ἀδικεῖν· ὁ δὲ πάντας Ἀθηναίους
ἐξηπατηκώς, καὶ προδοὺς τὴν πίστιν ἣν παρ' ὑμῶν
οὐκ ἄξιος ὢν ἔλαβε, καὶ τὸ καθ' αὑτὸν μέρος
ἅπαντ' ἀνατετροφὼς τὰ ἐν τῇ πόλει, οὗτος ἐπὶ τὴν
ἀπολογίαν ἥκειν φήσει τὴν ὑπὲρ τῆς αἰτίας τῆς εἰς
5 αὑτὸν² γεγενημένης; ἐγὼ δέ, ὦ ἄνδρες,³ εἰ δεῖ
τἀληθῆ λέγειν—δεῖ δέ—, οὐ⁴ τὰς ἀποφάσεις οἶμαι
νῦν κρίνεσθαι, πότερον ἀληθεῖς εἰσιν ἢ ψευδεῖς αἱ
κατὰ Φιλοκλέους γεγενημέναι, ἀλλὰ περὶ μόνης⁵
τῆς τιμωρίας ὑμᾶς δεῖν τῆς ἐν τῷ ψηφίσματι γε-
γραμμένης δικάσαι νῦν, πότερα δεῖ χρημάτων τιμῆσαι τῷ τηλικαῦτα ἠδικηκότι τὴν πόλιν, ἢ θανάτῳ
ζημιώσαντας, ὥσπερ οὗτος ἔγραψεν ἐν τῷ ψηφίσματι καθ' αὑτοῦ, [ἢ]⁶ δημεῦσαι τὴν οὐσίαν τὴν ἐκ
τοιούτων λημμάτων συνειλεγμένην.
6 Οἴεσθε τοῦτον νῦν πρῶτον ἐπὶ τούτων τῶν χρημάτων πονηρὸν γεγενῆσθαι, ἢ νῦν πρῶτον καθ'
ὑμῶν δῶρα εἰληφέναι; οὐκ ἔστι ταῦτα, ἀλλὰ πάλαι
τοιοῦτος ὢν ἐλάνθανεν ὑμᾶς, καὶ ηὐτυχήκαθ' ὅτι⁷
οὐκ ἐν μείζοσι καιροῖς ἐπύθεσθε τὴν αἰσχροκέρδειαν
αὐτοῦ· οὐ γάρ ἐστι χαλεπώτερον ἀνθρώπου τὴν
7 αὑτοῦ⁸ πονηρίαν ἀγνοουμένην ἔχοντος. οὐκ ἀποκτενεῖτε, ὦ Ἀθηναῖοι, πάντες ὁμοθυμαδὸν τὸν εἰς

---

¹ ἑνὸς hic add. Blass (iam post ἐναντίον Bake): ἑνί τινι pro
ἐναντίον Lipsius.
² αὑτὸν Baiter et Sauppe: αὐτὸν codd.
³ ἄνδρες A : Ἀθηναῖοι N.   ⁴ οὐ Maetzner: οὐδὲ codd.

of justice in the city, and has now come forward to explain that he is guilty of none of these things. So complete has been his contempt for your apathy. The law of the city, which binds us all, lays it down that if anyone breaks an agreement made in the presence of one of the citizens he shall be liable as an offender. Shall this man, who has deceived every Athenian, betrayed the trust which he did not deserve to receive from you, and so done everything in his power to ruin all the city's institutions, claim that he is coming to make his defence against the charge laid against him ? It is my personal opinion, Athenians, if I am to speak the truth,—as I must,—that there is no question whether the reports bearing on Philocles are true or false ; you have simply to consider now the punishment mentioned in the decree and to decide whether you ought to fine a man who has done the city so much harm or sentence him to death,— as he proposed in the decree against himself,—confiscating the property which he has amassed from perquisites like this.

Do you think that this question of the gold is the first occasion when Philocles has shown his dishonesty and that he has never taken bribes against you before ? You are wrong. He has been like this a long time, though you did not notice it ; indeed you have been fortunate not to have met with his venality on more important occasions ; for there is no greater menace than a man whose dishonesty passes unobserved. Athenians, will you not all unite in killing

---

⁵ μόνης Reiske : μὲν codd.
  ⁶ ἢ del. Reiske.
⁷ ηὐτυχήκαθ' ὅτι Vogel : ηὐτύχει καθότι A : εὐτύχει καθότι N.
  ⁸ αὐτοῦ N corr.² : αὐτὴν N pr. A, del. Maetzner.

DINARCHUS

τοσαύτην αἰσχύνην καὶ ἀδικίαν πολλοὺς τῶν πολιτῶν[1] ἐμβεβληκότα, τὸν ἀρχηγὸν γενόμενον τοῦ
διαδεδομένου χρυσίου καὶ εἰς αἰτίαν καθιστάντα[2]
πᾶσαν τὴν πόλιν; ἀλλ' ὑπομενεῖτ' ἀκούειν τοῦ
τοσαῦτα διαπεπραγμένου καθ' ὑμῶν, ὡς [ὅτι][3] τὸ
συνέδριον τὸ ἐν Ἀρείῳ πάγῳ ψευδεῖς πεποίηται τὰς
ἀποφάσεις, καὶ ὡς αὐτὸς μὲν δίκαιος καὶ χρηστὸς
καὶ ἀδωροδόκητός ἐστιν, ἡ δ' ἐξ Ἀρείου πάγου
βουλὴ ταῦτα πάντα προεῖται χάριτος ἢ λημμάτων[4]
8 ἕνεκα; ἆρ' ἴσθ' ὅτι ἐπὶ μὲν τῶν ἄλλων ἀδικημάτων
σκεψαμένους ἀκριβῶς δεῖ μεθ' ἡσυχίας καὶ τἀληθὲς
ἐξετάσαντας, οὕτως ἐπιτιθέναι τοῖς ἠδικηκόσι τὴν
τιμωρίαν, ἐπὶ δὲ ταῖς φανεραῖς καὶ παρὰ πάντων
ὡμολογημέναις προδοσίαις πρώτην[5] τετάχθαι τὴν
ὀργὴν καὶ τὴν μετ' αὐτῆς[6] γιγνομένην τιμωρίαν;
9 τί γὰρ τοῦτον οὐκ ἂν οἴεσθε ἀποδόσθαι τῶν ἐν τῇ
πόλει σπουδαιοτάτων, ὅταν ὑμεῖς ὡς πιστὸν αὐτὸν
καὶ δίκαιον φύλακα καταστήσητε; ποίας οὐκ ἂν
προδοῦναι τριήρεις τῶν ἐν τοῖς νεωρίοις; ἢ τίνος
ἂν φροντίσαι φυλακῆς, λήσειν ἐλπίσαντα καὶ λήψεσθαι[7] διπλάσιον οὗ νῦν εἴληφε χρυσίου; οὐδὲν
10 ὅ τι οὐκ ἂν ὁ τοιοῦτος, ὦ ἄνδρες, ποιήσειεν. ὅστις
γὰρ ἀργύριον καὶ χρυσίον περὶ πλείονος τῆς πρὸς
ὑμᾶς πίστεως ἡγεῖται[8] καὶ μήθ' ὅρκου μήτ' αἰσχύνης μήτε δικαίου πλείω λόγον ἢ τοῦ λαμβάνειν
ποιεῖται, οὗτος ἀποδώσεται τὸ καθ' αὑτὸν τὴν
Μουνιχίαν, ἂν ἔχῃ τὸν ὠνησόμενον, οὗτος ἐξαγγελεῖ

---

[1] τῶν πολιτῶν om. A.
[2] καθιστάντα Stephanus : καθίσαντα codd.
[3] ὅτι del. Maetzner.

294

one who has plunged many of our citizens into such deep disgrace and guilt, who first opened the way for the gold that has been distributed, exposing the whole of Athens to blame? Or will you consent to hear this man, who has done so much to harm you, argue that the council of the Areopagus has falsified the reports and that, while he is just and upright and incorruptible, it has published all this in return for favours or bribes? Do you realize that, although in the case of other offences you must first consider critically and with deliberation, discovering the truth, and only then administer punishment to the offenders, nevertheless, in cases of obvious and unquestioned treason, you should give first place to anger and the vengeance that goes with it? Do you think this man would refrain from selling any one of the things most vital in the city, when you, relying on his loyalty and honesty, had placed him in charge of it? Do you think that there are any triremes in the dockyards which he would not let go, or that he would trouble to keep anything safe, if there was a prospect of escaping detection and receiving double the amount of gold which he has now received? Nothing, gentlemen, is beyond a man of this type. For if anyone values silver and gold more highly than his loyalty to you and has no more regard for an oath or for honour and right than he has for making money, then that man, in so far as he is able, will sell Munichia if he has a buyer; he will signal to the enemy and

⁴ λημμάτων N : λήμματος A.
⁵ πρώτην Reiske : πρῶτον codd.
⁶ αὐτῆς Bekker : αὐτὴν codd.
⁷ λήψεσθαι A corr.² N corr.² : λήψεσθε A pr. N pr.
⁸ ἡγεῖται Baiter et Sauppe : αἱρεῖται codd.

τοῖς πολεμίοις σύνθημα φήνας καθ᾽ ὑμῶν, οὗτος
προδώσει τὴν¹ πεζὴν² καὶ ναυτικὴν δύναμιν.

11 Μὴ οὖν, ὦ Ἀθηναῖοι, τὴν τίμησιν ὑπὲρ τῶν
γεγενημένων μόνον ὑπὸ Φιλοκλέους ἀδικημάτων
ἡγεῖσθε μέλλειν ποιεῖσθαι, ἀλλὰ καὶ ὑπὲρ τῶν ἄλλων ὧν ἂν³ ἔπραξεν οὗτος κύριος γενόμενος. καὶ
τοῖς μὲν θεοῖς ἔχετε χάριν ὑπὲρ τοῦ μὴ παθεῖν τι
μεῖζον ὑπὸ τούτου δεινόν, ἐγνωκότες τοῦτον οἷός
ἐστιν· ἀξίως δ᾽ ὑμῶν αὐτῶν καὶ τῆς τοῦ κρινομένου
12 πονηρίας κολάσατε αὐτόν· ὃς, ὦ Ἀθηναῖοι, τρὶς
μὲν⁴ ἢ τετράκις ἱππαρχηκὼς ἀνδρῶν καλῶν κἀγαθῶν, πλεονάκις δ᾽ ἢ δεκάκις στρατηγὸς ὑφ᾽ ὑμῶν
κεχειροτονημένος οὐκ ἄξιος ὤν, τιμώμενος καὶ ζη-
λούμενος διὰ τὴν πρὸς ὑμᾶς πίστιν ἀπέδοτο καὶ
προέδωκε τὸ τῆς ἡμετέρας ἡγεμονίας⁵ ἀξίωμα, καὶ
εἰς τὸ αὐτὸ κατέστησεν ἑαυτὸν Ἀριστογείτονι,
καὶ μισθωτὸν καὶ προδότην ἀντὶ στρατηγοῦ ἐποίη-
13 σεν. ἔπειθ᾽ ὑποστείλασθαί τι δεῖ πρὸς τὸν τοιοῦτον ὑμᾶς,⁶ καὶ αἰσχυνθῆναι τοὺς ἠδικημένους, ὃς οὐκ
ᾐσχύνθη τοιαῦτα πράττων καθ᾽ ὑμῶν καὶ τῶν ἄλλων·
οὐχ οἱ τοιοῦτοι τῶν ἀνθρώπων ἐλεοῖντ᾽ ἂν εἰκότως
παρ᾽ ὑμῖν, ὦ Ἀθηναῖοι· πολλοῦ γε καὶ δεῖ· ἀλλ᾽ οἱ
[110] προδοθέντες ἂν ὑπὸ Φιλοκλέους, εἴ τιν᾽ οὗτος παρ-
έλαβε καιρὸν χρημάτων πολλῶν·⁷ ἐν οἷς καὶ ἡ ἀκτὴ
καὶ οἱ λιμένες εἰσὶ καὶ τὰ νεώρια, ἃ οἱ πρόγονοι
14 κατασκευάσαντες ὑμῖν⁸ κατέλιπον. ὧν ἀναμιμνη-
σκομένους ὑμᾶς, ὦ Ἀθηναῖοι, δεῖ μὴ παρέργως
ἔχειν πρὸς τὰς ὑπὸ τῆς βουλῆς γεγενημένας ἀπο-

---

¹ τὴν om. N.
² πεζὴν N : πεζικὴν Α.
³ ἂν add. A corr.²
⁴ μὲν om. Α.

reveal your secrets, he will betray your army and your
fleet.

Therefore, Athenians, do not imagine that, in
assessing the penalty, you are merely going to judge
of the crimes which Philocles has actually committed ;
you will bear in mind those which he would have
committed, had it been in his power. Thank the
gods, now that you know the defendant's character,
that you have suffered no more grievous harm at his
hands, and punish him as your duty and his baseness
demand. This man, Athenians, has held a cavalry
command, three or four times, over reputable men ;
he has been appointed a general by you more than
ten times, unworthy though he was, and has enjoyed
honour and aroused emulation because of his reputation for loyalty towards you. Yet he sold and betrayed
the dignity of a command conferred by us, reducing
himself to the level of Aristogiton and changing from
a general into a hireling and a traitor. Is this a reason
why you, the injured parties, should give way to
feelings of consideration for such a person when he
himself showed no consideration in treating you and
your fellows as he did ? Those who could justly
claim your pity, Athenians, are not the like of him,—
far from it,—they are those whom Philocles would
have betrayed if he had had the chance of a good
price ; and among them are the promontory and
harbours, and the dockyards which your ancestors
built and left you. You must remember these,
Athenians, and not make light of the reports pub-

---

⁵ ἡμετέρας ἡγεμονίας N : ἡγεμονίας ἡμῶν A.
⁶ ὑμᾶς Reiske : ὑμῖν codd.
⁷ χρημάτων πολλῶν infra post πρόγονοι transtulit Blass.
⁸ κατασκευάσαντες ὑμῖν N   ὑμῖν κατασκευάσαντες A.

φάσεις, ἀλλ' ἀκολούθως ταῖς πρότερον κεκριμέναις[1]·
αἰσχρὸν γὰρ ἀπειπεῖν τιμωρουμένους ἐστὶ τοὺς
προδότας τῆς πόλεως γεγενημένους, καὶ ὑπολεί-
πεσθαί τινας τῶν ἀδίκων καὶ πονηρῶν ἀνθρώπων,
ὅτε οἱ θεοὶ φανεροὺς ὑμῖν ποιήσαντες παρέδοσαν
τιμωρήσασθαι, ἑορακότες[2] τὸν δῆμον ἅπαντα κατήγορον τούτου γεγενημένον καὶ προκεχειρικότα
πρῶτον τῶν ἄλλων ἐπὶ τὸ[3] τὴν τιμωρίαν ἐν ὑμῖν
δοῦναι.

15 Ἀλλ' ἔγωγε, νὴ τὸν Δία τὸν σωτῆρα, αἰσχύνομαι,
εἰ προτραπέντας ὑμᾶς δεῖ[4] καὶ παροξυνθέντας ὑφ'
ἡμῶν[5] ἐπὶ τὴν τοῦ νῦν εἰσεληλυθότος[6] τὴν κρίσιν
τιμωρίαν ἐλθεῖν. [καὶ][7] οὐκ αὐτόπται ἐστὲ τῶν
ὑπὸ τούτου γεγενημένων ἀδικημάτων; καὶ ὁ μὲν
δῆμος ἅπας οὔτ' ἀσφαλὲς οὔτε δίκαιον νομίζων
εἶναι παρακαταθέσθαι τοὺς ἑαυτοῦ παῖδας ἀπεχει-
ροτόνησεν αὐτὸν ἀπὸ τῆς τῶν ἐφήβων ἐπιμελείας,

16 ὑμεῖς δ' οἱ τῆς δημοκρατίας καὶ τῶν νόμων φύλακες, οἷς[8] ἡ τύχη καὶ ὁ κλῆρος . . . ὑπὲρ τοῦ[9]
δήμου δικάσοντας ἐπέτρεψεν, φείσεσθε τοῦ τοιαῦτα
διαπεπραγμένου, καὶ τὸ πέρας ἔχοντες τῶν ἐν τῇ
πόλει ἁπάντων δικαίων ἀτιμώρητον ἀφήσετε τὸν
δωροδόκον καὶ πάντων τῶν γεγενημένων κακῶν
αἴτιον, ὅς, ὅπερ καὶ μικρῷ πρότερον εἶπον, μόνος

---

[1] Post κεκριμέναις lacunam indicavit Blass, qui καὶ ταύτην
κρίνειν deesse putavit.

[2] ἑορακότες Blass : ἐωρακότες NA : ἐωρακότας Stephanus.

[3] τὸ N : τῷ A.   [4] δεῖ A corr. ras. : δεῖν A pr. N.

[5] ἡμῶν A corr. : ὑμῶν A pr. N.

[6] εἰσεληλυθότος Blass (iam εἰσεληλυθότος [τὴν κρίσιν] Maetzner) : ἐκλελοιπότος NA.

[7] καὶ del. Baiter.

[8] οἷς Reiske : οὓς codd. : οἷς et δικάσαι infra pro δικάσοντας
Sauppe ; sed inter φύλακες et ἐπέτρεψεν nonnihil excidisse

298

lished by the council. ⟨Treat this case⟩ [a] as you treated those on which you have already passed judgement. For it is shameful to grow weary of punishing men who have proved traitors to the city, and shameful that any lawbreakers and reprobates should survive, when the gods have exposed them and surrendered them to you for punishment, having seen that the whole people had accused Philocles and handed him over first of all to meet with his deserts before you.

By Zeus the Saviour, I am ashamed that you should need us to encourage you and goad you on before you proceed to punish the defendant now on trial. Are you not eyewitnesses of the crimes he has committed? The whole people considered that it was not safe or right to trust him with their children and so rejected him as Supervisor of the Ephebi. Will you, the guardians of democracy and law, spare a man who has behaved like this; you to whom the fortune of lot has entrusted ⟨the protection⟩ [b] of the people by means of the judgement you will give? You are the supreme court of justice in the city. Will you acquit a man guilty of taking bribes and every other crime, who, as I said just now, is unique among criminals in that

---

[a] The sense of this passage is evident, though it is not clear whether Dinarchus is expressing himself loosely or whether, as Blass suggests, a few words have dropped out of the text.

[b] Some such meaning seems called for as is presumed by Reiske, but the actual Greek words supplied by him make the future participle δικάσοντας rather awkward.

---

videtur : post δικάσοντας lacunam indicavit Blass, qui οὓς retinuit : sensum ita supplet Reiske : οἷς ἡ τύχη . . . τὸ ὑπὲρ τοῦ δήμου ἀμύνεσθαι δικάσοντας ἐπέτρεψεν.

[9] τοῦ add. A corr.[2]

τῶν πονηρῶν πάντων τρὶς οὐχ ἅπαξ ἀποπέφανται,
καὶ τρὶς ἤδη δικαίως ⟨ἂν⟩[1] ἐζημιωμένος θανάτῳ
17 κατὰ τὸ αὑτοῦ ψήφισμα. τί οὖν ἀναμενεῖτ’, ὦ
Ἀθηναῖοι; καὶ ποῖα ἀδικήματα ζητεῖτε ἕτερα
μείζω τῶν εἰρημένων ἀκοῦσαι; οὐχ ὑμεῖς ἐστε
καὶ οἱ ὑμέτεροι πρόγονοι οἱ Τιμοθέῳ[2] Πελοπόννησον περιπλεύσαντι καὶ τὴν ἐν Κερκύρα ναυμαχίαν
Λακεδαιμονίους νικήσαντι καὶ Κόνωνος υἱεῖ τοῦ[3]
τοὺς Ἕλληνας ἐλευθερώσαντος[4] καὶ Σάμον λαβόντι[5]
καὶ Μεθώνην καὶ Πύδναν καὶ Ποτείδαιαν, καὶ πρὸς
ταύταις ἑτέρας εἴκοσι πόλεις, οὐδὲν τούτων ὑπόλογον ποιησάμενοι; οὐδὲ τῆς τότε ἐνεστώσης
κρίσεως καὶ τῶν ὅρκων οὓς ὀμωμοκότες φέρετε
τὴν ψῆφον ἀντικαταλλαξάμενοι τὰς τηλικαύτας
εὐεργεσίας, ἀλλ’ ἑκατὸν ταλάντων τιμήσαντες, ὅτι
χρήματ’ αὐτὸν Ἀριστοφῶν ἔφη παρὰ Χίων εἰληφέναι καὶ Ῥοδίων; τὸν δὲ μιαρὸν ἄνθρωπον καὶ
18 προδότην, ὃν οὐχ εἷς ἀνὴρ ἀλλὰ πᾶσα ἡ ἐξ Ἀρείου
πάγου βουλὴ ζητήσασα ἀποπέφαγκε χρήματ’ ἔχειν
καθ’ ὑμῶν, ὃς οὐσίαν ἔχων πολλὴν καὶ παίδων
ἀρρένων οὐκ ὄντων αὐτῷ, καὶ οὐδενὸς ἄλλου δεό-
μενος ὧν ⟨ἂν⟩[6] ἄνθρωπος μέτριος δεηθείη, οὐκ
ἀπέσχετο χρημάτων διδομένων κατὰ τῆς πατρίδος,
οὐδ’ ἀπεκρύψατο τὴν ἔμφυτον πονηρίαν, ἀλλ’ ἀνεῖλε
πᾶσαν τὴν γεγενημένην αὐτῷ πρὸς ὑμᾶς πίστιν,
καὶ οἷς πρότερον ἔφη διαφέρεσθαι, πρὸς τούτους

---

[1] ἂν add. Reiske.   [2] Cf. Dinarch. i, 14.
[3] τοῦ add. A corr.[2]

he has been reported not once merely but three times and might already have been rightly made liable three times to the death penalty by his own decree. Then why will you wait, Athenians ? What further crimes do you wish to hear of greater than those we have mentioned ? Was it not you and your ancestors who made no allowance for Timotheüs,[a] though he had sailed round the Peloponnese and beaten the Spartans in the sea-fight at Corcyra, though his father was Conon who liberated Greece and he himself had taken Samos, Methone, Pydna, Potidaea, and twenty cities besides ? You did not take this record into consideration at all, or allow such services to outweigh the case before you or the oaths which you swear before giving your verdict, but fined him a hundred talents, because Aristophon said he had been bribed by the Chians and Rhodians. ⟨Will you then acquit⟩[b] this abominable man, reported not by one individual but by the whole council of the Areopagus, after an investigation, to be holding bribes against you ; who, though he has ample means and no male heirs and lacks nothing else that a normal man could need, did not withhold his hand from the bribes offered against his country or suppress his natural depravity, but destroyed entirely his reputation for loyalty towards you, by ranging himself with

[a] This passage corresponds almost word for word with Dinarch. i. 14. See note on that.

[b] An apodosis conveying some such meaning as this, which is needed to complete the sense of the sentence, seems to have dropped out of the Greek text.

---

4 ἐλευθερώσαντος A corr.² : ἐλευθερώσαντι A pr. N.
5 λαβόντι N A pr. : λαβόντος A corr.²
6 ἂν add. Bekker.

ἔταξεν αὐτόν, καὶ ἐξήλεγξεν αὐτοῦ τὴν προσποίητον
καλοκαγαθίαν, ὅτι ψευδὴς ἦν.[1]

19 Ἃ χρὴ λογισαμένους ὑμᾶς πάντας,[2] ὦ Ἀθηναῖοι,
καὶ τῶν παρόντων καιρῶν ἀναμνησθέντας, οἳ πίστεως οὐ δωροδοκίας δέονται, μισεῖν τοὺς πονηρούς,
ἀνελεῖν ἐκ τῆς πόλεως[3] τὰ τοιαῦτα θηρία, καὶ δεῖξαι
πᾶσιν ἀνθρώποις ὅτι οὐ συνδιέφθαρται τὸ τοῦ δήμου
πλῆθος τῶν ῥητόρων καὶ τῶν στρατηγῶν τισιν,
οὐδὲ δουλεύει ταῖς δόξαις, εἰδότας[4] ὅτι μετὰ μὲν
δικαιοσύνης καὶ τῆς πρὸς ἀλλήλους ὁμονοίας ῥᾳδίως
ἀμυνούμεθα, θεῶν ἵλεων ὄντων, ἐάν τινες ἡμῖν[5]
ἀδίκως ἐπιτιθῶνται, μετὰ δὲ δωροδοκίας καὶ προδοσίας καὶ τῶν ὁμοίων τούτοις κακῶν, ἃ τοῖς τοιούτοις ἀνθρώποις πρόσεστιν, οὐδεμί᾽ ἂν[6] πόλις σωθείη.

20 μηδεμίαν οὖν δέησιν, ὦ Ἀθηναῖοι, μηδ᾽ ἔλεον εἰς
ὑμᾶς λαμβάνοντες[7] αὐτούς, μηδὲ τὴν ἐξ αὐτῶν τῶν
ἔργων καὶ τῆς ἀληθείας ἀποδεδειγμένην ὑμῖν κατὰ
τῶν κρινομένων ἀδικίαν[8] . . . ἄκυρον ποιήσαντες,
βοηθήσατε κοινῇ τῇ πατρίδι καὶ τοῖς νόμοις· ταῦτα
[111] γὰρ ἀμφότερα διαδικάζεται νῦν πρὸς τὴν τούτου
21 πονηρίαν. ὑπὲρ πάσης, ὦ Ἀθηναῖοι, τῆς χώρας
νῦν μέλλετε φέρειν τὴν ψῆφον, καὶ τῶν ἐν ταύτῃ
κατεσκευασμένων ἱερῶν καὶ τῶν ἀρχαίων νομίμων
καὶ τῆς παραδεδομένης ὑπὸ τῶν προγόνων ὑμῖν[9]
πολιτείας, οὐχ ὑπὲρ Φιλοκλέους μόνον· οὗτος μὲν[10]

---

1 Post ψευδὴς ἦν apodosin excidisse putant nonnulli.
2 πάντας add. N.
3 πόλεως N : πολιτείας A.
4 εἰδότας Ald. : εἰδότες NA.
5 ἡμῖν A corr.[2] : ὑμῶν A pr. N.
6 οὐδεμί᾽ ἂν Bekker : οὐδεμία codd.
7 λαμβάνοντες] del. Thalheim, qui post αὐτούς excidisse
προσεμένοι vel aliud simile putat.

those whom he once professed to oppose and proving
that his counterfeited honesty was sham ?

Let every one of you bear these points in mind,
Athenians, and remember the present circumstances,
which call for good faith, not corruption. You must
hate the wicked, wipe out such monsters from the city,
and show the world that the mass of people have not
been corrupted with a few orators and generals and
are not cowed by their reputation ; for they realize
that with integrity and agreement among ourselves
we shall easily triumph, by the grace of the gods, if
anyone unjustly attacks us, but that with bribery
and treason and the allied vices practised by men
like this no city could survive. Therefore, Athenians,
do not admit any request or plea for pity ; do not
⟨condone⟩ the guilt which you have seen fastened
upon the defendants in the plain light of facts, ⟨or
invalidate the council's report⟩ [a] ; but one and all
assist your country and the laws, since both are now
on trial against this man's iniquity. The whole
country will be affected by the verdict you are about
to give : the shrines which have been erected in it,
the agelong traditions, and the constitution which
your ancestors have handed down to you. It is not
a question of Philocles alone ; for he has condemned

---

[a] Some words have clearly dropped out from this passage.
No certain restoration is possible, although the general sense
is not difficult to conjecture. The restoration of Sauppe is
followed in the translation.

---

[8] Post ἀδικίαν lacunam indicavit Sauppe, qui totum locum
sic restituit : μηδ' ἔλεον ⟨δεξάμενοι⟩ μηδὲ τὴν ἐξ αὐτῶν κτλ. . . .
ἀδικίαν εἰς ὑμᾶς λαμβάνοντες αὐτοὺς ⟨μηδὲ τὴν τῆς βουλῆς ἀπό-
φασιν⟩ ἄκυρον ποιήσαντες κτλ.

[9] ὑμῖν Reiske : ὑμῶν codd.

[10] μὲν om. A.

DINARCHUS

γὰρ αὐτοῦ πάλαι θάνατον κατέγνωκε. ταῦθ᾽ ὑμᾶς
ἱκετεύων ἐγὼ δικαιοτέραν πολὺ δέησιν δέομαι τούτων τῶν τοιαῦτα[1] πεπραχότων, μὴ ἐγκαταλιπεῖν
ὑπὲρ ὧν οἱ πρόγονοι πολλοὺς ὑπέμειναν κινδύνους,
μηδ᾽ εἰς ἀδοξίαν αἰσχρὰν ἀγαγεῖν τὸ τῆς πόλεως
ἀξίωμα, μηδὲ ἀντικαταλλάξασθαι[2] τὴν πρὸς τούτους
χάριν τῶν νόμων καὶ τῶν τοῦ δήμου ⟨ψηφισμάτων⟩[3]
22 καὶ τῶν τῆς βουλῆς ἀποφάσεων. ἀκριβῶς γὰρ
ἴστε, ὦ Ἀθηναῖοι, ἀκριβῶς, ὅτι ὑμεῖς μὲν παρὰ
πᾶσιν ἀνθρώποις ἐπαινεῖσθε ταῖς γεγενημέναις ζητή-
σεσιν ὑπὲρ τούτων τῶν χρημάτων, οἱ δ᾽ ἐξεληλεγ-
μένοι κατὰ τῆς ἑαυτῶν πατρίδος δῶρα εἰληφότες
πονηροὶ καὶ ἄδικοι καὶ μισόδημοι νομίζονται εἶναι,
φιλεῖν ὑμᾶς φάσκοντες καὶ πράττειν ὑπὲρ τῶν τῆς
πόλεως ἀγαθῶν, καὶ δι᾽ ὑμᾶς ἔνδοξοι γεγενημένοι.[4]

---

[1] τοιαῦτα Blass : ταῦτα codd.
[2] ἀντικαταλλάξασθαι Hirschig : καταλλάξασθαι codd.
[3] ψηφισμάτων add. Maetzner.
[4] κατὰ φιλοκλέους subicit N : deesse quaedam putant
Baiter et Sauppe.

304

himself to death long ago. In addressing these entreaties to you I am urging a far juster plea than the men who have committed these shameful acts : I am asking you not to desert the things for which your ancestors faced many dangers, not to turn the city's honour into utter shame, and not to let personal regard for the defendants override your respect for the laws, the people's decrees, and the reports of the council. For let me make it quite clear to you, Athenians, quite clear, that you are being applauded universally in consequence of the inquiries held upon this money, and that men who have been convicted of taking bribes against their own country are regarded as wicked and injurious, haters of democracy, professing, as they do, to be your friends and to work for the city's interests, and having made their reputation thanks to you.[a]

[a] The concluding sentences of the speech are lost.

FRAGMENTS

INTRODUCTION

DINARCHUS was a prolific writer and, in the first century B.C., was credited with over a hundred and sixty speeches.[a] Eighty-seven of these were known to Dionysius of Halicarnassus, who, though rejecting twenty-seven as spurious, recorded the titles and opening words of all of them, dividing his list into four classes : genuine public, spurious public, genuine private, and spurious private orations.[b] To these we can add a further twelve, mentioned by different authors, thus giving a total of ninety-nine speeches which in antiquity were attributed to Dinarchus. Seven of them are still extant ; for besides the three printed in this volume four have survived among the works of Demosthenes.[c] The following selection includes only speeches whose titles have some his-

[a] By Demetrius of Magnesia. See Dion. *Dinarch.* 1.

[b] See Dion. *Dinarch.* 10 *sq.*

[c] These are : (1) *Against Theocrines* ([Dem.] lviii.), assigned by Callimachus to Demosthenes, by Dionysius to Dinarchus ; Harpocration was doubtful ; (2) *Against Boeotus for the Name* (Dem. xxxix.), a genuine speech of Demosthenes ; Dionysius recognized that it was too early to be the work of Dinarchus ; (3) *Against Mantitheüs on the Dowry* ([Dem.] xl.), also regarded by Dionysius as too early to be the work of Dinarchus ; (4) *Against Evergus and Mnesibulus* ([Dem.] xlvii.) ; Harpocration (*s.v.* Ἐκαλίστρουν) suggested that this might possibly be the work of Dinarchus.

torical interest together with those of which appreciable fragments exist. The bracketed numbers in the margin are those assigned to the fragments by Sauppe.[a]

[a] For a full list of titles see Blass, *Attische Beredsamkeit* iii. 2, pp. 298 *sq.*

A. ΔΗΜΟΣΙΟΙ ΛΟΓΟΙ ΓΝΗΣΙΟΙ

[i. 3. 3]   1. ΚΑΤΑ ΠΟΛΥΕΥΚΤΟΥ ΒΑΣΙΛΕΥΕΙΝ
ΛΑΧΟΝΤΟΣ

Ἀνθρώπου καὶ μισθωτοῦ καὶ πάντα τὰ ἐγκύκλια
ἀδικήματα ἠδικηκότος.   Priscian xviii. 23, p. 189 Kr.

Dionysius gives the titles of four speeches relating to
Polyeuctus, of which this is the first. To these Harpocration
appears to add another two, but Sauppe may be right in

2. ΚΑΤΑ ΠΟΛΥΕΥΚΤΟΥ ΑΠΟΦΑΣΙΣ

[ii. 5. 9]   Καὶ τὰς ἰδίᾳ παραγγελίας γεγενημένας καὶ τας
δεήσεις.   Harpocration, s.v. παραγγελία.

Title known from Harpocration. The speech is perhaps

3. ΚΑΤΑ ΠΥΘΕΟΥ ΠΕΡΙ ΤΩΝ ΚΑΤΑ
ΤΟ ΕΜΠΟΡΙΟΝ

[vi. 1. 16]   1. Ἐμπεπηδηκότων τῶν ῥητόρων ὥσπερ ἀπρότων εἰς τὸ ἐμπόριον.   Harpocration, s.v. ἀπρότων.
[vi. 2. 17]   2. Ἀλλ' οἶμαι ὥσπερ οἱ τοὺς καλλίας ἐν τοῖς
οἴκοις τρέφοντες.   Suidas ii. 1, p. 42.

310

A. *Public speeches* (*genuine*)

1. AGAINST POLYEUCTUS ON HIS APPOINTMENT BY LOT TO BE KING ARCHON

. . . Of a man who is a hireling and has committed all the lowest crimes.

regarding both titles as alternatives for the second speech given by Dionysius. The identity of Polyeuctus and the date and circumstances of the trial are not known.

2. AGAINST POLYEUCTUS, A DENUNCIATION

The canvassing and the requests made in private.

identical with the second in Dionysius' list. (See note on no. 1 above.) Date and circumstances not known.

3. AGAINST PYTHEAS CONCERNING THE AFFAIRS OF THE MARKET

1. When the orators had leapt into the emporium like ἄπροτοι.

2. But, I suppose, like men who keep monkeys in their houses, . . .

DINARCHUS

[vi. 12. 26]   3. Οὐδεὶς ὑπόλογος βουλῇ γέγονεν.   Harpocration, s.v. ὑπόλογον.

[vi. 13. 27]   4. Πάλιν παρ᾽ Αἰσχίνην ἀποφοιτήσας παρὰ
τουτῷ δῆλον ὅτι χρυσοχοεῖν ἐμάνθανεν, ἀλλ᾽ οὐ τὸ
προκείμενον αὐτῷ πράττειν ἢ πάσχειν.   Harpocration, s.v. χρυσοχοεῖν.

Date and circumstances not known.   The word ἄπροτοι
was regarded by Harpocration as a mistake for ἀλησίπων.

4. ΚΑΤΑ ΛΥΚΟΥΡΓΟΥ

[viii. 1. 31]   Καὶ τὰς σεμνὰς θεὰς αἷς ἐκεῖνος ἱεροποιὸς
καταστὰς δέκατος αὐτός.   Etym M. p. 469. 6.

Date and circumstances not known.   The speech may have

5. ΣΥΝΗΓΟΡΙΑ ΑΙΣΧΙΝΗΙ ΚΑΤΑ ΔΕΙΝΙΟΥ

[ix. 1. 35]   1. Ὅταν οὖν ἀπολογούμενος κλιμάζῃ καὶ παρ-
άγῃ τοὺς νόμους.   Harpocration, s.v. κλιμάζῃ.

[ix. 1. 35]   2. Οὗτος κλιμακίζει τοὺς νόμους.   Suidas, s.v.
κλιμακίζειν.

6. ΤΥΡΡΗΝΙΚΟΣ

[xii. 1. 46]   Μετὰ ταῦτα τοῦ Δάμωνος ἤδη περὶ ἀναγωγὴν
ὄντα καὶ περίστασιν ποιησαμένου[1] καὶ μαρτυρεῖν
ἀξιοῦντος.   Harpocration, s.v. περίστασιν.

Date and circumstances not known.   The speech was per-

[1] ποιησαμένου Bekker ; ποιήσουσιν οὐ A ; ποιήσαντος N.

312

3. No right of pardon has been granted to the Council.

4. Again, he left this master and resorted to Aeschines, under whom he clearly learnt to melt gold but not to discharge or endure the task before him.

He records a variant reading παρνόπων, πάρνοψ being a kind of locust. The word χρυσοχοεῖν was used proverbially to mean " fail in a tempting speculation " but the sense of this fragment is obscure.

4. AGAINST LYCURGUS

The awful goddesses for whom he was appointed overseer of sacrifices with nine others.

been written for the same trial as the Περὶ τῆς Διοικήσεως of Lycurgus. (See Lycurg. frag. 2 and note.)

5. DEFENCE OF AESCHINES AGAINST DINIAS

1. When therefore in his defence he distorts and misconstrues the laws.

2. This man distorts the laws.

Date and circumstances not known.

6. TYRRHENIAN SPEECH

After this, when I was on the point of putting to sea, since Damon gathered a group round me and asked me to give evidence . . .

haps concerned with the Athenian outpost against the Etruscans sent in 324 B.C. (see Hyp. frag. 8). The meaning of the word περίστασις is doubtful here.

DINARCHUS

7. ΚΑΤ' ΑΓΑΣΙΚΛΕΟΥΣ

[xvi. 3. 58]   1. Οἳ ἀντὶ σκαφηφόρων ἔφηβοι εἰς τὴν ἀκρόπολιν ἀναβήσονται, οὐχ ὑμῖν ἔχοντες χάριν τῆς
πολιτείας ἀλλὰ τῷ τούτου ἀργυρίῳ. Harpocration,
s.v. σκαφηφόροι.

[xvi. 4. 59]   2. Σκύθου[1] τοίνυν τοῦ προμετρητοῦ ἦν υἱὸς
ἐν δημοσίοις[2] γέγονε καὶ αὐτὸς[3] ἐν τῇ ἀγορᾷ προ-
μετρῶν διατετέλεκε καὶ ὑμεῖς ἐκλαμβανόμενοι[4]
παρ' αὐτοῦ τοὺς πυροὺς διατελεῖτε.[5] Harpocration
et Suidas, s.v. προμετρητής.

Date not known. According to Harpocration Agasicles
bribed the people of Halimus to enrol him in the deme and

8. ΚΑΤΑ ΚΑΛΛΙΣΘΕΝΟΥΣ[6]

[xviii. 1. 69] Μαρτύρομαι τὴν Ἑστίαν τὴν βουλαίαν.
Harpocration, s.v. βουλαία.

Date and circumstances not known. Harpocration quotes

9. ΚΑΤΑ ΑΓΝΩΝΙΔΟΥ[7] ΠΕΡΙ ΤΩΝ
ΑΡΠΑΛΕΙΩΝ

Date 323 B.C. Reiske's emendation is almost certainly
right. We know from Hyperides (v., col. 40) that Hagno-

10. ΚΑΤ' ΑΡΙΣΤΟΝΙΚΟΥ ΠΕΡΙ ΤΩΝ
ΑΡΠΑΛΕΙΩΝ

   [1] Σκύθου] ὁ Σκύθου Suidas.   [2] δημοσίοις] δημόταις Suidas.
   [3] αὐτὸς] ὁ αὐτὸς Suidas.
   [4] ἐκλαμβανόμενοι Sauppe : ἐκλαβόμενοι Suidas.
   [5] Verba ὑμεῖς usque ad διατελεῖτε om. Harpocration.
   [6] ΚΑΛΛΙΣΘΕΝΟΥΣ Meursius : ΚΛΕΙΣΘΕΝΟΥΣ codd.
   [7] ΑΓΝΩΝΙΔΟΥ Reiske : ΓΝΩΔΙΟΥ codd.

7. AGAINST AGASICLES

1. Who will go up on to the Acropolis as ephebi rather than as bowl-carriers, being obliged to this man's money rather than to you for their citizenship.

2. Moreover he was the son of a Scythian measurer. He has taken part in public life and has himself been a measurer up till now in the market, and you regularly receive the corn from him.

was therefore impeached. The case is mentioned by Hyp. iv. 3. For ephebi see Lycurg. *Leocr.* 76, note. σκαφήφοροι were metics who carried bowls in the Panathenaic procession. Evidently they sometimes paid others to perform this task for them.

8. AGAINST CALLISTHENES

I call to witness Hestia of the Council.

a number of words from the speech which show that it dealt with the subject of corn. Demosthenes (xx. 33) mentions a Callisthenes who was in charge of the corn supply in 357 B.C., but even if this speech concerns the same man it must belong to a considerably later date than this.

9. AGAINST HAGNONIDES, CONCERNING THE MONEY OF HARPALUS

nides was one of the accused in the Harpalus affair ; for which see the Introduction to Dinarch. *Against Demosthenes.*

10. AGAINST ARISTONICUS, CONCERNING THE MONEY OF HARPALUS

Date 323 B.C. Aristonicus also was involved in the Harpalus affair. See note on frag. 9 above.

DINARCHUS

B. ΔΗΜΟΣΙΟΙ ΛΟΓΟΙ ΨΕΥΔΕΠΙΓΡΑΦΟΙ

11. ΚΑΤΑ ΜΟΣΧΙΩΝΟΣ

[xxvii. 82] Εἰ φράτορες αὐτῷ καὶ βωμοὶ Διὸς ἑρκείου καὶ Ἀπόλλωνος πατρῴου εἰσίν. Harpocration, *s.v.* Ἑρκεῖος Ζεύς.

12. ΥΠΕΡ ΤΟΥ ΜΗ ΕΚΔΟΥΝΑΙ ΑΡΠΑΛΟΝ ΑΛΕΞΑΝΔΡΩΙ

Date 324 B.C. For the circumstances see the Introduction to Dinarch. *Against Demosthenes.* A speech with this title, possibly the same, was attributed to Demosthenes by Diony-

13. ΚΑΤΑ ΔΗΜΟΣΘΕΝΟΥΣ ΠΑΡΑΝΟΜΩΝ

Date and circumstances not known. The speech was

C. ΙΔΙΩΤΙΚΟΙ ΛΟΓΟΙ ΓΝΗΣΙΟΙ

14. ΚΑΤΑ ΠΡΟΞΕΝΟΥ

[xlii. 1. 85] 1. Δείναρχος Σωστράτου Κορίνθιος Προξένῳ ᾧ σύνειμι βλάβης, ταλάντων δύο. ἔβλαψέ με Πρόξενος ὑποδεξάμενος εἰς τὴν οἰκίαν τὴν ἑαυτοῦ τὴν ἐν ἀγρῷ, ὅτε πεφευγὼς Ἀθήνηθεν κατῄειν ἐκ Χαλκίδος, χρυσίου μὲν στατῆρας ὀγδοήκοντα καὶ διακοσίους καὶ πέντε, οὓς ἐκόμισα ἐκ Χαλκίδος,

316

B. *Public speeches (spurious)*

11. AGAINST MOSCHION

If he has clansmen and altars of Zeus of the Court and Apollo God of the Family, . . .

Date and circumstances not known. Dion. (*Dinarch.* 11) rejected this speech, on the grounds of internal evidence, as too early to have been written by Dinarchus.

12. ON THE REFUSAL TO SURRENDER HARPALUS TO ALEXANDER

sius (περὶ τῆς λεκτ. Δημ. δεινότητος 57). He would not admit the present one as the work of Dinarchus on stylistic grounds.

13. AGAINST DEMOSTHENES FOR ILLEGAL PROPOSALS

rejected as spurious by Dionysius on the same grounds as no. 12.

C. *Private speeches (genuine)*

14. AGAINST PROXENUS

1. I, Dinarchus, son of Sostratus of Corinth, claim for damage from Proxenus, with whom I am living, the sum of two talents. I sustained damage from Proxenus in the following manner. He received into his own house in the country, at the time of my return from Chalcis after I had been an exile from Athens, 285 gold staters, which to his knowledge I brought

εἰδότος Προξένου, καὶ εἰσῆλθον ἔχων εἰς τὴν οἰκίαν
αὐτοῦ, ἀργυρώματα δὲ οὐκ ἔλαττον¹ εἴκοσι μνῶν
ἄξια ἐπιβουλεύσας τούτοις. Dionysius, de Dinar-
cho 3.

[xlii. 2. 86] 2. Olim in adolescentia sedulo omnem gloriam
sectabar; at nunc in senectute summum me ambi-
tionum invasit odium. Tunc facile multis opitulabar;
nunc iam me ipsum tueri vix possum. Tunc mihi
beatissimus videbar, si quam plurimis benigne fecis-
sem; nunc contra vereor, ne quid mihi desit ad
necessarium aetatis meae cultum. Tunc ego ipse pro
republica fortiter arma capiebam; nunc praeterquam
laudare eos qui rempublicam armati defendunt nihil
valeo. Rutil. Lup. ii. 16.

15. ΚΑΤΑ ΚΛΕΟΜΕΔΟΝΤΟΣ

16. Ο ΥΣΤΕΡΟΣ

[lx. 1. 103] 1. Ἀναγνώσεται δὲ τῶν μὲν ἐπιδημούντων τὰς
μαρτυρίας, τῶν δὲ ἀποδημούντων τὰς ἐκμαρτυρίας.
Ammonius, de Diff. locut. p. 48.

[lx. 2. 104] 2. Πολλὰ κἀγαθά, ὦ ἄνδρες δικασταί, γένοιτο
ὑμῖν καὶ τῷ νομοθετήσαντι ἐξεῖναι τῶν ἀποδημούντων ἐκμαρτυρίας παρέχεσθαι. Idem, p. 91.

back from Chalcis and had with me when I entered
his house, together with silver plate worth not less
than 20 minas ; and all this he plotted to steal.

2. Once, in my youth, I eagerly sought after every
honour ; but now, in my old age, I have conceived
the greatest aversion towards wordly advancement.
In those days without trouble I helped many ; now I
am barely able still to protect myself. Then I counted
myself happiest if I had helped as many as I could ;
yet now I fear that I may lack the means to furnish
the care due to my age. Then in person I bravely
took up arms to defend the state ; now I have but the
strength to praise those others who defend the state
in arms.

This speech, written shortly after 292 B.C., when Dinarchus
returned from exile, was said to be the only one delivered by
himself. See Life of Dinarchus.

15 and 16. AGAINST CLEOMEDON
I AND II

1. He will read the evidence of those who were in
the city and the depositions taken, out of court, from
those who were away.

2. May you be richly rewarded, gentlemen of the
jury, you and the lawgiver who made it possible for
those who are away to furnish depositions out of
court.

Date not known. The case was one of assault. That
there were two speeches is shown by Eusebius (*Praep. Ev.* x. 3,
p. 466 c) who mentions the first. There is no means of telling
from which of the two these fragments come.

---

[1] ἔλαττον Reiske : ἐλάττω codd.

17. ΠΡΟΣ ΑΝΤΙΦΑΝΗΝ[1] ΠΕΡΙ ΤΟΥ ΙΠΠΟΥ

18. Ο ΥΣΤΕΡΟΣ

[lxiv. 2. 111] Ὠνοῦνταί μοι τὸν ἵππον τὸν ὀχεῖον. Harpocration, *s.v.* ὀχεῖον.

19. ΚΑΤΑ ΔΑΟΥ[2] ΥΠΕΡ ΑΝΔΡΑΠΟΔΩΝ

[lxvi. 112] Διοικῶν δὲ τὴν οὐσίαν αὐτοῦ Κεφαλίων μειρακιωδέστερον καὶ φύσει χρηστὸς ἦν καὶ εὐήθης. Galenus in Hippocr. *Prognost.* 1. 3, vol. 18. 2, p. 237.

D. ΙΔΙΩΤΙΚΟΙ ΛΟΓΟΙ ΨΕΥΔΕΠΙΓΡΑΦΟΙ

E.

20. ΥΠΕΡ ΕΥΘΥΓΕΝΟΥΣ

[lxxxi. 118] Ἀνέῳγεν πᾶς ὁ τόπος. Cramer, *Anecdot. Oxon.* 1, p. 52. 10.

21. ΚΑΤΑ ΛΕΩΧΑΡΟΥΣ

[lxxxv. 124] Περὶ τοῦ ταλαιπώρου Διδύμου νῦν πρὸς ὑμᾶς ἐρῶ· καί μοι δεῦρο αὐτοῦ τὸ παιδίον κάλεσον. Suidas, *s.v.* δεῦρο.

---

[1] ΠΡΟΣ ΑΝΤΙΦΑΝΗΝ add. Harpocration.
[2] ΚΑΤΑ ΔΑΟΥ] ΠΡΟΣ ΔΑΩΝΑ Galenus.

---

[a] The nine speeches listed by Dionysius under this head include two which have survived as the works of Demosthenes

320

17 and 18. AGAINST ANTIPHANES CONCERNING THE HORSE I AND II

They buy me the stallion.

The full title is preserved by Harpocration; Dionysius simply calls the speech "On the Horse." Date and circumstances not known. The fragment may belong to either speech.

19. AGAINST DAÜS CONCERNING SLAVES

In administering his property rather childishly Cephalio was honest and simple of character.

Date and circumstances not known.

D. *Private speeches (spurious)*[a]

E. *Speeches not mentioned by Dionysius*

20. IN DEFENCE OF EUTHYGENES

The whole place was open.

Date and circumstances not known.

21. AGAINST LEOCHARES

I will now tell you about the unfortunate Didymus. Will you please call his child up.

Date and circumstances not known.

(Dem. xxxix. and [Dem.] xl.). See Introduction to the Fragments. Of the other seven no fragments remain.

22. ΠΡΟΣ ΤΟΥΣ ΛΥΚΟΥΡΓΟΥ
ΠΑΙΔΑΣ

Title known from Harpocration, who quotes the word
ἀπονομή (portion), a technical term relating to the ownership
of mines. Date and circumstances doubtful, but the speech

23. ΚΑΤΑ ΜΕΝΕΣΑΙΧΜΟΥ

[lxxxvii. 126]   Αἱ γὰρ ἀπὸ τῶν κοινῶν ἔχθραι καὶ πραγ-
ματεῖαι αἴτιαι τῶν ἰδίων διαφορῶν καθεστήκασι.
Suidas, s.v. πραγματεία.

24. ΚΑΤΑ ΤΙΜΑΡΧΟΥ

[lxxxviii. 127]   Περίφοβος ἦν πρὸς ὑμᾶς εἰσελθεῖν.   Priscian
xviii. 26.

F. ΑΠΑΡΑΣΗΜΑ

[lxxxix. 1. 128]   1. Item Dinarchi [1] : Partim nostri silebant,
partim autem ingentem clamorem excitabant.   At
hi socii, praeclara nostra auxilia, neutrum poterant.
Neque constanti silentio neque forti clamore strenui [2]
quid agere [4] conabantur.   Huc accedebat ignavae
turbae [4] strepitus, qui nihil eorum mentes ad virtutem
erigebat.[5]   Rutil. Lup. i. 14.
[lxxxix. 2. 129]   2. Dinarchi :   Itaque ut familiares videban-

---

[1] *Dinarchi* Ruhnken : *dives avarus* codd. et Sauppe.
[2] *strenui* Iacob : *strenue* codd.

22. AGAINST THE CHILDREN OF LYCURGUS

may well have been written for the occasion when Menesaechmus prosecuted the children of Lycurgus shortly after
their father's death. See Life of Lycurgus.

23. AGAINST MENESAECHMUS

For the enmities and grievances which arise from
public life are the causes of private differences.

Date and circumstances not known. Compare however
Lycurg. frag. 4, with which this may possibly be connected.

24. AGAINST TIMARCHUS

He was very much afraid to come before you.

Date and circumstances not known.

F. *Fragments of uncertain origin*

1. Some of our men were silent; others raised a
loud shout. But these allies, our fine supporters,
could do neither. They made no attempt to offer
any active help either by keeping a steadfast silence
or by giving a brave shout. Moreover the craven
crowd set up a clamour, which did nothing towards
kindling their spirits with valour.

2. Therefore, as they seemed to be close acquain-

---

³ *agere* Stephanus : *agerent* codd.
⁴ *turbae* Capperonnius : *tubae* codd.
⁵ *erigebat* Heusinger : *exigebat* vel -*bant* codd.

tur, hos necessitudine opitulandi adstrinxit, hosque
ignotos iuxta benevolentiae causa illexit. Rutil.
Lup. ii. 20.

[lxxxix. 3. 130] 3. Περιπέτονται δὲ τῶν ταλαιπώρων ἄστυ
Θηβαίων χελιδόνες. Longinus, de Invent., vol. ix.
p. 585 Walz.

[lxxxix. 4. 131] 4. Ἀθέμιστα καὶ ἀνόσια δρᾷ. Bekker, Anecdota, p. 353.

tances, he impressed these with the need for helping, and others, who were almost strangers, he won over in the name of kindness.

3. Swallows fly round the city of the unhappy Thebans.

4. He does unholy and impious things.

DEMADES

LIFE OF DEMADES [a]

DEMADES was the son of a shipowner named Demeas and belonged to the deme Paeania. His birth, of which the date is not known, can hardly be placed later than 380 B.C., as he was already an old man at the time of his death in 319. Though perhaps the most brilliant speaker among the statesmen of his day, he was worthy of little esteem as a man. From the outset of his career he supported the interests of Macedon but was open to bribes from all parties and made no secret in Athens of his venality. " You think it remarkable," he once told a playwright, " that you have earned a talent by reciting. I was once paid ten by the king to keep quiet." The money which he thus acquired was largely squandered in self-indulgence, and as an old man he was described by Antipater as nothing else but tongue and stomach. Yet such was his ability that, despite grave reverses, he held a position at the head of affairs for twenty years and contrived to outlive all his chief opponents. [b]

[a] Sources for the Life of Demades. There is no ancient biography of Demades. The facts known about him have to be gathered from scattered references in the works of the orators Demosthenes, Hyperides, and Dinarchus, and in those of many other writers, of whom Plutarch, Diodorus and Athenaeus are the most valuable. Suidas' short note on him is very inaccurate.

[b] *Cf. CIA* ii. 804 b ; Plut. *Phoc.* 1 ; Gellius xi. 10 ; Athen. ii. 44 f ; Dinarch. i. 104.

DEMADES

Having had no special education during his youth Demades boasted that the Athenian platform had been his teacher. How he came to enter politics, after starting life in his father's trade and even performing the work of a common rower, is not known, but his exceptional gift for oratory no doubt made the way easier. Though he is said to have opposed Demosthenes over the Olynthian war in 349, we hear no more of him until the time of Chaeronea (338), when he was among the prisoners taken during the battle. After being dispatched to Athens as Philip's spokesman, he returned with Aeschines and Phocion to negotiate with the king the peace that bore his name.[a]

Henceforward Demades figured prominently in the pro-Macedonian party, though his fortunes varied with the mood of the people. The decade following Chaeronea witnessed his greatest successes; for, though prosecuted by Hyperides shortly after the battle for proposing honours for a certain Euthycrates who was in the pay of Philip, he was soon required again by Athens to intercede with Macedon, both in 336, when Alexander entered Thessaly, and also in 335, when, after sacking Thebes, the king demanded the surrender of the chief Athenian statesmen. With the help of Phocion Demades succeeded in averting this blow, and as a reward for his services, despite the opposition of Lycurgus, was granted a bronze statue in the market place and free meals in the Prytaneum. During the reconstruction period at Athens, after 334, when the rival parties in the city were temporarily

---

[a] Cf. Quintil. ii. 17. 12; Suidas, s.v. " Demades "; Stobaeus, Flor. xxix. 91 (frag. 22. 5); Plut. Dem. 10, 13; Diodor. xvi. 87; Plut. Phoc. 16; Dem. xviii. 285.

reconciled, Demades shared with Phocion the control
of external affairs and even accompanied his late
opponent Lycurgus on two missions, to Delphi in 330,
to dedicate a new temple, and to Oropus in 329, to
supervise some games, an errand for which he was
thanked by Demosthenes.[a]

In the years that followed, however, his popularity
seems to have declined. Like Demosthenes he was
convicted, in 323, of taking bribes from Harpalus and
fined accordingly, and, in the same year, the proposal
that Alexander should be deified cost him ten talents.
Being three times penalized for illegal proposals he
lost the right to take part in public affairs ; but this
disgrace was short-lived, since in 322 he was needed
again as a mediator and the prohibition was therefore
withdrawn. The Lamian war was now at its end and
Antipater threatened an invasion of Attica. Again
in conjunction with Phocion, Demades contrived to
placate him, and even, it seems, wrote secretly for
help to Perdiccas, a step which later caused his
downfall. For the present he collaborated with the
new oligarchy in Athens by proposing that the democratic leaders, who had fled when the city surrendered,
should be condemned to death ; and when the
measure was passed Antipater hastened to carry out
the sentence, including Demosthenes and Hyperides
among his victims.[b]

Demades himself had only three more years of life.
Going to Macedon in 319, with his son Demeas, to

<hr />

[a] Cf. Hyp. frag. 19 ; [Demad.] *On the Twelve Years* 14 ;
Plut. *Dem.* 23 ; Diodor. xvii. 15 ; Longinus, *de Invent. t.* ix.
p. 544 ; Dinarch. i. 101 ; Lycurg. frag. 14.

[b] Cf. Dinarch. i. Introd. and 89 ; Arrian, *Succ. Alex.* 13 ;
Aelian, *V.H.* v. 12 ; Paus. vii. 10. 1 ; Diodor. xviii. 18 and 48 ;
Plut. *Phoc.* 26 and *Dem.* 28.

ask for the withdrawal of the garrison which Antipater had placed in Munichia, he found that his letter to Perdiccas of three years before had been discovered. He was accordingly seized and sent back for trial to Athens, where the oligarchs condemned him to death and executed his son with him.[a]

Demades was regarded in antiquity as a talented speaker and the wittiest of all the Attic orators. Quintilian classed him with Pericles, and Theophrastus is supposed to have called him too great for the city, thus admitting his superiority over Demosthenes whom he described as merely worthy of it. It was in extempore debate that Demades chiefly excelled ; and, although he left no written works, some of his choicer sayings were remembered and are still preserved. The Byzantines even attributed to him entire works, now regarded as later compositions, of which the following speech is an example. These are the writings to which the grammarian Tzetzes refers ; a few of their titles are recorded by Suidas and as many as fourteen in the index of a Florentine manuscript. The speech *On the Twelve Years*, mentioned in both lists, is the only one of which any fragments have survived.[b]

[a] *Cf.* Plut. *Dem.* 31 and *Phoc.* 30 ; Athen. xiii. 591 f.
[b] *Cf.* Cic. *Orat.* xxvi. 90, *Brut.* ix. 36 ; Quintil. xii. 10. 49 ; Plut. *Dem.* 10 ; Tzetzes, *Chil.* vi. 16, 112 *sq.* (frags. 15 and 16) ; Suidas, *s.v.* " Demades " ; *Hermes*, vol. iii. p. 277.

ON THE TWELVE YEARS

INTRODUCTION

THE speech *On the Twelve Years* has survived in manuscripts as the work of Demades and was accepted as such by Suidas.[a] Its genuineness was however questioned as early as 1768 by Hauptmann, and it is now rejected by all as spurious on the strength of both external and internal evidence. This may be summarized briefly as follows. (*a*) *External.* Cicero and Quintilian state categorically that no works of Demades were extant in their day,[b] and there are no quotations from him in the writings of Harpocration or other lexicographers. (*b*) *Internal.* The speech itself is poorer than might be expected of a talented orator, being artificial and unimpressive in style ; the number of words and phrases occurring in it which cannot be paralleled in the writings of Attic orators is out of all proportion to its length,[c] and no facts are included which a later writer could not have known.

Whatever the real date of the work may be, it professes to give a defence, offered by the orator in about 326 B.C., for the previous twelve years of his career. The title was perhaps suggested by the speech *On the Ten Years* of Demetrius of Phalerum.[d]

---

[a] Suidas, *s.v.* " Demades."
[b] Cic. *Brut.* ix. 36 ; Quintil. ii. 17. 13.
[c] *e.g.* παρανάλωμα, λογογραφία, εἰς δίκας . . . ἔθηκα τὸν πόνον.
[d] Diog. Laert. v. 81.

ANALYSIS

[178]   Τῆς μὲν τῶν κινδυνευόντων σωτηρίας, ὦ ἄνδρες
Ἀθηναῖοι, καὶ τῆς τιμωρίας ὑμεῖς παρὰ τῶν νόμων
τὴν ἐξουσίαν εἰλήφατε· οὔτε δ᾽ ἰατρὸς ἐμπείρως
δύναται θεραπεῦσαι τοὺς κάμνοντας, ἂν μὴ τὴν
αἰτίαν τοῦ νοσήματος κατανοήσῃ, οὔτε δικαστὴς
ὁσίαν θεῖναι τὴν ψῆφον, ἐὰν μὴ τοῖς τῆς κρίσεως
2 δικαίοις σαφῶς[1] ᾖ παρηκολουθηκώς. ἐμπεσὼν δ᾽
αὐτὸς εἰς μέσην τὴν τῶν[2] ῥητόρων δυσμένειαν,
ὥσπερ τῆς παρὰ θεῶν, οὕτω τῆς παρ᾽ ὑμῶν δέομαι
τυχεῖν βοηθείας. διαβάλλουσι γάρ μου τὸν βίον,
οἰόμενοι τὸν λόγον ἄπιστον καταστήσειν. ἐγὼ δ᾽
ἀποθανὼν μὲν ἢ ζῶν οὐδέν εἰμι· τί γὰρ Ἀθηναίοις,
εἰ[3] παρανάλωμα[4] Δημάδης;[5] δακρύσει δέ μου τὴν
ἀπώλειαν οὐχ ὁ στρατιώτης[6]—πῶς γάρ; ὃν αὔξει
μὲν πόλεμος, εἰρήνη δ᾽ οὐ τρέφει—ἀλλ᾽ ὁ τὴν
χώραν γεωργῶν καὶ ὁ τὴν θάλατταν πλέων καὶ
πᾶς ὁ τὸν ἡσύχιον βίον ἠγαπηκώς, ᾧ τὴν Ἀττικὴν
ἐτείχισα, τοὺς ὅρους τῆς χώρας περιβαλὼν οὐ
3 λίθοις ἀλλὰ τῇ τῆς πόλεως ἀσφαλείᾳ. δεινὸν δέ
τι συμβαίνει πολλοῖς τῶν κρινόντων, ὦ ἄνδρες[7]
δικασταί. ὥσπερ γὰρ ἡ τῶν ὀφθαλμῶν νόσος τὴν
ὅρασιν συγχέασα κωλύει τὰ ἐμποδὼν κείμενα θεω-

---

[1] σαφῶς add. e.

[2] μέσην τὴν τῶν Sauppe : τὴν τῶν E : μέσην τῶν cett.

[3] εἰ] ἢ Stephanus.   [4] παρανάλωμα] παραναλοῦμαι Blass.

336

ON THE TWELVE YEARS

THE laws have given you the right, Athenians, to acquit or punish men on trial. A doctor cannot treat his patients skilfully if he has not discerned the cause of the disease, nor can a member of a jury give a fair vote unless he has followed intelligently the rights and wrongs of the case. Since I have myself become exposed to the full hatred of the orators, I am asking not only for divine assistance but for your help also. For they are casting aspersions on my personal history, thinking to undermine your confidence in my speech. I am of no consequence whether alive or dead; for what do the Athenians care if Demades is lost to them, too? No soldier will shed tears over my death—(How could he, when war brings him advancement and peace destroys his livelihood?); but it will be lamented by the farmer, the sailor, and everyone who has enjoyed the peaceful life with which I fortified Attica, encircling its boundaries, not with stone, but with the safety of the city. In many cases, gentlemen of the jury, when men are serving as judges they are seriously misled. For, just as a complaint of the eyes, by confusing the vision, prevents a man from seeing what lies before him, so an unjust

---

⁵ Post Δημάδης verba ἐμοῦ δὲ τὴν εἰρήνην συμβουλεύοντος add. e.   ⁶ στρατιώτης] στρατός e.
⁷ ὦ ἄνδρες X corr.: ωδε X pr.: ὦ N.

ρεῖν, οὕτως ἄδικος παρεισδύνων λόγος εἰς τὰς τῶν
δικαστῶν[1] γνώμας οὐκ ἐᾷ δι' ὀργὴν συνορᾶν τὴν
ἀλήθειαν. διὸ καὶ δεῖ συνορᾶν ὑμᾶς εὐλαβῶς ἐπὶ
τῶν κινδυνευόντων μᾶλλον ἢ τῶν ἐγκαλούντων· οἱ
μὲν γὰρ αὐτόθεν ἔχουσιν ἐκ τῆς πρωτολογίας
[179] ὁποῖον αὐτοὶ βούλονται τὸν δικαστήν, οἱ δ' ἀναγ-
κάζονται πρὸς ὠργισμένους κριτὰς τὴν διάνοιαν
4 ἀντιτάσσεσθαι. ἐὰν μὲν οὖν φαίνωμαι τοῖς ἐγ-
καλουμένοις ἔνοχος, καταψηφίσασθε, μὴ φείσησθε·
οὐ παραιτοῦμαι· ἂν δ' εὑρίσκωμαι τῶν ἐγκεκλη-
μένων κεχωρισμένος τῷ δικαίῳ, τοῖς νόμοις, τῷ
συμφέροντι, μὴ πρόησθέ με τῇ τῶν κατηγόρων
ὠμότητι. εἰ δὲ πάντως ἀποθανὼν συμβαλοῦμαί
τι πρὸς τὴν κοινὴν σωτηρίαν, ὡς οὗτοι λέγουσιν,
ἑτοίμως ἔχω τελευτᾶν· κτήσασθαι γὰρ ἰδίῳ θανάτῳ
δημοσίαν εὔνοιαν[2] καλόν, ἐὰν ἡ χρεία τῆς πατρίδος,
ἀλλὰ μὴ ὁ τούτων λόγος τὸ ζῆν[3] ἀφαιρήσηται.[4]
5 δότε δή μοι πρὸς θεῶν, ὦ ἄνδρες Ἀθηναῖοι, δότε
διαλεχθῆναι ὡς προαιροῦμαι πρὸς ὑμᾶς περὶ τῶν
δικαίων. δοκῶ μὲν γὰρ δύναμιν εἶναί μοι καὶ τοῖς
ἄλλοις βοηθεῖν· ἐν δὲ τούτοις ἐμποδίζει μου τὸν
λόγον ὁ φόβος. ἄλλως δ' οὐ τὸν ἔλεγχον τοῦ
πράγματος δέδοικα,[5] ἀλλὰ τὴν τῶν ἀντιδίκων διαβολὴν μόνον, ἥτις[6] οὐ κρίνει τοὺς ἀδικοῦντας, ἀλλὰ
6 φύεται τοῖς δοκοῦσι[7] λέγειν ἢ πράττειν. ἡ παρ'
ὑμῖν ἐλπὶς δὲ δικαία· οὐ μικρὰ ⟨γάρ⟩[8] ἐστι τῷ
κινδυνεύοντι ῥοπὴ πρὸς σωτηρίαν ἡ τῶν ἀκουόντων
βούλησις ταττομένη μετὰ τοῦ δικαίου. ἐὰν ταύτης

---

[1] δικαστῶν] δικαίων e.
[2] εὔνοιαν] εὐδαιμονίαν Sauppe.
[3] ζῆν Sauppe : νῦν codd.
[4] ἀφαιρήσηται C : ἀφαιρήσεται cett. : ἀφαιρῆται Bekker.

speech, insinuating itself into the minds of the jury,
prevents them in their anger from perceiving the
truth. You should therefore exercise more care in
dealing with the accused than with the plaintiffs.
For the latter, by virtue of speaking first, have the
jury in the mood which suits them, while the former
are compelled to plead their cause to judges already
prejudiced by anger. Now, if you hold me liable for
the charges, condemn me out of hand ; I ask no
pardon. But if, on considerations of justice, law, and
expediency, I prove to be innocent of these charges,
do not leave me to the savagery of my prosecutors.
If my death will contribute in the least, as these men
say, to the common safety, I am ready to die. For
it is a noble thing to win public esteem by the loss
of one's own life, so long as it is given in answer to
the country's need and not the argument of these
accusers. I entreat you by the gods, Athenians, give
me free scope to explain to you my claims to fair
treatment. I have, I believe, the power even to be
of assistance to others, but on this occasion fear
restrains my speech. Apart from that I am not
afraid that the facts will convict me ; all I fear is my
opponents' slander which, instead of bringing wrongdoers to justice, attaches to any with a reputation
as an orator or statesman. The hopes I place in you
are justified ; for the sympathy of his hearers, when
it is ranged on the side of justice, is no small factor
in securing the acquittal of the accused. If I gain

---

[5] δέδοικα om. codd. praeter C.

[6] τὴν τῶν ἀντιδίκων διαβολὴν μόνον, ἥτις C : τῇ τῶν ἀδίκων
μόνον, ὃς cett. : τὸν τῶν ἀντιδίκων φθόνον, ὃς Sauppe.

[7] δοκοῦσι] εὖ δοκοῦσι Bekker : δοκοῦσί τι Sauppe.

[8] γάρ add. Blass.

κατατύχω,[1] πάσας ἀπολύσομαι τὰς διαβολάς· ἄνευ
δὲ ταύτης οὔθ᾽ ὁ λόγος οὔθ᾽ οἱ νόμοι οὔθ᾽ ἡ τῶν
πραγμάτων ἀλήθεια σῶσαι δύνανται[2] τὸν ἀδίκως
κρινόμενον. οὐκ ἀγνοεῖτε δὲ ὅτι πολλοὶ πολλάκις
ἤδη τῶν ἐγκαλούντων ἀπὸ μὲν τῆς κατηγορίας
ἔδοξαν δίκαια λέγειν, παρατεθείσης δὲ τῆς ἀπολογίας εὑρέθησαν αὐτοὶ συκοφαντοῦντες· ὃ δὴ καὶ
νῦν πέπεισμαι τούτοις παρακολουθήσειν ὑμῶν
ἀκούειν προαιρουμένων μετ᾽ εὐνοίας.

7 Ἐπεὶ δὲ καὶ τῆς ἄλλης μου πολιτείας κατηγορεῖν
ἐπεχείρησαν, βραχέα βούλομαι περὶ αὐτῆς εἰπεῖν,
ἔπειθ᾽ οὕτως ἐπὶ τὴν λοιπὴν δικαιολογίαν ἀπελθεῖν,
ἵνα μὴ λάθωσιν ὑμᾶς παρακρουσάμενοι. γεγονὼς
γάρ, ὦ ἄνδρες Ἀθηναῖοι, Δημέου[3] πατρός, ὡς καὶ
ὑμῶν οἱ πρεσβύτεροι γινώσκουσι, τὸν μὲν ἄλλον
χρόνον οὕτως ἔζων ὡς ἐδυνάμην, οὔτε κοινῇ τὸν
δῆμον ἀδικῶν οὔτ᾽ ἰδίᾳ λυπῶν οὐδένα τῶν ἐν τῇ
πόλει, πειρώμενος δ᾽ ἀεὶ τοῖς ἰδίοις πόνοις τὴν
8 ἀσθένειαν τοῦ βίου διορθοῦσθαι. ἡ πενία δ᾽ ἴσως
δύσχρηστον μὲν ἔχει τι καὶ χαλεπόν, κεχώρισται δ᾽
αἰσχύνης, ὡς ἄν, οἶμαι, τῆς ἀπορίας ἐπὶ πολλῶν οὐ
τρόπου κακίαν ἀλλὰ τύχης ἀγνωμοσύνην ἐλεγ-
χούσης. προσελθὼν δὲ τοῖς κοινοῖς, οὐκ εἰς δίκας
καὶ τὴν ἀπὸ τῆς λογογραφίας ἐργασίαν ἔθηκα τὸν
πόνον, ἀλλ᾽ εἰς τὴν ἀπὸ τοῦ βήματος παρρησίαν
ἣ τοῖς[4] μὲν λέγουσιν ἐπισφαλῆ παρέχεται τὸν βίον,
τοῖς δ᾽ εὐλαβουμένοις[5] μεγίστην δίδωσιν ἀφορμὴν

---

[1] κατατύχω C : κατατυχών cett.
[2] δύνανται X : δύναται e : δύναιτ᾽ ἂν C.
[3] Δημέου Blass (iam Δημαίου Lhardy et Kiessling) : Δημάδου
codd.
[4] ἡ τοῖς] αὐτη δὲ τοῖς e.
[5] εὐλαβουμένοις] εὐλαβῶς ἀκροωμένοις Blass.

this I shall rebut all the calumnies; without it neither speech nor laws, nor the light of facts, can save a man unjustly brought to trial. I need not remind you that numerous prosecutors on many occasions in the past have, on the strength of their pleas, been thought to be urging a just case, but after a comparison with the defence they have been found to be themselves speaking falsely; and I am convinced that my accusers now will have the same experience, if you consent to grant me a favourable hearing.

As they attempted to question the rest of my administration, I wish to make a few points in connexion with it and then to pass on to the remainder of my defence in order to prove their dishonesty to you. I am the son of Demeas, Athenians, as the elder ones among you know, and the early part of my life I lived as best I could, neither doing harm to the community nor troubling any individual in the city. I merely persisted in trying, by my own efforts, to better my humble position. Penury may involve inconvenience and hardship but it carries with it no discredit, since poverty is frequently, I imagine, a mark not of weakness of character but of sheer misfortune. When I entered public life I did not concentrate on lawsuits or the perquisites to be derived from writing speeches but on speaking freely from the platform, a practice which makes the lives of orators dangerous but holds out the clearest opportunities of success, if men are careful *a*; for, though

---

a εὐλαβουμένοις clearly refers to the hearers, not to the orators, and therefore the sense is the same as that given by the words εὐλαβῶς ἀκροωμένοις, even if we do not adopt that emendation.

πρὸς κατόρθωσιν· οὐ γὰρ ἐν τῇ τοῦ λέγοντος χά-
ριτι δεῖ συνεκπίπτειν τὴν τῆς πατρίδος σωτηρίαν.
9 χιλίων ταφὴ Ἀθηναίων μαρτυρεῖ μοι, κηδευθεῖσα
ταῖς τῶν ἐναντίων χερσίν, ἃς ἀντὶ πολεμίων φιλίας
ἐποίησα τοῖς ἀποθανοῦσιν. ἐνταῦθα ἐπιστὰς τοῖς
πράγμασιν ἔγραψα τὴν εἰρήνην· ὁμολογῶ. ἔγραψα
καὶ Φιλίππῳ τιμάς· οὐκ ἀρνοῦμαι. δισχιλίους γὰρ
αἰχμαλώτους ἄνευ λύτρων καὶ χίλια πολιτῶν σώματα χωρὶς κήρυκος καὶ τὸν Ὠρωπὸν ἄνευ πρε-
10 σβείας λαβὼν ὑμῖν ταῦτ᾽ ἔγραψα. ἐπείληπτο δὲ
τῆς γραφούσης χειρὸς οὐχ ἡ δωροδοκία τῶν Μακεδόνων, ὡς οὗτοι πλαττόμενοι λέγουσιν, ἀλλ᾽ ὁ
καιρὸς καὶ ἡ χρεία καὶ τὸ τῆς πατρίδος συμφέρον
καὶ ἡ τοῦ βασιλέως φιλανθρωπία. ἐλθὼν γὰρ ἐπὶ
τὸν κίνδυνον ἐχθρὸς τῶν ἀγώνων φίλος ἐχωρίσθη,
τὸ τῶν νενικηκότων ἆθλον τοῖς σφαλεῖσι προσθείς.
11 πάλιν τοίνυν ἧκε τῇ πόλει καιρὸς ἕτερος, ἵνα τοὺς
μεταξὺ κινδύνους ἑκὼν ἐπιλάθωμαι· καὶ πάντες μὲν
οἱ τὴν Ἑλλάδα κατοικοῦντες τὸν Ἀλέξανδρον ἐπὶ
τὴν ἡγεμονίαν ἀνεβίβαζον, καὶ τοῖς ψηφίσμασιν
ἀναπλάττοντες φρόνημα μεῖζον τοῦ δέοντος ἀνδρὶ
νέῳ καὶ φιλοδόξῳ περιέθηκαν· λοιποὶ δ᾽ ἦμεν ἡμεῖς
καὶ Λακεδαιμόνιοι, πρόβλημα τῆς σωτηρίας ἔχοντες, οὐ χρημάτων πλῆθος, οὐχ ὅπλων παρασκευάς,
οὐχὶ πεζῶν[1] σύνταξιν, ἀλλ᾽ ἐπιθυμίαν μεγάλην, δύ-
12 ναμιν δ᾽ ἀσθενῆ καὶ ταπεινήν. ὧν μὲν γὰρ[2] ἐσύλησε
[180] τὴν ἰσχὺν ὁ περὶ Λεῦκτρα κίνδυνος, ὁ δὲ πρότερον
ἀπείρατος ὢν πολεμίας σάλπιγγος Εὐρώτας Βοιωτοὺς ἐν τῇ Λακωνικῇ στρατοπεδεύοντας εἶδεν[3]·

[1] οὐχὶ πεζῶν] οὐχ ἱππέων καὶ πεζῶν Blass.
[2] ὧν μὲν γὰρ] τῶν Λακεδαιμονίων e.
[3] εἶδεν Ald. : εἶχεν codd. et e.

they succumb to the speaker, their country's safety must not also fall a victim. I have, to bear me out, the burial of a thousand Athenians [a] performed by the hands of our adversaries, hands which I won over from enmity to friendship towards the dead. Then, on coming to the fore in public life, I proposed the peace. I admit it. I proposed honours to Philip. I do not deny it. By making these proposals I gained for you two thousand captives free of ransom, a thousand Athenian dead, for whom no herald had to ask, and Oropus without an embassy. The hand that wrote them was constrained, not by Macedonian gifts, as my accusers falsely allege, but by the need of the moment, the interest of my country, and the generosity of the king. For he entered the war as our foe but emerged from the struggle as a friend, awarding to the vanquished the prize of the victors. Again, there came a second crisis for the city ; for I deliberately ignore the intervening dangers. All other inhabitants of Greece were promoting Alexander to the rank of leader, and by remoulding him in their decrees they raised the aspirations of a young and ambitious man to an excessive pitch. We and the Spartans remained, with neither revenues nor armaments nor regiments of infantry to be the bulwark of our safety, yet fortified by a great desire, though our power was small and humble. The Spartans had been deprived of their strength by the battle of Leuctra,[b] and the Eurotas, which had never yet heard an enemy trumpet, saw Boeotians camping in

---

[a] It is said that after Chaeronea in 338 B.C. Philip was insulting his prisoners, until Demades, by his frank speech, won him over to a better attitude towards Athens. *Cf.* Diodor. xvi. 87.   [b] *Cf.* Dinarch. i. 73, note.

[DEMADES]

ἀπέκειρε γὰρ τὴν ἀκμὴν τῆς Σπάρτης ὁ Θηβαῖος,
καὶ τοὺς ὅρους τῆς Λακωνικῆς τεθειμένους, τὴν
ἀκμὴν τῶν νέων, συνέκλεισε ταῖς τέφραις. τὰς δ᾽
ἡμετέρας παρασκευὰς ἀνάλωσεν ὁ πόλεμος, καὶ
τὴν ἐλπίδα τῶν ζώντων συνέτριψεν ἡ συμφορὰ τῶν
13 ἀποθανόντων. Θηβαῖοι δὲ μέγιστον εἶχον δεσμὸν
τὴν τῶν Μακεδόνων φρουράν, ὑφ᾽ ἧς οὐ μόνον τὰς
χεῖρας συνεδέθησαν, ἀλλὰ καὶ τὴν παρρησίαν ἀφ-
ῄρηντο· τῷ γὰρ Ἐπαμινώνδου σώματι συνέθαψε
τὴν δύναμιν τῶν Θηβαίων ὁ καιρός. ἤκμαζον δὲ
τοῖς σύμπασιν[1] οἱ Μακεδόνες, οὓς ἤδη ταῖς ἐλπίσιν
ἐπὶ τὰ σκῆπτρα καὶ τοὺς Περσῶν[2] θησαυροὺς ἡ
14 τύχη διεβίβαζεν. ἐνταῦθ᾽ ὁμοίως Δημοσθένης μὲν
ἐκύρωσε πόλεμον, καλὴν μὲν τοῖς ὀνόμασιν, οὐ
σωτήριον δὲ τοῖς ἔργοις συμβουλίαν εἰσηγησάμενος
τοῖς πολίταις· ὡς δὲ πλησίον ἔστη τῆς Ἀττικῆς
ὁ πόλεμος,[3] ἡ χώρα δὲ εἰς τὴν πόλιν κατεκλείετο,
καὶ τὸ περιμάχητον καὶ θαυμαζόμενον ὑπὸ πάντων
ἄστυ βοῶν καὶ προβάτων ὥσπερ ἔπαυλις καὶ τῶν
βοσκημάτων[4] ἐπληροῦτο, βοηθείας δ᾽ οὐδαμόθεν
15 ἦν ἐλπίς, ἔγραψα τὴν εἰρήνην. ὁμολογῶ, καί φημι
καλῶς καὶ συμφερόντως πεπραχέναι τοῦτο· κρεῖττον γὰρ ἐπερχόμενον ἐκκλῖναι τὸ νέφος ἢ φερο-
μένῳ συναπενεχθῆναι τῷ ῥεύματι. ἀξιῶ δ᾽, ὦ
ἄνδρες Ἀθηναῖοι, τὴν ἐκ τῶν πραγμάτων λύπην
ἐμοὶ παρ᾽ ὑμῶν μηδεμίαν ἀπογεννῆσαι δυσμένειαν.

---

[1] σύμπασιν Blass : σώμασιν codd. et e.
[2] Περσῶν inter τὰ et σκῆπτρα transtulit Blass.
[3] ὁ πολέμιος add. e.
[4] καὶ τῶν βοσκημάτων om. e.

Laconia. For the Theban had cut off the bloom of
Sparta, enveloping in ashes the flower of her young
men, the established boundaries of Laconia. Our
own resources were spent with war and the hopes of
the survivors were oppressed by the fate of the dead.
The Thebans were suffering the closest restriction
in the Macedonian garrison[a] which bound their hands
together and had even deprived them of their freedom
of speech. Time buried the power of Thebes with
the body of Epaminondas. The Macedonians had
reached their full strength, and in their aspirations
Fortune was already leading them across the sea
against the throne and treasuries of Persia. Then
too Demosthenes decided upon war, offering to his
compatriots counsel which, though seemingly prudent,
was in reality fraught with danger.[b] When the enemy
was encamped near Attica and the country was being
confined in the town, when the city, worthy to be
striven for and marvelled at by all, was being filled
like a stable with oxen, sheep and flocks and there
was no hope of help from any quarter, I proposed the
peace. I admit it and I maintain that it is an honourable and expedient course to have taken. For it is
better to shun the cloud as it approaches than to be
swept away in the rush of the flood. I ask, Athenians,
that the grief occasioned by events shall not engender
in you any bitterness against me. For I have no

[a] *i.e.* the garrison established in the Cadmea by Philip
after Chaeronea.

[b] After the accession of Alexander in 336 B.C. Demosthenes
proposed a decree to honour Philip's murderer, and war was
imminent. But in the same year, when Alexander entered
Thessaly, Athens retracted. Demades apparently negotiated
the ensuing agreement, but we have no other evidence to
confirm the statement made in this passage.

[DEMADES]

οὐ γὰρ ἐγὼ κρατῶ τῆς τύχης, ἀλλ' ἡ τύχη τοῦ βίου, δι' ἣν κινδυνεύει. δεῖ δὲ τὸν σύμβουλον, καθάπερ τὸν ἰατρόν, οὐ τῆς νόσου τὴν αἰτίαν ἔχειν, ἀλλὰ τῆς 16 θεραπείας τὴν χάριν ἀπολαμβάνειν. καταχωρίσαντες οὖν τὰ συμβάντα διὰ τὰς ἔξωθεν αἰτίας, ψιλῶς ἐπὶ τῶν πραγμάτων γυμνὴν θεωρήσατέ μου τὴν πολιτείαν. μετὰ ταῦτα τοίνυν τῇ πόλει τρίτος ἐπήγετο[1] κίνδυνος πάντων χαλεπώτατος, οὐκέτι πεμφθεὶς ὑπὸ τῆς τύχης, ἀλλ' ὑπὸ τῶν τότε ῥητόρων 17 ἐπαχθείς. καί μοι τῶν πεπραγμένων ἀναμνήσθητε, ἡνίκα Δημοσθένης καὶ Λυκοῦργος τῷ μὲν λόγῳ παραταττόμενοι τοὺς Μακεδόνας ἐνίκων ἐν Τριβαλλοῖς, μόνον δ' οὐχ ὁρατὸν ἐπὶ τοῦ βήματος νεκρὸν τὸν Ἀλέξανδρον προέθηκαν, ἐν τῷ δήμῳ δ' ἀλείψαντες λόγοις εὐπρεπέσι Θηβαίων τοὺς παρόντας φυγάδων θυμοὺς ἐπ' ἐλπίδι τῆς ἐλευθερίας ἠκόνησαν, ἐμὲ δὲ στυγνὸν καὶ περίλυπον ἔφασκον εἶναι, μὴ συνευδοκοῦντα . . .

18 Ἔχει τι πικρὸν ὁ τῆς ἀληθείας λόγος, ἐπειδάν τις ἀκράτῳ παρρησίᾳ χρώμενος μεγάλων ἀγαθῶν προσδοκίαν ἀφαιρῆται· τὰ δὲ προσηνῆ κἂν ᾖ ψευδῆ πείθει τοὺς ἀκούοντας.

19 Προσδόκιμος ἦν εἰς τὴν Ἀττικὴν ὁ κίνδυνος.

20 Μετὰ βραχὺ δὲ καὶ αἱ τῶν Μακεδόνων ἐπιδοράτιδες ἥπτοντ' ἤδη τῆς Ἀττικῆς, καὶ γειτνιώσης τῆς συμφορᾶς καὶ τῆς Ἑλλάδος κατεπτηχυίας, ἔδει καταψᾶν καὶ τιθασεύειν[2] τὴν ὀργὴν τοῦ βασιλέως ἠρεθισμένην κατὰ τοῦ δήμου.

---

[1] ἐπήγετο X : ἐγένετο T : ἐπὶ N : ἐπεὶ Scheibe.
[2] τιθασεύειν Haupt : τιθασσεύειν cod.

346

mastery over Fortune ; it is Fortune which controls life and gives it its danger. The counsellor, like the doctor, must not take blame for the disease ; he must be thanked for the cure. Discount, therefore, what happened from extraneous causes and simply examine my policy naked in the light of facts. To resume then : after this the city was exposed to a third and paramount danger, not this time sent by Fortune but brought on us by the politicians of the day.[a] I would ask you to recall their conduct when Demosthenes and Lycurgus, side by side in their speeches, were defeating the Macedonians among the Triballi and almost exhibited the body of Alexander on the platform for us to see ; when, in the Assembly, they calmed the Theban exiles, who were present, with specious words and spurred on their minds to conceive a hope of freedom, protesting that I was gloomy and over pessimistic since I did not approve . . .

There is bitterness in the voice of truth, when the speaker with simple frankness takes away the expectation of great successes : while pleasant words, though they are false, convince those who hear them.

The danger was expected to reach Attica.

In a short time the Macedonian spearheads had already closed on Attica, and now that the catastrophe was on our borders and Greece was cowering we had need to soothe and tame the anger of the king, which had been roused against our people.

---

[a] The reference is to the events leading up to the destruction of Thebes in 335 B.C., after which Demades interceded with Alexander on behalf of Athens. See Dinarch. i. 10, note.

21 Οὐχ ἡ δόσις τῶν χρημάτων λυπεῖ, ἀλλ᾽ ἡ πρᾶξις τοῦ λαμβάνοντος, ἐὰν ᾖ κατὰ τοῦ συμφέροντος.

22 Ταῦτα λέγων τὸν τοῦ πολέμου πυρσὸν αἴρει, καὶ ὁ πολέμιος ἐπὶ τῶν πυλῶν στρατοπεδεύει.

23 Αἵματι τὸν πόλεμον διέκρινεν.

24 Οὐ γὰρ ἵνα λάβω χρυσίον, ὡς αὐτοὶ πλαττόμενοι λέγουσιν, ἀλλ᾽ ἵνα τόδε.

25 . . . σύμμαχον εἶχεν ὑποψίαν.

26 Ὄφελον καὶ Θηβαίους ἔχειν Δημάδην· ἔτι γὰρ ἂν ἦσαν αἱ Θῆβαι πόλις· νῦν δ᾽ εἰσιν οἰκόπεδον πόλεως καὶ λείψανα κακῶν ταῖς τῶν ἐχθρῶν χερσὶν εἰς ἔδαφος ἀχθεῖσαι.

27 Πολέμιον αἷμα καὶ Μακεδονικὸν πῦρ εἰς τὴν Ἀττικὴν ὑποδέχεσθαι ἦν οὐ καλόν, οὐδὲ σιωπᾶν καὶ καρτερεῖν ὁρῶντα καταδυομένην ὥσπερ ναῦν τὴν πόλιν.

28 Ἀλλ᾽ οἱ δείλαιοι σύμβουλοι ἐξαγαγόντες εἰς τὴν Βοιωτίαν τὴν ἀκμὴν τῆς πόλεως εἰσήγαγον εἰς πολυάνδριον.

29 Εἰρήνην[1] δεῖ καὶ οὐ λόγον ἀντιτάττειν τῇ τῶν Μακεδόνων φάλαγγι· ἄπρακτος γὰρ ἡ σπουδὴ τοῦ λόγου τῶν ἐλάττονα τῆς βουλήσεως ἐχόντων τὴν δύναμιν.

30 Πραΰνεται γὰρ ὁ τῶν ἠδικημένων θυμός, ἐπειδὰν ὁ τὴν αἰτίαν ἔχων μὴ φιλονικῇ, κριτὴν δὲ ποιῇ τῆς εἰς αὑτὸν φιλανθρωπίας τὸν ἀδικούμενον.

It is not the giving of the bribe that distresses us but the action of the man who takes it, if it is directed against our interests.

With these words he raises the firebrand of war and the enemy encamps at the gates.

He decided the war with bloodshed.

My purpose is not to get gold, as these men falsely allege ; it is this.

. . . had suspicion as an ally.

If only the Thebans had possessed a Demades ; for Thebes would then be still a city. Now it is but the site of a city, a remnant of catastrophe, razed to its foundations by enemy hands.

It was not honourable to admit enemy blood and Macedonian fire into Attica nor to be silent and endure the sight of the city sinking like a ship.

But the cowardly politicians, leading out the flower of the city to Boeotia, led them to a graveyard.

It is with peace, not argument, that we must counter the Macedonian phalanx ; for argument lacks power to take effect when urged by men whose strength is less than their desire.

The anger of those who have been wronged is appeased whenever he who is to blame refrains from contentiousness and lets the party wronged judge for himself the kindness he will show.

---

¹ εἰρήνην Haupt : εἰρήνης cod.

31 Τοὺς πρέσβεις εἰς φρέαρ κατέχωσαν, εὐγενῶς
μὲν τοῖς θυμοῖς παραστάντες, οὐκ εὐσεβῶς δὲ τῇ
τιμωρίᾳ χρησάμενοι.

32 Ἐπόνει τοῖς κακοῖς ἡ Σπάρτη.

33 Ὁ Δημοσθένης ὁ πικρὸς συκοφάντης διαστρέφων
τὸ πρᾶγμα τῇ δεινότητι τῶν ῥημάτων διέβαλεν.

34 Ἐγίνωσκον ἀκριβῶς τὸν μὲν τῶν πολιτευομένων
βίον εὐκίνητον ὄντα, τὸ δὲ μέλλον ἀόρατον, ποικίλας
δὲ τὰς τῆς τύχης[1] μεταβολάς, ἀκρίτους δὲ τοὺς τὴν
Ἑλλάδα κατέχοντας καιρούς· ὃν οὖν καθ᾽ ἑτέρων
ἤμελλον τίθεσθαι νόμον.

35 Οὐκ ἐγὼ ταῦτα συνεβούλευον, ἀλλ᾽ ἡ πατρίς, ὁ
καιρός, τὰ πράγματα διὰ τῆς ἐμῆς φωνῆς ἠξίου
ταῦτα πράττειν· οὐ δίκαιον οὖν τὸν σύμβουλον
καιρῶν εὐθύνας ὑπέχειν καὶ ὧν ἐν τῇ τύχῃ τὸ τέλος.

36 Αὐτοχειρὶ σφαγεὶς τὸν βίον ἐξέλιπεν.

37 Αἱ θυγατέρες Ἐρεχθέως τῷ καλῷ τῆς ἀρετῆς
τὸ θῆλυ τῆς ψυχῆς ἐνίκησαν, καὶ τὸ τῆς φύσεως
ἀσθενὲς ἔπανδρον ἐποίησεν ἡ πρὸς τὸ θρέψαν ἔδαφος
φιλοστοργία.

38 Πρεσβῦται φιλοψυχοῦσιν ἐπὶ δυσμαῖς τοῦ βίου.

39 . . . πολεμίῳ πυρὶ τὴν Ἑλλάδα περιέλαμψεν.

---

[1] τύχης Haupt : ψυχῆς cod.

[a] For the well-known story of the envoys of Darius, whom
the Spartans threw into a well and the Athenians into a pit,
see Herod. vii. 133.

They entombed the envoys in a well,[a] noble in so far as they stood by their resolution, but impious in the execution of the punishment.

Sparta was worn out with difficulties.

Demosthenes, bitter sycophant that he is, by the cleverness of his words distorted the fact and showed it in a bad light.

They came to realize clearly the changeability of the politician's life, the uncertainty of the future, the variety of fortune's changes, and the difficulty of gauging the crises that hold Greece in their grip. Therefore the law which they intended to direct against others . . .

It was not I that advised this course : my country, the occasion, the circumstances themselves, thought fit to use my voice to put the measures into effect. It is unjust therefore that an adviser should be held accountable for circumstances and for events whose outcome rested with fortune.

Killed by his own hand he departed this life.

The daughters of Erechtheus,[a] by nobility of virtue, triumphed over the woman's weakness in their hearts ; the frailty of their nature was made virile by devotion to the soil that reared them.

Old men shrink from death in the sunset of life.

. . . lit up Greece with the fire of war.

[b] For the story of the daughters of Erechtheus see Lycurg. *Leocr.* 98 and note.

351

40 Λόγος κενῶς μὲν ἐξενεχθεὶς θήγει τὰ ξίφη, δεξιῶς
δὲ τεθεὶς καὶ τὰς ἠκονημένας λόγχας ἀπαμβλύνει·
οἰκονομία δ' ἀνύει πλέον ἢ βία.

41 Ἐπίστευσεν ὁ βάρβαρος τὸν λόγον, οὐ τὸν νοῦν
ἠρεύνησεν· ἔκρινε γὰρ τοῖς ὠσὶ πρὸς ἡδονὴν τὴν
ἐπαγγελίαν, οὐ πρὸς ἀλήθειαν. τὰ δ' οὐκ ἦν λόγος,
ἀλλ' ἔργα εὐθέως ἠκολούθει.

42 Βίᾳ μὲν οὐδὲ τῶν ἐλαχίστων δύναται κρατεῖν
ἄνθρωπος, ἐπινοίᾳ δὲ καὶ μεθόδῳ ὑπέζευξε μὲν
ἀρότρῳ βοῦν πρὸς τὴν ἐργασίαν τῆς χώρας, ἐχα-
λίνωσε δὲ τὸν ἵππον, ἐλέφαντι δὲ παρέστησεν
ἐπιβάτην καὶ ξύλῳ τὴν ἀμέτρητον θάλασσαν δι-
επέρασεν. τούτων δὲ πάντων ἀρχιτέκτων καὶ δη-
μιουργός ἐστιν ὁ νοῦς, ᾧ δεῖ καθηγεμόνι χρωμένους
μὴ πάντα ζητεῖν πρὸς τὰς ἰδίας ὀξύτητας, ἀλλὰ
πρὸς τὰς τῶν πραγμάτων φύσεις καὶ μεταπτώσεις.
οὕτω κἀγὼ καθάπερ τι φοβερὸν θηρίον κεχαρισμέ-
νοις λόγοις τιθασεύσας τὸν Ἀλέξανδρον ἐποίησα
χειροήθη πρὸς τὸ μέλλον.

43 Ἄρρενα λόγον καὶ τοῦ τῶν Ἀθηναίων ὀνόματος
ἀξίαν παρρησίαν.

44 Μισῶ τοὺς δημαγωγούς, ὅτι ταράττουσι τὸν
δῆμον καὶ τὸ κτῆμα τῆς ἐμῆς πολιτείας τὴν εἰρήνην
ψηφίσματι πολέμου παραθραύουσιν.

45 Οἱ πρόγονοι τὴν πόλιν ἐκλιπόντες πόλιν ἔσχον
τὴν θάλατταν· ἡ δ' ἀπὸ τῆς ναυμαχίας ἧττα καὶ
τὴν πεζὴν δύναμιν συνέτριψεν.

46 Ἐλευθερία ὠτακουστὴν οὐκ εὐλαβεῖται.

A word, if rashly uttered, will sharpen the sword of war, and yet, if skilfully chosen, it will blunt the spear even though it is already whetted. There is more speed in management than in force.

The barbarian accepted the statement but did not probe its meaning. For his ears interpreted the message to conform with his own pleasure rather than with the truth. But this was no idle speech, for deeds followed hard upon it.

Force does not enable a man to master even the smallest things. It was inventiveness and system that made him yoke the ox to the plough for the tilling of the land, bridle the horse, set a rider on the elephant, and cross the boundless sea in boats of wood. The engineer and craftsman of all these things is mind, and we must use it as our guide, not always seeking to follow the subtleties of our own plans but rather the natural changes of events. This was the method by which I tamed Alexander, like some fearful beast, with flattering words and made him tractable for the future.

A manly utterance and a frankness worthy of the name Athenian.

I hate the popular leaders because they disturb the people and shatter the peace, the fruit of my administration, with a decree in favour of war.

Our ancestors left Athens and held the sea as a city, and the naval disaster shattered the land army also.

Freedom is not on guard against a spy.

47 Ὀλισθηραὶ δὲ καὶ συνεχεῖς αἱ παρὰ τῶν πραγμάτων γινόμεναι μεταβολαί.

48 Ψηφίσματι γὰρ εὐνοίας ὁ τῆς ἀθανασίας ἀφίδρυται βωμός.

49 Ἐπιστήσεις αὐτοῖς κήρυκα τὸν χρόνον φθεγγόμενον.

50 Ἀλέξανδρος ὁ τὰς ἐλπίδας συνάπτων πρὸς τὴν τῆς οἰκουμένης ἡγεμονίαν.

51 Ὁ Δημοσθένης ἀνθρωπάριον ἐκ συλλαβῶν καὶ γλώσσης συγκείμενον.

52 Ἐκεῖνοι γὰρ οἱ λόγοι τὴν ὀργὴν τοῦ βασιλέως ὥσπερ ὕπνῳ κατεκοίμησαν.

53 Ἔτι γὰρ ἤκμαζον αἱ δυνάμεις τῆς πόλεως καὶ τῆς Ἑλλάδος τὸ φρόνημα, καὶ συνέρρει ἡ τύχη τῷ δήμῳ· νῦν δ᾽ ἐξωστράκισται μὲν πᾶν τὸ χρήσιμον ἐκ τῶν πραγμάτων, ἐξήρηται δὲ τὰ νεῦρα τῶν πόλεων, εἰς ἄνεσιν δὲ καὶ τρυφὴν νενεύκασιν οἱ βίοι, τὰ δὲ τῆς ὁμονοίας οὐκέτι μένει, νόθαι δὲ γεγόνασιν αἱ τῶν φίλων ἐλπίδες.

54 Ὁ δὲ πόλεμος ὥσπερ νέφος ἐκ παντὸς τόπου τῆς Εὐρώπης ἐπήρτητο, καὶ συνέκλειέ μου τὴν ἐπὶ τῆς ἐκκλησίας παρρησίαν, καὶ τὴν μετ᾽ ἐλευθερίας καὶ δόξης φωνὴν ἀφῄρει.

55 Ἐκ τῶν πραγμάτων σκοπεῖτε τὴν ἀλήθειαν, καὶ μὴ ψευδεῖς αἰτίας ὁμολογουμένων ἔργων προκρίνητε.

The changes to which events are subject are treacherous and unceasing.

For it is by a resolution of goodwill that the altar of immortality has been erected.[a]

You will set over them time speaking as a herald.

Alexander who framed his hopes to gain world dominion.

Demosthenes, a little man made up of syllables and a tongue.

For those words as it were lulled to sleep the king's anger.

For the powers of the city and the pride of Greece were still at their height, and fortune favoured the people. But now every element of value in the political world has been ostracized and the cities' hamstrings removed ; men's lives have inclined to relaxation and luxury, the means of concord are no longer there, and the hopes of our friends have proved vain.

War, like a cloud, was threatening Europe from every quarter, suppressing my right to speak my mind in the assembly and taking away all power of free and noble utterance.

Examine the truth in the light of events and do not give more weight to false charges than to accepted facts.

[a] Apparently a reference to the deification of Alexander in 324 B.C.

[DEMADES]

56 . . . διὰ τῶν πραγμάτων πολέμιον πῦρ προαγο-
ρεύει. αὕτη ἡ Ἀλεξάνδρου[1] ἐπιστολὴ συνέτριβέ μου
τὴν διάνοιαν· αὕτη πόλεμον ἐν τύπῳ γραμμάτων
περιέχουσα μονονοὺκ ἐπιλαβομένη μου τῆς χειρὸς
ἐξήγειρεν· αὕτη πορευομένη διὰ τῶν λογισμῶν τὴν
ἡσυχίαν ἄγειν οὐκ ἐπέτρεψεν· ἐν πύλαις γὰρ ὁ
κίνδυνος.

57 Ἡ δ' ἐμὴ πολιτεία καὶ ὁ τότε θόρυβος συν-
επέστησε τὴν πόλιν, καὶ διεκώλυσεν ὥσπερ κῦμα
πανταχόθεν ἐπικλύσαι τὴν Ἀττικήν, καὶ τὴν ἐν
Βοιωτίᾳ παρασκευὴν ἔτρεψεν εἰς Πέρσας.

58 Οὐ τὴν αὐτὴν ἔχει φαντασίαν ἐφεστηκὼς καὶ
διαλλαγεὶς ὁ τοῦ πολέμου φόβος ὥσπερ γνόφος.

59 Διὸ καὶ πάντων δοκεῖ χαλεπώτατον, ἐν εἰρήνῃ
λόγον ὑποσχεῖν τῶν ἐν πολέμῳ πεπολιτευμένων·
κρίνει γὰρ ἕκαστος πρὸς τὴν παροῦσαν ἡσυχίαν,
οὐ πρὸς τὸν παρελθόντα κίνδυνον. ὅταν δέ τις
ἀνέλῃ τῶν πραγμάτων τὸν καιρόν, ἀνταναιρεῖται
καὶ τὸ δίκαιον τῆς πράξεως.

60 Ἕκαστον τῶν ἀδικημάτων ἰδίας ἔχει τὰς οἰκο-
νομίας· ἃ μὲν γάρ ἐστι δεόμενα τῆς ⟨ἐξ⟩[2] Ἀρείου
πάγου βουλῆς, ἃ δὲ τῶν ἐλαττόνων δικαστηρίων,
ἃ δὲ τῆς ἡλιαίας· πάντα δὲ ταῦτα διώρισται τοῖς
ὀνόμασι, τοῖς· πράγμασι, τοῖς χρόνοις, τοῖς ἐπιτιμίοις, ταῖς ἀγωγαῖς καὶ τῷ πλήθει τῶν δικαζόντων.

61 Ἀδίκους οἱ συκυφάνται μου ποιοῦνται τὰς

. . . by the course of events proclaims the fire of war. This letter of Alexander's broke my purpose.[a] This letter, embracing war in characters of ink, almost seized me by the hand and roused me. It travelled through my thoughts and did not let me rest in peace ; for the danger was at our gates.

My diplomacy and the clamour that greeted it combined to set the city on the watch, saved Attica from being swamped from every side as by a wave and turned the army in Boeotia against the Persians.[b]

Fear of war, like darkness, does not present the same aspect when it confronts us as when it has been averted.

It seems, therefore, the harshest imaginable rule that a man should be held accountable in time of peace for his administration during war. For every critic judges it with reference to the present calm, not to the danger that is over. And yet, if we make no allowance for the crisis, we are removing too the justification for the action.

Each offence is dealt with in its own particular way : some call for the council of the Areopagus, some for lesser courts, others for the Heliaea. All these are distinguished in name, circumstance, time, penalty, procedure, and in the number of the jury.

Those who malign me are making unwarranted

[a] Perhaps Alexander's letter demanding triremes from Athens (see Plut. *Phoc.* 21).
[b] After the fall of Thebes in 335 B.C.

---

[1] Ἀλεξάνδρου] secl. Blass.
[2] ἐξ add. Blass.

διώξεις· οὐ γὰρ βουλεύσεως ἐγκαλοῦσιν, οἷς ἀνώμοτος ἡ κακία· τοῖς δὲ δικασταῖς ἔνορκος ἡ κρίσις.

62 Ἄδικος κρίσις ἀδίκου τιμωρίας ὀνόματι μόνον διαφέρει.

63 Ὑποβρύχιον ὤσειν μ᾽ ὑπολαμβάνουσιν.

64 Οὐ δίκαιόν ἐστι τὴν τοῦ κινδυνεύοντος σωτηρίαν ἐφόδιον γενέσθαι συκοφαντίας τοῖς πάντα τολμᾶν προῃρημένοις, οὐδὲ τὴν ἐκ τῶν λόγων κατηγορίαν ἰσχυροτέραν ἡγεῖσθαι τῆς ἐκ τῶν πραγμάτων ἀπολογίας.

65 Ἑτερόφθαλμος γέγονεν ἡ Ἑλλὰς τῆς τῶν Θηβαίων ἀναιρεθείσης πόλεως.

accusations. They do not charge me with plotting, for their villainy is bound by no oath. But the jury's judgement is governed by an oath.

An unjust trial differs from an unjust punishment only in name.

They think that they will plunge me below the surface.

It is not right that the saving of a man in danger should provide fuel for the malicious charges of those who have abandoned all principle, nor that an accusation based on stories should be held stronger than a defence grounded on facts.

Greece has lost an eye in the destruction of the Thebans' city.

HYPERIDES

LIFE OF HYPERIDES [a]

HYPERIDES was born at Athens in 390 B.C. and executed by Antipater in 322. For the last forty years of his life he took part in politics and early espoused the anti-Macedonian cause, in loyalty to which he met his death. His character was one of marked contrasts. In public life, though he gained no crown and did not rank in popular esteem with either Demosthenes or Lycurgus, he showed himself not only active but also devoted, refusing the bribes of Harpalus and being said by some to have bitten out his tongue at the last to avoid betraying Athens. In his personal habits, however, he was notoriously self-indulgent, arousing comment by his affairs with courtesans and his addiction to good food and drink.[b] A varied experience of city life no doubt enhanced his powers as an advocate.

[a] Sources for the Life of Hyperides. The chief source for the life of Hyperides is the Pseudo-Plutarch's biography of him in the *Lives of the Ten Orators*, from which are taken nearly all the details given in the above account. He is also discussed by Hermippus, *The Pupils of Isocrates*, Book III, and Suidas has a short note on him (*s.v.* " Hyperides "). Brief references to him are to be found in the writings of numerous authors, in particular his contemporaries Demosthenes, Aeschines and Lycurgus, and of later writers, Plutarch, Pseudo-Plutarch, Lucian, Dionysius of Halicarnassus, Athenaeus and Alciphron.

[b] Athen. viii. 341 e.

HYPERIDES

Born of a good family, Hyperides studied as a young man under Plato and Isocrates [a] and began his career by writing speeches for others. Apart from the record of three prosecutions, those of the orator Aristophon in 362 B.C., the general Autocles shortly after and Diopithes of Sphettus at an uncertain date,[b] no trace of his public activities is discernible before the forties. In 343 he prosecuted Philocrates, who had proposed the recent peace with Philip,[c] and probably shortly after was chosen by the Areopagus to supplant Aeschines as Athenian spokesman in a dispute with Delos.[d] The people of that island had appealed to the Amphictyonic Council in order to obtain the temple of Apollo, which was still controlled by Athens. The case was heard before the Council and Hyperides was successful. In 341 we find him as the city's envoy in Chios and Rhodes seeking to form an alliance against Philip,[e] and on the latter's threat in 340 to take Euboea he sailed there with forty triremes, of which two were provided by himself. The following year he was again abroad as trierarch with the Athenian fleet at Byzantium.[f]

Though not himself present on the field of Chaeronea [g] Hyperides was active in Athens after the defeat. During that emergency he proposed that the women and children should be removed to the Piraeus, that aliens should be made citizens, and slaves released and armed to protect the city. Although

[a] Athen. viii. 342 c.
[b] For Aristophon and Diopithes see Hyp. iv. 28 and 29 and frag. 17, note ; for Autocles see frag. 14, note.
[c] See Hyp. iv. 29 and frag. 16, note.
[d] Dem. xviii. 134. See Hyp. frag. 1, note.
[e] See Hyp. frags. 5 and 6, notes.
[f] I.G. ii. 808 c.   [g] Lucian, Parasit. 42.

this measure was apparently carried, the more drastic of its clauses were not put into effect ; and as the tension eased, its proposer was accused by Aristogiton of having made proposals which violated the constitution. He secured his acquittal, however, on the grounds that the arms of Macedon had darkened his vision,[a] and soon after the battle seems to have visited some smaller states in search of help against Philip. To this time his Cythnian speech should probably be assigned.[b]

While Lycurgus was at the head of internal affairs, the activities of Hyperides, now a prominent figure of the anti-Macedonian party, continued unabated. His prosecutions of Demades [c] for illegality and Philippides for a pro-Macedonian measure belong to the period succeeding Chaeronea ; and as the defence of Euxenippus must be assigned to approximately 330 B.C. and the speech against Athenogenes to the early twenties, we may presume that until the Lamian War he was still practising as an advocate. In 324 he attacked Demosthenes over the Harpalus affair. The two men had long been friends, and Hyperides had even proposed that the other should be crowned for his services before Chaeronea. He may now have thought it his duty to put public interest before personal feelings ; for though Lucian credits him with lower motives,[d] we hear no mention of any earlier estrangement. According to tradition he was himself the only man of note who on that occasion had not received a bribe.

After the death of Alexander in 323 Hyperides toured the Peloponnese to rouse the cities against

---

[a] See Hyp. frag. 18 and note.
[b] See Hyp. frag. 4, note.
[c] See Hyp. frag. 19, note.
[d] Lucian, *Enc. Dem.* 31.

HYPERIDES

Antipater, and while on this journey, became reconciled with Demosthenes, who, though in exile, had come on the same errand. In the following year, as the leading orator in Athens, he shared with Leosthenes the conduct of the Lamian War and gave his Funeral Speech over the dead. But the project which he so wholeheartedly supported was doomed to failure, for before the end of the year Athens surrendered unconditionally. On the motion of Demades, Demosthenes, Hyperides and some others were condemned to death by the people, and the agents of Antipater lost no time in carrying out the sentence (322 B.C.).

As a speaker Hyperides had many gifts and was compared by one critic to a pentathlete, because in all the qualities of an orator he fell only just short of the best.[a] Though well able to deal with serious cases, he excelled particularly at the lighter type of oratory, being adroit in argument, often racy, and rather free with colloquialisms. The directness, grace and urbanity which recommended his writings in antiquity are still discernible, even in the fragmentary portions that remain.

[a] [Longinus], *De Sublim.* 34. Other criticisms are given by Dion. Hal. *De Imitat.* B, v. 6 and *De Dinarch.* 1, 6 and 7; Dio Chrys. xviii. 11; Hermogenes, Περὶ Ἰδεῶν B, p. 382; Cic. *de Orat.* iii. 28, *Orat.* 110; Quintil. *Inst. Or.* x. 1. 77.

NOTE ON THE TEXT

EXTENSIVE restoration has been necessary in the text of Hyperides, as a glance at the following pages will show, even to establish the present standard of completeness. In the indication of restored words and letters, by the usual square brackets, this volume follows a middle course between those of the Teubner and Oxford texts. The former, that of C. Jensen, printed in columns corresponding to those of the papyrus, marks all restorations and doubtful letters ; the latter is far more selective. In the present edition all restorations of two or more consecutive letters are marked, while the rest, with a few exceptions, are ignored. The critical notes, though incomplete, are intended to cover all important points and to pay a fair tribute to those scholars who have worked on the text. Even in Jensen's excellent *apparatus criticus* not all restorations are accounted for, and of those which were made early and universally accepted it has not always been possible to trace the authorship. In the case of some of the longer reconstructions, where the version printed is sometimes the result of combined labours, the critical note, for the sake of brevity, has occasionally been somewhat simplified.

By no means all the reconstructions accepted in this edition can be regarded as certain. The text, except for a few changes, is the same as that of

Jensen, who has admitted a moderate number of conjectural words ; and the Oxford edition, though differing often in detail, will be found to admit about the same proportion. Of the longer conjectural restorations, put forward by various scholars, most have not been adopted here, on the ground that they do not recapture the words of the speaker, though they may often convey their general sense. Readers will find in the recent Budé edition of G. Colin a text which is rather more venturesome in this respect.

No generally accepted order of arrangement has yet been established for the six speeches. The Teubner text presents them in the order in which they were discovered, while in the Budé edition and in the Oxford text they are arranged in the order in which the editors believe them to have been delivered. References to them in Liddell and Scott's Greek Lexicon are made according to titles, and, in the main, the section numbers of the Oxford text, which are adopted here. For the beginning of the *Lycophron*, however, and the *Demosthenes*, fragment numbers are quoted ; and where these differ in the Loeb edition, the Oxford number is given in brackets. The numbers assigned to the speeches in the chief editions are as follows.

	Number in the Loeb and Oxford Texts	Number in the Budé Edition	Number in the Teubner Text
In Defence of Lycophron	I	II	II
Against Philippides	II	I	IV
Against Athenogenes	III	IV	V
In Defence of Euxenippus	IV	III	III
Against Demosthenes	V	V	I
Funeral Speech	VI	VI	VI

I

SPEECH IN DEFENCE OF LYCOPHRON

INTRODUCTION

THE papyrus containing the Defence of Lycophron supplies a title for the speech but does not tell us who wrote it. There is, however, no reason to doubt its authorship, as the only speech of that name mentioned by ancient writers was the work of Hyperides, and Pollux [a] attributes to him a statement which, though not an actual quotation, clearly refers to a passage in the extant fragment.[b]

The year in which the trial took place cannot be determined with certainty. (a) Before the fragments of the second speech were discovered it was generally held that the date must fall prior to 338 B.C. on the strength of a passage in the first speech [b] where Hyperides asserts that in this type of indictment (εἰσαγγελία) the prosecutor ran no risk. It is known that subsequently in such cases the prosecutor had to pay a thousand drachmas if he failed to obtain one-fifth of the votes [a]; and it appears from a statement of Demosthenes in the speech on the Crown [c] that this provision was already in force shortly after the battle of Chaeronea (338). But if 338 is the latest possible date for the trial, it can hardly be placed

---

[a] Pollux viii. 52.   [b] § 8.

[c] Demosthenes (xviii. 250), speaking in 330 of trials which took place soon after Chaeronea, says : " you acquitted me and did not give the prosecutors their share of the votes [τὸ μέρος τῶν ψήφων]."

much earlier, since Dioxippus, who is mentioned in the speech as having been the strongest man in Greece [a] at the time of his sister's wedding, three years before the trial, was still regarded as such as late as 326 when he was performing for Alexander in India.[b] (b) An alternative and somewhat preferable line of argument, giving a date of 333, is based on a fragment of the second speech,[c] where we read that at the time of his sister's wedding Dioxippus was due to leave for the Olympic games where he became a victor. His Olympic victory has been dated on other grounds at 336 B.C., and as the trial took place some three years later we obtain the date of 333. In accepting this we must assume that in 333 the new provision, whereby a prosecutor in a case of εἰσαγγελία might incur a fine, had not yet come in, but that by 330, when Demosthenes made his speech on the Crown, it was already in force. The words of Demosthenes, in the passage mentioned above, would thus be appropriate to the time at which he was speaking but not strictly applicable to the conditions obtaining directly after the battle of Chaeronea.

Lycophron was an Athenian citizen and a keen breeder of horses. He served for three years as a cavalry commander in Lemnos, where he was crowned by the inhabitants in recognition of his merits.[d] At the age of fifty, while still in the island,[e] he was accused in Athens of adultery. The accusers were a certain Ariston, referred to in the speech as ὁ κατήγορος, and the orator Lycurgus, who brought an impeachment before the Assembly while Lycophron was still absent.

---

[a] § 5. [b] Diodor. xvii. 100-101.
[c] Frag. xiii. [d] See §§ 16 sq.
[e] This is inferred from what the speaker says in § 3.

The case was entrusted by the people to a special court, and meanwhile Lycophron's relatives wrote to Lemnos to acquaint him with the circumstances. He thus returned to Athens in time and secured the help of Hyperides for his defence.

The circumstances which led up to the trial are not altogether clear owing to the fragmentary state of the speech, but the available details can be pieced together to make a story which is probably substantially correct. We may conclude that most of the events mentioned took place about three years before the trial, since the accused was still in Athens at the time.

Lycophron was accused of adultery with an Athenian woman, a sister of Dioxippus the wrestler. Her first husband, whose name has not been preserved, was an invalid at the time of the affair and soon died, leaving her pregnant.[a] His will appointed a certain Euphemus [b] as guardian of the child with charge of the estate, so long as it was a minor. In the event of its death, at birth or later, certain relatives were to inherit the property. It seems probable that these relatives began by accepting the will, but that there were others who from the first disputed it.[c] After about three years, since the child had not died and seemed likely to succeed to the

_____

[a] See frag. iv. The first two letters of the husband's name were Χρ and the last two -ος; therefore neither Grenfell and Hunt's restoration of Chremes nor Colin's of Charisandros is satisfactory. Compare frag. i. of the second speech.

[b] Euphemus was probably a friend of the husband rather than a brother of the bride, as Blass thought; for in § 5 the speaker implies that the brother Dioxippus attended the wedding because he was the only person suitable to give away the bride.

[c] This is inferred from frag. iv.

whole estate, all the relatives united in an attempt to prove it illegitimate. They argued that Lycophron was the father and brought this action for adultery against him.[a]

Before Lycophron left Athens the woman had already married again, her second husband being an Athenian named Charippus. Euphemus had provided a dowry, and her brother, Dioxippus, had been present at the ceremony. Lycurgus alleged before the Assembly that Lycophron had asked the woman, even during the wedding procession,[b] not to consummate the marriage with Charippus, and in this way had ruined her future, since a respectable man would not retain her as his wife. He evidently claimed that adultery was a crime likely to undermine the life of the city [c] and so tried to justify himself for making the case one of impeachment (εἰσαγγελία), where a γραφὴ ὕβρεως before the Thesmothetae would have been the normal procedure.

Two speeches by Lycurgus against Lycophron are known to have been published.[d] The first was perhaps delivered in the Assembly and the second before the court. It is possible that Hyperides also wrote two, of which this, the more important, was to be spoken by Lycophron, while the second may have been intended for the orator himself or for some other advocate for the defence, such as Theophilus.[e] No second speech in defence of Lycophron, however, is

---

[a] Compare frag. i. of the second speech, from which it is clear that they accused Lycophron of having had an affair with the woman before the death of her first husband.

[b] See § 3.

[c] See § 12.

[d] Compare Lycurg. frags. 11 and 12.

[e] See § 20.

attributed to Hyperides by ancient writers, and on the whole it seems more probable that the second speech, though composed for this trial, was the work of another orator.

In what remains of the first speech Lycophron is made to attack Ariston and his kinsman by marriage, Theomnestus,[a] and to show that the charges made against him are absurd. He argues that his opponents are breaking the law by using the method of impeachment and that they are trying to prevent him from bringing forward his witnesses. The verdict is not known.

[a] It appears from frag. v. of the second speech that Theomnestus was related to Ariston by marriage.

ANALYSIS

Frags. i.-iii.   Appeal to the jury and prayer to the gods. The present case is not covered by the Impeachment Law.

Frag. iv.-§ 7.   The conduct of Lycophron's opponents has been inconsistent. Ariston is a sycophant. If Lycophron had behaved at the wedding as they allege, (a) Lycophron would have been killed, (b) Charippus would not have married the woman.

§§ 8-12.   The accuser has an unfair advantage over Lycophron and, to ensure his own safety, is violating the Impeachment Law.

§§ 13-18.   The charge that Lycophron ruins women is absurd, as his life story shows. As Hipparch he was crowned by the inhabitants of Lemnos.

§§ 19-20.   Appeal to the jury to give Lycophron's supporters a fair hearing.

ΑΠΟΛΟΓΙΑ ΥΠΕΡ ΛΥΚΟΦΡΟΝΟΣ

Frag. I[1]

[col. 41]   ... [καὶ ἰδίᾳ] ἕκαστος καὶ κοι[νῇ], ἔπειτα τῷ
νό[μῳ] καὶ τῷ ὅρκῳ, ὃς κε[λεύει] ὑμᾶς ὁμοίως
[ἀκούειν] τῶν τε κατη[γόρων[2] καὶ τῶ]ν ἀπο[λο-
γουμένων] καὶ ...

[Desunt col. 41 versus fere viginti unus et col. 42
fere tota.]

Frag. II

[col. 43]   τῇ κατηγορίᾳ χρῆσθαι, οὕτω καὶ ἐμὲ ἐᾶτε ὃν
τρόπον προῄρημαι καὶ ὡς ἂν δύνωμαι ἀπολογεῖσθαι.
καὶ μηδεὶς ὑμῶν ἀπαντάτω μοι μεταξὺ λέγοντι,
" τί τοῦθ᾽ ἡμῖν λέγεις; " μηδὲ προστίθετε τῇ
κατηγορίᾳ παρ᾽ ὑμῶν αὐτῶν μηδέν, ἀλλὰ [μᾶ]λλον
τῇ ἀπολογίᾳ ...

[Desunt col. 43 versus fere quindecim et col. 44
versus fere decem.]

Frag. III

[col. 44]   [οὐδ]ὲ ὁ νόμος συγκα[τηγο]ρεῖν[3] μὲν τῷ βου[λο-

---

[1] Hoc fragmentum restituit Kenyon.

IN DEFENCE OF LYCOPHRON

Frag. I

. . . each man in private and in public life,[a] and also in the law and in the oath which bids you give an equal hearing to the prosecution and to the defence . . .

Frag. II

. . . to conduct the prosecution,[b] allow me also in the same way to follow out, so far as I am able, the line of defence which I have chosen. I must ask you all, while I am speaking, to refrain from interrupting me with : " Why are you telling us this ? " And do not add anything of your own to the prosecution's argument ; rather ⟨attend⟩ to the defence . . .

Frag. III

. . . nor is it true that the law, while allowing

[a] Blass, comparing Aeschin. iii. 1, conjectured the sense to be : " I come before you now having put my trust both in the gods, on whom you all rely in private and in public life, and also in the law, etc."

[b] The sense is no doubt : " Since you allowed my opponents to conduct the prosecution as they wished, allow me also a fair hearing in my defence."

---

2 κατηγόρων Fuhr : κατηγορούντων Kenyon.
3 συγκατηγορεῖν Sauppe.

μ]ένῳ κατὰ τῶν [κριν]ομένων[1] ἐξου[σίαν] δίδωσι,
συναπολογεῖσθαι δὲ κωλύει. ἵνα δὲ μὴ πρὸ τοῦ
πράγματος πο[λλ]ο[ὺς] λόγους ἀναλ[ώσω],[2] ἐπ᾽
αὐτὴν τὴν [ἀπολογ]ίαν[3] πορεύσομαι, τοῖς μὲν θεοῖς
εὐξάμενος βοηθῆσαί μοι καὶ σῶσαι ἐκ τοῦ παρόντος
ἀγῶνος, ὑμᾶς δέ, ὦ ἄνδρες δικασταί, ἐκεῖνο παρ-
αιτησάμενος, πρῶτον . . .

[Deest col. 45 fere tota.]

Frag. IIIa (IV) [4]

ἢ νεωρίων προδοσίαν ἢ ἀρχείων ἐμπυρισμὸν ἢ
κατάληψιν ἄκρας . . . .

Frag. IV (V)

[Desunt col. 46 versus fere quindecim.]

[col. 46] . . . . . . ὁ Εὔ[φημος][5] . . . . . πρ]ῶτον[6] . . . .
ἐπε]ιδὴ[7] ἐτε[λεύτησεν ἐκ]εῖνος . . . . ρος ὁ
Φλυ[εύς,][7] . . . . . ἐξ αὐτοῦ . . . . . .

[Desunt col. 46 versus septem]

[col. 47] . . . . . ὅτι ἡ γυνὴ . . . . τον καὶ το[. . . . .]ατο
ἐκεῖνος [κυοῦ]σαν[8] τὴν γυναῖ[κα ἐξ] αὐτοῦ καταλέ-
[λοιπε]ν, οὐ παρὰ τοὺς ν[όμο]υς γενόμενον. [εἰ δ᾽
ὥσ]περ Ἀρίστων ἐ[ν τῇ ε]ἰσαγγελίᾳ γρά[φει],[9]
οὕτως ὑπέλα[βον τ]ὰ περὶ το[ύτων εἶν]αι,[10] οὐκ
ἔδει δήπ[ου αὐτ]οὺς κωλύειν [τοὺς ἐγγυ]τάτω[11]
γένου[ς ἐξά]γειν[8] τὸν Εὔφημον, ἀλλ᾽ ἐᾶν. νῦν δὲ

---

[1] κρινομένων Boeckh, Sauppe.
[2] ἀναλώσω Babington.
[3] ἀπολογίαν Boeckh, Sauppe.

freedom to join in the prosecution of men on trial,
denies the right to share in their defence. I do not
intend to waste words before coming to the point,
and shall therefore proceed to the actual defence,
after praying the gods to help me and bring me safely
through the present trial and requesting you, gentlemen of the jury, first . . .

Frag. IIIa (IV)

. . . either the betrayal of dockyards, the burning
of public buildings, or the seizure of the Acropolis . . .

Frag. IV (V)

. . . Euphemus . . . first . . . when the husband
died . . . of Phlya . . . from him . . . that the
woman . . . he had left his wife with child, which
did not entail any breach of the law. But if their
interpretation of this story tallied with that given
by Ariston in the impeachment, they [a] should not
surely have prevented the nearest relatives from
ejecting Euphemus. They ought to have let them do
so. Whereas now, by behaving as they did, they

---

[a] The reference seems to be to those relatives due to benefit
by the will in the event of the child's death. See Introduction.

---

4 Hoc fragmentum a Polluce (ix. 156) servatum huc inseruit
Blass.

5 Εὔφημος Blass.

6 πρῶτον Fuhr.

7 ἐπειδὴ usque ad Φλυεύς restituit Sauppe : ἐκεῖνος ὁ Χαρίσ-
ανδρος ὁ Φλυεύς Colin.

8 κυοῦσαν usque ad ἐξάγειν plerumque restituit Blass.

9 ὥσπερ et γράφει Kenyon.

10 τούτων εἶναι Jensen.   11 ἐγγυτάτω Boeckh.

τοῦτο ποιήσαντες ἔργῳ μεμαρτυρήκασιν αὐτοί, ὡς
ψευδής ἐστιν ἡ αἰτία κατ᾽ ἐμοῦ. πρὸς δὲ τούτοις
πῶς οὐκ ἄτοπον, εἰ μέν τι ἔπαθεν τὸ παιδίον ἢ
γιγνόμενον ἢ καὶ ὕστερον, ταύταις ταῖς διαθήκαις
ἰσχυρίζεσθαι ἂν αὐτούς, ἐν αἷς . . . . .

[Desunt col. 48 versus fere viginti.]

[col. 48] . . . . τὸν Εὐφη[μον] . . . . . .
ἐκώλυε . . . . [παρέ]χοντα[1] . . . . . . [μαρ]τυρίας[2]
. . . .

   .   .   .   .   .   .

Frag. IVa [3]

Οὔτε γὰρ τὴν ἑαυτοῦ χεῖρα δυνατὸν ἀρνήσασθαι.

   .   .   .   .

Frag. IVb [3]

νωθρεύεσθαι

   .   .   .   .   .   .

[col. 2] ᾽Αρίστωνος δὲ ἀνδ[ρά]ποδα εἶχεν ἐν το[ῖς] ἔργοις·
καὶ ταῦτα αὐτὸς ὑμῖν ἐμαρτύρησεν ἐπὶ τοῦ δικασ[τη]-
ρίου, ὅτ᾽ ἦν το[ύτ]ῳ ὁ ἀγὼν πρὸς ᾽Α[ρχε]στρατίδην.[4]
2 τοιο[ῦτο] γάρ ἐστι τὸ ᾽Αρίστ[ωνος][5] τουτουῒ πρᾶγμα·
[οὗ]τος[6] προσκαλεῖται μὲν περιὼν πάντας ἀνθρώπους, τῶν δ᾽ ὅσοι μὲν [ἂν] μὴ διδῶσιν αὐ[τῷ]
ἀργύριον, κρίν[ει καὶ] κατηγορεῖ, ὁπ[όσοι] δ᾽ ἂν
ἐθέλωσιν [ἀπο]τίνειν,[7] ἀφίησιν, [τὸ] δ᾽ ἀργύριον
Θεο[μνή]στῳ[5] δίδωσιν· ἐκ[εῖ]νος δὲ λαμβάνων ἀνδράποδα ἀγοράζει, καὶ παρέχει ὥσπερ τοῖς λῃσταῖς
ἐπισιτισμόν, καὶ δίδωσι τούτῳ ὑπὲρ ἑκάστου τοῦ

have by their own action furnished evidence that the charge against me is false. Besides, is it not strange that if anything had happened to the child at birth, or after, they would have adhered firmly to this will, in which . . .

Frag. IVa

. . . nor is it possible for him to deny his own handwriting . . .

Frag. IVb

. . . to be sluggish . . .

. . . and he had Ariston's slaves in his works. This fact he confirmed for you himself [a] in court when Ariston was bringing an action against Archestratides.[b] Let me explain the kind of method which this man Ariston employs. He issues a summons against everyone he meets, accusing and prosecuting those who do not give him money, but letting go all who are willing to pay. He gives the money to Theomnestus who takes it and buys slaves, providing Ariston with a livelihood, as is done for pirates, and

[a] The subject is probably Theomnestus.
[b] Nothing is known of this man. He may be the Archestratides against whom Hyperides composed a speech. Compare frag. 52.

---

[1] Εὔφημον et παρέχοντα Blass.   [2] μαρτυρίας Boeckh.
[3] Haec duo fragmenta a Polluce (ii. 152 et ix. 137) servata huc inseruit Blass.
[4] Ἀρχεστρατίδην Babington.
[5] Ἀρίστωνος usque ad Θεομνήστῳ plerumque restituit Schneidewin.
[6] οὗτος Shilleto : αὐτὸς Schneidewin.
[7] ὁπόσοι et ἀποτίνειν Babington.

HYPERIDES

[col. 3] ἀνδραπόδου ὀβολὸν τῆς ἡμέρας, ὅπως ἂν ᾖ ἀθάνατος
συκοφάντης.

3 Ἄξιον δ' ἐστίν, ὦ ἄνδρες δικασταί, κἀκεῖθεν
ἐξετάσαι τὸ πρᾶγμα, ἀφ' ὧν ἐν τῷ δήμῳ τὸ πρῶτον αὐτοὶ εὐθὺς ᾐτιάσαντο. ἐμοὶ γὰρ ⟨οἱ⟩[1] οἰκεῖοι
ἀπέστειλαν[2] γράψαντες τήν τε εἰσαγγελίαν καὶ τὰς
αἰτίας ἃς ἐν τῇ ἐκκλησίᾳ ᾐτιάσαντό με, ὅτε τὴν
εἰσαγγελί[αν] ἐδίδοσαν, ἐν α[ἷς ἦ]ν γεγραμμένον ὅτι
Λυκοῦργος λέγ[ει], φάσκω[ν τ]ῶν [ο]ἰκ[είω]ν ἀκ[η-
κ]οέναι,[3] ὡς ἐγὼ παρακολουθῶν, ὅτε Χάριππος
ἐγάμει τὴν γυναῖκα, παρεκελευόμην αὐτῇ ὅπως μὴ
[col. 4] πλησιάσει[4] Χαρίππῳ ἀλλὰ διαφυλάξει αὐτήν. ἐγὼ
4 δὲ ἃ καὶ πρὸς τοὺς ἐπιτηδείου[ς καὶ] πρὸς τοὺς
ο[ἰκείους][5] τοὺς ἐμαυτ[οῦ εὐθὺς][6] ἥκων ἔλεγ[ον, κ]αὶ
νῦν πρὸς ὑμ[ᾶς λέ]γω,[7] ὅτι, εἰ ἔστιν τ[αῦ]τα ἀληθῆ,
ὁμολ[ογ]ῶ καὶ τἆλλα πάν[τα π]εποιηκέναι τὰ [ἐν τῇ]
εἰσαγγελίᾳ γε[γραμ]μένα.[8] ὅτι δὲ [ψευδῆ][9] ἐστιν,
ῥᾴδιον [οἶμαι][10] εἶναι ἅπασι[ν ἰδεῖν].[11] τίς γὰρ οὕτω[ς
5 ἐστὶ][12] τῶν ἐν τῇ π[όλει] ἀλόγιστος, ὅσ[τις ἂν] πι-
στεύσαι τού[τοις τοῖς][12] λόγοις; ἀνάγ[κη γάρ],[13] ὦ
ἄνδρες δικ[ασταί,] πρῶτον μὲν ὀρεωκόμον καὶ
προηγητὴν ἀκολουθε[ῖν] τῷ ζεύγει, ὃ ἦγεν τὴν
[col. 5] γυναῖκα, ἔπειτα δὲ παῖδας τοὺς προπέμποντας αὐτὴν ἀκολουθεῖν καὶ Διώξιππον· καὶ γὰρ οὗτος
6 ἠκολούθει διὰ τὸ χήραν ἐκδίδοσθαι αὐτήν. εἶτ'

---

[1] οἱ add. Schneidewin.
[2] ἀπέστειλαν] ἐπέστειλαν Blass.
[3] οἰκείων ἀκηκοέναι Babington.
[4] πλησιάσει Schneidewin : πλησιάσῃ A.
[5] οἰκείους Babington.
[6] εὐθὺς Blass : τότε Babington.
[7] λέγω Schneidewin : ἐρῶ Babington.
[8] γεγραμμένα Babington.

382

paying him an obol a day for each slave, to enable him to continue permanently as a false informer.

When considering the matter, gentlemen of the jury, we ought to begin with the charges which my accusers themselves brought against me at the outset in the Assembly. My relatives communicated the impeachment to me by letter, and also the charges which they made against me in the Assembly when they brought the impeachment. Among these was recorded a statement of Lycurgus, who claimed to have been told by the relatives that during the wedding of Charippus to the woman I followed and tried to persuade her to reserve herself and have nothing to do with Charippus. Let me now repeat to you the answer which I gave to the relatives and also to my own relations directly I arrived, namely this. If these accusations are true, I agree to having done all the other things set down in the impeachment. But they are false, as is surely obvious to everyone. For who is there in Athens so uncritical as to believe these allegations? There must have been attenders, gentlemen of the jury, with the carriage that conveyed the bride : first a muleteer and a guide, and then her escort of boys, and also Dioxippus.[a] For he was in attendance, too, since she was a widow being given away in marriage. Was

---

[a] For Dioxippus, the athlete who accompanied Alexander to India (Diodor. xvii. 100. 2), see Introduction to the speech.

---

[9] ψευδῆ Schneidewin.
[10] οἶμαι Caesar.
[11] ἰδεῖν Caesar : γνῶναι Patakis.
[12] ἐστι et sq. Babington, sed τούτοις τοῖς Blass : τοιούτοις Babington.
[13] ἀνάγκη γὰρ ἦν Sauppe : ἦν om. Blass.

HYPERIDES

ἐγὼ εἰς τοῦτο ἀπονοίας ἦλθον, ὥστε ἄλλων τε
τοσούτων ἀνθρώπων συνακολουθούντων καὶ Διωξίπ-
που καὶ Εὐφραίου τοῦ προσγυμναστοῦ[1] αὐτοῦ, οἳ
τῶν Ἑλλήνων ὁμολογουμένως ἰσχυρότατοί εἰσιν,
οὔ[τ]' ἠσχυνόμην τοιούτους λόγους λέγων περὶ
γυναικὸς ἐλευθέρας πάντων ἀκουόντων, [οὔτ']² ἐδε-
δίειν μὴ πα[ραχρ]ῆμα ἀπόλωμαι [πνι]γόμενος;³
[col. 6] τίς [γὰρ] ἂν ἠνέσχετο [τοι]αῦτα περὶ τῆς αὑτοῦ
ἀδελφ[ῆς ἀκού]ων⁴ οἷά με ο[ὗτοι αἰτι]ῶνται εἰρη-
7 κ[έναι καὶ¹⁵ οὐ]κ ἂν ἀπέ[κτεινε⁶ τὸν] λέγοντα; [τὸ
δὲ κεφ]άλαιον⁴ ἀπ[άντων,⁷ ὡς]⁸ καὶ μικρῷ [πρό-
τερο]ν⁷ εἶπον, εἰς [τοῦτο⁹ ἀν]αισθησίας ὁ Χ[άριππ]ος,
ὡς ἔοικεν, [ἦλθε]ν, ὥστε πρότ[ερον] μέν, ὥς φασιν,
[τῆς γυν]αικὸς προλε[γούσης] ὅτι συνομωμο[κυῖα
εἴη πρὸς ἐμέ, πά[λιν δ]ὲ ἀκούων ἐμο[ῦ παρα]-
κελευομένο[υ αὐτῇ]⁹ ὅπως ἐμμ[είνειεν]¹⁰ τοῖς ὅρκοις
οἷ[ς ὤμο]σεν, ἐλάμβανε [τὴν]¹¹ γυναῖκα; καὶ ταῦ[τα
δο]κεῖ ἂν ὑμῖν ἢ ['Ορέστης]¹² ἐκεῖνος ὁ μαινόμενος
[col. 7] ποιῆσαι ἢ Μαργίτης ὁ πάντ[ων] ἀβελτερώτατος;
8 ['Αλ]λ' οἶμαι, ὦ ἄνδρε[ς δι]κασταί, πολλὰ πλεονεκ-
τοῦσιν ἐν τοῖς ἀγῶσιν οἱ κατήγοροι τῶν φευγόντων·
οἱ μὲν γὰρ διὰ τὸ ἀκίνδυνον αὐτοῖς εἶναι τὸν ἀγῶνα
ῥᾳδίως ὅ τι ἂν βούλωνται λέγουσι καὶ καταψεύ-
δονται, οἱ δὲ κρινόμενοι διὰ τὸν φόβον πολλὰ καὶ
τῶν πεπραγμένων αὐτοῖς εἰπεῖν ἐπιλανθάνονται.
9 ἔπειτα οἱ μὲν ἐπειδὰν πρότερον¹³ λόγον λάβωσιν,

---

¹ προσγυμναστοῦ] προγυμναστοῦ Westermann.
² οὔτ' . . . οὔτ' Sauppe : οὐκ . . . οὐδ' Blass.
³ πνιγόμενος Kenyon : ἀπαγόμενος Babington, Colin.
⁴ ἀπούων usque ad κεφάλαιον plerumque restituit Babington.
⁵ καὶ Schneidewin : ἆρ' Babington.
⁶ ἀπέκτεινε] ἀπεκώλυσε Colin.
⁷ ἀπάντων et πρότερον Sauppe.

384

I then so utterly senseless, do you think, that with all those other people in the procession, as well as Dioxippus and Euphraeus his fellow-wrestler, both acknowledged to be the strongest men in Greece, I had the impudence to pass such comments on a free woman, in the hearing of everyone, and was not afraid of being strangled on the spot? Would anyone have listened to such remarks about his sister as these men accuse me of having made, without killing the speaker? And to crown it all, as I said just now, are we to conclude that Charippus was so completely obtuse that he was still prepared to marry her, although in the first place she said beforehand, according to their story, that she was pledged to me and in the second place he heard me encouraging her to keep the promises she had made? Do you think that the mad Orestes, or Margites,[a] the greatest fool of all time, would act like that?

But then, in my opinion, gentlemen of the jury, the prosecutors in a trial have many advantages over the defendants. For them the case involves no risk,[b] and so they are free to talk and lie to their heart's content, while the men on trial are afraid and so forget to mention a great deal, even of what they have really done. Also, accusers, speaking first, do not confine

[a] Margites, the hero of an old comic epic early attributed to Homer, came to be regarded as the typification of a fool.
[b] For the importance of this statement for determining the date of the speech see Introduction.

---

[8] ὡς Blass : ὧν Colin.
[9] τοῦτο usque ad αὐτῇ Babington.
[10] ἐμμείνειεν Herwerden : ἐμμενεῖ ἐν Schneidewin.
[11] τὴν Babington : ὅμως Blass.
[12] Ὀρέστης Blass.
[13] πρότερον] τὸν πρότερον Colin : πρότεροι Patakis.

HYPERIDES

οὐ μόνον ἃ ἔχουσιν αὐτοὶ δίκαια περὶ τοῦ πράγματος
λέγουσιν, ἀλλὰ συσκευάσαντες λοιδορίας ψευδεῖς
κατὰ τῶν κρινομένων ἐξιστᾶσιν τῆς ἀπολογίας·
ὥστε συμβαίνειν αὐτοῖς δυοῖν τὸ ἕτερον, ἢ περὶ τῶν
[col. 8] ἔξωθεν διαβολῶν ἀπο[λογου]μένοις¹ τῆς [περὶ το]ῦ
πράγματος [ἀπολογία]ς ἀπολελ[εῖφθαι,² ἢ] μὴ
μεμνη[μένοις]³ τῶν⁴ προκ[ατηγορηθ]έντων, ο[ἴησι]ν⁵
καταλείπ[ειν παρ]ὰ τοῖς δικαστ[αῖς ὅτι] ἀληθῆ
10 ἐστιν [τὰ εἰρ]ημένα. πρὸς δ[ὲ τού]τοις τούς τε
μέ[λλοντα]ς βοηθεῖν το[ῖς φεύγ]ουσι⁶ προδιαβ[άλ-
λ]ουσι καὶ αὐτοῦ το[ῦ κριν]ομένου τὴν [ἀπολο]γίαν
διαστρ[έφουσιν]¹· οἷον καὶ Ἀ[ρίστων]⁷ οὑτοσὶ ἐν-
εχεί[ρησε⁸ ποιῆ]σαι⁹ ἐν τῇ κα[τηγορίᾳ,¹⁰ ὃ]ς οὐδ¹¹
ἀπολ[αύειν¹² δίδω]σι¹³ τῶν ἀ[ναβαινόν]των ὑπὲ[ρ
ἐμοῦ καὶ]¹³ συναπολ[ογησομέ]νων.¹⁴ δι[ὰ¹⁵ τί δ' οὑ]-
[col. 9] τοι] μὴ ἀπο[λογῶνται;]¹⁵ πότερ' οὐ δ[ίκαιόν ἐ]στι¹⁶
τοῖς κρινομένοις τοὺς οἰκείους καὶ τοὺς φίλους βοηθεῖν; ἢ ἔστιν τι τῶν ἐν τῇ πόλει τούτου δημοτικώ-
τερον, τοῦ τοὺς δυναμένους εἰπεῖν τοῖς ἀδυνάτοις
11 τῶν πολιτῶν κινδυνεύουσι βοηθεῖν; σὺ δὲ οὐ μόνον
περὶ τῶν συνηγόρων τοὺς λόγους πεποίησαι, ἀλλὰ
καὶ τὴν ἀπολογίαν τὴν ἐμὴν διατάττεις· καὶ παραγ-
γέλλεις τοῖς δικασταῖς περὶ ὧν δεῖ αὐτοὺς ἀκούειν
⟨καὶ⟩¹⁷ κελεύειν με ἀπολογεῖσθαι, καὶ περὶ ὧν μὴ

---

¹ ἀπολογουμένοις usque ad διαστρέφουσιν plerumque restituit Babington.
² ἀπολελεῖφθαι Schneidewin.
³ ἢ et μεμνημένοις Shilleto.
⁴ τῶν] περὶ τῶν Babington.
⁵ οἴησιν Schneidewin : οὕτω δόξαν Blass.
⁶ τοῖς φεύγουσι Caesar.
⁷ Ἀρίστων Sauppe.
⁸ ἐνεχείρησε Schneidewin.

386

themselves to putting the just arguments which support their case, but trump up baseless slanders about the accused and so deprive them of the means of defence. The latter are thus affected in one of two ways. Either they defend themselves against the extraneous charges and fall short in the relevant parts of their defence, or else they forget the accusations which have just been made, and so leave the jury with the impression that these are true. In addition to this the accusers create a prejudice against the advocates for the defence and distort the case of the accused himself; which is what Ariston here attempted to do, when speaking for the prosecution, since he does not even allow me to benefit from those who come forward to help me intending to share in my defence. What reason is there why they should not? Is it not right that men on trial should be supported by their relatives and friends? Or is there any custom in the city more democratic *a* than that which permits citizens capable of public-speaking to assist those who are incapable when they are in trouble? But you, Ariston, have not merely discussed my advocates; you even determine my own arguments and tell the jury what they must listen to, what line of defence they must prescribe for me, and

a Compare Hyp. iv. 11.

---

⁹ ποιῆσαι Blass : που Kenyon.
¹⁰ κατηγορίᾳ Babington.
¹¹ ὃς οὐδ' Blass : οὐδ' Kayser.
¹² ἀπολαύειν Sudhaus : ἀπολογίαν Blass.
¹³ δίδωσι usque ad καὶ Blass.
¹⁴ συναπολογησομένων Kayser.
¹⁵ διὰ usque ad ἀπολογῶνται Blass : ἀπολογήσονται Fuhr.
¹⁶ δίκαιόν ἐστι Sauppe.
¹⁷ καὶ add. Kayser : ἀκούειν del. Schneidewin.

ἐὰν λέγειν. καὶ τοῦτο πῶς καλῶς ἔχει, σὲ μὲν
ὅπως ἠβούλου τὴν κατηγορίαν ποιήσασθαι, προ-
[col. 10] ειδότα δὲ ἃ ἔχω ἐγὼ δίκαια λέγειν πρὸς τὰ παρὰ
σοῦ ἐψευσμένα, ὑφαιρεῖσθαί μου τὴν ἀπολογίαν;
12 καὶ ἐμὲ μὲν αἰτιᾷ ἐν τῇ εἰσαγγελίᾳ καταλύειν τὸν
δῆμον παραβαίν[ον]τα τοὺς νόμους, αὐ[τὸ]ς δ' ὑπερ-
πηδήσ[ας ἅπ]αντας¹ τοὺς ν[όμο]υς² εἰσαγγελία[ν δέ-
δ]ωκας ὑπὲρ ὧν [γρα]φαὶ πρὸς τοὺς θεσ[μοθ]έτας
ἐκ τῶν νό[μων] εἰσίν, ἵνα π[ρῶτον μ]ὲν ἀκίνδ[υνος
εἰσ]ίῃς εἰς τὸ[ν ἀγῶνα,] ἔπε[ιτ]α ἐξ[ῇ σοι³ τραγ]ῳ-
δίας² γρ[άψαι εἰς τὴ]ν⁴ εἰσαγγελ[ίαν οἵασ]περ⁵ νῦν
γέγρ[αφας, ὅς μ']⁶ αἰτιᾷ ὅτι [πολλὰς μὲν⁷ γ]υναῖκας
ποιῶ]⁸ ἀγάμ[ους ἔνδον κα]ταγηρ[άσκειν,⁹ πολλ]ὰς¹⁰
[col. 11] δὲ σ[υνοικεῖν ο]ἷς¹⁰ οὐ προσήκει παρὰ τοὺς νόμους.
13 οὐκοῦν¹¹ ἄλλην μὲν οὐδεμίαν τῶν ἐν τῇ πόλει γυναῖκα
ἔχεις εἰπεῖν, ᾗτινι ἐγὼ τούτων αἴτιός εἰμι, περὶ ἧς
δὲ νῦν τὴν κατηγορίαν πεποίησαι, πότερα ᾤου¹²
προσήκειν συνοικεῖν ἐκδεδομένην Χαρίππῳ, ἑνὶ
τῶν πολιτῶν, ἢ ἀνέκδοτον ἔνδον καταγηράσκειν,
ἢ εὐθὺς ἐξεδόθη τάλαντον ἀργυρίου προσθέντος

¹ ἅπαντας Blass.
² νόμους usque ad τραγῳδίας plerumque restituit Babington.
³ ἐξῇ σοι Kayser.   ⁴ γράψαι εἰς τὴν Blass.
⁵ οἵασπερ Kayser.
⁶ ὅς μ' Blass.
⁷ πολλὰς μὲν Sauppe.
⁸ ποιῶ Blass.
⁹ ἀγάμους ἔνδον καταγηράσκειν Babington.
¹⁰ πολλὰς usque ad οἷς Sauppe.
¹¹ οὐκοῦν Babington : οὔκουν Schneidewin.
¹² Post ᾤου add. οὐ Kirchhoff.

ᵃ A list of offences for which impeachments were appropriate is given in Hyp. iv. 8. The Thesmothetae were concerned mainly with crimes directed against the state, but

what they must not tolerate. Surely it is most unfair
that after conducting the prosecution as you wanted
you should rob me of my defence, because you know
already the honest answers I can offer to your lies.
And you accuse me in the impeachment of under-
mining the democracy by breaking the laws ; but
you override every law yourself, by presenting an
impeachment in a case where the laws require a
public charge before the Thesmothetae.^a Your object
was to run no risk in bringing in the action and also
to have the opportunity of writing tragic phrases ^b
in the impeachment, such as you have written now,
protesting that I am making many women grow old
unmarried in their homes and many live illegally
with men unsuited for them. The fact is that you
can instance no other woman in the city whom I have
wronged in this way, and as for the subject of your
present charge, what view did you take of her ? Was
she right to live with Charippus, an Athenian citizen
who was her husband ; or was she growing old unmarried in her home,^c she who was married at once,
as soon as Euphemus supplied a talent of silver as

they also dealt with cases of assault and adultery (ὕβρις and
μοιχεία). See Hyp. iv. 6 and Aristot. *Ath. Pol.* 59.
  ^b For this use of the noun τραγῳδία compare Hyp. iv. 26.
The verb τραγῳδέω is used with a similar sense by Demosthenes (*e.g.* xviii. 13).
  ^c This passage is not very clearly expressed in the Greek.
Lycophron is answering the charge that he causes women
(*a*) to grow old unmarried ; (*b*) to live with the wrong men.
Taking these points in the reverse order he retorts by asking
whether in the present case the woman is (*b*) doing wrong by
living with her legal husband or (*a*) growing old unmarried.
In view of the words οὐ προσήκει in § 12 above, a negative
before προσήκειν would make the sense of what follows much
clearer. Kirchhoff's suggested emendation is therefore
rather tempting.

389

αὐτῇ Εὐφήμου, δηλονότι οὐ διὰ πονηρίαν, ἀλλὰ
δι᾽ ἐπιείκειαν;

14 Τούτῳ μὲν οὖν ἔξεστιν, ⟨ὦ⟩¹ ἄνδρες δικασταί,
καὶ λέγειν ὅ τι ἂν βούληται καὶ καταψεύδεσθαι,
ὑμᾶς δ᾽ οἶμαι δεῖν οὐκ ἐκ τῶν τοῦ κατηγόρου δια-
[col. 12] βολῶν περὶ ἐμοῦ δικάζειν, ἀλλ᾽ ἐξ ἅπαντος τοῦ
βίου ὃν βεβίωκα ἐξετάσαντας. λαθεῖν γὰρ τὸ
πλῆθος τὸ ὑμέτερον οὐκ ἔνι οὔτε πονηρὸν ὄντα
οὐδένα τῶν ἐν τῇ πόλει οὔτε ἐπιεικῆ, ἀλλ᾽ ὁ παρελη-
λυθὼς χρόνος μάρτυς ἐστὶν ἑκάστῳ τοῦ τρόπου
ἀκριβέστατος, ἄλλως τε δὴ καὶ περὶ τούτων τῶν
15 αἰτιῶν οἷα αὕτη [ἐστ]ίν. ὅσα μὲν γὰρ [τῶ]ν ἀδικημάτων [ἐν ἁ]πάσῃ τῇ ἡλικίᾳ [τῇ]² τοῦ ἀνθρώπου
[ἐνδέ]χεται³ ἀδικῆ[σαι, τα]ῦτα μὲν δεῖ [σκοπεῖ]ν ἀπ᾽
αὐτοῦ τοῦ [ἐγκλή]ματος⁴ οὗ ἂν [ἔχῃ τις· μο]ιχεύειν
[δ᾽ οὐκ ἐνδέ]χεται ἀπὸ [πεντήκο]ντα ἐτῶν [ἄνθρω-
[col. 13] πον]⁵ ἀλλ᾽ ἢ πά[λαι τοιοῦτ]ός³ ἐστιν, ὃ δειξάτωσαν
16 οὗτοι, ἢ ψευδῆ τὴν αἰτίαν εἰκὸς εἶναι. ἐγὼ τοίνυν,
ὦ ἄνδρες δικασταί, μεθ᾽ ὑμῶν διατρίβων ἐν τῇ
πόλει τὸν ἅπαντα χρόνον, οὔτε αἰτίαν πονηρὰν
οὐδεμίαν πώποτ᾽ ἔλαβον, οὔτ᾽ ἔγκλημά μοι πρὸς
οὐδένα τῶν πολιτῶν γέγονεν, οὐδὲ πέφευγα δίκην
οὐδεμίαν, οὐδ᾽ ἕτερον δεδίωχα, ἱπποτροφῶν δὲ
διατετέλεκα φιλοτίμως τὸν ἅπαντα χρόνον παρὰ
δύναμιν καὶ ὑπὲρ τὴν οὐσίαν τὴν ἐμαυτοῦ. ἐστεφά-
νωμαι δ᾽ ὑπό τε τῶν ἱππέων πάντων ἀνδραγαθίας
17 ἕνεκα, καὶ ὑπὸ τῶν συναρχόντων. ὑμεῖς γάρ με,

---

¹ ὦ add. Babington, quod dubium an A supra versum
habeat.
² τῇ Sauppe.
³ ἐνδέχεται usque ad τοιοῦτος plerumque restituit Babington.

a dowry, obviously with no ulterior motive but simply out of kindness ? [a]

So Ariston may say whatever he pleases, gentlemen of the jury, and invent lies against me, but surely your verdict upon me must be based, not on the slanders of the prosecutor, but on a review of the whole of my life. No one in the city, whether good or bad, can deceive the community in which you live. Indeed the most reliable testimonial of character which a man can have is his past career, especially in refuting charges like the present. Where the crime is one which can be committed at any time during a man's life it should be considered in the light of the particular accusation made. But adultery is a practice which no man can begin after fifty. Either he has been a loose-liver for a long time—and let these men prove that that is true of me—or else the charge may be presumed false. Now I, gentlemen of the jury, have lived with you in Athens all my life. I have never been subjected to any discreditable charge, nor have I brought an accusation against another citizen. I have not been defendant or prosecutor in any lawsuit, but have always been a keen horsebreeder, consistently overtaxing my strength and my resources.[b] I have been crowned for bravery by the order of knights and by my colleagues in office.

[a] Probably Ariston had alleged that Euphemus was acting in collusion with Lycophron, but we have no details.

[b] Horsebreeding, which was carried on either for war or racing, was sometimes frowned on as a mark of wealth and ostentation. (Compare Lycurg. *Leocr*. 139). But here, though he admits extravagance, Lycophron is simply claiming to be doing his duty as a knight.

---

[4] ἐγκλήματος Blass : ἀξιώματος Babington.
[5] ἄνθρωπον olim Jensen : ἀρξάμενον Babington.

[col. 14] ὦ ἄνδρες δικασταί, πρῶτον μὲν φύλαρχον ἐχειρο
τονήσατε, ἔπειτα εἰς Λῆμνον ἵππαρχον· καὶ ἦρξα
μὲν αὐτόθι δύ' ἔτη τῶν πώποθ' ἱππαρχηκότων
μόνος, προσκατέμεινα δὲ αὐτόθι τὸν τρίτον ἐνιαυτόν,
οὐ βουλόμενος πολίτας ἄνδρας ἐπὶ κεφαλὴν εἰσπράτ
τειν τὸν μισθὸν τοῖς ἱππεῦσιν ἀπόρως διακειμένους.

18 καὶ ἐν τούτῳ μοι τῷ χρόνῳ ἔγκλημα μὲν οὐδεὶς
τῶν ἐκεῖ ἐνεκάλεσεν οὔτε ἰδίᾳ οὔτε δημοσίᾳ, στε
φάνοις δὲ τρισὶν ἐστεφανώθην ὑπὸ τοῦ δ[ήμ]ου τοῦ
ἐν Ἡφαισ[τί]ᾳ καὶ ἑτέροις ὑ[πὸ] τοῦ ἐν Μυρίνῃ· ἃ
[col. 15] [χρ]ὴ[1] τεκμήρια ὑμῖν ε[ἶν]αι[2] εἰς τοῦτον τὸν ἀγῶνα,
ὡς ψευδεῖς κατ' ἐμοῦ ⟨αἱ⟩[3] αἰτίαι εἰσίν. οὐ γὰρ
οἷόν τε τὸν Ἀθήνησι πονηρὸν ἐν Λήμνῳ χρηστὸν
εἶναι, οὐδ' ὑμεῖς ὡς τοιοῦτον ὄντα με ἀπεστέλλετε
ἐκεῖσε, παρακατατιθέμενοι δύο πόλεις τῶν ὑμε
τέρων αὐτῶν.

19 Ὅσα μὲν οὖν ἐγὼ εἶχον, ὦ ἄνδρες δικασταί, ὑπὲρ
ἐμαυτοῦ εἰπεῖν, σχεδὸν ἀκηκόατε. ἐπ[ει]δὴ δὲ ὁ
κατήγορος οὐκ ἀπείρως ἔχων τοῦ λέγειν, εἰωθὼς
δὲ πολλάκις ἀγωνίζεσθαι, ἐκάλει συνηγόρους τοὺς
συναπολοῦντάς τινα τῶν πολιτῶν ἀδίκως, δέομαι
ὑμῶν καὶ ἐγὼ καὶ ἀντιβολῶ κελεῦσαι κἀμὲ καλέσαι
[col. 16] τοὺς συνεροῦντας ἐμοὶ ὑπὲρ τηλικούτου ἀγῶνος,
καὶ ἀκοῦσαι εὐνοϊκῶς, εἴ τίς μοι ἔχει τῶν οἰκείων
20 ἢ τῶν φίλων βοηθῆσαι, πολίτῃ μὲν ὄντι ὑμετέρῳ,
ἰδιώτῃ δὲ καὶ οὐκ εἰωθότι λέγειν, ἀγωνιζομένῳ
δὲ καὶ κινδυνεύοντι οὐ μόνον περὶ θανάτου, ἐλά
χιστον γὰρ τοῦτό ἐστιν τοῖς ὀρθῶς λογιζομένοις,

---

[1] χρὴ Blass.   [2] εἶναι Sauppe.   [3] αἱ add. Babington.

---

[a] The ten phylarchs, one from each tribe, commanded the
cavalry of their own tribe under the hipparchs. Of these

For you appointed me, gentlemen of the jury, first as Phylarch and later as Cavalry Leader at Lemnos.[a] I held the command there for two years, the only cavalry leader who has ever done so, and prolonged my stay for a third, as I did not wish, in exacting the pay for the horsemen rashly, to burden citizens in financial straits. During that time no one there brought an action against me, either private or public. In fact I was crowned three times by the inhabitants of Hephaestia and as many times more by those of Myrine. These facts should satisfy you, in the present trial, that the charges against me are false. No man can be good in Lemnos if he is bad in Athens, and you had no poor opinion of me when you dispatched me there and made me responsible for two of your own cities.

Well, gentlemen of the jury, you have heard virtually all that I had to say in my own defence. The prosecutor, who is an experienced speaker and used to frequent litigation, summoned advocates [b] to help him in unjustly ruining a citizen. So I too am asking you, most earnestly, for your authority to summon my advocates in this important case, and I beg you to give a sympathetic hearing to any of my relatives or friends who can help me. I am a fellow-citizen of yours, an amateur unused to speaking, on trial now with the risk not only of losing my life—a minor consideration to men with a proper sense of values—but

there were two elected from the whole people. One of them was appointed to command a body of Athenian cavalry in Lemnos, after the Athenians gained control of the island by the Peace of Antalcidas in 387 B.C. Compare Aristot. *Ath. Pol.* 61. 6 ; Dem. iv. 27 ; *CIA* ii. 14 and 593.

[b] The chief of these advocates was the orator Lycurgus. See Introduction to the speech.

ἀλλ' ὑπὲρ τοῦ ἐξορισθῆναι καὶ ἀποθανόντα μηδὲ ἐν
τῇ πατρίδι ταφῆναι. ἐὰν οὖν κελεύητε, ὦ ἄνδρες
δικασταί, καλῶ τινα βοηθήσοντα. ἀνάβηθί μοι,
Θεόφιλε, καὶ σύνειπε ὅ τι ἔχεις· κελεύουσιν οἱ
δικασταί.

also of being cast out after death, without even the prospect of a grave in my own country. So if you will give the word, gentlemen of the jury, I will call an advocate. Will you please come up, Theophilus, and say what you can in my defence? The jury ask you to do so.

APPENDIX

SECOND SPEECH IN DEFENCE OF LYCOPHRON

INTRODUCTION

THE speech to which the following fragment belongs clearly bears on the same trial of Lycophron as that in which he was defended by Hyperides. What remains of it was discovered on papyrus in Egypt in 1905 and first published in 1919.[a] Out of more than forty fragments only those here given convey any coherent sense, but there is sufficient left of the speech to show the case with which it is concerned and to throw some light on the story. Not only are several proper names given, such as Lycophron, Theomnestus and Dioxippus, but the circumstances too are quite in keeping.

Since Lycurgus is known to have written two speeches for the prosecution,[b] Hyperides might be thought to have followed suit for the defence ; but among the many recorded titles of his works no second speech for Lycophron is included. Moreover the line of argument followed here is markedly different from that adopted in the first speech, and it therefore seems more reasonable to assume that this is the work of some other writer such as the advocate Theophilus.[c] The possibility that it is, after all,

---

[a] Oxyrhynchus Papyri, vol. xiii. no. 1607, edited by Grenfell and Hunt, who restored the text with the help of C. Hude and E. Lobel.

[b] See the introduction to Hyp. i., also Lycurg. frags. 11 and 12 and note. [c] See Hyp. i. 20.

only the exercise of some later imitator cannot be completely ruled out, but even so, the work may still supply us with valuable details ; for we may presume the writer to have read the speech of Hyperides in its entirety, and probably those of Lycurgus too, and thus to be in possession of all the relevant facts.

ΥΠΕΡ ΛΥΚΟΦΡΟΝΟΣ Β

[col. 1]   τοῦτο]ν δι[ο]ρύξαι τὸν [τοῖχο]ν τῆ[ς] πρὸς τὴν
[ἄνθρ]ωπον ὁμιλίας [ἕνε]κεν οὐδαμῶς [πιθ]ανόν
ἐστιν. οὔτε γὰ[ρ] ὡς ⟨πρὸς⟩ τοὺς πρότερον αὐτῷ
λειτουργοῦντας καὶ πᾶν ὅ τι κελεύ[οι] προθυμῶς
ὑπομένοντας διηνέχθη δεδήλωκεν, οὔθ᾽ ὅτι γενομένης πρὸς αὐτὸν ἁψιμαχίας ἐκεῖνοι τὴν χρείαν
[ἀ]πείπαντο, ὅθεν ὁ Λυκόφρων ἐπὶ τὸ τὸν τοῖχον
διορῦξαι κατηπ[είχθ]η, μηκέτι ⟨τῶν⟩ σω[μ]άτων
[. . . . . ὁ]μοίως τε [Desunt col. 1 versus fere sep-
[col. 2] tem] σθαι οὐκ ἂν διώρυξε τὸν τοῖχον. πό[θ]εν γὰρ
ἄνθρωπος [μ]ηδὲν κατεπειγό[μ]ενος ἀλλ᾽ ἔχων τὴν
[ἐ]ξουσίαν καὶ τὰ παρ᾽ ἐκείνης εἰδέναι καὶ τὰ παρ᾽
αὐτοῦ λέγειν [κ]αὶ [Desunt versus octo] καὶ το[ύτῳ
οὐδέ]ποθ᾽ ὁ Χρ . . . . . .¹ τὴν οἰκίαν ἀπ[εῖπεν?].
καὶ μὴν ἀδυν[άτο]υ γε εἶχεν τάξιν τὸ τὰς θεραπαίνας αὐτῆς πρὸς τοῦτον διαφέρεσθαι. τίς γὰρ ἂν
οὕτως ἐγενήθη θρασεῖα ὥστε ἢ τὰ παρὰ τούτου
ῥηθέντα ἢ τὰ παρ᾽ ἐκείνης πρὸς τοῦτον πα[ρα]-
σιωπῆσαι τῆς ἰδίας ἔχθρας [ἕν]εκα; πρό[χ]ει[ρος δὲ]
[col. 3] ἦν ὁ κίν[δυνος εἰ μ]ὲν γὰρ [Desunt versus sex] ἅπερ
οὗτοι π[ρούθεν?]το. νῦν δὲ ἐκ[ε]ῖν[ο]ν μὲν ἑώρων

SECOND SPEECH IN DEFENCE OF LYCOPHRON

Frag. I

As for his digging through the wall to have intercourse with the woman : that is quite incredible. For the accuser [a] has not shown either that he fell out with the people who had previously been serving him and readily submitting to any orders he gave them, or that they had a quarrel with him and so refused their services, thus inducing Lycophron to dig through the wall, as their persons were no longer . . . would not have dug through the wall. Why should a man who was not pressed for time and had the chance both of receiving news from her and giving his own messages and . . . and . . .[b] never forbade him (?) the house. Besides, it is almost out of the question for her servants to have quarrelled with him. Which one of them could have grown so rash as to withhold either his messages to her or hers to him, for reasons of personal spite ? For the danger was imminent, if . . . what these men assumed. In actual fact they

[a] Presumably Ariston.
[b] Evidently the invalid husband's name was given here, but it cannot be restored with certainty.

---

[1] Χρέμης Grenfell et Hunt.

κα[θ]' ὑπερβολὴν ἀσθ[ε]νῶς διακείμενον, ταύτην δὲ
τ[ὴν τ]ῆς ο[ἰ]κίας μ[έ]λλουσαν κυριεύε[ι]ν πολὺ πρὸ
ὀφθαλμῶν ἀνελάμβανον, μὴ παθόντος τι τούτου
τιμωρίαν ὑποσχῶσιν ὧν ἀντέπ[ρα]ξαν. οὔκουν οὔ-
τ[ε δ]ι⟨ο⟩ρυχθῆναι τὸν τοῖχον ὑπὸ τούτου πιθανόν,
οὔτε εἰώθει, καθάπ[ε]ρ λέγει, ταῖς θεραπαίναις διαλέγεσθαι. τ[ίνος] γὰρ ἕνεκεν; [τί ? πρὸς] αὐτὸν
τ[αύτας] διενεχ[θῆναι ἔδει ?], ὃν φιλο[φρονέστερον ?]
δὴ τῆς [δεσποίνης ?] προσφε[ρομένης αὐ]τῷ . . .

Frag. V

τίσιν οὖν τεκμ[η]ρίοις χρησάμε[νος] τούτους
κελεύ[ει] καταδικάζειν; χ[ρῆ]τ[α]ι νὴ Δία, ταῖ[ς
τῶν] κηδεστῶν μ[αρτυ]ρίαις Ἀνασχέτ[ου] καὶ Θεο-
μνήστ[ου καὶ] Κρίτωνος, ἃς καλῶς ἔχον ἐστίν, ὦ
ἄ[ν]δρες δικασταί, μ[ὴ] παρέρ[γως] ἐξετ[άσ]αι.
τὴν [γὰ]ρ ὅλη[ν κα]τηγορί[αν] ἐκ το[. . .

Frag. XIII

[col. 2] [τ]ῷ Χα[ρίπ]πῳ τὴν [ἀ]δελφὴ[ν ε]ἰς [Ὀ]λυ[μπίαν]
ἀποδημῆσα[ι] τὸν Δ[ι]ώξιππ[ο]ν στεφανώσ[ο]ντα
τὴν πόλιν. Λυκόφρονα δὲ τέως μὲν ‖λυ‖πέμποντα
ἐπισ[τολὰ]ς λέγειν . . .

saw their master in an extremely weak condi...
had their mistress, the future ruler of the househo...
constantly before their eyes as a reminder that, if
he died, they would be punished in return for what
they had done against her wishes. It is therefore
incredible that Lycophron dug through the wall ; nor
was he accustomed, as the accuser claims, to converse
with the servants. What reason would he have had
for doing so ? Why should they have quarrelled with
him, whom, as their mistress grew more favourably
disposed to him . . .

Frag. V

What then are the proofs on which he bases his
demand to the jury to condemn Lycophron ? He
actually bases it on the evidence of his kinsmen by
marriage, Anaschetus, Theomnestus [a] and Criton ;
and it would be as well for you, gentlemen of the jury,
to examine it carefully.   For the whole accusation . . .

Frag. XIII

. . . that [when he was about to marry ?] his sister
to Charippus, Dioxippus went away to Olympia where
he was to win a crown for his city, but that meanwhile
Lycophron sent letters saying . . .

[a] For Theomnestus compare Hyp. i. 2.

II
SPEECH AGAINST PHI-
LIPPIDES

INTRODUCTION

THE following fragment has neither title nor author's name attached to it, and even the word Philippides occurs in only one place where the letters -ili- have had to be restored. It is known, however, that Hyperides did compose a speech against Philippides,[a] and this fragment, on grounds of style and subject matter, has been accepted as the concluding part of it.

The date of the speech falls between 338 B.C., since it is subsequent to the battle of Chaeronea, and 336. It can hardly be placed much later than Philip's death in the latter year, for it includes a reference to him in language which suggests either that he was still alive when it was delivered or that he had only lately met his death.[b]

Philippides was a man of whom little is known. According to Athenaeus he was mentioned in comedy,[c] and it is clear from this speech that he had pro-Macedonian sympathies. The circumstances leading to his prosecution can be gathered from what Hyperides says.[d]

Shortly after the battle of Chaeronea, when Athens

---

[a] Athen. xii. 552 d.
[b] See § 8 and note.
[c] Athen. vi. 230 c, 238 c, etc.
[d] See §§ 4-6.

was temporarily cowed by Philip, a measure designed
to do honour to certain Macedonians was brought
before the Assembly, and despite a technical hitch
which rendered it illegal, the presidents allowed it
to be put to the vote and passed. They were never
impeached for doing so, as it was generally understood that they had acted under pressure from outside,
but later, when Philippides went a step farther and
moved that they should be crowned for doing their
duty towards the Athenian people and observing the
laws during their period of office,[a] the opponents of
Macedon intervened and prosecuted him for illegal
proposals.

Hyperides was one of the accusers, but only the
end of his speech is preserved. In the earlier part
of it he evidently referred to Philip and Alexander,
contrasting them with others who, in the past, had
established a greater claim to the city's gratitude.[b]
By the time that our fragment opens he is attacking
the Athenian supporters of Macedon, in particular
Philippides and Democrates of Aphidna, who were
no doubt confederates, and of whom the latter, as a
descendant of one of the tyrant-slayers, enjoyed
special privileges in Athens. The result of the trial
is not known.

[a] See § 6.   [b] See frag. vi.

ANALYSIS

ΚΑΤΑ ΦΙΛΙΠΠΙΔΟΥ

Frag. I [1]

. . . . ἐν] ἐλευθέρᾳ πό[λει τὰ τ]οῖς τυράννοις [συμ-
φέρο]ντα πραττον[τ . . . .]ν εἰς δουλεία[ν . . .

Frag. VI [2]

. . . . . καλῶ[ν πραγμάτων καὶ τῇ] πόλε[ι κ]αὶ
τοῖς Ἕλλησ[ιν αἴτι]ος ἐγένετο. τοι[γαροῦν][3] καὶ
παρ' ἡμῖν κα[ὶ παρὰ] το[ῖς] ἄλλοις πᾶσιν [τῶν
μεγίσ]των[4] δωρεῶ[ν ἔτυχεν . . . δ]ικαίως [. . . . . .
γ]ὰρ . . . . ὑπὸ

Frag. VIII (sub finem) [5]

. . . . δεῖ χάρι[ν ἡμᾶ]ς ἀ[ποδιδ]όναι Ἀλεξ[άνδ]ρῳ
[διὰ τοὺ]ς τελευτή[σαντ]ας . . . . ἐγὼ δὲ
[οἶμ]αι[6]. . . .

Frag. X [7]

. . . . ἐκεῖνος. ἔπειθ' [οὗτοι] ἐπεμβαίνουσιν τ[ῷ
δή]μῳ ἐν ταῖς ἀτυχ[ίαις. διό]περ καὶ πολὺ μᾶ[λλον

---

[1] Frag. I restituit Sudhaus.
[2] Frag. VI plerumque restituit Blass.
[3] τοιγαροῦν Jensen : τὸ παλαιὸν Blass.
[4] τῶν μεγίστων Fuhr : Κόνων (?) μεγίστων Blass.

AGAINST PHILIPPIDES

Frag. I

. . . in a free city furthering the interests of tyrants . . . towards slavery . . .

Frag. VI

. . . was responsible for actions which did credit to the city and to Greece.[a] Therefore both here and everywhere else he was paid the highest honours . . . rightly . . .

Frag. VIII (*sub finem*)

. . . we must thank Alexander on account of those who died . . . but I think . . .

Frag. X

Moreover these men trample on the people in their misfortune, and for this reason they deserve your

---

[a] The subject is perhaps Conon, an Athenian commander who was often praised in this way. Compare Dinarch. i. 14 and note.

---

[5] Frag. VIII hanc partem restituit Blass.
[6] οἶμαι Jensen.
[7] Frag. X e septem fragmentulis composuit Blass, qui pleraque restituit.

411

ἄξι]οί εἰσιν μισεῖσθ[αι. ὥσ]περ γὰρ τὰ σώματ[α
πλείσ]της¹ ἐπ[ιμ]ελείας ἐν [ταῖς] ἀρρωσ[τί]αις
δεῖται, οὕτως καὶ [αἱ] πόλεις πλείστης θερ[απ]είας
ἐν ταῖς ἀτυχίαις δ[έο]ντ[αι]. μόνοις δὲ τοῦτο[ις]²
. . . .

Frag. XI ³

Frag. XVa

. . . . [δί]δωσιν ἕκαστος αὐτῶν, ὁ μὲν ἐν Θήβαις, ὁ δ' ἐν Τανάγρᾳ, ὁ δ' ἐν τῇ ἐλευθε[⁴. . . . . . .
. . .]ατα τῶν . .

Frag. XVb ⁵

. . . . ἀ]παλλαγέντα; ἢ οὐκ εὔχεσθαι κα[ὶ τ]ἆλλα
πάντα τὰ ἐν τῇ ['Ελ]λάδι ἀνατραπῆναι, οἵ γ' ἀπὸ
τῶν ἀναιρουμένων πόλεων ἀπαρχὰς [λα]μ[βά]νου-
σιν; καὶ ὑμ[ᾶς μὲν ἀ]εὶ⁶ βούλεσθαι ἐν φ[όβῳ
καὶ]⁷ κινδύνοις εἶν[αι] . . . .

Frag. XXI ⁸

εὐτελὴς τὸ σῶμα διὰ λεπτότητα.

[col. 1] κατηγορίας ποιοῦνται, καὶ φανερὸν ποιοῦσιν ὅτι
οὐδὲ τότε φίλοι ὄντες Λακεδαιμονίων ὑπὲρ ἐκείνων
ἔλεγον, ἀλλὰ τὴν πόλιν μισοῦντες καὶ τοὺς ἰσχύον-
2 τας ἀ[εὶ]⁹ καθ' ὑμῶν θεραπεύοντες. ἐπεὶ δὲ νῦν ἡ

---

¹ πλείστης Kenyon : μεγίστης Blass.   ² τούτοις Kenyon.
³ Frag XI, cuius solum a sinistra parte exstat, sic
restituere tentavit Blass : δη]μοκρ[ατία. ἀφεὶς δὲ τὰ πολ]λὰ
περὶ [ὧν καὶ συνηγό]ρει Φιλί[ππῳ καὶ ἐστρα]τεύσατ[ο μετ'

hatred far more. For just as human bodies need most
care when they are sick, so it is with cities, which
need most attention in times of misfortune. To these
men (?) only . . .

Frag. XVa

. . . each of them gives, one in Thebes, another in
Tanagra . . .

Frag. XVb

Or that they do not pray for the overthrow of all
that is left in Greece, when they are deriving profits
from the cities that are being destroyed ? Or that,
while they wish you to spend your lives in fear and
danger . . .

Frag. XXI

Unimpressive in person on account of his thinness.

.   .   .   .

. . . make accusations. And they make it clear
that even when they were friends of the Lacedaemonians [a] their speeches were prompted not by love
for them but by hatred of Athens and a willingness
to flatter those whose power at any time threatened

---

[a] Hyperides may be alluding to the period from 378 to
371 B.C., when Athens and Thebes were at war with Sparta.

ἐκείνου ἐπὶ] τὴν χώ[ραν, ὅπερ μέγιστον,] τοῦτο δ[ηλώσω . . . . .
Φι]λιππο[. . . . . . ἐστρατεύ]σατο ἐφ' [ἡμᾶς καὶ τοὺς συμ]μάχους
[. . . . . ἀκρι]βῶς γε . . .

    4 Ἐλευθερίδι Kenyon : ἐλευθέρᾳ Blass.
    5 Frag. XVb e compluribus fragmentis composuit Blass.
    6 ὑμᾶς μὲν ἀεὶ Jensen.
    7 φόβῳ καὶ Blass.
    8 Frag. XXI ab Athenaeo xii. 552 d citatum est.
    9 Coll. 1 et 2 plerumque restituit Kenyon.

ἐκείνων δύναμις εἰς [τοῦτ]ον[1] μετέστη, τότε [δ]ὴ
[κο]λακεύειν προείλον[το[2]· κ]αὶ Δημοκράτη[ς[3] αὐ-
τ]οῖς ὁ Ἀφιδναῖος [ἀεὶ παρ]ακαθήμενος[4] καὶ ...ον
ἱστὰς[5] γελωτοπ[οιεῖ ἐ]πὶ τοῖς τῆς πόλεω[ς ἀ]τυχή-
μασιν, καὶ λο[ιδορεῖ]θ'[6] ὑμῖν μεθ' ἡμέρα[ν ἐν' τ]ῇ
ἀγορᾷ, εἰς ἑσπέρα[ν δὲ δε]ιπν[ή]σων ὡς ὑμ[ᾶς
ἔ]ρχεται. καίτοι, ὦ Δημ[όκρα]τες, μόνῳ σοι οὐκ
3 [ἔνι λέγ]ειν[8] περὶ τοῦ δήμου [φλα]ῦρον[9] οὐδέν· διὰ
[col. 2] τί; [ὅτι πρ]ῶτον μὲν οὐ παρ' ἑτέρου σ' ἔδει μαθεῖν
ὅτι ὁ δῆμος χάριτας ἀποδίδωσιν τοῖς εὐεργέταις,
ἀλλὰ παρὰ σαυτοῦ· αὐτὸς γὰρ ὑπὲρ ὧν ἕτεροι
εὐεργέτησαν νῦν τὰς τιμὰς κομίζει. ἔπειθ' ὅτι ἐν
νόμῳ γράψας ὁ δῆμος ἀπεῖπεν μήτε λέγειν ἐξεῖναι
[μηδενὶ] κακῶς Ἁρμόδιον καὶ Ἀρ[ισ]τογείτονα,
μήτ' ᾆσα[ι ἐ]πὶ[10] τὰ κακίονα. ᾗ[11] κ[αὶ] δεινόν ἐστιν
[ε]ἰ τοὺς μὲν σοὺς προγόνους ὁ δῆμος οὐδὲ μεθυ-
σθέντι ᾤετο δεῖν ἐξεῖναι κακῶς εἰπεῖν, σὺ δὲ νήφων
τὸν δῆμον κακ[ῶς] λέγεις.

4 [Βρ]αχέα δ' ἔτι πρὸς ὑμᾶς εἰπών, ὦ ἄνδρες δικασταί, [καὶ] ἀναλογισάμενος, κα[ταβ]ήσομαι. γραφὴ πα[ρα]νόμων ἐστὶν ὑπὲρ [ἧς τ]ὴν ψῆφον μέλλετε
[col. 3] [φέρ]ειν[12]· τὸ δὲ ψήφισμα τὸ κρινόμενον ἔπαινος

---

[1] τοῦτον Jensen : μικρὸν Blass, Kenyon.
[2] προείλοντο Blass.
[3] Post Δημοκράτης add. νῦν Kenyon : om. Jensen.
[4] παρακαθήμενος Jensen : συγκαθήμενος Kenyon.
[5] καὶ χορὸν ἱστὰς Blass.
[6] λοιδορεῖθ' Blass.
[7] ἐν Blass.
[8] ἔνι λέγειν Blass.
[9] φλαῦρον Crönert : φαῦλον Kenyon.
[10] ᾆσαι ἐπὶ Jebb.

you. And when the power recently shifted from
them to Philip they then chose to flatter him ; and
Democrates of Aphidna [a] who never leaves their
sides . . . makes jokes on the city's misfortunes,
abusing you in the market place by day and then
coming at evening to dine at your table. And yet
you, Democrates, are the one person who has no
right to say a single hard word against the state,
for two reasons : first because you needed no one
but yourself to show you that the city is grateful
to her benefactors, you who now enjoy the honours
for services which other men once rendered ; and
secondly because the people drew up a law forbidding anyone to speak ill of Harmodius and Aristogeiton or sing disparaging songs about them.[b] It is
therefore scandalous that, though the people saw fit
to prevent even a drunken man from abusing your
ancestors, you should be speaking ill of the state even
when you are sober.

I have a few more points to make, gentlemen of
the jury, and after summing up my argument will
leave the platform. The case in which you are going
to vote is an indictment for the proposing of illegal
measures and the decree under consideration is one

---

[a] Democrates of Aphidna was a politician whom Aeschines
mentions (ii. 17 ; cf. Isaeus vi. 22). He had quite a reputation for wit and some of his sayings are preserved. As a descendant of one of the tyrant-slayers, probably of Aristogiton,
who appears to have been a member of the tribe Aphidna,
he enjoyed free meals in the Prytaneum, a privilege to which
apparently only the eldest of each line was entitled (*CIA* i. 8 ;
ii. 240).

[b] Harmodius and Aristogiton are mentioned again in Hyp.
vi. 39. This particular privilege is not elsewhere recorded.

---

[11] ἦ Blass : ἤ L, Kenyon.   [12] φέρειν Blass.

προέδρων. ὅτι δὲ προσήκει τοὺς προέδρους κατὰ
τοὺς νόμους προεδρεύειν, οὗτοι δὲ παρὰ τοὺς νόμους
προηδρεύκασιν, αὐτῶν τῶν νόμων ἠκούετε ἀναγι-
5 γνωσκομένων. τὸ λοιπὸν ἤδη ἐστὶν παρ' ὑμῖν·
δείξετε γὰρ πότερα τοὺς παράνομα γράφοντας
τ[ιμ]ωρήσεσθε, ἢ τὰς τοῖς εὐε[ργέ]ταις ἀποδεδειγ-
μένας [τι]μὰς ταύτας δώσετε [το]ῖς ἐναντία τοῖς
νόμοι[ς πρ]οεδρεύουσιν, καὶ ταῦτα ὀμωμοκότες κατὰ
τοὺς νόμους ψηφιεῖσθαι. ἀλλὰ μὴν οὐδ' ἐξαπατηθῆναι ὑμῖν ἔνεστιν ὑπὸ τοῦ λόγου αὐτῶν, ἂν φῶσιν
ἀναγκαῖα εἶνα[ι τ]ῷ δήμῳ τὰ περὶ τῶν ἐπ[αίν]ων[1]
[col. 4] ψηφίζεσθαι· το[ὺς γ]ὰρ προέδρους οὐκ ἔνεστιν
6 εἰπεῖν ὡς ἀνάγκη τις ἦν στεφανῶσαι. πρὸ[ς δ]ὲ
τούτοις αὐτὸς ὑμῖν[2] ο[ὗ]τος ῥαδίαν πεποίηκ[εν] τὴν
γνῶσιν· ἔγραψεν γ[ὰρ] ὧν ἕνεκα ἐστεφάνω[σε]ν τοὺς
προέδρους, δι[κα]ιοσύνης τε τῆς εἰς τὸν δ[ῆμ]ον τὸν
Ἀθηναίων κα[ὶ δι]ότι κατὰ τοὺς νόμο[υς π]ροηδρεύ-
κασιν. ἐπὶ δ[ὴ[3] τ]αῦτ' ἄγετ' αὐτὸν ἀπολ[ογη]σό-
μενον, καὶ σύ, ὦ Φ[ιλι]ππίδη, δείξας ἀληθῆ εἶναι
τὰ περὶ τῶν προέδρων, ἃ ὑπέθου ἐν τῷ ψηφ[ίσ]ματι,
7 ἀπόφευγε. εἰ δ' ο[ἴει] κορδακίζων καὶ γελ[ωτ]ο-
ποιῶν, ὅπερ ποι[εῖν] εἴωθας,[4] ἐπὶ τῶν δικαστη[ρί]ων
ἀποφεύξεσθαι, ε[ὐήθ]ης εἶ, ἢ παρὰ τούτ[ο]ις[5] συγγνώμην ἢ ἔ[λεόν][6] τινα παρὰ τὸ δίκαι[ον ὑπ]άρ[χ]ειν.[7]

---

[1] ἐπαίνων Blass.
[2] Coll. 4 ad 8 plerumque restituit Kenyon, sed ὑμῖν Koehler:
ἡμῖν L.
[3] δὴ Blass.
[4] Post εἴωθας interpunxit Kenyon : infra, post δικαστηρίων
Blass.
[5] τούτοις Jenson : τούτων φὴς Kenyon.
[6] ἔλεόν Sandys.   [7] ὑπάρχειν Blass.

---

[a] In the 4th century B.C. the chairman of the πρυτάνεις

congratulating presidents.[a] Presidents should observe
the law during their period of office. These men have
broken it. As evidence for both these facts you heard
the actual laws read. The sequel now rests with you.
For you will make it plain whether you are going to
punish the proposers of illegal measures or whether
you intend to grant those honours, which till now have
been paid to your benefactors, to presidents whose
conduct is not lawful ; and that too when you have
sworn to observe the laws in giving your vote. There
is, however, one argument open to them, namely that
the people were compelled to pass the votes of
honour.[b] Even this cannot possibly mislead you ;
for it cannot be said that we were under any com-
pulsion to crown the presidents. Moreover the
defendant has himself made your decision easy, since
he stated in writing his reasons for crowning them.
They had, he said, been just towards the Athenian
people and observed the laws during their office.
That is a statement for which you must now summon
him to answer. And you, Philippides, show us that
what you assumed about the presidents in your decree
is true and you will be acquitted. But if you think
that your usual vulgarity and joking will secure your
pardon in court or win from these men any indulgence
or sympathy to which you are not entitled, you are

---

appointed these presidents by lot, one from each tribe except
that to which he himself belonged, for each meeting of the
Council or Assembly. After their appointment he drew lots
among them for their chairman (ἐπιστάτης). (See Aesch. i.
104, iii. 39, and Aristot. *Ath. Pol.* 44. 2.)

[b] *i.e.* the votes of honour for certain Macedonians. Hyperides argues that it may have been impossible to avoid
passing the votes of honour, but that there was no need to
congratulate the presidents for having done so.

[col. 5] πολλοῦ γε δ[εῖ. οὐ γ]ὰρ¹ ἀπέθου σαυτῷ εὔνοιαν
παρὰ τῷ δήμῳ, ἀλλ' ἑτέρωθι, οὐδὲ τοὺς σῶσαί σε
δυναμένους ᾤου δεῖν κολακεύειν, ἀλλὰ τοὺς τῷ
8 δήμῳ φοβεροὺς ὄντας. καὶ ἓν μὲν σῶμα ἀθάνατον
ὑπ[είλη]φας ἔσεσθαι, πόλεως δὲ τηλικαύτης θάνατον
κατέγνως, οὐδ' ἐκεῖνο συνιδών, ὅτι τῶν μὲν τυράννων οὐδεὶς πώποτε τελευτήσας ἀνεβίωσεν, πόλεις
δὲ πολλαὶ ἄρδην ἀναιρεθεῖσαι πάλιν ἴσχυσαν. οὐδὲ
τὰ ἐπὶ τῶν τριάκοντα ἐλογίσασθε, οὐδ' ὡς καὶ τῶν
ἐπιστρατευσάντων καὶ τῶν ἔνδοθεν συνεπιθεμένων
αὐτῇ περιεγένετο, ἀλλὰ φανεροὶ ἐγένεσθε καιρο-
φυλακοῦντες τὴν πόλιν εἴ ποτε δοθήσεται ἐξουσία
9 λέγειν τι ἢ πράττειν κατὰ τοῦ δήμου. εἶτα περὶ
[col. 6] καιρῶν αὐτίκα δὴ τολμήσετε λέγειν τοὺς κατὰ τῆς
πόλεως καιροὺς [[οὐ]]² παραφυλάξαντες; καὶ τὰ
παιδία ἥκεις ἔχων εἰς τὸ δικαστήριον, καὶ ἀναβι-
βάσας αὐτίκα δὴ ἀξιώσεις ὑπὸ τούτων ἐλεεῖσθαι;
ἀλλ' οὐ δίκαιον· ὅτε γὰρ ἡ πόλις ὑπὸ τῶν ἄλλων
ᾠκτείρετο διὰ τὰ συμβάν[τα], τόθ' ὑφ' ὑμῶν ἐξ-
υβρίζετο. καίτοι οὗτοι μὲν τὴν Ἑλλάδα σῴζειν
προελόμενοι ἀνάξια τῶν φρονημάτων ἔπασχον, σὺ
δὲ τὴν πόλιν εἰς τὰς ἐσχάτας αἰσχύνας ἀδίκως
10 καθιστὰς νυνὶ δικαίως τιμωρίας τεύξῃ. διὰ τί
γὰρ ⟨ἂν⟩³ τούτου φείσαισθε; πότερα διότι δημο-

---

¹ δεῖ. οὐ γὰρ Herwerden et Diels.
² οὐ del. Koehler : οὕτω Thalheim : ὡς οὐ ci. Kenyon : οἱ
Weil.   ³ ἂν add. Herwerden.

ᵃ This passage is important for determining the date of
the speech. It has been held, *e.g.* by Kenyon, that the remark
is a gibe, in which there would be no point unless Philip were
already dead. But the use of the perfect tense (ὑπείληφας)
seems to imply that he was still living when Hyperides spoke,
or had only just been killed.

a fool and very far from the mark. You see, you laid up popularity for yourself, not in Athens, but elsewhere. You thought fit to cringe before those whom the people feared rather than before the men who now have power to save you. You have concluded that one person will be immortal,[a] yet you sentenced to death a city as old as ours, never realizing the simple fact that no tyrant has yet risen from the dead, while many cities, though utterly destroyed, have come again to power. You and your party took no account of the history of the Thirty or of the city's triumph over her assailants from without and those within her walls who joined in the attack upon her.[b] It was well known that you were all watching the city's fortunes, waiting for the chance to say or do something against the people. Will you dare then presently to mention opportunities, when the opportunities you sought were for the city's ruin ? Have you brought your children with you into court, Philippides ?[c] Are you going to bring them soon on to the platform and so claim pity from the jury ? You have no right to pity. When others felt compassion for the city's misfortunes, you and your like were exulting over her.[d] They had resolved to save Greece in a spirit which ill deserved the fate they met. But you, who are unjustly bringing Athens into the depths of shame, deserve the punishment you are now about to suffer. Why should you spare this man, gentlemen ? Because he is a democrat ?

[b] The reference is to the return of the democrats to Athens in 403 B.C., under Thrasybulus, who had to contend both with the Spartans under Lysander and with the Thirty.

[c] For the bringing of children into court compare Hyp. iv. 41.

[d] At the time of Chaeronea (338 B.C.).

τικός ἐστιν; ἀλλὰ ἴστ' αὐτὸν τοῖς μὲν τυράννοις
δουλεύειν προελόμενον, τῷ δὲ δήμῳ προστάττειν
[col. 7] ἀξιοῦντα. ἀλλ' ὅτι χρηστός; ἀλλὰ δὶς αὐτοῦ
ἀ[δικί]αν κατέγνωτε. ναί, ἀ[λλ]ὰ χρήσιμος· ἀλλ' εἰ
χρήσ[εσ]θε τῷ ὑφ' ὑμῶν ὁμολ[ογ]ουμένως πονηρῷ
[κρ]ιθέντι, ἢ κρίνειν κακῶς δόξετε ἢ πονηρῶν [ἀν]-
θρώπων ἐπιθυμ[εῖν. ο]ὐκοῦν οὐκ ἄξιον τὰ [τούτ]ου
ἀδικήματα αὐτ[οὺς¹ ἀν]αδέχεσθαι, ἀλλὰ [τ]ιμω-
11 ρεῖ[σθ]αι τὸν ἀδικοῦν[τα]. καὶ ἀ[ν]² ἄρα λέγῃ τις
ἀναβὰς ὡς δὶς ἥλωκεν πρότερον παρανόμων, καὶ
διὰ τοῦτο φῇ δεῖν ὑμᾶς ἀποψηφίσασθαι, τοὐναντίον
ποιεῖτε κατ' ἀμφότερα. πρῶτον μὲν ὅ[τι ε]ὐτύχημά
ἐστιν τὸν ὁμολογουμένως τὰ παράνομα γράφοντα
τὸ τρίτον κρινόμενον λαβεῖν· οὐ γὰρ ὥσπερ ἀγαθοῦ
τινος φείδεσθαι προσήκει τούτου, ἀλλὰ τὴν ταχίστην ἀπηλλάχθαι, ὅς γε τοῦ τρόπου δὶς ἤδη ἐν ὑμῖν
[col. 8] βάσανον δέδωκεν. ἔπειτα δέ, ὥσπερ τοῖς τῶν
12 ψευδομαρτυρίων δὶς ἡλωκόσιν δεδώκατε ὑμεῖς τὸ
τρίτον μὴ μαρτυρεῖν μηδ' οἷς ἂν παραγένωνται,
ἵνα μηδενὶ τῶν πολιτῶν ᾖ τὸ ὑμέτερον πλῆθος
αἴτιον τοῦ ἠτιμῶσθαι, ἀλλ' αὐ[τὸ]ς α[ὑ]τῷ, ἂν μὴ
παύηται τὰ ψευδῆ μαρτυρῶν, οὕτω καὶ τοῖς ἡλω-

---

¹ αὐτοὺς Blass. ² ἂν Jenson : ἐὰν Kenyon.

ᵃ The penalties for illegal proposals and for giving false
witness seem to have been the same, although the exact rules
governing them in the 4th century B.C. are not quite clear.
In the 5th century a man three times convicted of false
witness was automatically disfranchised (v. Andocid. i. 74),
and the present passage suggests that in the 4th century too
a third conviction led to partial ἀτιμία. (Cf. Dem. li. 12 and
Plato, Laws 937 c, evidently inspired by current Athenian

420

Why, you are well aware that he has chosen to be the
slave of tyrants and is ready on the other hand to give
the people orders. Would it be because he is a good
man ? No ; for you twice condemned him as a
criminal. True, you may say, but he is useful.
Granted ; but if you use a man whom you are known
to have condemned as wicked, it will appear either
that your judgements are wrong or that you welcome
wicked men. It is not therefore right to take upon
yourselves this man's misdeeds. On the contrary :
the transgressor must be punished. And if anyone
comes forward with the plea that he has twice before
been convicted for illegal proposals and that therefore
you should acquit him,ᵃ please do just the opposite,
and that for two reasons. In the first place it is a
piece of good fortune, when a man is known to have
proposed illegal measures, that you should catch
him coming up for trial a third time. He is not a
good man and need not be spared as such. Indeed
you should rid yourselves of him as quickly as you
can, since he has twice already proved his character
to you. And secondly, compare the case of false
witness. If people have been twice convicted of
this, you have allowed them to refrain from giving
evidence a third time, even of events at which they
have themselves been present, so that, if anyone is
disfranchised, responsibility shall rest, not on the
people, but on the man himself, for continuing to bear
false witness. Similarly men convicted of illegal pro-

practice.) The actual penalty seems to have been a fine ; but
if this was not paid the prosecutor had the right to enforce
the judgement by a suit of ejection (δίκη ἐξούλης) and thus
partially disfranchise the culprit. (See Isocr. xvi. 47.) When
orators speak as if ἀτιμία were inevitable after any conviction
they are probably exaggerating.

κόσι παρανόμων ἔξεστιν μηκέτι γράφειν, εἰ δὲ μή,
δηλόν ἐστιν ὅτι ἰδίου τινὸς ἕνεκα τοῦτο ποιοῦσιν·
ὥστε οὐκ οἴκτου οἱ τοιοῦτοι ἄξιοί εἰσιν, ἀλλὰ
13 τιμωρίας. ἵνα δὲ μὴ προθέμενος πρὸς ἀμφορέα
ὕδατος εἰπεῖν μακρολογῶ, ὁ μὲν γραμματεὺς ὑμῖν
ἀναγνώσεται τὴν γραφὴν πάλιν· ὑμεῖς δὲ τῶν τε
[col. 9] κατηγορημένων μεμνημένοι καὶ τῶν νόμων ἀκούσαντες ἀναγιγνωσκομένων, τά τε δίκαια καὶ τὰ
συμφέροντα ὑμῖν αὐτοῖς ψηφίζεσθε.

posals need not bring forward proposals in future. If they do they are clearly actuated by some private motive. So that people of this type deserve punishment, not pity. I do not wish to speak too long after setting myself as a limit an amphora of water in the clock ; so the clerk will read you the indictment again. And now bear in mind the accusations and the laws which you heard read and bring in a verdict that will be just and also expedient for yourselves.

III

SPEECH
AGAINST ATHENOGENES

INTRODUCTION

ALTHOUGH the title for this speech is not preserved in the papyrus, the defendant's name appears repeatedly in the text, and as it is known from various writers that Hyperides did compose a speech against a certain Athenogenes and this work seems worthy of him, no doubts have been entertained regarding its authorship.

The date of the speech, which cannot be fixed precisely, evidently falls between 330 and 324 B.C., for while it is stated in § 31 that at the time of speaking the battle of Salamis (480) had taken place more than a hundred and fifty years before, it is clear from the same passage that Alexander's decree of 324, which restored Greek exiles to their native cities, had not yet been issued.

The plaintiff, for whom the orator wrote the speech, was a farmer, possibly named Epicrates,[a] and probably fairly young, since his father was still alive.[b] The circumstances of the case are known to us solely from his account of them.

Athenogenes, an Egyptian resident in Athens, owned three perfumery businesses, one of which was managed for him by a slave named Midas and his

---

[a] The name is by no means certain, since it depends on a restoration of the text in § 24, but it has been used in this account for the sake of clarity.   [b] See § 23.

two sons. Epicrates took a fancy to one of these boys and made Athenogenes an offer for his freedom. The latter, however, told the boy to insist that Epicrates should free his father and brother too ; and he employed a procuress named Antigone, who had once been his mistress, to persuade the young man to comply with the demand. This she did by using her charms on him and pretending to intercede with the owner on his behalf. Epicrates, who was completely duped, scraped together the money, forty minas,[a] and deposited it in a bank. Athenogenes then agreed to a meeting, said that Antigone had won him over, and consented to sell the three slaves. This meant that Epicrates, instead of paying for their freedom, would buy them formally and would have the choice of liberating them later if he wished. It also meant that he would assume responsibility for any debts standing to their names ; but, as though to compensate him for this, Athenogenes included in the bargain the perfume business, which he said was well stocked and would easily cover any liabilities.

Epicrates, eager to secure the boy, signed the purchase agreement without paying much attention to what was written in it or troubling to verify any details. In a short time he found himself in difficulties. Discovering that the business was in debt to the extent of five talents,[b] he collected his friends and examined the agreement more carefully, only to find that most of the debts were not mentioned in it. They then met Athenogenes in the market ; but in spite of a stormy scene, at which the bystanders supported them, they could make no impression on him, and so resolved to go to law.

[a] About £160.   [b] About £1200.

HYPERIDES

We cannot be certain what type of prosecution was employed, as the speaker could not rest his case on any particular law ; probably, as Blass thought, it was a suit for damage ($\delta i \kappa \eta$ $\beta \lambda \acute{a} \beta \eta s$). Hyperides composed two speeches for the plaintiff, of which this was the first and most important ; of the second, which he may have delivered himself, only a few words survive in quotations.[a] The verdict is not known and cannot easily be guessed. Legally Athenogenes, who was armed with the agreement, had the better position, but it is possible that the claims of equity proved too strong for him.

The case was well suited to the gifts of Hyperides. Though of no public importance, it involved an interesting variety of characters and was indefinite enough from a legal standpoint to need skilful handling. The speech, like the defence of Phryne, was regarded by ancient critics [b] as one of the best examples of his oratory.

[a] See Hyp. frag. 48.
[b] e.g. by [Longinus], De Subl. 34.

ANALYSIS

ΚΑΤ' ΑΘΗΝΟΓΕΝΟΥΣ

[col. 1] . . . . [αὐτ]ήν.[1] εἰπόντος δέ μου πρὸς αὐτὴν τά
τε [πραχθέ]ντα,[2] καὶ ὅτι μοι Ἀθηνογένης χαλε[πὸς]
εἴη καὶ οὐδὲν ἐθέλοι τῶν μετρίων [συγ]χωρεῖν,
τοῦτον μὲν ἔφη ἀεὶ τοιοῦτον [εἶν]αι, ἐμὲ δ' ἐκέλευε
2 θαρρεῖν· αὐτὴ γάρ μοι [πά]ντα συναγωνιεῖσθαι. καὶ
ταῦτ' ἔλεγεν [σπο]υδάζουσά τε τῷ ἤθει ὡς ἔνι
μάλιστα [καὶ] ὀμνύουσα τοὺς μεγίστους ὅρκους,
ἦ μὴν [με]τ' εὐνοίας τῆς ἐμῆς λέγειν καὶ ἐπὶ [πάση]ς
ἀληθείας· ὥστ' ἐμέ, ὦ ἄνδρες δικα[σταί, ῥηθ]ή-
σεται[3] γὰρ πρὸς ὑμᾶς τἀληθές, ταῦ[τα π]επεῖσθαι.
οὕτως, ὡς ἔοικεν, ἐξίστησιν [ἀνθρώπου][4] φύσιν
ἔρως, προσλαβὼν γυναι[κὸς συνεργ]ίαν.[5] ἐκείνη
γοῦν φενακίζουσα [ἄπαντ]α[6] ταῦτα προσπεριέκοψε[ν
α]ὐτῇ [ὡς δὴ][7] εἰς παιδίσκην τριακοσίας δραχμὰς
3 [εὐν]οίας ἕνεκα. ἴσως μὲν οὖν, ὦ ἄνδρες δι[κασ]ταί,
οὐδὲν [ὑπερ]θαυμαστόν[8] με ὑπὸ Ἀν[τιγόν]ας τὸν
τρόπον τουτονὶ παιδαγω[γηθῆ]ναι, γυναικὸς ἢ δει-
νοτάτη μὲν [τῶν] ἑταιρῶν, ὥς φασιν, ἐφ' ἡλ[ικί]ας
ἐγένε[το, διατ]ετέλεκε[9] δὲ πορνοβοσκοῦσα . . . .

---

[1] Primae litterae dubiae sunt. αὐτήν Jensen : om. Kenyon.
[2] πραχθέντα Revillout : πεπραγμένα Diels.

430

AGAINST ATHENOGENES

When I told her what had happened and explained that Athenogenes was rude to me and unwilling to come to any reasonable agreement, she said that he was always like that and told me not to worry, as she would support me in everything herself. Her manner when she said this could not have been more sincere, and she took the most solemn oaths to prove that she was thinking only of my welfare and was telling me the plain truth. So, to be quite honest with you, gentlemen of the jury, I took her at her word. That is how love, I suppose, upsets a man's natural balance when it takes a woman as its ally. She, at any rate, by this act of wholesale trickery pocketed, as a reward for her kindness, a further three hundred drachmas, ostensibly to buy a girl. Perhaps there is nothing very surprising, gentlemen of the jury, in my having been taken in like this by Antigone, a woman who was, I am told, the most gifted courtesan of her time and who has continued to practise as a procuress . . .

---

³ ῥηθήσεται Jensen : εἰρήσεται Kenyon.
⁴ ἀνθρώπου Blass : ἡμῶν τὴν Diels.
⁵ συνεργίαν Jensen : ποικιλίαν Kenyon : alii alia.
⁶ ἅπαντα Diels : τὰ μάταια Kenyon.
⁷ ὡς δὴ Diels : ἔτι Jensen.
⁸ ὑπερθαύμαστόν ci. Kenyon, qui tamen οὕτω θαυμαστόν habet : tantum θαυμαστόν Jensen.
⁹ διατετέλεκε Weil.

. . . . ἐν . . . . οἶκον
τοῦ Χολλίδου οὐ[δενὸς ἐλά]ττω¹ ὄντα ἀνῄρηκεν.
καίτοι [ὅπου καθ'² ἑ]αυτὴν οὖσα τοιαῦτα διεπράτ-
[τετο, τί οἴεσ]θ'³ αὐτὴν νῦν ἐν[νο]εῖν,⁴ προσ[λα-
[col. 2] βοῦσαν⁵ συ]ναγωνιστὴν Ἀθηνογένην, ἄνθρωπον
λογογράφον τε καὶ ἀγοραῖον, τὸ δὲ μέγιστον,
4 Αἰγύπτιον; τέλος δ' οὖν, ἵνα μὴ μακρολογῶ,
μεταπεμψαμένη γάρ⁶ με πάλιν ὕστερον εἶπεν ὅτι
πολλοὺς λόγους ἀναλώσασα πρὸς τὸν Ἀθηνογένην
μόλις εἴη συμπεπεικυῖα αὐτὸν ἀπολῦσαί μοι τόν
τε Μίδαν κα[ὶ τ]οὺς υἱεῖς ἀμφοτέρους τετταράκοντα
μνῶν, καὶ ἐκέλευέ με τὴν ταχίστην πορίζειν τὸ
5 ἀργύριον, πρὶν μεταδόξαι τι Ἀθηνογένει. συνα-
γαγὼν δ' ἐγὼ πανταχόθεν καὶ τοὺς φίλους ἐνοχλή-
σας καὶ θεὶς ἐπὶ τὴν τράπεζαν τὰς τετταράκοντα
μνᾶς ἧκον ὡς τὴν [Ἀντι]γόναν. κἀκε[ίνη] σ[υνή-
γα]γεν⁷ ἡμᾶς εἰς τὸ αὐτό, ἐμέ τε καὶ [Ἀθηνο]γ[έ]νην,
καὶ διή[λλ]αξε, καὶ παρεκελεύσατ[ο τ]οῦ λοιποῦ εὖ
ποιεῖν ἀλλήλους. καὶ ἔγωγ' ἔφην ταῦτα ποιήσειν,
καὶ Ἀθηνογένης οὑτοσὶ ὑπολαβὼν εἶπε[ν ὅ]τι τῶν
πεπραγμένων δεῖ με χάριν ἔχειν Ἀντιγόνα· καὶ
νῦν, ἔφη, ταύτης ἕνεκα ἤδη σοι ἐνδείξομαι ὅσα σε
ἀγα[θὰ] ποιήσω. σὺ μὲ[ν γάρ],⁸ ἔφη, [τὸ]⁸ ἀργύριον
ἐπ' ἐλευθερίᾳ καταβαλ[εῖ]ς⁹ το[ῦ¹⁰ Μίδο]υ¹¹ καὶ τῶν
παίδων, ἐγὼ δέ σοι ἀποδώσομαι αὐτοὺς ὠνῇ καὶ
πράσει, ἵνα πρῶτον μὲν μηδεὶς [παρε]νοχλῇ¹² μηδὲ

---

¹ οὐδενὸς ἐλάττω Jensen : οὐ φαῦλον οὕτω Blass.
² ὅπου καθ' in add. Jensen : ἥτις καθ' Blass : εἰ καθ' Weil.
³ τί οἴεσθ' Kenyon.
⁴ ἐννοεῖν Jensen : ἐπιτελεῖν Weil.
⁵ προσλαβοῦσαν Kenyon.
⁶ γάρ] del. Kenyon.
⁷ συνήγαγεν Revillout.   ⁸ γάρ et τὸ Diels.

has ruined the house of . . . of the deme Chollidae which was equal to any. And yet if that was how she behaved on her own, what do you think her plans are now when she has taken Athenogenes into partnership, who is a speechwriter, a man of affairs and, most significant of all, an Egyptian? At all events, to make a long story short, she finally sent for me again later and said that after a long talk with Athenogenes she had with difficulty managed to persuade him to release Midas and both his sons for me for forty minas.[a] She told me to produce the money as quickly as I could before Athenogenes changed his mind on any point. After I had collected it from every source and been a nuisance to my friends I deposited the forty minas in the bank and came to Antigone. She brought us both together, Athenogenes and myself, and after reconciling us asked us to treat each other as friends in future. I consented to this and Athenogenes, the defendant, replied that I had Antigone to thank for what had passed. "And now," he said, "I will show you how well I am going to treat you for her sake.[b] You are going to put down the money," he went on, "for the liberation of Midas and his sons. Instead I will sell them to you formally as your own, so that no one shall interfere with, or seduce the boy, and

---

[a] i.e. about £160. This was a high price for three slaves. Demosthenes tells us that the total cost of his father's fifty-two slaves (thirty-two swordsmiths and twenty couchmakers) was 230 minas, i.e. an average of just under eight pounds per head. (Dem. xxvii. 9.)

[b] For the explanation of this offer see Introduction.

---

[9] καταβαλεῖς Kenyon.
[10] τοῦ Weil : τῇ Diels.
[11] Μίδου Revillout.
[12] παρενοχλῇ Blass : σε ἐνοχλῇ Revillout.

διαφθείρῃ τὸν π[α]ῖδα, ἔ[π]ε[ι]τ᾽¹ αὐτοὶ [μὴ]² ἐγ-
6 χειρῶσι [πο]νηρε[ύε]σθαι³ μηδὲν διὰ τὸν φόβ[ον].⁴ τὸ
[col. 3] δὲ μέγιστον, νῦν μὲν ἂν δόξειαν δι᾽ ἐμὲ γεγονέναι
ἐλεύθεροι· ἐὰν δὲ πριάμενος σὺ ὠνῇ καὶ πράσει εἶθ᾽
ὕστερον, ὅτε ἄν σοι δοκῇ, ἀφῇς αὐτοὺς ἐλευθέρους,
διπλασίαν ἕξουσίν σοι τὴν χάριν. ὅσον μέντοι
ὀφείλουσιν ἀργύριον, μύρου τέ τινος τιμὴν Παγκά-
λῳ καὶ Προκλεῖ καὶ εἴ τι ἄλλο κατέθετό τις ἐπὶ
τὸ μυροπώλιον τῶν προσφοιτώντων, οἷα γίγνεται,
ταῦτα, ἔφη, σὺ ἀναδέξῃ· ἔστιν δὲ μικρὰ κομιδῇ
καὶ πολλῷ πλείω φορτία ἐστὶν τούτων ἐν τῷ ἐργα-
στηρίῳ, μύρον καὶ ἀλάβαστροι καὶ ζμύρνα, καὶ ἄλλ᾽
ἄττα ὀνόματα λέγων, ὅθεν πάντα ταῦτα δ[ιαλυθ]ή-
7 σε[ται]⁵ ῥᾳδίως. ἦν δέ, ὦ ἄνδρες δικασταί, ὡς
ἔοικεν, ἐνταῦθα ἡ ἐπιβουλὴ καὶ τὸ πλάσμα τὸ
μέγα. εἰ μὲν γὰρ ἐπ᾽ ἐλευθερίᾳ καταβάλλοιμι
αὐτῶν τὸ ἀργύριον, τοῦτο μόνον ἀπώλλυον ὃ δοίην
αὐτῷ, [ἀλλ᾽] οὐδὲν δεινὸν ἔπασχον· εἰ δὲ πριαίμην
ὠνῇ καὶ πράσει, ὁμολογήσας αὐτῷ τὰ χρέα ἀναδέξεσθαι,⁶ ὡς οὐθενὸς ἄξια ὄντα, δ[ιὰ] τὸ μὴ π[ρο]-
ειδέναι, ἐπάξειν μοι ἔμελλεν ὕστερον τοὺς χρ[ήσ]τας
καὶ τοὺς πληρωτὰς τῶν ἐράνων ἐν ὁμολογίᾳ λαβών·
8 ὅπερ ἐποίησεν. ὡς γὰρ εἰπόντος αὐτοῦ ταῦτα
ἐγὼ προσωμολόγησα, εὐθὺς ἐκ τῶν γονάτων λαβὼν
[τῶ]ν αὐτοῦ γραμματεῖόν τ[ι τὸ ἐγ]γεγραμ[μ]ένον⁷

¹ παῖδα, ἔπειτ᾽ Blass (secundum Jensen): Μίδαν, εἶτ᾽
Kenyon.   ² μὴ Blass.   ³ πονηρεύεσθαι Weil.
⁴ φόβον Kenyon.   ⁵ διαλυθήσεται Weil.
434

also so that the slaves themselves shall abstain from being troublesome, for fear of the consequences. But this is the chief advantage : under the present arrangement they would think that it was I who had freed them ; whereas, if you buy them formally first and then liberate them afterwards at your leisure, they will be doubly grateful to you. However," he said, " you will become responsible for what money they owe : a debt for some sweet oil to Pancalus and Procles [a] and any other sums which customers have invested in the perfumery in the ordinary course. It is a trifling amount and much more than counter-balanced by the stocks in the shop, sweet oil, scent-boxes, myrrh " (and he mentioned the names of some other things), " which will easily cover all the debts." There, so it seems, gentlemen of the jury, lay the catch, the real point of the elaborate plot. For if I used the money to buy their freedom I was simply losing whatever I gave him without suffering any serious harm. But if I bought them formally and agreed to take over their debts assuming, since I had no previous information, that these were negligible, he meant to set all his creditors and contributors [b] on me, using the agreement as a trap. And that is just what he did. For when I accepted his proposals he immediately took a document from his lap and began to read the contents, which were the text of

---

[a] The name is given as Polycles in § 10.
[b] *i.e.* friends who had made loans to the business. The money would be repaid in instalments free of interest. *Cf.* §§ 9 and 11.

---

[6] ἀναδέξεσθαι Blass : ἀναδέξασθαι P, ut vid. (sed littera α dubia), Kenyon, et in add. Jensen.
[7] τι τὸ ἐγγ . . Blass : τὸ ἐγγ . . Kenyon : τι προγ . . Colin.

[col. 4] ἀνεγίγνωσκ[εν]. ἦσαν δὲ αὗται συνθῆκαι πρὸς ἐμέ·
ὧν ἐγὼ ἀναγιγνωσκομένων μὲν ἤκουον, ἔσπευδον
μέντοι ἐφ' ὃ ἧκον τοῦτο διοικήσασθαι, καὶ σημαί-
νεται τὰς συνθήκας εὐθὺς ἐν τῇ αὐτῇ οἰκίᾳ ἵνα
μηδεὶς τῶν εὖ φρονούντων ἀκούσαι τὰ ἐγγεγραμ-
μένα, προσεγγράψας μετ' ἐμοῦ Νίκωνα τὸν Κη-
9 φισιέα. ἐλθόντες δ' ἐπὶ τὸ μυροπώλιον τὸ μὲν
γραμματεῖον τιθέμεθα παρὰ Λυσικλεῖ Λευκονοιεῖ,[1]
τὰς δὲ τετταράκοντα μνᾶς ἐγὼ καταβαλὼν τὴν
ὠνὴν ἐποιησάμην. τούτου δὲ γενομένου προσῄεσάν
μοι οἱ χρῆσται οἷς ὠφείλετο παρὰ τῷ Μίδᾳ καὶ
οἱ πληρωταὶ τῶν ἐράνων καὶ διελέγοντό μοι· καὶ
ἐν τρισὶν μησὶν ἅπαντα τὰ χρέα φανερὰ ἐγεγόνει,
ὥστ' εἶναί μοι [σὺ]ν τοῖς ἐράνοις, ὅπερ καὶ ἀρτίως
10 εἶπον, πε[ρὶ π]έντε τάλαντα. ὡς δ' ᾐσθόμην οὗ
ἦν κακοῦ, τότ' ἤδη τοὺς φίλους καὶ τοὺς οἰκείους
συνήγαγον καὶ τὰ ἀντίγραφα τῶν συνθηκ[ῶν] ἀνε-
γιγνώσκομεν· ἐν αἷς ἐγέγραπτο μὲν τὸ τοῦ Παγ-
κάλου καὶ τοῦ Πολυκλέους ὄνομα διαρρήδην, καὶ
ὅτι μύρων τιμαὶ ὠφείλοντο, ἃ ἦν βραχέα τε καὶ
ἐξῆν αὐτοῖς εἰπεῖν ὅτι τὸ μύρον ἄξιον εἴη τοῦ
ἀργυρίου τὸ ἐν τ[ῷ ἐ]ργαστηρίῳ, τὰ δὲ πολλὰ τῶν
χρεῶν καὶ τὰ μέγιστα οὐκ ἐνεγέγραπτο ἐπ' ὀνο-
[col. 5] μάτων, ἀλλ' ἐν προσθήκης μέρει ὡς οὐδὲν ὄντα,
11 "καὶ εἴ τῳ ἄλλῳ ὀφείλει τι Μίδας." καὶ τῶν
ἐράνων εἷς μὲν οὖν, ⟦Δικαιοκράτης⟧,[2] ἐνεγέγραπτο,
οὗ ἦσαν λοιπαὶ τρεῖς φοραί· οὗτος μὲν ἐπὶ τοῦ
Δικαιοκράτους ὀνόματος ἦν γεγραμμένος, οἱ δ'
ἄλλοι, ἐφ' οἷς εἰλήφει[3] πάντα ὁ Μίδας, νεοσύλλογοι

---

[1] Λευκονοιεῖ Kenyon : Λευκονοεῖ P.

[2] Δικαιοκράτης del. Weil.

[3] εἰλήφει] ὤφειλε Weil.

an agreement with me. I listened to it being read, but my attention was concentrated on completing the business I had come for. He sealed the agreement directly in the same house, so that no one with any interest in me should hear the contents, and added with my name that of Nicon of Cephisia. We went to the perfumery and deposited the document with Lysicles of Leuconoë, and I put down the forty minas and so made the purchase. When this was settled I was visited by the creditors, to whom Midas owed money, and the contributors too, who talked things over with me. In three months all the debts had been declared, with the result that, including repayment of contributions, I owed, as I said just now, about five talents.[a] When I realized what a plight I was in, at long last I called together my friends and relatives and we read the copy of the agreement in which the names of Pancalus and Polycles [b] were expressly written with the statement that certain sums were owing to them for sweet oil. These were small amounts, and they were justified in saying that the oil in the shop was equal in value to the money. But the majority of the debts, including the largest, were not given specifically ; they were mentioned as an unimportant item in a sort of footnote which ran : " and any debt which Midas may owe to any other person." Of the contributions one was noted of which three instalments for repayment were still outstanding.[c] This was given in the name of Dicaeocrates. But the others, on the strength of which Midas had acquired everything and which were of

---

[a] About £1200.

[b] The name is given as Procles in § 6. It is not known which is the correct form.

[c] See § 7, note.

HYPERIDES

δ' ἦσαν, τούτους δ' οὐκ ἐνέγραψεν ἐν ταῖς συνθή-
12 καις, ἀλλ' ἀπεκρύψατο. βουλευομένοις δ' ἡμῖν
ἔδοξεν πορεύεσθαι πρὸς τοῦτον καὶ διαλέγεσθαι.
καὶ καταλαβόντες αὐτὸν πρὸς τοῖς μυροπωλίοις
ἠρωτῶμεν εἰ οὐκ αἰσχύνοιτο ψευδόμενος κα[ὶ
ἐν]εδρεύσας ἡμᾶς ταῖς συνθήκαις, οὐ προειπὼν τὰ
χρέα. ὁ δ' ἀπεκρίνατο ἡμῖν ὡς οὔτε τὰ χρέα
γιγνώσκοι ἃ λέγομεν, οὔτε προσέχοι ἡμ[ῖν] τὸν
νοῦν, γραμματεῖόν τ' εἴη αὐτῷ κείμενον πρὸς ἐμὲ
περὶ τούτων. πολλῶν δ' ἀνθρώπων σ[υλλ]εγο-
μένων καὶ ἐπακουόντων τοῦ πράγματος, διὰ τὸ ἐν
τῇ ἀγορᾷ τοὺς λόγους γίγνεσθαι, καὶ κατατεμνόν-
των αὐτόν, κελευόντων τε [ἀπάγ]ειν[1] ὡς ἀνδρα-
ποδιστή[ν, τοῦτο μ]ὲν οὐκ ᾠόμεθα[2] δεῖν ποιεῖν,
πρ[οσεκαλεσά]μεθα δὲ αὐτὸν εἰς ὑμᾶς κατὰ [τὸν
νό]μον. πρῶτον μὲν οὖν ὑμῖν τὰς σ[υνθή]κας ἀνα-
γνώσεται· ἐ[ξ αὐτῶ]ν[3] γὰρ τ[ῶν] γεγρα[μμένων]
[col. 6] μαθήσεσθε τὴν ἐπιβουλὴν αὐτοῦ τούτου. λέγε τὰς
συνθήκας.

ΣΥΝΘΗΚΑΙ

13   Τὰ μὲν το[ίν]υν πεπραγμένα, ὦ ἄνδρες δικασταί,
καθ' ἓν ἕκαστον ἀκηκόατε. ἐρεῖ δὲ πρὸς ὑμᾶς
αὐτίκα μάλα Ἀθηνογένης ὡς ὁ νόμος λέγει, ὅσα
ἂν ἕτερος ἑτέρῳ ὁμολογήσῃ κύρια εἶναι. τά γε
δίκαια, ὦ βέλτιστε· τὰ δὲ μὴ τοὐναντίον ἀπαγορεύει
μὴ κύρια εἶναι. ἐξ αὐτῶν δέ σοι τῶν νόμων ἐγὼ
φανερώτερον ποιήσω. καὶ γὰρ οὕτω με διατέθεικας

---

[1] ἀπάγειν et sq. ad col. 6 finem plerumque restituit Blass.
[2] ᾠόμεθα Weil : οἰόμεθα P.
[3] ἐξ αὐτῶν Revillout.

---

[a] Summary arrest (ἀπαγωγή) by which the injured party

438

recent date, were not entered by him in the agreement but kept secret. On thinking it over we decided to go to Athenogenes and broach the matter. We found him near the perfume stalls and asked him whether he was not ashamed of being a liar and trapping us with the agreement by not declaring the debts beforehand. He replied that he did not know what debts we meant and that we made no impression on him ; he had in safe-keeping a document relating to me which covered the transaction. A crowd gathered and overheard the incident, as our altercation took place in the market. Although they gave him a slating and told us to arrest him summarily as a kidnapper,[a] we thought it best not to do so. Instead we summoned him before you, as the law permits. First of all then, the clerk shall read you the agreement ; for you shall have the actual text of the document as evidence of the plot, for which Athenogenes and no other is to blame. Read the agreement.

Agreement

Well, gentlemen of the jury, you have heard the facts in detail. But Athenogenes will presently tell you that in law whatever agreements one man makes with another are binding.[b] Yes, my friend, just agreements. But if they are unjust, the opposite is true : the law forbids that they be binding. I will quote the laws themselves to make this clearer to you.

seized the criminal and took him before the magistrate, could be used against various types of offender, e.g. thieves and kidnappers. Athenogenes was not actually a kidnapper, but he was driving a man to debt, which, though it did not lead to enslavement, might result in total ἀτιμία.

[b] This law is quoted elsewhere, e.g. by Dem. xlvii. 77.

HYPERIDES

καὶ περίφοβον πεποίηκας μὴ ἀπόλωμαι ὑπὸ σοῦ
καὶ τῆς δεινότητος τῆς σῆς, ὥστε τούς τε νόμους
ἐξετάζειν καὶ μελετᾶν νύκτα καὶ ἡμέραν, πάρεργα
14 τἄλ[λα π]άντα ποιησάμενον. ὁ μὲν τοίνυν εἷς νόμος
κελεύ[ει] ἀψευδεῖν ἐν τῇ ἀ[γορᾷ],[1] πάντων, οἶμα[ι,
π]αρά[γγελ]μα κάλ[λιστο]ν παραγγέλλων· σὺ [δὲ
ψε]υσάμενο[ς ἐν] μέσῃ τῇ ἀγορᾷ συν[θήκα]ς κατ'
ἐμ[οῦ ἔθ]ου. ἐπεὶ ἐὰν δ[είξῃς[2] προει]πὼν[3] ἐμ[οὶ
το]ὺς ἐράνους [καὶ τὰ χρέα, ἢ γράψας ἐν ταῖς
συν]θήκαις ὅσους [ἐπυθόμην, οὐδὲν[4] ἀντιλέ]γω σοι
15 ἀλλ' ὁμολογῶ [ὀφείλειν. μετὰ δὲ] ταῦτα ἕ[τερο]ς
[col. 7] νόμος [ἐστὶ περὶ ὧν ὁμολογοῦν]τες[5] ἀλλήλοις συμ-
βάλλουσιν, ὅταν τις πωλῇ ἀνδράποδον προλέγειν
ἐάν τι ἔχῃ ἀρρώστημα, εἰ δ[ὲ μ]ή, ἀναγωγὴ τούτου
ἐστίν. καίτοι ὅπου τὰ παρὰ τῆς τύχης νοσήματα
ἂν μὴ δηλώσῃ τις πωλῶν οἰκέτ[ην] ἀνάγειν ἔξεστι,
πῶς τά γε παρὰ σοῦ ἀδικήματα συσκευασθέντα
οὐκ ἀναδεκτέον σοί ἐστιν; ἀλλὰ μὴν τὸ μὲν ἐπί-
ληπτον ἀνδράποδον οὐ προσαπολλύει τοῦ πριαμένου τὴν οὐσίαν, ὁ δὲ Μίδας, ὃν σύ μοι ἀπέδου,
16 καὶ τὴν τῶν φίλων τῶν ἐμῶν ἀπολώλεκε. σκέψαι
δέ, ὦ Ἀθηνόγενες, μὴ μόνον περὶ τῶν οἰκετῶν,
ἀλλὰ καὶ περὶ τῶν ἐλευθέρων σωμάτων ὃν τρόπον
οἱ νόμοι ἔχουσιν. οἶσθα γὰρ δήπου καὶ σὺ καὶ ⟨οἱ⟩[a]

---

[1] ἀγορᾷ Revillout. [2] δείξῃς Weil.
[3] προειπὼν Revillout.
[4] ἐπυθόμην, οὐδὲν Fuhr.
[5] περὶ ὧν Weil: ὁμολογοῦντες Revillout: κεῖται περὶ ὧν οἱ
πωλοῦντες Volckmar.

For you have reduced me to such a state of fear lest I shall be ruined by you and your craftiness that I have been searching the laws night and day and studying them to the neglect of everything else. The first law, then, stipulates that people shall not tell lies in the market, which seems to me a most admirable provision.[a] Yet you lied in the middle of the market when you made the agreement to defraud me. But if you show that you declared to me beforehand the contributions and the debts, or that you wrote in the agreement the names of those whose existence I later discovered, I have no quarrel with you ; I admit that I owe the money. After this there is a second law, covering agreements between individuals, which states that whenever anyone sells a slave, he must declare in advance any physical disability from which the man suffers. Otherwise the slave in question can be returned to the vendor. And yet if a slave can be returned simply because of some weakness due to mischance which the master keeps secret at the time of the sale, how can you fail to take the responsibility for the crimes which you deliberately planned ? But the epileptic slave does not involve the buyer in fresh expense, whereas Midas, whom you sold to me, has even lost my friends' money. Consider the legal position, Athenogenes, as regards free persons as well as slaves. No doubt you know as everyone does

---

[a] The first of these two laws cited by the plaintiff is mentioned also by Dem. xx. 9. It was enforced by the ten agoranomoi, whose duty it was to guard against fraud in all questions of purchase. See Aristot. *Ath. Pol.* 51. For the second law compare Aeschin. iii. 249 and Plato, *Laws* 915 c.

---

[6] οἱ add. Blass.

ἄλλοι πάντες ὅτι οἱ ἐκ τῶν ἐγγυητῶν γυναικῶν
παῖδες οὗτοι γνήσιοί εἰσιν. ἀλ[λὰ] μὴ[ν¹ οὐκ
ἀ]πέ[χρ]ησε τῷ νομοθ[έτῃ] τὸ ἐγγ[υηθῆ]ναι τὴν
γυναῖκα ὑπὸ [τοῦ πατ]ρὸς [ἢ τοῦ ἀδ]ελφοῦ, ἀλλ'
ἔγραψε δι[αρρή]δην ἐν [τῷ νόμ]ῳ, [ἣν] ἂν ἐγγυήσῃ
τ[ις ἐπὶ δικαίοις δάμαρτα] ἐκ ταύτης εἶν[αι παῖδας
γνησίους,² καὶ οὐ]κ³ ἐάν τις ψευσ[άμενος ὡς θυγα-
τέρα⁴ ἐγ]γυήσῃ ἄλ[λην τινά. ἀλλὰ τὰς μὲν δι]καίας⁴
ἐγγύας κ[υρίας,⁵ τὰς δὲ μὴ δικαίας ἀκύρους] καθ-
17 ίστη[σιν.⁵ ἔτι δὲ καὶ ὁ περὶ] τῶν διαθηκῶν ν[όμο]ς
[col. 8] παραπλήσιος τούτοις ἐστίν· κελεύε[ι γὰρ ἐξεῖν]αι⁶
τὰ ἑαυτοῦ [δια]τίθεσθα[ι ὅπως ἄν]⁷ τις βούληται
πλὴν [ἢ γή]ρως ἕνε[κεν] ἢ νόσου ἢ μανιῶν ἢ γυ[ναι-
κὶ] πειθόμ[ενο]ν ἢ [ὑπὸ] δεσμοῦ ἢ ὑ[πὸ ἀνά]γκης
κ[ατ]αληφθ[έντ]α. ὅπου δὲ οὐδὲ [περὶ] τῶν αὑτοῦ
ἰδίων αἱ [μὴ δ]ίκαιαι⁸ διαθῆκαι κύριαί εἰσιν, πῶς
Ἀθηνογένει γε κα[τὰ τῶ]ν⁹ ἐμῶν συνθεμένῳ τοιαῦ-
18 τα δεῖ [κύρι]α εἶναι; καὶ ἐὰν μέν τι[ς] ὡς ἔοικ[ε]ν
τῇ ἑαυτοῦ γυναικὶ πειθόμενος διαθήκας [γρά]-
ψῃ¹⁰ ἄκυροι ἔσο[νται], εἰ δ' ἐγὼ τῇ Ἀθηνογ[ένο]υς
ἑταίρᾳ ἐπείσθην, προσαπολωλέναι [με]¹¹ δεῖ, ὃς ἔχω
μ[εγίσ]την¹¹ βοήθειαν τὴν ἐν τῷ νόμῳ γεγραμμένην,

---

¹ ἀλλὰ μὴν et sq. ad col. 8 finem plerumque restituit
Revillout.
² εἶναι παῖδας γνησίους Weil.
³ καὶ οὐκ Blass : ἀλλ' οὐκ Weil.
⁴ ὡς θυγατέρα usque ad δικαίας Fuhr.
⁵ κυρίας usque ad καθίστησιν Blass.
⁶ γὰρ ἐξεῖναι Blass.   ⁷ ὅπως ἄν Fuhr.
⁸ μὴ δίκαιαι Blass.   ⁹ κατὰ τῶν Kenyon.
¹⁰ γράψῃ Diels.   ¹¹ με et μεγίστην Weil.

that the children of married women are legitimate. Yet the mere act of betrothing a woman on the part of a father or brother was not enough for the law-maker. On the contrary, he wrote expressly in the law *a* : " whomsoever any man has lawfully betrothed as wife, her children shall be legitimate " ; not : " if any man has betrothed some other woman on the pretence that she is his daughter." He lays it down that just betrothals shall be valid and unjust ones invalid. Moreover the law dealing with wills is very similar to this.*b* It allows a man to bequeath his property as he wishes unless he is affected by old age, illness or insanity, and provided he is not influenced by a woman or imprisoned or otherwise coerced. But if even our own personal property cannot be administered according to an unjust will, surely Athenogenes who is disposing of my property through his agreement cannot enforce such terms. Apparently if a man respects the wishes of his own wife in making his will it will be invalid. Then must I, who was influenced by the mistress of Athenogenes, accept the contract and be ruined too,*c* even though I can claim the very powerful help of the law, having been com-

---

a This law is mentioned by Demosthenes (xliv. 49) and quoted in [Dem.] xlvi. 18, from which the text is here reconstructed.

b This law is quoted in [Dem.] xlvi. 14. Compare Isaeus vi. 10 ; Aristot. *Ath. Pol.* 35. As Colin points out, the comparison between συνθῆκαι (an agreement) and διαθήκη (a will) seems closer in Greek than in English.

c The argument is rather condensed ; the contrast is this : A will may be otherwise just and yet it becomes invalid when made under the influence of a wife. Therefore, *a fortiori*, this contract becomes invalid because (1) it was not just in other respects, (2) it was made under the influence of a woman less reputable than a wife.

ἀναγκασθεὶς ὑπὸ τούτων ταῦτα συνθέσθαι; εἶτα
σὺ ταῖς συνθήκαις ἰσ[χυρί]ζῃ ἃς ἐνεδρεύσαντές με
σὺ καὶ ἡ ἑ[ταίρα] σο[υ¹ ἐσ]ημήνασθε, καὶ ὑ[πὲρ ὧν²
οἱ νόμοι] β[ου]λεύσεως ὑμᾶς κε[λεύουσιν αἰτίου]s
εἶναι, ἐπὶ τούτοις προσ[λαμβάνειν τι ἀξιοῦ]τε.²
καὶ οὐ[χ ἱ]κανόν σοι [ἦν τὰς³ τεττεράκοντα] μνᾶς
εἰληφέναι [ὑπὲρ τοῦ μυροπωλίου, ἀ]λλὰ καὶ πέντε
[τάλαντα προσαφείλου⁴] με ὥσπερ [ὑ]πο⁵ . . . . . .
. . . . κατ]ε[ι]λημμένον . . . .
19 . . . . . s οὐκ ᾔδε[ι] . . . . Μίδαν
αδ . . . . σθέντα αλ . .
[col. 9] σ . . . . εἰς τὰ ἐν ἀγορᾷ, ἀτρέ[μα]⁶ δ᾽ [ἔχων ἐν
τρισὶ]⁷ μησὶν ἅπαντα τὰ χρέα καὶ τ[οὺς ἐράν]ους
ἐπυθόμην, οὗτ[ος] δέ, ὁ ἐκ τριγονίας [ὢν] μυροπώλης,
καθ[ήμε]νος δ᾽ ἐν τῇ ἀγο[ρᾷ] ὅσαι ἡμέραι, τρία [δὲ
μυ]ροπώλια κεκτη[μένος], λόγους δὲ κατὰ μῆνα
λαμβάνω[ν, οὐκ] ᾔδει τὰ χρέα. ἀλλ᾽ ἐν μὲν τοῖς
ἄλλοις οὐκ ἰδιώτης ἐστίν, πρὸς δὲ τὸν οἰκέτην
οὗτ[ως ε]ὐήθης ἐγένετο, καί τινα μὲν τῶν χρ[εῶ]ν,
ὡς ἔοικεν, ᾔδει, τὰ δέ φησιν οὐκ εἰδέναι, ὅσα μὴ
20 βούλεται. ὁ δὲ τοιοῦτο[ς αὐτοῦ]⁸ λόγος, ὦ ἄνδρες
δ[ικασ]ταί, οὐ[κ ἀπολόγημ]α⁹ ἐστιν, ἀλλ᾽ ὁμολόγημα
ὡς οὐ δεῖ [με τὰ χρέα διαλ]ύειν. ὅταν γὰρ φῇ μὴ
εἰδέναι [ἅπαντα]¹⁰ τὰ ὀφειλόμενα, οὐκ ἔστιν αὐτῷ
δήπου [τόδ᾽]¹¹ εἰπεῖν ὡς προεῖπέ μοι περὶ τῶν
χρε[ῶν· ὅσα δ᾽ ο]ὐκ¹² ἤκουσα παρὰ τοῦ πωλοῦντος
[ταῦ]τ[α οὐ δίκαιός] εἰμι διαλύειν. ὅτι μὲν οὖν

¹ ἑταίρα σου Diels.
² ὑπὲρ ὧν usque ad ἀξιοῦτε Jensen in add. : alii alia.
³ ἦν τὰς Weil.
⁴ προσαφείλου Kenyon : ἀπεστερήκατε Weil.
⁵ ὑποχείριον ἐν ποδοστράβῃ κατειλημμένον Revillout, coll. Har-
pocratione s.v. ποδοστράβη : ὑπὸ θηρευτοῦ κτλ. Richards.

pelled by these people to conclude the agreement?
Do you insist on the agreement when you and your
mistress laid a trap for me to get it signed? In circumstances where the laws relating to conspiracy
proclaim that you are guilty, are you expecting
actually to make a profit? You were not content
with the forty minas for the perfumery. No; you
robbed me of a further five talents as though I were
caught . . .ᵃ the affairs of the market, but by simply
waiting I discovered all the debts and loans in three
months. Whereas this man had two generations of
perfume sellers behind him; he used to sit in the
market every day, was the owner of three stalls and
had accounts submitted to him monthly and still he
did not know his debts. Though an expert in other
matters he was a complete simpleton in dealing with
his slave, and though he knew, apparently, of some
of the debts, he pleads ignorance of others—to suit
his convenience. In using an argument like this,
gentlemen of the jury, he is accusing, not excusing,
himself, since he is admitting that I need not pay the
debts. For if he says that he did not know the full
amount owing, surely he cannot claim that he informed me of the debts beforehand; and I am not
bound to pay those of which the seller did not notify

ᵃ The exact words cannot be restored but the sense is:
" It is absurd for Athenogenes, a shrewd business man, to
plead ignorance, when I with no experience of the market
discovered the facts so soon without effort."

---

⁶ Coll. 9, 10, 11 plerumque restituit Blass. ἀτρεκὲς δὴ ἐγὼ
Kenyon.   ⁷ ἐν τρισὶ Weil.
⁸ αὐτοῦ Revillout : οἶμαι Kenyon.
⁹ ἀπολόγημά Reinach.   ¹⁰ ἅπαντα Revillout.
¹¹ τόδ' Kenyon.   ¹² ὅσα δ' οὐκ Revillout.

ἤ[δεις, ὦ ᾿Αθηνό]γενες, ὀφείλοντα Μ[ίδαν] τ[ὰ
χρήματα ταῦτα] οἶμαι πᾶσιν εἶναι δῆλ[ον ἐξ ἄλλων
τε πολλ]ῶν καὶ ἐκ τοῦ αἰτεῖν [σε τὸν Νίκωνα ὑπὲρ
ἐ]μοῦ ἐγγυητ[ή]ν, εἰ . . . . [τ]ὰ
χρέα ὄντα ἱκανό[ν] . . . . νο. οὐ μὲν
δὴ ἐγὼ . . . . [τῷ] λόγωι σοῦ τού-
21 τ[ῳ] . . . . ος καὶ οὐκ εἰλ . . . . . .
. . . . νος καὶ τω . . . . τουτονὶ
[col. 10] τὸν τ[ρόπον. εἰ] σὺ μὲν διὰ τὸ μὴ εἰδέναι μὴ προ-
εἶπάς [μοι]¹ πάντα τὰ χρέα, ἐγὼ δὲ ὅσα σου ἤκουσα
ταῦτα μόνον οἰόμενος εἶναι τὰς συνθήκας ἐθέμην,
πότερος δίκαιός ἐστιν ἐκτεῖ[σα]ι, ὁ ὕστερος πριάμενος ἢ [ὁ π]άλαι κεκτημένος ὅτ᾽ ἐδανείζετο; ἐγὼ μὲν
γὰρ οἴομαι σέ. εἰ δ᾽ ἄρ᾽ ἀντιλέγομεν περὶ τούτου,
διαιτητὴς ἡμῖν γενέσθω ὁ νόμος, ὃν οὐχ οἱ ἐρῶντε[ς
ο]ὐδ᾽ οἱ ἐπιβουλεύοντες τοῖς [ἀλλ]οτρίοις ἔθεσαν,
22 ἀλλ᾽ ὁ δημοτικώτα[τος] Σόλων· ὃς εἰδὼς ὅτι πολλαὶ
ὠναὶ [γίγνον]ται ἐν τῇ πόλει ἔθηκε νόμον δίκαι[ον,
ὡς] παρὰ πάντων ὁμολογεῖται, τὰς ζη[μίας ἃς ἂν]
ἐργάσωνται οἱ οἰκέται καὶ τὰ ἀ[δικήμ]ατα² διαλύειν τὸν δεσπότην παρ᾽ ᾧ [ἂν ἐργάσ]ωνται³ οἱ
οἰκέται. εἰκότως· καὶ γὰρ [ἐάν τι ἀγ]αθὸν³ πράξῃ
ἢ ἐργασίαν εὕρ[ῃ] ὁ ο[ἰκέτης το]ῦ κεκτημένου αὐτὸν
γ[ίγ]νετ[αι. σὺ δὲ τὸν ν]όμον ἀφεὶς περὶ συνθ[ηκῶν

---

¹ μοι Diels.
² ἀδικήματα Jensen olim : ἀναλώματα Revillout.
³ ἂν ἐργάσωνται et ἐάν τι ἀγαθὸν Weil.

ᵃ This passage was restored by Blass, partly following
Revillout, to give the following meaning : ". . . because you

446

me. You knew that Midas owed this money, Athenogenes, as I think we all realize for several reasons,
and chiefly because you summoned Nicon to give
security for me *a* . . . in this way. If ignorance
prevented you from informing me in advance of all
the debts, and if I thought when I concluded the
agreement that your statement covered them all,
which of us has to pay them ? The subsequent pur-
chaser, or the man who owned the business originally,
when the money was borrowed ? Personally I think
that you are liable. But if it turns out that we dis-
agree on this, let the law be our arbiter, which was
made neither by lovers nor men with designs on
other people's property but by that great democrat
Solon. He knew that sales are constantly taking
place in the city and passed a law, which everyone
admits to be just, stating that any offences or crimes
committed by a slave shall be the responsibility of
the master who owns him at the time.*b* This is only
fair ; for if a slave gains any success or brings in
earnings, his owner enjoys the benefits. But you
ignore the law and talk about agreements being

a summoned Nicon to give security for me, knowing that I
could not meet the debts alone without his help. And indeed
I cannot, but I want to get to grips with this claim of yours
that you did not know who had invested what sums, or what
the individual debts were. Let us consider it in this way."
For Nicon see § 8.

b This law, which does not seem to be mentioned elsewhere,
is not strictly applicable here, since the plaintiff had agreed
in his contract to assume responsibility for Midas's debts.
However, it was a fair law, and if Athenogenes had not intended to take advantage of the plaintiff he would have been
willing to observe it. ζημίαν ἐργάζεσθαι, which appears to be
an old legal phrase, is variously understood. Other inter-
pretations than that adopted in the translation are : (1) to
incur loss, (2) to incur a fine.

παραβαιν]ομένων¹ διαλέγῃ. καὶ ὁ [μὲν Σόλων
οὐδ' ὃ] δικαίως ἔγραφεν ψήφ[ισμά τις τοῦ νόμου]²
οἴεται δεῖν κυριώ[τερον εἶναι, σὺ δὲ καὶ³ τ]ὰς ἀδίκους
συνθ[ήκας ἀξιοῖς κρατεῖν³ πάντων⁴ τ]ῶν νόμων.
23 καὶ π[ρὸς τούτοις, ὦ ἄνδρες δικαστ]αί, τῷ τε
πατ[ρὶ τῷ ἐμῷ καὶ τοῖς ἄλλοις ἐπιτ]ηδείοις ἔλ[εγεν
ὡς . . . . εθελ . . . .
[col. 11] . . . . δ]ωρεὰν . . . . κε . . . . τὸν δὲ
Μίδαν κελεύσ[ας]⁵ ἐᾶν αὐτῷ καὶ μὴ ὠνεῖσθαι· ἐμὲ
δ' οὐκ ἐθέλειν ἀλλὰ βούλεσθαι πάντας πρίασθαι.
καὶ ταῦτα καὶ πρὸς ὑμᾶς αὐτόν, φασίν, μέλλει⟨ν⟩
λέγειν, ἵνα δὴ δοκοίη μέτριος εἶναι, ὥσ[πε]ρ πρὸς
ἠλιθίους τινὰς διαλεξόμενος καὶ οὐκ αἰσθησομένους
24 τὴν τούτου ἀναίδ[εια]ν. τὸ δὲ γενόμενον δεῖ ὑμᾶς
ἀκοῦσα[ι· φαν]ήσεται γὰρ ἀκόλουθον ὂν τῇ ἄλλῃ
αὐτῶν ἐπιβο[υλῇ.] τὸν μὲν γὰρ παῖδα, ὅνπ[ερ
ἀρ]τίως εἶπο[ν, ἔπε]μπέ μοι λέγοντα ὅτι οὐκ [ἂν
συ]νείη μ[οι, εἰ μὴ λ]ύσομαι⁶ αὐτοῦ τὸν πατ[έρ]α καὶ
τὸν [ἀδελφ]όν.⁷ ἤδη δ' ἐμοῦ ὡμολ[ογη]κότος [αὐτῶν
κα]ταθήσειν, τριῶν ὄν[των], τὸ ἀ[ργύριον,⁸ προσ]-
ελθὼν ὁ Ἀθηνογένης πρός [τινας⁹ τῶν] φίλων τῶν
ἐμῶν " [τί] βού[λ]ετ[αι]," ἔφη, " Ἐπ]ικρατὴς¹⁰ πράγ-
25 ματα ἔχειν [ᾧ ἔξεστι λα]βόντι τὸν παῖδα [χρ]ῆσθ[αι]¹¹

¹ παραβαινομένων Diels.   ² ψήφισμά τις τοῦ νόμου Jensen.

448

broken. Solon did not consider that a decree, even when constitutionally proposed, should override the law.[a] Yet you maintain that even unjust agreements take precedence over all the laws. Besides this, gentlemen of the jury, he was saying to my father and my other relatives that . . .[b] telling me to leave Midas for him instead of buying him, but that I refused and wanted to buy them all. I gather that he is even going to mention these points to you with the idea of convincing you of his moderation, if you please. He must think that he is going to address a set of fools who will not realize his effrontery. You must hear what happened; for you will see that it fits in with the rest of their plot. He sent me the boy, whom I mentioned just now, with the message that he could not stay with me unless I freed his father and brother. When I had already agreed to put down the money for the three of them, Athenogenes approached some of my friends and said : " Why does Epicrates want to give himself extra trouble when he could take the boy and use . . . ? " I am not a seller

---

[a] This provision of Solon is mentioned by Andoc. i. 87 and by Dem. xxiii. 87.

[b] The sense evidently is : " that he offered me the one boy as a present and asked me to leave Midas." *Cf.* § 27.

---

[3] σὺ δὲ καὶ et ἀξιοῖς κρατεῖν Jensen : σὺ δὲ οἴει et δεῖν κρατεῖν Blass.

[4] πάντων Revillout.

[5] κελεύσας Jensen : κελεύοι με Weil.

[6] εἰ μὴ λύσομαι Kenyon : ἂν μὴ ὠνῶμαι Weil.

[7] ἀδελφόν Weil.

[8] ἀργύριον Revillout.

[9] τινας Diels.

[10] ἐβούλετο γενόμενος ἐπικρατὴς Kenyon.

[11] Post χρῆσθαι add. ὅ τι ἂν ἐθέλῃ Hager.

. . . . τὴν μὲν συκοφα[ντίαν . . . .
ἐ]ποιεῖτο τῷ δὲ λ[. . . . . ἀ]δικημά-
των κα[. . . . . ἐπ]ίστευσα [ὦ]s ἐ[. . . . .
. . . . . . τὸ]ν μὲν παῖδα δι[. . . . .
. . . . .]ν οὐκ ἤθελο[ν . . . .]
οὖν τετ[ταράκοντα¹ μνᾶς . . . . πέν]τε τάλα[ντα¹
. . . .

[Desunt versus duo.]

[col. 12]
26 [οὔτε μυροπώλη]s² εἰμὶ οὔτ' ἄλλην τέχνην ἐργά-
ζο[μαι, ἀλ]λ' ἅπερ ὁ πατήρ μοι ἔδωκεν χωρία
. . . . . τα]ῦτα³ γεωργῶ, πρ[ὸς δὲ τούτων ε[ἰς τὴν]
ὠνὴν ἐνεσείσθην. πότερα [γὰρ εἰκός ἐσ]τιν, ὦ
'Αθηνόγενες, ἐμὲ τῆς σῆς [τέχνης⁴ ἐπιθ]υμῆσαι,
ἧς οὐ[κ] ἤμην ἔμπει[ρος, ἤ σε καὶ τ]ὴν⁵ ἑταίραν
τοῖς ἐμοῖς ἐπι[βουλεῦσαι];⁶ ἐγὼ μὲν γὰρ οἴομαι
ὑμᾶς. δι[όπερ, ἄνδρες] δικασταί, ἐμοὶ μὲν ἂν εἰ[κό-
τως συγγνώ]μην ἔχο[ιτ' ἀ]πα[τη]θῆναι⁷ . . . . . .
καὶ ἀτυχῆσαι τ[οιού]τῳ [ἀνθρώπῳ περ]ιπεσόντα⁸
'Αθην[ογένει δὲ .].⁹

[Desunt versus fere sedecim.]

[col. 13]
27 ενε[. . . . . π]άντα¹⁰ ἐμοὶ εἶναι, τὰ δὲ τῆς ἀπάτ[ης
κέρδη αὐτ]ῷ¹¹· καὶ τὸν μὲν Μίδαν τὸν τολ . . . . . .
ξαι,¹² ὃν ἄκων φησὶν ἀ[πο]λῦσαι, τοῦτ[ον . . . . . .
λα]βεῖν,¹³ τοῦ δὲ παιδὸς [ὃν] τότε προῖκ[ά μοί φησιν¹⁴]
διδόναι, νῦν αὐτ[ὸν λ]αβεῖν ἀργύρ[ιον πολὺ πλε]ῖον
τῆς ἀξίας, οὐχ ὥστε ἐμὸν εἶ[ναι, ἀλλ' ὥστε ὑ]φ'

---

¹ τετταράκοντα usque ad τάλαντα Diels.
² Coll. 12 et 13 plerumque restituit Blass : οὔτε μυροπώλης
Diels.
³ ταῦτα Jensen.

of perfume [a] and I do not practise any other trade. I simply farm the property which my father gave me, and I was landed in the purchase by these people. Which is more probable, Athenogenes, that I set my heart on your trade in which I was not proficient, or that you and your mistress had designs on my money? Personally, I think that you are indicated. Therefore, gentlemen of the jury, you could fairly excuse me for being cheated by . . . and for having had the misfortune to fall in with a man like this, but to Athenogenes . . . all to be mine and the profits of the fraud to be his. . . . that I took Midas . . . whom he says he was reluctant to let go. But for the boy whom, we are told, he originally offered me for nothing, he has now been paid a far higher price than he is worth; and yet in the end the boy will not be my property but will be freed on

---

[a] The general sense of this mutilated passage is restored by Colin, in his translation, as follows: "Despite his dishonest purpose, I accepted his word, and when he offered me the boy, raised no objection over the price. I thus agreed to pay 40 minas, but I now find I must produce five talents for a perfumery in which I have no interest."

---

4 τέχνης Weil.
5 ἤ σε καὶ τὴν Weil.
6 ἐπιβουλεῦσαι Diels.
7 ἔχοιτ' ἀπατηθῆναι de Ricci, qui ὑπ' Ἀντιγόνας addit.
8 περιπεσόντα Diels.
9 Ἀθηνογένει δὲ Hager, qui ὀργίζοισθε addit. Huc inserunt quidam editores fragmentum extremae alicuius columnae quod ad finem orationis dedi.
10 ἕνεκα πάθη πάντα Colin.
11 ἀπάτης κέρδη αὐτῷ Revillout.
12 τολμῶντα συμπρᾶξαι Vogt.
13 τοῦτον συγχωρῶ λαβεῖν Blass.
14 φησιν Blass : ἔφη Kenyon.

28 [ὑμῶν] τῇ ψήφῳ ἐλεύθερον ἀφ[ίεσθαι.[1] αὐτὸς[2] μέ]ν-
τοι οὐκ ἀξιῶ πρὸς [τοῖς ἄλλοις καὶ ἀτι]μωθῆναι[3]
ὑπ᾽ Ἀθηνογέν[ους. καὶ γὰρ ἂν][4] δεινὸν [συ]μβαίνοι
μ[οι, ὦ ἄνδρες δικασ]ταί,[5] εἰ μ . . . . . ος
εισ . . . . ον ἥμαρτο[ν] . . . . . . δι . . . . κ . . . .
μία δὲ κ . . . . ου . . . . ιο . . [ἠδί]κηκεν
. . . . θε . . . . ἀ]δικήσαντ . . . .
. . . . τ]ιμήματι δ . . . . π
. . . . . ται πολιτ . . . . νος
ἐνίοτε . . . . .

[Desunt versus fere decem.]

[col. 14]

29 ώτατοι τῶν μετοίκων ἀφυ[λάκτως ἔρ]χεσθαι.[6] ἐν
δὲ τῷ πολέμῳ τῷ πρὸς Φίλιππον μικρὸν πρὸ τῆς
μάχης ἀπέ[λιπε][7] τὴν πόλιν, καὶ μεθ᾽ ὑμῶν μὲν οὐ
συνεστρατεύσ[ατ]ο εἰς Χαιρώνειαν, ἐξῴκησε δὲ εἰς
Τ[ροι]ζῆνα, παρὰ τὸν νόμον ὃς κελεύει ἔνδ[ειξιν]
ε[ἶ]ναι καὶ ἀπαγωγὴν τοῦ ἐξοικήσαντος [ἐν] τῷ
πολέμῳ, ἐὰν πάλιν ἔλθῃ. καὶ ταῦ[τ᾽ ἐποί]ει τὴν

---

[1] ἀφίεσθαι Jenson : ἀφεθῆναι Blass.
[2] αὐτὸς Diels.
[3] ἀτιμωθῆναι Weil.
[4] καὶ γὰρ ἂν Fuhr : λίαν γὰρ ἂν Diels.
[5] μοι, ὦ ἄνδρες δικασταί Revillout.
[6] Coll. 14, 15, 16 plerumque restituit Revillout : ἀφυλάκτως
ἔρχεσθαι Jensen.
[7] ἀπέλιπε Revillout : ἀπέδρα Kenyon.

---

[a] The point of this remark is not clear. The plaintiff might
mean that if he wins his case the boy will be freed, since he
never intended to buy him as a slave ; but the following
sentence suggests that he has in mind at present the consequences of his condemnation.

the strength of your verdict.[a] However I do not think myself that in addition to my other troubles I deserve to be disfranchised by Athenogenes.[b] For I should be receiving harsh treatment indeed, gentlemen of the jury, if . . . of the metics to come unguarded. During the war against Philip he left the city just before the battle and did not serve with you at Chaeronea. Instead, he moved to Troezen, disregarding the law [c] which says that a man who moves in wartime shall be indicted and summarily arrested if he returns. The reason for the move, it seems, was

[b] Disfranchisement could only follow upon condemnation if the plaintiff failed to obtain one-fifth of the votes and so became liable to pay ἐπωβελία, i.e. compensation to Athenogenes at the rate of one-sixth of the sum in question. On failure to pay this he would become liable to prosecution again (δίκη ἐξούλης) and if condemned would have to pay a fine to the state too. Finally as a state debtor he would be liable to loss of civic rights (ἀτιμία). The payment of ἐπωβελία certainly obtained in mercantile, and some other cases, and probably in cases of damage also. See Andoc. i. 73; Dem. xxi. 44, xxvii. 67, xxviii. 21, xlvii. 64; Aeschin. i. 163.

[c] This law, which is not mentioned by any other writer, appears to be the same as the one subsequently read out (§ 33) which forbade resident aliens to emigrate in time of war. It is not clear, however, why the clause quoted here should relate to an attempted return on the part of the law-breaker rather than to his actual departure. If the plaintiff is making a valid point we must assume that the law existed before the battle of Chaeronea, since it was then that Athenogenes left Athens. If so, it must have applied to resident aliens only (as indeed appears from § 33 to have been the case); for had it applied to citizens, Lycurgus would surely have mentioned it in his speech against Leocrates, as he was there concerned with just this question. It is possible, however, that Hyperides is alluding to some provision which did not come into force until the time of emergency after Chaeronea, but is attempting to impose on the ignorance of his hearers.

μὲν ἐκείνων πόλιν, ὡς ἔοικ[ε, περιέ]σε[σθ]αι[1] ὑπο-
λαμβ[άνω]ν, τῆς δὲ ἡμε[τέρας θά]να[το]ν κατα-
γνο[ύς].[2] καὶ τὰς θυγα[τέρας ἐν][3] τῆ παρ' ὑμῖν
εὐδα[ιμον]ίᾳ ἐκθρέψα[ς][4] . . . . ἐξέδωκ[εν]
. . . . . ὡς[5] πάλιν η . . . . ἐργασόμε[νος
30 ἐπ]εὶ εἰρήνη γέ[γονεν]. τ[αῦτ]α[6] γὰρ ὑμῖ[ν . . . . .]α-
σιν οἱ χρησ . . . . ο]ὖτοι ποι . . . . . . τῆ
εἰρήνῃ χρ . . . . πω . . . . . ἐν τοῖς κινδ[ύ-
νοις] . . . . π . . . . . μὲν ἐν Πλατα[ιαῖς]
. . . . δήσαντες ο . . . .
. . . . 'Αθη]νογ[ένη]s . . π . . . .
. . . . χειν . . . . . νω . . . .
το . . . . . . υθ . . . .

[Desunt versus fere sex.]

[col. 15]
31 [τὰς] κοινὰς τῆς πόλεως συνθήκας παραβὰς ταῖς
ἰδίαις πρὸς ἐμὲ ἰσχυρίζεται, ὥσπερ ἄν τινα πει-
σθέντα ὡς ὁ τῶν πρὸς ὑμᾶς δικαίων καταφρονήσας
οὗτος ἂν τῶν πρὸς ἐ[μὲ][7] ἐφρόντιζεν· ὃς οὕτω
πονηρός ἐστι καὶ πανταχοῦ ὅμοιος ὥστε καὶ εἰς
Τροιζῆνα ἐλθὼν καὶ ποιησαμένων αὐτὸν Τροιζηνίων
πολίτην, ὑποπεσὼν Μνησίαν τ[ὸν] Ἀργεῖον καὶ
ὑπ' ἐκείνου κατασ[τα]θεὶς [ἄρχω]ν, ἐξέβαλεν τοὺς
πολίτας ἐκ τῆς [πόλ]εως, ὡς ὑμῖν αὐτοὶ μαρτυρή-
32 σουσιν· ἐνθάδε γὰρ φεύγουσιν. καὶ ὑμεῖς μέν, ὦ
ἄνδρες δικασταί, ἐκπεσόντας αὐτοὺς ὑπεδέξασθε
καὶ πολίτας ἐποιήσασθε καὶ τῶν ὑμετέρων ἀγαθῶν
πάντων μετέδοτε, ἀπομνημονεύσαντες τὴν εὐερ-
γεσίαν τ[ὴν] πρὸς τὸν βάρβαρον δι' ἐτῶν πλειόνων

---

[1] περιέσεσθαι Weil.   [2] ἡμετέρας θάνατον καταγνούς Blass.
[3] θυγατέρας ἐν Vogt.

454

this : he thought that the city of Troezen would survive, whereas he had passed a sentence of death on
ours. His daughters whom he had brought up in the
prosperity which you provided . . . he married off
. . . with the intention of returning later to carry
on his business when peace was established. . . .
after disregarding the agreement which we all make
with the state, he insists on his private contract with
me, as if anyone would believe that a man who made
light of his duty to you would have cared about his
obligations to me. He is so degraded and so true to
type wherever he is, that even after his arrival at
Troezen when they had made him a citizen he became
the tool of Mnesias the Argive [a] and, after being
made a magistrate by him, expelled the citizens from
the city. The men themselves will bear witness to
this ; for they are here in exile.[b] And you, gentlemen
of the jury, took them in when they were banished ;
you made them citizens and granted them a share
of all your privileges. Remembering, after more
than a hundred and fifty years,[c] the help they gave
you against the barbarian, you felt that when men

[a] Mnesias the Argive is mentioned as a traitor by Demosthenes. (See Dem. xviii. 295, where, however, the name is
spelt Μνασέας.)
[b] As these men were still in Athens, Alexander's decree of
424 B.C., providing that exiles should return, cannot yet have
been issued. Hence we have a *terminus ante quem* for the
speech.
[c] The Athenians sent women and children to Troezen
before the battle of Salamis. (See Cic. *de Offic.* iii. 11. 48.)
Hence we have a rough *terminus post quem* for the speech.

---

[4] Post ἐκθρέψας add. ἐν τῇ ἀτυχίᾳ Colin, post ἐξέδωκεν add.
ἄλλοσε Weil.
[5] ως incertum : ὃς πάλιν ἦκεν ὑμῖν παρεργασόμενος Colin.
[6] ταῦτα Kenyon.   [7] ἐμέ Diels.

[ἢ¹ πε]ντήκοντα κ[αὶ] ἑκατόν, καὶ οἰόμενοι [δεῖν]
τοὺς ἐν τοῖς κινδύνοις ὑμῖν χρησίμους [γε]νομένους
τούτους ἀτυχοῦντ[ας περ]ισ[ωθῆναι]² ὑφ᾽ ὑμῶν. οὗτος δὲ ὁ μιαρός, [ὁ] ἀφεὶς [ὑμᾶς κἀ]κεῖ ἐγγραφ[εί]ς,
οὔτε τῆς πολιτεί[ας οὔτε³ τοῦ ἤθο]υς τῆς πόλεως
οὐδὲν [ἐ]πετή[δευεν ἄξι]ον³ ἀλ[λ᾽ οὕτ]ως ὠμῶς τοῖς
ὑπο[δεξαμένοις α]ὑτὸν⁴ [ἐχρ]ήσατο ὥστε [μ]ετα . . .
. . . . το ἐν τῇ ἐκκλησίᾳ . . . .
. . . . . κατὰ τοῦτ[ο] . . . .
[col. 16] . . . . ραν δεδ[ιὼς . . . . . .]ιν κατέφ[υγ]εν.
33 καὶ ταῦτα ὅτι ἀληθῆ λέ[γω, ἀνα]γνώσεται ὑμῖν
πρῶτον μὲν τὸν νόμον [ὃς] οὐκ ἐᾷ τοὺς μετοίκους
ἐξοι[κεῖ]ν ἐ[ν τῷ π]ολέμῳ, ἔπειτα τὴν Τροιζη[νίων]
μαρ[τυ]ρίαν, πρὸς δὲ τούτοις τὸ τῶν [Τροιζηνίω]ν⁵
ψήφισμα ὃ ἐψηφίσαντ[ο τῇ πόλει τῇ ὑμ]ετέρᾳ,⁶ δι᾽
ὃ ὑμεῖς αὐτοὺς [ὑπεδέξασθε] καὶ πολίτας ἐποιήσασθε. ἀνά[γνωθι].

[ΝΟΜΟΣ] ΜΑΡΤΥΡΙΑ [ΨΗΦΙΣΜ]Α

34 λα[βὲ δή μοι⁷ καὶ τὴ]ν τοῦ κηδ[εστ]οῦ αὐτοῦ μα[ρ-
τυρίαν]⁸ . . . . . . μεν ουσια . . . . . ι λατ . . . πα
. . . . κα]ταλειφ[θέντα . . . .
αδ . . . . [ἐ]ξῆς πάλιν ω . . . . . α
. . . . . π . . . . . . [τὴ]ν Ἀντιγόν[αν] . . . .
. . . . . ε . . . . μαρτ[υρ] . . . . .
. . . .

[Desunt versus fere decem.]

35
[col. 17] [πρα]χθέντα⁹ καὶ ὃν [τρ]όπον ἐ[πιβεβούλευκέν]¹⁰ μοι
Ἀθηνογένης, καὶ ὡς ὑμῖν π[ροσενήνεκ]ται.¹¹ τὸν
δὴ καὶ ἰδίᾳ πονηρὸν [καὶ τῆς πόλε]ως¹² τὴν σωτηρίαν
456

had been of service to you in times of danger you should protect them in their misfortune. But this abandoned wretch, who forsook you and was enrolled at Troezen, engaged in nothing that was worthy either of the constitution or the spirit of that city. He treated those who had welcomed him so cruelly that . . . in the Assembly . . . fled.[a] To prove that what I say is true the clerk will read you first the law, which forbids metics to move in war time, then the evidence of the Troezenians and also the Troezenians' decree passed by them in honour of your city, in return for which you welcomed them and made them citizens. Read.

The Law, the Evidence and the Decree

Now take the evidence of the father-in-law [b] . . . the way in which Athenogenes has plotted against me and also his behaviour towards you. If a man has been vicious in his private life and given up hope of

---

[a] The sense appears to be, as Colin suggests, that he was accused in the Assembly of the Troezenians and, fearing punishment, fled back to Athens.

[b] Revillout suggests that the defendant called for the father-in-law to give evidence that Athenogenes had been lavishing all his money on Antigone.

---

[1] ἢ Kenyon. [2] περισωθῆναι Jensen in add.
[3] οὔτε usque ad ἄξιον Jensen.
[4] ὑποδεξαμένοις αὐτὸν Blass.
[5] Τροιζηνίων Blass : αὐτῶν ἐκείνων Kenyon.
[6] τῇ πόλει τῇ ὑμετέρᾳ Diels.
[7] δή μοι Blass : μοι νῦν Revillout.
[8] μαρτυρίαν Blass.
[9] Col. 17 plerumque restituit Blass.
[10] ἐπιβεβούλευκέν Weil. [11] προσενήνεκται Sudhaus.
[12] καὶ τῆς πόλεως Diels.

ἀπελπίσαν[τα καὶ ὑμᾶς¹] ἐγκαταλιπόντα, καὶ παρ'
οὓς ἐξ[ῴκησεν] ἀναστάτους ποιήσαντα, [τοῦτον²
36 ὑμεῖς συν]ειληφότες³ οὐ κολάσετε; κ[αὶ ἐγώ,
ὦ ἄνδρες δι]κασταί, δέομαι ὑμῶν [καὶ ἀντιβολῶ
ἐλεῆσαί]⁴ με, ἐκεῖνο σκεψαμέ[νους, ὅτι προσήκει ἐν
τα]ύτῃ τῇ δίκῃ . . . . ιν ἐλεεῖν οὐ τὸν
φ . . . . [ἐὰ]ν ἁλῷ οὐδὲν πάσχε[ιν]
. . . . δε τοτ . . τι παλ . . . . . .
. . . . . . δ' ἂν ἀ[πο]φύγῃ με . . . .
[ἀπολο]ῦμαι.⁵ οὐ γὰρ ἂν δ[υναίμην] . . . .
ψ . . ν οὐδὲ [π]ολλοστ[ὸν μέρος] . . . .
αν . . . . . αιαχ . . . . ὦ]
ἄνδρ[ες δικ]αστ[αί, ... ς ἐξ . . . .
α[ὑτ]ῶν τ . . . .

[Desunt versus octo vel minus.]

Fragmentum⁶

. . . . αντησο . . . . λεκεν ἄλλοι[ς]
. . . . [τα]ῦτα πέπονθεν τ . . . . ων ἀνα-
λωμ[άτων] . . . . αλυσιτ
. . . . [ὀ]φείλουσ[ι] . . . . ὅποτε
ἀπέλυσεν . . . . . . [ὦ ἄνδ]ρες δικασ[ταί, ο]ὐδεὶς
ὑ[μῶν] . . . . του . . . . κατα

his city's safety ; if he has deserted you and expelled the citizens from the town of his adoption, will you not punish him when he is in your power ? For my part, gentlemen of the jury, I beg you most earnestly to show me mercy. Remember in this trial that you ought to have pity . . . suffer nothing if he is convicted . . .

---

[1] καὶ ὑμᾶς Revillout.
[2] τοῦτον Weil.
[3] συνειληφότες Sudhaus : νῦν εἰληφότες Blass.
[4] ἐλεῆσαί Hager.
[5] ἀποφύγῃ et ἀπολοῦμαι Diels.
[6] Hoc fragmentum in extrema duodecima columna locandum censebat Blass.

IV

SPEECH IN DEFENCE OF EUXENIPPUS

INTRODUCTION

THE Defence of Euxenippus is contained in the same papyrus as that of Lycophron and, like the latter, has been preserved without the name of its author. No specific reference to the speech occurs in ancient writers, but there are three passages in it which, taken together, are sufficient to establish it as the work of Hyperides.[a] The speaker tells us first that, at the trial of Polyeuctus, he was one of ten advocates from the tribe Aegeïs, and secondly that he prosecuted Aristophon of Hazenia and Philocrates of Hagnus.[a] It is known from other sources that Hyperides belonged to the tribe Aegeïs and that he prosecuted a certain Aristophon, probably the Hazenian, and Philocrates also.[b] Thirdly there is a reference in the speech to Agasicles whom Hyperides is known to have mentioned.[c]

The exact date of the speech is uncertain, but it cannot be much earlier than 330 B.C., the approximate date when Olympias obtained control of Molossia, or later than 324 B.C., since the orator Lycurgus, who took part in the trial, died in that year.

Euxenippus was a wealthy Athenian, probably a mine-owner. We learn from the speech that he took

---

[a] § 12, §§ 28 and 29.
[b] Schol. on Aeschin. i. 64. Dem. xix. 116.
[c] § 3. Harpocration, s.v. Ἀγασικλῆς.

no part in politics and was already elderly at the time of the trial, so that he cannot be identified with the Euxenippus recorded as archon for 305 B.C. The circumstances which led to his being accused were as follows.

After the battle of Chaeronea in 338 B.C. Philip restored Oropus to the Athenians. Such land as belonged to the town which was not consecrated ground was divided into five portions among the ten tribes. When the division had been made suspicion arose that a certain mountain, assigned to the tribes Hippothoöntis and Acamantis, was really sacred to the god Amphiaraüs. Accordingly three citizens, including Euxenippus, were appointed to sleep in the God's temple at Oropus in the hope that the truth would be revealed to them. After carrying out this duty Euxenippus reported that he had had a dream, which, it appears, was slightly in favour of the two tribes. There must, however, have remained some room for doubt ; for a certain Polyeuctus, probably of Cydantidae,[a] proposed a measure providing that Hippothoöntis and Acamantis should surrender the land to the God and that the other eight tribes should compensate them for their loss. The bill was defeated and Polyeuctus was fined twenty-five drachmas. It is not known why the penalty was so small ; perhaps the jury were influenced by the fact that Lycurgus supported the bill. In any case, Polyeuctus persisted in his efforts. This time, still with the help of Lycurgus, he sought to impeach Euxenippus, using a fresh argument to the effect that he had been bribed by the two tribes to report the dream in their favour.

[a] Mentioned by Dinarch. i. 58.

HYPERIDES

The speeches for the prosecution are not extant, but they clearly included a number of personal charges, of which the chief were that Euxenippus had pro-Macedonian sympathies and that he had made his money dishonestly. Hyperides assisted the defence and probably spoke second.[a] The jury's verdict is not known.

This speech is the only work of Hyperides which we possess in its entirety. Though in no way exceptional, it is clear and well-balanced, and has enabled modern critics to form a good opinion of its author's powers.

---

[a] The general tone of the speech and especially the words ὁ πρότερος ἐμοῦ λέγων in § 15 support this view. Comparetti's arguments against it are unconvincing. He claims that Hyperides spoke first for the defence, directly following Polyeuctus, the first accuser. Lycurgus, he argues, had not yet spoken, since Hyperides makes no reference to him. ὁ πρότερος ἐμοῦ λέγων he takes to refer to the advocate for the defence at the previous trial, when Polyeuctus incurred his fine. The objection to this argument is that at a public trial both, or all, the accusers spoke first and the defence followed. (See scholiast on Dem. xxii. *init.*) Therefore in this case Lycurgus must have preceded Hyperides; and the first advocate for the defence had probably already answered him when Hyperides rose to speak.

ANALYSIS

465

ΥΠΕΡ ΕΥΞΕΝΙΠΠΟΥ ΕΙΣΑΓΓΕΛΙΑΣ
ΑΠΟΛΟΓΙΑ ΠΡΟΣ ΠΟΛΥΕΥΚΤΟΝ

[col. 1] 'Αλλ' ἔγωγε, ὦ ἄνδρες δικασταί, ὅπερ καὶ πρὸς
τοὺς παρακαθημένους ἀρτίως ἔλεγον, θαυμάζω εἰ
μὴ προσίστανται ἤδη ὑμῖν αἱ τοιαῦται εἰσαγγελίαι.
τὸ μὲν γὰρ πρότερον εἰσηγγέλλοντο παρ' ὑμῖν
Τιμόμαχος καὶ Λεωσθένης καὶ Καλλίστρατος καὶ
Φίλων ὁ ἐξ 'Αναίων[1] καὶ Θεότιμος ὁ Σηστὸν ἀπ-
ολέσας καὶ ἕτεροι τοιοῦτοι· καὶ οἱ μὲν αὐτῶν ναῦς
αἰτίαν ἔχοντες προδοῦναι, οἱ δὲ πόλεις 'Αθηναίων,
2 ὁ δὲ ῥήτωρ ὢν λέγειν μὴ τὰ ἄριστα τῷ δήμῳ. καὶ
οὔτε τούτων πέντε ὄντων οὐδεὶς ὑπέμεινε τὸν
ἀγῶνα, ἀλλ' αὐτοὶ ᾤχοντο φεύγοντες ἐκ τῆς πό-
[col. 2] λεως, οὔτ' ἄλλοι πολλοὶ τῶν εἰσαγγελλομένων,
ἀλλ' ἦν σπάνιον ἰδεῖν ἀπ' εἰσαγγελίας τινὰ κρινόμενον ὑπακούσαντα εἰς τὸ δικαστήριον· οὕτως
ὑπὲρ μεγάλων ἀδικημάτων καὶ περιφανῶν αἱ εἰσαγγελίαι τότε ἦσαν. νυνὶ δὲ τὸ γιγνόμενον ἐν τῇ
3 πόλει πάνυ καταγέλαστόν ἐστιν. Διογνίδης μὲν καὶ

---

[1] ἐξ 'Αναίων] Αἰξωνεὺς ci. Schneidewin.

---

[a] The opening words are the same as those of the speech
against Demosthenes.

[b] Timomachus was an Athenian general who failed in his
command against Cotys of Thrace (c. 361 B.C.), and on his

466

IN DEFENCE OF EUXENIPPUS

PERSONALLY, gentlemen of the jury, as I was just saying to those seated beside me,[a] I am surprised that you are not tired by now of this kind of impeachment. At one time the men impeached before you were Timomachus, Leosthenes, Callistratus, Philon of Anaea, Theotimus who lost Sestos, and others of the same type.[b] Some were accused of betraying ships, others of giving up Athenian cities, and another, an orator, of speaking against the people's interests. Though there were five of them, not one waited to be tried; they left the city of their own accord and went into exile. The same is true of many others who were impeached. In fact it was a rare thing to see anyone subjected to impeachment appearing in court. So serious and so notorious were the crimes which at that time led to an impeachment. But the present practice in the city is utterly absurd. Diog-

return to Athens was condemned either to death or to a heavy fine. See Dem. xix. 180, and the scholiast on Aeschin. i. 56. Leosthenes, who led an Athenian fleet against Alexander of Pherae (c. 361 B.C.), lost five triremes, was condemned to death at Athens and went into exile. See Aeschin. ii. 124, and Diodor. xv. 95. 2. For Callistratus, a prominent orator, exiled at about the same time and later put to death, see Lycurg. Leocr. 93. Theotimus, also about the year 361, was impeached for losing Sestos to Cotys. Of Philon nothing further is known.

Ἀντίδωρος ὁ μέτοικος εἰσαγγέλλονται ὡς πλέο-
νος μισθοῦντες τὰς αὐλητρίδας ἢ ὁ νόμος κελεύει,
Ἀγασικλῆς[1] δ' ὁ ἐκ Πειραιέως ὅτι εἰς Ἁλιμουσίους
ἐνεγρά[φη,] Εὐξένιππος δ' [ὑπ]ὲρ τῶν ἐνυπνί[ων]
ὧν φησιν ἑω[ρακέ]ναι· ὧν οὐδεμ[ία] δήπου τῶν
[col. 3] αἰτιῶν τούτων οὐδὲν κοινωνεῖ τῷ εἰσαγγελτικῷ
νόμῳ.

4 Καίτοι, ὦ ἄνδρες δικασταί, ἐπὶ τῶν δημοσίων
ἀγώνων οὐ χρὴ τοὺς δικαστὰς πρότερον τὰ καθ'
ἕκαστα τῆς κατηγορίας ὑπομένειν ἀκούειν, πρὶν
⟨ἂν⟩[2] αὐτὸ τὸ κεφάλαιον τοῦ ἀγῶνος καὶ τὴν ἀντι-
γραφὴν ἐξετάσωσιν εἰ ἔστιν ἐκ τῶν νόμων ἢ μή·
οὐ μὰ Δία οὐχ ὥσπερ ἐν τῇ κατηγορίᾳ Πολύευκτος
ἔλεγεν, οὐ φάσκων δεῖν τοὺς ἀπολογουμένους ἰσχυρίζεσθαι τῷ εἰσαγγελτικῷ νόμῳ, ὃς κελεύει κατὰ
τῶν ῥητόρων αὐτῶν τὰς εἰσαγγελίας εἶναι περὶ τοῦ
λέγειν μὴ ⟦οὖ⟧[3] τὰ ἄριστα τῷ δήμῳ, οὐ κατὰ
[col. 4] πάντων Ἀθηναίων. ἐγὼ δὲ οὔτε πρότερον οὐδενὸς
5 ἂν μνησθείην ἢ τούτου, οὔτε πλείους οἶμαι δεῖν
λόγους ποιεῖσθαι περὶ ἄλλου τινὸς ἢ ὅπως ἐν
δημοκρατίᾳ κύριοι οἱ νόμοι ἔσονται, καὶ αἱ εἰσαγγελίαι καὶ αἱ ἄλλαι κρίσεις κατὰ τοὺς νόμους
εἰσίασιν[4] εἰς τὸ δικαστήριον. διὰ τοῦτο γὰρ ὑμεῖς
ὑπὲρ ἁπάντων τῶν ἀδικημάτων, ὅσα ἔστιν ἐν τῇ
πόλει, νόμους ἔθεσθε χωρὶς περὶ ἑκάστου αὐτῶν.
6 ἀσεβεῖ τις περὶ τὰ ἱερά· γραφαὶ[5] ἀσεβείας πρὸς
τὸν βασιλέα.—φαῦλός ἐστι πρὸς τοὺς ἑαυτοῦ γονεῖς·

[1] Ἀγασικλῆς Babington : Ἀγησικλης A.
[2] ἂν add. Schneidewin.
[3] οὖ del. Babington.
[4] εἰσίασιν edd. : εἰσίσασιν A.

nides and Antidorus the metic are impeached on a
charge of hiring out flute-girls at a higher price than
that fixed by law, Agasicles of Piraeus [a] because he
was registered in Halimus, and Euxenippus because
of the dreams which he claims to have had ; though
surely not one of these charges has anything to do
with the impeachment law.

And yet in public trials, gentlemen of the jury, the
jury should refuse to listen to the details of the
prosecution until they have first considered the point
at issue, and also the written statement of the
accused, to see if the pleas are legally valid. It
is certainly wrong to maintain, as Polyeuctus did
in his speech for the prosecution, that defendants
should not insist on the impeachment law ; which
lays it down that impeachments shall be reserved
for the orators themselves, when they speak against
the interests of the people, but shall not apply to
every Athenian. With me this law would have first
claim to notice ; and a point, I think, which should
be dwelt on as much as any, is how to ensure that the
laws in a democracy are binding and that impeachments and other actions brought into court are legally
valid. It was with this in view that you made separate
laws covering individually all offences committed in
the city. Suppose someone commits a religious
offence. There is the method of public prosecution
before the King-Archon. Or he maltreats his parents.

---

[a] Agasicles, according to Harpocration and Suidas (*s.v.*
Ἀγασικλῆς), though an alien, bribed the people of Halimus
to enrol him in their deme. The former adds that Dinarchus
wrote a speech prosecuting him for this. See Dinarch.
frag. 7.

---

[5] γραφαὶ] γράφεται Schneidewin : post γραφαὶ add. εἰσιν
Cobet.

ὁ ἄρχων ἐπὶ τούτου κάθηται.—παράνομά τις ἐν τῇ
[col. 5] πόλει γράφει· θεσμοθετῶν συνέδριον ἔστι.—ἀπα-
γωγῆς ἄξια ποιεῖ· ἀρχὴ τῶν ἔνδεκα καθέστηκε.—
τὸν αὐτὸν δὲ τρόπον καὶ ἐπὶ τῶν ἄλλων ἀδικημάτων
ἁπάντων καὶ νόμους καὶ ἀρχὰς καὶ δικαστήρια τὰ
7 προσήκοντα ἑκάστοις αὐτῶν ἀπέδοτε. ὑπὲρ τίνων
οὖν οἴεσθε¹ δεῖν τὰς εἰσαγγελίας γίγνεσθαι; τοῦτ'
ἤδη καθ' ἕκαστον ἐν τῷ νόμῳ ἐγράψατε, ἵνα μὴ
ἀγνοῇ μηδείς· " ἐάν τις," φησί, " τὸν δῆμον τὸν
Ἀθηναίων καταλύῃ"—εἰκότως, ὦ ἄνδρες δικασταί·
ἡ γὰρ τοιαύτη αἰτία οὐ παραδέχεται σκῆψι[ν ο]ὐ-
[col. 6] δεμίαν οὐδενὸς οὐδ' ὑπωμοσίαν, ἀλλὰ τὴν ταχίστην
8 αὐτὴν δεῖ εἶναι ἐν τῷ δικαστηρίῳ·—ἢ " συνίῃ ποι
ἐπὶ καταλύσει τοῦ δήμου ἢ ἑταιρικὸν συναγάγῃ,
ἢ ἐάν τις πόλιν τινὰ προδῷ ἢ ναῦς ἢ πεζὴν ἢ ναυτικὴν στρατιάν, ἢ ῥήτωρ ὢν μὴ λέγῃ τὰ ἄριστα
τῷ δήμῳ τῷ Ἀθηναίων χρήματα λαμβάνων"· τὰ
μὲν ἄνω τοῦ νόμου κατὰ πάντων τῶν πολιτῶν
γράψαντες (ἐκ πάντων γὰρ καὶ τἀδικήματα ταῦτα
γένοιτ' ἄν), τὸ δὲ τελευταῖον τοῦ νόμου κατ' αὐτῶν
τῶν ῥητόρων, παρ' οἷς ἔστιν καὶ τὸ γράφειν τὰ
9 ψηφίσματα. ἐμαίνεσθε γὰρ ἄν, εἰ ἄλλον τινὰ
τρόπον τὸν νόμον τοῦτον ἔθεσθε ἢ οὕτως· εἰ τὰς
[col. 7] μὲν τιμὰς καὶ τὰς ὠφελίας ἐκ τοῦ λέγειν οἱ ῥήτορες
καρποῦνται, τοὺς δὲ κινδύνους ὑπὲρ αὐτῶν τοῖς

¹ οἴεσθε] ὤεσθε Cobet.

ᵃ The King-Archon, who supervised all religious ceremonies
of state, judged all cases connected with religion, while the
Archon himself dealt with family law. (See Aristot. *Ath.
Pol.* 57. 2 and 56. 6.) For the Thesmothetae compare Hyp.
i. 12 and note. Summary arrest could be legally employed

The Archon presides over his case. Someone makes illegal proposals in the city. There is the board of Thesmothetae ready. Perhaps he does something involving summary arrest. You have the authority of the Eleven.[a] Similarly, to deal with every other offence you have established laws, offices, and courts appropriate to each. In what cases then do you think impeachments should be used ? Your answer has already been embodied in detail in the law, so as to leave no room for doubt. " If any person," it says, " seeks to overthrow the democracy of the Athenians." Naturally, gentlemen of the jury ; for a charge like that admits of no excuse from anyone nor of an oath for postponement.[b] It should come directly into court. " Or if he attends a meeting in any place with intent to undermine the democracy, or forms a political society ; or if anyone betrays a city, or ships, or any land, or naval force, or being an orator, makes speeches contrary to the interests of the Athenian people, receiving bribes." The opening provisions of the law were made applicable by you to the entire citizen body, since those are offences which anyone might commit ; but the latter part is directed against the orators themselves, in whose hands the proposing of measures rests. You would have been insane if you had framed the law in any other way ; if, when the orators enjoy both the honours and the profits of speaking, you had exposed the ordinary citizen

---

[a] against three classes of criminal. Of these, two were tried by the Eleven and one by the Thesmothetae. (See Aristot. *Ath. Pol.* 52. 1.)

[b] A man due to be tried could offer the court an excuse (σκῆψις) and provide a second party to take an oath (ὑπωμοσία) that this excuse was true. In such cases the jury might grant a postponement.

ἰδιώταις ἀνεθήκατε. ἀλλ' ὅμως Πολύευκτος οὕτως
ἐστὶν ἀνδρεῖος, ὥστε εἰσαγγελίαν διώκων οὐκ ἔφη
δεῖν τοὺς φεύγοντας τῷ εἰσαγγελτικῷ νόμῳ χρῆ-
10 σθαι. καὶ οἱ μὲν ἄλλοι πάντες κατήγοροι, ὅταν
οἴωνται δεῖν ἐν τῷ προτέρῳ λόγῳ ὑφελεῖν τῶν
φευγόντων τὰς ἀπολογίας, τοῦτο παρακελεύονται
τοῖς δικασταῖς, μὴ ἐθέλειν ἀκούειν τῶν ἀπολογου-
μένων, ἐάν τινες ἔξω τοῦ νόμου λέγωσιν, ἀλλ'
ἀπαντᾶν πρὸς τὰ λεγόμενα καὶ κελεύειν τὸν νόμον
[col. 8] ἀναγιγνώσκειν· σὺ δὲ τοὐναντίον τὴν εἰς τοὺς
νόμους καταφυγὴν ἐκ τῆς ἀπολογίας οἴει δεῖν
ἀφελέσθαι Εὐξενίππου.

11　Καὶ πρὸς τούτοις οὐδὲ βοηθεῖν οὐδένα φῂς δεῖν
αὐτῷ οὐδὲ συναγορεύειν, ἀλλὰ παρακελεύῃ τοῖς
δικασταῖς μὴ θέλειν ἀκούειν τῶν ἀναβαινόντων.
καίτοι τί τού⟨του⟩ τῶν¹ ἐν τῇ πόλει βέλτιον ἢ
δ[ημο]τικώτερόν ἐστι, πολλῶν καὶ ἄλλων καλῶν
ὄντων, ἢ ὁπόταν τις ἰδιώτης εἰς ἀγῶνα καὶ κίνδυνον
καταστὰς μὴ δύνηται ὑπὲρ ἑαυτοῦ ἀπολογεῖσθαι,
τούτῳ τὸν βουλόμενον τῶν πολιτῶν ἐξεῖναι ἀνα-
βάντα βοηθῆσαι καὶ τοὺς δικαστὰς ὑπὲρ τοῦ πράγ-
[col. 9] ματος τὰ δίκαια διδάξαι; ἀλλὰ νὴ Δία αὐτὸς
12 τοιούτῳ πράγματι οὐ κέχρησαι, ἀλλ' ὅτ' ἔφευγες
τὸν ἀγῶνα ὑπ' Ἀλεξάνδρου τοῦ ἐξ Οἴου, δέκα μὲν
συνηγόρους ἐκ τῆς Αἰγηΐδος φυλῆς ᾐτήσω, ὧν καὶ
ἐγὼ εἷς ἦν αἱρεθεὶς ὑπὸ σοῦ, ἐκ δὲ τῶν ἄλλων
Ἀθηναίων ἐκάλεις ἐπὶ τὸ δικαστήριον τοὺς βοηθή-
σοντάς σοι. καὶ τὰ μὲν ἄλλα τί δεῖ λέγειν; αὐτῷ
δὲ τούτῳ τῷ ἀγῶνι πῶς κέχρησαι; οὐ κατηγό-

to the risks that go with them. Nevertheless, Polyeuctus is bold enough to assert, though he is bringing in an impeachment, that defendants must not make use of the impeachment law. All other prosecutors who think it necessary, when speaking first, to steal the defendants' arguments from them encourage the jury to refuse to listen to any defendant who does not keep within the scope of the law, to challenge his statements and tell the clerk to read the law. The opposite is true of you : it is recourse to law of which you think you should deprive Euxenippus in his defence.

You also maintain that no one should even help him or be his advocate, and you exhort the jury to refuse a hearing to those who come up to speak. And yet, of the many good institutions of the city, what is better or more democratic [a] than our custom, when some private person is facing the danger of a trial and cannot conduct his own defence, of allowing any citizen who wishes to come forward to help him and give the jury a fair statement of the case ? You will claim, no doubt, that you have never worked on such a principle. Yet when you were prosecuted by Alexander of Oeon,[b] you asked for ten advocates from the tribe Aegeïs, and I was one of them, chosen by yourself. You also summoned men from other tribes into the court to help you. But why should I mention other instances ? Take your handling of the present trial. Did you not make as many accusa-

---

[a] Compare Hyp.: i. 10.
[b] Nothing further is known of this trial. For other occasions on which Hyperides opposed Polyeuctus compare Fragments 24 and 25.

---

[1] τούτου τῶν Cobet : τοῦ τῶν A.

ρησας ὁπόσα ἐβούλου; οὐ Λυκοῦργον ἐκάλεις
συγκατηγορήσοντα, οὔτε τῷ λέγειν οὐδενὸς τῶν ἐν
τῇ πόλει καταδεέστερον ὄντα, παρὰ τούτοις τε
13 μέτριον καὶ ἐπιεικῆ δοκοῦντα εἶναι; εἶτα σοὶ μὲν
[col. 10] ἔξεστι καὶ φεύγοντι τοὺς βοηθήσοντας καλεῖν καὶ
διώκοντι τοὺς συγκατηγόρους ἀναβιβάσασθαι, ὃς
οὐ μόνον ὑπὲρ σεαυτοῦ δύνασαι εἰπεῖν, ἀλλὰ καὶ
ὅλῃ¹ πόλει πράγματα παρέχειν ἱκανὸς εἶ, Εὐξενίππῳ δ' ὅτι ἰδιώτης ἐστὶ καὶ πρεσβύτερος οὐδὲ
τοὺς φίλους καὶ τοὺς οἰκείους ἐξέσται βοηθεῖν, εἰ
δὲ μή, διαβληθήσονται ὑπὸ σοῦ;
14 Νὴ Δία, τὰ γὰρ πεπραγμένα αὐτῷ δεινά ἐστι
καὶ ἄξια θανάτου, ὡς σὺ λέγεις ἐν τῇ κατηγορίᾳ.
σκέψασθε δή, ὦ ἄνδρες δικασταί, καθ' ἓν ἕκαστον
αὐτῶν ἐξετάζοντες. ὁ δῆμος προσέταξεν Εὐξενίππῳ τρίτῳ αὐτῷ ἐγκατακλιθῆναι εἰς τὸ ἱερόν,
[col. 11] οὗτος δὲ κοιμηθεὶς ἐνύπνιόν φησιν ἰδεῖν, ὃ τῷ
δήμῳ ἀπαγγεῖλαι. τοῦτ' εἰ μὲν ὑπελάμβανες
ἀληθὲς εἶναι, καὶ ὃ εἶδεν ἐν τῷ ὕπνῳ τοῦτ' αὐτὸν
ἀπαγγεῖλαι πρὸς τὸν δῆμον, τί καὶ ἀδικεῖ, ἃ ὁ θεὸς
αὐτῷ προσέταττε ταῦτ' ἐξαγγείλας πρὸς Ἀθη-
15 ναίους; εἰ δέ, ὥσπερ νυνὶ λέγεις, ἡγοῦ αὐτὸν
καταψεύσασθαι τοῦ θεοῦ καὶ χαριζόμενόν τισι μὴ
τἀληθῆ ἀπηγγελκέναι τῷ δήμῳ, οὐ ψήφισμα ἐχρῆν
σε πρὸς τὸ ἐνύπνιον γράφειν, ἀλλ' ὅπερ ὁ πρότερος
ἐμοῦ λέγων εἶπεν, εἰς Δελφοὺς πέμψαντα πυθέσθαι
παρὰ τοῦ θεοῦ τὴν ἀλήθειαν. σὺ δὲ τοῦτο μὲν οὐκ
ἐποίησας, ψήφισμα δὲ αὐτοτελές. ἔγραψας κατὰ

¹ Post ὅλῃ add. τῇ Cobet.

ª I follow Colin's interpretation of the word αὐτοτελής in
this passage, although it was often used technically to

tions as you wished ? Did you not call Lycurgus to join you in the prosecution, a speaker who is the equal of any in the city and who has the reputation among these gentlemen of being sound and honourable ? If you then, as a defendant, may summon advocates, or as a prosecutor may bring in co-prosecutors—you who are not merely capable of speaking for yourself but well able to give a whole city trouble —is Euxenippus, because he is not a professional speaker and is now advanced in years, even to be denied the help of friends and relatives, on pain of their being abused by you ?

Yes ; for in the words of your indictment, his conduct has been scandalous and deserves the death penalty. Gentlemen of the jury, will you please review it and scrutinize it point by point ? The people ordered Euxenippus, as one of three, to lie down in the temple ; and he tells us that he fell asleep and had a dream which he reported to them. If you assumed, Polyeuctus, that this was true and that he reported to the people what he actually saw in his sleep, why is he to blame for notifying the Athenians of the commands which the god had been giving him ? If on the other hand, as you now maintain, you thought that he misrepresented the god and, out of partiality for certain persons, had made a false report to the people, rather than propose a decree disputing the dream you ought to have sent to Delphi, as the previous speaker said, and inquired the truth from the god. But instead of doing that, you proposed a decree, entirely conceived by yourself,[a] against two

describe a decree laid before the people without previous consideration by the Council (see Hesychius, *s.v.* αὐτοτελὲς ψήφισμα).

[col. 12] δυοῖν φυλαῖν οὐ μόνον ἀδικώτατον, ἀλλὰ καὶ ἐναντίον αὐτὸ ἑαυτῷ· δι' ὅπερ ἥλως παρανόμων, οὐ δι'
Εὐξένιππον.

16 Ἐξετάσωμεν δὲ περὶ αὐτοῦ τουτονὶ τὸν τρόπον.
αἱ φυλαὶ σύνδυο γενόμεναι τὰ ὅρη τὰ ἐν Ὠρωπῷ
διείλοντο, τοῦ δήμου αὐταῖς δόντος. τοῦτο τὸ ὅρος
ἔλαχεν[1] Ἀκαμαντὶς καὶ Ἱπποθοωντίς. ταύτας τὰς
φυλὰς ἔγραψας ἀποδοῦναι τὸ ὅρος τῷ Ἀμφιαράῳ
καὶ τὴν τιμὴν ὧν ἀπέδοντο, ὡς πρότερον τοὺς
ὁριστὰς τοὺς πεντήκοντα ἐξελόντας αὐτὸ τῷ θεῷ
καὶ ἀφορίσαντας, καὶ οὐ προσηκόντως τὰς δύο
17 φυλὰς ἐχούσας τὸ ὅρος. μικρὸν δὲ διαλιπὼν ἐν
ταὐτῷ ψηφίσματι γράφεις τὰς ὀκτὼ φυλὰς πορί-
[col. 13] σαι[2] τοῖν[3] δυοῖν φυλαῖν τὰ διάφορα καὶ ἀποδοῦναι,
ὅπως ἂν μὴ ἐλαττῶνται. καίτοι εἰ μὲν ἴδιον ⟨ὂν⟩[4]
τῶν φυλῶν ἀφῃροῦ τὸ ὅρος, πῶς οὐκ ὀργῆς ἄξιος
⟨εἶ⟩;[5] εἰ δὲ μὴ προσηκόντως εἶχον αὐτό, ἀλλὰ τοῦ
θεοῦ ὄν, διὰ τί τὰς ἄλλας φυλὰς ἔγραφες αὐταῖς
προσαποδιδόναι ἀργύριον; ἀγαπητὸν γὰρ ἦν αὐταῖς εἰ τὰ τοῦ θεοῦ ἀποδώσουσιν καὶ μὴ προσ-
αποτείσουσιν ἀργύριον.

18 Ταῦτ' ἐν τῷ δικαστηρίῳ ἐξεταζόμενα οὐκ ὀρθῶς
ἐδόκει γεγράφθαι, ἀλλὰ κατεψηφίσαντό σου οἱ δικασταί. εἶτ' εἰ μὲν ἀπέφυγες τὴν γραφήν, οὐκ
ἂν κατεψεύσατο οὗτος τοῦ θεοῦ, ἐπειδὴ δὲ συνέβη
σοι ἀλῶναι, Εὐξένιππον δεῖ ἀπολωλέναι; καὶ σοὶ
[col. 14] μὲν τῷ τοιοῦτο ψήφισμα γράψαντι πέντε καὶ εἴκοσι

---

[1] ἔλαχεν] ἔλαχον Cobet.
[2] πορίσαι Cobet : ποιῆσαι A.
[3] τοῖν Westermann : ταν A.
[4] ὂν add. Cobet.
[5] εἶ add. Schneidewin.

tribes, a measure not only most unjust but self-contradictory also. This was what caused your conviction for illegal proposals. It was not the fault of Euxenippus.

Let us consider it in this way. The tribes, formed into groups of two, shared out the mountains in Oropus awarded to them by the people. This mountain fell to the lot of Acamantis and Hippothoöntis. You proposed that these tribes should restore the mountain to Amphiaraüs and the price of produce from it which they had sold; your reason being that the fifty boundary officials had selected it beforehand and set it apart for the god, and that the two tribes had no right to be holding it. A little later in the same decree you propose that the eight tribes shall provide compensation and pay it to the other two so that they shall not suffer unfairly. But if the mountain really belonged to the two tribes and you tried to take it from them, surely we are entitled to be angry. Alternatively, if they had no right to be occupying it and it belonged to the god, why were you proposing that the other tribes should actually pay them compensation? They should have been well content that when restoring the property of the god they did not also pay a fine in cash.

These proposals, when examined in court, were considered unsatisfactory, and the jury condemned you. So if you had been acquitted in your trial, Euxenippus would not have misrepresented the god: because you happened to be convicted, must ruin fall on him? [a] And when you, who proposed a decree like

___
[a] Apparently it was loss of prestige which caused Polyeuctus to be resentful against Euxenippus, since the actual fine was negligible.

δραχμῶν ἐτιμήθη, τὸν δὲ κατακλιθέντα εἰς τὸ ἱερὸν
τοῦ δήμου κελεύσαντος μηδ' ἐν τῇ Ἀττικῇ δεῖ
τεθάφθαι;

19 Ναί[1]· δεινὰ γὰρ ἐποίησεν περὶ τὴν φιάλην, ἐάσας
Ὀλυμπιάδα ἀναθεῖναι εἰς τὸ ἄγαλμα τῆς Ὑγιείας.
τοῦτο γὰρ ὑπολαμβάνεις, ἐφόδιον ἑαυτῷ εἰς τὸν
ἀγῶνα τὸ ἐκείνης ὄνομα παραφέρων καὶ κολακείαν
ψευδῆ κατηγορῶν Εὐξενίππου, μῖσος καὶ ὀργὴν
αὐτῷ συλλέξειν παρὰ τῶν δικαστῶν. δεῖ δέ, ὦ
βέλτιστε, μὴ ἐπὶ τῷ Ὀλυμπιάδος ὀνόματι καὶ τῷ
[col. 15] Ἀλεξάνδρου τῶν πολιτῶν τινα ζητεῖν κακόν τι
20 ἐργάσασθαι, ἀλλ' ὅταν ἐκεῖνοι πρὸς τὸν δῆμον τὸν
Ἀθηναίων ἐπιστέλλωσι μὴ τὰ δίκαια μηδὲ τὰ
προσήκοντα, τότε ἀναστάντα ὑπὲρ τῆς πόλεως
ἀντιλέγειν καὶ πρὸς τοὺς ἥκοντας παρ' αὐτῶν
δικαιολογεῖσθαι καὶ εἰς τὸ κοινὸν τῶν Ἑλλήνων
συνέδριον πορεύεσθαι βοηθήσοντα τῇ πατρίδι. σὺ
δ' ἐκεῖ μὲν οὐδεπώποτε ἀνέστης οὐδὲ λόγον περὶ
αὐτῶν ἐποίησω, ἐνθάδε δὲ μισεῖς Ὀλυμπιάδα ἐπὶ
21 τῷ ἀπολέσαι Εὐξένιππον, καὶ φῂς κόλακα αὐτὸν
εἶναι ἐκείνης καὶ Μακεδόνων· ὃν ἐὰν δείξῃς ἀφιγ-
[col. 16] μένον πώποτε εἰς Μακεδονίαν, ἢ ἐκείνων τινὰ ὑπο-
δεξάμενον εἰς τὴν αὐτοῦ οἰκίαν, ἢ χρώμενον τῶν
ἐκεῖθέν τινι ἢ ἐντυγχάνοντα, ἢ λόγους καὶ οὑστι-
νασοῦν ἢ ἐπ' ἐργαστηρίου ἢ ἐν τῇ ἀγορᾷ ἢ ἄλλοθί
που περὶ τούτων τῶν πραγμάτων εἰρηκότα, καὶ μὴ
κοσμίως καὶ μετρίως τὰ αὐτοῦ πράττοντα ὥσπερ

---

[1] τεθάφθαι. Ναί Kayser (coll. Hyp. ii. 10 ; Dinarch i. 7) :
τεταφναι A (litteris θαι in margine additis).

---

[a] Olympias, mother of Alexander the Great, was sent by
him about 331 B.C. to Epirus, where her brother Alexander
was king. On the death of the latter she became regent for
478

that, were fined a mere twenty-five drachmas, is the man who lay down in the temple at the people's request even to be refused a grave in Attica ?

Yes, you say ; for he committed a serious crime in regard to the cup which he allowed Olympias to dedicate to the statue of Health.[a] You think that if you bring her name irrelevantly into the case to serve your own ends and accuse Euxenippus of deceitful flattery, you will bring down the jury's hatred and anger upon him. The thing to do, my friend, is not to use the name of Olympias and Alexander in the hope of harming some citizen. Wait till they send the Athenian people some injunctions which are unjust or inappropriate. Then is the time for you to get up and oppose them in the interests of your city, disputing the cause of justice with their envoys and resorting to the Congress of the Greeks[b] as the champion of your country. But you never stood up or spoke about them there ; it is only here that you hate Olympias so that you can ruin Euxenippus by alleging that he flatters her and the Macedonians. If you show us that he has ever been to Macedon or entertained any of the people in his own home, that he knows a Macedonian intimately or meets any of them ; if you prove that he has said one word about such matters, either in a shop or in the market or anywhere else, instead of quietly and modestly mind-

---

the young prince Neoptolemus and so controlled Molossia, which had been attached to the kingdom by Philip in 343 B.C. The statue of Health stood on the Acropolis. (See Paus. i. 23. 5.) It is not known how Euxenippus was connected with this affair.

[b] The Congress, which united all Greek states except Sparta, was founded by Philip after the battle of Chaeronea in 338 B.C.

εἴ τις καὶ ἄλλος τῶν πολιτῶν, χρησάσθωσαν αὐτῷ
22 οἱ δικασταὶ ὅ τι βούλονται. εἰ γὰρ ταῦτα ἦν ἀληθῆ
ἃ κατηγορεῖς, οὐκ ἂν σὺ μόνος ᾔδεις, ἀλλὰ καὶ οἱ
ἄλλοι πάντες οἱ ἐν τῇ πόλει· ὥσπερ καὶ περὶ τῶν
ἄλλων ὅσοι τι ὑπὲρ ἐκείνων ἢ λέγουσιν ἢ πράτ-
[col. 17] τουσιν, οὐ μόνον αὐτοί,[1] ἀλλὰ καὶ οἱ ἄλλοι Ἀθηναῖοι
ἴσασι καὶ τὰ παιδία τὰ ἐκ τῶν διδασκαλείων καὶ
τῶν ῥητόρων τοὺς παρ' ἐκείνων μισθαρνοῦντας καὶ
τῶν ἄλλων τοὺς ξενίζοντας τοὺς ἐκεῖθεν ἥκοντας
καὶ ὑποδεχομένους καὶ εἰς τὰς ὁδοὺς ὑπαντῶντας
ὅταν προσίωσι·[2] καὶ οὐδαμοῦ ὄψει οὐδὲ παρ' ἑνὶ
23 τούτων Εὐξένιππον καταριθμούμενον. σὺ δ' ἐκείνων μὲν οὐδένα κρίνεις οὐδ' εἰς ἀγῶνα καθίστῃς,
οὓς πάντες ἴσασι ταῦτα πράττοντας, κατ' Εὐξενίππου δὲ κολακείαν κατηγορεῖς, οὗ ὁ βίος τὴν
[col. 18] αἰτίαν οὐ παραδέχεται. καίτοι, εἰ νοῦν εἶχες, περί
γε τῆς φιάλης τῆς ἀνατεθείσης οὔτ' ἂν Εὐξένιππον
ᾐτιῶ, οὔτ' ἂν ἄλλον λόγον οὐδένα ἐνταῦθα ἐποιήσω·
οὐ γὰρ ἁρμόττει. διὰ τί; καί μου τὸν λόγον, ὦ
ἄνδρες δικασταί, ἀκούσατε, ὃν μέλλω λέγειν.

24 Ὑμῖν Ὀλυμπιὰς ἐγκλήματα πεποίηται περὶ τὰ
ἐν Δωδώνῃ οὐ δίκαια, ὡς ἐγὼ δὶς ἤδη ἐν τῷ δήμῳ
ἐναντίον ὑμῶν καὶ τῶν ἄλλων Ἀθηναίων πρὸς τοὺς
ἥκοντας παρ' αὐτῆς ἐξήλεγξα οὐ προσήκοντα αὐτὴν
ἐγκλήματα τῇ πόλει ἐγκαλοῦσαν. ὑμῖν γὰρ ὁ Ζεὺς
ὁ Δωδωναῖος προσέταξεν ἐν τῇ μαντείᾳ τὸ ἄγαλμα
[col. 19] τῆς Διώνης ἐπικοσμῆσαι· καὶ ὑμεῖς πρόσωπόν τε
25 ποιησάμενοι[3] ὡς οἷόν τε κάλλιστον καὶ τἆλλα πάντα

---

[1] αὐτοί] οὗτοι Cobet.
[2] προσίωσι] προΐωσι Cobet.
[3] ποιησάμενοι Kayser : κοσμησάμενοι A : κομισάμενοι Comparetti.

480

ing his own business as much as any other citizen,
the jury may do what they like with him. For if
these charges of yours were true, not only you but
everyone else in the city would know the facts, as
is the case with all the others who speak or act in the
interests of Macedon. Their conduct is no secret.
The rest of Athens, even the schoolchildren, know
the orators who take Macedonian money and the
other persons who put up Macedonian visitors, either
secretly making them welcome or going into the
streets to meet them when they arrive. You will not
see Euxenippus classed with a single one of these men
anywhere. But you do not prosecute or bring to
trial any of the people who are universally known
to be doing these things, and yet you accuse Euxenippus of flattery when his manner of life disproves the
charge. And yet if you had any sense, you would
neither be blaming Euxenippus for the dedication of
the cup nor have made any further mention of the
affair, since it is impolitic to do so. Why is that ?
Will you please listen, gentlemen of the jury, to the
account which I am going to give ?

Olympias has made complaints against you about
the incident at Dodona,[a] complaints which are unfair,
as I have twice already proved in the Assembly before
yourselves and the rest of Athens. I explained to
her envoys that the charges she brings against the
city are not justified. For Zeus of Dodona commanded
you through the oracle to embellish the statue of
Dione. You made a face as beautiful as you could,
together with all the other appropriate parts ; and

---

[a] Dodona in Epirus was, second to Delphi, the most famous
oracle of Greece. Dione, a consort of Zeus, was often wor-
shipped in his temples.

τὰ ἀκόλουθα, καὶ κόσμον πολὺν καὶ πολυτελῆ τῇ
θεῷ παρασκευάσαντες, καὶ θεωρίαν καὶ θυσίαν
πολλῶν χρημάτων ἀποστείλαντες, ἐπεκοσμήσατε
τὸ ἕδος τῆς Διώνης ἀξίως καὶ ὑμῶν αὐτῶν καὶ τῆς
θεοῦ. ὑπὲρ τούτων ὑμῖν τὰ ἐγκλήματα ἦλθε παρ'
Ὀλυμπιάδος ἐν ταῖς ἐπιστολαῖς, ὡς ἡ χώρα εἴη
ἡ Μολοττία[1] αὐτῆς, ἐν ᾗ τὸ ἱερόν ἐστιν· οὔκουν
26 προσήκειν[2] ἡμᾶς τῶν ἐκεῖ οὐδὲ ἓν κινεῖν. ἐὰν μὲν
τοίνυν τὰ περὶ τὴν φιάλην γεγονότα ἐν ἀδικήματι
[col. 20] ψηφίσησθε εἶναι, τρόπον τινὰ καὶ ἡμῶν αὐτῶν
καταγιγνώσκομεν ὡς τὰ ἐκεῖ οὐκ ὀρθῶς ἐπράξαμεν·
ἐὰν δ' ἐπὶ τοῦ γεγενημένου ἐῶμεν, τὰς τραγῳδίας
αὐτῆς καὶ τὰς κατηγορίας ἀφῃρηκότες ἐσόμεθα.
οὐ γὰρ δήπου Ὀλυμπιάδι μὲν τὰ Ἀθήνησιν ἱερὰ
ἐπικοσμεῖν ἔξεστιν, ἡμῖν δὲ τὰ ἐν Δωδώνῃ οὐκ
ἐξέσται, καὶ ταῦτα τοῦ θεοῦ προστάξαντος.
27 Ἀλλ' οὐκ ἔστιν, ὦ Πολύευκτε, ὡς ἐμοὶ δοκεῖς,
ὅθεν κατηγορίαν οὐκ ἂν ποιήσαιο. καίτοι σε ἐχρῆν,
ἐπείπερ προῄρησαι πολιτεύεσθαι, καὶ νὴ Δία καὶ
δύνασαι, μὴ τοὺς ἰδιώτας κρίνειν μηδ' εἰς τούτους
[col. 21] νεανιεύεσθαι, ἀλλὰ τῶν ῥητόρων ἐάν τις ἀδικῇ,
τοῦτον κρίνειν, στρατηγὸς ἐάν τις μὴ τὰ δίκαια
πράττῃ, τοῦτον εἰσαγγέλλειν· παρὰ γὰρ τούτοις
ἐστὶ καὶ τὸ δύνασθαι βλάπτειν τὴν πόλιν, ὅσοι ἂν
αὐτῶν προαιρῶνται, οὐ παρ' Εὐξενίππῳ οὐδὲ τῶν
28 δικαστῶν τούτων οὐδενί. καὶ οὐ σὲ μὲν οὕτως
οἴομαι δεῖν πράττειν, αὐτὸς δὲ ἄλλον τινὰ τρόπον
τῇ πολιτείᾳ κέχρημαι, ἀλλ' οὐδ' αὐτὸς ἰδιώτην
οὐδένα πώποτε ἐν τῷ βίῳ ἔκρινα, ἤδη δέ τισι καθ'

having prepared a great deal of expensive finery for the goddess and dispatched envoys with a sacrifice at great expense, you embellished the statue of Dione in a manner worthy of yourselves and of the goddess. These measures brought you the complaints of Olympias, who said in her letters that the country of Molossia, in which the temple stands, belonged to her, and that therefore we had no right to interfere with anything there at all. Now if you decide that the incidents relating to the cup constitute an offence, we are in a sense condemning ourselves as being wrong in what we did at Dodona. But if we acquiesce in what has been done we shall have taken away her right to these theatrical complaints and accusations. For I presume that when Olympias can furnish ornaments for shrines in Athens we may safely do so at Dodona, particularly when the god demands it.

However, it seems to me, Polyeuctus, that there is nothing which you would not use as grounds for an accusation. But from the time when you decided to play a part in public life, for which I admit you are well fitted, you should not have prosecuted private individuals or made them the victims of your impudence. Wait for an orator to commit a crime and then prosecute him, or for a general to do wrong and then impeach him. These are the men who have power to harm the city, all of them who choose to do so, not Euxenippus or any member of this jury. It is not as if I were prescribing one line of conduct for you having followed another in my own public life. I myself never in my life prosecuted any private citizen, and there are some whom before now I have

---

[1] Μολοττία Lightfoot : Μολοσσία A : del. Cobet.
[2] προσήκειν Cobet : προσῆκεν A.

ὅσον ἐδυνάμην ἐβοήθησα. τίνας οὖν κέκρικα καὶ εἰς
ἀγῶνα καθέστακα; ᾿Αριστοφῶντα τὸν ᾿Αζηνιέα,[1]
[col. 22] ὃς ἰσχυρότατος ἐν τῇ πολιτείᾳ γεγένηται (καὶ οὗτος
ἐν τούτῳ τῷ δικαστηρίῳ παρὰ δύο ψήφους ἀπ-
29 έφυγε)· Διοπείθη τὸν Σφήττιον, ὃς δεινότατος
ἐδόκει[2] εἶναι τῶν ἐν τῇ πόλει· Φιλοκράτη τὸν
᾿Αγνούσιον, ὃς θρασύτατα καὶ ἀσελγέστατα τῇ πολιτείᾳ κέχρηται. τοῦτον εἰσαγγείλας ἐγὼ ὑπὲρ ὧν
Φιλίππῳ ὑπηρέτει ⟦καὶ⟧[3] κατὰ τῆς πόλεως, εἷλον
ἐν τῷ δικαστηρίῳ, καὶ τὴν εἰσαγγελίαν ἔγραψα δικαίαν καὶ ὥσπερ ὁ νόμος κελεύει, '' ῥήτορα ὄντα
λέγειν μὴ τὰ ἄριστα τῷ δήμῳ τῷ ᾿Αθηναίων χρήματα λαμβάνοντα καὶ δωρεὰς παρὰ τῶν τἀναντία
30 πραττόντων τῷ δήμῳ''· καὶ οὐδ᾿ οὕτως ἀπέχρησέ
[col. 23] μοι τὴν εἰσαγγελίαν ⟦ἂν⟧[4] δοῦναι, ἀλλ᾿ ὑποκάτω
παρέγραψα· '' τάδ᾿ εἶπεν οὐ τὰ ἄριστα τῷ δήμῳ
χρήματα λαβών,'' εἶτα τὸ ψήφισμα αὐτοῦ ὑπέγραψα·
καὶ πάλιν, '' τάδε εἶπεν οὐ τὰ ἄριστα τῷ δήμῳ
χρήματα λαβών,'' καὶ τὸ ψήφισμα παρέγραφον.
καὶ ἔστι μοι πεντάκις ἢ ἑξάκις τοῦτο γεγραμμένον·
δίκαιον γὰρ ᾤμην δεῖν τὸν ἀγῶνα καὶ τὴν κρίσιν
ποιῆσαι. σὺ δ᾿ ἃ μὲν εἰπεῖν Εὐξένιππον φῂς οὐ
τὰ ἄριστα τῷ δήμῳ, οὐκ εἶχες γράψαι εἰς τὴν
εἰσαγγελίαν, ἰδιώτην δ᾿ ὄντα κρίνεις ἐν τῇ τοῦ
31 ῥήτορος τάξει. μικρὰ δὲ περὶ τῆς ἀντιγραφῆς
[col. 24] εἰπών, ἑτέρας αἰτίας καὶ διαβολὰς ἥκεις φέρων

---

[1] ᾿Αζηνιέα Schaefer : αιζηνιεα A.
[2] ἐδόκει Schaefer : δόκει A.
[3] καὶ del. Blass : ὑπηρετήκει Schoemann.
[4] ἂν del. Babington.

---

[a] Of the three orators here mentioned Aristophon was
prosecuted by Hyperides in 362 B.C., Diopithes at an un-

484

done my best to help. What men, then, have I prosecuted and brought to trial ? Aristophon of Hazenia,[a] now a most influential person in public life—he was acquitted in this court by two votes only ; Diopithes of Sphettus, thought to be the most formidable man in the city ; Philocrates of Hagnus, whose political career has been marked by the utmost daring and wantonness. I prosecuted that man for his services to Philip against Athens and secured his conviction in court. The impeachment which I drew up was just and in accordance with the law, referring to him as " an orator giving counsel against the best interests of the people and receiving money and gifts from those working against them." Even so I was not satisfied to bring in the impeachment before I had added underneath : " These proposals he made against the best interests of the people, because he had taken bribes." And I wrote his decree underneath. And again I added : " These further proposals he made against the best interests of the people, because he had taken bribes." And I wrote the decree alongside. Indeed this statement is written down five or six times in my speech ; for I thought that I must make the trial and the prosecution just. But you could not include in your impeachment the things which you allege Euxenippus to have said against the best interests of the people. Yet, though he is a private citizen, by your mode of prosecution you class him as an orator. After a scanty reference to the defendant's written statement you are now bringing fresh charges and incriminations against him, mentioning, amongst other similar allegations,

known date, and Philocrates in 343. See further, notes on Fragments 17, 15, and 16.

κατ᾽ αὐτοῦ, λέγων ὡς Φιλοκλεῖ τὴν θυγατέρα
ἐδίδου καὶ Δημοτίωνος δίαιταν ἔλαβεν, καὶ ἄλλας
τοιαύτας κατηγορίας, ἵν᾽ ἐὰν μὲν ἀφέμενοι[1] τῆς
εἰσαγγελίας περὶ τῶν ἔξω τοῦ πράγματος κατηγορηθέντων ἀπολογῶνται, ἀπαντῶσιν αὐτοῖς οἱ δι-
κασταί· τί ταῦθ᾽ ἡμῖν λέγετε; ἐὰν δὲ μηδένα λόγον
περὶ αὐτῶν ποιῶνται, ὁ ἀγὼν αὐτοῖς χείρων γίγνη-
ται. τῶν γὰρ κατηγορηθέντων τὸ μὴ λαβὸν ἀπολογίαν ὑπὸ τῇ ὀργῇ τῶν δικαστῶν καταλείπεται.

32 καὶ τὸ πάντων δειν⟨ότ⟩ατον τῶν ἐν τῷ λόγῳ λεγο-
[col. 25] μένων ὑπὸ σοῦ, ὃ σὺ ᾤου λανθάνειν ὧν ἕνεκα λέγεις,
οὐ λανθάνων, ὁπότε παραφθέγγοιο ἐν τῷ λόγῳ
πολλάκις, ὡς πλούσιός ἐστιν Εὐξένιππος, καὶ
πάλιν διαλιπών, ὡς οὐκ ἐκ δικαίου πολλὴν οὐσίαν
συνείλεκται· ἃ εἰς μὲν τὸν ἀγῶνα τοῦτον οὐδὲν
δήπου ἐστίν, εἴτε πολλὰ οὗτος κέκτηται εἴτε ὀλίγα,
τοῦ δὲ λέγοντος κακοηθία καὶ ὑπόληψις εἰς τοὺς
δικαστὰς οὐ δικαία, ὡς ἄλλοθί που οὗτοι τὴν
γνώμην ἂν σχοίησαν ἢ ἐπ᾽ αὐτοῦ τοῦ πράγματος,
καὶ πότε[ρον] ἀδικεῖ ὑμᾶς ὁ κριν[όμ]ενος ἢ οὔ.

33 Κακ[ῶς] μοι[2] δοκεῖς εἰδ[έν]αι, ὦ Πολύευκτε, σ[ύ
τε][3] καὶ οἱ ταὐτὰ γι[γνώσκο]ντες,[4] ὅτι οὔ[τε δῆμός][5]
[col. 26] ἐστιν οὐδ[ὲ εἶ]ς[6] ἐν τῇ οἰκουμένῃ οὔτε μόναρχος
οὔτε ἔθνος μεγαλοψυχότερον τοῦ δήμου τοῦ Ἀθηναίων, τοὺς δὲ συκοφαντουμένους τῶν πολιτῶν ὑπό
τινων ἢ καθ᾽ ἕνα ἢ ἀθρόους οὐ προΐεται ἀλλὰ βοηθεῖ.

---

[1] Post ἀφέμενοι excidisse οἱ ὑπὲρ αὐτοῦ ἀπολογούμενοι vel
simile aliquid suspicatus est Kenyon.
[2] Κακῶς μοι Blass : Κακῶς ἐμοὶ Cobet.
[3] σύ τε Cobet.
[4] γιγνώσκοντες Müller.
[5] οὔτε δῆμός Cobet.
[6] οὐδὲ εἷς Blass.

that he tried to marry his daughter to Philocles, that he undertook an arbitration for Demotion, and other similar charges.[a] Your intention is that, if the defence neglect the main indictment and deal with the irrelevant allegations, the jury shall interrupt them by calling : " Why do you tell us this ? " and if they ignore the additional points entirely their case shall be weakened. For any charge that is not refuted is left to be fastened on by the anger of the jury. The most outrageous feature of your speech was the fact that often during the argument you let fall the remark—you thought that your motive in doing so passed unnoticed, though it was obvious—that Euxenippus was rich, and again, a little later, that he had amassed great wealth dishonestly. It has surely nothing to do with this case whether he is a man of large means or small, and to raise the matter is malicious and implies an unfair assumption regarding the jury, namely that they would base their verdict on other considerations than the point at issue and the question whether the man on trial is offending against you or not.

You do not realize, Polyeuctus, it seems to me, you and those who share your views, that there is not in the world a single democracy or monarch or race more magnanimous than the Athenian people, and that it does not forsake those citizens who are maligned by others, whether singly or in numbers, but supports them. Let me give an instance. When

---

[a] Nothing is known of Philocles and the reference to Demotion is obscure. He was clearly an unpopular character, perhaps the parasite feeder satirized by comedians (see Athen. vi. 243 b). The translation of the phrase Δημοτίωνος δίαιταν ἔλαβεν is doubtful ; it might mean: " adopted the method of life of Demotion."

34 καὶ πρῶτον μὲν Τείσιδος τοῦ Ἀγρυλῆθεν ἀπογρά
ψαντος τὴν Εὐθυκράτους οὐσίαν ὡς δημοσίαν
οὖσαν, ἣ πλεόνων ἢ ἐξήκοντα ταλάντων ἦν, καὶ
μετ᾽ ἐκείνην πάλιν ὑπισχνουμένου τὴν Φιλίππ[ου]
καὶ Ναυσικλέους ἀ[πο]γράψειν, καὶ λέγο[ντ]ος ὡς
ἐξ ἀναπογρ[άφ]ων μετάλλων π[επλ]ουτήκασι, τοσ
ο[ῦτον¹ οὗ]τοι ἀπέλιπον [τοῦ πρ]οσέσθαι² τινὰ
[col. 27] τ[οιοῦτο]ν³ λόγον ἢ τῶν ἀλλοτρίων ἐπιθυμεῖν, ὥστε
τὸν ἐγχειρήσαντα συκοφαντεῖν αὐτοὺς εὐθὺς ἠτί
μωσαν, τὸ πέμπτον μέρος τῶν ψήφων οὐ μετα
35 δόντες. τοῦτο δ᾽, εἰ βούλει, τὸ πρώην ὑπὸ τῶν
δικαστῶν πραχθὲν τοῦ ἐξελθόντος μηνὸς πῶς οὐ
μεγάλου ἐπαίνου ἄξιόν ἐστι; φήναντος γὰρ Λυσ
άνδρου τὸ Ἐπικράτους μέταλλον τοῦ Παλληνέως⁴
ἐντὸς⁵ τῶν μέτρων τετμημένον, ὃ ἠργάζετο μὲν
ἤ[δη] τρία ἔτη, μετεῖχον δ᾽ αὐτοῦ οἱ πλουσι[ώ]
τατοι σχεδόν τι τῶν ἐν τῇ πόλει, ὁ δὲ Λ[ύσα]νδρος
ὑπισχνεῖτ[ο τρι]ακόσια τάλαντα εἰσ[πράξει]ν⁶ τῇ
[col. 28] πόλει (τ[οσαῦτα]⁷ γὰρ εἰληφέναι α[ὐτοὺς⁸ ἐ]κ τοῦ
36 μετάλλου)· ἀλλ᾽ ὅμως οἱ δικασταὶ οὐ πρὸς τὰς τοῦ
κατηγόρου ὑποσχέσεις ἀποβλέποντες, ἀλλὰ πρὸς
τὸ δίκαιον, ἔγνωσαν ἴδιον εἶναι τὸ μέταλλον, καὶ
τῇ αὐτῇ ψήφῳ τάς τε οὐσίας αὐτῶν ἐν ἀσφαλείᾳ
κατέστησαν, καὶ τὴν ὑπόλοιπον ἐργασίαν τοῦ με
τάλλου ἐβεβαίωσαν. τοιγαροῦν αἱ καινοτομίαι⁹
πρότερον ἐκλελειμμέναι διὰ τὸν φόβον νῦν ἐνεργοί,
καὶ τῆς πόλεως αἱ πρόσοδοι αἱ ἐκεῖθεν πάλιν αὔ-

---

¹ τοσοῦτον Caesar.　　² τοῦ προσέσθαι Spengel.
³ τοιοῦτον Babington.
⁴ Post Παλληνέως add. ὡς Cobet.
⁵ ἐντὸς] ἐκτὸς Cobet, et apud Dem. xxxvii. 36.
⁶ εἰσπράξειν Schneidewin.　　⁷ τοσαῦτα Babington.

Tisis of Agryle brought in an inventory of the estate
of Euthycrates, amounting to more than sixty talents,
on the grounds of its being public property, and again
later promised to bring in an inventory of the estate
of Philip and Nausicles saying that they had made
their money from unregistered mines, this jury were
so far from approving such a suggestion or coveting
the property of others that they immediately disfranchised the man who tried to slander the accused
and did not award him a fifth part of the votes.[a]   Or
take a recent instance, if you like, the verdict given
by the jury last month, surely a most commendable
decision.   I refer to the case of Lysander, who reported that the mine of Epicrates of Pallene had been
bored beyond the boundaries.   It had already been
worked for three years and virtually the richest men
in Athens had shares in it.   Lysander promised to
secure three hundred talents for the city, since that,
he claimed, was the sum which they had made from
the mine.   In spite of this the jury were governed,
not by the accuser's promises, but by the claims of
justice.   They decided that the mine was within its
proper limits, and in one and the same verdict assured
the safety of the men's estates and guaranteed their
working of the mine for the remainder of the period.
That is why the excavation of new mines, neglected
previously because men were afraid, is now in pro-
gress, and the city's revenues from these are again

---

[a] No other details are known of the cases mentioned here.
An Epicrates of Pallene is known to have been trierarch in
342 B.C. (*I.G.* ii. 803 e), and may be the man referred to in
connexion with the second of the two trials.

---

[8] αὐτοὺς Cobet : αὐτὸν Babington.
[9] Post καινοτομίαι add. αἱ Cobet.

ξονται, ἃς ἐλυμήναντό τινες τῶν ῥητόρων ἐξ[απ]α-
τήσαντες τὸν δῆμον καὶ δασμολ[ογή]σαντες τοὺς
37 ἐκ[εῖθεν].¹ ἔστι γάρ, ὦ ἄνδρ[ες δι]κασταί, οὐχ
[col. 29] οὗτος [χρη]στὸς² πολίτης, ὅ[στις] μικρὰ δοὺς πλείω
βλάπτει τὰ κοινά, οὐδ᾽ ὅστις εἰς τὸ παραχρῆμα
ἐξ ἀδίκου πορίσας κατέλυσε τῆς πόλεως τὴν ἐκ
δικαίου πρόσοδον, ἀλλ᾽ ὅτῳ μέλει καὶ τῶν εἰς τὸν
ἔπειτα χρόνον ὠφελίμων τῇ πόλει καὶ τῆς ὁμονοίας
τῶν πολιτῶν καὶ τῆς δόξης τῆς ὑμετέρας· ὧν ἔνιοι
οὐ φροντίζουσιν, ἀλλὰ τῶν ἐργαζομένων ἀφαιρού-
μενοι πόρους φασὶ τούτους πορίζειν, ἀπορίαν ἐν τῇ
πόλει παρασκευάζοντες. ὅταν γὰρ ᾖ³ φοβερὸν τὸ
κτᾶσθαι καὶ φείδεσθαι, τίς βουλήσεται κινδυνεύειν;

38 Τούτους μὲν οὖν ἴσως οὐ ῥᾴδιόν ἐστι κωλῦσαι
[col. 30] ταῦτα πράττειν· ὑμεῖς δέ, ὦ ἄνδρες δικασταί, ὥσπερ
καὶ ἄλλους πολλοὺς σεσώκατε τῶν πολιτῶν ἀδίκως
εἰς ἀγῶνας καταστάντας, οὕτω καὶ Εὐξενίππῳ
βοηθήσατε, καὶ μὴ περιίδητε αὐτὸν ἐπὶ πράγματι
οὐδενὸς ἀξίῳ καὶ εἰσαγγελίᾳ τοιαύτῃ, ᾗ οὐ μόνον
οὐκ ἔνοχός ἐστιν, ἀλλὰ καὶ αὐτὴ παρὰ τοὺς νόμους
ἐστὶν εἰσηγγελμένη, καὶ πρὸς τούτοις ὑπ᾽ αὐτοῦ
39 τοῦ κατηγόρου τρόπον τινὰ ἀπολελυμένη. εἰσήγ-
γελκε γὰρ αὐτὸν Πολύευκτος λέγειν μὴ τὰ ἄριστα
τῷ δήμῳ τῷ Ἀθηναίων χρήματα λαμβάνοντα καὶ
δωρεὰς παρὰ τῶν τἀναντία πραττόντων τῷ δήμῳ
[col. 31] τῷ Ἀθηναίων. εἰ μὲν οὖν ἔξωθεν τῆς πόλεώς
τινας ᾐτιᾶτο εἶναι, παρ᾽ ὧν τὰ δῶρα εἰληφότα
Εὐξένιππον συναγωνίζεσθαι αὐτοῖς, ἦν ἂν αὐτῷ
εἰπεῖν ὅτι, ἐπειδὴ ἐκείνους οὐκ ἔστι τιμωρήσασθαι,
490

being increased, revenues which some of our orators impaired by misleading the people and subjecting the mine-workers to tribute. The good citizen, gentlemen of the jury, is not a man to make some small additions to the public funds in ways which cause an ultimate loss, nor one who, by dishonestly producing an immediate profit, cuts off the city's lawful source of revenue. On the contrary, he is the man who is anxious to keep what will be profitable to the city in the future, to preserve agreement among the citizens and safeguard your reputation. There are some who disregard these things. By taking money from contractors they claim that they are providing revenue, although it is the lack of it that they are really causing in the city. For when anxiety is attached to earning and saving, who will want to take the risk?

Now perhaps it is not easy to prevent these men from acting as they do; but you, gentlemen of the jury, have saved many other citizens who were unjustly brought to trial. Then help Euxenippus in the same way, rather than desert him over a trivial matter, and in an impeachment like the present: an impeachment to which he is not liable, which has been framed in defiance of the laws, and which moreover has been partly invalidated by the prosecutor himself. For Polyeuctus has impeached Euxenippus for speaking against the best interests of the people of Athens, being in receipt of money and gifts from those acting against the people of Athens. Now if he were arguing that there were men outside the city with whom Euxenippus was co-operating on receipt of bribes, he would then be able to say that, since these persons

---

¹ ἐκεῖθεν Lightfoot.　　　　² χρηστὸς Meuss.
³ ᾗ Babington : ἦν A.

δεῖ τοὺς ἐνθάδε αὐτοῖς[1] ὑπηρετοῦντας δίκην δοῦναι. νῦν δὲ ᾿Αθηναίους φησὶν εἶναι παρ᾽ ὧν τὰς δωρεὰς εἰληφέναι αὐτόν. εἶτα σύ, ἔχων ἐν τῇ πόλει τοὺς ὑπεναντία πράττοντας τῷ δήμῳ, οὐ τιμωρῇ, ἀλλ᾽ Εὐξενίππῳ πράγματα παρέχεις;

40 Βραχὺ δ᾽ ἔτι εἰπὼν περὶ τῆς ψήφου ἧς ὑμεῖς μέλλετε φέρειν καταβήσομαι. ὅταν γὰρ μέλλητε, [col. 32] ὦ ἄνδρες δικασταί, διαψηφίζεσθαι, κελεύετε ὑμῖν τὸν γραμματέα ὑπαναγνῶναι τήν τε εἰσαγγελίαν καὶ τὸν νόμον τὸν εἰσαγγελτικὸν καὶ τὸν ὅρκον τὸν ἡλιαστικόν· καὶ τοὺς μὲν λόγους ἁπάντων ἡμῶν ἀφέλετε, ἐκ δὲ τῆς εἰσαγγελίας καὶ τῶν νόμων σκεψάμενοι ὅ τι ἂν ὑμῖν δοκῇ δίκαιον καὶ εὔορκον εἶναι, τοῦτο ψηφίσασθε.

41 ᾿Εγὼ μὲν οὖν σοί, Εὐξένιππε, βεβοήθηκα ὅσα εἶχον. λοιπὸν δ᾽ ἐστὶ δεῖσθαι τῶν δικαστῶν καὶ τοὺς φίλους παρακαλεῖν καὶ τὰ παιδία ἀναβιβάζεσθαι.[2]

---

[1] αὐτοῖς Babington : αὐτοὺς A.
[2] Subscriptio in A : ὑπὲρ Εὐξενίππου εἰσαγγελίας ἀπολογία πρὸς Πολύευκτον.

could not be punished, their servants in the city must be brought to justice. But, in fact, he says that it is from Athenians that Euxenippus has had the gifts. For shame, sir ; when you have here in the city the men who act against the people, do you let them be and choose instead to harass Euxenippus ?

I will say a few words more about the vote which you are going to give and then leave the platform. When about to go to the ballot, gentlemen of the jury, tell the clerk to read you the impeachment, the impeachment law and the oath sworn by jurymen. Dispense with the arguments of us all ; let the impeachment and the laws govern your decision and give whatever verdict you consider to be just and in keeping with your oath.

And now, Euxenippus, I have done all in my power to help you. It remains for you to ask the jury's permission to summon your friends and bring your children to the bar.

V

SPEECH AGAINST DEMO-
STHENES

INTRODUCTION

When the papyrus fragments of the speech against Demosthenes came to light, although the reconstruction and interpretation of them presented many difficulties, enough was already known of the case [a] to enable the work to be identified. The speech was delivered in 323 B.C.

Hyperides was one of the ten accusers chosen by the Athenian people in the Harpalus case, of which a brief account has been given earlier in this volume.[b] At least two orators, Stratocles and the client of Dinarchus, preceded him. Nevertheless, his speech is a moderately long one, though it is clear from the existing fragments that he repeated some of the arguments used by previous speakers.

The mutilated condition of the text makes any attempt at analysis difficult, but the gist of the argument can be surmised from what is known of the case from other writers. The following summary is based on G. Colin's reconstruction of the speech.[c]

[a] e.g. from Pseudo-Plutarch's Lives of the Ten Orators (Hyp. § 8, etc.) ; and from Dinarch. Against Demosthenes.
[b] See Dinarch. Against Demosthenes, Introduction.
[c] G. Colin, Le Discours d'Hypéride contre Démosthène, Paris, 1934, and Budé Hyperides, 1946.

ANALYSIS

grown rich in public life. Unlike private citizens, who suffer for every lapse, orators are favoured. Yet Demosthenes shows no gratitude for this ; he is careless of the fortunes of the state. Cols. 34. 8-end. The acquittal of these men might involve a war merely to protect their gains. Appeal to the jury to do their duty and condemn the defendants.

ΚΑΤΑ ΔΗΜΟΣΘΕΝΟΥΣ ΥΠΕΡ ΤΩΝ
ΑΡΠΑΛΕΙΩΝ

Frag. I

[col. 1] 'Αλλ' ἐγώ, ὦ [ἄνδρες][1] δικασταί, [ὅπερ καὶ] πρὸς
τοὺ[ς παρακαθη]μένους [ἀρτίως ἔλ]εγον, θαυ[μάζω][2]
τουτὶ τὸ πρᾶ[γμα, εἰ δ]ὴ³ νὴ Δία κατὰ [Δημ]ο-
σθένους μό[νου τ]ῶν ἐν τῇ πόλει [μήτε] οἱ νόμοι
ἰσχύου[σιν, οἱ] κελεύοντες κύ[ρια εἶν]αι ὅσα ἄν τις
[αὐτ]ὸς καθ' αὑτοῦ διάθηται, μήτε τὰ ψηφίσματα
τοῦ δήμου, καθ' ἃ ὑμεῖς μὲν ὀμωμόκατε τὴν
ψῆφον οἴσειν, ἔγραψεν δὲ αὐτὰ οὐδεὶς τῶν ἐχθρῶν
τῶν Δημοσθένους, ἀλλ' αὐτὸς οὗτος, ἐψηφίσατο
δὲ ὁ δῆμος [το]ύτου κελεύο[ντο]ς⁴ [καὶ μόνον] οὐχ
ἑκου[σίως αὐτὸν ἀπο]λλύ[οντος] [Desunt col. 1
[col. 2] versus fere tres.] [καίτοι τὸ] δίκαιον, ὦ ἄνδρες
δικασταί, ἁπλοῦν ὑπολαμβάνω ἡμῖν εἶναι πρὸς
Δημοσθένη. ὥσπερ γὰρ ἐπὶ τῶν ἰδίων ἐγκλημάτων
πολλὰ διὰ προκλήσεων κρίνεται, οὕτως καὶ τουτὶ
τὸ πρᾶγμα κέκριται. σκέψασθε γάρ, ὦ ἄνδρες
δικασταί, οὑτωσί. ᾐτιάσατό σε, ὦ Δημόσθενες,
ὁ δῆμος εἰληφ[έναι] εἴκοσι τάλαντ[α ἐπὶ] τῇ πολιτείᾳ
κ[αὶ τοῖς] νόμοις. ταῦτα σ[ὺ ἔ]ξαρνος ἐγένου μὴ
λαβεῖν, καὶ πρόκλησιν γράψας ἐν ψηφίσματι προσ-

AGAINST DEMOSTHENES

Frag. I

PERSONALLY, gentlemen of the jury, as I was just saying to those seated beside me, what surprises me is this. Is it really true that Demosthenes, unlike any other man in Athens, is exempt from the laws which enforce an agreement made by a person against his own interests ? Is he unaffected by the people's decrees, which you have sworn to observe in voting, decrees which were proposed, not by any of his enemies, but by Demosthenes himself, and which the people carried on his motion, almost as though he deliberately sought to destroy himself . . . and yet the just verdict, gentlemen of the jury, is, as I see it, simple : it is in our favour against Demosthenes. In private suits differences are often settled by challenge, and that is how this affair also has been settled. Look at it in this way, gentlemen. The people accused you, Demosthenes, of having accepted twenty talents illegally, against the interests of the state. You denied having done so and drew up a challenge, which you laid before the people in the

---

[1] Coll. 1 et 2 plerumque restituit Blass.
[2] θαυμάζω Jensen : θαῦμα τηλικουτὶ νομίζω Blass.
[3] εἰ δὴ Jensen : εἰ μὴ Blass.
[4] κελεύοντος Sauppe.

HYPERIDES

ἤνεγκας τῷ δήμῳ, ἐπιτρέπων ὑπὲρ ὧν τὴν αἰτίαν
ἔσχες τῇ βουλῇ τῇ ἐξ Ἀρείου πά[γου] . . . .
[Desunt col. 2 versus fere tres et col. 3 versus
fere quattuordecim.]

Frag. II

[col. 3] [Καὶ συκοφαντεῖς τὴν βουλήν, προκλήσεις ἐκ-
τιθεὶς καὶ ἐρωτῶν ἐν ταῖς προκλήσεσιν, πόθεν
ἔλα]βε[ς¹ τὸ χρυσίον, καὶ τίς] ἦν σο[ι ὁ] δούς, καὶ
ποῦ². τελευτῶν² δ᾽ ἴσως ἐρωτήσεις καὶ ὅ τι³ ἐχρή-
σω λαβὼν⁴ τῷ χρυσίῳ, ὥσπερ τραπεζιτικὸν λόγον
παρὰ τῆς βουλῆς ἀπαιτῶν. ἐγὼ δ[ὲ τ]οὐναντίον

[col. 4] [ἡδέως ἂ]ν παρὰ σοῦ [πυθοίμ]ην, τίνος [ἂν ἕν]εκα⁵
ἡ ἐξ Ἀρείου [πάγου βου]λὴ⁵ ἔφη . . . . ις
ἀδίκ[ως] . . . . τατοχρυ . . . φησι του . . . . . ωτατις.
. . . . ε δικαστ . . . . ἂν ενοι . . . . . .
εσθαι εμ . . . . δι]καίως τω . . . ι . . . .
[Desunt col. 4 versus fere viginti et col. 5 versus
fere decem.]

Frag. III

[col. 5] . . . τὰς ἀποφάσεις. οὐκ ἔστι ταῦτα, ἀλλὰ πάντων
φανήσον[τα]ι μάλιστα δημο[τικώ]τατα⁶ τῷ πράγ-
μα[τι κ]εχρημένοι· τοὺς [μὲ]ν γὰρ ἀδικοῦντας [ἀπ]-
έφηναν, καὶ ταῦ[τ᾽ οὐ]χ ἑκόντες, ἀλλ᾽ ὑπὸ [τοῦ δ]ήμου
πολλάκις [ἀναγ]καζόμενοι· τὸ [δὲ κο]λάσαι τοὺς
ἀδι[κοῦντα]ς⁶ οὐκ ἐφ᾽ αὑτοῖς [ἐποί]ησαν,⁷ ἀλλ᾽ ὑμῖν
[ἀπέδ]οσαν τοῖς κυρίοις. Δ[ημοσθένης]⁷ δ᾽ οὐ μό-

[col. 6] νον ἐπὶ τοῦ αὐτοῦ ἀγῶνος οἴεται δεῖν ὑμᾶς παρακρούσασθαι διαβαλὼν τὴν ἀπόφασιν, ἀλλὰ καὶ τοὺς
ἄλλους ἀγῶνας ἅπαντας ἀφελέσθαι ζητεῖ τοὺς τῆς
πόλεως· ὑπὲρ οὗ δεῖ ὑμᾶς νυνὶ βουλεύσασθαι προσ-

502

form of a decree entrusting the matter on which you were accused to the council of the Areopagus. . . .

Frag. II

. . . and you malign the Areopagus and publish challenges, in which you ask how you came by the gold, who gave it you, and where. Perhaps you will end by asking what you used it for after you obtained it, as though you were demanding a banker's statement from the Areopagus. I, on the other hand, should like to know from you why the council of the Areopagus said . . .

Frag. III

. . . the reports. On the contrary they have shown, as you will recognize, an exceptionally democratic spirit in handling the affair. They reported the guilty persons ; even this was not done from choice but in answer to repeated pressure from the people ; and they did not undertake to punish them on their own responsibility but rightly left it to you, with whom the final authority rests. It is not only his own trial which Demosthenes has in mind when he determines to mislead you by abusing the report ; he wishes also to frustrate all the other prosecutions which the city has in hand. That is a point to be

---

¹ Coll. 3 et 4 composuit et plerumque restituit Blass : verba συκοφαντεῖς usque ad ἀπαιτῶν citat Alexander Numen, Περὶ σχημ. viii. 457 Walz.

² ποῦ et τελευτῶν A : πῶς et τελευταῖον Alexander.

³ ὅ τι] εἰ Alexander.   ⁴ λαβὼν om. Alexander.

⁵ ἕνεκα et βουλὴ Egger.

⁶ δημοτικώτατα usque ad ἀδικοῦντας Sauppe.

⁷ ἐποίησαν usque ad Δημοσθένης Blass.

HYPERIDES

ἔχοντας τὸν νοῦν, καὶ μὴ τῷ λόγῳ ὑπὸ τούτου
ἐξαπατηθῆναι. τὰς γὰρ ἀποφάσεις ταύτας τὰς
ὑπὲρ τῶν χρημάτων ῾Αρπάλου πάσας ὁμοίως ἡ
βουλὴ πεποίηται καὶ τὰς αὐτὰς κατὰ πάντων, καὶ
οὐδεμιᾷ προσγέγραφεν διὰ τί ἕκαστον ἀπο[φαί]νει,
ἀλλὰ ἐπὶ κεφαλαίου γράψασα ὁπόσον ἕκαστος εἴληφεν χρυσίον, τοῦτ᾽ οὖν [ὀφε]ιλέτω.¹ [ἢ] ἰσχύ[σει
[col. 7] Δημοσθ]ένης παρ᾽ ὑμ[ῖν² τῆς κατ᾽ αὐτοῦ] ἀπο-
[φάσεως² μεῖζον];³ οὐκ ἐσ . . . . ἀπογι . . . .
. . . . . . ἀπόφα . . . . ἔλαβεν . . . . . . σι καὶ οἱ
ἄ[λλοι πάντες·] οὐ γὰρ δή[που⁴ Δημο]σθένει [μόνῳ
τοῦ]το ἰσχυρὸ[ν⁴ ἔσται, τοῖς] δ᾽ ἄλλοις ο[ὔ. καὶ
γὰρ] οὐχ ὑπὲρ [εἴκοσι⁵ τα]λάντων δ[ικάζετε], ἀλλ᾽
ὑπὲρ τ[ετρακο]σίων,⁶ οὐδ᾽ ὑ[πὲρ ἑνὸς] ἀδικήμ[α-
τ]ο[ς,⁶ ἀλλ᾽ ὑ]πὲρ ἁπάντ[ων. ἡ γὰρ]⁷ σὴ ἀπόνο[ια, ὦ
Δημό]σθενες, ὑπ[ὲρ ἁπάντων] τῶν ἀδικούντων νῦν
προκινδυνεύει καὶ προαναισχ[υν]τεῖ. ἐγὼ δ᾽ ὅτι
μὲν ἔλαβες τὸ χρυσίον ἱκανὸν οἶμαι εἶν[αι] σημεῖον
τοῖς δικασταῖς τὸ τὴν βουλήν σου καταγνῶναι,
[col. 8] [ἢ σαυτὸν⁸ ἐ]πέτρεψας· [τίνων δὲ ἔ]νεκα ἔλαβες,
[καὶ ἐπὶ⁹ τί]σιν αἰτίαις [πᾶσαν τὴ]ν πόλιν κα
. . . . ενος . . . . χρυσί . . . .
τος τοὺς . . . . ὥσ]περ εἰ . . . . [φανερ]ὸν
ποι[ήσω.¹⁰ ἐπ]ειδὴ γὰρ ἦλ[θεν, ὦ ἄν]δρες δικα[σταί,

---

¹ ὀφειλέτω Boeckh.
² Col. 7 plerumque restituit Sauppe, sed ὑμῖν usque ad ἀποφάσεως Blass.   ³ μεῖζον Fuhr : μᾶλλον Blass.
⁴ δήπου usque ad ἰσχυρὸν Kenyon, sed μόνῳ Jensen (μὲν
Kenyon).   ⁵ εἴκοσι Boeckh.
⁶ τετρακοσίων usque ad ἀδικήματος Boeckh : τριακοσίων
Sauppe.   ⁷ ἡ γὰρ Blass.
⁸ Col. 8 composuit Sauppe et Blass, plerumque restituit
Blass.

504

carefully borne in mind and you must not be deceived by the defendant's argument. For these reports concerning the money of Harpalus have all been drawn up by the Areopagus on an equal footing. They are the same for all the accused. In no case has the council added the reason why it publishes a particular name. It stated summarily how much money each man had received, adding that he was liable for that amount. Is Demosthenes to have more weight with you than the report given against him ? . . .[a] For of course this argument, if it protects Demosthenes, will also protect the rest. The sum on which you are pronouncing judgement is not twenty, but four hundred,[b] talents. You are judging all the crimes, not one. For your mad conduct, Demosthenes, has made you champion of all these criminals, foremost in danger as you are in impudence. In my opinion the fact that you took the gold is proved to the jury well enough by your being condemned by the council to which you entrusted yourself. . . .[c] When Harpalus arrived in Attica, gentlemen of the

[a] The sense of the missing words appears to be : " If you discredit the report, you thereby admit that no one took the money, and all the others are acquitted."

[b] The figure mentioned later, in column 10, is 350 talents, which is confirmed by Pseudo-Plutarch, *Dem.* 846 b. Hence Boeckh suggested the reading 400 in this passage, on the grounds that Hyperides would be more likely to exaggerate than otherwise.

[c] Although the missing Greek words cannot be restored with certainty, the sense appears to be : " I shall now produce the evidence relating to the gold which you previously accepted, and, as I said, explain why you took the money and for what reasons you disgraced the whole city."

---

[9] καὶ ἐπὶ Jensen : ἔτι δὲ Blass.   [10] ποιήσω Fuhr.

"Άρπα]λος εἰς τὴν ['Αττική]ν, καὶ οἱ πα[ρὰ Φιλο-
ξέ]νου ἐξαι[τοῦντες αὐ]τὸν ἅμα [προσήχθησ]αν πρὸς
[τὸν δῆμον, τότε παρελθὼν¹ Δημ]οσθένης [διεξῆλθεν]
μακρὸν [λόγον, φά]σκων² οὔτε [τοῖς παρ]ὰ Φιλο-
ξέ[νου ἐλθο]ῦσι καλῶς [ἔχειν τὸν] "Αρπαλον [ἐκ-
δοῦναι² τ]ὴν πόλιν, [οὔτε δεῖν] αἰτίαν οὐ[δεμίαν τ]ῷ
δήμῳ [δι' ἐκεῖνο]ν παρ' 'Α[λεξάνδρο]υ καταλεί-
[col. 9] πεσθαι, ἀσφαλέστατον δ' εἶναι τ[ῇ πόλει]³ τά τε
χρήματα [καὶ τὸν] ἄνδρα φυλάτ[τειν], καὶ ἀναφέρει[ν
τὰ χρή]ματα ἅπα[ντα] εἰς [τὴν] ἀκρόπολιν, ἃ ἦλθε[ν
ἔ]χων "Αρπαλος εἰ[ς τὴν] 'Αττικήν, ἐν τῇ αὔρι[ον]
ἡμέρᾳ. "Αρπαλο[ν δ' ἤ]δη⁴ ἀποδεῖξαι τὰ [χρή]ματα,
ὁπόσα ἐστ[ίν]· οὐχ ὅπως πύθο[ιτο] τὸν ἀριθμὸν
αὐτῶν, ὡς ἔοικεν, ὁπόσα ἦν, ἀλλ' ἵνα εἰδῇ ἀφ' ὅσων
αὐτὸν δεῖ τὸν μισθὸν πράττεσθαι. καὶ καθήμενος
κάτω ὑπὸ τῇ κατατομῇ, οὗπερ [εἴω]θε κα[θῆσ]θ[αι],
ἐκέλευ[ε Μνησ]ίθεον⁵ τὸν χορευτὴν ἐρωτῆσαι τὸν
"Αρπαλον, ὁπόσα εἴη τὰ χρήματα τὰ ἀνοισθησόμενα
εἰς τὴν ἀκρόπολιν. ὁ δ' ἀπεκρίνατο ὅτι ἑπτα-
[κόσια τάλαντα] [Desunt col. 10 versus duode-
[col. 10] cim.] [τὰ χρήματα εἶναι τη]λικ[αῦτα]⁶ αὐτὸς ἐν
τῷ δ[ήμῳ] πρὸς ὑμᾶς ε[ἰπών], ἀναφερομέν[ων
τρια]κοσίων ταλά[ντων] καὶ πεντ[ήκοντα ἀν]θ'
ἑπτακοσίων, λ[αβὼν] τὰ εἴκοσι τάλα[ντα οὐ]δένα

¹ τότε παρελθὼν Jensen : μέμνησθε ὡς τότε Blass.
² φάσκων et ἐκδοῦναι Kenyon.
³ Col. 9 composuit Sauppe et Kenyon, plerumque restituit
Kenyon.
⁴ δ' ἤδη Schaefer : δὲ δὴ Sauppe.
⁵ Μνησίθεον Blass.
⁶ Col. 10 plerumque restituit Blass.

jury, and the envoys from Philoxenus demanding him were, at the same time, brought into the Assembly, Demosthenes came forward and made a long speech in which he argued that it was not right for Athens to surrender Harpalus to the envoys from Philoxenus,[a] and that Alexander must not be left with any cause for complaint, on his account, against the people; the safest course for the city was to guard the money and the person of Harpalus, and to take up all the money, with which Harpalus had entered Attica, to the Acropolis on the following day, while Harpalus himself should announce then and there how much money there was. His real purpose, it seems, was not simply to learn the figure, but to find out from how large a sum he was to collect his commission. Sitting below in his usual place in the niche,[b] he told Mnesitheüs the dancer to ask Harpalus how much money there would be to take up to the Acropolis. The answer given was seven hundred talents. . . .[c] He had told you himself in the Assembly that that was the correct figure; and yet when the total brought up to the Acropolis was three hundred and fifty talents instead of seven hundred, having by then received his twenty, he did not utter

[a] Philoxenus, one of Alexander's generals, was governor of Cilicia at the time.

[b] It is not known what niche is meant. It may have been a cutting in the side of the Pnyx. The word κατατομή is cited by Harpocration as occurring in this speech.

[c] In the missing lines Hyperides probably explained that the Assembly was then dismissed and not summoned again until the following day, when the money had been paid over. Pseudo-Plutarch, *Dem.* 846 B, says that Demosthenes was accused of having taken bribes because he had not reported the amount of money brought to the Acropolis or the carelessness of those in charge of it.

λόγον ἐπ[οιήσα]το [Desunt versus tres.] ἐν τῷ
δήμῳ ἑ[πτα]κόσια φήσας εἶν[αι] τάλαντα, νῦν τὰ
[col. 11] ἡ[μί]ση ἀναφέρεις, κα[ὶ . . . .]ω ὅτι[1] τοῦ
[. . . . ἀν]ενεχθῆναι . . . . εἰς ἀκρόπολιν [. . . . . . .
τα]ῦτα τὰ πρά[γματα] [Desunt versus quattuor.]
. . . . ονλι . . . . . ἔκρινον τ[ὸν . . . . οὔτ᾽] ἂν ἐπρί[ατο
Ἅρπαλ]ος τὰς φε[. . . . . . . ο]ὔτ᾽ ἂν ἡ πόλις [ἐν
αἰτίαις] καὶ διαβο[λαῖς ἦν.] ἀλλὰ πάν[τω]ν τούτων,
ὦ Δημό[σθενες] . . . . ἐστίν . . . . . .
μως ἐγ . . . . στους [. . . . . . . .α]ἰσχυν . . . .
. . . . νει . . . . . [χρ]υσίον . . . . . γὰρ ὅτι . . . . . .
νοιω . . . . . του . . . . . πεν
[col. 12] σ]τατῆρας ἔλαβε· σὺ δ᾽ ὁ τῷ ψηφίσματι τοῦ σώματος αὐτοῦ τὴν φυλακὴν καταστήσας καὶ οὔτ᾽
ἐκλειπομένην ἐπανορθῶν οὔτε καταλυθείσης τοὺς
αἰτίους κρίνας, προῖκα δηλονότι τὸν καιρὸν τοῦτον
τεταμίευσαι; καὶ τοῖς μὲν ἐλάττοσι ῥήτορσιν ἀπ-
έτινεν ὁ Ἅρπαλος χρυσίον, τοῖς θορύβου μόνον καὶ
κραυγῆς κυρίοις, σὲ δὲ τὸν τῶν ὅλων πραγμάτων
ἐπιστάτην παρεῖδεν; καὶ τῷ τοῦτο πιστόν; τοσοῦτον δ᾽, ὦ ἄνδρες δικασταί, τοῦ πράγματος κατα-
πεφρόνηκεν Δημοσθένης, μᾶλλον δέ, εἰ δεῖ μετὰ
παρρησίας εἰπεῖν, ὑμῶν καὶ τῶν νόμων, ὥστε τὸ
[col. 13] μὲν πρῶτον, ὡς [ἔοι]κεν, ὁμο[λογεῖν[2] μὲν εἰληφέ]ναι[3]
τὰ χρήματ[α, ἀλλὰ] κατακεχρῆσθαι αὐτὰ ὑμῖν προ-

---

[1] Col. 11 om. Kenyon.
[2] Col. 13 plerumque restituit Blass.
[3] εἰληφέναι Boeckh.

[a] The sense of the mutilated column 11 appears to be: " You
did not reflect that if the whole amount originally mentioned
was not taken up to the Acropolis someone must have em-
bezzled. You were interested solely in your own fee ; for

a word. . . . After saying before the Assembly that
there were seven hundred talents you now bring
up half. . . .[a] Harpalus would not have bought . . .
nor would the city be exposed to accusation and reproach. But of all these things, Demosthenes . . .
It was you who decreed that a guard should be posted
over the person of Harpalus. Yet when it relaxed
its vigilance you did not try to restore it, and after it
was disbanded you did not prosecute those responsible. I suppose you went unpaid for your shrewd
handling of the crisis ? If Harpalus distributed
his gold among the lesser orators, who had nothing
to give but noise and shouting, what of you who
control our whole policy ? Did he pass you over ?
That is incredible. So supreme is the contempt,
gentlemen of the jury, with which Demosthenes
has treated the affair, or to be quite frank, you and
the laws, that at the outset, it seems, he admitted
having taken the money but said that he had used
it on your behalf and had borrowed it free of interest[b]

you cannot persuade us that you received nothing when we
know that Demades was paid 5000 staters." For the bribe
paid to Demades see Dinarch. i. 89.

[b] There does not seem to be an exact parallel for this use
of the word προδανείζομαι, and there are two possible inter-
pretations. (1) The active προδανείζω apparently has the
sense of " lend without interest " in Pseudo-Plutarch, *Lives
of the Ten Orators* 852 B, and in Aristot. *Ath. Pol.* 16. If the
translation given above is correct, Demosthenes claimed to
have borrowed the money from Harpalus and to have
advanced it to the Athenian people. (2) On the other hand
the noun προδανειστής is used in a Delian inscription with
the sense of " one who borrows for another." On this analogy
we might translate προδεδανεισμένος as " having borrowed
for the people." Demosthenes would thus be claiming to
have acted as an intermediary in accepting a loan from
Harpalus to the state.

509

δεδανεισμένος εἰς τὸ θεωρικόν· καὶ περιὼν Κνωσίων
καὶ οἱ ἄλλοι φίλοι αὐτοῦ ἔλεγον ὅτι ἀναγκάσουσι
τὸν ἄνθρωπον οἱ αἰτιώμενοι εἰς τὸ φανερὸν ἐνεγκεῖν
ἃ οὐ βούλεται, καὶ εἰπεῖν ὅτι τῷ δήμῳ προδεδάνει-
στ[αι] τὰ χρήματα εἰς τὴν διοίκησιν. ἐπειδὴ δ' ὑμῶν
οἱ ἀκούσαντες πολλῷ μᾶλλον ἠγανάκτουν ἐπὶ τοῖς
κατὰ τοῦ πλήθους τοῦ ὑμετέρου λόγοις, εἰ μὴ
μόνον ἱκανὸν εἴη αὐτῷ ἰδίᾳ δεδωροδοκηκέναι, [ἀλλὰ
καὶ τὸν δῆμο]ν [οἴοιτο δεῖν ἀνα]πιμ[πλάναι [De-
sunt col. 13 versus unus et col. 14 versus octo.]

[col. 14] λέγων καὶ αἰτιώ[με]νος,[1] ὅτι 'Αλεξάνδρῳ χαριζο-
μένη ἡ βουλὴ ἀνελεῖν αὐτὸν βούλεται· ὥσπερ οὐ
πάντας ὑμᾶς εἰδότας, ὅτι οὐδεὶς τὸν τοιοῦτον
ἀναιρεῖ, ὃν ἔστιν πρίασθαι, ἀλλ' ὅντινα μήτε πεῖσαι
ἔστιν μήτε χρήμασιν διαφθεῖραι, τοῦτον δ[ὴ][2] σ]κο-
ποῦσιν ὅπω[ς ἐ]κ παντὸς τρόπ[ου ἐκ]ποδὼν ποιήσουσιν. κίνδυνος δ' ὡς ἔ[οι]κεν ἐστίν, μὴ σύ, ὦ
Δημόσθενες, ἀπαραίτητος καὶ ἄπειστος εἶ πρὸς
[col. 15] δωροδ[οκίαν];[2] μὴ νομίζ[ετε δὲ[3] διὰ] τῆς τούτω[ν
δωρο]δοκίας τὰ τυ[χόντα τῶν][4] πραγμάτω[ν ἀλί-
σ]κεσθαι.[5] ο[ὐ γὰρ ἄδηλόν][6] ἐστιν ὅτι [πάντες][6] οἱ
ἐπιβουλεύοντες τοῖς 'Ελληνικοῖς πράγμασιν τὰς μὲν
μικρὰς πόλεις τοῖς ὅπλοις συσκευάζονται, τὰς δὲ
μεγάλας τοὺς δυναμένους ἐν αὐταῖς ὠνούμε[νοι,
ο]ὐδ' ὅτι Φίλιππος [τηλικ]οῦτος[7] ἐγένετο [ἐξ ἀρχ]ῆς[7]
χρήματα δια[πέμψα]ς[8] εἰς Πελο[πόννη]σον καὶ Θετ-

---

[1] Col. 14 composuit Sauppe et Blass : αἰτιώμενος Blass.
[2] δὴ usque ad δωροδοκίαν Kenyon.
[3] μὴ νομίζετε δὲ Colin : ἢ μὴ νομίζῃ τις Kenyon.
[4] τυχόντα τῶν Boeckh.   [5] ἁλίσκεσθαι Blass.
[6] ἄδηλόν et πάντες Sauppe.
[7] τηλικοῦτος et ἐξ ἀρχῆς Boeckh.
[8] διαπέμψας Sauppe.

510

for the Theoric fund. Cnosion [a] and his other friends went about saying that Demosthenes would be compelled by his accusers to publish facts which he wished kept secret and to admit that he had borrowed the money free of interest for the state to meet expenses of government. Since the anger of those of you who heard this statement was greatly increased by these aspersions cast on your democracy, on the grounds that he was not content to have taken bribes himself but thought fit to infect the people too . . .[b] speaking and complaining that the Areopagus was seeking favour with Alexander and for that reason wanted to destroy him. As if you did not all know that no one destroys the kind of man who can be bought. On the contrary, it is the opponent who can be neither persuaded nor corrupted with bribes that men contrive to be rid of by any means in their power. There is some likelihood, it seems, that you, Demosthenes, are deaf to prayers and not to be persuaded into taking bribes ? Do not imagine, gentlemen, that only trivial matters are affected by the venal conduct of these men. For it is no secret that all who conspire for power in Greece secure the smaller cities by force of arms and the larger ones by buying the influential citizens in them ; and we know that Philip reached the height he did because, at the outset, he sent money to the Pelopon-

[a] Cnosion, a boy with whom Demosthenes was friendly, is mentioned also by Aeschin. ii. 149, and by the scholiast on that passage.
[b] The gist of the missing lines was probably that Demosthenes changed his tactics and began to plead a different excuse.

HYPERIDES

[ταλίαν] καὶ τὴν ἄλλην [ʽΕλλάδα], καὶ τοὺς ἐν [δυ-
νάμει]¹ ὄντας ἐν [ταῖς πόλε]σιν καὶ προ[εστῶτας]¹
. . . . .

[Desunt col. 15 versus quinque et col. 16 fere tota.]

Frag. IV (V)

[col. 17] . . .[τερα]τεύῃ,² καὶ οὐχ ἅπασιν οἴει φανερὸν εἶναι
ὅτι φάσκων ὑπὲρ τοῦ [δήμου]³ λέγειν ὑπὲρ [ʼΑλεξ-
ά]νδρου φανερῶς [ἐδημηγ]όρεις·⁴ ἐγὼ γὰρ [οἶμαι
καὶ] ἔμπροσθεν [γνῶναι]⁴ ἅπαντας ὅτι [τοῦτ᾽ ἐ]ποίη-
σας καὶ περὶ Θη[βαί]ων καὶ περὶ τῶν [ἄλ]λων
ἁπάντων, καὶ ὅτι χρήματα εἰς [ταῦτα] δοθέντα ἐκ
τῆς [ʼΑσίας αὐ]τὸς σαυτῷ [ἰδίᾳ περιπ]οιησάμε[νος⁵
κατανήλω]σας τὰ [πολλά, καὶ νῦν δὲ ναυ]τικοῖς
ἐργάζῃ χ[ρήμα]σιν⁶ καὶ ἐκδόσεις δί[δως], καὶ πριάμενος ο[ἰκί]αν . . . .μο⁷ . . . . .υπα . . . .ν τω . . . . .
ρωι, οὐκ οἰκεῖς ἐ[ν Π]ειραιεῖ, ἀλλ᾽ ἐξορμεῖς ἐκ τῆς
πόλεως. δεῖ δὲ τὸν δίκαιον δημαγωγὸν [σω]τῆρα
τῆς [ἑαυτοῦ⁸ πατρίδος εἶναι,⁹ μὴ¹⁰ δραπέτην. ἐπειδὴ
[col. 18] δὲ νῦν ʽʼΑρπαλος οὕτως ἐξαίφνης]¹⁰ πρὸς τὴν ʽΕλλάδα
προσέπεσεν ὥστε μηδένα προαισθέσθαι, τὰ δ᾽ ἐν
Πελοποννήσῳ καὶ τῇ ἄλλῃ ʽΕλλάδι οὕτως ἔχοντα
κατέλαβεν ὑπὸ τῆς ἀφίξεως τῆς Νικάνορος καὶ
τῶν ἐπιταγμάτων ὧν ἧκεν φέρων παρ᾽ ʼΑλεξάν-

---

¹ δυνάμει usque ad προεστῶτας Blass.
² Col. 17 plerumque restituit Blass.
³ δήμου Babington.
⁴ ἐδημηγόρεις usque ad γνῶναι Sauppe.
⁵ περιποιησάμενος Sauppe.
⁶ χρήμασιν Jensen.
⁷ Colin sic restituit : ὕφορμον, ὅποι ὑπάγοις ἐν τῷ καιρῷ.

512

nese, Thessaly, and the rest of Greece, and those
with power in the cities and authority. . . .[a]

Frag. IV (V)

. . . you tell us marvellous stories, little thinking
that your conduct is no secret : you professed to be
supporting the people's interests but were clearly
speaking on behalf of Alexander. Personally I believe
that even in the past everyone knew that you acted
in this way over the Thebans, and over all the rest,
and that you appropriated money, which was sent
from Asia to buy help,[b] for your own personal use,
spending most of it ; and now you engage in sea
commerce and make bottomry loans, and having
bought a house . . . you do not live in the Piraeus
but have your anchorage outside the city.[c] A popular
leader worthy of the name should be the saviour of
his country, not a deserter. When Harpalus recently
descended on Greece so suddenly that he took everyone by surprise, he found affairs in the Peloponnese
and in the rest of Greece in this condition owing to
the arrival of Nicanor with the orders which he

---

[a] The words " he bribed " should probably be added to
complete the sense.

[b] Compare Dinarch. i. 10, note and 18-22 ; Aeschin. iii.
239-240. Demosthenes was said by his opponents to have
accepted money from Persia for use against Macedon, but
to have withheld it when Alexander destroyed Thebes in
335 B.C.

[c] The house in the Piraeus is mentioned by Dinarch. i. 69 ;
and Aeschin. iii. 209 uses these exact words.

---

[8] ἑαυτοῦ Jensen.
[9] πατρίδος εἶναι Kenyon.
[10] μὴ usque ad ἐξαίφνης Blass.

δρου περί τε τῶν φυγάδων καὶ περὶ τοῦ τοὺς
κοινοὺς συλλόγους Ἀχαιῶν τε καὶ Ἀρκάδων [καὶ
Β]οιωτῶν[1] [Desunt col. 18 versus fere duodecim.]

[col. 19] ταῦτα[2] σὺ πα[ρεσκεύ]ακας[3] τῷ ψηφ[ίσματι], συλ-
λαβὼν τὸ[ν Ἅρπα]λον, καὶ τοὺς μὲ[ν Ἕ]λληνας
ἅπαντας [πρεσ]βεύεσθαι πεπ[οίη]κας ὡς Ἀλέξ-
ανδ[ρον], οὐκ ἔχοντας ἄλλ[ην] οὐδεμίαν ἀποσ[τρο]-
φήν, τοὺς δὲ σ[ατράπας],[4] οἳ αὐτοὶ ἂν ἧκο[ν ἑκόν]τες
πρὸς ταύτη[ν τὴν] δύναμιν, ἔχοντες τὰ χρήματα
καὶ τοὺς στρατιώτας ὅσους ἕκαστος αὐτῶν εἶχεν,
τούτους σύμπαντας οὐ μόνον κεκώλυκας ἀποστῆναι
ἐκείνου τῇ συλλήψει τῇ Ἁρπάλου, ἀλλὰ καὶ . . . . .
[ἕ]καστον [αὐτῶν].[5]

[Desunt col. 19 versus fere sex et col. 20 versus
fere undecim.]

Frag. V (VI)

[col. 20] . . . [ὑπὸ[6] Δη]μοσθένο[υς ἀπο]σταλείς, παρὰ [δ᾽
Ὀλυμ]πιάδι Καλλίας ὁ [Χαλ]κιδεύς, ὁ Ταυρο-
σθένους ἀδελφός· τούτους γὰρ ἔγραψε Δημοσθένης
Ἀθηναίους εἶναι καὶ χρῆται τούτοις πάντων μάλιστα. καὶ οὐδὲν θαυμαστόν· οὐδέποτε γὰρ οἶμαι
ἐπὶ τῶν αὐτῶν μένων εἰκότως φί[λους] τοὺς ἀπ᾽
Εὐρίπου κέκτηται. εἶτα σὺ περὶ [φιλ]ίας πρὸς ἐμὲ

---

[1] Βοιωτῶν Blass : τοιούτων Colin.
[2] Col. 19 plerumque restituit Boeckh.
[3] παρεσκεύακας Jensen : παρῆρησαι Blass.
[4] σατράπας Sauppe.
[5] αὐτῶν Jensen.
[6] Coll. 20 et 21 plerumque restituit Blass.

brought from Alexander relating to the exiles ^a and
to the . . . of the Achaean, Arcadian, and Boeotian
Leagues. . . . You have contrived this situation by
means of your decree, because you arrested Harpalus.
You have induced the whole of Greece to send envoys
to Alexander, since they have no other recourse,
and have prevented all the satraps, who by themselves
would willingly have joined forces with us, each with
money and all the troops at his disposal, not merely
from revolting from him, by your detention of Harpalus, but also . . . each of them . . .^b

Frag. V (VI)

. . . sent by Demosthenes,^c and with Olympias
Callias the Chalcidian, the brother of Taurosthenes.
For these men were made Athenian citizens on the
motion of Demosthenes and they are his special
agents. Naturally enough ; for being perpetually
unstable himself, I suppose he might well have friends
from the Euripus.^d Will you dare then presently to

^a Dinarch. i. 82 also refers to this event, which took place
in 324 B.C. Nicanor, the son-in-law of Aristotle, was sent by
Alexander to Olympia to proclaim his demand for the return
to their cities of all Greek exiles except the Thebans.

^b The general sense appears to be: " All the satraps
united with Alexander. You yourself are now a supporter of
his and have your agents with every important Macedonian."

^c Sauppe suspected that the man here referred to was
Aristion of Samos, a friend of Demosthenes who, according
to Harpocration (*s.v.* ᾿Αριστίων), was mentioned in this speech
and was sent by Demosthenes to Hephaestion in order to
reach an understanding with him. For Callias and Taurosthenes of Chalcis compare Dinarch. i. 44 and note.

^d A comparison between the Euripus, a very changeable
strait, and the character of Callias is made also by Aeschin.
iii. 90.

τολ[μήσεις αὐτίκα μά]λα [λέγειν]   [Desunt col. 20
[col. 21] versus fere unus et col. 21 unus.]   [ταύτην τὴν
φιλίαν διέ]λυσας αὐ[τό]ς, ὅ[τε χρ]υσίον κατὰ τῆς
[πατρ]ίδος[1] ἔλαβες καὶ [μετ]εβάλο[υ]. καὶ κατα-
[γέλα]στον[2] μὲν σαυ[τὸν] ἐποίησας, κατῄ[σχυν]ας
δὲ τοὺς ἐκ τῶν [ἔμπρ]οσθεν[1] χρόνων [τῶν α]ὐτῶν
τί σοι προ[ελομέ]νους· καὶ ἐξὸν [ἡμῖν] λαμπροτάτοις
[εἶναι] παρὰ τῷ δήμῳ [καὶ τὸ]ν ὑπόλοιπον [βίον
ὑ]πὸ δόξης χρη[στῆς πα]ραπεμφθῆ[ναι, ἄπα]ντα
ταῦτα ἀνέτρ[εψας, κα]ὶ οὐκ αἰσχύνει νυνὶ τηλικοῦ-
τ[ος] ὢν ὑπὸ μειρακίων κρινόμενος περὶ δωροδοκίας.
καίτοι ἔδει τοὐναντίον ὑφ' ὑμῶν παιδεύεσθαι τοὺς
νεωτέρους τῶν ῥητόρων, καὶ [εἴ] τι προπετέστερον
[col. 22] ἔπραττον ἐπιτιμᾶσθαι καὶ κολάζεσθαι.   νῦν δὲ
τοὐναντίον οἱ νέοι τοὺς ὑπὲρ ἑξήκοντα ἔτη σωφρο-
νίζουσιν. διόπερ, ὦ ἄνδρες δ[ικα]σταί, δικαίως
ἂν ὀργίζοι[σθ]ε Δημοσθένει, εἰ καὶ δόξης ἱκανῆς
[καὶ] πλούτου πολλοῦ δ[ι' ὑ]μᾶς[3] μετεσχηκὼς μηδ'
ἐπὶ γήρως [ὀ]δῷ[4] κήδεται τῆς πατρίδος. ἀλλ'
ὑμεῖς μὲν ᾐσχύνεσθε ἐπὶ . ησ . . . . υ τοὺς
περιεστηκότας [τῶ]ν Ἑλλήνων, ὅτε [τινῶ]ν[5] κατ-
εχειρο[τον]εῖτε, εἰ τοιούτο[υς καὶ] δημαγωγοὺς κα[ὶ
στρ]ατηγοὺς καὶ φύλα[κα]ς τῶν πραγμ[άτων] . . .

[Desunt col. 22 versus quattuor et col. 23 fere tota.]

Frag. VI (VII)

[col. 24]   Οὐ γάρ ἐστιν ὁμοίως [δεινό]ν,[6] εἴ τις ἔλα[βεν],
ἀλλ' εἰ ὅθεν μὴ [δεῖ, ο]ὐδέ γ' ὁμοίως [ἀδι]κοῦσιν οἱ

---

[1] πατρίδος et ἔμπροσθεν Boeckh.
[2] καταγέλαστον Babington.   [3] δι' ὑμᾶς Sauppe.
[4] ὀδῷ Babington, coll. Polluce ii. 15.

speak to me of friendship . . . you yourself broke
up that friendship when you accepted bribes against
your country and made a change of front. You made
yourself a laughing stock and brought disgrace on
those who had ever shared your policy in former
years. When we might have gained the highest
distinction in public life and been accompanied for
the remainder of our lives by the best of reputations,
you frustrated all these hopes, and you are not
ashamed, even at your age,[a] to be tried by youths for
bribery. And yet the positions ought to be reversed :
your generation ought to be training the younger
orators, reproving and punishing any over-impetuous
action. But the fact is just the opposite : the youths
are taking to task the men of over sixty. Therefore,
gentlemen of the jury, you have a right to feel resentful towards Demosthenes ; for after gaining a toler-
able reputation and great riches, all through you,
even on the threshold of old age he has no loyalty to
his country. But you used to be ashamed . . . the
Greeks who were standing round, when you passed
sentence on certain persons,[5] to think that such
popular leaders and generals and guardians of your
affairs . . .[b]

Frag. VI (VII)

. . . For to take money is not so serious as to take
it from the wrong source, and the private individuals

---

[a] Demosthenes was just over sixty.
[b] The sense of this passage is probably : " Since you
condemned such generals as Timotheüs, though you shrank
from doing so, you should not hesitate to condemn Demosthenes." Compare Dinarch. i. 16.

---

[5] τινῶν Blass.
[6] Col. 24 plerumque restituit Sauppe.

ἰδιῶται [οἱ¹ λαβ]όντες τὸ χρυσίον [καὶ]² οἱ ῥήτορες
καὶ οἱ [στρατ]ηγοί. διὰ τί; ὅτι τοῖς [μὲν]² ἰδιώταις Ἅρπα[λος ἔ]δωκεν φυλάτ[τειν τ]ὸ χρυσίον, οἱ
δὲ [στρατη]γοὶ καὶ οἱ ῥήτο[ρες πρ]άξεων ἕνεκα
[εἰλή]φασιν.³ οἱ δὲ νό[μοι τ]οῖς μὲν ἀδικοῦ[σιν
ἁπλ]ᾶ,⁴ τοῖς δὲ δω[ροδοκοῦσι]ν δεκαπλᾶ [τὰ ὀφλ]ή-
ματα προστάτ[τουσιν]⁴ ἀποδιδόναι· [ὥσπερ οὖ]ν
τὸ τίμη[μα τιμῆ]σαι ἔστιν ἐκ [τῶν νό]μων τούτοις
. . . . . s, οὕτω καὶ . . . . . αι παρ' ὑμῶν . . . . σι
κατ' αὐτῶν . . . . αι. ὅπερ γὰρ [καὶ ἐν τ]ῷ δήμῳ
εἶ[πον, π]ολλὰ ὑμεῖς, ὦ [ἄνδρ]ες δικασταί, δί[δοτε
[col. 25] ἑ]κόντες τοῖς στρατηγοῖς καὶ τοῖς ῥήτορσιν ὠφε-
λεῖσθαι, οὐ τῶν νόμων αὐτοῖς δεδωκότων τοῦτο
ποιεῖν, ἀλλὰ τῆς ὑμετέρας πραότητος καὶ φιλαν-
θρωπίας· ἓν μόνον παραφυλάττοντες, ὅπως δι' ὑμᾶς
καὶ μὴ καθ' ὑμῶν ἔσται τὸ λαμβανόμενον. καὶ
Δημοσθένη καὶ Δημάδην ἀπ' αὐτῶν τῶν ἐν τῇ
πόλει ψηφισμάτων καὶ προξενιῶν οἶμαι πλείω ἢ
ἑξήκοντα τάλαντα ἑκάτερον εἰληφέναι, ἔξω τῶν
βασιλικῶν καὶ τῶν παρ' Ἀλεξάνδρου. οἷς δὲ μήτε
ταῦτα ἱκανά ἐστιν μήτ' ἐκεῖνα, ἀλλ' ἤδη ἐπ' αὐτῷ
τῷ σώματι τῆς πόλεως δῶρα εἰλήφασι, πῶς οὐκ
ἄξιον τούτους κολ[άζ[ειν ἐστίν; ἀλλὰ τῶν μὲν
[col. 26] ἰδιωτῶν ὑμῶν ἐάν τις ἀρχήν τιν[α ἄρχων]⁵ δι'
ἄγνοιαν ἢ [δι' ἀπει]ρίαν⁶ ἁμάρτη τ[ι, οὗτος]⁷ ὑπὸ
τούτων κ[αταρρη]τορευθεὶς⁷ ἐν τῷ [δικα]στηρίῳ ἢ

¹ οἱ Blass.
² καὶ usque ad μὲν Boeckh.
³ εἰλήφασιν Babington.
⁴ ἁπλᾶ usque ad προστάττουσιν Blass.
⁵ ἄρχων Boeckh.
⁶ δι' ἀπειρίαν Babington.
⁷ οὗτος et καταρρητορευθεὶς Sauppe.

who took the gold are not so culpable as the orators and generals. Why is that ? Because the private individuals were given the money by Harpalus for safe-keeping, but the generals and orators have accepted it with some policy in view. The laws prescribe that ordinary offenders shall pay a simple fine but that men accepting bribes shall pay ten times the usual sum.[a] Therefore, just as we can lawfully fix the penalty for these men, so also . . . from you against them. . . . It is as I said in the Assembly. You give full permission, gentlemen of the jury, to the orators and generals to reap substantial rewards. It is not the laws which grant them this privilege but your tolerance and generosity. But on one point you insist : your interests must be furthered, not opposed, with the money they receive. Now Demosthenes and Demades, from actual decrees passed in the city and from proxenies, have each received, I believe, more than sixty talents, quite apart from the Persian funds and money sent from Alexander. If neither of these sources suffices for them, and they have now accepted bribes which threaten the city's life itself, can we doubt our right to punish them ? Suppose that one of you, mere private individuals, during the tenure of some office, makes a mistake through ignorance or inexperience ; he will be overwhelmed in court by the eloquence of these men and will either lose his life

---

[a] The term ἀδικεῖν seems to be used in this context to describe the milder breaches of the law, and is used in the same sense by Aristot. *Ath. Pol.* 54. 2, where κλέπτειν, δῶρα λαμβάνειν, and ἀδικεῖν are distinguished as punishable with a tenfold fine, a tenfold fine, and a simple fine respectively. Dinarchus is misleading when he refers (i. 60) to a double fine. A simple fine was doubled only when it was not paid up within a fixed time.

ἀπο[θανεῖ]ται ἢ ἐκ τῆς πατ[ρίδος] ἐκπεσεῖται·
αὐτ[οὶ δὲ] τηλικαῦτα ἀδικ[ήσαν]τες τὴν πόλιν οὐδε-
μιᾶς τιμωρία[ς τεύ]ξονται; καὶ Κόν[ων][1] μὲν ὁ
Παιανιεύς, [ὅτι][2] ὑπὲρ τοῦ υἱοῦ ἔλαβ[εν] τὸ θεωρικὸν
ἀπ[οδη]μοῦντος, πέντ[ε δρα]χμῶν ἕνεκεν [ἱκε]τεύων
ὑμᾶς τάλαντον ὤφλεν ἐν τῷ δικαστηρίῳ, τούτων
κατηγορούντων· καὶ Ἀριστόμαχος ἐπιστάτης γενόμενος τῆς Ἀκαδημείας, ὅτι σκαφεῖον ἐκ τῆς παλαί-
στρας μετενεγκὼν εἰς τὸν κῆπον τὸν αὑτοῦ πλησίον
ὄντα ἐχρῆτο καὶ ἔφη . . .

[Desunt col. 27 fere tota et col. 28 versus septem.]

Frag. VII (VIII)

[col. 28] [Οὐ μέντοι][3] ἡμᾶς ὁ δῆμ[ος ἐν τῷ] μετὰ ταῦτα
χρ[όνῳ] οὐκ εἴα προσ[ιέναι] αὐτῷ οὐδὲ δια[λέγε]-
σθαι, ἀλλὰ καὶ συ[μβούλοις ἐχ]ρῆτο καὶ σ[υνηγόροις]
[Desunt versus fere duo.] τοῦ δ]ὲ ἐπιόν[τος][4] . . . . .
ἐ]πὶ τὴν δι[οίκησιν τῶ]ν αὐτοῦ ἅπασαν [ταμ]ίαν[5]
ἐχειροτόνησ[εν], ὑπ]ολαμβάνων χάριν αὐτῷ παρ'
ἡμῶν ὀφείλεσθαι, ὅπερ δίκαιον ἦν. καὶ πρὸς τούτοις ἀγώνων ἡμῖν ὕστερον πολλῶν γεγενημένων
[col. 29] [ἐξ ἐ]κείνων[6] τῶν [πραγ]μάτων[6] [καὶ αὐτοῦ][7] τοῦ
π]ολέμου, οὐδε[πώποτε ἡ]μ[ῶ]ν οὗτοι [κατε]ψηφί-
σαντο, ἀλλ' ἐκ πάντων ἔσωσαν, [ὅπερ μ]έγιστον
καὶ [ἀξιοπι]στότατον[8] τῆς [τοῦ δήμ]ου [εὐ]νοίας[9]

---

[1] Κόνων Boeckh.　　　　　[2] ὅτι Babington.
[3] Coll. 28 et 29 plerumque restituit Blass.
[4] τοῦ δ' ἐπιόντος ἔτους ci. Jensen.　　　[5] ταμίαν Kenyon.
[6] ἐξ ἐκείνων et πραγμάτων Kenyon.
[7] καὶ αὐτοῦ Jensen : καὶ περὶ Blass.
[8] ἀξιοπιστότατον Kenyon.
[9] εὐνοίας Fuhr : διανοίας Blass.

or be banished from his country. Shall they themselves, after harming the city on such a scale, escape unscathed ? Conon of Paeania took theoric money for his son who was abroad.[a] He was prosecuted for it by these men in court, and though he asked your pardon, had to pay a talent, all for taking five drachmas. Aristomachus also, because, on becoming principal of the Academy, he transferred a spade from the wrestling school to his own garden near by and used it and . . .

Frag. VII (VIII)

. . . However during the period which followed [b] the people did not forbid us to approach them or to discuss with them ; instead they used us as counsellors and advisers . . . and elected him next . . . as treasurer with full control of their finances, considering, quite rightly, that we owed him a debt of gratitude. Later, too, though we were often brought to trial on the strength of that policy and the war itself, these men did not vote against us once but brought us safely through everything ; and one could not have a more impressive, or a surer sign of popular

---

[a] Conon is perhaps the banker to whom Dinarchus refers (i. 43), and the incident which he mentions later in the speech (i. 56) is possibly the same as that to which Hyperides is alluding here, though according to Dinarchus it was the Areopagus who accused the culprit. Compare Dinarch. i. 56, note. The story of Aristomachus is not known.

[b] Hyperides is referring to the period which followed Chaeronea, and the statesman in question is Lycurgus. Demosthenes also speaks of the number of trials which took place at this time (Dem. xviii. 249). Hyperides himself was prosecuted by Aristogiton. Compare Fragment 18 and note.

[σημεῖον. καὶ γρά]ψαι, ὦ [Δημόσθενες] [Desunt aliquot versus.] . . . . ὑ]πὸ¹ το[ῦ ψη]φίσματος [ἠλωκέ]ναι σε αὐτόμ[ατον, οὐ]κ ἐποίησαν . . . .

[col. 30] γενομεν [Desunt aliquot versus.] [ὁ δῆ]μος² ἐποίησεν, ὥστ' αὐτὸς ὑπὸ τῆς τύχης ἀφαιρεθεὶς τὸν στέφανον, ἡμῶν ὃν ἔδωκεν οὐκ ἀφείλετο. οὕτως οὖν ἡμῖν τοῦ δήμου προσενηνεγμένου, οὐ πάντα ⟨τὰ⟩ δί[κα]ι᾽ ἂν αὐτῷ ἡμεῖς [ὑπη]ρετοῖμεν³ καὶ εἰ δ[έοι⁴ ἀ]ποθνήσκοιμεν [ὑπὲρ] αὐτοῦ; ἐγὼ [μὲν οἶμαι· ἀλλὰ σ]ὺ κατὰ [τοῦ δήμου] . . . [Desunt aliquot versus.] . . . σ]θαι εὐεργετήματα⁵· οὐ γὰρ τὴν ἑτέρων πατρίδα εὖ ποιεῖν [αὐ]τοὺς ἀλλὰ τὴν

[col. 31] ἑαυ[τῶν, ο]ὐδὲ [Desunt aliquot versus.] . . . αν καὶ λόγου δύναμιν ἀποδεικνύμενος διατετέλεκας· καὶ ὅτε μὲν ἡγοῦ τὴν βουλὴν ἀποφανεῖν τοὺς ἔχοντας τὸ χρυσίον, πολεμικὸς ὢν καὶ ταράττων τὴν πόλιν, ἵνα τὴν ζήτησιν ἐκκρούοις· ἐπειδὴ δὲ ἀναβάλοιτο τὸ ἀποφῆναι ἡ βουλή, οὔπω φάσκουσα εὑρηκέναι, τότ' ἐν τῷ δήμῳ συγχωρῶν Ἀλεξάνδρῳ καὶ τοῦ Διὸς καὶ τοῦ Ποσειδῶνος εἶ[ναι εἰ βούλ]οιτο,⁶ [κα]ὶ ἀφι[κομένου]⁷ . . . .

[Desunt col. 31 versus fere decem.]

[col. 32] . . . . . οστους . . . . ἐβούλετ[ο⁸ . . . .] στῆσαι εἰκό[να Ἀλεξάν]δρου βασι

---

¹ Hoc fragmentum, quod ad finem orationis habet Kenyon, huc inseruit Blass.
² Col. 30 plerumque restituit Fuhr.
³ ὑπηρετοῖμεν Blass.
⁴ δέοι Boeckh.

522

favour. . . .[a] the people so behaved that though deprived themselves by fortune of their crown of glory, they did not take from us the wreath which they had granted. When the people have acted thus towards us should we not render them all due service, and if need be die for them ? I believe we should, but you, against the people . . .[b] benefits. For them to serve their own, and not some other's country . . . you have continued to display the power of your eloquence. When you thought that the Areopagus would report those who had the gold you became hostile and created a disturbance in the city so as to obstruct the inquiry. But when the Areopagus postponed its statement on the grounds that it had not yet discovered the truth, you conceded in the Assembly that Alexander might be the son of Zeus and Posidon too if he wished . . .[c] wished . . . to set up a statue

[a] The sense of the mutilated passage beginning with the words καὶ γράψαι has been restored by Blass and Colin as follows : " Although you, Demosthenes, dared to propose the death penalty for yourself if the council reported that you had received anything from Harpalus, when it made its report and you were *ipso facto* convicted by the terms of the decree, these gentlemen did not take account of the circumstance but allowed you a special trial. For the people have always behaved in such a way towards us orators, etc."

[b] The sense appears to be : " You oppose the people and forget that there are men who wish to serve their own country instead of other people's. You have continued to be disloyal and to display your eloquence."

[c] Compare Dinarch. i. 94.

---

[5] Hoc fragmentum, quod ad finem orationis habet Kenyon, huc inseruit Blass.

[6] εἶναι εἰ βούλοιτο Sauppe.

[7] ἀφικομένου ci. Blass, τοῦ Νικάνορος add. Colin.

[8] Coll. 32 et 34 plerumque restituit Sauppe.

HYPERIDES

λ[έως τοῦ ἀνι]κήτου θε[οῦ . . . .
. . . . καὶ . . . .
. . . . . [ἀγ]γελίαν¹ . . . . . ['Ολυμ]πίας.¹ . . . .
. . . . ἀπήγ[γειλε
τῷ δή]μῳ . . . . . .

[Desunt col. 32 versus fere quattuordecim et
col. 33 fere tota.]

Frag. VIII (IX)

[col. 34] . . . [τῶν ἐγ]κλημάτων, καὶ κήρυγμα περὶ [τού]των
ἐποιήσατο· οἱ δ᾽ [ἀντὶ] τοῦ ἀποδόντες ἃ ἔλαβον
ἀπηλλάχθαι τιμωρίας καθ᾽ αὑτῶν καὶ ζητήσεις
ἔγραφον. τοὺς δὴ τὸ μὲν ἐξ ἀρχῆς ἀδικήσαντας
καὶ δωροδοκήσαντας, ἀδείας δ᾽ αὐτοῖς δοθείσης
μὴ ἀποδόντας τὸ χρυσίον τί χρὴ ποιεῖν; ἐᾶν ἀτι-
μωρήτους; ἀλλ᾽ αἰσχρόν, ὦ ἄνδρες δικαστ[αί,
ἰ]δίων ἕνεκα ἐγκ[λη]μάτων πόλεως σωτηρίαν κιν-
[δυ]νεύειν· οὐ γὰρ ἔ[στι]ν ὑμᾶς τούτων [ἀπ]οψη-
φίσασθαι, μὴ [ἐθέλοντας]² ἀναδέξα[σθαι καὶ τὰ²
ἀδική]μα[τα] [Desunt col. 34 versus fere quattuor
[col. 35] et col. 35 versus fere undeviginti.] μ[ὴ³ τοίνυν,
ὦ ἄνδρες] δικασ[ταί, προτιμᾶτε] τὴν τούτω[ν πλεο-]
νεξίαν τ[ῆς ὑμετέ]ρας αὐτῶν [σωτηρί]ας· μηδὲ
λη[μμάτων] αἰσχρῶν ἕν[εκα τὸν] πόλεμον, ἀλ[λὰ
[col. 36] πρα]γμάτων ἀξιω[τέρων καὶ] μεταλ[λ]α[γῆς ἀμεί-
νονος] ποιή[σησθε]. . . .

[Desunt col. 36 versus fere viginti sex et col. 37
versus quinque.]

¹ ἀγγελίαν et 'Ολυμπίας Blass.
² ἐθέλοντας et καὶ τὰ Thalheim.
³ Col. 35 restituit Blass.

524

of Alexander, the king and god invincible . . .
Olympias . . . announced to the people . . .

Frag. VIII (IX)

. . . of the charges and made a proclamation about
them.[a] And they, instead of returning what they
had received and being quit of the affair, were proposing penalties and inquiries directed against themselves. How ought we to treat men who began by
doing wrong and taking bribes and then, when
exemption was offered them, did not give back the
gold ? Should we let them go unpunished ? No ;
for it would be a shameful thing, gentlemen of the
jury, to jeopardize the safety of the city because of
charges brought against individual men. You cannot
acquit these men themselves unless you are willing
also to assume responsibility for their crimes. . . .
Then do not indulge their love of gain, gentlemen of
the jury, at the expense of your own security. Do
not let your motive for making war be love of sordid
gain ; let it be rather a wish for a more creditable
record and a change to better fortunes. . . .

[a] Dinarchus makes no clear reference to this proclamation.
Compare Dinarch. i. 4.

HYPERIDES

Frag. IX (X)

[col. 37] . . . . εσαλε . . . . [ὑ]πὲρ αὐτῶν

ε . . . . οις τὴν εἰρή[νην ἐπ]οιησάμεθα . . . .

. . . . βουλευω . . . . ων χρη

. . . . εν χε [Desunt versus fere

[col. 38] sedecim.] . . . αὐτῷ παρ' ἑκάστου ἡμῶν γίγνεσθαι,
καὶ τὸ μὲν κατηγορεῖν ἐν τῷ δικαστηρίῳ καὶ
ἐξελέγχειν τοὺς εἰληφότας τὰ χρήματα καὶ δεδωρο-
δοκηκότας κατὰ τῆς πατρίδος ἡ[μῖν]¹ προσ[έτ]αξεν
[τοῖς ᾑρημένοις] κατη[γόροις]· τὸ δ' ἀ[ποφῆναι τοὺς
ε]ἰληφότας [ἀπέδωκεν τ]ῇ βουλῇ [τῇ ἐξ Ἀρείου]
πάγου, ἢ [τούτους εἰς τ]ὸν δῆ[μον ἀπέδει]ξεν·
τὸ [δὲ κολάσαι τ]οὺς [ἀδικοῦντας² ὑμῖν] [Desunt

[col. 39] versus fere undecim.] [ἐξ Ἀρείου] πάγου. ἐὰν
δὲ ἡ ψῆφος μὴ ἀκόλουθος γένηται τοῖς νόμοις
καὶ τοῖς δικαίοις, τοῦτο δή, ὦ ἄνδρες δικασταί,
παρ' ὑμῖν ἔσται καταλελειμμένον. διόπερ δεῖ πάντας ὑμᾶς³ [Desunt versus fere quattuor.] [τὴ]ν
σωτη[ρίαν τῆς π]όλεως καὶ τὴν ἄλ[λη]ν [[τὴν]]⁴
εὐδαιμονίαν τὴν ὑπάρχουσαν ὑμῖν ἐν τῇ χώρᾳ καὶ
κοινῇ πᾶσι καὶ ἰδίᾳ ἑνὶ ἑκάστῳ, καὶ εἰς τοὺς τάφους
τοὺς τῶν προγόνων, τιμωρήσασθαι τοὺς ἀδικοῦντας
ὑπὲρ ἁπάσης τῆς πόλεως, καὶ μήτε λόγου παρά-

[col. 40] κλησιν [Desunt versus tres.] [τοὺς εἰληφό]τας⁵
δῶ[ρα κατὰ τῆς] πατρίδος καὶ τ[ῶν] νόμων· μη-
δ[ὲ τοῖς] δακρύοις τοῖς Ἁγ[νω]νίδου προσέχετε
[τὸν] νοῦν, ἐκεῖνο λο[γιζό]μενοι, ὅτι ἀτυχ[ήσαν]τι
μὲν [Desunt versus fere decem.] οὗτος δ' ἂν
[κλαίων]⁶ οὐ δίκαια ποιήσ[ειεν],⁶ ὥσπερ καὶ οἱ

526

AGAINST DEMOSTHENES

Frag. IX (X)

. . . on behalf of them . . . we made peace.
. . . to be rendered to it by each of us. The prosecuting in court and the exposing of those who had
received the money and taken bribes against their
country it allotted to us, the chosen accusers. The
reporting of the names of the recipients it assigned
to the Areopagus, who gave these men's names to
the people. Punishment of the criminals . . . to
you . . . the Areopagus. If the vote goes contrary
to law or justice, that is a responsibility, gentlemen
of the jury, which will rest with you. You must all
therefore . . . the safety of the city and the good
fortune which in other ways you all enjoy in this
country both collectively and individually. Remember the tombs of your ancestors and punish the
offenders in the interests of the whole city. Do not
allow their plausibility in argument . . . the men
who have taken bribes against their country and
defied the laws. And do not let the tears of Hagnonides [a] affect you. Remember this . . . but this man
would have no right to shed tears, any more than

---

[a] Hagnonides, who is described by Plutarch as a sycophant, and against whom, if Reiske's emendation is correct,
Dinarchus composed a speech, was probably acquitted. He
fled from Athens after the Lamian war but later returned
and was condemned to death. Compare Dinarch. frag. 9 ;
Plut. *Phoc.* 38.

---

[1] Col. 38 plerumque restituit Blass.
[2] τοὺς ἀδικοῦντας Fuhr : τοῖς δικάσταις Blass.
[3] Post ὑμᾶς add. ἀποβλέψαντας εἰς Boeckh.
[4] τὴν del. Blass.
[5] Col. 40 plerumque restituit Boeckh, sed τοὺς εἰληφότας
Sauppe.
[6] κλαίων et ποιήσειεν Blass.

HYPERIDES

λ[ησταὶ] οἱ ἐπὶ τοῦ τροχ[οῦ κλαί]οντες, ἐξὸν αὐ[τοῖς]
μὴ ἐμβαίνε[ιν εἰς] τὸ πλοῖον. οὕτω καὶ Δη[μο]-
σθένης τί προσ[ῆκον]¹ κλαιήσει, ἐ[ξὸν² αὐτῷ] μὴ
λαμ[βάνειν] . . .

Citationes ³

[a]   Ἀλλὰ τοὺς νεωτέρους ἐπὶ βοήθειαν καλεῖς, οὓς
ὕβριζες καὶ ἐλοιδοροῦ ἀκρατοκώθωνας ἀποκαλῶν;

────────

[b]   Εἰ μέν τις ἀκρατέστερον ἔπιεν, ἐλύπει σε.

────────

[c]   Οὐδὲ μέχρι παραγραφῆς.

────────

[—]   Ἄνανδρος.

¹ προσῆκον Blass.

528

pirates who cry upon the wheel when they need not have embarked in the boat. The same is true of Demosthenes. What excuse will he have for tears when he need not have accepted . . .

Citations

But you call upon the younger men, though you used to abuse and insult them with the name of wine-swillers.

Anyone who drank rather freely used to vex you.

Not even within a limited time.

Cowardly.

---

[2] ἐξὸν Sauppe : δέον Blass.
[3] Accedunt quattuor fragmenta quae ex hac oratione citant Priscianus xviii. 235 ; Athenaeus x. 424 d ; Harpocration, s.v. παραγραφή ; Photius, p. 116, 22 (Reitz).

VI

FUNERAL SPEECH

INTRODUCTION

THE funeral speech of Hyperides, delivered in 322 B.C. over the Athenian dead in the Lamian war, is mentioned more than once by ancient authors [a]; so that the text, when it was at last recovered, was identified despite the absence of title.

When the news of Alexander's death reached Greece in 323, the Athenians immediately voted for war with Macedon. Lycurgus, who for years had husbanded the city's strength, had died too soon to see the results of his work; Demosthenes was in exile, Demades disfranchised, and Phocion, though still taking part in public affairs, had pleaded in vain for peace. It was therefore natural that Hyperides, always a vigorous opponent of Macedon, should be the leading spokesman of the war.

The first active step which the Athenians took was to send for a general named Leosthenes, to us an unknown figure, and to provide him with the money necessary to secure mercenaries; of which as it happened there were eight thousand at Cape Taenarum waiting to be employed.[b] Leosthenes, who had perhaps seen service under Alexander, was clearly an outstanding man. More than a mere soldier, for Hyperides ascribes to him the city's policy, he proved himself an able leader in the coming summer.

---

[a] *e.g.* Diodor. xviii. 13; *Lives of the Ten Orators*, 849 F.
[b] See § 11.

FUNERAL SPEECH

The war, which was to end a year later in disaster, began well for Athens, since the first few months brought three victories in the field. Sailing first with his mercenaries to Aetolia in quest of allies, Leosthenes subsequently occupied Thermopylae, and turning back from there defeated a Macedonian force under the commander of the Cadmea garrison who was trying to prevent the arrival of Athenian reinforcements. This was the first success.[a] Meanwhile Antipater prepared to move. Forced, in his capacity as regent for Alexander, to bear the brunt of the war, he sent to Asia to make good his shortage of men and then marched south into Thessaly, there to encounter Leosthenes already north of Thermopylae. In the battle which followed the Athenians scored their second triumph, and Antipater was beleaguered in the town of Lamia. Leosthenes rejected all offers of peace but proved unable to storm the place ; and the siege which dragged on through the winter finally cost him his life. His place was taken by Antiphilus, who, though forced to withdraw from Lamia, succeeded in killing Leonnatus, the satrap of Phrygia, who had come to relieve the town.[b] Antipater, now freed, withdrew to Macedonia, leaving Athens the victor in the first round of the contest ; for the Athenian fleet, of which Hyperides makes no mention, had probably not yet sustained its first defeat at the hands of Cleitus off Abydos.

At this stage of the war, in the early spring of 322,[c]

[a] See § 17.   [b] See § 14.

[c] The exact chronology is uncertain, but the tone which Hyperides adopts suggests that neither the naval defeat off Abydos nor the drawn battle of Crannon, dated by the *Cambridge Ancient History* to the spring and summer of 322 respectively, had taken place at the time he spoke.

according to the custom which Thucydides has described,[a] the Athenian dead were buried at a public funeral and Hyperides was chosen to pronounce the oration over them. A funeral speech, to judge from those which have survived,[b] was bound to observe certain rigid conventions. The speaker confessed his inadequacy for the task, and besides praising the dead and consoling the bereaved, paid tribute to the prowess of their ancestors and the glory of the city. Hyperides discharged all these duties but in his own way. It was unusual to give to one man the prominence which he here gives to Leosthenes ; and there is no surviving parallel to the passage in which the leader is depicted in Hades as welcomed by the heroes of old. The speech was counted a remarkable one in antiquity,[c] and despite a few faults of inaccuracy and certain rhetorical features which modern readers may think inappropriate, it still claims admirers, and is probably the orator's best known work.

[a] Thucyd. ii. 34.

[b] The other extant funeral speeches are : those of Pericles (Thucyd. ii. 35 *sq.*), Lysias (ii.), Plato (*Menexenus*), and [Demosthenes] (lx.).

[c] [Longinus], *de Sublim.* 34. 2 ; *Lives of the Ten Orators*, 849 F.

ANALYSIS

535

[col. 1] Τῶν μὲν λόγων τ[ῶν μελ]λόντων[1] ῥηθήσεσ[θαι
ἐπὶ] τῷδε τῷ τάφῳ [περί τε][2] Λεωσθένους τοῦ
στ[ρατη]γοῦ καὶ περὶ τῶν ἄ[λλων] τῶν μετ᾽ ἐκείνου
[τετελ]ευτηκότων ἐν τ[ῷ πολ]έμῳ, ὡς ἦσαν ἄν[δρες
ἀ]γαθοί, μά[ρτυς][3] αὐτὸς ὁ χ]ρόνος[4] ὁ σ . . . . . .
. . . . . . ωι τὰς πρ[άξεις][5] . . . .]ς ἀνθρω[π
. . . . . ν] πω κα[. . . . . ἑ]ώρακε ωρ . . . .
[ἐν τῷ π]αντὶ αἰῶ[νι . . . . γ]εγενη[. . . . . . .
οὔτε] ἄνδρας [ἀμείνους τῶν] τετελευτ[ηκότων] οὔτε
2 πρ[άξεις μεγαλ]οπρεπεστ[έρας. διὸ] καὶ μάλιστα
[νῦν φοβοῦ]μαι,[6] μή μοι συμ[βῇ τὸν λ]όγον ἐλάττ[ω
φαίν]εσθαι τῶν ἔρ[γων] τῶν γεγενη[μέ]νων. πλὴν
κατ᾽ [ἐκεῖ]νό γε πάλιν θα[ρρῶ ὅ]τι τὰ ὑπ᾽ ἐμοῦ
⟨ἐ⟩κ[λει]πόμενα[7] ὑμεῖς οἱ ἀκούοντες προσθήσετε·
οὐ γὰρ ἐ⟨ν⟩ τοῖς τυχοῦσιν οἱ λόγοι ῥηθήσονται,
[col. 2] ἀλλ᾽ ἐν αὐτοῖς τοῖς μάρτυσι τῶν ⟨ἐκ⟩είνοι[ς π]ε-
3 πραγμένων. ἄξιον δέ [ἐσ]τιν ἐπαινεῖν ⟨τ⟩ὴν μὲν
[πό]λιν ἡμῶν ⟨τ⟩ῆς προαιρέ[σεω]ς ἕνεκεν, τὸ προ-
ε[λέσθ]αι ὅμοια καὶ ἔτι σε[μνό]τερα καὶ καλλίω
τῶν [πρότ]ερον αὐτῇ πεπρα[γμέ]νων, τοὺς δὲ τε-
τε[λευ]τηκότας τῆς ἀνδρείας τῆς ἐν τῷ πολέμῳ,
τὸ μὴ καταισχῦναι τὰς τῶν προγόνων ἀρετάς, τὸν

---

[1] Col. 1 plerumque restituit Blass.
[2] περί τε Cobet.
[3] μάρτυς Buecheler.

FUNERAL SPEECH

THE words to be pronounced above this grave, a
tribute to Leosthenes the general and the others who
have perished with him in the war, for the courage
they have shown, have as their witness time itself . . .[a]
nor better men than these now dead nor more re-
splendent actions. Indeed my greatest doubt to-day
is lest my speech may prove unworthy of their
exploits. I am, however, taking heart in this assurance : that what I leave unsaid will be supplied by
you who hear me ; for my listeners will be no random
audience but the persons who themselves have witnessed the actions of these men. While praise is due
to Athens for her policy, for choosing as she did a
course not only ranking with her past achievements
but even surpassing them in pride and honour, and
to the fallen also for their gallantry in battle, for
proving worthy of their forbears' valour, to Leosthenes

[a] The missing words were restored by Sudhaus so as to
give the following sense : ". . . time itself which holds the
record of their deeds. For no man known during the history
of the world has seen in any land a nobler choice than this
or better men, etc."

⁴ αὐτὸς ὁ χρόνος Kenyon.
⁵ τὰς πράξεις Babington : τὰ ὅπλα Kenyon.
⁶ νῦν φοβοῦμαι Jensen in add. (φοβοῦμαι iam Babington) :
πεφόβημαι Herwerden.
⁷ ἐκλειπόμενα Sudhaus : παραλειπόμενα Sauppe.

δὲ στρατηγὸν Λεωσθένη διὰ ἀμφότερα· τῆς τε γὰρ
προαιρέσεως εἰσηγητὴς τῇ πόλει ἐγένετο, καὶ τῆς
στρατείας ἡγεμὼν τοῖς πολίταις κατέστη.

4 Περὶ μὲν οὖν τῆς πόλεως διεξιέναι τὸ καθ᾽ ἕκαστον ὧν[1] πρό[τε]ρον πᾶσαν τὴν Ἑλλά[δα] ⟨εὐερ-
γέτηκεν⟩[2] οὔτε ὁ χρόνος ὁ παρὼν ἱκανός, οὔτε ὁ
και[ρὸ]ς ἁρμόττων τῷ μα[κρ]ολογεῖν, οὔτε ῥᾴδι[ον]
ἕνα ὄντα τοσαύ[τας] καὶ τηλικαύτας πρά[ξεις]
[ἐπ]ελθεῖν[3] καὶ μνη[μο]νεῦσαι· ἐπὶ κεφαλαί[ου δ]ὲ
5 οὐκ ὀκνήσω εἰπεῖν [περ]ὶ αὐτῆς. ὥσπερ [γὰρ] ὁ
[col. 3] ἥλιος πᾶσαν τὴν οἰκουμ[ένη]ν ἐπέρχεται, τὰ[ς μὲν][4]
ὥρας διακρίνων [εἰς τὸ π]ρέπον[5] καὶ καλῶ[ς πάντα
καθ]ιστάς,[6] τοῖς δὲ σ[ώφροσι][7] καὶ ἐπ]ιεικέσι τ[ῶν
ἀνθρώπ]ων ἐπιμ[ελ]ούμενος κ]αὶ γεν[έσεως καὶ
τροφῆ]ς καὶ [καρπ]ῶν κ[αὶ τῶν ἄ]λλων[7] ἁ[πά]ντων
τῶν εἰς τὸν β[ίο]ν χρησίμων, οὕτως καὶ ἡ πόλις
ἡμῶν διατελε[ῖ το]ὺς μὲν κακοὺς κολάζο[υσα, τοῖς]
δὲ δικαίοις β[οηθοῦσα], τὸ δὲ ἴσον ἀν[τὶ τῆς ἀδι]-
κίας[8] ἅπασιν [ἀπονέμουσα,[9] τ]οῖς δὲ ἰδί[οις κινδύνοις κα]ὶ δαπάναι[ς κοινὴν ἄδει]αν τοῖς Ἕλλη[σιν
6 παρασκευ]άζουσα. [περὶ μὲν οὖ]ν τῶν κοινῶ[ν
ἔργων τῆς πόλ]εως[10] ὥσπερ [προεῖπον[11] φρά]σαι[12]
⟨παρ⟩αλείψω,[13] πε[ρὶ δὲ Λεωσθέν]ους καὶ τῶν
ἄ[λλων τοὺς λόγ]ους ποιήσομ[αι. νῦ]ν δὲ πόθεν
ἄρξωμα[ι λέγων],[14] ἢ τίνος πρῶτον μνησθῶ; πότερα περὶ τοῦ γένους αὐτῶν ἑκάστου διεξέλθω;
7 ἀλλ᾽ εὔηθες εἶναι ὑπολαμβάνω· τὸ⟨ν⟩ μὲν ⟨γὰρ⟩[15]

---

[1] ὧν Blass olim : τῶν S, ret. Cobet.
[2] εὐεργέτηκεν add. Blass olim : πεπραγμένων suppl. Cobet qui ἀνὰ post πρότερον add.
[3] ἐπελθεῖν Babington : ἀπελθεῖν S.

the general it is doubly due ; the city's guide in framing her decision, he was besides the citizens' commander in the field.

In the case of Athens, to recount in detail the benefits which she has previously conferred upon the whole of Greece would be a task too great to compass in the time we have, nor is the occasion one for lengthy speaking. Indeed it is not easy for a single man, faced with so many noble actions, to recall the full story to your minds. I shall, however, venture one general comment on her. Compare her with the sun which visits the whole world and duly separates the seasons, disposing all things for the best, with provision, where men are virtuous and prudent, for their birth and nurture, the crops and all the other needs of life ; for so our city never fails to punish the wicked, help the just, mete out to all men fairness in place of wrong, and at her individual peril and expense assure the Greeks a common safety. To deal with the achievements of the city as a whole is, as I said before, a task which I shall not attempt, and I will here confine myself to Leosthenes and his companions. At what point, then, shall I take up the story ? What shall I mention first ? Shall I trace the ancestry of each ? To do so would, I think, be

---

[4] Col. 3 plerumque restituit Babington.

[5] εἰς τὸ πρέπον Blass.

[6] πάντα καθιστάς Cobet.

[7] σώφροσι usque ad ἄλλων Blass.

[8] ἀδικίας Jensen : πλεονεξίας anon. ap. Babington.

[9] ἀπονέμουσα Kaibel : φυλάττουσα Blass.

[10] ἔργων τῆς πόλεως Sauppe et Tell.

[11] προεῖπον Blass. [12] φράσαι Kayser.

[13] παραλείψω Buecheler : αλιφω S.

[14] λέγων Sauppe.

[15] τὸν μὲν γὰρ Schäfer.

[col. 4] ἄλλους τινὰς ἀνθρώπους ἐγκωμιάζοντα, οἳ πολλαχόθεν εἰς μίαν πόλιν συνεληλυθότες οἰκοῦσι γένος
ἴδιον ἕκαστος συνεισενεγκάμενος, τοῦτον¹ μὲν δεῖ
κατ᾽ ἄνδρα γενεαλογεῖν ἕκαστον· περὶ δὲ ᾽Αθηναίων
ἀνδρῶν τοὺ⟨ς⟩ λόγου⟨ς⟩ ποιούμενον,² οἷς ἡ κοινὴ
γένεσις α[ὐτόχ]θοσιν οὖσιν ἀνυπέρβλητ[ον] τὴν εὐ-
γένειαν ἔχει, περίεργον ἡγοῦμαι εἶναι ἰδίᾳ [τὰ] γένη
8 ἐγκωμιάζειν. ἀλλὰ [πε]ρὶ τῆς παιδείας αὐτῶν ἐπι-
[μνη]σθῶ, καὶ ὡς ἐν πολλῇ σ[ωφρο]σύνῃ παῖδες
ὄντ[ες ἐτρά]φησαν καὶ ἐπαιδε[ύθησαν]³ ὅπερ εἰώ-
θασίν [τινες ποι]εῖν;⁴ ἀλλ᾽ οἶμαι π[άντας] εἰδέναι
ὅτι τούτο[υ ἕνεκα]⁵ τοὺ⟨ς⟩ παῖδας παιδεύο[μεν],⁵
ἵνα ἄνδρες ἀγαθοὶ γ[ένων]ται·⁶ τοὺς δὲ γεγενη-
μ[ένους] ἐν τῷ πολέμῳ ἄνδρ[ας] ὑπερβάλλοντας τῇ
ἀ[ρετῇ], πρόδηλόν ἐστιν ὅτι πα[ῖδ]ες ὄντες καλῶς
9 ἐπαιδε[ύθη]σαν. ἁπλούστατον ο[ὖν ἡ]γοῦμαι εἶναι
τὴν ἐν τῷ πολέμῳ διεξελθεῖν ἀρετήν, καὶ ὡς πολλῶν ἀγαθῶν αἴτιοι γεγένη⟨ν⟩ται τῇ πατρίδι καὶ
τοῖς ἄλλοις ῞Ελλησιν. ἄρξομαι δὲ πρῶτον ἀπὸ τοῦ
10 στρατηγοῦ· καὶ γὰρ δίκαιον. Λεωσθένης γὰρ ὁρῶν
τὴν ῾Ελλάδα πᾶσαν τεταπεινωμένην καὶ⁷ . . . . .
[col. 5] ἐπτη[χυ]ῖαν, κατεφθαρμένην ὑπὸ [τῶν] δωροδοκούντων παρὰ Φι[λίπ]που καὶ ᾽Αλεξάνδρου κατὰ
[τῶν] πατρίδων τῶν αὐτῶν, [καὶ τ]ὴν μὲν πόλιν
ἡμῶν [δεομέ]νην⁸ ἀνδρός, τὴν δ᾽ ῾Ελλά[δα πᾶ]σαν
πόλεως, ἥτις προστῆ[ναι δυν]ήσεται⁹ τῆς ἡγεμονίας, [ἐπέδ]ωκεν¹⁰ ἑαυτὸν μὲν τῇ [πατρί]δι, τὴν δὲ
11 πόλιν τοῖς ῞Ελλη[σιν] εἰς τὴν ἐλευθερίαν· καὶ ξενικὴν

---

¹ τοῦτον Cobet : τούτων S.
² ποιούμενον] ποιούμενος Cobet.
³ ἐπαιδεύθησαν Babington.

foolish. Granted, if one is praising men of a different
stamp, such as have gathered from divers places into
the city which they inhabit, each contributing his
lineage to the common stock, then one must trace
their separate ancestry. But from one who speaks of
Athenians, born of their own country and sharing a
lineage of unrivalled purity, a eulogy of the descent
of each must surely be superfluous. Am I then to
touch upon their education, and, as other speakers
often do, remind you how as children they were
reared and trained in strict self-discipline ? None of
us, I think, is unaware that our aim in training children is to convert them into valiant men ; and that
men who have proved of exceptional courage in war
were well brought up in childhood needs no stressing.
The simplest course, I think, will be to tell you of
their courage under arms, revealing them as authors
of many benefits conferred upon their country and
the rest of Greece. First I shall take the general, as
is his due. For Leosthenes perceived that the whole
of Greece was humiliated and . . . cowed, corrupted
by men who were accepting bribes from Philip and
Alexander against their native countries. He realized
that our city stood in need of a commander, and
Greece herself of a city, able to assume the leadership, and he gave himself to his country and the city
to the Greeks, in the cause of freedom. After raising

---

⁴ τινες ποιεῖν Jensen (ποιεῖν iam Lightfoot) : παιδεύειν
Sauppe.

⁵ ἕνεκα et παιδεύομεν Sauppe.

⁶ γένωνται Babington.

⁷ Post καὶ add. ὥσπερ Kenyon.

⁸ δεομένην Babington, qui coll. 5 et 6 plerumque restituit.

⁹ δυνήσεται Schäfer.

¹⁰ ἐπέδωκεν Kayser : ἀπέδωκεν Babington.

μὲν δύναμιν ⟨συ⟩στησάμενος, τῆς δὲ πολιτικῆς
ἡγεμὼν καταστάς, τοὺς πρώτους ἀντιταξαμένους
τῇ τῶν Ἑλλήνων ἐλευθερίᾳ Βοιωτοὺς καὶ Μακεδόνας καὶ Εὐβοέας καὶ τοὺς ἄλλους συμμάχους
12 αὐτῶν ἐνίκησε μαχόμενος ἐν τῇ Βοιωτίᾳ. ἐντεῦθεν
δ' ἐλθὼν εἰς Πύλας καὶ καταλαβὼν τὰς [πα]ρόδους,[1]
δι' ὧν καὶ πρότερον ἐ[πὶ τ]οὺς Ἕλληνας οἱ βάρβαροι
ἐ[πο]ρεύθησαν, τῆς μὲν ἐπὶ [τὴν] Ἑλλάδα πορείας
Ἀντίπατρον ἐκώλυσεν, αὐτὸν δὲ [κα]ταλαβὼν ἐν
τοῖς τόποις τού[τοι]ς καὶ μάχῃ νικήσας, ἐπολι[όρ]κει
13 κατακλείσας εἰς Λαμίαν. Θετταλοὺς δὲ καὶ
Φωκέας καὶ [Αἰ]τωλοὺς καὶ τοὺς ἄλλους ἅπαντας
τοὺς ἐν τῷ τόπῳ συμμάχους ἐποιήσατο, καὶ ὧν
Φίλιππος καὶ Ἀλέξανδρος ἀκόντων ἡγούμενοι ἐσεμ-
νύνοντο, τούτων Λεωσθένης ἑκόντων τὴν ἡγεμονίαν
ἔλαβεν. συνέβη δ' αὐτῷ τῶν μὲν πραγμάτων ὧν
[col. 6] προείλετο κρατῆσαι, τῆς δὲ εἱ[μαρ]μένης οὐκ ἦν
14 περιγενέ[σθαι.] δίκαιον δ' ἐστὶν μὴ μ[όνον] ὧν
ἔπραξεν Λεωσθέν[ης ἀε]ὶ[2] χάριν ἔχειν αὐτῷ πρ[ώ-
τῳ,[3] ἀ]λλὰ καὶ τῆς ὕστερον [γενομέν]ης μάχης μετὰ
τ[ὸν ἐκείνο]υ[4] θάνατον, καὶ τῶν [ἄλλων ἀγ]αθῶν
τῶν ἐν τῇ σ[τρατείᾳ τ]αύτῃ συμβάντων [τοῖς Ἑλ]-
λησιν· ἐπὶ γὰρ τοῖς ὑπὸ [Λε]ωσθένους ⟨τε⟩θεῖσιν
θεμελίοις οἰκοδομοῦσιν οἱ νῦν τὰς ὕστερον πράξεις.
15 καὶ μηδεὶς ὑπολάβῃ με τῶν ἄλλων πολιτῶν [μη]δένα
λόγον ποιεῖσθαι, [ἀλλὰ][5] Λεωσθένη μόν⟨ον⟩ ἐγκω-
[μιάζ]ειν.[5] συμβαίνει γὰρ [τὸν Λε]ωσθένους ἔπαινον
[ἐπὶ ταῖ]ς μάχαις ἐγκώμιον [τῶν ἄλ]λων[6] πολιτῶν
εἶναι· το[ῦ μὲν] γὰρ βουλεύεσθαι καλ[ῶς ὁ στρα]-
τηγὸς αἴτιος, τοῦ δὲ νι[κᾶν μαχ]ομένους οἱ κινδυ-

a mercenary force he took command of the citizen
army and defeated the first opponents of Greek
freedom, the Boeotians, Macedonians and Euboeans,
together with their other allies, in battle in Boeotia.
Thence he advanced to Pylae [a] and occupied the pass
through which, in bygone days as well, barbarians
marched against the Greeks. He thus prevented the
inroad of Antipater into Greece, and overtaking him
in that vicinity, defeated him in battle and shut him
into Lamia, which he then besieged. The Thessalians,
Phocians, Aetolians, and all the other peoples of the
region, he made his allies, bringing under his control,
by their own consent, the men whom Philip and
Alexander gloried in controlling against their wish.
The circumstances subject to his will he mastered,
but fate he could not overpower. Leosthenes must
have first claim upon our gratitude for ever, not only
for the acts performed by him, but also for the later
battle, fought after his death, and for those other
triumphs which the Greeks have gained in this
campaign. For on the foundations laid by Leosthenes
the subsequent success of his survivors rests. Let no
one fancy that I disregard the other citizens and keep
my eulogy for him alone. The praise bestowed upon
Leosthenes for these engagements is in fact a tribute
to the rest. For though sound strategy depends upon
the leader, success in battle is ensured by those who

---

[a] In fact Leosthenes seems to have occupied Thermopylae
before his victory in Boeotia.

---

[1] παρόδους Spengel.
[2] ἀεὶ Jensen (sed in add. καὶ): ζῶν Kenyon.
[3] πρώτῳ Blass.
[4] ἐκείνου Müller.
[5] ἀλλὰ et ἐγκωμιάζειν Sauppe.
[6] τῶν ἄλλων Jensen.

HYPERIDES

ν[εύειν ἐθ]έλοντες τοῖς σώμασ[ιν· ὥστ]ε ὅταν ἐπαι-
ν[ῶ τὴν γ]εγονυῖαν νίκην, ἅμα τ[ῇ Λε]ωσθένους ἡγε-
μονίᾳ καὶ [τὴν τ]ῶν ἄλλων ἀρετὴν ἐγκωμ[ιάσ]ω.[1]

16 τίς γὰρ οὐκ ἂν δικα[ίως] ἐπαινοίη τῶν πολιτῶ[ν
το]ὺς ἐν τῷδε τῷ πολέμῳ [τε]λευτήσαντας, οἳ τὰς
ἑα[υτῶ]ν ψυχὰς ἔδωκαν ὑπὲρ τῆ[ς τῶ]ν Ἑλλήνων
ἐλευθερίας, [φα]νερωτάτην ἀπόδειξιν τ[αύτ]ην ἡγούμενοι εἶναι τοῦ [βούλ]εσθαι τῇ Ἑλλάδι [τὴν] ἐλε[υ-
[col. 7] θερ]ίαν περιθεῖναι, τὸ μαχομ[ένους][2] τελευτῆσαι

17 ὑπὲρ αὐτῆ[ς. μ]έγα δ᾽ αὐτοῖς συνεβάλετ[ο εἰ]ς τὸ
προθύμως ὑπὲρ τῆς ['Ελλά]δος[3] ἀγωνίσασθαι τὸ ἐν
τῇ [Βοιω]τίᾳ τὴν μάχην τὴν π[ροτέραν][3] γενέσθαι.
ἑώρων γὰ[ρ τὴν μὲν π]όλιν τῶν Θηβαίων οἰκτ[ρῶς
ἠφα]νισμένην ἐξ ἀνθρώπων, [τὴν δὲ ἀ]κρόπολιν
αὐτῆς φρουρου[μένην] ὑπὸ τῶν Μακεδόνων, τὰ δὲ
σώματα τῶν ἐνοικούντων ἐξηνδραποδισμένα, τὴν
δὲ χώραν ἄλλους διανεμομένους, ὥστε πρὸ ὀφθαλμῶν ὁρώμενα αὐτοῖς τὰ δεινὰ ἄοκνον π[αρ]εῖχε
τόλμα⟨ν⟩ εἰς τὸ κινδυνεύειν [πρ]οχείρως.

18   Ἀλλὰ μὴν τήν γε π[ερὶ Π]ύλας[4] καὶ Λαμίαν
μάχην γεν[ομέν]ην οὐχ ἧττον αὐτοῖς ἔνδο[ξον γεν]-
έσθαι συμβέβηκεν ἧς [ἐν Βοιω]τοῖς ἠγωνίσαντο,
οὐ μόνον [τῷ μαχο]μένους νικᾶν Ἀντίπατρον [καὶ
τοὺς σ]υμμάχους, ἀλλὰ καὶ τῷ τόπῳ [τῷ ἐ]νταυθοῖ
γεγενῆσθαι τὴν μ[άχην.] ἀφικνούμενοι γὰρ οἱ Ἕλλη[νες ἅπα]ντες δὶς τοῦ ἐνιαυτοῦ εἰς [τὴν Πυλ]αίαν,
θεωροὶ γενήσοντ[αι] τῶν ἔργων τῶν π[επρα]γμένων

---

[1] ἐγκωμιάσω Stahl : ἐγκωμιάζω Sauppe.
[2] μαχομένους Sauppe : μαχόμενοι Babington.
[3] Col. 7 plerumque restituit Babington : sed Ἑλλάδος et
προτέραν Sauppe.   [4] περὶ Πύλας Cobet.

544

are prepared to risk their lives ; and therefore, in the praise that I bestow upon the victory gained, I shall be commending not merely the leadership of Leosthenes but the courage of his comrades too. For who could rightly grudge his praise to those of our citizens who fell in this campaign, who gave their lives for the freedom of the Greeks, convinced that the surest proof of their desire to guarantee the liberty of Greece was to die in battle for her ? One circumstance did much to reinforce their purpose as champions of Greece : the fact that the earlier battle was fought in Boeotia.[a] They saw that the city of Thebes had been tragically annihilated from the face of the earth, that its citadel was garrisoned by the Macedonians, and that the persons of its inhabitants were in slavery, while others parcelled out the land among themselves. And so these threats, revealed before their eyes, gave them an undaunted courage to meet danger gladly.

Yet the action fought near Pylae and Lamia has proved to be as glorious for them as the conflict in Boeotia, not solely through the circumstances of victory in the field, over Antipater and his allies, but on the grounds of situation also. The fact that this has been the battle's site will mean that all the Greeks, repairing twice a year to the council of the Amphictyones, will witness their achievements ; for

---

[a] The points which Hyperides makes in this and in the following section will not bear examination. For (1) the first victory was gained in the territory of Plataea, not within sight of Thebes ; (2) the second battle was probably fought near Heraclea in Trachis, and its site could not be seen from Anthela where the Amphictyonic council met. Moreover, the council met there only once a year and could hardly be called representative of the whole of Greece.

αὐτοῖς· ἅμα γὰρ εἰς τὸ[ν τό]πον ἀθροισθήσονται
19 καὶ τῆ[ς το]ύτων ἀρετῆς μνησθήσοντ[αι. ο]ὐδένες
γὰρ πώποτε τῶν γεγονότων οὔτε περὶ καλλιόνων
οὔτε πρὸς ἰσχυροτέρους οὔτε μετ' ἐλαττόνων ἠγωνίσαντο, τὴν ἀρετὴν ἰσχὺν καὶ τὴν ἀνδρείαν πλῆθος,
ἀλλ' οὐ τὸν πολὺν ἀριθμὸν τῶν σωμάτων εἶναι
κρίνοντες. καὶ τὴν μὲν ἐλευθερίαν εἰς τὸ κοινὸν
πᾶσιν κατέθεσαν, τὴν δ' εὐδοξίαν ⟨τὴν⟩[1] ἀπὸ τῶν
[col. 8] πράξεων ἴδιον στέφανον τῇ πατρίδ[ι περι]έθηκαν.[2]
20 Ἄξιον τοίνυν συλλογίσασθαι καὶ τί ἂν συμβῆναι
νομίζομεν[3] μὴ κατὰ τρόπον τούτων ἀγωνισαμένων.
ἆρ' οὐκ ἂν ἑνὸς μὲν δεσπότου τὴν οἰκουμένην ὑπ-
ήκοον ἅπασαν εἶναι, νόμῳ δὲ τῷ τούτου τρόπῳ
ἐξ ἀνάγκης χρῆσθαι τὴν Ἑλλάδα; συνελόντα δ' εἰπεῖν, τὴν Μακεδόνων ὑπερηφανίαν καὶ μὴ τὴν τοῦ
δικαίου δύναμιν ἰσχύειν παρ' ἑκάστοις, ὥστε μήτε
γυναικῶν μήτε παρθένων μήτε παίδων ὕβρεις . . . . .
21 ἀνεκλείπτους[4] ἑκάστοις καθεστάναι. φανερὸν δ' ἐξ
ὧν ἀναγκαζόμεθα καὶ νῦν ἔτι[5]· θυσίας μὲν ἀνθρώποις γ[ιγνο]μένας[6] ἐφορᾶν, ἀγάλμ[ατα δὲ] καὶ βωμοὺς καὶ ναοὺς τοῖ[ς μὲν] θεοῖς ἀμελῶς, τοῖς δὲ
ἀνθρώ[ποις] ἐπιμελῶς συντελούμενα, καὶ τοὺς
⟨τού⟩των[7] οἰκέτας ὥσπερ ἥρωας τιμᾶν ἡμᾶς ἀναγ-
22 καζομένους. ὅπου δὲ τὰ πρὸς ⟨τοὺς⟩[8] θεοὺς ὅσια
διὰ τὴν Μακεδόνων τόλμαν ἀνῄρηται, τί τὰ πρὸς
τοὺς ἀνθρώπους[9] χρὴ νομίζειν; ἆρ' οὐκ ἂν παν-
τελῶς καταλελύσθαι; ὥστε ὅσῳ δεινότερα τὰ

---

[1] τὴν add. Blass.
[2] περιέθηκαν Sauppe.
[3] νομίζομεν Kayser : νομίζοιμεν S.
[4] ἀνεκλείπτους plerique edd., qui lacunam indicant : ἂν
ἐκλείπτους (verbum ignotum) S : post ἑκάστοις add. μὴ Colin.
[5] ἔτι Kayser : ἐστι Cobet : ἐὰν Caffiaux.

546

by the very act of gathering in that spot they will
recall the valour of these men. Never before did men
strive for a nobler cause, either against stronger
adversaries or with fewer friends, convinced that
valour gave strength and courage superiority as no
mere numbers could. Liberty they gave us as an
offering for all to share, but the honour of their deeds
they have bestowed upon their country as a wreath
for her alone.

Now we might well reflect what, in our opinion, the
outcome would have been, had these men failed to do
their duty in the struggle. Must we not suppose that
the whole world would be under one master, and
Greece compelled to tolerate his whim as law ? In
short that Macedonian arrogance, and not the power
of justice, would lord it among every people. . . .[a]
The practices which even now we have to countenance
are proof enough : sacrifices being made to men ;
images, altars, and temples carefully perfected in
their honour, while those of the gods are neglected,
and we ourselves are forced to honour as heroes the
servants of these people. If reverence for the gods
has been removed by Macedonian insolence, what
fate must we conclude would have befallen the rules
of conduct towards man ? Would they not have been
utterly discounted ? The more terrible therefore

[a] Various attempts have been made to restore this corrupt
passage, from which some words seem to have dropped out,
but none is wholly satisfactory. In any case the sense appears
to be that outrages on women, girls, and children would continue without pause in every city.

---

[6] γιγνομένας Cobet.
[7] τούτων Cobet.
[8] τοὺς add. Cobet.
[9] Post ἀνθρώπους add. δίκαια Fritzsche.

HYPERIDES

προ⟨σ⟩δοκῶμεν' ἂν γενέσθαι κρίνομεν,[1] τοσούτῳ
μειζόνων ἐπαίνων τοὺς τετελευτηκότας ἀξίους χρὴ
23 νομίζειν. οὐδεμία γὰρ στρατεία τὴν ⟨τῶν⟩[2] στρα-
τευομένων ἀρετὴν ἐνεφάνισεν μᾶλλον τῆς νῦν γεγενημένης, ἐν ᾗ γε παρατάττεσθαι μὲν ὁσημέραι
ἀναγκαῖον ἦ⟨ν⟩, πλείους δὲ μάχας ἠγωνίσθαι διὰ
[col. 9] μιᾶς στρατ[είας] ἢ τοὺς ἄλλους πάντας πληγὰς[3]
λαμβάνειν ἐν τῷ παρεληλυθότι χρόνῳ, χειμώνων
δ' ὑπερβολὰς καὶ τῶν καθ' ἡμέ[ρα]ν ἀναγκαίων
ἐνδείας τοσ[αύ]τας καὶ τηλικαύτας οὕτως [ἐγ]κρα-
τῶς ὑπομεμ⟨ε⟩νηκένα[ι, ὥσ]τε καὶ τῷ λόγῳ χαλεπὸν
[εἶν]αι φράσαι.
24 Τὸν δὴ τοιαύτας καρτερίας ἀόκνως ὑπομεῖναι
τοὺ⟨ς⟩ πολίτας προτρεψάμενον Λεωσθένη, καὶ τοὺς
τῷ τοιούτῳ στρατηγῷ προθύμως συναγωνιστὰς
σφᾶς αὐτοὺς παρασχόντας, ἆρ' οὐ διὰ τὴν τῆς
ἀρετῆς ἀπόδειξιν εὐτυχεῖς μᾶλλον ἢ διὰ τὴν τοῦ
ζῆν ἀπόλειψιν ἀτυχεῖς νομιστέον; οἵτινες θνητοῦ
σώματος ἀθάνατον δόξαν ἐκτήσαντο, καὶ διὰ τὴν
ἰδίαν ἀρετὴν τὴν κοινὴν ἐλ[ευ]θερίαν τοῖς Ἕλλησιν
25 ἐβεβαίωσαν. φέρει γὰρ πᾶσαν εὐδαιμονίαν[4] . . . . . .
ἄνευ τῆς αὐτονομίας. ο⟨ὐ⟩ γὰρ ἀνδρὸς ἀπειλήν,
ἀλλὰ νόμου φωνὴν κυριεύειν δεῖ τῶν εὐδαιμόνων,
οὐδ' αἰτίαν φοβερὰν εἶναι τοῖς ἐλευθέροις, ἀλλ'
ἔλεγχον, οὐδ' ἐπὶ τοῖς κολακεύουσιν τοὺς δυνάστας
καὶ διαβάλλουσιν τοὺ⟨ς⟩ πολίτας τὸ τῶν πολιτῶν
ἀσφαλές, ἀλλ' ἐπὶ τῇ τῶν νόμων πίστει γενέσθαι.
26 ὑπὲρ ὧν ἁπάντων οὗτοι πόνους πόνων διαδόχους
ποιούμενοι, καὶ τοῖς καθ' ἡμέραν κινδύνοις τοὺ⟨ς⟩

---

[1] κρίνομεν Kayser : κρίνοιμεν S.
[2] τῶν add. Babington.
[3] πληγὰς] del. Cobet.

we think the consequences would have been, the greater must be the praise which we believe the dead have earned. For no campaign has better shown the courage of the soldiers than this last, when they had daily to be arrayed for combat, to fight, on but one expedition, more battles than the combats which any soldier of the past endured,[a] and face extreme severities of weather and many hard privations in the daily needs of life with an endurance almost beyond description.

Such trials Leosthenes induced the citizens to brave undaunted, and they gave up their persons gladly to share the struggle with so great a leader. Should they not then be counted fortunate in their display of valour rather than unfortunate in their sacrifice of life ? For in exchange for a mortal body they gained undying glory, safeguarding by their personal courage the universal liberty of Greece. . . .[b] If men are to be happy, the voice of law, and not a ruler's threats, must reign supreme ; if they are free, no groundless charge, but only proof of guilt, must cause them apprehension ; nor must the safety of our citizens depend on those who slander them and truckle to their masters but on the force of law alone. Such were the aims with which these men accepted labour upon labour, and with the dangers of the passing hour

---

[a] The exaggeration of this remark has led some editors to doubt the reading.

[b] The Greek words which follow here cannot be translated as they stand. Fritzsche's emendation probably restores the correct sense, namely : " Nothing brings complete happiness without self-government." But the Greek wording is uncertain.

---

[4] Intercidisse aliquid videtur : ante πᾶσαν add. οὐδὲν Fritzsche : alii alia.

εἰς τὴν ἅπαντα χρόνον φόβους τῶν πολιτῶν καὶ τῶν
Ἑλλήνων παραιρούμενοι, τὸ ζῆν ἀνήλωσαν εἰς τὸ
27 τοὺς ἄλλους καλῶς ζῆν. διὰ τούτους πατέρες
ἔνδοξοι, μητέρες περίβλε⟨π⟩τοι τοῖς πολίταις γεγόνασι, ἀδελφαὶ γάμων τῶν προσηκόντων ἐννόμως
τετυχήκασι καὶ τεύξονται, παῖδες ἐφόδιον εἰς τὴν
πρὸς τὸν δῆμον ε[ὔνοι]αν[1] τὴν τῶν οὐκ ἀπολωλό-
[col. 10] των ἀρετήν, οὐ γὰρ θεμιτὸν τούτου τοῦ ὀνόματος
τυχεῖν τοὺς οὕτως ὑπὲρ καλῶν τὸ⟨ν⟩ βίον ἐκλιπόν-
τας, ἀλλὰ τῶν τὸ ζῆν ⟨ε⟩ἰς αἰώνιον τάξιν μετηλ-
28 λα[χό]των ἕξουσιν. εἰ γὰρ [ὁ τοῖ]ς[2] ἄλλοις ὢν
ἀνιαρ[ότ]ατος[3] θάνατος τούτοις ἀρχηγὸς μεγάλων
ἀγαθῶν γέγονε, πῶς τούτους ο⟨ὐ⟩κ εὐτυχεῖς κρίνειν
δίκαιον, ἢ πῶς ἐκλελοιπέναι τὸν βίον, ἀλλ᾽ οὐκ ἐξ
ἀρχῆς γεγονέναι καλλίω γένεσιν τῆς πρώτης ὑπαρ-
ξάσης; τότε μὲν γὰρ παῖδες ὄντες ἄφρονες ἦσαν,
29 νῦν δ᾽ ἄνδρες ἀγαθοὶ γεγόνασιν. καὶ τότε μὲν ⟨ἐν⟩
πολλῷ[4] χρόνῳ καὶ διὰ πολλῶν κινδύνων τὴν ἀρετὴν
ἀπέδειξαν· νῦν δ᾽ ἀπὸ ταύτης ἀρξα⟨μένους ὑπάρ-
χει⟩[5] γνωρίμους πᾶσι καὶ μνημονευτοὺς διὰ ἀνδρα-
30 γαθίαν γεγονέναι. τίς ⟨γὰρ⟩[6] κα⟨ι⟩ρὸς ἐν ᾧ τῆς
τούτων ἀρετῆς οὐ μνημονεύσομεν; τίς τόπος ἐν
ᾧ ζήλου καὶ τῶν ἐντιμοτάτων ἐπαίνων τυγχάνον-
τας οὐκ ὀψόμεθα; πότερον οὐκ ἐν τοῖς τῆς πόλεως
ἀγαθοῖς; ἀλλὰ τὰ διὰ τούτους γεγονότα τ[ίνας]
ἄλλους ἢ τούτους ἐπαινεῖσθ[αι] καὶ μνήμης τυγχάνειν ποιήσει; ἀλλ᾽ οὐκ ἐν ταῖς ἰδίαις εὐπραξίαις;
ἀλλ᾽ ἐν τῇ τούτων ἀρετῇ βεβαίως αὐτῶν ἀπολαύ-
31 σομεν. παρὰ ποίᾳ δὲ τῶν ἡλικιῶν οὐ μακαριστοὶ

¹ εὔνοιαν Cobet.   ² ὁ τοῖς Cobet.
³ ἀνιαρότατος Babington.
⁴ ἐν πολλῷ Babington : πολλῶν S.

dispelled the terrors which the whole future held for citizens and Greeks, sacrificing their lives that others might live well. To them we owe it that fathers have grown famous, and mothers looked up to in the city, that sisters, through the benefit of law, have made, and will make, marriages worthy of them, that children too will find a passport to the people's hearts in these men's valour ; these men who, far from dying—death is no word to use where lives are lost, as theirs were, for a noble cause—have passed from this existence to an eternal state. For if the fact of death, to others a most grievous ill, has brought to them great benefits, are we not wrong indeed to count them wretched or to conclude that they have left the realm of life ? Should we not rather say they have been born anew, a nobler birth than the first ? Mere children then, they had no understanding, but now they have been born as valiant men. Formerly they stood in need of time and many dangers to reveal their courage ; now, with that courage as a base, they have become known to all, to be remembered for their valour. On what occasion shall we fail to recollect the prowess of these men, in what place fail to see them win their due of emulation and the highest praise ? What if the city prospers ? Surely the successes, which they have earned, will bring their praises, and none other's, to our lips and to our memories. Shall we then forget them in times of personal satisfaction ? We cannot ; for it is through their valour that we shall have the safe enjoyment of those moments. Will there be men of any

---

5 ἀρξαμένους ὑπάρχει Kenyon: αξαθαι S : ἄξαντας ἦν Jensen in add. : ὑπάρχει εὐθὺς Cobet.
6 γὰρ add. Cobet.

HYPERIDES

[col. 11] γενήσο[νται; πότερον οὐ πα]ρὰ¹ τοῖς π[ρεσβυ-
τέροις,² οἳ ἄ]φοβον ἄ[ξειν τὸν λοιπὸν] βίον κα[ὶ ἐν
τῷ ἀσφαλεῖ] γεγενῆσ[θαι νομίζουσι]³ διὰ τούτ[ους;
ἀλλ' οὐ παρὰ τοῖς] ἡλικιώτ[αις; . . . . . . τελευτὴ
φ . . . . καλῶς ὠ . . . .
παρὰ πο . . . . αι γεγον . . . . ; [ἀλλ'
32 οὐ παρὰ τοῖς] νεωτέρο[ις καὶ παισίν; ἔπει]τα οὐ
τὸν [θάνατον ζηλώσου]σιν αὐτ[ῶν, καὶ αὐτοὶ σπου]-
δάσουσιν [μιμεῖσθαι ὡς πα]ράδειγμ[α τὸν τούτων
33 βίον, ἀνθ'] οὗ τὴν ἀ[ρετὴν καταλελοί]πασι; οὐκ-
[οῦν ἄξιον εὐδαιμονί]ζειν αὐ[τοὺς ἐπὶ τοσαύτῃ τι]μῇ,
ἢ τίνε[ς . . . .]φοι λει . . . .
Ἕλλην . . . . τῶν πε . . . .
παρὰ πο[. . . . . τῆς] Φρυγῶν κ[ρα-
τησάσης στρα]τείας ἐγ[κωμιασθήσεται; . . . . .] δὲ
τῆς ἐλ . . . . τάτοις ε . . . .
ἅπασιν κ[αὶ λόγοις καὶ ᾠ]δαῖς⁴ ἐπα[ιν . . . .
34 ἀμφό]τερα⁵ γὰρ ε . . . . περὶ Λεωσ[θένους . . . .]
καὶ τῶν τ[ελευτησάντων] ἐν τῷ πολ[έμῳ.⁵ εἰ μὲν
γὰρ]⁶ ἡδονῆς ἕν[εκεν μνημονεύ]ουσιν τὰς τ[οιαύτας
καρ]τερίας, τί γέ[νοιτ' ἂν τοῖς Ἕλ]λησιν ἥδι[ον ἢ
ἔπαινος τῶν] τὴν ἐλευθερί[αν παρασκευα]σάντων
ἀ[πὸ τῶν Μακεδό]νων;⁶ εἰ δὲ [ὠφελείας ἕνε]κεν⁷
[col. 12] ἡ τοια[ύτη μνήμη]⁸ γίγνεται, τίς ἂν λόγος ὠφελή-
σειεν μᾶλλον τὰς τῶν ἀκουσόντων⁹ ψυχὰς τοῦ τὴν
ἀρετὴν ἐγκωμιάσαντος¹⁰ καὶ τοὺς ἀγαθοὺς ἄνδρας;

¹ Col. 11 plerumque restituit Blass.
² πρεσβυτέροις Cobet : γεραιτέροις Sauppe.

552

age who will not count them blessed ? What of the older generation, who think that through the efforts of these men they have been placed in safety and will pass the rest of their lives free from dread ? Consider their compeers . . .[a] Think, too, of the younger men and boys. Will they not envy their death and strive themselves to take as an example these men's lives, in place of which they have left behind their valour ? Ought we then to count them happy in so great an honour ?[b] . . . For if it is for pleasure that men recall such feats of courage, what could be more pleasing to Greeks than the praise of those who gave them freedom from the Macedonian yoke ? Or if it is desire for profit that prompts such recollections, what speech could be of greater profit to the hearts of those about to hear it than one which is to honour courage and brave men ?

---

[a] The sense is supplied by Kenyon as follows : " To them it has been given, because these died in battle, to enjoy their lives in honour and safety."

[b] The missing passage from ἤ τίνες to τῷ πολέμῳ has been tentatively restored by Blass and Kenyon to give the following sense : " Neither poets nor philosophers will be in want of words or song in which to celebrate their deeds to Greece. Surely this expedition will be more famed in every land than that which overthrew the Phrygians. Throughout all time in every part of Greece these exploits will be praised in verse and song. Leosthenes himself and those who perished with him in the war will have a double claim to be revered."

---

[3] νομίζουσι Jensen : ἡγήσονται Blass.
[4] καὶ λόγοις καὶ ᾠδαῖς Cobet.
[5] ἀμφότερα usque ad πολέμῳ Cobet.
[6] εἰ μὲν γὰρ usque ad Μακεδόνων post Cobet et alios Blass.
[7] ὠφελείας ἕνεκεν Babington.
[8] μνήμη Cobet.
[9] ἀκουσόντων] ἀκουόντων Sauppe.
[10] ἐγκωμιάσοντος] ἐγκωμιάζοντος Sauppe.

35 Ἀλλὰ μὴν ὅτι παρ' ἡμῖν καὶ τοῖς λοιποῖς[1] πᾶσιν
εὐδοκιμεῖν αὐτοὺς ἀναγκαῖον, ἐκ τούτων φανερόν
ἐστιν· ἐν Ἅιδου δὲ λογίσασθαι ἄξιον, τίνες οἱ τὸν
ἡγεμόνα δεξιωσόμενοι τὸν τούτων. ἆρ' οὐκ ἂν
οἰόμεθα ὁρᾶν Λεωσθένη δεξιουμένους καὶ θαυμά-
ζοντας τῶν † ἡμιθέων καλουμένων†[2] τοὺς ἐπὶ
Τροίαν στρατεύσαντας,[3] ὧν οὗτος ἀδελφὰς πράξεις
ἐνστησάμενος τοσοῦτον διήνεγκε, ὥστε οἱ μὲν μετὰ
πάσης τῆς Ἑλλάδος μίαν πόλιν εἷλον, ὁ δὲ μετὰ
τῆς ἑαυτοῦ πατρίδος μόνης πᾶσαν τὴν τῆς Εὐρώπης
καὶ τῆς Ἀσίας ἄρχουσαν δύναμιν ἐταπείνωσεν.
36 κἀκεῖνοι μὲν ἕνεκα μιᾶς γυναικὸς ὑβρισθείσης
ἤμυναν, ὁ δὲ πασῶν τῶν Ἑλληνίδων τὰς ἐπιφερο-
μένας ὕβρεις ἐκώλυσεν, μετὰ τῶν συνθαπτομένων
37 νῦν αὐτῷ ἀνδρῶν.[4] τῶν ⟨δὲ⟩[5] μετ' ἐκείνους μὲν
γεγενημένων, ἄξια δὲ τῆς ἐκείνων ἀρετῆς διαπεπραγμένων, λέγω δὴ τοὺς περὶ Μιλτιάδην καὶ
[col. 13] Θεμιστοκλέα καὶ τοὺς ἄλλους, οἳ τὴν Ἑλλάδα
ἐλευθερώσαντες ἔντιμον μὲν τὴν πατρίδα κατέστη-
38 σαν, ἔνδοξον ⟨δὲ⟩[6] τὸν αὐτῶν βίον ἐποίησαν, ὧν
οὗτος τοσοῦτον ὑπερέσχεν ἀνδρείᾳ καὶ φρονήσει,
ὅσον οἱ μὲν ἐπελθοῦσαν τὴ⟨ν⟩ τῶν βαρβάρων δύναμιν
ἠμύναντο, ὁ δὲ μηδ' ἐπελθεῖν ἐποίησεν. κἀκεῖνοι
μὲν ἐν τῇ οἰκ⟨ε⟩ίᾳ τοὺς ἐχθ⟨ρ⟩οὺς ἐπεῖδον ἀγωνιζο-
μένους, οὗτος δὲ ἐν τῇ τῶν ἐχθρῶν περιεγένετο τῶν
ἀντιπάλων.

---

[1] λοιποῖς Babington : λόγοις S.
[2] ἡμιθέων καλουμένων Cobet : δεηγορμένων καλουμένους S :
διηγμένων καὶ ὑμνουμένων in obelis Kenyon : τῶνδε ἡγούμενον
καὶ καλουμένους ci. L. A. Post.
[3] τοὺς ἐπὶ Τροίαν στρατεύσαντας Babington : τοὺς ἐπὶ
στρατείαν στρασαντ . s S.

With us and all mankind, it is clear, in the light of these reflections, that their fame is now assured, but what of the lower world? Who, we may well ask ourselves, are waiting there to welcome the leader of these men? Are we not convinced that we should see, greeting Leosthenes with wonder, those of the so-called demi-gods who sailed against Troy : heroes whom he so far excelled, though his exploits were akin to theirs, that they with all Greece at their side took but one city, while he with his native town alone brought low the whole power which held Europe and Asia beneath its sway? They championed one lone woman wronged, but he staved off from all Greek women the violence coming upon them, aided by these men who now are being buried with him. Remember the figures who,[a] born after the heroes of old, yet rivalled their deeds of valour, the followers of Miltiades and Themistocles, and those others who, by freeing Greece, brought honour to their country and glory to their lives ; whom Leosthenes so far outdid in bravery and counsel, that where they beat back the barbarian power as it advanced, he even forestalled its onslaught. They saw a struggle with the foe in their own land, but he defeated his opponents on the foe's own soil.

[a] This sentence is awkward in Greek because, though τῶν γεγενημένων is genitive, dependent on ὑπερέσχεν, the writer has inserted ὧν which is not needed. The difficulty can be avoided by placing a comma after ἀνδρῶν and the full stop after διαπεπραγμένων, but then λέγω δὴ makes an abrupt beginning to the new sentence.

---

[4] Sic interpunxit Sauppe ; ἀνδρῶν, et διαπεπραγμένων. Cobet.

[5] δὲ add. Sauppe.

[6] δὲ add. Babington.

39 Οἶμαι δὲ καὶ ⟨τοὺς⟩[1] τὴν πρὸς ἀλλήλους φιλίαν
τῷ δήμῳ βεβαιότατα ἐνδειξαμένους, λέγω δὲ Ἁρμόδιον καὶ Ἀριστογείτονα, † οὐθένας[2] οὕτως αὑτοῖς
οἰκειοτέρους ὑμῖν εἶναι νομίζειν ὥς†[2] Λεωσθέ⟨ν⟩η
καὶ τοὺς ἐκείνῳ συναγωνισαμένους, οὐδ' ἔστιν οἷς ἂν
μᾶλλον ἢ τούτοις πλησιάσειαν ἐν Ἅιδου. εἰκότως·
οὐκ ἐλάττω γὰρ ἐκείνων ἔργα διεπράξαντο, ἀλλ'
εἰ δέον εἰπεῖν, καὶ μείζω. οἱ μὲν γὰρ τοὺς τῆς
πατρίδος τυράννους [κα]τέλυσαν, οὗτοι δὲ τοὺς τῆς
40 Ἑλλάδος ἁπάσης. ὦ καλῆς μὲν καὶ παραδόξου
τόλμης τῆς πραχθείσης ὑπὸ τῶνδε τῶν ἀνδρῶν,
ἐνδόξου δὲ καὶ μεγαλοπρεποῦς προαιρέσεως ἧς
προείλοντο, ὑπερβαλλούσης δὲ ἀρετῆς καὶ ἀνδραγαθίας τῆς ἐν τοῖς κινδύνοις, ἣν οὗτοι παρασχό-
μενοι εἰς τὴν κοινὴν ἐλευθερίαν τῶν Ἑλλήνων . . .

* * * * * * *

41 Χαλεπὸν[3] μὲν ἴσως ἐστὶ τοὺς ἐν τοῖς τοιούτοις
ὄντας πάθεσι παραμυθεῖσθαι. τὰ γὰρ πένθη οὔτε
λόγῳ οὔτε νόμῳ κοιμίζεται, ἀλλ' ἡ φύσις ἑκάστου
καὶ φιλία πρὸς τὸν τελευτήσαντα ⟨τὸν⟩[4] ὁρισμὸν
ἔχει τοῦ λυπεῖσθαι. ὅμως δὲ χρὴ θαρρεῖν καὶ τῆς
λύπης παραιρεῖν[5] εἰς τὸ ἐνδεχόμενον, καὶ μεμνῆσθαι μὴ μόνον τοῦ θανάτου τῶν τετελευτηκότων,
42 ἀλλὰ καὶ τῆς ἀρετῆς ἧς καταλελοίπασιν. εἰ[6] γὰρ

---

[1] τοὺς add. Babington.
[2] οὐθένας usque ad ὡς locus corruptus : οὐδένας οὕτως
αὑτοῖς οἰκείους ἂν εἶναι Sauppe : οὐδαμῶς αὑτοὺς οἰκειοτέρους
ὑμῖν εἶναι νομίζειν ἢ Kenyon : οἰκείους ἑτέρους pro οἰκειοτέρους
ci. L. A. Post. Alii alia.
[3] Epilogus apud Stobaeum, Florileg. cxxiv. 36 servatus est.

Those too, I fancy, who gave the people the surest token of their mutual friendship, Harmodius and Aristogiton,[a] do not regard . . . as Leosthenes and his comrades in arms ; nor are there any with whom they would rather hold converse in the lower world than these. We need not wonder ; for what these men did was no less a task than theirs ; it was indeed, if judgement must be passed, a greater service still. Those two brought low the tyrants of their country, these the masters of the whole of Greece. Noble indeed beyond our dreams was the courage these men attained, honourable and magnificent the choice they made. How supreme was the valour, the heroism in times of peril, which they, dedicating to the universal liberty of Greece . . .

It is hard no doubt to offer consolation to those borne down with griefs like these. For sorrows are not stilled by word or law ; only the individual's temper, and the measure of his feeling for the dead, can set the limit to his mourning. Yet we must take heart, and restricting our grief as best we may, bear in our minds, with the thought of death, the glorious name which the fallen have left behind them. For

---

[a] The sense appears to be that they regard no one as so suitable to rank with themselves as Leosthenes and his comrades. Harmodius and Aristogiton, who in 514 B.C. plotted to assassinate the two sons of Pisistratus, and after killing one, Hipparchus, were captured and put to death, were later looked upon as liberators of the city. They and their descendants, who enjoyed special privileges, are not infrequently referred to by the orators. Compare Dinarch. i. 63 and 101 ; Hyp. ii. 3.

---

⁴ τὸν add. Sauppe.
⁵ παραιρεῖν Gesner : παραινεῖν codd.
⁶ εἰ Leopardi : οὐ codd.

θρήνων ἄξια πεπόνθασιν, ἀλλ᾽ ἐπαίνων μεγάλων
πεποιήκασιν. εἰ δὲ γήρως θνητοῦ μὴ μετέσχον,
ἀλλ᾽ εὐδοξίαν ἀγήρατον εἰλήφασιν, εὐδαίμονές τε
γεγόνασι κατὰ πάντα. ὅσοι μὲν γὰρ αὐτῶν ἄπαιδες
τετελευτήκασιν, οἱ παρὰ τῶν Ἑλλήνων ἔπαινοι
παῖδες αὐτῶν ἀθάνατοι ἔσονται. ὅσοι δὲ παῖδας
καταλελοίπασιν, ἡ τῆς πατρίδος εὔνοια ἐπίτροπος
43 αὐτοῖς τῶν παίδων καταστήσεται. πρὸς δὲ τούτοις, εἰ μέν ἐστι τὸ ἀποθανεῖν ὅμοιον τῷ μὴ γενέσθαι, ἀπηλλαγμένοι εἰσὶ νόσων καὶ λύπης καὶ τῶν
ἄλλων τῶν προσπιπτόντων εἰς τὸν ἀνθρώπινον βίον·
εἰ δ᾽ ἔστιν αἴσθησις ἐν Ἅιδου καὶ ἐπιμέλεια παρὰ
τοῦ δαιμονίου, ὥσπερ ὑπολαμβάνομεν, εἰκὸς[1] τοὺς
ταῖς τιμαῖς τῶν θεῶν καταλυομέναις βοηθήσαντας
πλείστης κηδεμονίας[2] ὑπὸ τοῦ δαιμονίου τυγχάνειν. . . .

[1] εἰκὸς Toup : εἶναι vel εἴη codd.

though their fate deserves our tears, their conduct claims the highest praise. Though they have failed to reach old age in life, they have achieved a fame which knows no age, and have attained the height of satisfaction. For all who were childless at their death the praises of the Greeks will be immortal children. For all who have children alive the good-will of their country will be the children's guardian. And furthermore, if death means non-existence, they have been released from sickness and from grief, and from the other ills which vex our human life. But if in Hades we are conscious still and cared for by some god, as we are led to think, then surely those who defended the worship of the gods, when it was being overthrown, must receive from him the greatest care of all. . . .

---

[2] κηδεμονίας Ruhnken : ἐπιμελείας vel εὐδαιμονίας codd. : ἐπιμελείας καὶ κηδεμονίας Fuhr.

FRAGMENTS

FRAGMENTS

INTRODUCTION

HYPERIDES was credited with seventy-seven speeches in antiquity, of which the Pseudo-Plutarch accepted fifty-two as genuine.[a] Seventy-one titles have survived and of these fifteen are certainly open to question. As in the case of Lycurgus, the list is based on the testimony of Harpocration, Suidas and other writers. The speech on the Treaty with Alexander, which has survived among the writings of Demosthenes, was thought by Libanius [b] to resemble in style the work of Hyperides.

In the present volume the titles are arranged according to the classification given by Blass in *Attische Beredsamkeit* and all surviving fragments except single words are given. The bracketed numbers in the margin are those assigned to the fragments in the Oxford text.

[a] [Plut.] *Lives of the Ten Orators* 849 D.
[b] Arg. ad [Dem.] xvii.

A. ΛΟΓΟΙ ΔΗΜΗΓΟΡΙΚΟΙ ΚΑΙ ΠΡΕΣΒΕΥ-ΤΙΚΟΙ

1. ΔΗΛΙΑΚΟΣ

[67]   1. Λέγεται γὰρ τὴν Λητὼ κυοῦσαν τοὺς παῖδας ἐκ Διὸς ἐλαύνεσθαι ὑπὸ τῆς Ἥρας κατὰ πᾶσαν γῆν καὶ θάλατταν[1]· ἤδη δὲ αὐτὴν βαρυνομένην καὶ ἀποροῦσαν ἐλθεῖν εἰς τὴν χώραν[2] τὴν ἡμετέραν, καὶ λῦσαι τὴν ζώνην ἐν τῷ τόπῳ, ὃς νῦν Ζωστὴρ καλεῖται.   Syrian, in Hermog., ed. Rabe i. p. 37, and Max. Planud. v. 481. 10 etc.

[68]   2. Ἐνταυθοῖ θύεται τῷ Ἀπόλλωνι ὁσημέραι καὶ μερὶς αὐτῷ καὶ δεῖπνον παρατίθεται.   Priscian xviii. 251.

[69]   3. Καὶ τὸν κρατῆρα τὸν Πανιώνιον κοινῇ οἱ Ἕλληνες κεραννύουσιν.   Athen. x. 424 e.

[70]   4. Ἀφίκοντό τινες εἰς Δῆλον ἄνθρωποι Αἰολεῖς πλούσιοι, χρυσίον ἔχοντες πολύ, κατὰ θεωρίαν τῆς Ἑλλάδος ἀποδημοῦντες ἐκ τῆς ἑαυτῶν· οὗτοι ἐφάνησαν ἐν Ῥηνείᾳ ἐκβεβλημένοι τετελευτηκότες· τοῦ δὲ πράγματος περιβοήτου ὄντος, ἐπιφέρουσι Δήλιοι τοῖς Ῥηνεῦσιν αἰτίαν, ὡς αὐτῶν ταῦτα πεποιηκότων, καὶ γράφονται τὴν πόλιν αὐτῶν ἀσεβείας.   οἱ δὲ Ῥηνεῖς ἠγανάκτηνταί τε τῷ πράγματι, καὶ προσκαλοῦνται Δηλίους τὴν αὐτὴν δίκην.

564

A. *Speeches written for delivery in the assembly or on embassies*

1. THE DELIAN SPEECH

1. It is said that Leto, who was about to give birth to the children of Zeus, was driven by Hera over land and sea.[1] And when she was already weary and distressed she came to our country and loosened her girdle in the place now called Zoster.[2]

2. There a sacrifice is daily made to Apollo and a portion is set aside for him with a meal.

3. And the Greeks together mix the Panionian bowl.

4. Some Aeolians arrived at Delos. They were rich, carried a lot of gold, and were away from their country making a tour of Greece. These men were discovered cast up on Rhenea dead. The news was noised abroad, and the Delians accused the people of Rhenea of the crime and indicted their city for impiety. The Rheneans, who resented the action, brought the same charge against the Delians. When

---

[1] Text Syrian : κατὰ γῆν καὶ κ. θ. Max. Planud., Kenyon.
[2] Text Syrian : εἰς τὴν γῆν ἐλθεῖν Max. Planud., Kenyon.

HYPERIDES

οὔσης δὲ τῆς διαδικασίας,[1] ὁπότεροί εἰσιν οἱ τὸ
ἔργον πεποιηκότες, ἠρώτων οἱ Ῥηνεῖς τοὺς Δηλίους, δι᾽ ἣν αἰτίαν[2] ὡς αὐτοὺς[3] ἀφίκοντο· οὔτε γὰρ
λιμένας εἶναι παρ᾽ αὐτοῖς οὔτε ἐμπόριον οὔτε ἄλλην
διατριβὴν οὐδεμίαν· πάντας δὲ ἀνθρώπους ἀφικνεῖ-
σθαι πρὸς τὴν Δῆλον ἔλεγον, καὶ αὐτοὶ τὰ πολλὰ
ἐν Δήλῳ διατρίβειν. τῶν δὲ Δηλίων ἀποκρινομένων
αὐτοῖς, ὅτι ἱερεῖα ἀγοράσοντες[4] οἱ ἄνθρωποι διέβησαν εἰς τὴν Ῥήνειαν, διὰ τί οὖν, ἔφασαν οἱ
Ῥηνεῖς, εἰ ἱερεῖα ἧκον ὠνησόμενοι,[4] ὥς φατε, τοὺς
παῖδας τοὺς ἀκολούθους οὐκ ἤγαγον τοὺς ἄξοντας
τὰ ἱερεῖα, ἀλλὰ παρ᾽ ὑμῖν ἐν Δήλῳ κατέλιπον, αὐτοὶ
δὲ μόνοι διέβησαν; πρὸς δὲ τούτοις τριάκοντα
σταδίων ὄντων ἀπὸ τῆς διαβάσεως πρὸς τὴν πόλιν
τὴν Ῥηνέων, τραχείας οὔσης ὁδοῦ, δι᾽ ἧς ἔδει
αὐτοὺς πορευθῆναι ἐπὶ τὴν ἀγορασίαν, ἄνευ ὑποδη-
μάτων διέβησαν, ἐν Δήλῳ δ᾽ ἐν τῷ ἱερῷ ὑπο-
δεδεμένοι περιεπάτουν; Sopat. ad Hermog. iv.
p. 445 sq.

[71] 5. Σύνταξιν ἐν τῷ παρόντι οὐδενὶ διδόντες,
ἡμεῖς δέ ποτε ἠξιώσαμεν λαβεῖν. Harpocration,
s.v. σύνταξις.

---

[1] διαδικασίας Blass : δικασίας codd.
[2] αἰτίαν ⟨ἂν⟩ ὡς Blass, Kenyon.
[3] αὐτοὺς Blass : αὑτοὺς codd.

566

the debate to discover the guilty party took place,
the Rheneans asked the Delians why the men had
come to them, since they had no harbours or market
or anything else worth a visit. Everyone, they
argued, went to Delos and they themselves often
stayed there. When the Delians answered that the
men crossed to Rhenea to buy sacred victims, the
Rheneans said : " If, as you say, they came to buy
victims, then why did they not bring the slaves, who
attended them, to take back the victims, instead of
leaving them in Delos and crossing alone ? Besides,
it is thirty stades from the landing-place to the city
of Rhenea ; and, although it is a rough road along
which they would have had to go to make the purchase, did they cross with nothing on their feet,
whereas in Delos, in the temple, they used to walk
about with shoes on ? "

5. Now paying tribute to no one, while we once
claimed it from others.

Date *c.* 343 B.C. The Delians had been expelled from their
island by the Athenians in 422 B.C. They were restored a
year later at the instigation of the Delphic oracle, but never
regained control of the temple of Apollo despite their efforts
to do so. Finally, in 346 B.C., when Philip was admitted
by the Amphictyones, they laid their grievance before this
council, hoping that the king would help them. The
Athenians appointed Aeschines to plead their cause, but the
Areopagus, who had the final authority in such matters, sent
Hyperides instead (see Dem. xviii. 134), probably because
they suspected Aeschines for his pro-Macedonian sympathies.
Hyperides appears to have won his case, as the Athenians
remained masters of the temple. We are told that he dwelt
much on mythology, which explains the reference to Leto.
The subject of fragment 4 may be the crime for which the
Athenians expelled the Delians. (See Thucyd. v. 1.)

---

4 ἀγοράσοντες . . . ὠνησόμενοι Sauppe ; ἀγοράσαντες . . .
ὠνησάμενοι codd.

HYPERIDES

2. ΠΡΟΣ ΘΑΣΙΟΥΣ

[107] 1. Εὐθὺς δὲ καρπεύειν ἀγαθὴν καὶ πλείστην χώραν. Pollux vii. 149.

Date and circumstances doubtful. This speech may have been delivered in connexion with a quarrel between Thasos

3. ΥΠΕΡ ΚΑΛΛΙΠΠΟΥ ΠΡΟΣ ΗΛΕΙΟΥΣ

Title known from Harpocration. Date 332 B.C. Callippus, an Athenian athlete, was accused of bribing his opponents at the Olympic games. Hyperides failed to clear him of the

4. ΚΥΘΝΙΑΚΟΣ

[117] 1. Οἱ μὲν θρασεῖς ἄνευ λογισμοῦ πάντα πράττουσιν· οἱ δὲ θαρραλέοι μετὰ λογισμοῦ τοὺς προσπεσόντας κινδύνους ἀνέκπληκτοι ὑπομένουσιν. Suidas i. 2, p. 1109. 13.

Date and circumstances doubtful. After the battle of Chaeronea (338 B.C.) Athens sent for help to various small

5. ΡΟΔΙΑΚΟΣ

Title quoted in Bekker, *Anecdota*. Date 341 B.C. Hyperides went on an embassy to Chios and Rhodes to secure

6. ΧΙΑΚΟΣ [?]

Title perhaps quoted by the scholiast on Aristophanes, but

7. ΠΕΡΙ ΤΟΥ ΠΟΛΥΕΥΚΤΟΝ ΣΤΡΑΤΗΓΕΙΝ

[156] 1. Τῶν τόπων τὴν ἀλιμενίαν. Pollux i. 101.

2. AGAINST THE THASIANS

And immediately to enjoy the produce of a large stretch of fertile country.

and Maronea over Stryme. The dispute is mentioned in Philip's letter (341 B.C.) as being already over ; it was settled by discussion at the instigation of Athens. (See Dem. xii. 17.)

3. IN DEFENCE OF CALLIPPUS AGAINST THE ELEANS

charge, although the Pseudo-Plutarch (*Hyp.* 850 B) says that he succeeded. (See Pausanias v. 21. 3.)

4. CYTHNIAN SPEECH

Rash men do everything without reflection ; but courageous men reflect on the dangers they encounter and meet them unafraid.

states (see Lycurg. *Leocr.* 42), and it is possible that this speech was composed then.

5. RHODIAN SPEECH

the islands as allies for Athens against Philip. (See [Plut.] *Hyp.* 850 A.)

6. CHIAN SPEECH

the word Χιακῷ is an emendation for χαλκῷ. Date 341 B.C. (See note on fragment 5 above.)

7. ON THE APPOINTMENT OF POLYEUCTUS AS GENERAL

1. The absence of harbours in the region.

[157]   2. Τὸ μὲν οὖν τῶν ἐλαυνόντων πλῆθος καὶ τὸν
τοῦ ῥοθίου ψόφον καὶ τὸ μέγεθος τοῦ σκάφους
ἐκπεπληγμένοι δεινῶς ἦσαν.   Suidas ii. 2, p. 622.

Date and circumstances not known.   The Polyeuctus con-

8. ΠΕΡΙ ΤΗΣ ΦΥΛΑΚΗΣ ΤΩΝ ΤΥΡΡΗΝΩΝ

Title known from Harpocration.   Date 324 B.C.   In this
year Athens founded a colony on the Adriatic to protect her

9. ΠΛΑΤΑΙΚΟΣ

10. ΠΕΡΙ ΤΩΝ ΣΤΡΑΤΗΓΩΝ [?]

Title known from the Pseudo-Plutarch.[b]   Date 335.   The
speech concerned the generals whose surrender Alexander

11. ΠΕΡΙ ΤΩΝ ΤΡΙΗΡΩΝ [?]

Title known from the Pseudo-Plutarch.[b]   Date c. 335.   The
speech probably concerned the twenty ships which the

12. ΥΠΕΡ ΧΑΡΗΤΟΣ ΠΕΡΙ ΤΟΥ ΕΠΙ ΤΑΙΝΑΡΩΙ ΞΕΝΙΚΟΥ [?]

Title known from the Pseudo-Plutarch.[b]   Date and circumstances not known.   The general Chares who, we are
told, was a friend of Hyperides, was no longer alive in 323 ;

---

[a] Plut. *Moral.* 350 B.

2. They were extremely alarmed at the number of the rowers, the noise of the oars splashing and the size of the ship.

cerned is probably Polyeuctus of Cydantidae, the prosecutor of Euxenippus. (See *Hyp.* iv.)

8. ON THE OUTPOST AGAINST THE ETRUSCANS

trade against Etruscan pirates and to ensure a supply of corn. The measure was prompted by the famine of 330 B.C.

9. PLATAEAN SPEECH

Title known from Plutarch.[a] Date and circumstances not known.

10. ON THE GENERALS

demanded after the fall of Thebes. It is not known whether the work was ever published.

11. ON THE TRIREMES

Athenians sent to Alexander to assist him in the conquest of Persia. (See Plut. *Phoc.* 21.) It is not known whether the speech was published.

12. IN DEFENCE OF CHARES ON THE MERCENARY FORCE AT TAENARUM

therefore this speech must be dated before then. Some have wished to read Leosthenes for Chares, giving a date of 323 B.C. It is not known whether the speech was published.

[b] [Plut.] *Hyp.* 848 E.

13. ΥΠΕΡ ΑΡΠΑΛΟΥ

[45] 'Εκπηδήσαντες ἐκ τῶν περδικοτροφείων. Pollux
x. 159.

Β. ΛΟΓΟΙ ΔΙΚΑΝΙΚΟΙ

Ι. ΛΟΓΟΙ ΔΗΜΟΣΙΟΙ

14. ΚΑΤ' ΑΥΤΟΚΛΕΟΥΣ ΠΡΟΔΟΣΙΑΣ

[55] 1. Καὶ Σωκράτην οἱ πρόγονοι ἡμῶν ἐπὶ λόγοις
ἐκόλαζον. Greg. Corinth. *ad Hermog.* vii. p. 1148,
ed. Walz.

2. Ἔργα νέων, βουλαὶ δὲ μέσων, εὐχαὶ δὲ γερόν-
των.
Mich. apost. *Prov. cent.* vii. 90 L.

Title known from Harpocration, etc. Date *c.* 360 B.C.
Autocles, an Athenian general, failed to support a Thracian

15. ΚΑΤΑ ΔΙΟΠΕΙΘΟΥΣ [?]

Title known from Hyperides.[a] Date and circumstances

16. ΚΑΤΑ ΦΙΛΟΚΡΑΤΟΥΣ [?]

Title known from Hyperides.[a] Date 343 B.C. Philocrates
of Hagnus proposed the peace with Philip in 348 B.C. The
exact circumstances of this trial are not known, but Demo-

---

[a] Hyp. iv. 29.

13. IN DEFENCE OF HARPALUS

Jumping out of the partridge-coops.

Pollux doubts if the speech is genuine. For Harpalus see Dinarch. i., Introduction.

B. *Speeches written for delivery in a court of law*

I. *Public cases*

14. AGAINST AUTOCLES FOR TREASON

1. Our ancestors punished Socrates for what he said.

2. Labours are the part of the young, counsels of the middle-aged, prayers of the old.

prince Miltocythes in his revolt against Cotys, and was tried on his return. (See Dem. xxiii. 104.) The second fragment, either the whole line or the first two words, was quoted by Hyperides as a proverb from Hesiod.

15. AGAINST DIOPITHES

not known. Diopithes of Sphettos, an Athenian orator whom Demosthenes [b] mentions, was trierarch in 349/8. (See *IG.* iv. 2, 802 b.)

16. AGAINST PHILOCRATES

sthenes mentions it in 343 B.C. as having just happened.[c] Philocrates was condemned and went into exile. (See Dinarch. i. 28 and Aeschin. ii. 6.)

[b] Dem. xviii. 70.   [c] Dem. xix. 116.

HYPERIDES

17. ΚΑΤΑ ΑΡΙΣΤΟΦΩΝΤΟΣ
ΠΑΡΑΝΟΜΩΝ

[41] 1. Οἶδε γὰρ αὑτῷ δεδομένην ἄδειαν καὶ πράττειν
καὶ γράφειν ὅ τι ἂν ἔμβραχυ βούληται. Schol.
Plat. Hip. Min. 365 d.

[44] 2. Nam cum ceterorum opinionem fallere conaris,
tu tete frustraris. Non enim probas, cum te pro astuto
sapientem appelles, pro confidente fortem, pro illi-
berali diligentem rei familiaris, pro malivolo severum.
Nullum est enim vitium, quo[1] virtutis laude gloriari
possis.[1] Rutil. Lup. i. 4. *Cf.* Quintilian ix. 3. 65.

Date 362 B.C. Aristophon of Hazenia, a distinguished
orator, was active at the end of the Peloponnesian war. As
an old man he defended the law of Leptines and is often
mentioned by the orators. (See Dinarch. i. 14, iii. 17.)
Hyperides refers to this trial in a context which suggests that

18. ΠΡΟΣ ΑΡΙΣΤΟΓΕΙΤΟΝΑ

[27] 1. Quid a me saepius his verbis de meo[2] officio re-
quiris? Scripsisti, ut servis libertas daretur?[3]
Scripsi[4]; ne liberi servitutem experirentur. Scripsisti, ut exules restituerentur? Scripsi[4]; ut ne quis
exilio afficeretur. Leges igitur, quae prohibebant
haec, nonne legebas?[5] Non poteram; propterea
quod literis earum arma Macedonum opposita officiebant.[6] Rutil. Lup. i. 19.

¹ *quod . . . possit* Madvig.
² *meo* Stephanus : *medio* codd.
³ *daretur* Stephanus : *detur* codd.
⁴ *scripsi . . . scripsi* Ruhnken : *scripsisti . . . scripsisti*
codd.
⁵ *nonne legebas* Ruhnken : *non negligebas* codd.
⁶ *officiebant* Ruhnken : *obsistebant* codd.

17. AGAINST ARISTOPHON FOR ILLEGAL PROPOSALS

1. For he knows that he has been given freedom to please himself in virtually all his actions and proposals.

2. For by trying to deceive the minds of others you defeat your own ends. In fact you are unconvincing when you call yourself wise instead of cunning, brave instead of conceited, careful of your money instead of mean, and stern instead of disagreeable. There is no fault of which you can boast simply by praising virtue.

it was a case of indictment for illegal proposals, and says that the accused was acquitted by two votes.[a] The passage in a scholiast which says that he was condemned is probably textually corrupt.[b] According to Aeschines (iii. 194), Aristophon boasted that he had escaped seventy-five such trials.

18. AGAINST ARISTOGITON

1. Why do you persist in putting these questions to me about my time of office : " Did you propose that slaves should be free ? " I did propose it; to prevent free men from experiencing slavery. " Did you propose that exiles should be restored ? " I did ; so that none should suffer by being exiled. " Then did you not read the laws forbidding such proposals ? " I could not do so, because the Macedonian arms before me blotted out their letters.[c]

[a] Hyp. iv. 28.
[b] Schol. Aeschin. i. 64.
[c] Most of these statements are given in Greek by various writers ; see especially [Plut.] Hyp. 849 A.

[28]   2. Οὐκ ἐγὼ τὸ ψήφισμα ἔγραψα, ἡ δ᾽ ἐν Χαιρωνείᾳ μάχη.   [Plut.] *Vit. X Or.* 849 A.

[29]   3. Ὅπως πρῶτον μὲν μυριάδας πλείους ἢ ιε´
τοὺς ⟨δούλους τοὺς⟩ ἐκ τῶν ἔργων τῶν ἀργυρείων
καὶ τοὺς κατὰ τὴν ἄλλην χώραν, ἔπειτα τοὺς
ὀφείλοντας τῷ δημοσίῳ καὶ τοὺς ἀτίμους καὶ τοὺς
ἀπεψηφισμένους καὶ τοὺς μετοίκους.¹   Suidas i. 1,
p. 562. 19.

[30]   4. Καὶ οὐδὲ ἐκ τῆς παροιμίας δύνασαι μανθάνειν
τὸ μὴ κινεῖν κακὸν εὖ κείμενον.   Schol. Plat. p. 254
H.

[31]   5. Καὶ ἔφασαν ἐν Οἰνόῃ ἀκοῦσαι, ὅτι μάχη εἴη
γεγονυῖα.   Harpocration, *s.v.* Οἰνόη.

[32]   6. Καὶ τὰ χρήματα τά τε ἱερὰ καὶ τὰ ὅσια.
Harpocration, *s.v.* ὅσιον.

[39]   7. Ὀρθῆς δὲ τῆς πόλεως οὔσης ἐπὶ τούτοις.

8. Nam disputandi aut suadendi est aliud idoneum
tempus : cum quidem adversarius armatus praesto
est, resistendum est huic non verbis sed armis.   Rutil. Lup. ii. 2.   *Cf.* Quintil. x. 3. 75.

19. ΚΑΤΑ ΔΗΜΑΔΟΥ ΠΑΡΑΝΟΜΩΝ

[76]   1. Ἃ μὲν γὰρ οὗτος εἰσκεκόμικεν, οὐκ ἔχει
τὰς ἀληθεῖς αἰτίας τῆς προξενίας· ἐγὼ δέ, εἰ δεῖ
πρόξενον ὑμῖν αὐτὸν γένεσθαι, δι᾽ ἃ τούτου² τεύξεται γράψας εἰσφέρω. (ἔπειτα τὸ ψήφισμα
εἰσφέρει·) δεδόχθαι αὐτὸν εἶναι πρόξενον, ὅτι τὰ
Φιλίππῳ συμφέροντα καὶ λέγει καὶ ποιεῖ, ὅτι γενό-

¹ μετοίκους Schmidt : ἀποίκους codd.
² δι᾽ ἃ τούτου Bake : διὰ τούτων vel διὸ τούτου codd.

2. It was not I that proposed the decree, but the battle of Chaeronea.

3. That in the first place the slaves both from the silver mines and up and down the country, more than a hundred and fifty thousand in number, and secondly the public debtors, the disfranchised, those struck off the roll of citizens, and the metics.

4. And you cannot even learn from the proverb to let sleeping dogs lie.[a]

5. They said that they had heard at Oenoë that a battle had been fought.

6. And the money, both sacred and public.

7. When the city was alert at this news.

8. For there is another time for debate and counsel; but when an armed enemy is at the gates he must be resisted with arms and not with words.

Date c. 338 B.C. After Chaeronea Hyperides proposed that the slaves and unprivileged classes should be freed of their disabilities and armed to defend the city. For this he was afterwards prosecuted by Aristogiton but acquitted. (See Lycurg. Leocr. 36, [Plut.] Hyp. 848 F.) Two short passages from Aristogiton's speech are quoted by Gregory of Corinth.[b]

19. AGAINST DEMADES FOR ILLEGAL PROPOSALS

1. The arguments which Demades has brought forward do not give the real reasons for the appointment. If Euthycrates is to be your proxenus, let me submit to you in writing a statement of the services for which this will be his reward. " It has been resolved that he shall be proxenus, because he speaks and acts in the interests of Philip; because, as

---

[a] Literally : to leave a bad thing that is harmlessly placed.
[b] Ad Hermog. t. vii. p. 1272.

μενος ἵππαρχος τοὺς Ὀλυνθίων ἱππέας προὔδωκε
Φιλίππῳ, ὅτι τοῦτο πράξας αἴτιος τοῦ Χαλκιδέων
ὑπῆρξεν ὀλέθρου, ὅτι ἁλούσης Ὀλύνθου τιμητὴς
ἐγένετο τῶν αἰχμαλώτων, ὅτι ἀντέπραξε τῇ πόλει
περὶ τοῦ ἱεροῦ τοῦ Δηλίων, ὅτι τῆς πόλεως περὶ
Χαιρώνειαν ἡττηθείσης οὔτε ἔθαψε τῶν τεθνεώτων
τινὰς οὔτε τῶν ἁλόντων οὐδένα ἐλύσατο.   Apsines
ix. p. 547 W.

Εἰ τἀληθῆ Δημάδης ἐβούλετο περὶ Εὐθυκράτους
εἰπεῖν τοιοῦτον αὐτὸν ἔδει ψήφισμα γράψαι¹ . . .
δι' ἣν Εὐθυκράτην πρόξενον ἐποίησεν. ἐγὼ ⟨δὴ⟩²
τὰ πεπραγμένα αὐτῷ, ἐπιγράψας τὸ τούτου ὄνομα,
ἀναγνώσομαι. (καὶ πλάττεται τοιοῦτον ψήφισμα·)
Δημάδης Δημέου³ Παιανιεὺς εἶπεν· ἐπειδὴ Εὐθυ-
κράτης προὔδωκε τὴν ἑαυτοῦ πατρίδα Ὄλυνθον
καὶ αἴτιος ἐγένετο τὰς πόλεις τῶν Χαλκιδέων οὔσας
τετταράκοντα ἀναστάτους γενέσθαι . . . Johannes,
ad Hermog. περὶ μεθόδου δεινότητος f. 481 v.

[77]   2. Ἀλκίμαχον καὶ Ἀντίπατρον Ἀθηναίους καὶ
προξένους ἐποιησάμεθα. Harpocration, s.v. Ἀλκί-
μαχος.

[78]   3. Μήτε πόλεως μήτε πολιτείας ἐπηβόλους γενέσθαι. Etym. Magn. p. 357. 25 ; Porphyr. Quaest.
Hom. c. 1.

[79]   4. Περὶ οὗ πολλῷ ἂν δικαιότερον ἐν τοῖς ὀξυθυ-
μίοις ἡ στήλη σταθείη ἢ ἐν τοῖς ἡμετέροις ἱεροῖς.
Harpocration, s.v. ὀξυθύμια.

[80]   5. Εἶναι δὲ τοὺς ῥήτορας ὁμοίους τοῖς ὄφεσι·
τούς τε γὰρ ὄφεις μισητοὺς μὲν εἶναι πάντας, τῶν
δὲ ὄφεων αὐτῶν τοὺς μὲν ἔχεις τοὺς ἀνθρώπους
ἀδικεῖν, τοὺς δὲ παρείας αὐτοὺς τοὺς ἔχεις κατ-
εσθίειν. Harpocration, s.v. παρεῖαι ὄφεις.

cavalry commander, he betrayed the Olynthian cavalry to Philip and through this act was responsible for the destruction of the Chalcidians ; because, on the capture of Olynthus, he assessed the prices of the prisoners ; because he opposed the city's interests concerning the temple at Delos, and, when the city was defeated at Chaeronea, neither buried any dead nor ransomed any prisoners."

If Demades had wished to speak the truth about Euthycrates, he ought to have proposed a decree like the following . . . on account of which he made Euthycrates proxenus. I will draw up a record of his conduct in Demades' name and read it to you. " Demades, son of Demeas of the Deme Paeania, proposed that, whereas Euthycrates betrayed his own city, Olynthus, to Philip, and was responsible for the destruction of the forty cities of the Chalcidians, etc."

2. We made Alcimachus and Antipater Athenian citizens and proxeni.

3. To have neither city nor citizenship.

4. For whom the column would be more suitably erected among the refuse at the crossroads than in our temples.

5. That orators are like snakes, in that all snakes are hateful, though some of them, the adders, are harmful to men, while others, the brown snakes, eat the adders.

---

[1] Lacunam indicavit Brinkmann : δι' ἥντινα αἰτίαν suspicit Rabe.   [2] δὴ supplevit dubitanter Rabe.
[3] Δημέου Fuhr : Δημάδου codd.

[86]   6. 'Ραδιεστέραν τὴν πόλιν.   Athen. x. 424 d.

Date c. 337 B.C. Demades had proposed to make the
Olynthian, Euthycrates, an Athenian proxenus, although, in
348 B.C., he had betrayed his city to Philip. (See Dem. xix.
265, Suidas, s.v. " Demades.") For this Hyperides attacked

20. ΠΡΟΣ ΔΙΩΝΔΑΝ

Title from Eusebius,[b] etc. Date c. 339 B.C. Just before
Chaeronea Hyperides proposed to crown Demosthenes for

21. ΠΕΡΙ ΤΩΝ ΕΥΒΟΥΛΟΥ ΔΩΡΕΩΝ

Title known from Harpocration. Date between 343 and
330 B.C. Eubulus was financial administrator at Athens from
355 B.C. onwards and worked for accord with Philip.   Hyperides opposed a motion proposing certain honours to him

22. ΚΑΤΑ ΜΕΙΔΙΟΥ ΠΑΡΑΝΟΜΩΝ

The Pseudo-Plutarch says that Hyperides prosecuted
Midias for proposing that honours should be paid to
Phocion ; but Plutarch is probably right in attributing this

23. ΥΠΕΡ ΤΩΝ ΛΥΚΟΥΡΓΟΥ ΠΑΙΔΩΝ

[118]   Τίνα φήσουσιν οἱ παριόντες αὐτοῦ τὴν τάφον;
οὗτος ἐβίω μὲν σωφρόνως, ταχθεὶς δὲ ἐπὶ τῇ διοική-
σει τῶν χρημάτων εὗρε πόρους, ᾠκοδόμησε τὸ
θέατρον, τὸ ᾠδεῖον, τὰ νεώρια, τριήρεις ἐποιήσατο,

580

6. The city easier.

him in a speech which Plutarch [a] says was full of abuse. The verdict is not known. The word ὀξυθύμια in No. 4 is difficult. It appears to denote refuse which was apparently carted to crossroads and burnt there.

20. AGAINST DIONDAS

his services to the state. For this he was prosecuted by Diondas for illegal proposals but easily acquitted. (See [Plut.] Hyp. 848 F, Dem. xviii. 222.)

21. ON THE HONOURS FOR EUBULUS

after his death, the exact date of which is not known. It is known from Aeschines (ii. 8) that he was still alive in 343 B.C., and from Demosthenes (xviii. 162) that he was dead by 330 B.C. (See Schol. on Aeschin. ii. 8.)

22. AGAINST MIDIAS FOR ILLEGAL PROPOSALS

speech to Hyperides' son, Glaucippus. Date not known. (See [Plut.] Hyp. 850 B, Plut. Phoc. 4.)

23. IN DEFENCE OF THE CHILDREN OF LYCURGUS

How will they speak who pass his grave? " This man led a virtuous life. When appointed to administer the treasure he found means of revenue, and built the theatre, the Odeum and the docks. He constructed triremes and harbours. This was the

[a] Plut. Moral. 810 c and D.
[b] Euseb. Praepar. Evang. x. 3, p. 466 a.

HYPERIDES

λιμένας· τοῦτον ἡ πόλις ἡμῶν ἠτίμωσε καὶ τοὺς
παῖδας ἔδησεν αὐτοῦ. Apsines, τέχν. ῥητ. ix. p.
545 Walz.

Date c. 324 B.C. After the death of Lycurgus, Menesaechmus prosecuted his children on the grounds that their father

24. ΚΑΤΑ ΠΟΛΥΕΥΚΤΟΥ ΠΕΡΙ ΤΟΥ ΔΙΑΓΡΑΜΜΑΤΟΣ

[147]   1. Ἡγεμὼν συμμορίας. Harpocration, *s.v.* ἡγε-
μών.

[149]   2. Μετοικικῆς συμμορίας ταμίας. Pollux viii.
144.

[150]   3. Οὗτοι πολλάκις ἀγορὰς ποιοῦνται. Harpocration, *s.v.* ἀγοράς.

25. ΠΡΟΣ ΠΟΛΥΕΥΚΤΟΝ

[159]   Εἰσὶ γὰρ ἐν τῇ συμμορίᾳ ἑκάστῃ ιε΄ ἄνδρες.
Harpocration, *s.v.* συμμορία.

Title known from Harpocration. Date and circumstances
not known. The speech is perhaps identical with the last.
The defendant was probably Polyeuctus of Cydantidae, the

26. ΚΑΤΑ ΔΗΜΕΟΥ ΞΕΝΙΑΣ

Title known from Harpocration, who doubts whether the
speech is genuine. Date and circumstances not known.
Sauppe assigned to this speech a saying of Hyperides recorded by Athenaeus (xiii. 591 f.) : " Won't you be quiet, boy ?

27. ΥΠΕΡ ΔΗΜΟΠΟΙΗΤΟΥ

Title known from Harpocration, who doubts if the speech
is genuine. Date and circumstances not known.

man whom our city degraded and whose children she imprisoned.''

was a state-debtor. Hyperides and Demosthenes defended them successfully. (See [Plut.] *Lycurg.* 842 ε, Dem. *Ep.* iii. 1 *sq.*)

24. AGAINST POLYEUCTUS ON THE REGISTER

1. The leader of a naval board.
2. The treasurer of a metics' naval board.
3. These men frequently hold markets.

Title known from Harpocration. Date and circumstances not known. The register referred to was a list of the sums which citizens were liable to pay to defray the cost of the navy.

25. AGAINST POLYEUCTUS

There are fifteen men on each naval board.

prosecutor of Euxenippus, since Harpocration quotes the word Κυδαντίδης as occurring in the speech.

26. AGAINST DEMEAS FOR USURPING CITIZEN RIGHTS

You're more long-winded than your mother.'' Demeas was the son of Demades and his mother was a flute player.

27. IN DEFENCE OF ONE ADMITTED TO CITIZENSHIP

HYPERIDES

28 et 29. ΚΑΤ' ΑΡΙΣΤΑΓΟΡΑΣ
ΑΠΡΟΣΤΑΣΙΟΥ ΛΟΓΟΙ Β΄

[13] 1. "Ωστε Λαΐς μὲν ἡ δοκοῦσα τῶν πώποτε
διενηνοχέναι τὴν ὄψιν καὶ "Ωκιμον καὶ Μετάνειρα.
Athen. xiii. p. 587 c.

2. Ἐπεὶ καὶ ὁ τῆς δωροξενίας νόμος ἁρμόττων
ἐστὶ τῷ νῦν ἀγῶνι παραχθῆναι· εἰ γὰρ καὶ τοὺς ἀπο-
φυγόντας ξενίας εἴρηκεν ἐξεῖναι τῷ βουλομένῳ πάλιν
γράψασθαι, ἐὰν μὴ δοκῶσι δικαίως τὸ πρῶτον ἀπο-
πεφευγέναι, πῶς οὐ φανερόν ἐστι κατ' Ἀρισταγό-
ρας τὸ δίκαιον; Harpocration, s.v. δωροξενία.

[21] 3. "Ωστε κελευστέον τοὺς μαρτυροῦντας τὰ τοιαῦτα καὶ τοὺς παρεχομένους . . . ⟨μὴ⟩¹ μάτην
ἀπατᾶν ὑμᾶς, ⟨ἐὰν⟩² μὴ τυγχάνωσι δικαιότερα λέγοντες καὶ νόμον ὑμῖν ἀναγκάζετε παρέχεσθαι, τὸν
κελεύοντα μὴ νέμειν προστάτην. Suidas, s.v. νέμειν
προστάτην. Cf. Harpocration, s.v. προστάτης.

[24] 4. Καὶ πάλιν τὰς Ἀφύας καλουμένας τὸν αὐτὸν
τρόπον ἐκαλέσατε. Athen. xiii. p. 586 a.

Date and circumstances not known. It seems probable that
the Aristagora in question was the woman of that name whom
Pseudo-Plutarch mentions as Hyperides' mistress ([Plut.]
Hyp. 849 D). The existence of the second speech is known

30. ΥΠΕΡ ΦΡΥΝΗΣ ΑΣΕΒΕΙΑΣ

[172] 1. Οὐ γὰρ ὅμοιόν ἐστι τὸν μὲν ὅπως σωθήσεται
ἐκ παντὸς τρόπου ζητεῖν, τὸν δὲ ὅπως ἀπολέσει.³
Syrian, *ad Herm.* iv. p. 120 Walz.

¹ μὴ add. Coraes.
² Post ὑμᾶς lacunam suspicatus est Wilamowitz : ἐὰν supplevit Sauppe : ἀλλ' ἀποδεικνύαι ὅτι Blass, Kenyon.
³ ἀπολέσει Walz : ἀπολέσειεν codd.

28 and 29. AGAINST ARISTAGORA FOR FAILURE TO OBTAIN A PATRON I AND II

1. So that Laïs, thought to be fairer of face than any mortal woman, and Ocimon and Metanira.

2. The law relating to the bribery of the jury by aliens may suitably be quoted at the present trial. For since it lays down that even when aliens are acquitted on a charge of usurping citizen rights, whoever wishes may indict them again, if on the first occasion they seem not to have deserved their acquittal, surely there can be no doubt what is legal in the case of Aristagora.

3. So that you must instruct those who give this type of evidence and produce . . . not to waste time deceiving you, if they have not a better case to put. Make them produce for you the law which forbids the registering of a patron.

4. And again in the same way you summoned the so-called Aphyae.

from Athenaeus (xiii. 587 c), and it is thought that the first was composed for a previous trial when Aristagora was acquitted. An alien resident in Athens had to have a citizen as his patron. Fragment 1 includes the names of three courtesans, all of whom are mentioned by Athenaeus. Laïs lived at Corinth about 420 b.c. Metanira was said to be loved by Socrates. (See Athen. xiii. 588 e, 567 c, 584 f, etc.)

30. IN DEFENCE OF PHRYNE ON A CHARGE OF IMPIETY

1. There is a difference between one man striving for her (?) acquittal and another doing his best to ruin her (?).

[173] 2. Τί γάρ ἐστιν αἰτία αὕτη, εἰ Ταντάλῳ ὑπὲρ τῆς κεφαλῆς λίθος κρέμαται; Alex. *de Schem.* viii. p. 458 Walz.

Date not known. The defence of Phryne was one of the most celebrated of the cases which Hyperides undertook and the speech which he composed for it one of his finest. (See [Longinus,] *de Sublim.* 34. 3, Quintil. x. 5. 2). Phryne was a courtesan, a well-known beauty, who included among her lovers Hyperides and Praxiteles the sculptor. The

31. ΥΠΕΡ ΦΟΡΜΙΣΙΟΥ

32. ΚΑΤΑ ΠΑΤΡΟΚΛΕΟΥΣ ΠΡΟΑΓΩΓΕΙΑΣ

[139] 1. Οἱ δὲ ἐννέα ἄρχοντες εἰστιῶντο ἐν τῇ στοᾷ, περιφραξάμενοί τι μέρος αὐτῆς αὐλαίᾳ. Pollux iv. 122.

[—] 2. Ἀδούλευτον ἢ βάρβαρον πριάσθω. Phot. ed. Reitz, p. 33. 1 *sq.*

[143] 3. Πάνδημος Ἀφροδίτη. Harpocration.

[144] 4. Κλίνη παράβυστος . . . ὑπὲρ τοῦ τὴν παῖδα μὴ ἀθυμῆσαι. Pollux iii. 43.

Title known from various writers, including Harpocration,

33. ΠΡΟΣ ΔΗΜΕΑΝ

34 et 35. ΥΠΕΡ ΧΑΙΡΕΦΙΛΟΥ ΠΕΡΙ ΤΟΥ ΤΑΡΙΧΟΥΣ

[181] 1. Ἀφεὶς τὴν ὑπέραν τὸν πόδα διώκει. Harpocration et Suidas, *s.vv.* ἀφέντες et ἀφείς.

586

2. Why is she to blame if a stone hangs over the head of Tantalus ?

former defended her, when she was accused of impiety by a certain Euthias, and is said to have secured her acquittal by displaying her bosom to the jury at a critical point in the trial. (See [Plut.] *Hyp.* 849 E.) Athenaeus has another version of the story (xiii. 591 e).

31. IN DEFENCE OF PHORMISIUS

Title known from Harpocration. Date and circumstances not known.

32. AGAINST PATROCLES FOR PROCURING

1. The nine archons were banqueting in the portico, having screened off a part of it with a curtain.

2. Let him buy a man who has never been a slave, or buy a barbarian.

3. Everyman's Aphrodite.

4. A stuffed couch to prevent the girl from losing heart.

who doubts if it is genuine. Date and circumstances not known.

33. AGAINST DEMEAS

Title known from Pollux (x. 15) and Harpocration. The Demeas in question was probably the son of Demades. (*Cf.* frag. 26.) Date and circumstances not known.

34 and 35. IN DEFENCE OF CHAEREPHILUS ON THE SALT FISH I AND II

1. He lets go the ship's brace and clutches at the sheet.

[182] 2. Καὶ τῆς Πυκνὸς τοσοῦτον εὑρισκούσης. Harpocration, s.v. Πυκνί.

[184] 3. Μετὰ ταῦτα ὕστερον ἦλθον ἀναθησόμενοι τὸ
τάριχος. Priscian xviii. 169.

Title known from Harpocration and others. Date and
circumstances not known. Chaerephilus was a dealer in salt

II. ΛΟΓΟΙ ΙΔΙΩΤΙΚΟΙ

(i) Αἰκείας

36. ΚΑΤΑ ΔΩΡΟΘΕΟΥ

[97] 1. Ἀκούω γὰρ Αὐτοκλέα τὸν ῥήτορα πρὸς Ἱππόνικον τὸν Καλλίου περὶ χωρίου τινὸς ἀμφισβητήσαντα,[1] καὶ λοιδορίας αὐτοῖς γενομένης ῥαπίζειν
τὸν[2] Ἱππόνικον ἐπὶ κόρρης . . . ἔπειτα Ἱππόνικος
ὑπ᾽ Αὐτοκλέους μόνον ἐρραπίσθη τὴν γνάθον· ἐγὼ
δ᾽ ὑπὸ τούτων τῶν τριχῶν εἰλκόμην, κονδύλους
ἔλαβον. Etymolog. Laurentianum, ed. E. Miller, p. 121
et Harpocration, s.v. ἐπὶ κόρρης.

[98] 2. Πρὸς τὸ πρόσωπον προσπτύειν. Pollux viii.
76.

[99] 3. Ἐν αὐτῷ[3] ὥσπερ τὸ ἀτιμότατον θεράπιον.
Pollux iii. 74.

37. ΚΑΤΑ ΜΑΝΤΙΘΕΟΥ

[120] 1. Ἔθεσαν οὐ μόνον ὑπὲρ τῶν ἐλευθέρων, ἀλλὰ
καὶ ἐάν τις εἰς δούλου σῶμα ὑβρίσῃ, γραφὰς εἶναι
κατὰ τοῦ ὑβρίσαντος. Athen. vi. p. 267 a.

---

[1] ἀμφισβητήσαντα Hager : ἀναμφισβητήσαντος codd.: ἀμφισ-
βητῆσαι Sauppe.

2. And when the Pnyx found so much.

3. After this they came later to put on the salt fish.

fish who was given Athenian citizenship on the proposal of Demosthenes. (See Dinarch. i. 43 and note.) Probably on this occasion he had been accused of breaking the law when importing and selling his goods. Fragments 1 and 2 are from the first speech ; fragment 3 may be from either.

II. *Private cases.*

(i) *Cases of Assault*

36. AGAINST DOROTHEÜS

1. I am told that the orator Autocles had a dispute with Hipponicus the son of Callias about some land, that they began to abuse each other and that Autocles slapped him on the cheek . . . Hipponicus, then, only had his cheek slapped by Autocles, but I was dragged along by the hair by these men and hit with their fists.

2. To spit in the face.

3. In it like the meanest slave.

Title known from Harpocration, who assigns the speech to Hyperides or Philinus. Autocles was an able orator (Xenophon, *Hell.* vi. 3. 7), and is perhaps the same man who figures in Frag. 14.

37. AGAINST MANTITHEÜS

1. They legislated not only for free men but for slaves too, ruling that if anyone did violence to the person of a slave there should be an indictment against the party guilty of violence.

---

² τὸν Blass : αὐτὸν codd.
³ ἐν αὐτῷ codd. : ἐν ταὐτῷ Blass, Kenyon.

HYPERIDES

[121] 2. Ἄγων Γλυκέραν τε τὴν Θαλασσίδος, ζεῦγος
ἔχων. Athen. xiii. p. 586 b.

[124] 3. Σκευοποιοῦντα τὸ πρᾶγμα. Harpocration, *s.v.*
σκευοποιοῦντα.

Title known from Athenaeus, etc. Date and circumstances
not known. The law mentioned in fragment 1 illustrates the
fact that a slave at Athens was allowed some of the rights

(ii) *Λόγοι ἐπιτροπικοὶ καὶ ὀρφανικοί*

38. ΚΑΤ' ΑΝΤΙΟΥ

39. ΠΡΟΣ ΧΑΡΗΤΑ

[192] Ἐπεὶ δὲ ἐνεγράφην ἐγὼ καὶ ὁ νόμος ἀπέδωκε
τὴν κομιδὴν τῶν καταλειφθέντων τῇ μητρί, ὃς
κελεύει κυρίους εἶναι τῆς ἐπικλήρου καὶ τῆς οὐσίας
ἁπάσης τοὺς παῖδας,[1] ἐπειδὰν ἐπὶ διετὲς ἡβῶσιν.
Harpocration, *s.v.* ἐπὶ διετὲς ἡβῆσαι.

(iii) *Λόγοι κληρικοί*

40 et 41. ΠΕΡΙ ΤΟΥ ΙΠΠΕΩΣ ΚΛΗΡΟΥ
ΛΟΓΟΙ Β΄

Title known from Harpocration, who quotes from the

42. ΠΕΡΙ ΤΟΥ ΠΥΡΡΑΝΔΡΟΥ ΚΛΗΡΟΥ

Title known from Harpocration, who does not give the
author. Sauppe inferred, however, from what Harpocration

[1] παῖδας Valesius : ἄπαιδας codd.

590

2. Bringing Glycera, daughter of Thalassis, in a carriage.

3. Contriving the affair.

of a human being. Thus a free man who killed a slave was liable for manslaughter, though not for murder.

(ii) *Cases relating to Guardians or Orphans*

38. AGAINST ANTIAS

Title known from Harpocration, who says that this was an orphan case. Date and circumstances not known.

39. AGAINST CHARES

When I was registered and duly obtained control over the money left to my mother by the law which provides that the sons of an heiress shall be responsible for her and all her property as soon as they have completed their second year after puberty.

Title known from Harpocration and Pollux. Date and circumstances not known.

(iii) *Inheritance Cases*

40 and 41. ON THE INHERITANCE OF HIPPEUS I AND II

second speech, thus showing that there were two. Date and circumstances not known.

42. ON THE INHERITANCE OF PYRRHANDRUS (?)

says later that Hyperides' name had here dropped out of the text. Date and circumstances not known.

HYPERIDES

(iv) Περὶ ἀντιδόσεως

43. ΚΑΤΑ ΠΑΣΙΚΛΕΟΥΣ

[134] 1. Ἕως μὲν οἱ πλουσιώτατοι παρακρουόμενοι τὴν πόλιν σὺν πέντε καὶ ἐξ τριηραρχοῦντες μέτρια ἀνήλισκον, ἡσυχίαν ἦγον οὗτοι· ἐπειδὴ δὲ ταῦτα κατιδὼν Δημοσθένης νόμον ἔθηκε τοὺς τ᾿ τριηραρχεῖν καὶ βαρεῖαι γεγόνασιν αἱ τριηραρχίαι, νῦν ὁ Φορμίων αὐτὸν ἐκκλέπτει. Harpocration, *s.v.* συμμορία.

[135] 2. Ἄξιοι μισεῖσθαι τῇ πόλει. Priscian xviii. 24, § 191.

[136] 3. Ἐὰν δέ τις ἔκδεια γένηται. Harpocration, *s.v.* ἔκδεια.

Title known from Harpocration, etc. Date and circumstances not known. The speech is perhaps identical with No. 44. The richer citizens at Athens might be compelled to undertake at their own expense at least one public service (λειτουργία) per year. If anyone thought his nomination for this duty unfair, on the grounds that a more suitable person had been overlooked, he might appeal for an exchange

44. ΠΡΟΣ ΠΑΣΙΚΛΕΑ

[137] Τὴν οἰκίαν τὴν μεγάλην τὴν Χαβρίου καλουμένην καὶ τὸ ἄμφοδον. Pollux ix. 36.

592

(iv) *Speeches in Cases of Exchange*

43. AGAINST PASICLES

1. While the very rich were trierarchs with five or six others and defrauded the city by spending only moderate sums, these men kept quiet. But after Demosthenes perceived this abuse and introduced a law providing that the Three Hundred should be trierarchs, now that the trierarchy has become a burden, Phormio stealthily withdraws himself.

2. Deserving the city's hatred.

3. If any deficiency occurs.

(ἀντίδοσις), *i.e.* he could challenge the other to undertake the service instead of himself or to exchange properties. The other might prove his right to exemption and the case be dismissed. Otherwise an exchange might be effected. No certain details of the Trierarch Law mentioned in fragment 1 are available except those given by Demosthenes (xviii. 104). Between 357 and 340 B.C. the twelve hundred richest citizens bore the costs of the trierarchy among them, irrespective of variation in wealth. Thus even a rich man might share the cost of one ship not only with five or six, but even with fifteen others. But by Demosthenes' law of 340 B.C. the burdens were distributed according to wealth and one rich man alone might have to pay for two ships. The Three Hundred was a term used to describe the group of richest men liable for property tax (εἰσφορά), and it probably applied to the trierarchy too.

44. AGAINST PASICLES FOR EXCHANGE

The big house called Chabrias' and the alley beside it.

The title, which is known from Pollux, may refer to the same speech as No. 43. Date and circumstances not known.

HYPERIDES

(v) ’Αποστασίου

45. ΚΑΤΑ ΔΗΜΗΤΡΙΑΣ

Title known from Harpocration. Date and circumstances not known. A freedman (ἀπελεύθερος), like a metic, had a

(vi)

46. ΠΡΟΣ ΑΠΕΛΛΑΙΟΝ ΠΕΡΙ ΤΟΥ ΘΗΣΑΥΡΟΥ

[10]   Ἐξέδωκε τὴν πρόγονον τὴν αὑτοῦ.   Pollux iii. 27.

Title known from Harpocration, etc. Date and circumstances not known.

47. ΠΡΟΣ ΕΠΙΚΛΕΑ ΠΕΡΙ ΟΙΚΙΑΣ

[103]   Ὑπερῷα ἐπαίρειν . . . στέφειν τὰ οἰκήματα εἰς τὴν ὁδόν . . . τὰς πλίνθους ἀναβάλλειν πρὸς ἀριθμόν . . . ὑπερῷα ἐγεῖραι.   Pollux vii. 119, 125.

48. ΚΑΤ’ ΑΘΗΝΟΓΕΝΟΥΣ Β΄

[1]   Τὰ τῶν φωρῶν κρείττω.   Harpocration, s.v.

Title known from Harpocration, who quotes the above proverb, which he says refers to prosperous criminals. For the date (between 330 and 324 B.C.) and circumstances see

49. ΠΕΡΙ ΤΩΝ ΟΡΙΩΝ

50. ΠΕΡΙ ΟΧΕΤΟΥ

Title known from Pollux. Date and circumstances not known.

(v) Cases of Neglect of a Patron

45. AGAINST DEMETRIA FOR NEGLECT OF HER PATRON

patron, usually his former master. If convicted of neglect of him (ἀποστασίου) he might be sold back into slavery.

(vi) Other Types of Private Suit

46. AGAINST APELLAEUS ON THE TREASURE

He gave in marriage his daughter by a former wife.

47. AGAINST EPICLES CONCERNING A HOUSE

To raise the upstairs rooms . . . to crown the rooms towards the street . . . to lay the courses of bricks in line . . . to erect the upstairs rooms.

Title known from Harpocration, etc. Date and circumstances not known.

48. AGAINST ATHENOGENES II

The lot of a thief is better.

Introduction to the first speech against Athenogenes (Hyp. iii).

49. ON THE BOUNDARIES

Title known from Bekker, *Anecdota*. Date and circumstances not known.

50. ON THE WATER PIPE

HYPERIDES

C. ΛΟΓΟΙ ΑΔΗΛΟΙ

51. ΥΠΕΡ ΑΚΑΔΗΜΟΥ

52. ΚΑΤ᾽ ΑΡΧΕΣΤΡΑΤΙΔΟΥ

[50] Οἱ τοὺς ἰθυφάλλους ἐν τῇ ὀρχήστρᾳ ὀρχούμενοι.
Harpocration, s.v. ἰθύφαλλοι.

Title known from Harpocration. Date and circumstances
not known. The Ithyphalli was a dance which accompanied
the phallic procession at the festival of Bacchus. The name

53. ΠΡΟΣ ΔΑΜΙΠΠΟΝ

Title known from Harpocration. Date and circumstances
not known.

54. ΚΑΤΑ ΚΟΝΩΝΟΣ

[114] Ἐν Διομείοις Ἡράκλειον. Harpocration, s.v.

55. ΥΠΕΡ ΚΡΑΤΙΝΟΥ

[115] Ἀπόκριναί μοι, Ἑρμεία, ὥσπερ κάθῃ. Zonaras,
Lex. p. 1168.

56. ΠΡΟΣ ΛΥΣΙΔΗΜΟΝ

Title known from Pollux. Date and circumstances not
known.

57. ΥΠΕΡ ΜΙΚΑΣ

[125] Ἐμισθώσατο τυλυφάντας. Pollux vii. 191 et x.
39.

596

C. *Unclassified speeches*

51. IN DEFENCE OF ACADEMUS

Title known from Harpocration. Date and circumstances not known.

52. AGAINST ARCHESTRATIDES

Those who dance the Ithyphalli in the dancing ring.

Archestratides appears also in the speech for Lycophron (Hyp. i. 1).

53. AGAINST DAMIPPUS

54. AGAINST CONON

Feast of Heracles in the deme Diomea.

Title known from Harpocration. Date and circumstances not known.

55. IN DEFENCE OF CRATINUS

Answer me, Hermeas, from your seat.

Title known from Bekker, *Anecdota*. Date and circumstances not known.

56. AGAINST LYSIDEMUS

57. IN DEFENCE OF MICA

She (?) hired weavers of cushion-covers.

Title known from Pollux. Date and circumstances not known.

HYPERIDES

58. ΥΠΕΡ ΞΕΝΙΠΠΟΥ

Title known from Harpocration. The speech may, as
Schaefer conjectured, be the same as the following one.
Date and circumstances not known.

59 et 60. ΥΠΕΡ ΞΕΝΟΦΙΛΟΥ ΛΟΓΟΙ Β΄

61. ΠΡΟΣ ΠΑΓΚΑΛΟΝ

Title known from Harpocration. Date and circumstances
not known.

62. ΥΠΕΡ ΣΙΜΜΙΟΥ ΠΡΟΣ ΠΥΘΕΑΝ
ΚΑΙ ΛΥΚΟΥΡΓΟΝ

63. ΣΥΝΗΓΟΡΙΚΟΣ

64. ΠΡΟΣ ΤΙΜΑΝΔΡΑΝ

[164] Καταλειφθέντων γὰρ τούτων, δυοῖν ἀδελφαῖν,
ὀρφανῶν καὶ πρὸς πατρὸς καὶ πρὸς μητρὸς καὶ
παιδαρίων.[1] Suidas ii. 2, p. 157.

Title known from Suidas. Demetrius (*On Style* 302) speaks
of the prosecutor of Timandra as though he did not know

[168]   ## 65. ΠΡΟΣ ΥΓΙΑΙΝΟΝΤΑ

Ἔνη καὶ νέα. Harpocration, *s.v.*

Title known from Harpocration. Date and circumstances

---

[1] καταλλαχθέντων, δυαῖν, ὀρφαναῖν, παιδαρίων παίδων codd. :
correxit Blass : δυοῖν ἀδελφοῖν καὶ δυοῖν ἀδελφαῖν habet Kenyon.

58. IN DEFENCE OF XENIPPUS

59 and 60. IN DEFENCE OF XENOPHILUS I AND II

Title known from Harpocration, who tells us that there were two speeches. (See Harpocration, *s.v.* κεραμεῖς, though the reading is doubtful.) Date and circumstances not known.

61. AGAINST PANCALUS

62. IN DEFENCE OF SIMMIAS AGAINST PYTHEAS AND LYCURGUS

Title known from Harpocration. Date and circumstances not known.

63. THE ADVOCATE'S SPEECH

Title known from Pollux. Date and circumstances not known.

64. AGAINST TIMANDRA

For when these children, two sisters and only little girls, were left without either father or mother.

his identity, which casts some doubt on the authenticity of the work. Date and circumstances not known.

65. AGAINST HYGIAENON

The old and the new day.

not known. The name " old and new " was given to the last day of the month. By Solon's regulation every other month began half-way through the day. The name " old and new " properly applied only to days of this kind, but in fact it was used to denote the last day of every month.

D. ΑΠΑΡΑΣΗΜΑ

[195]   1. ῟Α δ' ἐστὶν ἀφανῆ, ἀνάγκη τοὺς διδάσκοντας τεκμηρίοις καὶ τοῖς εἰκόσι ζητεῖν. Clem. Alex. Strom. vi. 625 A, Sylb. ii. 18. 3 Stählin.

[196]   2. Χαρακτὴρ οὐδεὶς ἔπεστιν ἐπὶ τοῦ προσώπου τῆς διανοίας τοῖς ἀνθρώποις. Clem. Alex. Strom. vi. 625 c, Sylb. ii. 18. 8 Stählin.

[197]   3. Τῷ μὲν τοίνυν Διί, ὦ ἄνδρες δικασταί, ἡ ἐπωνυμία γέγονε τοῦ ἐλευθέριον προσαγορεύεσθαι διὰ τὸ τοὺς ἐξελευθέρους τὴν στοὰν οἰκοδομῆσαι τὴν πλησίον αὐτοῦ. Harpocration, s.v. Ἐλευθέριος Ζεύς.

[198]   4. Ἐγὼ δὲ οὔτε δᾳδούχου θυγατέρα ἔχω οὔτε ἱεροφάντου. Harpocration, s.v. ἱεροφάντης.

[200]   5. Κρεμάσας ἐκ τοῦ κίονος ἐξέδειρεν, ὅθεν καὶ μωλώπων ἔτι νῦν τὸ δέρμα μεστὸν ἔχει. Pollux iii. 79.

[201]   6. Καὶ τῷ σκέλει με ἠρέμα ἔκρουσεν. Antiatt. in Bekker, Anecdota 101. 23.

[202]   7. Καὶ ἐμοὶ μὲν συμβάσης ἀρρωστίας καὶ ὑπομοσθείσης ταύτης τῆς γραφῆς ἀνεβλήθη ὁ ἀγών. Schol. Aristoph. Plut. 725.

[204]   8. Ἀρχομένων δεῖ τῶν ἀδικημάτων ἐμφράττειν τὰς ὁδούς· ὅταν δ' ἅπαξ ῥιζωθῇ κακία καὶ παλαιὰ γένηται καθάπερ σύντροφος ἀρρωστία, χαλεπὸν αὐτὴν κατασβέσαι. Stobaeus, Flor. xlvi. 63.

[205]   9. Δεῖ τὴν ἐκ τῆς οἰκίας ἐκπορευομένην ἐν τοιαύτῃ καταστάσει εἶναι τῆς ἡλικίας, ὥστε τοὺς ἀπαντῶντας πυνθάνεσθαι, μὴ τίνος ἐστὶ γυνή, ἀλλὰ τίνος μήτηρ. Stobaeus, Flor. lxxiv. 33.

[206]   10. Τοὺς μὲν πρὸς τὸν ἄνδρα τὸν ἑαυτῆς γυναικὶ

600

D. *Fragments of uncertain origin*

1. When a question is obscure teachers must examine it in the light of evidence and probability.

2. There is no sign of a man's principles in his face.

3. The name Eleutherios, the freer, has been given to Zeus, gentlemen of the jury, because the Exeleutheroi, the freedmen, built the portico near him.

4. I have neither torchbearer's, nor initiating priest's, daughter.

5. He hung him from the pillar and thrashed him, with the result that his skin is still covered with weals.[a]

6. And tapped me lightly with his leg.

7. As I was taken ill the term of this indictment was prolonged on oath and the trial postponed.

8. It is in the early stages of crime that the avenues to it must be barred. When once evil has taken root and grown old like a congenital complaint it is hard to extinguish it.

4. If a woman goes out of her house she should have reached a time of life when those who meet her will ask not whose wife she is but whose mother.[b]

10. It is right for a woman to adorn herself as she

---

[a] Assigned to the speech against Dorotheüs (No. 36) by Sauppe.

[b] Assigned to the speech against Aristagora (No. 28) by Westermann.

καλλωπισμοὺς ὅπως βούλοιτο χρὴ γίγνεσθαι· τοὺς
μέντοι περὶ τὰς ἐξόδους οὐκέτι πρὸς τὸν ἄνδρα
ἀλλὰ πρὸς τοὺς ἑτέρους ⟨γιγνομένους⟩[1] φοβητέον.
Stobaeus, *Flor.* lxxiv. 34.

[208] 11. Δεῖ τὸν ἀγαθὸν ἐπιδείκνυσθαι ἐν μὲν τοῖς
λόγοις ἃ φρονεῖ, ἐν δὲ τοῖς ἔργοις ἃ ποιεῖ. Max.
Conf. *Loci Comm.* col. 729 Migne.

[210] 12. Διὰ δύο προφάσεις τῶν ἀδικημάτων οἱ ἄνθρωποι ἀπέχονται, ἢ διὰ φόβον ἢ διὰ αἰσχύνην. Max.
Conf. *Loci Comm.* col. 753 Migne.

[211] 13. Πάντων ἀπαιδευτότατον (ἔφη) τὸ λοιδορεῖν.
Dionys. Antiochi, *Epist.* 79.

[213] 14. Sume hoc ab iudicibus nostra voluntate, nemi-
nem illi propiorem cognatum quam te fuisse ; con-
cedimus officia tua in illum nonnulla exstitisse ;
stipendia vos una fecisse aliquamdiu nemo negat :
sed quid contra testamentum dicis, in quo scriptus
hic est ? Rutil. Lup. i. 19.

[214] 15. Non enim simile est vivere in aequa civitate,
ubi ius legibus valeat,[2] et devenire sub unius tyranni
imperium, ubi singularis libido dominetur. Sed
necesse est, aut legibus fretum meminisse libertatis,
aut unius potestati traditum quotidiano[3] commentari[4]
servitutem. Rutil. Lup. ii. 2.

[215] 16. Quid si tandem iudice natura hanc causam
ageremus, quae ita divisit ⟨virilem et⟩[5] muliebrem
personam, ut suum cuique opus atque officium dis-
tribueret, et ego hunc ostenderem muliebri[6] ritu esse
suo corpore abusum[6] : nonne vehementissime admi-
raretur, si quisquam non gratissimum munus arbi-

may please for her husband, but when she does so for going out there is cause for alarm, since that is not for her husband but for other men.

11. A good man should express himself sincerely in word and deed.

12. There are two things which restrain men from crime, fear and shame.

13. Nothing is so uncultured as abusiveness.

14. Let the jury grant with my consent that you were as near a relative to the deceased as any. We admit that you had done him an occasional kindness. No one denies that you had been together for some time in the army. But why do you take exception to the will in which my client is mentioned?

15. Living in a democratic state where justice is established by the laws is different from passing into the power of one tyrant when the caprice of an individual is supreme. We have either to put our trust in laws and so remember freedom or else to be surrendered to the power of one man and brood daily over slavery.

16. Just suppose that in conducting this case we had Nature to judge us, who when dividing man and woman assigned special tasks and duties to each; and suppose I were to show that this man by acting as a woman had misused his body; would not Nature be exceedingly surprised that anyone had failed to count it the most welcome privilege to be born a man

---

¹ γιγνομένους add. Nauck.
² valeat Aldina : vallat codd.
³ quotidiano Ruhnken : quotidianam codd.
⁴ commentari Stephanus : commentare codd.
⁵ virilem et add. Ruhnken.
⁶ muliebri . . . abusum Stephanus : tui liberi . . . adlusum codd.

traretur, virum se natum, sed depravato naturae
beneficio in mulierem convertere properasset?
Rutil. Lup. ii. 6.

[216]   17. Nam hominis avari atque asoti unum idemque
vitium est : uterque enim nescit uti atque utrique
pecunia dedecori est. Quare merito utrique pari
poenia afficiuntur, quos pariter non decet habere.
Rutil. Lup. ii. 9.

[217]   18. Cogis me iniuriae tuae causam proferre ?
Nihil agis ; non dicam. Sed ipsum tempus eam
patefaciet. Rutil. Lup. ii. 11.

[218]   19. Sed ego iam, iudices, summum ac legitimum,
quod exposui, meae causae ius omitto ; vobis quod
aequissimum videatur ut constituatis permitto. Non
enim vereor, quin, etiamsi sit[1] novum vobis instituen-
dum, libenter id quod postulo propter utilitatem
communis consuetudinis sequamini. Rutil. Lup. ii. 17.

[219]   20. Δοκεῖς γὰρ αὐτὸν εἰπεῖν. Herodianus, περὶ
σχημ. viii. 598 Walz.

[219a]   21. Παραπέμπει γὰρ ἡμᾶς ἡ ἐλπίς· αὕτη δὲ
ἀτυχούντων ἐστὶν ἐφόδιον. Herodianus, περὶ σχημ.
viii. 601 Walz.

[221]   22. Τὸν ἀγήρατον χρόνον.   Pollux ii. 14.

[240]   23. Ἔμμηνοι δίκαι.   Harpocration, s.v.

[241]   24. Κατηγόρησεν ἐνδόσιμα.   Pollux viii. 143.

[242]   25. Ἐπιβασίαν τῇ δίκῃ.   Pollux ii. 200.

[249]   26. Τὰ ὄντα καταβέβρωκεν.   Pollux vi. 39.

[251]   27. Ἐπὶ κεφαλὴν σπεύδειν.   Pollux ii. 42.

[261]   28. Τοῦ παροδίου τοίχου.   Pollux vii. 121.

[264]   29. Λείαν περιεσύραντο.   Pollux i. 162.

[273]   30. Τοκίζεται αὐτῷ ἀργύριον.   Pollux iii. 85.

[275]   31. Οἱ δὲ φρονηματισθέντες ὑπὸ τῶν δεδηλω-
μένων ἕτοιμοι ἦσαν.   Suidas, s.v. φρονηματισθῆναι.

and had abused Nature's kindness by hastening to change himself into a woman ?

17. The miser and the debauchee are guilty of one and the same fault. Both are incapable of using money ; both are disgraced by it. Therefore both are rewarded with a similar punishment, and rightly, since neither is suited to be a possessor.

18. Are you forcing me to announce the reason for your doing the wrong ? You are unsuccessful. I shall not say, but time itself will reveal it.

19. But now, gentlemen of the jury, I am leaving the rights of my case which, as I have shown, have the fullest legal justification, and allowing you to give the verdict which you think fairest. For I have no doubt that even if you have to create a new precedent you will grant what I ask because of the service to public morality.

20. You think that he said.

21. For we are escorted by hope which is the maintenance of the unfortunate.

22. Ageless time.[a]

23. Monthly lawsuits.

24. He made his accusation conform.

25. A stepping-stone to justice.[b]

26. Has devoured the property.

27. To hurry headlong.

28. The wall facing the street.

29. They swept off the booty.

30. Money is lent to him at interest.

31. And they, made proud by what had been explained, were ready.

---

[a] Referred to the *Funeral Speech* by Sauppe.
[b] The exact meaning of this phrase is not known.

---

[1] *etiamsi sit* Ruhnken : *etiam sit* codd.

INDEX OF PROPER NAMES

INDEX OF PROPER NAMES

INDEX OF PROPER NAMES

INDEX OF PROPER NAMES

INDEX OF PROPER NAMES

INDEX OF PROPER NAMES

INDEX OF
SELECTED GREEK WORDS

FOR VOLUMES I AND II

An.=Antiphon, As.=Andocides, L.=Lycurgus, D.=Dinarchus, De.= Demades, H.=Hyperides, fr.=fragments, An. app.=appendix of vol. I (pp. 314-317), H. app.=appendix to Hyperides i in vol. II (pp. 400-402). References are to the titles and Greek text of the speeches (by sections unless otherwise stated) and the fragments, as numbered.

ἀγορά, An. v. 10, vi. 39 ; As. i. 36, 45, 76, ii. 8, iv. 14, fr. ii ; L. 5, 51, 142, fr. 10. 1 ; D. i. 32, 43, 101, fr. 7. 2 ; H. ii. 2, iii. 12, 14, 19, iv. 21

ἄδεια, An. v. 77 ; As. i. 11 sq., 15, 20, 22, 34, 77, ii. 23, 27 ; L. 104 ; H. v. 34, vi. 5, fr. 17. 1

ἀλιτήριος, An. iv a 3, 4, β 8, γ 7, δ 10 ; As. i. 51, 130, 131 ; L. 117

ἀνάγειν, H. iii. 15

ἀναγωγή, H. iii. 15

ἀναυμαχίου, As. i. 74

ἀντιγραφή, H. iv. 4, 31

ἀντομνύναι, An. i. 8

ἀπάγειν, An. v. 38, 85 ; As. i. 94, 105, iv. 18 ; L. 121 ; D. ii. 9, 10 ; H. iii. 12

ἀπαγωγή, An. v. 9 ; As. i. 88, 91 ; H. iii. 29, iv. 6

ἀπογράφειν, As. i. 13, 15, 17, 19, 34, 43, 47, 67 ; H. iv. 34

ἀπογράφεσθαι, An. vi. 35, *passim*

ἀπογραφή, As. i. 23

ἀποδοκιμάζειν, D. i. 79, ii. 10

ἀποικία, As. iii. 9, 15

ἀποφαίνειν, D. i. 3, *passim*, ii. 2, *passim*, iii. 16, 18 ; H. v cols. 5, 6, 31, 38

ἀπόφασις, D. i. 1, *passim*, ii. 1, *passim*, iii. 5, *passim*, fr. 2 tit. ; H. v cols. 5, 6, 7

ἀρά, As. i. 31 ; L. 31 ; D. i. 46 sq., ii. 16

ἄρχειν (hold office), As. i. 73, 87 sq., 93, 96, 99, 147 ; D. ii. 10 ; H. i. 17

ἀρχή (office), An. v. 48, fr. B 1. 2 ; As. i. 73, 79, 83 sq., 90, 96, 147 ; D. ii. 10 ; H. iv. 6, v col. 26

ἄρχων, An. v. 47 ; As. iv. 14,

615

INDEX OF GREEK WORDS

INDEX OF GREEK WORDS

617

INDEX OF GREEK WORDS

ἐρήμην δίκην, An. ii α 8, v. 13
ἔρημον ἀγῶνα, L. 117
ἑταιρεία, As. i. 100
ἑταῖρος, As. iv. 4, 14
εὔθυναι, An. vi. 43, fr. B 1. 2 ;
  As. i. 73, 78, 90 ; L. fr. 3
  tit.
εὔθυνος, As. i. 78
ἐφέται, As. i. 78
ἔφηβος, L. 76 ; D. iii. 15, fr.
  7. 1

ζητηταί, As. i. 65

ἡλιαία, An. vi. 21 ; De. 60

θεσμοθέται, An. vi. 21, 35,
  app. A ; As. i. 28, 79 ; L.
  121 ; H. i. 12, iv. 6

ἱεροσυλεῖν, An. v. 10 ; L. 65,
  90, 136
ἱερῶν κλοπή, An. ii α 6
ἱππαρχεῖν, D. iii. 12 ; H. i. 17
ἵππαρχος, H. i. 17, fr. 19. 1
ἱπποτροφεῖν, L. 139 ; H. i. 16

κάκωσις, L. 147 ; cf. As. i.
  74 ; D. ii. 18
καταλύειν τὸν δῆμον, As. i. 95
  sq., 101 ; iii. 4, 6, 10, 12 ;
  L. 124 sq. ; D. i. 76
κατάλυσις τοῦ δήμου, As. i. 36,
  iii. 6, 12 ; L. 126, 147 ;
  D. i. 94 ; H. iv. 8
κλέπτειν, An. ii γ 4, v. 38 ; L.
  65, 90 ; D. i. 70, ii. 10
κλέπτης, An. v. 9 ; D. i. 41,
  ii. 10
κλῆρος, L. 103 (Homer) ; D.
  iii. 16 ; H. frs. 40 & 41
  tit., 42 tit.

κληρουχία, An. fr. B 8
κλοπή, An. ii α 6 ; As. i. 74

ληξιαρχικὸν γραμματεῖον, L. 76
λῃτουργεῖν, As. i. 132
λῃτουργία, An. v. 77 ; As. iv.
  42 ; L. 139
λιπεῖν τὴν τάξιν, As. i. 74 ; L.
  20, 76, 77 ; D. i. 12, 71, 81
λιποταξίου, L. 147

μεσεγγυᾶσθαι, An. vi. 50
μετοικεῖν, L. 133
μέτοικος, As. i. 15, 144 ; H.
  iii. 28, 33, iv. 3, fr. 18. 3
μυστήρια, As. i tit., 10, passim

νομίμων εἴργεσθαι, An. vi. 34
  sq., 40

ὅρκος, An. v. 11, 90, 96, vi.
  25, 49, 51 ; As. i. 8, passim, iii. 22, 34, iv. 3, 21,
  39 ; L. 76 sq., 80 sq., 127 ;
  D. i. 14, 71, iii. 2, 17 ; H.
  i fr. i, iii. 2, iv. 40
ὁρκωτής, An. vi. 14
ὄρυγμα, L. 121 ; D. i. 62
ὀστρακίζειν, As. iii. 3, iv. 3,
  36. Cf. ἐξοστρακίζειν

παράνομα, An. fr. B 5 tit. ;
  As. i. 17, 22 ; L. 7 ; D. i.
  100 sq., ii. 12 ; H. ii. 4, 5,
  11, 12, iv. 6, 15, fr. 17 tit.,
  19 tit.
πάρεδρος, As. i. 78
πέμπτον μέρος τῶν ψήφων,
  As. i. 33, iv. 18 ; D. i. 54
πεντεδραχμία, D. i. 56
πεντηκοστή, As. i. 133 ; L.
  19, 58

INDEX OF GREEK WORDS

619

INDEX OF GREEK WORDS

Printed in Great Britain by R. & R. CLARK, LIMITED, Edinburgh

THE LOEB CLASSICAL LIBRARY

VOLUMES ALREADY PUBLISHED

LATIN AUTHORS

AMMIANUS MARCELLINUS. J. C. Rolfe. 3 Vols. (*2nd Imp. revised.*)

APULEIUS: THE GOLDEN ASS (METAMORPHOSES). W. Adlington (1566). Revised by S. Gaselee. (*7th Imp.*)

ST. AUGUSTINE, CONFESSIONS OF. W. Watts (1631). 2 Vols. (Vol. I *7th Imp.*, Vol. II *6th Imp.*)

ST. AUGUSTINE: SELECT LETTERS. J. H. Baxter. (*2nd Imp.*)

AUSONIUS. H. G. Evelyn White. 2 Vols. (*2nd Imp.*)

BEDE. J. E. King. 2 Vols. (*2nd Imp.*)

BOETHIUS: TRACTS AND DE CONSOLATIONE PHILOSOPHIAE. Rev. H. F. Stewart and E. K. Rand. (*6th Imp.*)

CAESAR: CIVIL WARS. A. G. Peskett. (*5th Imp.*)

CAESAR: GALLIC WAR. H. J. Edwards. (*10th Imp.*)

CATO AND VARRO: DE RE RUSTICA. H. B. Ash and W. D. Hooper. (*3rd Imp.*)

CATULLUS. F. W. Cornish: TIBULLUS. J. B. Postgate; and PERVIGILIUM VENERIS. J. W. Mackail. (*12th Imp.*)

CELSUS: DE MEDICINA. W. G. Spencer. 3 Vols. (Vol. I *3rd Imp. revised*, Vols. II and III *2nd Imp.*)

[CICERO]: AD HERENNUM. H. Caplan.

CICERO: BRUTUS AND ORATOR. G. L. Hendrickson and H. M. Hubbell. (*3rd Imp.*)

CICERO: DE FATO; PARADOXA STOICORUM; DE PARTITIONE ORATORIA. H. Rackham. (With De Oratore, Vol. II.) (*2nd Imp.*)

1

THE LOEB CLASSICAL LIBRARY

Cicero : De Finibus. H. Rackham. (4th Imp. revised.)

Cicero : De Inventione, etc. H. M. Hubbell.

Cicero : De Natura Deorum and Academica. H. Rackham. (2nd Imp.)

Cicero : De Officiis. Walter Miller. (6th Imp.)

Cicero : De Oratore. E. W. Sutton and H. Rackham. 2 Vols. (2nd Imp.)

Cicero : De Republica and De Legibus. Clinton W. Keyes. (4th Imp.)

Cicero : De Senectute, De Amicitia, De Divinatione. W. A. Falconer. (6th Imp.)

Cicero : In Catilinam, Pro Murena, Pro Sulla, Pro Flacco. Louis E. Lord. (3rd Imp. revised.)

Cicero : Letters to Atticus. E. O. Winstedt. 3 Vols. (Vol. I 6th Imp., Vols. II and III 4th Imp.)

Cicero : Letters to his Friends. W. Glynn Williams. 3 Vols. (Vols. I and II 3rd Imp., Vol. III 2nd Imp. revised and enlarged.)

Cicero : Philippics. W. C. A. Ker. (3rd Imp.)

Cicero : Pro Archia, Post Reditum, De Domo, De Haruspicum Responsis, Pro Plancio. N. H. Watts. (3rd Imp.)

Cicero : Pro Caecina, Pro Lege Manilia, Pro Cluentio, Pro Rabirio. H. Grose Hodge. (3rd Imp.)

Cicero : Pro Milone, In Pisonem, Pro Scauro, Pro Fonteio, Pro Rabirio Postumo, Pro Marcello, Pro Ligario, Pro Rege Deiotaro. N. H. Watts. (2nd Imp.)

Cicero : Pro Quinctio, Pro Roscio Amerino, Pro Roscio Comoedo, Contra Rullum. J. H. Freese. (2nd Imp.)

Cicero : Tusculan Disputations. J. E. King. (4th Imp.)

Cicero : Verrine Orations. L. H. G. Greenwood. 2 Vols. (Vol. I 3rd Imp., Vol. II 2nd Imp.)

Claudian. M. Platnauer. 2 Vols.

Columella : De Re Rustica. 2 Vols. Vol. I. Books I-IV. H. B. Ash. Vol. II. Books V-IX. E. M. Forster and E. Heffner. (Vol. I 2nd Imp.)

Curtius, Q. : History of Alexander. J. C. Rolfe. 2 Vols.

Florus. E. S. Forster ; and Cornelius Nepos. J. C. Rolfe. (2nd Imp.)

Frontinus : Stratagems and Aqueducts. C. E. Bennett and M. B. McElwain. (2nd Imp.)

Fronto : Correspondence. C. R. Haines. 2 Vols. (Vol. I 3rd Imp., Vol. II 2nd Imp.)

2

THE LOEB CLASSICAL LIBRARY

GELLIUS. J. C. Rolfe. 3 Vols. (*2nd Imp.*)

HORACE: ODES AND EPODES. C. E. Bennett. (*14th Imp. revised.*)

HORACE: SATIRES, EPISTLES, ARS POETICA. H. R. Fairclough. (*8th Imp. revised.*)

JEROME: SELECT LETTERS. F. A. Wright. (*2nd Imp.*)

JUVENAL AND PERSIUS. G. G. Ramsay. (*7th Imp.*)

LIVY. B. O. Foster, F. G. Moore, Evan T. Sage and A. C. Schlesinger. 14 Vols. Vols. I-XIII. (Vol. I *4th Imp.*, Vols. II, III, V and IX *3rd Imp.*, Vols. IV, VI-VIII, X-XII *2nd Imp. revised.*)

LUCAN. J. D. Duff. (*3rd Imp.*)

LUCRETIUS. W. H. D. Rouse. (*7th Imp. revised.*)

MARTIAL. W. C. A. Ker. 2 Vols. (Vol. I *5th Imp.*, Vol. II *4th Imp. revised.*)

MINOR LATIN POETS: from PUBLILIUS SYRUS to RUTILIUS NAMATIANUS, including GRATTIUS, CALPURNIUS SICULUS, NEMESIANUS, AVIANUS, with "Aetna," "Phoenix" and other poems. J. Wight Duff and Arnold M. Duff. (*3rd Imp.*)

OVID: THE ART OF LOVE AND OTHER POEMS. J. H. Mozley. (*3rd Imp.*)

OVID: FASTI. Sir James G. Frazer. (*2nd Imp.*)

OVID: HEROIDES AND AMORES. Grant Showerman. (*4th Imp.*)

OVID: METAMORPHOSES. F. J. Miller. 2 Vols. (Vol. I *10th Imp.*, Vol. II *8th Imp.*)

OVID: TRISTIA AND EX PONTO. A. L. Wheeler. (*3rd Imp.*)

PETRONIUS. M. Heseltine; SENECA: APOCOLOCYNTOSIS. W. H. D. Rouse. (*8th Imp. revised.*)

PLAUTUS. Paul Nixon. 5 Vols. (Vols. I and II *5th Imp.*, Vol. III *3rd Imp.*, Vols. IV-V *2nd Imp.*)

PLINY: LETTERS. Melmoth's translation revised by W. M. L. Hutchinson. 2 Vols. (*6th Imp.*)

PLINY: NATURAL HISTORY. H. Rackham and W. H. S. Jones. 10 Vols. Vols. I-VI and IX. (Vol. I *3rd Imp.*, Vols. II-IV *2nd Imp.*)

PROPERTIUS. H. E. Butler. (*6th Imp.*)

PRUDENTIUS. H. J. Thomson. 2 Vols.

QUINTILIAN. H. E. Butler. 4 Vols. (*3rd Imp.*)

REMAINS OF OLD LATIN. E. H. Warmington. 4 Vols. Vol. I (Ennius and Caecilius). Vol. II (Livius, Naevius, Pacuvius, Accius). Vol. III (Lucilius, Laws of the XII

3

Tables). Vol. IV (Archaic Inscriptions). (Vol. IV 2nd Imp.)

SALLUST. J. C. Rolfe. (3rd Imp. revised.)

SCRIPTORES HISTORIAE AUGUSTAE. D. Magie. 3 Vols. (Vol. I 3rd Imp., Vols. II and III 2nd Imp. revised.)

SENECA: APOCOLOCYNTOSIS. Cf. PETRONIUS.

SENECA: EPISTULAE MORALES. R. M. Gummere. 3 Vols. (Vol. I 4th Imp., Vols. II and III 3rd Imp. revised.)

SENECA: MORAL ESSAYS. J. W. Basore. 3 Vols. (Vol. II 3rd Imp. revised, Vols. I and III 2nd Imp. revised.)

SENECA: TRAGEDIES. F. J. Miller. 2 Vols. (Vol. I 4th Imp., Vol. II 3rd Imp. revised.)

SIDONIUS: POEMS AND LETTERS. W. B. Anderson. 2 Vols. Vol. I. (2nd Imp.)

SILIUS ITALICUS. J. D. Duff. 2 Vols. (Vol. I 2nd Imp., Vol. II 3rd Imp.)

STATIUS. J. H. Mozley. 2 Vols. (2nd Imp.)

SUETONIUS. J. C. Rolfe. 2 Vols. (Vol. I 7th Imp., Vol. II 6th Imp.)

TACITUS: DIALOGUS. Sir Wm. Peterson; and AGRICOLA AND GERMANIA. Maurice Hutton. (6th Imp.)

TACITUS: HISTORIES AND ANNALS. C. H. Moore and J. Jackson. 4 Vols. (Vols. I and II 3rd Imp., Vols. III and IV 2nd Imp.)

TERENCE. John Sargeaunt. 2 Vols. (7th Imp.)

TERTULLIAN: APOLOGIA AND DE SPECTACULIS. T. R. Glover; MINUCIUS FELIX. G. H. Rendall. (2nd Imp.)

VALERIUS FLACCUS. J. H. Mozley. (2nd Imp. revised.)

VARRO: DE LINGUA LATINA. R. G. Kent. 2 Vols. (2nd Imp. revised.)

VELLEIUS PATERCULUS AND RES GESTAE DIVI AUGUSTI. F. W. Shipley. (2nd Imp.)

VIRGIL. H. R. Fairclough. 2 Vols. (Vol. I 18th Imp., Vol. II 13th Imp. revised.)

VITRUVIUS: DE ARCHITECTURA. F. Granger. 2 Vols. (Vol. I 2nd Imp.)

GREEK AUTHORS

ACHILLES TATIUS. S. Gaselee. (2nd Imp.)

AENEAS TACTICUS, ASCLEPIODOTUS AND ONASANDER. The Illinois Greek Club. (2nd Imp.)

THE LOEB CLASSICAL LIBRARY

AESCHINES. C. D. Adams. (*2nd Imp.*)

AESCHYLUS. H. Weir Smyth. 2 Vols. (Vol. I 6*th Imp.*, Vol. II 5*th Imp.*)

ALCIPHRON, AELIAN AND PHILOSTRATUS: LETTERS. A. R. Benner and F. H. Fobes.

APOLLODORUS. Sir James G. Frazer. 2 Vols. (Vol. I 3*rd Imp.*, Vol. II 2*nd Imp.*)

APOLLONIUS RHODIUS. R. C. Seaton. (4*th Imp.*)

THE APOSTOLIC FATHERS. Kirsopp Lake. 2 Vols. (Vol. I 8*th Imp.*, Vol. II 6*th Imp.*)

APPIAN'S ROMAN HISTORY. Horace White. 4 Vols. (Vol. I 3*rd Imp.*, Vols. II, III and IV 2*nd Imp.*)

ARATUS. *Cf.* CALLIMACHUS.

ARISTOPHANES. Benjamin Bickley Rogers. 3 Vols. (Vols. I and II 5*th Imp.*, Vol. III 4*th Imp.*) Verse trans.

ARISTOTLE: ART OF RHETORIC. J. H. Freese. (3*rd Imp.*)

ARISTOTLE: ATHENIAN CONSTITUTION, EUDEMIAN ETHICS, VIRTUES AND VICES. H. Rackham. (3*rd Imp.*)

ARISTOTLE: GENERATION OF ANIMALS. A. L. Peck. (2*nd Imp.*)

ARISTOTLE: METAPHYSICS. H. Tredennick. 2 Vols. (3*rd Imp.*)

ARISTOTLE: METEOROLOGICA. H. D. P. Lee.

ARISTOTLE: MINOR WORKS. W. S. Hett. " On Colours," " On Things Heard," " Physiognomics," " On Plants," " On Marvellous Things Heard," " Mechanical Problems," " On Indivisible Lines," " Situations and Names of Winds," " On Melissus, Xenophanes, and Gorgias." (2*nd Imp.*)

ARISTOTLE: NICOMACHEAN ETHICS. H. Rackham. (5*th Imp. revised.*)

ARISTOTLE: OECONOMICA AND MAGNA MORALIA. G. C. Armstrong. (With Metaphysics, Vol. II.) (3*rd Imp.*)

ARISTOTLE: ON THE HEAVENS. W. K. C. Guthrie. (3*rd Imp.*)

ARISTOTLE: ON THE SOUL, PARVA NATURALIA, ON BREATH. W. S. Hett. (2*nd Imp. revised.*)

ARISTOTLE: ORGANON. H. P. Cooke and H. Tredennick. 3 Vols. Vol. I. (2*nd Imp.*)

ARISTOTLE: PARTS OF ANIMALS. A. L. Peck; MOTION AND PROGRESSION OF ANIMALS. E. S. Forster. (3*rd Imp.*)

ARISTOTLE: PHYSICS. Rev. P. Wicksteed and F. M. Cornford. 2 Vols. (Vol. I 2*nd Imp.*, Vol. II 3*rd Imp.*)

ARISTOTLE: POETICS and LONGINUS. W. Hamilton Fyfe;

THE LOEB CLASSICAL LIBRARY

DEMETRIUS ON STYLE. W. Rhys Roberts. (*5th Imp. revised.*)

ARISTOTLE: POLITICS. H. Rackham. (*4th Imp.*)

ARISTOTLE: PROBLEMS. W. S. Hett. 2 Vols. (*2nd Imp. revised.*)

ARISTOTLE: RHETORICA AD ALEXANDRUM. H. Rackham. (With Problems, Vol. II.)

ARRIAN: HISTORY OF ALEXANDER AND INDICA. Rev. E. Iliffe Robson. 2 Vols. (Vol. I *3rd Imp.*, Vol. II *2nd Imp.*)

ATHENAEUS: DEIPNOSOPHISTAE. C. B. Gulick. 7 Vols. (Vols. I, V and VI *2nd Imp.*)

ST. BASIL: LETTERS. R. J. Deferrari. 4 Vols. (*2nd Imp.*)

CALLIMACHUS AND LYCOPHRON. A. W. Mair; ARATUS. G. R. Mair. (*2nd Imp.*)

CLEMENT OF ALEXANDRIA. Rev. G. W. Butterworth. (*3rd Imp.*)

COLLUTHUS. *Cf.* OPPIAN.

DAPHNIS AND CHLOE. *Cf.* LONGUS.

DEMOSTHENES I: OLYNTHIACS, PHILIPPICS AND MINOR ORATIONS: I-XVII AND XX. J. H. Vince. (*2nd Imp.*)

DEMOSTHENES II: DE CORONA AND DE FALSA LEGATIONE. C. A. Vince and J. H. Vince. (*3rd Imp. revised.*)

DEMOSTHENES III: MEIDIAS, ANDROTION, ARISTOCRATES, TIMOCRATES, ARISTOGEITON. J. H. Vince. (*2nd Imp.*)

DEMOSTHENES IV-VI: PRIVATE ORATIONS AND IN NEAERAM. A. T. Murray. (*2nd Imp.*)

DEMOSTHENES VII: FUNERAL SPEECH, EROTIC ESSAY, EXORDIA AND LETTERS. N. W. and N. J. DeWitt.

DIO CASSIUS: ROMAN HISTORY. E. Cary. 9 Vols. (Vols. I and II *3rd Imp.*, Vols. III and IV *2nd Imp.*)

DIO CHRYSOSTOM. 5 Vols. Vols I and II. J. W. Cohoon. Vol. III. J. W. Cohoon and H. Lamar Crosby. Vols. IV and V. H. Lamar Crosby. (Vols. I-III *2nd Imp.*)

DIODORUS SICULUS. 12 Vols. Vols. I-VI. C. H. Oldfather. Vol. VII. C. L. Sherman. Vols. IX and X. Russel M. Geer. (Vols. I-III *2nd Imp.*)

DIOGENES LAERTIUS. R. D. Hicks. 2 Vols. (Vol. I *4th Imp.*, Vol. II *3rd Imp.*)

DIONYSIUS OF HALICARNASSUS: ROMAN ANTIQUITIES. Spelman's translation revised by E. Cary. 7 Vols. (Vols. I-IV *2nd Imp.*)

6

THE LOEB CLASSICAL LIBRARY

EPICTETUS. W. A. Oldfather. 2 Vols. (*2nd Imp.*)

EURIPIDES. A. S. Way. 4 Vols. (Vols. I and II *7th Imp.*, Vols. III and IV *6th Imp.*) Verse trans.

EUSEBIUS: ECCLESIASTICAL HISTORY. Kirsopp Lake and J. E. L. Oulton. 2 Vols. (Vol. I *3rd Imp.*, Vol. II *4th Imp.*)

GALEN: ON THE NATURAL FACULTIES. A. J. Brock. (*4th Imp.*)

THE GREEK ANTHOLOGY. W. R. Paton. 5 Vols. (Vols. I and II *5th Imp.*, Vol. III *4th Imp.*, Vols. IV and V *3rd Imp.*)

THE GREEK BUCOLIC POETS (THEOCRITUS, BION, MOSCHUS). J. M. Edmonds. (*7th Imp. revised.*)

GREEK ELEGY AND IAMBUS WITH THE ANACREONTEA. J. M. Edmonds. 2 Vols. (Vol. I *3rd Imp.*, Vol. II *2nd Imp.*)

GREEK MATHEMATICAL WORKS. Ivor Thomas. 2 Vols. (*2nd Imp.*)

HERODES. *Cf.* THEOPHRASTUS: CHARACTERS.

HERODOTUS. A. D. Godley. 4 Vols. (Vols. I-III *4th Imp.*, Vol. IV *3rd Imp.*)

HESIOD AND THE HOMERIC HYMNS. H. G. Evelyn White. (*7th Imp. revised and enlarged.*)

HIPPOCRATES AND THE FRAGMENTS OF HERACLEITUS. W. H. S. Jones and E. T. Withington. 4 Vols. (*3rd Imp.*)

HOMER: ILIAD. A. T. Murray. 2 Vols. (*6th Imp.*)

HOMER: ODYSSEY. A. T. Murray. 2 Vols. (*8th Imp.*)

ISAEUS. E. S. Forster. 2 Vols. (*2nd Imp.*)

ISOCRATES. George Norlin and LaRue Van Hook. 3 Vols. (Vols. I and III *2nd Imp.*)

ST. JOHN DAMASCENE: BARLAAM AND IOASAPH. Rev. G. R. Woodward and Harold Mattingly. (*3rd Imp. revised.*)

JOSEPHUS. H. St. J. Thackeray and Ralph Marcus. 9 Vols. Vols. I-VII. (Vol. V *3rd Imp.*, Vol. VI *2nd Imp.*)

JULIAN. Wilmer Cave Wright. 3 Vols. (Vols. I and II *3rd Imp.*, Vol. III *2nd Imp.*)

LONGUS: DAPHNIS AND CHLOE. Thornley's translation revised by J. M. Edmonds; and PARTHENIUS. S. Gaselee. (*3rd Imp.*)

LUCIAN. A. M. Harmon. 8 Vols. Vols. I-V. (Vols. I and III *3rd Imp.*, Vols. II, IV and V *2nd Imp.*)

LYCOPHRON. *Cf.* CALLIMACHUS.

LYRA GRAECA. J. M. Edmonds. 3 Vols. (Vol. I *4th Imp.*, Vols. II and III *3rd Imp.*)

LYSIAS. W. R. M. Lamb. (*2nd Imp.*)

THE LOEB CLASSICAL LIBRARY

MANETHO. W. G. Waddell; PTOLEMY: TETRABIBLOS. F. E. Robbins. (*2nd Imp.*)

MARCUS AURELIUS. C. R. Haines. (*4th Imp. revised.*)

MENANDER. F. G. Allinson. (*3rd Imp. revised.*)

MINOR ATTIC ORATORS. 2 Vols. K. J. Maidment and J. O. Burtt. (Vol. I *2nd Imp.*)

NONNOS: DIONYSIACA. W. H. D. Rouse. 3 Vols. (Vol. III *2nd Imp.*)

OPPIAN, COLLUTHUS, TRYPHIODORUS. A. W. Mair. (*2nd Imp.*)

PAPYRI. NON-LITERARY SELECTIONS. A. S. Hunt and C. C. Edgar. 2 Vols. (*2nd Imp.*) LITERARY SELECTIONS. Vol. I (Poetry). D. L. Page. (*3rd Imp.*)

PARTHENIUS. *Cf.* LONGUS.

PAUSANIAS: DESCRIPTION OF GREECE. W. H. S. Jones. 5 Vols. and Companion Vol. arranged by R. E. Wycherley. (Vols. I and III *2nd Imp.*)

PHILO. 10 Vols. Vols. I-V. F. H. Colson and Rev. G. H. Whitaker; Vols. VI-IX. F. H. Colson. (Vols. I-III, V-IX *2nd Imp.*, Vol. IV *3rd Imp.*)
Two Supplementary Vols. Translation only from an Armenian Text. Ralph Marcus.

PHILOSTRATUS: THE LIFE OF APOLLONIUS OF TYANA. F. C. Conybeare. 2 Vols. (Vol. I *4th Imp.*, Vol. II *3rd Imp.*)

PHILOSTRATUS: IMAGINES; CALLISTRATUS: DESCRIPTIONS. A. Fairbanks. (*2nd Imp.*)

PHILOSTRATUS AND EUNAPIUS: LIVES OF THE SOPHISTS. Wilmer Cave Wright. (*2nd Imp.*)

PINDAR. Sir J. E. Sandys. (*7th Imp. revised.*)

PLATO I: EUTHYPHRO, APOLOGY, CRITO, PHAEDO, PHAEDRUS. H. N. Fowler. (*4th Imp.*)

PLATO II: THEAETETUS AND SOPHIST. H. N. Fowler. (*4th Imp.*)

PLATO III: STATESMAN, PHILEBUS. H. N. Fowler; ION. W. R. M. Lamb. (*4th Imp.*)

PLATO IV: LACHES, PROTAGORAS, MENO, EUTHYDEMUS. W. R. M. Lamb. (*3rd Imp. revised.*)

PLATO V: LYSIS, SYMPOSIUM, GORGIAS. W. R. M. Lamb. (*5th Imp. revised.*)

PLATO VI: CRATYLUS, PARMENIDES, GREATER HIPPIAS, LESSER HIPPIAS. H. N. Fowler. (*4th Imp.*)

THE LOEB CLASSICAL LIBRARY

PLATO VII : TIMAEUS, CRITIAS, CLITOPHO, MENEXENUS, EPI-
STULAE. Rev. R. G. Bury. (3rd Imp.)

PLATO VIII : CHARMIDES, ALCIBIADES, HIPPARCHUS, THE
LOVERS, THEAGES, MINOS AND EPINOMIS. W. R. M. Lamb.
(2nd Imp.)

PLATO : LAWS. Rev. R. G. Bury. 2 Vols. (3rd Imp.)

PLATO : REPUBLIC. Paul Shorey. 2 Vols. (Vol. I 5th Imp.,
Vol. II 3rd Imp.)

PLUTARCH : MORALIA. 14 Vols. Vols. I-V. F. C. Babbitt ;
Vol. VI. W. C. Helmbold ; Vol. X. H. N. Fowler. (Vols.
I, III and X 2nd Imp.)

PLUTARCH : THE PARALLEL LIVES. B. Perrin. 11 Vols.
(Vols. I, II, VI, VII and XI 3rd Imp., Vols. III-V and
VIII-X 2nd Imp.)

POLYBIUS. W. R. Paton. 6 Vols. (2nd Imp.)

PROCOPIUS : HISTORY OF THE WARS. H. B. Dewing. 7 Vols.
(Vol. I 3rd Imp., Vols. II-VII 2nd Imp.)

PTOLEMY : TETRABIBLOS. Cf. MANETHO.

QUINTUS SMYRNAEUS. A. S. Way. (2nd Imp.) Verse trans.

SEXTUS EMPIRICUS. Rev. R. G. Bury. 4 Vols. (Vols. I and
III 2nd Imp.)

SOPHOCLES. F. Storr. 2 Vols. (Vol. I 9th Imp., Vol. II 6th
Imp.) Verse trans.

STRABO : GEOGRAPHY. Horace L. Jones. 8 Vols. (Vols. I,
V and VIII 3rd Imp., Vols. II-IV, VI and VII 2nd Imp.)

THEOPHRASTUS : CHARACTERS. J. M. Edmonds ; HERODES,
etc. A. D. Knox. (3rd Imp.)

THEOPHRASTUS : ENQUIRY INTO PLANTS. Sir Arthur Hort.
2 Vols. (2nd Imp.)

THUCYDIDES. C. F. Smith. 4 Vols. Vol. I 4th Imp., Vols.
II-III 3rd Imp.)

TRYPHIODORUS. Cf. OPPIAN.

XENOPHON : CYROPAEDIA. Walter Miller. 2 Vols. (Vol. I
4th Imp., Vol. II 3rd Imp.)

XENOPHON : HELLENICA, ANABASIS, APOLOGY, AND SYMPO-
SIUM. C. L. Brownson and O. J. Todd. 3 Vols. (Vols. I
and III 3rd Imp., Vol. II 4th Imp.)

XENOPHON : MEMORABILIA AND OECONOMICUS. E. C. Marchant. (3rd Imp.)

XENOPHON : SCRIPTA MINORA. E. C. Marchant. (2nd Imp)

(For Volumes in Preparation see next page.)

THE LOEB CLASSICAL LIBRARY

VOLUMES IN PREPARATION

GREEK AUTHORS

ARISTOTLE: DE MUNDO, etc.   D. Furley and E. S. Forster.
ARISTOTLE: HISTORY OF ANIMALS.   A. L. Peck.
PLOTINUS.   A. H. Armstrong.

LATIN AUTHORS

ST. AUGUSTINE: CITY OF GOD.
CAESAR: AFRICAN, ALEXANDRINE AND SPANISH WARS.
A. S. Way.
CICERO: PRO SESTIO, IN VATINIUM, PRO CAELIO, DE PROVINCIIS CONSULARIBUS, PRO BALBO.   J. H. Freese and R. Gardner.
PHAEDRUS AND OTHER FABULISTS.   B. E. Perry.

DESCRIPTIVE PROSPECTUS ON APPLICATION

LONDON
WILLIAM HEINEMANN LTD
Cloth 15s.

CAMBRIDGE, MASS.
HARVARD UNIV. PRESS
Cloth $2.50